FOR REFERENCE ONLY
DO NOT REMOVE FROM LIBRARY

Encyclopedia of VIRGINIA

THOMAS JEFFERSON

Encyclopedia of VIRGINIA

-a volume of
ENCYCLOPEDIA OF THE UNITED STATES

SOMERSET PUBLISHERS
200 PARK AVENUE, 303E
NEW YORK, NEW YORK 10017

Copyright 1992© by Somerset Publishers

All rights reserved. No part of this work may be reproduced or utilized in any form or by any means, electronic or mechanical, or by any information storage and retrieval system, without permission in writing from the publisher.

Printed in the United States of America

```
           Library of Congress Cataloging-in-Publication Data


The encyclopedia of Virginia.
       p.   cm. -- (Encyclopedia of the United States)
    Includes bibliographical references and index.
    ISBN 0-403-09902-1
    1. Virginia--Encyclopedias.   I. Series.
  F226.E53   1992
  975.5'003--dc20                                              92-6629
                                                                  CIP
```

FOREWORD

Information on this state is available from many other sources. Histories and geographies abound; there are place-name books, guidebooks and biographical references; many excellent atlases provide map detail; government registers contain in-depth coverage of the political organization.

It is the existence of so many varied sources of information that makes a systematic, encyclopedic reference necessary — a single source for the most useful information about Virginia.

A secondary purpose of this volume is to play a part in a national reference on all of the states, a systematic approach to referencing the entire nation — an *Encyclopedia of the United States* with each volume following a planned outline that matches each other volume in the series — with exceptions in the format made only when necessary.

This goal was partly achieved during the Great Depression years with the publication of the WPA Federal Writers' Project State and City Guidebooks, which we are proud to have republished in recent years in their original form. While containing a wealth of interesting and still useful information, they are outdated for most of the reference needs of today. And they were essentially *tour-guides* rather than general reference books. They were, however, very useful in the planning of this new work.

By providing consistency in format throughout the series of volumes in this Encyclopedia, researchers, whether they are academic scholars or occasional public library users, will be aided in knowing that a source exists for information on any of the states.

It is our hope that this Encyclopedia series will have a permanence through the issuance of revised editions at intervals to be determined by a careful watch on the availability of new material. Undoubtedly changes in the concept will be reflected in later editions as a result of feedback from users and the observations and introspection of our editors.

We wish to acknowledge with great appreciation the co-operation of the many state and local government offices that have furnished or reviewed material.

We are further grateful to the many librarians who have made their facilities so available during the years that this project has been in process.

The Editor

CONTENTS

INTRODUCTION 1
GEOGRAPHICAL CONFIGURATION 11
PRE-HISTORY AND ARCHEOLOGY 25
HISTORY 33
CHRONOLOGY OF VIRGINIA 71
DIRECTORY OF STATE SERVICES 91
COLONIAL GOVERNORS 97
GOVERNORS 131
U.S. SENATORS FROM VIRGINIA 201
DICTIONARY OF PLACES 221
PICTORIAL SCENES 317
GUIDE TO HISTORICAL PLACES 336
HISTORICAL PLACES 337
CONSTITUTION OF VIRGINIA 495
BIBLIOGRAPHY 547
INDEX 557
MAP OF VIRGINIA 588

INTRODUCTION TO VIRGINIA

Northern Virginia has always been endowed with special historical, cultural and social significance. Here is an almost perfectly balanced region. 18th century townhouses dominate the cobblestone streets. Famous men have walked this land. George Washington was born here. Mount Vernon, the most famous home in America still stands. Dulles Int'l Airport is located here.
 Tidewater is the oldest part of Virginia and one of the liveliest sections of the state. There are miles and miles of golden beaches, to years and years of rich and colorful history.
 Eastern Shore is 70-mile-long peninsula once visited by Blackbeard the pirate. One side of the Eastern Shore is bathed by the Atlantic Ocean, the other by the Chesapeake Bay.
 Central-Southside is the heart of Virginia. It encompasses the spirited old capital city of Richmond, dramatic Civil War battlefields, Kings Dominion theme park, famous historic homes. Shenandoah: it is a name famous in legend and song, an Indian word meaning "daughter of the stars." To follow the Skyline Drive across the highest crests of the Blue Ridge Mountains is literally to ride along the very top of the state. This region is known as Virginia's crowning glory. The Shenandoah Valley is 200-miles-long. Robert E. Lee's office is exactly the way he left it on the day he died.
 Highlands-this is the land that was once the American frontier. The Blue Ridge, the Allegheny and the Cumberland mountains are all here.
 The outline of the State is roughly the shape of a triangle. The total area of Virginia is 42,627 square miles of which 2,365 square miles are water surface. Along the southern boundary from the Atlantic to Cumberland Gap the maximum length of the State is about 432 miles. Its maximum width north and south is 200 miles.

Encyclopedia of Virginia

STATE SYMBOLS

THE NAME

Historians generally agree that Virginia was named by Queen Elizabeth herself in commemoration of her unmarried state. The name was given about 1584 or 1585.
Thomas Nelson Page says:
Queen "Elizabeth graciously accorded the privileges proposed by Raleigh, giving to this new land a name in honour of her maiden state, and it was called Virginia. Raleigh was knighted for his service and given the title of 'Lord and Governor of Virginia.'"
As to the naming of Virginia, Henry Howe says:
"The glowing description given by the adventurers, on their return, of the beauty of the country, the fertility of the soil, and pleasantness of the climate, delighted the queen, and induced her to name the country of which she had taken possession, Virginia, in commemoration of her unmarried life."
The origin of the word Virginia is accounted for as follows: It is a Latin name generally considered to be derived from the Latin word *Virgo*, meaning *a virgin*, but in reality it is the feminine form of the masculine noun *Virginius Verginius*, the name of a Roman gens.

NICKNAMES

Virginia is nicknamed the *Ancient Dominion*, the *Cavalier State, Down Where the South Begins*, the *Mother of Presidents*, the *Mother of States*, the *Mother of Statesmen*, and *The Old Dominion*.
The names, the *Ancient Dominion* and *The Old Dominion*, are still widely applied to Virginia, having originated in Colonial days. About the year 1663, after Charles Stuart had become King of England, he quartered the Arms of Virginia on his royal shield; thus ranking Virginia along with his other four dominions, England, Scotland, France, and Ireland. Historians say that the new king elevated Virginia to the position of a dominion "by quartering its arms (the old seal of the Virginia Company) on his royal shield with the arms of England, Scotland, and Ireland, **and that** the burgesses were very

Introduction

proud of this distinction and, remembering that they were the oldest as well as the most faithful of the Stuart settlements in America, adopted the name of 'The Old Dominion.'" Colonel Richard Lee, of the Colony of Virginia, is said to have visited Charles Stuart while he was in exile in the city of Brussels, about 1658. Charles was proclaimed King Charles II of England on May 8, 1660, and the Virginians accepted him as their king on September the 20th following his ascension. This pleased King Charles so much that he referred to the people of this colony as "the best of his distant children," and elevated the colony of Virginia to the position of a dominion.

Fiske says that "after the restoration of Charles II, a new seal for Virginia, adopted about 1663, has the same motto *En dat Virginia quintam* the effect of which was to rank Virginia by the side of his Majesty's other four dominions, England, Scotland, 'France,' and Ireland. We are told by the younger Richard Henry Lee that in these circumstances originated the famous epithet 'Old Dominion.'"

Virginia's nickname, the *Cavalier State*, is derived from the name of the Cavaliers who came over and settled there during, and shortly after the time of Charles I.

Because Virginia is the most southern of the Middle Atlantic States, located south of the Potomac river, radio broadcasters call it *Down Where the South Begins*.

Her sobriquet, the *Mother of Presidents*, alludes to the fact that so many of the early presidents of the United States were native Virginians.

Virginia was called the *Mother of States* because she was the first of the states to be settled.

The original territory of Virginia was split up to make West Virginia, Ohio, Kentucky, Illinois, Indiana, Wisconsin and a part of Minnesota; hence she came to be known as the *Mother of Statemen*.

The Virginians are nicknamed *Beagles* or *Beadles*, *Cavaliers*, *F. F. V's*, *Sorebacks*, and *Tuckahoes*. The sobriquet *Beadles* or *Beagles* originated during colonial days, due to the fact that the Virginians, following the English custom, used beadles in their courts. The second nickname, *Cavaliers*, alludes to Virginia's English Cavalier settlers, and *F. F. V.'s* stands for the *First Families of Virginia*, of which the people of the State have been and are very proud. "The abbreviation was of northern origin, and was in common use prior to the Civil War.

Tradition gives two accounts of the origin of the nickname *Soreback* applied to Virginians. One is that the Virginians are so hospitable that they slap one another on the backs until their backs become sore; the other is that the people in the southern part of the state raise so much cotton that it makes their backs sore to pick it. The North Carolinians seem to be the originators of this account. The nickname *Tuckahoes* was originally applied only to the poorer white people living in the lower part of the State.

This nickname was often heard during the Civil War because poverty often drove these Virginians to eat tuckahoe.

THE FLAG

An act of the legislature of Virginia, approved March 24, 1930, says:

"The Flag of the Commonwealth shall hereafter be made of bunting or merino. It shall be a deep blue field, with a circular white centre of the same material. Upon this circle shall be painted or embroidered, to show on both sides alike, the coat-of-arms of the State, as described in section twenty-seven of the Code of Virginia, as amended by this act, for the obverse of the great seal of the State; and there shall be a white silk fringe on the outer edge, furthest from the flag-staff. This shall be known and respected as the flag of Virginia.

Introduction

THE STATE MOTTO

Virginia's motto is *Sic Semper Tyrannis*, meaning *Thus Ever to Tyrants Thus Always to Tyrants*. This is the original motto recommended for the seal of Virginia by George Mason to the Virginia Convention in 1776. It was probably made up by him and his associates.

The obverse of the seal of Virginia has *Virtus* with her foot on a prostrate tyrant, and the motto suggests that all tyrants will meet with such treatment. Robert Hay in speaking of Virginia's seal said: "Its motto, *Sic semper tyrannis*, so appropriate for Richard Henry Lee, had a melancholy fame in connection with the murder of Lincoln."

On the exergon of the reverse of the first seal of Virginia adopted by the convention of delegates held at Williamsburg in July 1776, appeared the motto, *Deus Nobis Pace Olim Fecit*. This motto is found in Virgil's *Eclogues*, Book 1, line 6. It means *God gave us this freedom*. The motto was changed to the word *Perse verando* by an act of the General Assembly passed in October 1779.

THE GREAT SEAL

The present seals of the Commonweath of Virginia were adopted by an act of the General Assembly of the State of Virginia, approved March 24, 1930.

The act reads:

"Be it enacted by the general assembly of Virginia. That sections twenty-seven and thirty-one of the Code of Virginia, be amended and re-enacted so as to read as follows:

"Section 27. The great seal of the Commonwealth of Virginia shall consist of two metallic discs, two inches and one-fourth of an inch wide, with such words and figures engraved thereon as will, when used, produce impressions to be described as follows: On the obverse, Virtus, the genius of the Commonwealth, dressed as an Amazon, resting on a spear in her right hand, point downward, touching the earth; and holding in her left hand, a sheathed sword, or parazonium, pointing upward; her head erect and face upturned; her left foot on the form of Tyranny represented by the prostrate body of a man, with his head to

her left, his fallen crown near by, a broken chain in his left hand, and a scourge in his right. Above the group, and within the border conforming therewith shall be the word Virginia, and in the space below, on a curved line, shall be the motto, sic semper tyrannis. On the reverse, shall be placed a group consisting of Libertas, holding a wand and pileus in her right hand; on her right, Aeternitas, with a globe and phoenix in her right hand; and on the left of Libertas, Ceres, with a cornucopia in her left hand, and an ear of wheat in her right; over this device in a curved line, with word perseverando.

"(a) The governor is hereby authorized and directed to cause a new great seal of the Commonwealth to be constructed and engraved, with all reasonable dispatch, in strict conformity with the foregoing description, by artists and engravers of high rank in their profession and under the supervision of the art commission of Virginia, and when completed, to also have constructed and engraved a new lesser seal of the Commonwealth in accordance with section twenty-eight of the Code of Virginia. The governor shall, after said seals shall have been completed, and approved by him, proclaim the same, by such means as he may deem sufficient, to be the true great seal and lesser seal of the Commonwealth.

"(b) The great and lesser seals now in use in the office of the secretary of the Commonwealth are hereby declared to be the true great and lesser seals of the Commonwealth for the time being, and to so continue and be used as such, until the new seals shall be completed and proclaimed as herein provided for, and all official acts done thereunder, in the name of the Commonwealth, are hereby declared to be valid in so far as the affixing of the

Introduction

seal of the State thereto, may have been, or may be, a necessary part of the due execution, or performance thereof.

"(c) Any and all seals now under the care of the secretary of the Commonwealth shall, after the completion and proclamation of the new seals herein provided for, be cancelled by quartering the same with two straight lines crossing at right angles at the center of the discs, and cut at least as deep as the figures thereon, which seals so cancelled shall be safely kept in the office of the secretary of the Commonwealth and at least three clear impressions thereof filed with the State librarian to be by him duly indexed and safely kept in a suitable place.

"(d) The new, and permanent, seals of the Commonwealth, herein provided for shall, when completed, be kept and used as provided by law, and at least three clear impressions thereof shall be made and filed with the State librarian to be by him kept and displayed in some suitable place in the State library, for public inspection.

"(e) A sum sufficient, not to exceed fifteen hundred dollars, is hereby appropriated, out of any money in the treasury not otherwise appropriated, to meet the necessary expenses of carrying out the provisions of this act."

The *Proclamation by the Governor*, proclaiming the new seal of the Commonwealth of Virginia says:

"Whereas it is provided by section twenty-eight of the Code of Virginia that 'The lesser seal of the Commonwealth shall be one and nine-sixteenth inches in diameter, and have engraved thereon the device and inscriptions contained in the obverse of the great seal,'"

"Now, therefore, in confirmity with the provisions of section twenty-seven of the Code of Virginia, I do hereby proclaim the first of the said seals, herein above described, to be the great seal of the Commonwealth, and the second of the said seals, to be the lesser seal of the Commonwealth.

"Given under my hand and under the lesser seal of the Commonwealth, at Richmond, this 2nd day of December, in the year of our Lord one thousand, nine hundred and thirty-one, and in the one hundred and fifty-sixth year of the Commonwealth."

By the Governor: "Jno. Garland Pollard, Governor, Peter Saunders, Secretary of the Commonwealth."

Encyclopedia of Virginia

THE STATE FLOWER

Virginia, by an act of her General Assembly on March 6, 1918, declared the American dogwood, (*Cornus florida*), to be the floral emblem of the State. It was selected as the State flower because it is so prevalent in the State and because it adds beauty to the Virginia landscape, especially in the spring. The blossom of the American dogwood, (*Cornus florida*), varies in color from white to rose-red, and both the white and the pink varieties are found growing in the State. The act adopting the Virginia floral emblem does not specify what the color shall be, but the dogwood with white flowers is more generally found throughout the State.

THE STATE SONG

A musical composition often used in some parts of the Commonwealth at public gatherings or patriotic occasions is *Call of Virginia*, with words written by Lillian Smith and music composed by B. T. Gilmer. This song was published and copyrighted by B. T. Gilmer, Draper, Virginia, in 1926.

Another musical composition, very popular and widely used in Virginia is *Old Virginia*, the words of which were composed by Dr. John W. Wayland, and the music written by Will H. Ruebush. This song was first published by the Ruebush-Kieffer Company, Dayton, Virginia as a special feature for a collection of State and National songs entitled *Songs of the People*. The State Teachers College at Harrisonburg, Virginia, has published and is distributing free of charge for the use of their students, and for the use of teachers and pupils in Virginia, a special edition of this song.

One of the most familiar and best loved songs dealing with Virginia is the composition entitled *Carry Me Back to Old Virginia*, with music composed by James Bland. This production is found in many song collections; but it may be bought from Oliver Ditson Company, 179 Tremont Street, Boston, Massachusetts, or from Charles H. Ditson and Company, 10 East 34th Street, New York City.

Introduction

THE STATE BIRD

The cardinal is the state bird. Prior to 1912 there was a law passed protecting the robin.
The act says:
"1. Be it enacted by the General Assembly of Virginia, That it shall be unlawful for any person to shoot at, kill, or capture robins at any time, or to take or destroy their nests or eggs.
"2. Any person violating any of the provisions of this act shall be deemed guilty of a misdemeanor, and shall be punished by a fine of not less than five nor more than fifty dollars."
The robin is discussed under the topic *Michigan*.

THE STATE TREE

The state tree is the flowering dogwood which was designated in 1956.

THE CAPITOL BUILDING

The site of the Virginia capitol is at Richmond. The central building, begun in 1785, was completed in 1792. The wings were added in 1902. Thomas Jefferson designed this building. It represents the Classical type of architecture, which Thomas Jefferson designated as cubic architecture. Jefferson patterned this structure after the Maison Quarree of Nismes, an ancient Roman temple. This structure is one hundred and forty-six feet long, eighty-four and one-half feet wide, and fifty-three feet high, not including the wings added in 1906. The cost of the original building was about one hundred and twelve thousand dollars.

GEOGRAPHICAL CONFIGURATION

Although three centuries of political change have gradually reduced the vast range of Virginia's original domain, the topography of the State is still unusually varied. As chartered in 1609, the Old Dominion extended from the Atlantic to the Pacific, and from the approximate latitude of Columbia, South Carolina, to a parallel above the southern boundary of the present State of Pennsylvania. Until 1784 it stretched far northwest of the Ohio River and west of the Mississippi. Kentucky was part of Virginia until 1792; West Virginia became a separate State in 1863. But, notwithstanding this contraction, Virginia retains its characteristic trend 'across the grain' of the continent and also a diversity of geographic, topographic, and geologic features somewhat different from that of other Atlantic seaboard States.

The outline of the State is roughly the shape of a triangle. Its base is the almost straight southern boundary, which divides Virginia from North Carolina and Tennessee. With slight variation, this line follows parallel 36 22' from the Atlantic shore to Cumberland Gap, at 83 41' west longitude. The little village of Cumberland Gap on the Virginia-Tennessee border is about 25 miles farther west than the meridian of Detroit, Michigan. On the western side of the triangle the jagged and tortuous ridge lines of some of the Appalachian ranges demark Virginia from Kentucky and West Virginia as far northeast as latitude 39 28'. The eastern boundary of the mainland is defined by the Potomac River, Chesapeake Bay, and the Atlantic Ocean. Below the mouth of the Potomac the line crosses Chesapeake Bay to cut off from Maryland a long outer peninsula known as the Eastern Shore.

The total area of Virginia is 42,627 square miles, of which 2,365 square miles are water surface. Along the southern boundary from the Atlantic to Cumberland Gap the maximum length of the State is about 432 miles. Its maximum width north and south is 200 miles. By highway, Cumberland Gap is about 510 miles from Washington, D.C. The extreme airline distance diagonally across the State from the northeast corner of Accomac County on the Eastern Shore peninsula to Cumberland Gap is about 470 miles.

Virginia is divided physiographically into five distinct provinces-the Coastal Plain, the Piedmont Province, the Blue Ridge Province, the Valley and Ridge Province, and the Appalachian Plateau.

Encyclopedia of Virginia

Coastal Plain : 'Tidewater' is the name generally given to the broad belt of undulating and river-gashed plain that borders the eastern seaboard of Virginia from the Potomac to the North Carolina line. This province decreases in width from 120 miles near Bowling Green, 35 miles north of Richmond, to 80 miles near Norfolk in the south, and is traversed by great estuaries, which drain into Chesapeake Bay. The interstream ridges are narrow and relatively flat. In general the plain descends gently from an altitude of 300 feet at its western edge near Washington to sea level, at a rate of less than three feet to the mile. Tidal channels of four rivers sever the northern and central part of the plain into three long peninsulas, whose eastern extremities-with the peninsula of the Eastern Shore-border the lower Chesapeake Bay and form a magnificent system of natural harbors. This pattern of bays, deep tidal rivers, and long intervening necks of arable land has had a profound influence upon the social and commercial life of Tidewater Virginia.

Piedmont Province : There is no sharp line of division between the Coastal Plain and the Piedmont Province, which broadens southward from a width of 40 miles at the north to about 185 miles at the North Carolina line. Imperceptibly rising toward the foothills of the Blue Ridge, the province ranges in altitude from about 300 feet at the east to from 500 to 1,000 feet at the base of the mountains, reaching its greatest height in the southwestern part. The surface has been so channeled by streams that, with a few notable exceptions, flat areas are few. Hills or ridges dot the general surface near the western border. Some of these are outlying spur ridges and foothills of the Blue Ridge; others are isolated ridges and low mountains. They rise to altitudes as great as 2,200 feet.

Blue Ridge Province : The Blue Ridge rises rather abruptly above the western part of the Piedmont. In the northern half of the State it is a distinct ridge, bordered here and there on each side by subordinate ridges and with numerous deep coves in each slope. Some of the peaks have altitudes of more than 4,000 feet. In its southern part the Blue Ridge Province is a high, broad, somewhat rugged plateau-a region of rolling uplands, deep ravines, and high peaks. The highest mountains in Virginia, Mount Rogers (5,719 feet) and Whitetop (5,520 feet), are in the extreme southwestern part. At the North Carolina line the Blue Ridge Plateau is about 60 miles wide, with a general elevation of about 1,500 feet above the Piedmont upland.

Most of Virginia west of the Blue Ridge Province lies in the Appalachian Valley, commonly called the Valley of Virginia. The width of the province in the north, between the Blue Ridge and the West Virginia line, is about 35 miles; along the Tennessee line it is about 100 miles. Altitudes vary from approximately 300 feet above sea level at Harper's Ferry, on the Potomac, to 4,500 feet at the highest points of numerous ridges. In length, the Valley of Virginia extends 360 miles from the Potomac River southwestward to Tennessee. It is in reality a series of elongate

Geographical Configuration

valleys separated by transverse ridges, plateaus, or narrow gaps. The largest and best known of its principal units, Shenandoah Valley at the north, is about 150 miles long and from 10 to 20 miles wide. It contains a number of natural wonders. Above its center this valley is divided into two parts by Massanutten Mountain, a long high ridge. Other units in the Valley of Virginia, from north to south, are Fincastle Valley, Roanoke (Salem) Valley, Dublin Valley, Abingdon Valley, and Powell Valley. Dublin and Abingdon valleys, in the southwestern part, are from 2,100 to 2,400 feet above sea level.

Appalachian Plateau : Designated by some geographers as the Southwestern Plateau, the Appalachian Plateau in Virginia embraces parts of the Cumberland and Kanawha plateaus, which extend a relatively short distance into Virginia and Kentucky. The general elevation is between 2,700 and 3,000 feet, but the plateau is channeled by streams into a maze of deep narrow ravines and winding ridges. Cumberland Mountain, overlooking Powell Valley, marks the eastern boundary. Other mountains lie along the boundary farther northeast. In place of the elongate conformations of the Valley and Ridge Province, there is a multitude of irregular hills and peaks. The rock formations, in a few places, dip sufficiently to create more or less definite northeast-southwest ridges, but in general the only elevations that have a directional trend are inter-stream ridges.

CLIMATE

Virginia's climate is on the whole mild and equable, with refreshing seasonal changes that vary somewhat in different areas.

Southeastern Tidewater, within a 50-mile radius of Norfolk, has a particularly even climate. Thermometer readings in winter are rarely lower than 15 above zero, and the average temperature of the coldest winter month is about 40 above. This lower Chesapeake region has an average of about 258 days of sunshine a year and an average growing season of 200 days. Summer temperatures are only a little warmer than in the Piedmont Tidewater zone to the north and west.

In the remainder of the Tidewater and in the Piedmont, average summer and winter temperatures are slightly lower than in the Norfolk region. The coldest winter temperatures in Piedmont are from 5 to 15 above zero; the summer maximum of from 105 to 107 is infrequently reached.

In the Appalachian zone, which includes the mountain and valley regions to the west and the upper reaches of Piedmont near the Blue Ridge, zero weather is frequent in winter. The average temperature for December, January, and February ranges around freezing point. Summer temperatures in the Shenandoah Valley average a little above 75 with an occasional 'high' of 90; but the nights are cool because of mountain breezes that dispel the quickly radiated heat of the lower levels.

Encyclopedia of Virginia

Rainfall in Virginia averages from 40 to 45 inches a year, and is well distributed. There is ample precipitation from May to September, when rain is needed for growing crops. June, July, and August are months of greatest rainfall, and November is the driest month.

Snowfalls are moderate over most of the State and melt quickly, except in the mountain section and the northern part of the Shenandoah Valley, where the annual snowfall is from 25 to 30 inches a year. In the southeastern Tidewater the fall is commonly less than 10 inches; in the Piedmont it is 18 inches or more.

Midwinter days (from sunrise to sunset) in the latitude of Richmond are about half an hour longer than in the latitude of Boston and Detroit; midsummer days are about half an hour shorter. Clear days are most frequent in the fall and spring and average 12 a month throughout the year. Cloudy days average 9 a month, and partly cloudy 10 a month.

In the eastern section, fogs are frequent during the cooler season. They are likely to occur in the early morning and to disperse in a few hours. Heavy summer fogs occur in the mountain and valley regions about three times a month.

Virginia in general escapes both the rigorous cold of States farther to the north and the debilitating summer heat of more southerly regions. The climate fosters a well-balanced variety of agricultural products and has attracted to the State many industries to which conditions of temperature and humidity are important.

GEOLOGY

The mystery obscuring the pre-Cambrian eras-dim ages of the early geologic past that were longer, possibly, than all subsequent time-is not clarified by their rock remains in Virginia. If life existed during the vast era of creation known as the Archeozoic, it was of a nature too primal and transitory to leave traces. In looking for clues among the next younger Algonkian rocks, too, the geologist is baffled by a profound metamorphism that reduces theory to conjecture. Rocks in the Piedmont and the Blue Ridge prove that the surface-formed materials of the pre-Cambrian eras included both sedimentary strata and lava flows.

The story becomes more legible in the fossil-bearing strata of the Paleozoic era, deposited long before the present Appalachian Mountains were formed. During most of the era the portion of Virginia west of the Blue Ridge, as well as a part of the Piedmont, was submerged in great inland seas that advanced in the Cambrian period over the Mississippi Valley. Erosion of the Piedmont uplands supplied sediment that was spread over the beds of the seas to the west. Enormous volumes of lime silt accumulated in these seas, giving rise later to the limestone valleys, such as the Shenandoah. Great coal swamps existed during the later Paleozoic era. Later a series of great lateral thrusts from

Geographical Configuration

the southeast uplifted the sea beds of sediment to mountainous heights, folding and faulting the strata and expelling the sea from the interior of Virginia.

Here, at the close of Paleozoic time, occurred one of the greatest revolutions in the earth's history. The shrinkage of the earth had produced accumulated stresses that crumpled the weaker sediments in the sea trough, pushed up the old Appalachian mountain system, and drove the interior seas from the continent, never to return over such a vast area. The Appalachian Mountains as they are now known, however, were not produced until the Mesozoic and Cenozoic eras.

In the Triassic period, first of the Mesozoic era, erosion of the recently elevated mountains furnished a large amount of debris to be carried down the eastern slopes and deposited in the deltas and on flood plains of rivers flowing toward the Atlantic and in numerous down-warped basins. Triassic muds and sands (Newark series) of Virginia were laid down in various basins of the central Piedmont. The drainage of the Cretaceous period deposited sands, muds, and some limy materials in lakes, swamps, and estuaries over much of the Coastal Plain.

The Cenozoic era, during which forms of modern life first appeared on the earth, embraces the Eocene, Miocene, and Pliocene epochs of the Tertiary or mammal age. Most geologists include in this era the 'age of man,' the Quaternary, or ice age; by others this period is designated as the first in the Psychozoic era. Invading the land from the east, the Atlantic laid the Tertiary deposits of sediment at least as far westward as the present fall line and over the whole of what is now the Coastal Plain. Later in the Cenozoic era, rivers spread sand and gravel widely over the Tertiary sediments.

The recent chapters of the geologic story of western Virginia are written in topography rather than in sedimentary deposits. Yielding to erosion, the mountainous surface of the region diminished in Mesozoic time to a nearly flat surface, slightly above sea level. A vertical uplift in the late Cretaceous period raised this plain to a height of from 1,000 to 2,000 feet above the sea, and another vertical uplift of approximately the same force toward the close of the Tertiary age further increased the altitude without folding the strata. Erosion by the rejuvenated streams carved valleys in the softer limestone and shales and left the resistant beds standing high as great elongate mountain ridges.

The geologic divisions of Virginia today coincide with the physiographic divisions. Each of the provinces is distinguished by characteristic groups of rocks-sedimentary, igneous, and metamorphic-and its boundaries are delimited chiefly by the character and structure of its rocks.

The geologic structure of the Coastal Plain is simple. Beds of sedimentary rock dip gently seaward and are exposed in wide belts of successively older rocks from the coast to the fall line. Clays, sandstones, greensands, diatomaceous earth, and shell marl (Cretaceous and Tertiary) range from loose to well-indurated

Encyclopedia of Virginia

materials. The province contains true rocks in the geologic sense, although few of the formations are well consolidated. Superficial mantels of sand and gravel (Quaternary) occur along the main streams and the coast. Dismal Swamp, southwest of Norfolk, is underlain by peat.

By deep borings (2,251 feet) it has been proved that the basement rocks of the Coastal Plain are crystalline, like those of the Piedmont Province.

The Piedmont is predominately an area of very old (pre-Cambrian) crystalline rocks, both igneous and metamorphic. It abounds in granites, gneisses, schists, and greenstones. Slate (early Paleozoic), soapstone, and marble occur in many places. Metamorphic rocks have been so changed from their earlier condition that the character of many of the original rocks is indeterminate. The major types of rock masses extend northeast and southwest in long and relatively narrow belts. Broad elongate lowlands of general southwest trend are underlain by much younger (Triassic) red sandstone and shale. The most extensive belt of these formations occurs in the northwestern part of the Piedmont Province and in the Richmond Basin southwest of Richmond. The latter contains important bodies of coal and some natural coke.

While simple in its broad outlines, the structural arrangement of crystalline rocks in the Piedmont Province is complex in detail. The prevailing dip of foliation in the metamorphic rocks is toward the southeast. In places the schists and gneisses are much contorted. Granites and other igneous rocks have been intruded more or less along the trend (strike) of the foliation or grain of the older rocks. The grain of the province is northeast and southwest, with the different rocks in a somewhat belted type of arrangement. Numerous faults occur in parts of the province.

Rocks in the Blue Ridge Province are chiefly crystalline, such as granite, gneiss, and greenstone. Schists and altered rhyolite occur in the southwestern plateau portion. The northwest flank is covered by sandstone and quartzite (early Paleozoic) that dip under the Valley of Virginia.

The geologic structure, especially in the plateau part of the Blue Ridge, is somewhat similar to that of the Piedmont region, except that more of the rocks are in massive crystalline bodies, like granite and greenstone. The ridge part of the province in the north is a huge uphold of granite and greenstone that has been thrust northwestward for miles along a great fault.

The Valley and Ridge Province is underlain by sedimentary rocks (Paleozoic). The Valley of Virginia is dominantly a limestone (Paleozoic) region, although broad belts of shale are common. Adjoining ridges and those within the valley are capped with hard sandstone. Anthracitic coal occurs in the middle part, particularly in the vicinity of New River and Roanoke. In the Valley and Ridge sections to the west, beds of hard sandstone support the ridges along their crests. There are outcroppings of limestone and shale along their slopes, and most of the intermontane valleys are on shale or sandstone. Some valleys are dominantly limestone. Formations in the Appalachian Valley have a total thickness of about eight miles.

Geographical Configuration

Laterally the sedimentary strata of the Appalachian Valley have been squeezed into a series of great anticlines (upfolds) and synclines (downfolds), the folds generally being overturned toward the northwest and trending southwest parallel to the ridges and valleys. Many of them have been broken into great fractures or faults, so that large blocks or long thick horizontal slices of the earth's crust have been shoved miles to the northwest. These faults cause a marked repetition in the outcrop of various limestones and other formations and add to the valley's complexity of structure and diversity of topography.

In the order of their formation, the bedrocks of Virginia represent most of the periods in the four more recent eras of geologic time. The oldest, or pre-Cambrian rocks of igneous and metamorphic origin, are found at the surface only in the Piedmont region and in the Blue Ridge. An analysis of radioactive mineral from the Blue Ridge indicated that some of the rocks are eight hundred million years old. Paleozoic rocks are west of the Blue Ridge, except for small areas of older Paleozoic in the Piedmont. The upper Cambrian and part of the subsequent Ordovician limestone are sometimes designated collectively as 'valley limestone.' The Mesozoic rocks in Virginia crop out only in the Piedmont and along the western edge of the Coastal Plain. The Cenozoic is represented by Tertiary marine deposits and Quaternary sand and gravel. Most of the Coastal Plain is covered by unconsolidated Tertiary sands, clays, gravels, and marls, chiefly of Miocene age. To the Quaternary age belong upland sands and gravels scattered over the higher lands, as do lower terrace sands and gravels of the Chesapeake Bay region and the estuaries.

Fossil remains of marine invertebrates, such as corals, snails, clams, and crustacea, occur in many of the Paleozoic shales and limestones and the Valley and Ridge Province. Some of the limestones contain colonies of fossil seaweed. Of the Mesozoic era, when reptiles dominated land and sea, Virginia's fossils records are meager. Dinosaur footprints have been preserved in Triassic sandstones of Loudoun County. Scant records, too, exist of the vertebrates of the Cenozoic age, which saw the rise and dominance of mammals-although the sediments of the Coastal Plain have yielded teeth and vertebrae of whales, and there are fragmental remains of elephants in western Virginia. Some beds abound in invertebrate shells, the cliffs near Yorktown having yielded more than 100 species.

Fossil plants in Virginia are confined mainly to coal beds (the remains of swamp vegetation) and to the shales associated with such beds. They include types of ferns, rushes, and conifers that have, in the main, become extinct. One of the formations in the Coastal Plain contains a peculiar and industrially valuable earth, diatomite, composed of millions of tiny plants called diatoms.

Encyclopedia of Virginia

NATURAL RESOURCES

The diversified geography and topography of Virginia account for natural resources that are both varied and abundant. Many types of soils are present; water resources range from rushing mountain streams and underground reservoirs to deep navigable outlets to the sea; mineral deposits are numerous; plant and animal life thrives in great variety.

Soils : The soils of the Coastal Plain are of three general types. The most fertile is the black stiff loam of tidal lowgrounds. Though boggy in wet weather and impregnably hard in dry weather, this soil requires little fertilization. The light sandy loams just west of the lowgrounds are easily cultivated and yield readily to fertilization for the growing of truck crops. The still higher clay and sand loams of the Coastal Plain, even though impoverished, react favorably to crop rotation and produce a wide variety of staple and special crops.

The Virginia Piedmont lands are generally fertile. The limestone and a part of the clay lands produce bluegrass, grains, and fruits. Virginia's tobacco belt lies in the central and southern portions of the Piedmont. Limestone soils predominate in the valley areas west of the Blue Ridge. Toward the north in the Shenandoah Valley is the apple country of the State. Here also, along with grain, hay, and vegetables, are raised fine beef cattle, and poultry production is a profitable enterprise. In the southwestern section, the raising of livestock is of chief agricultural importance.

Soil conservation in Virginia has been largely concerned with the rehabilitation of lands impoverished by tobacco culture. Tidewater soils, exhausted in the Colonial period by intensive tobacco cultivation, were saved from utter ruin by the introduction of crop rotation and the use of marl as a neutralizing agent.

The present soil conservation problem centers in the Piedmont, where soils were depleted by the production of bright tobacco. Used in cigarette manufacture the world over, bright tobacco afforded an annual harvest of gold until the serious decline of prices in the late 1920's. The land on which tobacco had been grown, moreover, was unfit for subsistence crops. In limiting the tobacco crop to raise prices, some of the land was retired, hills were terraced, dikes were built in water courses, and legume crops were planted on acres once devoted to tobacco.

Erosion does comparatively little damage to the soils of the flat Coastal Plain or in the mountain region where outcropping strata and the quickgrowing bluegrass hold the precious top soil; but many clay hills of the Piedmont have been washed of their former fertility.

Water : Virginia has a tidal shore line of 1,280 miles and contains all or part of eight river systems. About 2,365 square miles of its area are covered with water.

The Potomac River-including the north and south forks of its tributary, the Shenandoah-has a drainage area of 5,960 square miles, and its tidal section is 117 miles long. The Rappahannock

Geographical Configuration

River system, of which the Rapidan is chief tributary, lies entirely in Virginia, with its headwaters in the Blue Ridge and a course stretching 105 miles to the fall line. All the James River system, descending from high Allegheny ridges to Hampton Roads, is in Virginia, except a few headwater creeks that extend into West Virginia. While the Chowan River itself lies in the Tidewater region of North Carolina, its three main tributaries, the Meherrin, the Nottoway, and the Blackwater, are Virginia streams. The Roanoke River, with the Dan as its principal tributary, also flows into North Carolina but has a course of 240 miles in Virginia, from the Valley of Virginia to the southeastern Piedmont. The New River (paradoxically one of the oldest rivers in North America) rises in western North Carolina and flows north and west to cut through the Valley Ridges across the Blue Ridge Plateau and the Valley of Virginia into West Virginia. The Holston, Clinch, and Powell Rivers, draining the southern part of the Valley of Virginia southwestward, are the State's principal tributaries of the Tennessee River system.

Uniform rainfall gives the numerous streams of Virginia a fairly even flow, and all the nontidal waters are suitable for ordinary industrial use. The steep gradient from headwaters in the mountains makes Virginia's larger streams a potential source of hydroelectric development with an estimated capacity of 459,000 horsepower.

Mineral Resources : Coal, the State's most important commercial mineral resources, occurs in three principal areas. The largest of these, the southwest Virginia field, on the eastern side of the Allegheny Plateau, covers 1,550 square miles and contains some 30 billion tons of bituminous coal. Next in importance is the Valley Field, in the Valley of Virginia, which covers 100 square miles and contains more than a billion tons of semianthracite coal. This latter field was the first to be mined in the United States (1750) but has been worked little since the opening of mines in the mountains (1880). Natural gas in commercial quantities is found in the southwestern part of the Valley of Virginia.

Next in importance is a wide variety of nonmetallic minerals used in building and manufacturing. Principally, these are limestone, dolomite, shale, and sandstone in the Valley and Ridge regions; granite on the eastern Blue Ridge slope, in the central Piedmont, and along the fall line; calcareous marl in the Tidewater; and brick clays widely distributed throughout the State.

Other nonmetallic minerals, not so general in their distribution, are salt and gypsum in southwest Virginia; glass sand in the Valley region; barite in southwest Virginia and the Piedmont; kaolin and black marble in the Shenandoah Valley; greenstone, slate, soapstone, and talc in the central Piedmont; feldspar, mica, and cyanide in the southern Piedmont; ocher in southwest Virginia and the Tidewater regions; and diatomite in the Tidewater.

Iron occurs in great quantities in Virginia than does any other metal, lower grades of ore being widespread in the Valley

Encyclopedia of Virginia

Ridges, the central Blue Ridge, and the western edge of the central and southern Piedmont. Manganese ores are common in the Valley Ridges and western Piedmont. Gold, the first to be mined in the United States, occurs in a middle belt through the northeastern Piedmont and at one place in the Blue Ridge Plateau. Lead and zinc occur in southwest Virginia; pyrite and pyrrhotite in the southern Blue Ridge Plateau and central Piedmont; and titanium in the Piedmont. Copper occurs in the southern Piedmont; arsenic, asbestos, and graphite in the southern and central Piedmont; nickel and cobalt in the southern Blue Ridge; and tin in the central Blue Ridge; but none of these appears in commercial quantities.

FLORA AND FAUNA

On the Coastal Plain in Virginia are vast stretches of pine woods, interspersed with hardwood trees and splashed in early spring by flowering redbud and dogwood. Broomsedge covers many impoverished field, and near the tidal rivers and inlets are acres of waving marsh grass. Hardwood and pine areas extend throughout the Piedmont, broken by hillsides where broomsedge and weeds provide scant coverings. In the mountains are great slopes and ridges of hardwood and small tracts of pine, spruce, and hemlock. At the higher levels, rhododendron and mountain laurel abound; and bluegrass carpets the uncultivated fields of the valleys.

Though the original timber has long since been cut and the subsequent growth periodically exploited, more than 65 per cent of Virginia's area still consists of woodland. Among the varieties of trees found in the State are twelve kinds of oak, five of pine, four of hickory, three each of cedar, maple, birch, and elm, and two each of walnut, locust, gum, and poplar. In the Coastal Plain, pines are of first commercial importance, but other trees having general distribution are oak, red, cedar, gum, poplar, beech, hickory, persimmon, ash, walnut, locust, dogwood, and redbud, with cypress and southern white cedar in isolated areas. The Piedmont forests contain oak, poplar, beech, gum, walnut, dogwood, redbud, persimmon, locust, and (less generally) red cedar and pine. The mountain forests are also principally of hardwood, containing oak, poplar, maple, beech, basswood, hickory, locust, walnut, red cedar, ash, dogwood, redbud, and cucumber magnolia. Pine, hemlock, and red spruce, though important, are less common in the mountains.

An adequate system of forest fire control has been developed. Individuals, corporations, and the State collectively maintain lookout towers and employ fire fighters. Two National forests, a National Park, and six State parks hold a vast area of the State's woodland in reserve.

The principal native grasses of Virginia are marsh, crab, wire, and blue grass. Marsh grass, limited to the salt flats of the Coastal Plain, serves as a natural protection against erosion caused by encroachment of the sea and provides valuable grazing.

Geographical Configuration

Crab grass on the arable lands of the coast is cut for hay. The wire grass indigenous to all sections and bluegrass in the mountains provide grazing and help prevent erosion.

Many wild flowers are indigenous to Virginia. On mountain and cliff are trailing arbutus, rhododendron, many kinds of azaleas, and mountain laurel. Peculiar to the Alleghenies are the Canby's mountain lover, an evergreen; St. John's wort, with its large pale-yellow blossom; the mountain spurge, its purple blooms hidden under low leaves; mountain mint or Virginia thyme with its lavender-tipped white flowers; and trailing wolfsbane. Among the more notable flowers characteristic of the lowland woods and fields are the abundant blue lobelia, which originated in Virginia; prolific and dainty quaker-ladies or bluets; sturdy erect blue lupine with blossoms similar to those of the wisteria vine, which is also abundant throughout the State; the poison-rooted May apple; the rare spring beauty; false rue anemone; morning glory; chicory, the root of which is often blended with coffee; lowland laurel; and delicate yellow dogtooth, Confederate, and wood violets.

Though Virginia's animal life is still varied and plentiful, civilization has levied a costly toll upon many species of earlier fauna. Some mountainous regions in the western part of the State are still primitive enough to shelter a small herd of elk, a few black bears, and an occasional wildcat; and the Dismal Swamp is still the habitat of bears and wildcats. But the bison that once fed on Virginia bluegrass are gone; beavers, wolves, and panthers are extinct. The otter and the mink have dwindled to an alarming degree and survive mainly along isolated water courses. Deer, because of conservation measures and their own shy habits, are increasing; and the prolific muskrat is safe despite much trapping. The fox, raccoon, opossum, squirrel, mole, rat, and mouse have adapted themselves to civilization; and so, in a more limited way, have the skunk and the ground hog. Public opinion and restricted fox hunting protect the red and gray fox. Protective laws have saved the raccoon from extinction, and the unobtrusive opossum has managed to survive in spite of the epicures who would garnish him with sweet potatoes. By canny foraging on farm gardens, the rabbit still maintains a comfortable livelihood.

Game birds flourish under a protective conservation program. The bobwhite is widely distributed throughout the State, the wary turkey still inhabits the woods; the ruffed grouse is found in hilly areas; mourning doves and woodcock, though reduced in number, exist in nearly every section of the State; and sora appear annually in the coastal marshes.

Although only a few game waterfowl nest in Virginia, others migrating to the South either spend the winter or find an intermediate resting place here. Gray and black mallards, as well as wood or summer ducks, nest in the State or pass through on their semiannual journeys; canvasbacks, shovelers, goldeneyes, redheads, scaups or bluebills, and many of the lesser diving ducks winter in Virginia waters; the mallard, black duck, and pintail are plentiful in marshes and shallow waters; Canada geese and brant remain all winter on coastal feeding grounds. Of nongame waterfowl, bitterns, herons, several varieties of gulls, and numerous shore birds haunt the tidal waters and marshes.

Bald and golden eagles are now restricted to a few coastal and mountain areas. Virginia has more than a dozen species of hawks, ranging from the large marsh hawk to the diminutive sparrow hawk; and eight species of owls, from the great horned to the small screech owl. Hawks and owls are commonly killed without discrimination in Virginia, though only five of the hawk species and one of the owl are considered more destructive than beneficial. The turkey buzzard and the black buzzard, despite their attacks on small farm animals and their reputation as spreaders of disease, are tolerated as scavengers.

Great numbers of song birds make Virginia their home. The belligerent English sparrow dominates bird life near human habitation, and his many cousins are common over the countryside. The mockingbird sings both night and day; but his cousin, the catbird, is a temperamental artist who varies his monotonous grating cry only on special occasions. Robins and bluebirds are ever present in the fields and woods. Other birds common in Virginia are the crow, bluejay, cowbird, meadow or field lark, oriole, purple martin, cliff and barn swallows, house and marsh wrens, nuthatch, titmouse, several species of woodpecker and tanager, chuck-will's-widow, whippoorwill, nighthawk or bullbat, chimney swift, hummingbird, kingbird or bee martin, starling, wood thrush, and the glorious cardinal or redbird.

Virginia's poisonous snakes are the pit viper or rattlesnake, the copperhead, the cottonmouth moccasin, and the water moccasin. The rattlesnake, found in the western mountains and in some isolated eastern regions, is a dark brown or yellowish color with contrasting darker spots. The bronze and yellow-banded copperhead has a rather wide distribution and is the State's most treacherous serpent. The cottonmouth moccasin, short, thick, and vicious-looking, is restricted to the Dismal Swamp.

Of the nonpoisonous group, the black snake is the most common, but blue and black races are particularly prevalent. These constrictors are valuable as enemies of small rodents. The black chicken snake, the mountain or pilot black snake, and the corn snake, all larger than the racer, are found in the mountains. The king snake, another of the constrictor group, feeds on other snakes as well as on rodents. Other harmless serpents are two species of garter snake, the milk snake or cowsucker, green snake, water snake, ringneck snake, spreading adder or puff snake, and pine snake-largest of all Virginia snakes.

In the category of turtles, the diamondback terrapin, green sea turtle, and snapping turtle are prized as food. More common are several kinds of mud turtles and the dry-land box turtle. Among the frogs are the spring peeper, green frog, tree frog, toad-frog, and bullfrog. Several kinds of lizards and salamanders inhabit the state.

Inland waters contain bass of three kinds-the rock bass or redeye, the smallmouthed black bass in the clear highland streams, and the largemouthed black bass in the sluggish rivers

Geographical Configuration

and ponds of the flat country. Throughout the entire State are bream, silver and yellow perch, pike, carp, and common catfish. Only in the New River, however, is found the giant Mississippi catfish. Speckled and rainbow trout are restricted to certain mountain streams, as are the few pickerel in the State.

The salt-water fish, besides being of great commercial importance, include several varieties caught for sport. Most common in tidal waters are the croaker, hogfish, spot, white perch, gray and spotted trout, striped bass or rockfish, alewife, menhaden, flounder, bluefish, shad, catfish, eels, angelfish, dogfish, and shark. Sturgeon and sheepshead, once common, are now scarce. The shellfish of importance are oysters, clams, scallops, blue crabs, and shrimps. All the salt-water bottoms contain oyster beds. Clams are restricted to the lower regions of Chesapeake Bay, and scallops to the seacoast inlets. Blue crabs and shrimp are found in tidal waters.

PRE-HISTORY
AND ARCHEOLOGY

At the dawn of the seventeenth century, three distinct groups of Indian tribes, representing three different linguistic stocks, occupied the territory that is now Virginia. Along the coast and up the tidal rivers to their falls were the many palisaded settlements of the Algonquian group, the Powhatan confederacy, enemy of the Siouan stock composed of the Monacan and Manahoac federations that spread from the banks of the upper James and the headwaters of the Potomac and Rappahannock Rivers to the Allegheny Mountains. The bellicose and scattered Iroquoian stock was represented by the Conestoga (Susquehanna) tribe of nearly 600 warriors living in fortified towns near the headwaters of the Chesapeake Bay; the Rickohockan, or Rechahecrian (who are identified with the Cherokee by most ethnologists, as the Yuchi by John Reed Swanton), occupying the mountain valleys of the southwest; and the Nottoway in the southeast. During their first years in Virginia the colonists of the London Company found along the rivers and coast some 200 villages under the leadership of Wahunsonacock, known to the colonists as Powhatan. This chief of an Algonquian confederation, which consisted of about 2,400 warriors, had inherited the territories of the Powhatan, Arrowhatock, Appamatuck, Pamunkee, Youghtanund, and Mattapament, to which, by later conquest, he had added other tribes, bringing the number under his dominion up to 30. Of the 36 'King's howses' or tribal capitals, Werowocomoco, on the left bank of the York River, was Powhatan's favorite, and the one in which, as a prisoner in 1608, Captain John Smith first saw the powerful chieftain.

> Arriving at *Weramocomoco* (Werowocomoco) their Emperour proudly lying uppon a Bedstead a foote high, upon tenne or twelve Mattes, richly hung with manie Chaynes of great Pearles about his necke, and covered with a great Covering of *Rahaughcums*. At (his heade sat a woman, at his feete another; on each side sitting uppon a Matte uppon the ground, were raunged his chiefe men on each side the fire, tenne in a ranke, and behinde them as many yong women, each (with) a great Chaine of white Beades over their shoulders, their heades painted in redde: and (Powhatan) with such a grave Maiesticall countenance, as drave me into admiration to see such state in a naked Salvage.

Displacement of the Indians began almost simultaneously with the finishing of the first stockade at Jamestown. Before the colony was two years old, the principal Indian settlements had been seized, Powhatan had withdrawn to a remote town on the Chickahominy River, and the Indians were so intent on revenge that no Englishman was safe outside the fort. Temporary suspension of hostilities, however, was established by the marriage of John Rolfe and Powhatan's daughter, Pocahontas, in 1614, after which the colonists 'had friendly trade and commerce, as well with *Powhatan* himselfe, as all his subjects.'

In the treaty of peace that followed, the Indians acknowledged the British as their masters. But the chief of the Pamunkey tribe, Opechancanough, who succeeded Powhatan in reality though not nominally, was determined to annihilate the white invaders. In 1622 his carefully planned attack resulted in the massacre of some 350 settlers. The colonists who escaped, forewarned by a converted Indian boy, retaliated at once, and during the autumn of 1622 and the following winter killed so many Indians and destroyed so many of their settlements that for more than 20 years there was a truce. But in 1644, Opechancanough, now old and feeble, decided upon a last effort. In the uprising that began on April 18 with a sudden massacre along the whole border, the Indians were routed and Opechancanough was captured and brought to Jamestown, where he was murdered by an outraged colonist. In October 1646 his successor made a treaty of submission by which the Indians agreed to abandon everything below the falls of the James and Pamunkey Rivers and to restrict themselves on the north to the territory between the York and the Rappahannock.

The Jamestown settlers' contact with the Indians of Siouan stock was limited. A week after landing, on May 21, 1607, Captain John Smith with a party of 23 pushed up the James to the falls, where they were told by Pawatah (Powhatan) that it was a 'Daye and a halfe Iorney to Monanacah . . . his Enmye,' who 'came Downe at the fall of the leafe and invaded his Countrye.' In the autumn of 1608 Captain Christopher Newport, 'with 120 chosen men,' went up 'fortie myles' past the falls and discovered on the south bank of the James two Monacan towns. The first, Mowhemenchouch (Mowhemcho), was an open settlement, through which John Lederer passed in 1670, calling it Mahock, which Francis Louis Michel, a visitor in 1672, called Maningkinton, and which a Huguenot colony took possession of in 1699. It later became Monacan Town. The second village, 14 miles distant, was Massinacack. In August 1608 Captain Smith with 12 men and the Indian guide Mosco, 'a lusty Salvage of *Wighcocomoco,*' ascended the Rappahannock, had an encounter with Manahoac Indians (of whom some 12 tribes wandered over the Rapidan-Rappahannock area of the Piedmont section), and from an Indian named Amoroleck received the information about the Siouan tribes that is contained in his *Description of Virginia* 1612): Upon the head of the river of *Toppahanock* (Rappahannock) is a people called *Mannahoacks.* To these are contributers the *Tauxanias,* the *Shackaconias,* the *Ontponeas,* the *Tegninatoes,* the *Whonkenteases,* the *Stegarakes,* the *Hassinnungaes,* and divers others; all confederats with the *Moncacans,* though many different in language, and be very barbarous, living for most part of wild beasts and fruits.

Pre-History and Archeology

The Monacan confederacy, dwelling 'upon the head of the Powhatans' along the James above the falls, consisted, according to Smith's enumeration, of the Monacan proper, 'the *Mowhemenchughes,* the *Massinnacacks,* the *Monahassanughs,* the *Monasickapanoughs,* ' together with other tribes not named. The 'chiefe habitation ' of this confederacy of five tribes, whose generic name of Monacan applied also to the territory they occupied, was Rasauweak (Rassawek), at the confluence of the James and Rivanna Rivers. The allied Monacan and Manahoac confederacies were constantly at war with the Powhatan and the Iroquois (the Massawomek of John Smith and the Massawomees of Jefferson), 'their most mortall enemies.'

Banded into a league late in the sixteenth century, the powerful Iroquois began thereafter their gradual descent upon these weaker tribes of the south, annihilating some and causing others to flee, eventually to merge for protection-thus completely shattering the tribal pattern existing in 1607. About 1656, 'the Mahocks and Nahyssans,' according to Lederer, but more probably the Shackoconian tribe of the Manahoac confederacy, seeking a new dwelling place, 'sett downe near the falls of James river, to the number of six or seaven hundred.' In an attempt to dispel them, the English, who were joined by the Pamunkey under Totopotomoi, precipitated what was perhaps the bloodiest Indian battle ever fought on the soil of Virginia, the last great fight between Siouan and Algonquian tribes. The Powhatan, who had suffered even more at the hands of the English than at those of the Iroquois, became by 1665 mere dependents of the colony, submissive to the stringent laws enacted that year, which compelled them to accept chiefs appointed by the governor. After the Treaty of Albany in 1684, the Powhatan confederacy all but vanished.

The exploratory trip made in 1670 by John Lederer, a German who received a 'commission of discovery' from Governor Berkeley, lifted the veil that had so long covered the activity of these Siouan tribes. Drastic changes, caused by the hostile wedge formed by the Iroquois in the north and by the English in the east, had taken place among the confederations in a little more than half a century. Leaving the falls of the James, Lederer went southwest 'toward the Monakins,' then 'from Mahock' (Mohemcho), the tribe's town, 'into the province of Carolina,' finding in 'these parts . . . formerly possessed by the Tacci, alias Dogi,' the tribe of Nahyssan (the Monahassanugh of John Smith) still living at their village on the James. This tribe, called Hanohaskie by Thomas Batts (1671), became in later narratives the Tutelo (Totero or Todirish-roone), a generic Iroquoian name applicable to all Siouan tribes in Virginia and Carolina. A subtribe of the Tutelo was the Saponi (the Monasickapanough of John Smith), who had moved from the Rivanna to a tributary of the upper Roanoke, where their town of Sapon was visited first by Lederer and then by Batts. Other tribes of Siouan stock were the Nuntaneuck (the Tauxanias of Smith); the Akenatzy (Occaneechi), who lived on an island in the Roanoke River; the Managog (Manahoac), who had but lately roamed the upper Piedmont region; and the Monakin or Monacan, who occupied the village of Mohemcho. All these tribes were of Siouan stock.

Encyclopedia of Virginia

Between 1671 and 1701 the Saponi and Tutelo tribes withdrew from their position at the base of the mountains, directly in the path of the Iroquois, and settled on two islands in the Roanoke River near the one inhabited by their kinsmen the Occaneechi, an important tribe whose island was the great trading center 'for all the Indians for at least 500 miles.' The Occaneechi's wealth, however, was their undoing. In 1676, the Susquehanna (Conestoga), driven from their Chesapeake Bay home by the Iroquois and the English, fled to the Occaneechi, whom they tried to dispossess. In the battle that ensued, the Susquehanna were driven from the island. In May of the same year, Nathaniel Bacon, Jr., with 200 Virginians, arrived there in pursuit of the Susquehanna, joined the Occaneechi, and put the Susquehanna to flight. The latter settled near the Nottoway tribe, their Iroquois kinsmen, and became the Meherrin. Afterwards the whites turned on the Occaneechi, whereupon this tribe abandoned its island home, fled into Carolina, and eventually combined with the Saponi, Tutelo, and other tribes of Siouan stock in a body numbering about 750 persons. In 1705, according to Robert Beverley, the Indian population within the explored portions of Virginia numbered fewer than 500 able-bodied men, of whom 350 were remnants of tribes once belonging to the Powhatan confederacy.

Through the persuasion of Governor Spotswood, who hoped to protect them from the Iroquois and at the same time to make them a barrier between the Virginia settlements and the hostile southern tribes, the Saponi, Tutelo, ' Stukarocks,' and federated tribes moved in a consolidated group from Carolina to the vicinity of Fort Christanna, shortly after the opening of the Tuscarora War (1711-12). Here Spotswood, to secure the fidelity of the smaller tribes, began a school to which were admitted as pupils-and hostages-the children of chiefs. But this seed of civilization fell on sterile ground. The Saponi, or, as they were then commonly called, the Christanna Indians, were still at war. Quarrels persisted between them and the neighboring Nottoway and Meherrin; while the more distant Iroquois, who cherished toward these people 'so inveterate an enmity' that it could be 'extinguished ' only by their 'total Extirpation,' continued their attacks.

Finally, Governor Spotswood, hoping to put an end to the warfare between the Iroquois and the southern tribes, in 1722 promoted the Albany (N.Y.) Conference, at which a peace treaty was signed by the Five Nations of the Iroquois and their allies, the Tuscarora, Shawnee, and others on the one hand, and by Virginia and its tributary Indians on the other. Thus the long war ended and peace finally came in Virginia to 'the Nottoways, Meherrins, Nansemonds, Pamunkeys, Chichominys, and the Christanna Indians'-called 'Todirich-roones' by the Iroquois, and comprising 'the *Saponies, Ochineechees, Stenkenocks* (Stegarakes), *Meipontskys, (Ontponeas) & Toteroes,* ' all of whom were grouped at 'Sapponey Indian town,' which was 'about a musket-shot from the fort.' Dissatisfied with the proximity of white settlements and at peace with the Iroquois, the restless Saponi, Tutelo, and such allied tribes as the Occaneechi and the

Pre-History and Archeology

Stegarake (only survivor of the Manahoac confederacy) abandoned the settlement near Fort Christanna about 1740, went first to Pennsylvania and then to New York, where they placed themselves under the protection of their traditional enemy, becoming in 1753 a part of the Six Nations.
 During the first half of the eighteenth century the Shenandoah Valley-last frontier of Virginia-was the hunting ground of such nonresident Indian tribes as the Delaware, Catawba, and Shawnee, among whom there was continual warfare. After the completion of a chain of forts along the border for the protection of white settlers, the Indians suddenly withdrew from the valley in 1754, but returned in 1756 at the beginning of the French and Indian War. Depredations continued until the end of the war in 1763, after which the valley was left in peace. The Cherokee, as the white settlements pressed upon them in their mountain fastness, moved gradually westward.
 In 1768, Governor Francis Fauquier, answering a question propounded by the Lords of Trade and Plantation, revealed the state to which the aborigines of Virginia had been reduced. 'The number of Indians residing in the known parts of this Colony,' he wrote, 'is very small, there being only some remains of the Eastern Shore and Pamunkey Indians, who are so far civilized as to wear European dress, and in part follow the customs of the common Planters.
 Besides these there are some of the Nottoways, Meherins, Tuncaroras and Saponeys; who tho' they live in peace in the midst of us, lead in great measure the Life of wild Indians. The number of all these decrease very fast owing to their great fondness for Rum.'
 These remnants were the amalgamation of some of the numerous tribes that had roamed the forests of Virginia. The Nottoway, strong during the first, settlement period and greatly outnumbering the Powhatan in the provincial census of 1669, were by 1820 reduced to 27 persons, of whom only three spoke, the tribal language. The Meherrin, the other Virginia tribe of Iroquoian stock, equaled in number the Pamunkey-originally the strongest tribe of the Powhatan confederacy-in 1699, after which they rapidly vanished. The Nansemond tribe of the Powhatan confederacy, composed of some 300 warriors in 1622, had dwindled to 45 men by 1669. In 1744 they joined the Nottoway. Today, in Virginia, there are several groups and scattered families of Indian descent, comprising 779 persons. The State recognized three tribes: the Pamunkey, the Mattaponi, and the Chickahominy.
 Description of the sedentary Powhatan Indians in their 'pallizadoed townes' formed much of the substance of early writings on Virginia. 'Their habitations or townes' were 'for the most part by the rivers, or not far distant from fresh springs, commonly upon a rise of a hill.' Many settlements, particularly those on the Bay, were protected by encircling palisades, as depicted in the water-color drawings of Secotan and Pomeioc (in Carolina) made in 1585 by 'Maister Jhon White, an English paynter.' Where there was less danger of attack, the habitations of the Algonquian spread out unprotected on the river shore. Werowocomoco, Powhatan's favorite, village, and Kecoughtan (at

or near the present site of Hampton) were typical. '*Kegquouhtan* . . *Virginia,* 'pleasantly seated upon three acres of ground, uppon a plaine, halfe invironed with a great Bay of the great River . . . the Towne adioyning to the maine by a necke of Land of sixtie yardes.' 'Placed' under the covert of trees,' the houses-all alike, 'scattered without forme of a street,' and 'warm as stoves, albeit very smoakey'--were like 'garden arbours.' A framework of poles was set in two parallel rows inclosing the floor space. Opposite poles were bent over and lashed to one another in pairs to form a series of arches of equal height, and these arches were joined by horizontal poles placed at intervals and securely tied together 'with roots, bark, or the green wood of the white oak run into thongs.' Each of the flat ends had a door hung with mats. Outside stood a wooden mortar and pestle for grinding corn. The smoke from the fire kindled on the ground inside escaped through a small vent in the roof. The coverings were generally of bark or mats of rushes, occasionally of boughs. The ordinary dwelling, which housed from 6 to 20 people, contained but one room, on each side of which were platforms or bedsteads about a foot high and covered with 'fyne white mattes' and skins. In 'square plotts of cleered grownd' near these bark-covered houses, the women raised tobacco and such vegetables as corn, beans, an herb called 'melden,' squash, 'pumpons and a fruit like unto a musk millino.' Maize was so important that platforms were erected in the fields, where watchers were stationed to protect the crop from birds, and the shelled corn filled storage baskets that took 'upp the best part of some of their houses.' Among the roots used for food were groundnuts *(Apios tuberosa)* and tuckahoe *Peltandra Virginica* and *Orontium aquaticum).* In March and April the Powhatan lived on their 'weeres,' feeding on 'fish, turkies and squirrells,' the fish being caught in fish dams or shot with 'long arrows tyed in a line'; in May they 'set their corne'; and in the 'tyme of their huntings' they gathered 'into companyes' with their families and went 'toward the mountaines,' where there was 'plenty of game.'

The empire ruled over by Powhatan was reduced to subdivisions, each with a governmental hierarchy consisting of the *cockarouse* or sachem, the *werowance* or war leader, the tribal council, and the priests. Nor did the scheme vary under Opechancanough. 'This revolted Indian King with his squaw,' wrote Thomas Martin in 1622, 'commaundeth 32 Kingdomes under him. Everye Kingdome contayneigne ye quantitie of one of ye shires here in England. Everye such Kingdome hath one speciall Towne seated upon one of ye three greate Rivers . . . ' Dwellings and gardens were owned privately, but all other property was held in common.

Typical of the Iroquoian type of town was the village of the Nottoway, which William Byrd visited in 1728. A strong palisade, about 10 feet high, surrounded a quadrangle dotted with long communal 'cabins . . . arched at the top, and covered with bark.' Inside there was no furniture except 'hurdles' for repose. The fortification served as a place of refuge for members of the tribe living in outlying districts. The towns of the Siouan tribes were

Pre-History and Archeology

similar. Within the inclosure of those that were palisaded stood the prominent round 'town house' surrounded by the 'arbour-like' dwellings of the people. The Cherokee towns spread out along the banks of mountain streams or in a valley. Close by the dwellings of logs chinked with clay stood a conical earth-covered lodge known as the 'winter hot house.' On an artificial mound in the center of the village was the large oblong 'council house,' center of all tribal ceremonies.

The male Indian costume consisted of garments of skins or woven fiber and moccasins; the women wore skirts of fringed deerskin or woven silkgrass fiber (silk weed or Indian hemp, *Asclepias pulchra*), which reached from the waist to the middle of the thigh. Members of both sexes wore in winter mantles made of skins and feathers. Feathered headgear, necklaces of clam shells, beads, or pearls, copper pendants, wampum head rings, and body tattooing completed the garish personal decoration. 'The Siouan Indians of 'Sapponey Town,' visited by Byrd in 1728, had probably varied little since early days in their traditional war dress. With 'feathers in their hair and run through their ears, their faces painted with blue and vermillion, their hair cut in many forms,' they were 'really . . . very terrible.' Both men and women greased their bodies and heads with bear's oil or walnut oil mixed with paint, either of which yielded an 'ugly smell.' The 'sweating-houses,' little huts built with wattles, were also tribal survivals. Heated by red-hot pebbles, they were used by sick Indians to sweat out maladie,'a remedy . . . for all distempers.'

The handicrafts were exclusively womans' province---the making of wooden dishes and trays, 'earthern pottes,' and the thread spun from 'barks of trees, deare sinews, or a kind of grasse they call *Pemmenaw,* ' which was used variously as 'lines for angles,' 'nets for fishin,' sewing the deerskin mantles, and the making of baskets and 'aprons . . . women wear about their middles, for decency's sake.'

In their monotheistic religion, according to Lederer, the Indians worshiped *Okee,* called also *Mannith,* the 'creator of all things.' 'To him alone the high priest or *Periku'* offered sacrifices. 'The government of mankind' was assigned to 'lesser deities, as *Quiacosough* and *Tagkanysough* -that is, good and evil spirits.' Smith, however, says 'their chief God' was 'the Devil, him they call Okee.'

Burial customs varied among the different tribes. Within most of the temples were the image of Okee and the sepulchers of kings. The Algonquian buried ordinary members of the tribe in pits; while the bodies of the chiefs were disemboweled, dried, stuffed with sand, wrapped in skins and mats, and then laid in the temple. Henry Spelman, who lived among tribes along the Potomac prior to 1610, described a burial resembling the type used by Indians of the Plains. The body, wrapped in mats, was laid on a scaffold about three or four yards high. Ossuaries were common among the southern Algonquian and the Siouan tribes of the Piedmont. The bones of the dead, in a reburial ceremony, were deposited in great pits until a huge mound was formed.

Today, along the shores of Chesapeake Bay and the banks of many of its tributaries are heaps of oyster shells, containing bits of pottery and stone implements, which mark the position of many ancient Algonquian settlements, some having flourished long after 1607. Westward, along the valley of the James from the falls to the mountains, in the section once dominated by the Siouan tribes, are traces of their village and campsites on the banks of streams, where fragments of pottery and stone implements are scattered over the surface. The same district contains soapstone quarries and occasionally a macabre ossuary. In the Rappahannock-Rapidan area most of the mortars, long cylindrical pestles, hammers, discoidal stones, and pipes have been garnered; but occasionally axes, projectile points, and bits of pottery are brought to the surface by freshets or turned up by the plow.

HISTORY

When on May 14, 1607 the *Sarah Constant, Goodspeed,* and *Discovery* landed at Jamestown the colonists sent by the Virginia Company of London, years of futile effort to achieve British colonization in America were terminated in the establishment of a permanent settlement in the New World. All North America not Spanish or French was then called Virginia, in honor of the Virgin Queen. In 1578 Sir Humphrey Gilbert had obtained authority from Elizabeth to colonize lands on the Western Hemisphere not already claimed by any Christian prince or people, but he had failed to plant an enduring settlement. Groups of adventurers sent out by Sir Walter Raleigh either returned disheartened to England or mysteriously disappeared.

In 1606, however, King James granted a joint charter to two companies, one, with headquarters in London, authorized to settle southern Virginia; and the other, with headquarters in Plymouth, authorized to settle northern Virginia; but neither to plant within 100 miles of the other. The expeditions sent out by the Plymouth Company met with failure, but the London Company established the settlement at Jamestown. The years between 1607 and 1624, encompassing the overlordship of the Virginia Company of London, assured the permanence of the first English colony in America.

On April 26, 1607 (O.S.) the colonists landed on a point of land they called Cape Henry, opposite another point they named Cape Charles, honoring two sons of their king. An indication of future trouble came toward evening when a band of Indians arrived 'creeping upon all foure from the Hills, like Beares, with their Bowes in their mouthes.' The adventurers ascended the river and landed at a place they named 'James Towne' to honor the king himself.

Leadership aboard the three little boats left much to be desired; the men had quarreled grievously among themselves; malaria lurked in the marshy lands; and supplies were insufficient. John Smith, the most able man in the company and the one fitted for almost any emergency by a life of incredible adventure, was in chains when the little band reached Virginia. Fortunately, however, the opening of the sealed orders of the king named him a member of the council along with Edward Maria Wingfield, Christopher Newport, Bartholomew Gosnold, John Ratcliffe, John Martin, and George Kendall. The incompetent Wingfield was made president of the council. Smith demanded trial for the charges that had been preferred against him, was released, and by force of personality became the acknowledged leader. On June 22, Newport sailed for England, leaving in Virginia 100 men, more than half of whom were 'gentlemen,' unfit for the tasks involved in making a wilderness habitable. Bickering was the order of the day. In September Wingfield was deposed; and Ratcliffe, who subsequently proved himself unequal to the responsibility, was elected president of the council. Whether or not credence can be given to the story of Pocahontas's saving John Smith's life, there is no doubt that Smith became the hero of Jamestown, exploring the new land, wheedling supplies from the Indians, and effectively using the strong arm in emergencies.

The London Company, with stockholders looking toward gains that might be derived from the finding of a passage to the South Sea and from the discovery of precious metals in the New World, was guilty of inadequate stewardship. The 'First Supply,' brought by Newport on January 2, 1607 (January 12, 1608, N.S.), contained insufficient provisions and 70 new colonists. Likewise Newport's 'Second Supply,' arriving in September of the same year, bringing again some 70 settlers, added little to the welfare of the colony. Then it was that John Smith, having been chosen president of the council, composed the letter known as 'Smith's Rude Answer,' in which he replied to the London Company's demand that the colonists send commodities sufficient to pay the cost of the voyage, a lump of gold, assurance that they had found the South Sea, and one member of the lost Roanoke Colony. He wrote:

"When you send againe I entreat you rather send but thirty Carpenters, husbandmen, gardiners, fishermen, blacksmiths, masons and diggers up of trees, roots, well provided; than a thousand of such as we have: for except wee be able both to lodge them and feed them, the most will consume with want of necessaries before they can be made good for anything."

Chiefly because of Smith's leadership, most of the 200 settlers survived the winter and in the spring set about planting and building cheerfully enough. In August seven of the nine ships that had left England with Sir Thomas Gates landed their colonists at Jamestown. In October John Smith, having been severely injured, returned to England for medical treatment, and the settlers faced the long and terrible winter of 1609-10 without competent leadership. Supplies were soon exhausted; no one was capable of intimidating or cajoling the Indians; the water was unfit for drinking; 'sicknesse' took its ghastly toll. In May when Gates, whose ship had been wrecked on the Bermudas, reached Jamestown as first governor, he found only a few wrecked survivors. Five hundred strong at the beginning of winter, the colonists, numbering but 65 pitiable creatures, started back to England on June 7, 1610. They had reached Mulberry Island, 14 miles distant, when Lord De la Warre arrived with supplies and new settlers. All turned back, weary but determined to carry on.

The kindly De la Warre, returning to England in the spring of 1611, left as deputy governor George Percy, succeeded soon by Sir Thomas Dale, whose absolution the colonists found difficult to endure. Meanwhile, by two clever strokes, John Rolfe became the

History

savior of Virginia: in 1612 he introduced the cultivation of tobacco, ending the futile search for gold; and in 1614 he married Pocahontas, effecting a convenient alliance with the Powhatan confederacy. George Yeardley, who became deputy governor in 1616, set up the first windmill in America, imported a herd of blooded cattle, turned his attention to the fertilization of the soil, and encouraged the cultivation of tobacco. But Sir Samuel Argall, appointed in May 1617 virtually reduced the colonists to the status of slaves until his flagrant misconduct caused his removal.

By April 1619 the colony under Sir George Yeardley, now governor, had apparently achieved a degree of stability that augured well for continued prosperity. Plantations had been established eastward and westward on both sides of the James River. A few women had crossed the Atlantic to convert the wilderness into a home, and plans were afoot for the sending of 150 maids, who arrived by 1621 to become wives of the settlers. From a Dutch man-of-war were obtained in 1619 the first blacks landed in Virginia, 20, who were received as indentured servants and not as slaves for life.

VIRGINIA ACHIEVES REPRESENTATIVE GOVERNMENT

But the most far-reaching event of 1619 was the meeting of the House of Burgesses, the first democratically-elected legislative body to convene in the New World. Each of the 11 duly constituted plantations sent two members to represent it in this epoch making body. The early deliberations of the burgesses centered about education. In 1618 the City of Henricus had been selected as suitable site for a proposed university. The East India School, which was to be established at Charles City Point, was planned to prepare students for the college; money had been subscribed for both institutions; and the revenues from an iron foundry at Falling Creek were to be used for the support of the university.

Representative government in Virginia, however, had come through an evolutionary process. The charter of 1606, giving to the Plymouth and London Companies authority to colonize Virginia between 34 and 45 north, provided for a superior council in England appointed by the king, and a local governing council appointed by the superior council, the local council to elect its own president. The charter gave to the colonists small hope of gain, for the property, held in common stock, belonged to the London Company. The second charter, however, obtained on May 23, 1609, and drafted by Sir Edwin Sandys, leader of the Liberal Party in Parliament, gave the London Company direct administration of the colony and power to prescribe the form of government to be established, but was less democratic than the first in that the governor was to be appointed by the council in London and not by the council in Virginia. The territory, redefined, had a frontage 200 miles south and 200 miles north of Point Comfort, and extended 'up into the land, throughout from sea to sea, west and northwest.'

Almost at once the government of the colonists became the talking point of liberals in Parliament, who wanted to increase the rights enjoyed by British subjects in the face of Stuart absolutism. It was under the more Liberal charter of 1612, also drafted by Sandys, that the colonists were able to achieve representative government. More important, however, were the reaffirmation of those privileges the second charter had granted and the clear statement that all laws governing Virginia, were to be made by the London Company. The execution of the order was delayed, however, by Argall, who arrived as deputy governor in May 1617; connived with Sir Robert Rich in England to plunder the 'common stock'; and continued martial law in the colony. As Lord De la Warre, sent by the London Company with authority to arrest Argall, died on his way across the ocean, it was not until the arrival of Yeardley, on April 19, 1619, that the new government was put into effect, incorporating the principles of 'the Great charter of privileges, orders, and laws' drawn up in 1618 by Sir Edwin Sandys and Sir Thomas Smyth. Settlers were given their own tracts of land; martial law and common holding came to an end; lands to be tilled by servants during indentureship were laid out for the support of officials, in order to relieve the people of taxation 'as much as may be'; four 'corporacouns' were constituted, each with a proposed capital city; and through the creation of the House of Burgesses the colonists shared in making the laws.

Soon after affairs had begun to run smoothly in the colony, Virginia narrowly escaped all invasion of the Pilgrim Fathers, whose expedition, financed mainly by members of the London Company, was authorized to settle south of the Hudson River in southern Virginia. Thrown off their course, the Pilgrims set foot on a rock off the coast of northern Virginia. So did chance take a hand in determining the course of history.

A 'deadly stroake' was dealt the southern colony in 1622 when the Indians attempted by wholesale butchery to rid the country of white invaders. From the marriage of John Rolfe and Pocahontas in 1614, till the death of Powhatan in 1618, a state of comparative peace had emboldened the colonists to spread their plantations along both banks of the James River and to neglect their stockades. But the implacable Opechancanough, who had succeeded Powhatan as chief of the Indian confederacy, was scheming with diabolical cleverness. On March 22, 1622, at precisely the same hour the Indians struck along a 140-mile front. Three hundred and forty-seven colonists were killed instantly and 18 died later, reducing the settlement by more than a third. Jamestown suffered less, however, than the outlying plantations, for Chanco, a converted Indian, working at the plantation of Richard Pace across the river, informed his master of the plot. Though the surviving settlers did not desert Virginia and though others arrived almost at once, it was many years before the colony recovered from the disaster. Plans were abandoned for the East India School and the university, which were to be established to Christianize and educate the Indians.

History

The days of the Virginia Company of London, moreover, were numbered. The widening breach between the liberals and the king had been reflected in James's denunciation of Sir Edwyn Sandys. In answer to the king's command in 1620, 'Choose the devil if you will, but not Sir Edwin Sandys' as company treasurer, Sandys stepped aside in favor of his friend, the Earl of Southampton, whom the king found equally unacceptable. It was Sandys, however, who drew up the liberal instrument known as the Virginia Constitution of 1621. In 1622 the king granted the London Company a monopoly of the sale of tobacco in England. The condition that 40,000 pounds of Spanish tobacco be also imported was not satisfactory to Spain, whose favor James sought as he looked toward an alliance between his son and the Infanta. Through the scheming of the wily Count of Gondomar, Spanish ambassador, all investigation was ordered of the London Company both in England and Virginia. When the commission returned from the colony in June 1624 with an unfavorable report, only partially true, the King's Bench revoked the charter of the London Company and Virginia became a royal colony, extending from modern Pennsylvania to Florida and indefinitely westward.

Anglo-Saxon love of personal liberty continued to express itself in the Virginia colony. All the revolutionary pronouncements that emanated from Virginia between 1763 and 1776 had their antecedents in the period that immediately followed the dissolution of the London Company. Just before the revocation of the company's charter the general assembly had resolved, forecasting the words of Parliament's petition to Charles five years later and in amazing prophecy of the doctrine condemning taxation without representation, that 'the governor shall not lay any taxes or impositions upon the colony, their lands or commodities, other than by authority of the General Assembly . .

The king's failure to provide for a House of Burgesses in the governmental plans he instituted after the demise of the London Company had little effect upon the progress of the democratic principle. After James had commissioned a council to take charge of affairs in Virginia, had appointed the governor, and, forthwith, had died, Virginians sent Yeardley across the ocean to urge the king to 'avoid the oppression of governors in colonial affairs' and to continue the general assemblies. Until royal recognition of the House of Burgesses came in 1628, Governors Francis Wyatt, George Yeardley, and Francis West were wise enough to allow the burgesses to assist the council unofficially in the passing of 'proclamations, ordinances, and orders.' The principle of taxation by representation was reiterated in resolutions passed in 1631, in 1632, in 1642, in 1652, and many other times before a Virginian gave the Declaration of Independence to the world.

The behavior of liberty-loving Virginians must have sorely tried the royal Stuarts, whose edicts brought forth either argument or disobedience. During the investigation of the London Company, the clerk of the council had lost his ears for giving the king's commissioners certain official papers. Virginians dared to ask that the charter of the London Company be renewed. Other evidences of insubordination followed. There was, for instance, Virginia's protest against Lord Baltimore's proprietary, carved from Virginia territory by royal grant in 1632. For some strange reason there had been no trouble when Sir Robert Heath had received patent in 1629 to that part of southern Virginia styled 'Carolana.' Chief among the agitators against Lord Baltimore was William Claiborne, who, anticipating the grant, had established on the Isle of Kent within the Maryland territory a trading post and colony. The conflict, however, was not between Virginia and Lord Baltimore, but was a contest that Claiborne carried on with the aid of his settlers.

Interposed in the general confusion was the not inconsiderable matter of 'thrusting' a royal governor out of Virginia. Sir John Harvey was appointed in 1628. His arrival having been delayed, the council continued Captain Francis West as acting governor and the assembly convened. It refused to agree to the king's demand regarding English monopoly of Virginia tobacco and sent West abroad as the first of a long line of agents who presented the colony's cause to the king. Dr. John Pott was then named acting governor. When Harvey finally reached Virginia, in 1630, he discredited Pott, usurped the powers of the general assembly, and refused to forward to the king the general assembly's 'denial' of the tobacco monopoly. Finally, when the governor dissolved the assembly, the house of burgesses defiantly continued its sessions. In peaceful revolution the governor was 'thrust out,' and the council in 1635 named John West his successor. Though Harvey took his appeal to the king, who ruled that the deposed governor must return to Virginia as governor if just for a day, Virginia's first popular revolution was successful. In 1639 the king appointed Sir Francis Wyatt governor.

In the meantime new governmental machinery had been installed. In 1634 the four 'corporacouns' that had been created in 1619 gave place to eight shires, later designated as counties. All free male citizens had the right to vote for members of the house of burgesses and for county officers.

Then came Sir William Berkeley, who supplanted Wyatt in 1641 and continued in office until 1652. Though the staunchest of royalists, Sir William endeared himself to Virginians at once by exercising justice and good sense. After the massacre of 1644, led by the aged Opechancanough, had wiped out about 300 colonists, Berkeley dealt with the Indians courageously and promptly. The civil war in England was reflected, however, in Berkeley's intolerance toward dissenters. When three pastors from the Massachusetts Bay colony accepted Captain Richard Bennett's invitation to settle in Virginia, they were ordered to return 'with all convenience.' The oppressive act against nonconformists passed in 1647 caused many Puritans in Virginia to migrate to more tolerant Maryland.

Berkeley's intense loyalty to the Crown furnishes the key to his character. He went to England to offer aid to Charles I; after the execution of his sovereign, he refused to recognize Cromwell;

History

and he extended to Charles II an invitation to make his home in Virginia. When Virginia was at last 'reduced' to Parliament, the loyal servant of the king retired to Green Spring near Jamestown.

Under the Commonwealth, Virginia enjoyed almost complete political freedom. Fortunately, the Navigation Act, first passed in 1651 limiting colonial trade to England and her possessions, was not strictly enforced. That Virginians had learned to govern themselves was attested by the averting of a civil war that was threatened by the inhabitants of the eastern shore. These isolated settlers, in a protest drawn up on March 30, 1652, embodying a complaint that dated back to 1647, based their refusal to pay taxes on the grounds that, since they had received no summons for election of burgesses, they considered themselves 'disjointed and sequestered from the rest of Virginia.' Moreover, without authority from the general assembly, they had made their own reprisals against the Dutch among them, who they claimed had been selling arms to the Indians. No blood was shed in the settlement of the difficulty, and the eastern shore, then Northhampton County, remained within Virginia.

The Restoration ushered in one of Virginia's darkest eras. The chaotic situation in England and the death of Governor Mathews in 1660 caused Virginia to turn again to their old leader. Accordingly, the House of Burgesses elected Sir William Berkeley governor, and soon thereafter Charles II reappointed him.

Though it was quite another Berkeley who resumed office, he worked at first in the interest of the colonists. The Navigation Act of 1660, more thoroughly enforced than Cromwell's, imposed real hardship upon Virginia planters by requiring all trade with Virginia to pass through English ports with payment of high duties. Governor Berkeley traveled to England in 1661 to make personal protest against the obnoxious regulation that was reducing the price of Virginia tobacco, and in 1664 he, endeavored to obtain the cooperation of Carolina and Maryland in concerted restriction of tobacco planting. The governor also had a hand in the general assembly's inauguration of a works program, by means of which factories were established both to provide employment and to furnish the colonists with needed commodities.

His philosophy, however, was that of the benevolent despot, who would brook no opposition to his authority. Satisfied with the representative whose election he had influenced in 1661, when reaction against the Commonwealth had increased his popularity, he issued no other writ for an election until forced to do so by the rebellion that ended his career. Accordingly, control of the colony fell into the hands of an oligarchy that controlled Virginia for 15 years. Restriction of the franchise to 'freeholders and housekeepers' who were 'answerable . . . for levies' further strengthened the throttle hold of Berkeley's political machine. Charles II's grant of the Northern Neck, the area lying between the Potomac and the Rappahannock from the Chesapeake back to the headwaters of both rivers, to four royal favorites in 1669 was deeply resented by Virginians.

Encyclopedia of Virginia

VIRGINIA'S FIRST REBELLION

In 1674 a young man came out of England with courage to defy autocratic rule. His name was Nathaniel Bacon; his family was old and distinguished; he had been educated at Oxford, and he had traveled extensively. Upon taking up lands in Virginia, he was almost at once made a member of the council. Though the fundamental cause of unrest in Virginia was economic and brought about by dire distress of the small farmers, liberty-loving Anglo-Saxons were holding responsible for their plight the arrogant rule of the governor, who they believed had deprived them of the freeman's right to petition for redress. The immediate occasion of what is known as Bacon's Rebellion was an Indian uprising, which Berkeley failed to handle with dispatch.

Following depredations of the Susquehannock in northern Virginia in 1675, which Berkeley had sent troops to punish, and the unfortunate killing of Indians who came bearing a flag of truce, the Susquehannock had sought revenge upon the whites and had enlisted other tribes as allies. Although the governor authorized an expedition to be led by Sir Henry Chicheley, suddenly disbanding the militia, he remained inactive while atrocities continued. When Virginians petitioned for commanders to lead them in defense of their 'lives and estates,' the governor not only refused but forbade further requests 'under great penalty.' Then it was that Nathaniel Bacon assumed leadership and sent messengers to the governor asking that he be given a commission. When Berkeley lost no time in refusing and in declaring Bacon a rebel, the affair took on the nature of an insurrection. An autocratic governor had arrogantly offended a man who became, over night, the spokesman of the aroused masses.

While fighters flocked to Bacon's ranks, the governor issued a writ for the election of a new House of Burgesses. Having already dealt summarily with the Indians, Bacon was elected a burgess. Though Berkeley had dubbed him 'the greatest rebel that ever was in Virginia,' he was pardoned and again took his seat as a member of the council. The rebellion was not at an end, however. Soon Bacon, hearing that Berkeley plotted against him, left Jamestown, again without a commission to proceed against the Indians. Thenceforth the rebels concentrated their attack upon Berkeley's government. With his motley followers, Bacon appeared again at Jamestown and forced the governor to sign the commission so long sought. Under Bacon's influence the burgesses liberalized the laws of the colony. The unhappy governor left Jamestown, finally going to the eastern shore, and Nathaniel Bacon was, for a time, the virtual head of government. From Middle Plantation, now Williamsburg, he issued a proclamation calling upon Virginians to 'consult with him for the present settlement of His Majesty's distressed colony.' The people came and 'none or very few' failed to sign an oath that pledged them to aid in the Indian war, to oppose the governor, and to resist any effort that England might make to suppress Bacon until the king could be acquainted with the 'grievances' of the colony.

History

The young leader then made his fatal mistake. He seized the British guardship, put two of his lieutenants in command, and sent it across the bay to capture Berkeley without first removing the British captain. Upon arrival at the eastern shore, the captain delivered the ship to the governor, and Bacon's men were held captive. When Berkeley returned to Jamestown, Bacon followed and stormed the capital. Berkeley fled to the guardship, and Bacon set fire to Jamestown. From Berkeley's home, Green Spring, 100 years before another Virginian phrased the Declaration of Independence, Bacon issued a proclamation declaring that, should Berkeley be upheld by England, Virginians must defend their liberties or abandon the colony. The young leader then set out upon a grand tour of Virginia. In Gloucester County he was stricken with a fever and died before his leadership could be challenged by the king.

Virginia's second rebellion against autocracy ended with the terrible vengeance of an old man who believed that the divine right he represented had been defied. In demented fury Berkeley hanged, without trial, more than 20 men and confiscated the property of many others. Charles II snorted in disgust upon hearing the news: 'That old fool has hanged more men in that naked country than I have done here for the murder of my father.' Recalled to England, Sir William Berkeley died within a year. In Virginia, however, a fire had been rekindled, which succeeding decades of conservatism were powerless to extinguish.

Although self-government in Virginia was immediately threatened, the uprising served as a warning to other governors and prepared Virginia to accept joyfully the expulsion of James II. In particular the experience created among the poorer planters a sense of solidarity. Bacon's Rebellion was the first organized and violent resistance on a large scale to British authority in America.

Out of the confusion following Berkeley's departure emerged a succession of even more incompetent governors who, as royal agents through the decade preceding the 'Glorious Revolution,' despoiled the colony and sought to destroy popular government in Virginia. Against even the determination of James II, however, the burgesses successfully defended their two most precious prerogatives: control over general taxation and initiation of legislation.

After the trying first years, life in Virginia had soon taken on, except for the effects of Black slavery and eighteenth-century affluence, the character it retained in Tidewater even after the newer colonists of Piedmont and the Valley altered radically the total picture. In the seventeenth century Virginia society had been divided into three main classes: a small group, privileged and secure, if not wealthy; the vastly preponderant yeomen, who were to become a true middle class after slavery had been thoroughly introduced; and the indentured servants. Static among the nonfree laborers was the Black minority. Members of the miniature aristocracy owned large, but rarely enormous, tracts of land, stretching back from the wooded banks of the great rivers or on navigable tributary creeks, and lived in comfortable houses. No one had very many slaves or the more usual indentured servants. A few leaders managed a little better, usually by doing something besides raising tobacco. Planter William Fitzhugh practiced law and engaged in trade; William Byrd I traded and speculated in frontier land. These big planters monopolized the seats in the governor's council and, with him, ran the colony. M. Durand, a Huguenot forerunner of the French to come later, observed in 1687: 'There are no lords, but each is a sovereign on his own plantation. The gentlemen called Cavaliers are greatly esteemed and respected, and are very courteous and honorable. They hold most of the offices in the country.'

Mention of books from the earliest days and the existence later of fair-sized libraries indicate a respectable level of education among the few. Many small collections of books were recorded during this period. In 1667 a Mr. Mathew Hubard died in possession of more than 30 volumes, including John Smith's *Historie of Virginia* and the poetry of John Donne; and an inventory of Colonel Ralph Wormeley's library in 1701 listed above 500 titles. The office-holding planters of substance had their children taught at home and frequently sent eldest sons to schools in England. In 1681 there had been an abortive attempt to establish a printing press in the colony.

Without luxury and reduced to bare necessities for the majority, life in seventeenth-century Virginia was not, however, without merriment. There was time for a good deal of drinking, it seems, and a good deal of convivial visiting. And everybody smoked. A decade after Bacon's Rebellion, M. Durand could say in a pamphlet designed to attract his persecuted coreligionists: 'The land is so rich and so fertile that when a man has fifty acres of ground, two men-servants, a maid and some cattle, neither he nor his wife do anything but visit among their neighbors... When a man squanders his property he squanders his wife's also, and this is fair, for the women are foremost in drinking and smoking.'

In 1682 another rebellion was launched by Virginians. Bumper crops and the failure of the government to authorize a year's cessation brought the price of tobacco in London down to the point of crisis. Taking cessation into their own hands, desperate planters rode through the night tearing up tens of thousands of young plants. It took several months and the execution of six 'plant-cutters' to discourage the practice. Robert Beverley, formerly a loyalist, suspected of instigating the riots, was imprisoned. This unofficial crop control was only a temporary and slight tonic. Lord Culpeper, a proprietor of the Northern Neck and then governor, wrote the Privy Council in 1683, the year following the Tobacco Riots: I soe encouraged the planting of tobacco that if the season continue to favorable... there will bee a greater cropp by far than ever grew since its first seating. And I am confident that Customs next year from thence will be 50,000 more than ever heretofore in any one year.' Though admitting that 'the great Cropp then in hand would most certainly bring that place (Virginia) into the utmost exigencies again,' he promised to put

History

down any disturbances that might result. The effect on the Exchequer of the consequent decline in price of tobacco was offset by raising the rate of customs, already over 300 per cent. Taxes in Virginia were also raised.

In 1689, however, Virginia made a fresh start. Amid rumors of a projected Indian-Catholic massacre and threats of another revolt, the happy news arrived of the expulsion of James II and the peaceful accession of William and Mary. Later that year the passage in England of the Bill of Rights cleared the way for Anglo-American progress. In 1693 education was given a real impetus in Virginia by the founding of the College of William and Mary, the second college in America. Finally, the beginning of the new era was marked symbolically by the removal in 1699 of the capital from Jamestown to Williamsburg. By 1700, when the population had reached about 70,000, the most important new trends were under way: quantity production of tobacco on a vast scale; the consequent growth of slavery as the foundation of the colony's economy with the parallel suppression of Virginia's sturdy yeomanry; the immigration of new racial elements; and westward expansion.

The essential history of Virginia from 1690 to 1776 is a record of the economic and territorial expansion of a maturing colony.

Henceforward tobacco dominated Colonial Virginia. A comparatively prosperous decade following the Revolution in England was terminated by the War of the Spanish Succession (Queen Anne's War), which virtually closed most of the ports of Europe to British trade and thus deprived Virginia of a world market. Cut into by export duties in Virginia and the tax on tobacco entering England, 600 percent by 1705, profits almost vanished. It became clear that America's real enemy, responsible for adverse legislation, was the middle class in England, made up of businessmen who were determined to force empire trade through English channels at all costs.

Black slavery was the inevitable answer to Virginia's economic impasse. After 1690, and especially after 1710, the proportion of Black immigration rose sharply. Black slaves increased from about 5 percent of the population in 1670 to 9 percent in 1700, 25 percent in 1715, when they numbered about 23,000 against a total population of about 95,000, and to about 40 percent by the middle of the century. Having prospered briefly after 1689, the hardy, independent 'peasantry' never recovered from the blow inflicted by the Spanish War. Many migrated to other colonies, particularly Pennsylvania, but most of them either sank to become the new class of 'poor whites' or rose to become petty, slaveholding planters.

The colony did not come into its 'great days' easily. Overproduction soon resulted from the importation of too many slaves, and a semiprohibitive duty was imposed in 1710. Many attempts to limit or prohibit the slave trade were obstructed by the British government, which acquired a monopoly of the valuable traffic in slaves in 1713 by the Treaty of Utrecht. Tobacco depressions gave a slight encouragement to the development of manufactures, in spite of opposition in England, and to the export of naval stores and other raw materials. Governor Spotswood established the first successful smelting furnace in 1715, and other furnaces were set up a few years later in the Valley of Virginia. Except for coarse 'Virginia cloth' and farm implements, however, manufacturing made small headway in Colonial Virginia, without skilled artisans or an invigorating climate. During this period pirates also interfered with trade, but Governor Spotswood did much to discourage piracy when he destroyed Blackbeard and his crew in 1718.

Regulation of the tobacco trade became a necessity. From about one and a third million pounds in 1640, exportation had risen to more than 18,000,000 pounds by 1688, to considerably more by 1699, and, after the war slump had climbed back to about 20,000,000 pounds in 1731. A new inspection law, enacted in 1730 through the efforts of Sir John Randolph sent to London by the general assembly, to present the case of Virginia planters, brought about an era of prosperity by providing for the issuance of notes in receipt for crops stored in public warehouses. In 1755, when there were about 175,000 whites and 120,000 blacks in the colony, more than 42,000,000 pounds of tobacco were exported.

Geographic, racial, religious, and social changes marked the first half of the eighteenth century. Steadily new plantations were developed as the frontier was pushed westward. Governor Spotswood and a cavalcade mixing business with pleasure paid the first formal visit to the Valley in 1716. As early as 1650-51, however, Abraham Wood and Edward Bland, seeking a new fur-trading field distant from the encroachments of Maryland, had made into the southwest a journey of exploration, which was followed sporadically by other pilgrimages. In 1728 William Byrd II headed a commission that surveyed the Virginia-North Carolina line from the ocean about 240 miles westward. By this time pioneers from Tidewater had begun to take up Piedmont land. Large grants, made in 1749 to the Loyal Company and the Ohio Company, threw much of the western territory into the hands of speculators and stimulated exploration. That year Christopher Gist reached the falls of the Ohio, the site of the present Louisville.

During the period 1699-1755 several racial strains, other than the African, were added to the English stock of Virginia. From the beginning, small groups of foreigners had come to the colony; eight 'Dutch-men' and Poles, sent over in 1608 to make 'soap-ashes' and glass; a few Frenchmen in 1620 to help found a silk industry; and from time to time a sprinkling of Swedish, Polish, German, and other artisans. Elias Legardo, Joseph Moise, Rebecca Isaacke, who arrived from England in 1624, were the first Jews to reach Virginia. The last of many convicts, felons or rebellious victims of oppression, who were shipped out frequently over a period of about 60 years against the protest of Virginians, were 52 Scottish prisoners in 1678, probably Covenanters. Throughout the seventeenth century small groups of intransigent Irish had been sent over as political prisoners. In 1699, however, members of the

History

first large influx of foreigners began to come: French Huguenot refugees fleeing from persecution following the Revocation of the Edict of Nantes in 1685. The small groups of Germans, who came in 1714 and 1717 to settle at Germanna, the site of Governor Spotswood's iron furnaces, later joined their compatriots in the Valley. Scottish immigrants constituted another valuable ingredient in Virginia's new 'melting-pot.' Having previously ventured across the Atlantic in search of religious freedom, these Presbyterians came freely after the Toleration Act was passed in 1689 and on equal terms with the English after 1707, when the Union of Scotland with England was accomplished.

By far the largest and most far-reaching infusion into Virginia's racial stock, however, was the invasion of the tramontane Valley by Germans, Scotch-Irish, English Quakers, and a scattering of Welsh Baptists, who had settled in Penn's tolerant colony. About 1730, just when outpost settlement advancing from Tidewater had reached the mountains on the east, these people, industrious merchants, yeomen, and peasants, began a migration into the Valley that continued in full spate beyond the middle of the century. These nonconformists brought a dissent that was to destroy the Anglican establishment and a tough philosophy that was later to override Tidewater and take the lead in revolt against British oppression.

HEYDAY OF COLONIAL LIFE

By the middle of the eighteenth century Colonial Virginia had achieved its heyday. Affluence had polished the manners and enriched the life of old Tidewater and newer Piedmont gentry, while a 'hardy race had settled in the Valley; and beyond the mountains hunters and pioneers were pushing toward the Ohio.' Estates had expanded along with tobacco production and slavery until several nabobs held vast domains. Upon these rose the great Georgian Colonial houses of eastern Virginia, most of which were built between 1730 and 1760. Libraries grew in number and size. William Byrd II, with nearly 4,000 volumes, owned the largest, perhaps, in America at the time. As early as 1724 the Reverend Hugh Jones was recording: 'good Families . . . live in the same neat manner, dress after the same Modes, and behave themselves exactly as the Gentry in London; most Families of any Note having a Coach, Chariot, Berlin, or Chaise.'

Virginians preferred the country. The well-known mansion of brick or stone, with its various outbuildings, was the center of an almost self-sufficient community. Poor farmers lived in small houses of frame or brick, far more numerous than the 'great' houses. Stories were long told of remote planters haunting the nearest roadside to watch for the weekly stage, hoping to find a traveler who could be persuaded to stop over for a day or a week or a month. Early in the century Governor Spotswood had 'showed small Concern in reporting that upon an official Occasion he had entertained four Hundred Guests at Supper.' Colonel James Gordon of Lancaster County noted one day in his diary: 'No company, which is surprising.'

Encyclopedia of Virginia

During this mid-eighteenth-century period, life in the Valley was vastly different from that in the Tidewater. The Germans, who peopled the lower region, and the Scotch-Irish, whose province became the upper Valley, brought traditions of hard work from their native lands. They built small stone houses that were strongholds against the Indians, still inhabiting this frontier country. Just behind the vanguard of these industrious folk sprang up mills, furnaces, forges, and even small factories. The rich land was turned rapidly into profitable farms. Nonconformist churches soon flourished here, and education was not far behind.

Defense of Virginia's western frontier in the 1750's provided a seminary for the Revolution. The French and Indian War, begun in 1754, schooled Americans to fight British regulars and thrice baptized in leadership their future commander in chief. Land was behind it all. The Anglo-Americans were pushing farther and farther westward into the 'Great Woods'; while, the French, having long intended to make the Alleghenies, if not eventually the ocean, their eastern boundary, were setting up outposts in territory already granted to the new land companies. By 1753 French had begun stirring up unfriendly Indian tribes and pushing eastward to implement their claim to the Allegheny westward. On the basis of the royal charters of 1606, 1609, and 1612, Virginia laid claim, later established, to the West and Northwest as far as British territory extended. Twice Governor Dinwiddie had sent George Washington out to protect the interests of Virginia and the land companies, the first time to deliver a formal protest and soon afterwards to join Colonel Joshua Fry's small force. Washington fell into command when Colonel Fry was killed accidentally. A fort, originally planned by the British at the site of the present Pittsburgh, had been built by the French and named Duquesne. The French, advancing from their stronghold, forced Washington to evacuate Fort Necessity, which he had built at the present Farmington, Pennsylvania. Because the British Government was eager to prevent backdoor encroachments of the French, General Edward Braddock and British troops were sent to Virginia in 1755 to lead an offensive. With two complete regiments of regulars, several companies from Virginia and two other colonies, and with Washington on his staff, Braddock reached a spot near Fort Duquesne in July. The general led his redcoats forward in formation to engage the French and Indians. Surrounded by an enemy hidden behind trees, his men were cut to pieces as they fled, and General Braddock was mortally wounded in the rout.

Washington, left once more in command, was soon recommissioned as a colonel and made commander in chief of Virginia forces. Troops were collected and drilled and forts were built along the immediate frontier. Though attempts were made to take Fort Duquesne, it was not occupied until late in 1758 and then only after the French, deserted by their Indian allies and hotly engaged farther north by the British, had blown it up. Washington and his Virginians were first to enter the smoking ruins. This war, which ended in America the following year on the Plains of Abraham and was formally closed by the Treaty of Paris in 1763,

History

marked Virginia's coming of age. The defeat of the British leadership and British regulars in 1755 had vindicated 'bush-fighting' and given Americans a new self confidence. Events during these war years had revealed also the need and the value of intercolonial cooperation.

The West had become a permanent scene of action. No sooner was the Treaty of Paris signed than George III issued his restrictive proclamation of 1763, prohibiting trade with the Indians or grants of land beyond the Alleghenies. This challenge trod on too many Virginia toes to be taken seriously, but settlement was further opposed by a renewal of border warfare with the Indians. Other troubles were in store for Virginia. In 1769-70 the Walpole Company was formed by associates in England and France, as well as in America, who began negotiations for a tract on a scale that would have dwarfed its predecessors. When it became generally known that 20,000,000 acres within Virginia's domain were involved, and that the king contemplated a new colony to be known as Vandalia, opposition flared. Even reactionary Governor Dunmore, who arrived in 1771, took Virginia's part in protests that ran on into 1773-74 and forestalled the enterprise.

A long series of frontier 'outrages' became general war again in 1774. Governor Dunmore led a detachment of Virginia troops into the West and ordered Major Andrew Lewis forward with another. While the governor was negotiating peace with the Indians at a point some distance away, the Battle of Point Pleasant took place on October 10 at the junction of the Ohio and Great Kanawha Rivers, and the Indians were driven back across the river. The whole campaign may have been intended to divert public attention from the political crisis then at hand. Nevertheless, pacification followed speedily in the West, and it was possible to form the County of Kentucky in 1776, before troubles, incident to the Revolution, broke out again on the frontier.

VIRGINIA DEFIES THE KING

No sooner had the curtain fallen on the prologue, with the Treaty of Paris in 1763, than it rose on the first act of the pre-Revolutionary drama. Young Patrick Henry shouted the first frank challenge at the king. Failure of the tobacco crop had obliged the Virginia assembly in 1758 to pass Two Penny Act, providing that for 12 months obligations should be paid in currency at the rate of two pence per pound of tobacco, the price of which had then risen to six pence per pound. The clergy complained to the Board of Trade and Plantations and, after the king vetoed the act, brought suit for their usual quantity of tobacco and for damages. When Patrick Henry appeared for the defense in the Parsons' Cause in Hanover County in 1763, he spoke so eloquently, declaring that 'by this conduct the King, from being the father of his people, had degenerated into tyrant and forfeited all his right to his subjects obedience,' that the crowd broke into a tumult. The jury's award of only one penny damages to the plaintiff amounted to denying the right of the king's action. Already the old order was on the way out.

Although Anglo-American economic rivalry was the basic cause, expenses resulting from the war and consequent taxes became the occasion for the quarrels with the British Government, which believed itself justified in taxing America to help pay its own debt. The colonies held an opposite opinion. The Sugar Bill in 1764 was the first of many attempts to tax the colonies without their consent. The Virginia assembly was the first legislative body to take an official step in facing the Stamp Act issue. Burgesses and council protested against both the Sugar Bill and a proposed stamp tax as violations of constitutional rights, asserting that no subjects of Great Britain could justly be made subservient to laws passed without their consent.

The Stamp Act, passed in March 1765, evoked an immediate response from Virginia. Patrick Henry on May 29 stirred the, Virginia assembly to pass the Virginia Resolves on the following day, setting forth Colonial rights according to constitutional principles, and carried mainly by the representatives of a united interior, voting against those from eastern Virginia. 'Caesar had his Brutus,' cried the young orator, 'Charles I his Cromwell, and George Ill, may profit by their example. If this be treason, make the most of it.' Governor Fauquier was obliged to dissolve the assembly, but the die had been cast. Governor Hutchinson of Massachusetts declared, 'Nothing extravagant appeared in the papers till an account was received of the Virginia Resolves.' Nine years later Edmund Burke in his speech on Colonial taxation gave Virginia credit for arousing the general resistance to the Stamp Tax.

In the decade that began in 1764 Virginia continued to lead constitutional opposition to the new British policy. On February 8, 1766, the Act was flatly outlawed by the Northampton County court, which declared that 'the said act did not bind, affect, or concern the inhabitants of this colony, inasmuch as they conceive the same to be unconstitutional, and that the said several officers may proceed to the execution of their respective offices, without incurring any penalties by means thereof.' On February 27 the outstanding planters of northeastern Virginia, led by Richard Henry Lee, met at Leedstown in the Northern Neck, 115 strong, and leveled against the Stamp Act resolutions that embodied the principles later written into the Declaration of Independence. Another association in Norfolk, the 'Sons of Liberty,' met on March 31 and made similar protests. The most important single instrument, however, to form American opinion during this period was probably *An Enquiry into the Rights of the British Colonies*, a pamphlet in which Richard Bland presented in March 1766 the first printed argument that Virginia, like the other colonies, was 'no part of the Kingdom of England,' but united with the British Empire solely through its allegiance to the Crown-doctrine the American people afterwards accepted as the ground upon which they resisted Parliament. This was a remarkable statement of the political theory actually underlying the Empire but not recognized by statute until 165 years later.

History

Virginians were delighted at the repeal of the Stamp Act on March 18, 1766. After more than a year of surface tranquility, the Revenue Act was signed by the king on June 29, 1767. This external tax on glass, paper, white lead, painters' colors, and tea gave rise to memorials from burgesses and council and to protests from county after county.

In the autumn of 1768 Lord Botetourt arrived as Virginia's new governor. Leadership was slipping into the hands of a new element from Piedmont and farther west. When news reached Williamsburg early in 1769 of the order to transport the Boston rioters to London for trial, Virginians were incensed. The assembly, meeting in May, drafted resolutions condemning the attempt to transport Americans across the sea for trial, claiming the right of the colonies to concerted action and appeal, reiterating the exclusive right of the colony's assembly to levy taxes. Sympathetic Governor Botetourt was obliged to dissolve the disloyal burgesses, who withdrew to the Raleigh Tavern, where they signed a strict agreement not to import any slaves, wines, or British manufactures. The Non-Importation Agreement was soon adopted in all the colonies. The British Government was forced to give up the idea of transporting the patriots of Massachusetts for trial and by April 12, 1770, had rescinded all except the tax on tea and the principle involved. Beloved Governor Botetourt having died, haughty Lord Dunmore reached Virginia late in 1771. A royal order forbidding assent to any restriction of the slave trade led the Virginia assembly in February 1772 to send the king a petition, in which the trade was castigated as a 'great inhumanity' and one endangering 'the very existence of your Majesty's American dominions.'

Early in 1773 Virginia took a step that was to organize revolution. Renewal of the threat to transport Americans for trial in England emphasized the need for greater cooperation among the colonies. Led by Richard Henry Lee, a group of legislators, including Thomas Jefferson, Patrick Henry, and George Mason, proposed, and the legislature created, a standing committee of correspondence, representing the lower house, to inform the other colonies through similar committees, which they recommended be set up, of Virginia's reaction to the latest moves of the British ministry, to receive theirs in return, and to keep in touch with Virginia's London agent. Unlike the local and unofficial committees of correspondence, originated by Samuel Adams a year earlier to consolidate anti-British sentiment in the faction-torn townships of Massachusetts, this Virginia committee was an official, centralized body modeled on the permanent standing committee originated in 1759 to correspond on similar business with an agent in London. This committee, active until 1772, left four of its members to the new committee. The effort to transport Americans for trial was abandoned, and before the year was out Parliament repealed the duty on tea, not without retaining, however, the three-penny custom collectable in American ports. Associations against tea drinking were revived. Virginia had its 'tea-party' near Yorktown, similar to the one that took place in the Boston harbor.

Encyclopedia of Virginia

From the moment in May 1774 that news reached the colonies of the Boston Port Bill, closing that harbor in punishment of the tea dumpers, events moved swiftly to successive climaxes. The Virginia assembly resolved to set aside June 1, when the bill was to take effect, as a day of fasting and prayer. Governor Dunmore dissolved the legislature, and members gathered the next day at the Raleigh Tavern, declared common cause with Massachusetts, recommended that a general congress be held annually, that no East India Company commodity be imported, and advocated a general commercial boycott of Great Britain. Revolution was in the air when Virginia's first convention met in Williamsburg on August 1, pledged supplies to Boston, suspended transatlantic debts and commerce, and elected delegates to a continental congress.

Peyton Randolph of Virginia was made president of the First Continental Congress held in Philadelphia in September. Here Washington, without pretensions of eloquence, shone as a man of 'solid judgment and information.'

At the Second Virginia Convention, opening on March 20, 1775, Patrick Henry again was the central figure of high drama. Giving his impassioned plea for 'embodying, arming and disciplining ' Virginia militia, he closed with the fiery words:
Gentlemen may cry 'Peace! Peace!' but there is no peace. The war is actually begun! . . . Is life so dear or peace so sweet as to be purchased at the price of chains and slavery? Forbid it, Almighty God! I know not what course others may take, but, as for me, give me liberty, or give me death!

Patrick Henry's resolution was adopted and steps were taken for establishing manufactories to make both arms and other commodities that had formerly been imported from England.

On April 20 Governor Dunmore provoked the first armed resistance in Virginia by ordering the gunpowder stored in the public magazine in Williamsburg to be removed to a warship. Although the governor filled his palace with marines and threatened to 'proclaim liberty to the slaves and reduce Williamsburg to ashes' if he or his affairs suffered any injury, he was forced by the approach of Patrick Henry at the head of troops from Hanover and other counties to pay 320 for the powder. As soon as the little army had dispersed, his lordship declared Henry an outlaw, matching Governor Berkeley's treatment of Bacon just a century earlier. The burgesses, called by Lord Dunmore to consider Lord North's proposals, met once more on June 1. They rejected the 'Olive Branch' and, to defray the expense of the late Indian war, proposed a tax of 5 per head on imported slaves. To protect the slave trade the king's representative exercised his veto power for the last time in Virginia. When the burgesses were ready for his assent to bills passed, the governor refused to leave the *Fowey*, the ship to which he had fled on the night of June 8, and the burgesses adjourned on June 20, never to meet formally again. On June 15 the Continental Congress had elected George Washington commander in chief of American forces. The Third Virginia Convention, meeting in July, quickly provided for a committee of safety, for the raising of regular regiments, and for dividing the colony into 16 military districts. Lord Dunmore retired to Norfolk, where, lacking troops, he remained inactive for several months among a nest of Tories.

Meanwhile the Fourth Virginia Convention passed scathing resolutions condemning Lord Dunmore and announcing that the people of Virginia were ready to protect themselves 'against every species of despotism.' In November the ex-governor had declared the colony to be in revolt and had proclaimed all slaves in Virginia free. On December 9 his defending forces were routed at Great Bridge by 'shirt men,' militia acting under the Committee of Safety.

Having taken to his ships, he bombarded Norfolk on New Year's Day. It was not until the following July, however, that he was finally driven from the Chesapeake. Washington, having invested Boston in November, drove out the British under General Howe by March 1776. Virginia had sent up supplies as well as Daniel Morgan with his frontier marksmen, who could pick off captains at 'double the distance of common musket shot.' Morgan had soon gone on to distinguish himself before Quebec, carrying Virginia's offensive far afield.

Virginians remained ideologically in the forefront of opposition. Radicals were at the helm when the Fifth Virginia Convention opened in Williamsburg on May 6, 1776. Declaring on May 15 the colony a free and independent State, the Convention instructed Virginia delegates in Congress to propose separation from Great Britain. Tn obedience to the mandate from his State Richard Henry Lee rose in Congress on June 7 and proposed independence, contraction of foreign alliances, and establishment of a plan of confederation. Three days later, a committee was appointed to draft a declaration of independence. On June 12 the Virginia Convention, serving as a legislative body, adopted George Mason's Bill of Rights and on June 29 approved a constitution. The bill of rights and the constitution were to serve as patterns for other States and for the Nation itself. Lee's resolutions were adopted on July 2, 1776 and, when Jefferson's Declaration of Independence was approved by Congress on July 4, the United States of America was born.

For the next three years, while the war was being waged north and south and Virginia was contributing her full share of men and treasure and defending the western frontier, her legislators were laying the foundations of a new society. The progressives, led by crusading Thomas Jefferson, went far toward destroying the old regime. The new government, which endured without change for 54 years, consisted of a house of delegates, with the sole power to originate legislation; a senate, in place of the former council; a council of eight, limited to an executive function; and a chief magistrate. Both council and governor were chosen, the governor yearly, by the two houses voting together. When the legislature met in October 1776 several courts were set up immediately, and Jefferson, Pendleton; and Wythe were given the task of revising the whole body of Virginia law in conformance with the new constitution. By a legislative act of 1778 Virginia became the first State in the world to make a person engaged in the slave traffic guilty of a criminal offense. An amendment, however, that proposed freedom for all children born to slaves after the enactment of the bill was defeated. The laws of entail and primogeniture, legal basis of a social hierarchy, were abolished by bills that Jefferson presented now and that were passed a few years later.

Besides sending aid to the theaters of conflict north and south, Virginia began waging singlehanded a war in the West, where the British occupied a chain of forts from Detroit to Kaskaskia. On the strength of the battle of Saratoga, in which Daniel Morgan and his riflemen were important factors, Virginia sent into the Northwest George Rogers Clark in command of four companies. On July 4, 1778, General Clark surprised the fort at Kaskaskia and shortly afterward entered Vincennes without opposition from the friendly French residents. Later, during Clark's absence, Vincennes was retaken by British Governor Hamilton. On February 24, 1779, Clark returned, surprised the small garrison, and sent Hamilton to Williamsburg as a prisoner. Forts built to the mouth of the Ohio enabled Clark to hold the territory until the end of the war.

In May 1779 actual conflict was carried into the heart of Virginia, when Sir George Collier sailed into Hampton Roads with 2,000 troops. Using Portsmouth as their base, they raided surrounding country, destroyed the navy yard at Gosport (Portsmouth) and large quantities of stores. When reinforcement from Sir Henry Clinton in New York failed to arrive, the attempted blockade of Virginia was abandoned, and the colony's trade with the West Indies, now an American lifeline, continued.

Following a summer of American reverses on several fronts, rumor spread in 1780 that dismemberment of the Continental union and devastation of Virginia were planned. In October, General Alexander Leslie, having entered the Chesapeake with 3,000 troops, made Portsmouth his base. Upon news of the British defeat at King's Mountain, however, Leslie went south to join Cornwallis. At the end of December, Benedict Arnold with about 1,000 troops appeared in the Bay, advanced by water and land to Richmond, where he burned stores, and then established his base at Portsmouth. General William Phillips, joining forces with Arnold, undertook raids on a larger scale. At Petersburg, Phillips died a week before Cornwallis's arrival there on May 20, 1781. After General Nathanael Greene's move into the Deep South had left Virginia uncovered, General La Fayette, commanding part of the Continental Army, came to Virginia, advancing southward as far as Petersburg. Nearly 7,000 strong and well armed, the British began their pursuit of La Fayette, who retreated toward Fredericksburg, was joined by General Anthony Wayne, and then continued southwestward. Cornwallis dispatched Colonel John G. Simcoe with 500 men to Point of Fork to destroy an arsenal and stores that General von Steuben was unable to defend, and Colonel Banastre Tarleton with 350 men to Charlottesville to capture Thomas Jefferson and the Virginia legislature. Reunited without

History

these prizes at Elk Hill, the British moved eastward toward Williamsburg, followed by La Fayette, whose troops numbered about 5,000 after General von Steuben had joined him. On July 4 Cornwallis left Williamsburg, paused near Jamestown, where a part of his forces fought the inconsequential Battle of Greenspring, crossed the James, and proceeded to Portsmouth and thence to Yorktown, which he entrenched as a naval base.

With the arrival of 3,000 French regulars from the fleet under Admiral de Grasse, the initiative slipped irretrievably into the hands of the patriots, who strung themselves out across the peninsula. Washington and General Rochambeau arrived on September 15, and seven days later the Continental Army reached Jamestown by water from the North. While the French fleet prevented the arrival of British re-enforcements, the combined American and French forces began on September 28 to converge on Yorktown. The siege ended on October 19, with General Cornwallis's surrender.

VIRGINIANS IN THE MAKING OF THE CONSTITUTION

In the movement toward stronger union that resulted in the adoption of the Constitution, Virginia again played the leading part. Under the Articles of Confederation the Government was without power to regulate trade, raise revenue, or make foreign treaties, all pressing needs. James Madison, justly called the father of the Constitution, introduced into the Virginia general assembly in 1785 the resolution inviting commissioners from Maryland to meet with commissioners from Virginia to discuss common problems of trade and navigation. The conference, which opened in March at Alexandria and was continued at Mount Vernon, resulted in a plan for the two States' joint regulation of commerce and was the first step toward permanent union of the thirteen commonwealths. On January 21, 1786, the general assembly of Virginia adopted resolutions inviting all other States to meet for the purpose of considering the trade of the United States. Five States sent commissioners to the Annapolis Convention of September 11-14, 1786. Though navigation and commerce were still the points at issue, Washington and Madison were seeing the meeting of representatives of the several States as another step toward a stronger union. At Annapolis the Virginians were reinforced by Alexander Hamilton of New York. The convention adopted Hamilton's address that pledged the delegates to endeavor 'to procure the concurrence of the other states in the appointment of commissioners, to meet at Philadelphia, on the second Monday in May next to take into consideration the situation of the United States.'

George Washington was elected president of the convention that opened in Philadelphia on May 14, 1787. Governor Edmund Randolph of Virginia presented the 'Virginia Plan,' which incorporated James Madison's ideas and furnished the basis of deliberations. Madison spoke more frequently than any other

Encyclopedia of Virginia

delegate, kept copious notes that have enlightened historians, and wrote 20 of the 85 Federalist papers, which created a public opinion favorable to the adoption of the Constitution. The seven Virginia delegates, George Washington, George Wythe, George Mason, James Madison, Edmund Randolph, John Blair, and James McClurg, fought for the inclusion of a bill of rights, for the immediate cessation of the slave traffic, and for a progressive program of abolition. Because a bill of rights was omitted, because the Deep South and New England traders forced a compromise that continued the slave traffic until 1808 and failed to provide for the ultimate abolition of slavery, and because a mere majority of Congress was permitted to determine tariff policies, George Mason and Edmund Randolph refused to sign the instrument. James McClurg and George Wythe were absent. George Washington, James Madison, and John Blair signed, believing that the faults could be corrected immediately by amendments.

Virginia was the tenth State to ratify the Constitution. Meeting on June 2, 1788, the rank and file of delegates to the State convention split on sectional lines, Tidewater and the northwest favoring ratification, while Piedmont and the slaveless southwest, refusing to sanction the compromise between commercial North and plantation South over slavery and the tariff, fought for a second convention and revision. Among the leaders, Mason and Henry, encouraged by Richard Henry Lee writing from Chantilly, directed the opposition; Madison, Wythe, Pendleton, Henry Lee, and even Randolph, backed up by Washington's letters from Mount Vernon, conducted a successful defense. The attempt by the Northeastern States, acting through John Jay in 1786, to surrender navigation on the Mississippi to Spain had aroused such suspicion of New England's intentions that it took all of visionary Madison's persuasive talents to win ratification at last on June 26 by a small margin, and then only with the assurance that the first Congress would submit to the States amendments constituting a bill of rights, and with the clear proviso that the people of Virginia could cancel ratification setting up the Union 'whenever the powers granted unto it should be perverted to their injury or oppression.' The convention suggested 40 amendments, which were the bases of the 10 that became the Bill of Rights in the Constitution, the first nine introduced by James Madison and the tenth by Richard Henry Lee.

Meanwhile Virginia had been undergoing important geographical changes. Byrd's line between Virginia and North Carolina was extended west in 1779, although the exact location was disputed for another century; and the north-south boundary between Virginia and Pennsylvania, agreed upon that same year, was run in 1784-85. Within a year of the peace treaty, which recognized Virginia's claims, the Old Dominion surrendered the entire Northwest Territory, the vast section between the Ohio River and the Canadian border west from Pennsylvania to the Mississippi, and including the Great Lakes area, to the United States. In 1792 Kentucky became a State, thus fixing the limits Virginia preserved until 1861. Meanwhile, an interior change of

History

territorial status had taken place, the disappearance of the great proprietary of the Northern Neck. Taken up first in 1673 by Thomas, Lord Culpeper, who acquired five-sixths of the territory from the original grantees, the proprietary had passed in 1689 by marriage into the family of the fifth Lord Fairfax and was abolished by the general assembly in 1786.

George Washington, who took office as first President under the new Government on April 30, 1789, exerted a calming influence upon a decade of growing pains and political turmoil. Back from Paris in December 1789, Thomas Jefferson was appalled at the anti-democratic spirit he found in the highest places. Three months later Washington chose him Secretary of State. In opposition to Secretary of the Treasury Alexander Hamilton, he began to marshal the growing ranks of antifederal extremists who were to overthrow the conservatives in 1800. In the meantime the conservatives were ascendent. Led by Hamilton, they forced through the Assumption Bill in 1790, which Virginia and the other Southern States, with the exception of South Carolina, opposed on the ground that their debts were almost paid and the Government's assuming the debts of the Northern States inflicted an unfair hardship upon the South. As a sop to the agrarian opposition, they threw in the Southern choice of a site on the Potomac for the National capital, for which Virginia had already ceded territory. The next year Jefferson fought Hamilton's creation of the Bank of the United States. When war broke out between England and France in 1793 and John Jay negotiated a thoroughly Federalist treaty with England, attitudes split squarely; the banking and commercial imperialists, led by Hamilton, sympathized with England; the agrarian progressives, led by Jefferson, remained true to the cause of revolution and to America's old ally. In 1796 President Washington, having served two terms, retired to Mount Vernon, expressing regret that the 'increasing weight of years' admonished him 'to decline being considered among the number of those out of whom a choice is to be made,' but over Adams's administration he watched benevolently. In 1798 the Federalists enacted the infamous Alien and Sedition Laws, which made it possible to deport persons of less than 14 years' residence and to throw into jail others who should express un-American sentiments, in other words, ideas openly and severely in opposition to administration policies.

THE VIRGINIA DYNASTY

The accomplishments of Thomas Jefferson's administration, antithetical to that of Adams, were the clear articulation of democratic philosophy, the acquisition of a vast territory, and the futile enunciation of the principle that peace was more to be desired than the profits of commerce.

This man who had sprung from privileged aristocracy had from his youth espoused the cause of the masses. Upon assuming office, he discarded the monarchical rituals that had characterized the first two administrations and at once abolished from public entertainments all precedents as to rank and distinction. Opposed to the aristocratic doctrines of Alexander Hamilton and distressed because of Washington's conservatism, he had left the cabinet in 1794. As vice president during Adams's administration he had fought the Alien and Sedition Laws and had drafted the Kentucky Resolutions that eloquently protested the silencing, as he said, 'by force and not by reason the complaints and criticisms, just or unjust, of our citizens against the conduct of our agents.' The first of the alien laws, raising the number of years for naturalization from 5 to 14, was repealed in April 1802; the third, permitting the President to order 'dangerous' aliens out of the country, died at the end of the two-year period to which it was originally limited; and the sedition law, classifying as a crime criticism of the Government and of Federal officials, expired in March 1801. The establishment of a citizen's right to expatriation was a further expression of Jeffersonian democracy.

In acquiring the Louisiana Territory, Thomas Jefferson exceeded his constitutional authority to the great advantage of the United States. Robert R. Livingston, whom Jefferson had appointed minister to France, had expressed naive faith in existing treaties and apparently did not share Jefferson's belief that French occupation of Louisiana would be 'very ominous to us.' An ocean, moreover, separated Jefferson from Livingston, and letters were in danger of interception. So the President sent to France as an envoy extraordinary and minister plenipotentiary another Virginian, his trusted friend, James Monroe, without written authorization to purchase the whole territory. Livingston, somewhat piqued, tried to consummate the purchase while Monroe was on the ocean, but failed. So, to the vision of Thomas Jefferson and the immediate diplomacy of James Monroe belongs the credit for striking the bargain by which the United States almost doubled its area for the sum of $15,000,000. Though the Constitution gave the Federal Government no authority to buy and hold territory, Jefferson decided to postpone asking Congress to pass an amendment lest Napoleon change his mind. Jefferson sent two Virginians, Meriwether Lewis and William Clark, to explore the vast western territory. The expedition started from the mouth of the Missouri in the spring of 1804, and the explorers returned to the vicinity of St. Louis in the fall of 1806, having reached the mouth of the Columbia River.

Napoleon's Berlin and Milan Decrees and the British orders in Council, three decrees that restricted American trade and led to the impressment of American soldiers and the search and seizure of American ships, brought about the Embargo Act of 1807, which Jefferson considered preferable to war. Off the Virginia capes the American *Chesapeake* had been fired upon by the British *Leopard,* with consequent fatalities and the impressment of American sailors. When the money changers cried for war, Thomas Jefferson substituted economic sanctions. America's experiment was doomed to failure, however, for the New England traders and owners of vessels were so vociferous in protest that Congress in 1809 repealed the Embargo Act and, hoping to stimulate home manufactures, passed in its stead the Non-Intercourse Act.

History

Jefferson's mantle fell in 1809 upon the shoulders of another Virginian, James Madison. The peace policies of Jefferson collapsed during Madison's administration, chiefly because the popular demand for war made inroads upon the thinking of cabinet members and lawmakers. In June 1812 Congress declared a state of war to exist between the United States and Great Britain. Again the Virginia coast became a British target. In February 1813 Admiral George Cockburn, commanding British vessels, entered the Chesapeake, made headquarters at Lynnhaven Bay, landed a force of 1,800 men, and plundered coastal plantations. In April the British *St. Domingo* captured the *U.S.S. Dolphin* in the Rappahannock River. In June, though Cockburn had been reinforced by Admiral Borlasse Warren, the enemy fleet was repulsed in its effort to take Norfolk and Portsmouth. A few days later, however, Cockburn successfully pillaged the little town of Hampton, but soon thereafter turned his attention to the Carolinas. Despite Cockburn's return to the Chesapeake Bay in August 1814, Virginia suffered during the rest of the war little more than the shock of seeing Washington burned and President Madison and his plumply pretty wife Dolly seek refuge on its soil. The ratification of the Treaty of Ghent in February 1815, establishing the principle of the freedom of the seas, brought peace to the last year of Madison's second term, and sounded the death knell of the Federalist party, which had been expiring for some time with painful gasps. In addition, it paved the way for the 'era of good feeling' coincident with the two terms of James Monroe, the last of the Virginia dynasty.

As President of the United States, Monroe prevented the fortification of the Canadian border, acquired the Floridas, was party to the Missouri Compromise, and enunciated the great doctrine that has continued to dominate the foreign policy of the United States. Madison had wanted war vessels removed from the Great Lakes. Monroe all but achieved the goal. He sent to the British ministry 'a precise project for limiting the force'; in January 1817 Lord Castlereagh accepted the proposal; the actual reduction became effective the following year. The powers agreed to the maintenance of but one vessel on Ontario, two on the upper lakes, and one on Champlain. Thus the unfortified border made possible permanent peace between Canada and the United States and proved that disarmament promotes good will and security.

In annexing all Florida Monroe merely completed the task he had set out to accomplish when he went to France as Jefferson's special representative in 1803 and again in 1804. When Napoleon had sold the Louisiana Territory, he had said clearly that West Florida was included. Both Monroe and Livingston thought that the entire area had been purchased, only to be rudely awakened soon after the bargain was sealed. Later an uprising of the Seminoles, which was speedily, though unauthoritatively, quelled by General Andrew Jackson, expedited the settlement of the Florida question. On February 22, 1819, Secretary John Adams arranged the treaty that effected the purchase from Spain of all East and West Florida.

Encyclopedia of Virginia

The Missouri Compromise, framed by Virginia, born Henry Clay, was passed in March 1820. Jefferson had consistently opposed slavery; Madison had spoken of it as a 'dreadful calamity.' Monroe took steps toward the repatriation of the blacks to Africa. In Liberia, where the town of Monrovia still bears his name, several colonization projects were undertaken with his encouragement.

On December 2, 1823, Monroe sent to Congress his annual message that embodied the principles later known as the Monroe Doctrine, The Holy Alliance, created to suppress liberalism, was about to interfere with the new republics in South America. Jefferson, who had stood consistently against entangling alliances, corresponded with Monroe immediately before the message was written. Thus the doctrine protesting future European colonization in America and the extension on this hemisphere of such systems as those the Holy Alliance promoted was the contribution of both Thomas Jefferson and James Monroe.

The treaty with Russia signed on January 11, 1825, establishing the northwest boundary of the United States, was one of the last significant accomplishments of Monroe's administration.

Meanwhile sectionalism in Virginia had reared its head in a contest between a cismontane and a tramontane people. Unbalanced political representation between the two parts of Virginia led to threats of State dismemberment. In 1816, the year of James Monroe's presidential election, a compromise was reached by which the west 'obtained a representation in the Senate based upon white numbers in exchange for a law equalizing land values for purpose of assessment.' Slavery agitation subsided, internal improvements began, and a crop of young politicians matured.
The rising spirit of nationalism was typified by the American System, which had crept into Virginia with the demand for better means of communication between the eastern and western sections.

Partly because of this system Virginia moved into an epoch of solidification and construction. The general assembly authorized in 1816 the President and Directors of Public Works. The whole State united in 1819 against the establishment of Federal banks. But with agriculture, the case was different. Between 1817 and 1830 the eastern part of the State experienced a great industrial decline and loss of population. Tobacco planters gave up their impoverished farms to briars and broomsedge and moved to the western frontiers or into the new Southern cotton states. Fairfax County by 1833 had become a ruin; Norfolk, said Henry Ruffner in 1847, had lost half its commerce in 25 years. In much of the Piedmont and Tidewater, plantations were so run down that they could support only their owners; land values fell from $206,000,000 to $90,000,000 from 1817 to 1830; the total increase in the white population was only 91,213 in the decade following 1820. Similarly, the decrease of Virginia's exported goods fell from $8,212,860 in 1817 to $3,340,185 in 1828. The eastern part of the State was left with only the resource of surplus blacks.

History

During the years following 1818 Virginia was enveloped in one of America's periodic depressions. The planters of Tidewater and Piedmont discarded tobacco for cotton and tried to rejuvenate wornout land. They attributed their failure to the American System's doctrine that a high protective tariff was essential for making the nation self-supporting. Western Virginia, however, was developing rapidly. Wheat, sheep, and iron were coming to the front as economic products. But the inefficiency of the State in supplying this section with adequate means of communication brought dissatisfaction. Unable to fit slavery into their industrial scheme, the mountaineers turned against the American System just at the time that the depleted land of the east was being brought back to fertility and the sale of slaves had become an important economic factor.

Sectionalism was nowhere so apparent as in education. Only on the promise that free schools should later be established did the western part of Virginia consent to an annual appropriation of $15,000 for a proposed university. When the University of Virginia was founded in 1819, the site chosen was close to the mountains.

The Missouri Compromise had thrown the balance of political power to the North. The slavery question was dimmed, however, by agitation that centered about the tariff. The 'Tariff of Abominations,' enacted in 1828, caused the South to unite solidly against the North and brought about talk of secession.

SECTIONAL STRIFE AND SLAVE BREEDING

Although Andrew Jackson, elected in 1828, was against the American System, he did nothing at first toward lowering the high tariff. After South Carolina's Nullification Act, Governor John Floyd announced that any attempt to cross Virginia's territory would be met with armed resistance. Talk of secession was temporarily suspended by the passage of Clay's compromise tariff, providing for a gradual reduction of rates until 1841, and after 1842 for no duties above 20 per cent.

At the Whig Convention of 1839, presided over by James Barbour of Virginia, were nominated the party's first successful candidates, William Henry Harrison and John Tyler, both Virginians. Tyler, who followed Harrison's short tenure of office (March 4 to April 4, 1841), pursued the policies of the Virginia dynasty and fought the attempted revival of the American System. During Tyler's administration the Treaty of Washington was signed (1842), fixing the Canadian boundary as far west as the Rocky Mountains, and Texas was annexed. Though Governor William Smith called out three regiments for participation in the Mexican War (1846-48) and only one was accepted, the war's two heroes were Virginians, Zachary Taylor and Winfield Scott.

The question of slavery now dominated the scene. With the exhaustion of Tidewater soil and the rise of King Cotton, eastern Virginians were, driven into a nefarious traffic, that of supplying the new South's demand for more slaves. As the interstate slave trade increased, Virginia was dubbed the 'breeder of slaves.' In the western part of the State, abolitionists came to the front. In Virginia the slave industrial system was in a death grapple with the free industrial system. Nat Turner's slave insurrection of 1831 crystallized sentiment for and against abolition. Citizens flocked to one of three standards: removal of free blacks from the Tidewater and Piedmont sections; deportation of the entire black population; and a plan for gradual emancipation. In the legislature of 1832 an act that provided for colonization of free Blacks and another that would have brought about emancipation were lost by narrow margins. Later the 'Atherton Gag,' preventing discussion of slavery, was passed by the National House.

The Wilmot Proviso intensified hatred and misunderstanding. Virginia declared itself against the proposed exclusion of slavery from all territory to be acquired from Mexico. A crisis was averted, however, by Clay's Compromise of 1850. During 1852, the year *Uncle Tom's Cabin* was published, the Virginia branch of the American Colonization Society sent 243 Blacks to Liberia. The slavery question was revived in 1854 by the Kansas-Nebraska Bill, allowing local option as to slavery in new Territories; and in 1857 by the Dred Scott Decision. On the night of October 16, 1859, John Brown's band seized the United States arsenal at Harpers Ferry. At night 100 marines under Colonel Robert E. Lee arrived, surrounded the arsenal, and captured the raiders. In a swift trial, John Brown was convicted of murder and treason and hanged.

But Virginia remained union minded and declined South Carolina's proposal for a Southern convention. By 1860, however, the State needed only the shot fired at Fort Sumter by Edmund Ruffin, a Virginian, to crystallize. anti-union sympathies. When Lincoln issued a call for troops on April 15, 1861, Governor John Letcher refused to supply Virginia's quota. On the 17th the State Convention voted to secede from the Union, On April 23 Governor Letcher placed Robert E. Lee in command of Virginia troops. On the 25th Virginia joined the Confederate States. On May 21, 1861, Richmond was made the capital of the Confederacy.

The Virginia that seceded from the Union retained the forms, if not the substance, established during the half century that ended with the inauguration of John Quincy Adams. The caste system placed its entire weight on slavery. Just above the slave was the free black, fettered with legal restrictions, despised by 'poor whites,' that great mass of miserable people strewn about the Tidewater and Piedmont. In contrast were the poor 'mountain whites,' primitive, rugged, proud. Above these was the yeoman farmer class, independent, self-respecting, deeply religious. The planter class, at the top, had its own strata, 'the rabble of small planters,' possessing few slaves; the middle-class planters; and lastly a handful of upperclass planters. In 1860 out of a white population of 1,047,299 only 52,128 persons owned slaves; half of these held from one to four, and only 114 individuals owned as many as 100 slaves.

History

In mid-century, Virginia shared with the rest of the States in the spate of immigration that followed, the collapse of liberal movements in Europe when the revolutions of 1848 failed. Among the newcomers, who settled chiefly in Richmond, were many Jews. Although they had filtered into the colony from the beginning and there were 26 heads of families in Richmond who organized in 1789 Virginia's first Jewish congregation, Jews had not been attracted to agrarian Virginia. By the end of the eighteenth century they were coming in steady, if thin, streams, which swelled abruptly in 1848.

Except for the few towns, Virginia's Tidewater and Piedmont landscape was a patchwork of farms wedged between plantations. In the 'big house' the table was weighted with food and wines, and entertaining was on a grand scale. As many as 20 people often dined at Bolling Hall and remained the night, subjected only to a little 'doubling up.' Henry Barnard, who visited Shirley in 1833, left a minute description. At eight o'clock the family had breakfast, a cup of coffee or tea drunk 'fashionably,' cold ham 'of the real Virginia flavor,' and a variety of hot breads. About one o'clock the invited guests arrived, the gentlemen consumed 'grog,' and at three o'clock dinner was served. After champagne, the upper cloth was removed for the elaborate desserts. 'When you have eaten this, off goes the second table cloth, and then upon a bare mahogany table is set the figs, raisins, and almonds and . . . 2 or 3 bottles of wine.' The planter, as a rule oft-married and sire of many children, bought his whiskey by the barrel, fraternized at the tavern, went to barbecues, hunted, and took his daily tour of the plantation.

The slaves, grouped together in the 'quarter,' had plenty of fuel and a daily ration of a quart of corn meal and half a pound of salt pork for each adult, supplemented by vegetables in season. Coarse winter clothing, shoes, and blankets were issued in October; and medical attention was provided. They had their dances, baptizings, 'preaching,' house-raisings, and hunted rabbit, 'coon, and 'possum. The plantation was a factory, a school, a parish, a matrimonial bureau, a nursery, and a divorce court.

After 1835, the growing of wheat began to predominate south of the James, particularly in Tidewater; and farm land increased enormously in value, rising from $216,401,543 in 1850 to $371,761,661 in 1860. Industry's output in Virginia rose from $29,602,5077 in 1850 to $50,602,507 in 1860.

BATTLE GROUND OF THE 'SIXTIES

Virginia was the central battle ground of the war. Hoping for a quick subjugation, Federal armies occupied Alexandria and western Virginia (admitted as a separate State on June 20, 1863), reinforced the garrison at Fort Monroe, and threatened to enter the Valley near Harpers Ferry. Outmaneuvered north of Winchester and decisively defeated at Manassas on July 21, 1861, the North began molding a finer military organization; while the South, except for unsuccessful efforts to recover western Virginia, awaited the next Federal move.

Encyclopedia of Virginia

Declaration of martial law around Richmond, the Hampton Roads posts, and other threatened zones, early in March 1862, followed by the battle between the *Monitor* and the *Merrimac* on March 9, the evacuation of Norfolk on May 9, and preparations for the evacuation of Richmond the following week, was the result of Federal activities in the fall of 1861 and the winter following. Union forces took the forts at Cape Hatteras in August and those at Roanoke Island in February, thereby opening the back door to Norfolk. The coast of South Carolina below Charleston was occupied in November. Fort Henry on the Tennessee River and Fort Donelson on the Cumberland were captured in February, leading to the loss of Kentucky, half of Tennessee, and of Nashville, for the duration of the war. The *Trent Affair*, purely naval, in November and December almost culminated in war between the United States and Great Britain and momentarily raised Confederate hopes. The capture of New Orleans in April closed the mouth of the Mississippi. The battle of Shiloh on April 6 and 7 resulted in the loss of General Albert Sidney Johnston. The loss of Island No. 10 on April 8 opened the upper stretches of the Mississippi to the Union fleet and resulted in the subsequent evacuation of Corinth and Fort Pillow and in the Battle of Memphis and the consequent destruction of the Confederate river fleet.

Military movements on a large scale began in Virginia in March 1862. General Joseph E. Johnston withdrew from the vicinity of Washington to the Rappahannock. McClellan transferred his army to the vicinity of Fort Monroe and in May began an advance on Richmond, retarded by Johnston, now on the Peninsula; and Jackson's Valley campaign kept Washington on tenterhooks. The Federal fleet steamed up the James River to aid in taking Richmond, but on May 14, was effectively stopped at Drewry's Bluff -a fortification never taken.

After the indecisive battle of Seven Pines on May 31-June 1, 1862, Lee was placed in command of the Army of Northern Virginia. He defeated McClellan and relieved Richmond and began to withdraw to strike at Pope in northern Virginia. In August a decisive victory at Manassas over Pope, now commanding most of McClellan's army as well as his own, produced a near panic in Washington and necessitated the hurried restoration of McClellan to command. Lee's invasion of Maryland, coincident with Confederate advances in Kentucky, culminated in the indecisive battle of Sharpsburg, or Antietam, on September 17 and gave Lincoln his opportunity to claim a Northern victory and to announce on September 22 his purpose to proclaim emancipation. McClellan followed Lee back to Virginia, but his inertia again proved his undoing. He was supplanted by Burnside on November 7, 1862. Burnside was effectively disposed of at Fredericksburg on December 13, 1862, and Hooker, who succeeded him, ended an energetic campaign ingloriously at Chancellorsville in May 1863, though there the South sustained the irreparable loss of Stonewall Jackson.

History

When Lee's army invaded Pennsylvania in June 1863, panic reigned throughout the North. With Gettysburg, July 1-4, came defeat and the Confederacy's loss of all hope that European powers might intervene. Lee returned slowly to Virginia, followed by Meade who temporized throughout the fall and winter, unwilling to tilt lances again with an always dangerous foe.
 The last phase of the war began in March 1864. Then Grant, who had numerous successes in the west, including Vicksburg in July 1863, and Chattanooga in November, was placed in command of all Union armies. Under his plan Sherman began the march across the near South to cut off supplies from Virginia, Sigel moved down the Valley of Virginia for the same purpose, Butler advanced from Fort Monroe toward Richmond, and Grant remained with Meade to oppose Lee. Butler's and Sigel's movements came to naught. After Grant and Meade crossed the Rapidan on May 4, 1864, the battles of the Wilderness, Spotsylvania, North Anna River, Totopotomoy Creek, Cold Harbor, and the assault on Petersburg followed in rapid succession, all indecisive. General Early, whom Lee sent from Cold Harbor to the Valley, advanced to Washington and Baltimore, in July, but returned to the Valley when additional troops arrived to protect the Federal capital. When Sheridan, placed in command in the Valley in August, defeated Early at Winchester and at Fisher's Hill in September and at Cedar Creek in October, the Valley was lost to the South. Grant reached Petersburg in June, having suffered more than 60,000 casualties on the way, and attempted encirclement of the city and the cutting of rail communications. Heavy blows, failing to break Lee's lines, pushed the Federal lines gradually westward. The Crater fiasco, six months' work on the Dutch Gap Canal undertaken to permit entrance of the fleet, several efforts to break through east of Richmond, attempts to destroy the Virginia Central Railroad and the James River Canal, and repeated drives against the roads south and west of Petersburg were all unsuccessful. Federal failures in Virginia, from the beginning of the war until the final breaking of Lee's lines, repeatedly depressed Northern spirits. Sheridan's victories in the Valley and Sherman's march through Georgia, however, were of sufficient brilliance to re-elect Lincoln. Though heavy operations ceased, the winter proved hard for the ill-equipped and ill-fed Southern army. On February 3, 1865, a conference in Hampton Roads between Lincoln and Seward and Confederate commissioners effected nothing.
 With the coming of spring, Sheridan returned from the Valley, Grant became active along his entire line, and on the morning of April 2, 1865, Lee's lines broke southwest of the city. During the following night Richmond and Petersburg were evacuated; and Lee moved westward in an attempt to join Johnston in North Carolina. Grant sent one corps into Richmond, left another near Petersburg, and with the remainder, four corps and Sheridan's cavalry, began a running fight with Lee that terminated at Appomattox on April 9, 1865. With the surrender of Lee, the struggle ceased in Virginia, and the Confederacy collapsed.

Encyclopedia of Virginia

At last it was over -the strange, intangible thing for which men had fought and women had sacrificed and suffered. The privileged minority knew perhaps that they had been protecting the wealth ancestors had accumulated at the price of black men's liberty; the small planters had blindly followed an example they had seldom questioned; and from the ranks of the poor whites men and boys had enlisted, or later had been drafted. They had fought a good fight. Now it was over, and few were sorry. Soldiers would return to the hearth and the plow. The favored minority had lost much; the masses could continue to dig a living out of the soil that had not failed their forefathers.

VIRGINIA ACCEPTS RECONSTRUCTION

But a different South, a different Virginia, lay about them. Great houses had been burned; churches and courthouses were heaps of ashes; rare books, valued records had been destroyed. People were filled with awe and bewilderment, planters who had once been rich, poor whites, Blacks. Adversity had leveled the great and the small. And the conquerors had come down to take possession of Virginia. The war was over, but days of Reconstruction were at hand.

The State was without civil government; farms were ruined, and farmers had no implements, stock, seeds, or money; factories were reduced to ruins; merchandise was depleted and credit was gone; railways were in a state of dilapidation, and the canal was scarcely serviceable; Black labor had uncertain status and white labor was scarce; West Virginia, now a new State, had assumed no part of the *ante-bellum* debt, now $48,567,040, an increase of $16,628,896 since 1860, and Virginia $27,709,319 in unproductive stocks. The total loss, exclusive of slaves, amounted to $104,205,720.53.

The Federal army assumed command of the State and remained in virtual control until 1870. On May 9, 1865, President Johnson recognized the 'Restored Government' of Virginia, the Government had consented to a division of the State, and on May 26 Governor F.H. Pierpont moved from Alexandria to Richmond. On June 15 the Bureau of Refugees, Freedmen, and Abandoned Lands set up offices in the State. On June 27 all Virginia, except Fairfax County, became the Military Department of Virginia under command of General Alfred H. Terry.

Governor Pierpont was conservative. Through his action in securing sanction for a revision of the Alexandria Constitution of 1864 to enfranchise disqualified Confederates, he incurred the animosity of the radicals, who wished to gain control through the Black vote. When his term expired on April 4, 1868, his successor was appointed by military order.

In the spring of 1865 there were about 500,000 Blacks in the State and about 700,000 whites. Most cities had their Black population doubled almost overnight; around rural Bureaus squalid villages arose; and the mortality rate among blacks in-

History

creased appallingly. Independent courts were instituted in which all complaints, generally against whites, were heard. Authorized to function for one year after the declaration of peace, the Freedmen's Bureau was extended to January 1, 1869, though its educational and financial activities continued until June 20, 1872. Blacks did not gain suffrage until late in 1869 and radicals never controlled the State.

The failure of legislators in Virginia and other Southern States to ratify the Fourteenth Amendment gave a radical Congress excuse for severity. By the Reconstruction Act, passed on March 2, 1867, and supplemented on March 23, Virginia became Military District No. 1, commanded by General John M. Schofield.

The constitutional convention, for which the act had provided, convened in Richmond on December 3, 1867. Two-thirds of its 105 members were radicals, 25 of these blacks. Judge John C. Underwood, who had gained notoriety by impaneling a mixed jury and presiding at the attempted trial of Jefferson Davis in May 1867, was elected president. Two clauses of the constitution drafted by the convention effected the undoing of the radical element: one provided for the disfranchisement of a large number of military officers and governmental officials; the other prohibited from holding public office any person who had voluntarily aided the South during the war. General Schofield, addressing the convention on April 17, 1868, the day the instrument was approved by that body, and failing to prevent the insertion of these clauses, refused to authorize the expenditure of funds necessary for ratification.

President Grant having recommended to Congress that the people be allowed to vote on the objectionable clauses separately, the election, held on July 6, 1869, resulted in the adoption of the constitution without the two disfranchising clauses. Gilbert C. Walker of New York, a conservative Republican, was elected governor; and the legislators were two-thirds conservative, of 181 Senators and delegates 55 were radicals of which 24 were Blacks; three Blacks were conservative. The legislature convened on October 5 and on October 8 ratified the Fourteenth and Fifteenth Amendments. Virginia had complied with the terms of the Reconstruction Act. On January 26, 1870, the Old Dominion ceased to be Military District No. 1.

FROM COMMEMORATION TO ACHIEVEMENT

Then the State began its slow climb to recovery. The slave system had produced unhealthy economic conditions, false standards, and gross inequalities; and the war had brought about destitution. On March 2, 1870, a start was made toward the goal set by Thomas Jefferson almost 100 years before; a department of public education was established with Dr. William H. Ruffner as superintendent. Though impoverishment caused progress to be slow, by the turn of the century the State had laid the foundations for a system of secondary education, had somewhat strengthened its colleges for men, and had provided two normal schools, one for women and another for blacks . Within the three decades railroads relaid their trackage, built new lines to connect remote areas with centers of population, and established great terminals. Steamships, increasing in numbers, carried commercial tonnage on inland waterways and north and south from coastal ports. Factories began to add an industrial economy to the almost wholly agrarian economy that had formerly characterized Virginia.

The attempt to fund the State's *ante-bellum* debt gave rise to a powerful political party that stirred racial hatreds, ran the gamut of political passions, dragged Virginia through State and National courts, and died with the downfall of its principal figure, General William Mahone. An act of the assembly in 1871 provided for funding the State debt of more than $45,000,000 and tentatively assigned one-third to West Virginia. Mahone, the first postwar railroad magnate, entered the political field in 1873. Under the Democratic banner he virtually nominated the successful candidate for governor and, during the next four years, built up a small following on the debt question. Failing, however, to secure the gubernatorial nomination in 1877, he organized the Readjuster Party and built up in two years a powerful machine composed chiefly of Blacks and disgruntled Democrats. In 1879, having elected a legislature that sent him to the United States Senate, he began to institute throughout the State a spoils system strong enough to survive the downfall of its creator. Later Mahone allied himself openly with the Republican party, elected a Readjuster governor in 1881, and dispensed Federal patronage in Virginia. The dispute that had to do with the State debt became more violent and involved; fights and riots occurred; some laws were defeated, and others that were passed were vetoed or fought in the courts; and corruption prevailed. In 1883, however, control was wrested from Mahone's machine. The financial difficulties were adjusted in 1891-92 to the satisfaction of the State's creditors. It was not until 1915, however, that the Supreme Court of the United States rendered the opinion that West Virginia must assume its proportion of those obligations incurred when it was a part of Virginia.

But the Constitution of 1868 continued to be a thorn in the flesh of white Virginians. It did not discourage blacks from voting, and it had made possible as late as 1888 the election from the Fourth Congressional District of a black to the National House of Representatives. The delegates to the constitutional convention that assembled on June 12, 1901, wrote into the new instrument the 'understanding clause,' which was to be effective until 1904 and then to be superseded by an intelligence test which required voters to interpret the constitution. The payment of three years' poll tax six months before general elections was also made a prerequisite to voting, an imposition that has decreased the size of both the white and the black electorate. The constitution was not ratified by the voters but 'proclaimed' by the convention and 'approved ' by the legislature.

History

In the constitution of 1902 special provision was made for Virginia cities in line with the old precedent, reminiscent of England, by which they were politically independent of counties. Despite various inducements to found towns, Colonial Virginians had preferred to live on plantations. Each of the four 'corporacouns' constituted in 1619 was to have a capital city; in 1662 an act provided for the building of five towns; acts passed in 1680 and 1691 sought to establish towns. Though a few towns came into existence, the majority of Virginians continued to live on plantations. The political independence of the Virginia city had its origin in the act of 1705, which authorized 16 towns and provided that a community might become a ' free borough ' when it had accumulated as many as 30 families, and after the acquisition of 60 families that its constitution should 'be held perfect' and that it might then send a representative to the general assembly. Yet during the Colonial period only three municipalities had their own burgesses: Jamestown, the first capital; Williamsburg, the second; and Norfolk, the only free borough. Richmond, when rechartered with city status in 1842, became under the commonwealth the first independent municipality. Now there are in Virginia 24 cities that administer their own affairs and bear to counties only geographic relationships.

The constitution written largely to its liking, Virginia saw the end of its commemorative era that had been characterized by mourning, monuments to the illustrious dead, and nostalgia for the days that were no more, and launched upon twentieth-century accomplishments. The State was not crushed by the panic of 1907; the depression of 1921 had no serious State-wide consequences; and the cataclysm of the early 1930's was far less devastating than in most other States. The explanation is to be found in Virginia's small bonded indebtedness and the diversification of the industries that were established during the first third of the century. Between 1899 and 1929 the value of products manufactured in Virginia rose from $108,644,150 to $745,910,075, and the number of industrial workers was almost doubled. The foundation, accordingly, was laid for a solid prosperity that made progress possible in many fields. Virginia began in 1922 to lift itself literally out of the mud with the reorganization of a highway department under a competent commissioner, and has achieved a system of roads comparable to any other in the country. The more than 8,000 miles of hard-surfaced roads in the State have been brought about without a bond issue and by means of a gasoline tax imposed in 1926. And no 'nuisance' taxes have been imposed in Virginia. The $4,000,000 annual revenue from the sale of alcoholic beverages in State-owned stores has been in a measure an antidote for depression.

Woodrow Wilson, another Virginia-born President, was inaugurated in 1913. His administration was marked not only by high idealism and emphasis upon human welfare but also by a sound fiscal and economic policy. The Owen-Glass Federal Reserve Bank Act, credited with preventing the old type of money panic, was the handiwork of Virginians. Robert L. Owen of

Encyclopedia of Virginia

Oklahoma, chairman of the Senate Committee on Currency and Banking, was born in Virginia; and Carter Glass, then representative from Virginia, was serving as chairman of the House Committee on Currency and Banking.

The old wounds of the unreconstructed rebels within the State, salved by the Spanish-American War, were completely healed during the World War. A Democratic President, born in the Old Dominion, was at the helm; the Nation and Virginia held common cause in what the people believed to be an honest effort to safeguard those principles of self-government for which the oldest one of the United States had stood since the settlers at Jamestown demanded representative government. War brought prosperity to Virginia: factories; munitions plants; Camp Lee, where 50,000 soldiers were trained; Camp Humphreys for engineers; Camp Stuart for embarkation; and Langley Field for aviators. With the signing of the Armistice, cities that had come into existence or doubled their size almost overnight found a way to recover from the postwar slump through the establishment of new industries.

Virginia's principal progress during the twentieth century, however, has been made in relation to human welfare, particularly owing to the emphasis laid upon it by Governor Westmoreland Davis (1918-22). Though the State still lags far behind in education, the May Campaign of 1905, which had the essential characteristics of a religious revival, immediately resulted in better rural schools and more emphasis everywhere upon secondary education. Consolidated high schools, a start toward vocational education in cities and counties, a better State university that since 1920 has admitted women to its graduate and professional departments, the second oldest institution of learning in America converted into a coeducational State college, an agricultural and polytechnic institute that is sending its tentacles into many fields, a military institute that possesses traditions close to the hearts of Virginians, new buildings made possible to a large extent through Federal aid, and public insistence upon increased appropriations bear testimony to the progress made in the first four decades of the twentieth century. In 1916 foundations were laid for a modern public health program, which has steadily grown in the years that have followed. The State Board of Public Welfare, modestly established in 1908 as the Board of Charities and Corrections, received its new name in 1922. Its functions, consistently broadened, now include the administration of the eleemosynary and penal work of the State. The prisons, the four reform schools, the asylums for the insane, the sanitaria for tubercular patients, aid to dependent children, old age assistance, and much else come under its jurisdiction.

During the gubernatorial administration of Harry Flood Byrd the government of Virginia underwent complete reorganization. A commission on the simplification of State government had been appointed by Governor E. Lee Trinkle, in 1924 and had recommended changes that became the basis of the new plan. The reorganization act of 1927 provided that only three State officers be

History

elected by the people, the governor, lieutenant governor, and the attorney general. State government functions under 12 major departments: Taxation, Finance, Highways, Education, Corporations, Labor and Industry, Agriculture and Immigration, Conservation and Development, Health, Public Welfare, Law, and Workmen's Compensation. The heads of all these, with the exception of the department of law, are appointed by the governor. The governor may inspect all records and, when the legislature is not in session, may suspend any State executive officer except the lieutenant governor.

Republicans made significant gains during the 1963 elections, due in a large part to support from Black voters. However, in 1965 loyalty switched and a Democrat, Mills E. Goodwin, was elected Governor.

The late 1940's brought major developments in the progress of Black representation in government. W. Laurence became the first Black county supervisor (Nansemond County.)

The legislatures greatly increased funding for education and health from new sales taxes. A commission was also established to prepare for a major revision of the constitution. The new document took effect July 1, 1971. (See Constitution.)

In 1977 Richmond elected its first Black mayor, Henry L. Warsh, III. Then in 1989 a major development saw the election of L. Douglas Wilder as the nation's first elected Governor. In September, 1991 he announced his intention to run for U. S. President in the 1992 elections.

Between the industrial North and the still mostly agrarian South, between political left and right wings, between extremes of poverty and wealth, between the advocates of States' rights and the proponents of centralized government, Virginia, even now, stands on middle ground. Its democratic forms are sound; and, more than ever before, Virginia is aware of the necessity to raise educational standards and to ameliorate the condition of its vast submarginal population. Virginia still cherishes the heritage passed down from liberty-loving first settlers, who defied British kings; from Nathaniel Bacon and Patrick Henry, who roused the people against autocracy; from Thomas Jefferson, who enunciated the principles of democracy; from Robert E. Lee, who could turn defeat into spiritual victory. The weary travelers who disembarked at Jamestown established not only the first permanent English settlement in America, but a democratic ideal that may wane but will never die.

CHRONOLOGY OF VIRGINIA

1585 — August 17.— Sir Walter Raleigh's first settlers reach Roanoke Island in 'Virginia'.

1591 — Roanoke Island settlers having disappeared, the colony is abandoned.

1606 — April 10.— James I grants joint charter to two companies to colonize 'Virginia.'

1607 — May 14.— First permanent English settlement in the New World established at Jamestown.

1607 — August.— Colonists of Plymouth Company land at Kennebec (Maine) but make only temporary settlement.
December.— Captain John Smith saved by Pocahontas.

1608 — January 12.— Arrival of 'First Supply.'

1609 — May 23.— London Company granted second charter.

1609-10 — 'Starving Time'; between September and June population drops from about 500 to 60.

1610 — May 23.— Sir Thomas Gates, first governor, arrives at Jamestown.
June 8.— Colonists having abandoned Jamestown, return upon arrival of Thomas West, Lord Delaware, at Point Comfort.

1611 — March 12.— London Company granted third charter. (March 22, 1612, n.s.)

Encyclopedia of Virginia

1612 — John Rolfe introduces the cultivation of tobacco for export.

1614 — April 5.— John Rolfe marries Pocahontas at Jamestown.

1619 — July 30.— First representative legislature in America-House of Burgesses-meets in Jamestown.
August 30.— First Blacks arrive in Jamestown.
First foundry in America established on Falling Creek.

1620 — First shipload of 'maids' arrives to become wives of settlers.
December 11.— Pilgrims, authorized to settle in southern Virginia, land at Plymouth, having been thrown off course.

1622 — March 22.— Indian massacre wipes out about one third of colonists.

1624 — June 16.— London Company's charter revoked by King's Bench; Virginia becomes royal colony.
Doctrine of no taxation without representation is first asserted in Virginia by burgesses.

1628-29 — Population about 3,000.

1629 — October 30.— Province of Carolina carved from Virginia by royal grant to Sir Robert Heath.

1632 — Province of Maryland carved from Virginia by royal grant to Lord Baltimore.

1634 — First eight counties formed.
February 12.— Syms Free School endowed-first educational institution endowed and oldest free school in the United States.

1635 — Population about 5,000.
Sir John Harvey 'thrust out' by council and burgesses, who make first assertion of colonists' right to order own government.

Chronology

1644 — April 18.— Second Indian massacre kills about 300 colonists.

1649 — Virginians assert their allegiance to Charles II.

1650 — Population about 20,000.
Southwest Virginia explored by Abraham Wood and Edmund Bland.
October.— First navigation act passed by Parliament, banishing Dutch vessels from Virginia.

1651 — March 12.— Virginia capitulates to the Commonwealth.— (March 22, 1652, n.s.)

1652-60 — Only period of almost complete self-government in Colonial Virginia.

1652 — May 5.— Burgesses declare that 'the right of election of all officers of the Colony appertain to the Burgesses."

1659 — March 13.— Burgesses declare the 'Supreme power of the government' in Virginia rests in them; Berkeley elected governor.

1660 — July 31.— Charles II reappoints Berkeley as royal governor.

1670 — Population about 40,000.

1673 — Northern Neck of Virginia, granted to Lord Hopton and associates in 1649 by Charles II, actually becomes a proprietary when Lord Culpeper assumes control. Proprietary rights to all Virginia are bestowed upon Lord Arlington and Lord Culpeper.

1675 — Susquehannock Indian War.

1676 — Bacon's Rebellion.

1680 — An act for the establishment of one town for each county passed by general assembly; Charles II suspends its operation.

Encyclopedia of Virginia

1682 — Tobacco Riots.

1691 — General assembly re-enacts law providing for towns, but suspends operation of the act in 1693.

1693 — February 8.— The College of William and Mary, second institution of higher learning in America, founded at Middle Plantation (Williamsburg).

1699 — Seat of government moved to Middle Plantation.
Act for religious tolerance passed.
First group of Huguenots reach Virginia.

1700 — Population about 70,000.

1705 — Basis of independence from counties of Virginia's future cities laid by general assembly.

1716 — First theater in United States built in Williamsburg.

1722 — Williamsburg, capital of the colony, becomes first incorporated municipality in Virginia.

1730 — Population 114,000.

1736 — August 6.— First newspaper in Virginia founded at Williamsburg.

1749 — In transmontane Virginia 500,000 acres granted to Ohio Company and 800,000 to Loyal Company; Christopher Gist explores Ohio tract to falls of Ohio River (present Louisville).

1754 — George Washington with Virginia troops advances against the French in the Ohio Valley, precipitating French and Indian War.

1755 — March 23.— Patrick Henry delivers 'liberty or death' speech in Second Virginia Convention in Richmond.
June 15.— Washington chosen commander in chief of Continental Army.
October 24.— First bloodshed of Revolution in Virginia at Hampton.

Chronology

1755 — July 9.— Upon fatal wounding of General Edward Braddock, Washington rallies British regulars and Colonials near Fort Duquesne.

1755-56 — Population 294,000.

1758 — November 25.— Fort Duquesne occupied.

1759 — General assembly creates standing committee of correspondence to exchange information with colony's agent in London.

1763 — December 1.— Patrick Henry flouts British rule in the Parsons' Cause.
French and Indian War ends; transmontane region ceded to British.
Royal proclamation forbids further grants west of Alleghenies.

1765 — May 29.— Patrick Henry, protesting the Stamp Act, delivers in house of burgesses 'Caesar-Brutus' speech.

1766 — February 27.— One hundred and fifteen patriots sign Leedstown Resolutions embodying principles later incorporated in Declaration of Independence.

1769 — First 'lunatic asylum' in America established at Williamsburg.

1773 — March 14.— Burgesses meet in Raleigh Tavern, call convention, and propose congress of the Colonies.
June 1.— Virginia observes Fast Day in protest of Boston Port Bill.
August 1.— First Virginia Convention meets, chooses delegates to Continental Congress.
September 5.— Peyton Randolph of Virginia elected president of First Continental Congress.
October 10.— General Andrew Lewis defeats Shawnee at Point Pleasant (now West Virginia).

1776 — May 6-June 29.— Fifth Virginia Convention meets in Williamsburg, declares Virginia independent State, instructs Virginia's delegates to Continental Congress

75

to propose independence; adopts George Mason's declaration of rights and first constitution of a free and independent state, and elects Patrick Henry first governor of Commonwealth.
June 7.— Richard Henry Lee offers in Continental Congress resolutions for independence, foreign alliances, and a form of confederacy.
July 2.— Lee's resolutions adopted by Congress.
July 4.— Declaration of Independence, phrased by Thomas Jefferson, adopted by Congress.
December 5.— Phi Beta Kappa Society, first intercollegiate fraternity in United States, founded at Williamsburg.
Kentucky established as a county of Virginia.

1778 — July 9.— Virginia ratifies Articles of Confederation.

1779 — February 25.— George Rogers Clark with Virginia troops takes Vincennes.
May 9.— First formal invasion of Virginia by British who came by sea.
First law school in America established at College of William and Mary, which that year became first American university.

1780 — April 30.— Governor Jefferson moves executive office to Richmond.
December 30.— Benedict Arnold with 27 ships arrives in James River.

1781 — April 29.— La Fayette reaches Richmond.
May 20.— Cornwallis reaches Petersburg, taking command of combined British forces.
May 24.— La Fayette begins retreat before Cornwallis.
June 4.— Warned by Jack Jouette, Jefferson and Virginia Legislature escape Colonel Tarleton, who arrives in Charlottesville.
October 19.— Cornwallis surrenders at Yorktown.

1782 — Population 567,114.

1784 — March 1.— Virginia cedes Northwest Territory to United States.

Chronology

1785 — Virginia Statute for Religious Liberty passes legislature.
March 28.— Mt. Vernon Conference, called by Virginia Legislature, results in movement toward Constitutional Convention.

1786 — September 11.— Annapolis Convention meets at invitation of Virginia Legislature-second step toward Constitutional Convention.

1787 — May 25.— George Washington elected president of Constitutional Convention, meeting at Philadelphia.
May 29.— Governor Edmund Randolph submits to Convention Madison's Virginia Plan-basis of deliberations.

1788 — June 26.— Virginia ratifies Federal Constitution, 89 to 79.

1789 — April 30.— George Washington inaugurated first President of the United States.
December 3.— Virginia cedes to United States part of area for seat of government.

1790 — Population 747,610.
Virginia Legislature remonstrates against Assumption Bill-first remonstrance of a state against a Federal Act.

1791 — December 15.— America's Bill of Rights added to the Constitution when nine amendments offered by James Madison and tenth by Richard Henry Lee are ratified.

1798 — December 21.— Legislature adopts 'Virginia Resolutions,' protesting Alien and Sedition laws.

1799 — First ship constructed by the Federal Government-the Chesapeake-is built at the Gosport Navy Yard.

1800 — Population 880,200.

1801 — March 4.— Thomas Jefferson inaugurated President.

Encyclopedia of Virginia

1803 — February 23.— Chief Justice John Marshall of Virginia hands down opinion asserting U.S. Supreme Court's right of Judicial review.
April 30.— James Monroe, Jefferson's emissary, concludes treaty with France for Purchase of Louisiana Territory.

1804 — May 14.— Lewis and Clark, commissioned by Jefferson, begin exploration of Louisiana Territory.

1807 — May 22.— Trial of Aaron Burr begins in Richmond.
June 22.— British frigate *Leopard* attacks *Chesapeake* off Virginia capes.
December 22.— Congress passes Jefferson's Embargo Act.

1809 — March 4.— James Madison inaugurated President.

1810 — Population 974,600.

1812 — June 18.— President Madison signs Congressional act declaring war upon England.

1813 — British fleet ravages areas contiguous to Virginia waters.

1814 — August 24.— President and Mrs. Madison flee to Virginia before British entering Washington.

1816 — August 19-23.— Western Virginians, meeting at Staunton, demand new State constitution equalizing representation.

1817 — March 4.— James Monroe inaugurated President.

1819 — January 25.— University of Virginia established.
February 22.— President Monroe's envoys conclude treaty with Spain for acquisition of Floridas.

1820 — Population 1,065,366.

1823 — April 24.— Stephen F. Austin of Virginia obtains grant of land in Texas from Mexico for colonization.
December 2.— President Monroe promulgates the 'Monroe Doctrine.'

Chronology

1825 — January 11.— President Monroe's signature concludes treaty with Russia establishing Northwest boundary.
March 4.— End of 'Virginia Dynasty.'

1829 — February 21.— Legislature condemns 'Tariff of Abominations' as unconstitutional.

1830 — Population 1,211,405.

1831 — August 21.— Nat Turner's slave insurrection.

1832 — Bill to abolish slavery in Virginia lost in house of delegates by vote of 67 to 60.

1835 — Edgar Allan Poe becomes editor of *Southern Literary Messenger,* in which his first short stories have already appeared.

1836 — October 22.— Sam Houston of Virginia elected first President of Republic of Texas.

1840 — Population 1,239,797.

1841 — March 4.— William Henry Harrison of Virginia inaugurated President.
April 4.— John Tyler of Virginia inaugurated President.

1842 — January 24.— Thomas Walker Gilmer of Virginia moves that Congress censure John Quincy for presenting petition from abolitionists for peaceful dissolution of Union.

1845 — March 1.— President Tyler signs bill annexing Texas.

1846 — May 1.— Southern Methodists, meeting in Petersburg, organize Methodist Episcopal Church, South.

1847 — September 13.— General Winfield Scott of Virginia takes Mexico City.

1849 — March 4.— Zachary Taylor of Virginia inaugurated President.

Encyclopedia of Virginia

1850 — Population 1,421,661.

1851 — October 23-25.— New constitution, providing liberal white male franchise, ratified by big majority.

1859 — October 16.— John Brown and band seize U.S. Arsenal at Harpers Ferry, are later suppressed by troops under Colonel R.E. Lee.
December 2.— John Brown hanged.

1860 — Population 1,596,318.

1861 — February 4.— 'Peace Conference,' called by Virginia Legislature, meets in Washington, attended by representatives of 21 states.
February 13.— State Convention (Secession Convention) meets, but refuses to consider secession until peace overtures are exhausted.
April 17.— State Convention votes for secession 88 to 55.
April 25.— Virginia joins the Confederate States.
May 21.— Richmond chosen capital of Confederacy.
July 21.— First Battle of Manassas.

1862 — March 9.— Battle between *Monitor* and *Merrimac* in Hampton Roads.
March 23.— Battle of Kernstown (beginning of Jackson's Valley Campaign).
June 26.— Seven Days' Battles around Richmond begin.
August 29-30.— Second Battle of Manassas.
December 13.— Battle of Fredericksburg.

1863 — May 2-3.— Battle of Chancellorsville; Jackson mortally wounded.
June 20.— Virginia divided; West Virginia admitted as a State.

1864 — May 5-6.— Battle of Wilderness.
May 8-18.— Battle of Spotsylvania Courthouse.
June 3.— Second Battle of Cold Harbor.
June 15-18.— Battle of Petersburg; siege begins.

Chronology

1865 — April 2-3.— Richmond and Petersburg evacuated by Confederates.
April 9.— Lee surrenders at Appomattox.
May 22.— Jefferson Davis imprisoned at Fort Monroe.

1867 — March 2.— Virginia designated as Military District No.1 under Reconstruction Act.
May 13.— Jefferson Davis, arraigned in Richmond and indicted for treason, is admitted to bail.

1869 — July 6.— New State constitution ratified.
October 8.— Fourteenth and fifteenth amendments to Constitution ratified.

1870 — Population 1,225,163.
January 26.— Virginia readmitted to Union.

1880 — Population 1,512,565.

1889 — April 24.— Simpson dry dock, largest in world, opened at Newport News.

1890 — Population 1,655,980.

1894 — March.— Legislative Act provides for secret balloting.

1900 — Population 1,854,184.
May 12.— Legislature passes 'Jim Crow' law.

1902 — July 10.— New State constitution, effective by proclamation, improving public education and governmental efficiency and virtually eliminating Black vote through poll tax and 'understanding clause.'

1907 — April 26.— Jamestown Exposition opens to commemorate 300th anniversary of first landing of English settlers at Cape Henry.
December 16.— Atlantic Fleet, commanded by Rear Admiral Robley D. Evans of Virginia, leaves Hampton Roads for World Cruise.

1908 — Staunton, Virginia, is first city to adopt city manager form of government.

Encyclopedia of Virginia

1910 — Population 2,061,612.

1913 — March 4.— Woodrow Wilson of Virginia inaugurated President.

1914 — November 18.— Wilson signs Federal Reserve Bank Act, fathered by Congressman Carter Glass of Virginia.

1915 — June 14.— U.S. Supreme Court decision places upon West Virginia obligation to share Virginia's *antebellum* State debt.

1917 — April 6.— President Wilson signs Congressional Act declaring war upon Germany.
Hampton Roads becomes great naval and military base.

1918 — The College of William and Mary admits women.
The budget system, sponsored by Governor Westmoreland Davis, is adopted.

1920 — Population 2,309,187.
Women admitted to graduate and professional schools of University of Virginia.
November 2.— Virginia women vote, though Virginia had voted against ratification of Nineteenth Amendment.

1922 — February 27.— State Board of Public Welfare evolves from State Board of Charities and Corrections.
March 24.— State Highway Commission created.
March 27.— Juvenile and Domestic Relations Court established.

1924 — March 20.— Act provides for sterilization of persons committed to State institutions.

1927 — April 27.— Act for reorganization of State government, sponsored by Governor Harry Flood Byrd, passes general assembly.

Chronology

1930 — Population 2,421,851.
March 17.— Legislative act exempts new manufactories from taxation for five years under specified conditions.

1936 — December 18.— Act approved, in conformity with Federal Social Security Act, creating Unemployment Compensation Commission.

1938 — March 31.— Public newspaper, founded.
Public Asistance Act revised and approved, in conformity with Federal Social Security Act, to render old age assistance, aid to dependent children, aid to the blind, and for general relief.

1940 — Population 3,967,000.
Ten new buildings dedicated at Virginia Polytechnic Institute in Blacksburg.

1942 — January. 22.— C.W. Darden Jr. sworn in as Governor.
Students at the University of Virginia work for the war effort.

1943 — The city of Richmond proposes using Black policemen in Black city districts.

1944 — July.— 325th anniversary of the first meeting of the legislature in Jamestown.
World War II servicemen allowed to vote in elections without registering or paying poll tax.

1946 — February.— Legislature passes bill prohibiting strikes by state, municipal or county employees.
December.— State of emergency declared as result of coal strike.

1947 — November.— W. Lawrence becomes the first Black elected to the County Supervisors Board, Nansemond County.
340th anniversary of the settlement of Jamestown.

1948 — More than 50,000 Blacks register to vote in Richmond area. Black candidates run for city posts.

Encyclopedia of Virginia

1949 — Governor Tuck declares a state of emergency due to coal strike; orders seizure of the mine.

1950 — January 19.— Population 3,319,000.
J.S. Battle inaugurated as Governor.

1951 — U.S. Supreme Court upholds Virginia's poll tax law.
Executes seven Blacks, one white man for rape.

1952 — March.— Rioting University students burn one building; three students held in connection with the fire.
School segregation laws upheld.
Ex-Governor Peery dies.

1953 — Democratic campaign manager Kellam resigns after indictment on Federal income tax charge.
Stanley elected Governor.

1954 — January.— T. B. Stanley inaugurated as Governor.
Supreme Court Justice Campbell dies.

1955 — December.— State Legislature approves a referendum to decide whether Virginia should hold a Constitutional Convention to draw up an amendment to circumvent the U.S. Supreme Court edict on school segregation.
Hit by floods; federal relief sought.

1956 — March.— Memorial to World War II and Korean War dead dedicated in Richmond.
September.— Legislative Committee established to probe racial litigation and public school integration.

1957 — November.— J. L. Almond, proponent of racial segregation, elected Governor.
Norfolk organizers begin a drive to increase Black voter registration.

1958 — Furor over segregation issue continues; 26 white adults and children sue Governor Almond and State

Chronology

Administration to enjoin 'massive resistance' laws against racial integration of public schools.

1959 — Coal mine shutdown causes depression in Southwestern part of the state.

November.— Segregation moderates win in most key races for the State Legislature.

1960 — Population 3,967,000.

1961 — Government urged to modernize to keep up with the states shift from a rural to an urban economy.

1962 — January.— Harrison inaugurated as Governor.

October.— H. R. Adams becomes first Black admitted to University of Virginia, Martinsville.

1963 — Republicans make the biggest gains in a century during the November elections; resurgence is due in large part to support from Black voters.

1964 — December.— Appeals Court rules Virginia counties must end tuition grants to white students in segregated private schools.

February 13.— John Paul, 80, federal judge 1931-60 dies. He issued the first integration order (for Charlottesville public schools in July 1956).

1965 — November.— Democrat Mills E. Godwin, Jr. elected Governor with strong support from Blacks and organized labor.

Prince Edward Action Group in Prince Edward County, Virginia was granted $90,193. for a 3-month remedial reading program for Black children who had been without schooling from 1959-1964. (The county's public school system had been abolished during that period to avoid compliance with the 1954 Supreme Court school integration ruling, and white children had attended a private academy.)

1966 — Business interest expands in the state as a record number of new manufacturing plants are built.

March.— U.S. Supreme Court rules Virginia poll tax unconstitutional.

1967 — Dr. William Ferguson Reid (D), 42, a physician, became the first Black to be elected to the General Assembly since 1891.

1968 — January.— First Black member of the State Legislature since 1891 sworn in; J. N. Bradby becomes Sheriff and Mrs. I. W. Adkins becomes clerk of Charles City County, the first Blacks to hold these posts in the state. Sheriff Bradby found dead in March; death is ruled suicide.

April.— 300 students at Virginia Union University take over administration building to protest the University's system of testing.

1969 — November.— L. Holton elected first Republican Governor in 84 years.

1500 University of Virginia students protest to demand admission of Black Assistant Admissions Dean, and more Black coaches and athletes; students demonstrate against U.S. involvement in Vietnam.

1970 — Population 4,651,000.
Anti-war protests continue on University campuses.
January 13.— Governor-elect Linwood Holton announced the appointment of William B. Robertson, as an executive assistant on his staff--first Black to serve in a Virginia governor's office.

1971 — Industrial development surges with the expansion or establishment of 164 manufacturing plants.

1972 — Hurricane Agnes strikes Richmond; area declared flood disaster area.

1973 — November.— Former Governor, the Republican conservative, Mills .E. Godwin wins the gubernatorial race in a close election against independent liberal H. E. Howell.

Chronology

1974 — June 4.— Pope Paul VI creates new diocese at Arlington to end bitter struggle between conservative priests and progressives.

1975 — Death penalty restored.

October 26.— Anwar Sadat began a 10-day visit to the U.S. to seek economic and military aid for Egypt and to explain his policies to the American people. He stayed overnight in Williamsburg, Virginia.

1976 — Restored historical buildings displayed for the nation's Bicentennial.

1977 — Charles S. Robb, son-in-law of President Lyndon Johnson, elected Lieutenant Governor.

March 8.— Richmond City Council elected Henry L. Marsh 3rd as the first Black mayor.

1978 — November.— John W. Warner elected to the Virginia Senate with campaign help from his wife, Elizabeth Taylor.

1979 — September 7.— Hurricane David causes tornado flurries and torrential flood damage.

1980 — Population 5,347,000.

Legislature proclaims January 16 "Roy Clark Day" in honor of the country singer from Maherrin, Virginia.

Virginia Electric and Power Company considers switching two partially built nuclear power plants to coal due to problems with nuclear power.

1981 — John W. Hinckley, Jr. was being held at U.S. Marine Corps Stockade at Quantico, Virginia on charges of attempting to kill President Reagan.

1982 — November.— Charles Robb elected Governor; first Democrat in twelve years.

Edwin P. Wilson a former CIA official was convicted on seven federal counts involving illegal transportation of firearms to the Libyan government. A federal jury in Alexandria, Virginia found Wilson guilty of masterminding the conspiracy.

Encyclopedia of Virginia

1983 — Town of Surrey develops plans for emergency evacuation in the event of a nuclear accident at the nearby Virginia Electric and Power Company nuclear power plant.

1984 — CIA admits having two meetings at their agency in Langley, Virginia with Lyndon H. LaRouche in which matters of national security were discussed.

1985 — November.— L. Douglas Wilder elected Lieutenant Governor; first Black to hold a statewide post since the reconstruction.

Sue Terry becomes the first woman Attorney General of Virginia.

1986 — April.— Hurricane Charley batters the Virginia coast causing deaths and property damage; resulting in over $7 million dollars worth of damage along the North Carolina, Virginia and Maryland coasts.

1987 — January.— Winter storm, with high tides and gale force winds causes extensive damage along Virginia coast.

February.— Grand jury indicts 16 followers of Lyndon LaRouche on charges of securities fraud and other offenses.

1988 — August.— Virginia Electric & Power Company fined $100,000 because of "significant weaknessess" in radiation safety at its Surry nuclear plant. It was the second fine of the year.

December.— LaRouche and six others were convicted of mail fraud and conspiracy to commit mail fraud. LaRouche was also found guilty of conspiring to defraud the IRS.

1989 — January 27.— Lyndon H. LaRouche Jr. was sentenced in an Alexandria, Virginia courthouse to 15 years in federal prison.

September 21.— Hurricane Hugo hit Charleston, late in the evening, with winds of 135 miles per hour, setting off a 17-foot tidal surge that swept into Charleston harbor.

Chronology

	November 27.— L. Douglas Wilder was the winner of the state's gubernatorial election. Wilder won 897,139 votes, or 50.19%.
1990 —	Population 6,187,358. August 6-7.— Deployment of F-15 fighters from Langley Air Force Base, Virginia was ordered by President Bush. They took off for Saudi Arabia. The plan was dubbed operation "Desert Shield".

President Bush gave his first address on AIDS since taking office. He urged compassion and an end to discrimination against individuals infected with the AIDS virus. He spoke in Alexandria, Virginia.

L. Douglas Wilder was sworn in as governor of Virginia. Wilder became the first elected black governor ever to take office in the U.S.

1991 — January 9.— Governor L. Douglas Wilder asked state legislature for the authority to require furloughs without pay for up to 100,000 state employees.

Appeals court ruled that Jim Bakker be resentenced by a different judge since a North Carolina judge allowed his personal feelings to influence his decision.

DIRECTORY OF STATE SERVICES

ADJUTANT GENERAL, OFFICE OF
501 E. Franklin Street, Richmond, VA 23219.

ADMINISTRATION, DEPARTMENT OF
9th Street Office Bldg., 9th and Grace Streets, P.O. Box 1475, Richmond, VA 23212.

AERONAUICS, OFFICE OF 4508 S. Laburnman Ave., Richmond, VA 23231.

AGING, DEPARTMENT OF
700 E. Franklin St., 10th Fl., Richmond, VA 23219-2327.

AGRICULTURE, DEPARTMENT OF
Washington Bldg., Rm. 210, Capitol Sq., 1100 Bank St., P.O. Box 1163, Richmond, VA 23209.

AIR POLLUTION CONTROL, DEPARTMENT OF
9th Street Office Bldg., Rm. 801, 9th & Grace Streets, P.O. Box 10089, Richmond, VA 23240.

ALCOHOLISM
Division of Mental Health, 2901 Hermitage Road, P.O. Box 27491, Richmond, VA 23261.

ARCHIVES AND RECORDS, DEPARTMENT OF
State Library Bldg., 10th St. at Capitol Sq., Richmond, VA 23219-3491.

ARTS & HUMANITIES COMMISSION
James Monroe Bldg., 101 N. 14th St., Richmond, VA 23219.

ATTORNEY GENERAL, OFFICE OF
Department of Law, 101 N. Eighth Street, Richmond, VA 23219.

AUDIT, DEPARTMENT OF
James Monroe Bldg., Rm. 800, 101 N. 14th Street, P.O. Box 1295, Richmond, VA 23210.

AVIATION, DEPARTMENT OF
4508 S. Laburnum Ave., P.O. Box 7716, Richmond, VA 23231.

Encyclopedia of Virginia

BUDGET, DIVISION OF
Department of Finance, 9th Street Office Bldg., Rm. 412, 9th & Grace Streets, P.O. Box 1422, Richmond, VA 23211.

CHILD WELFARE SERVICES
Ratcliff Bldg., Rm. 212, 1602 Rolling Hills Drive; Mail: Blair Bldg., 8007 Discovery Drive, Richmond, VA 23229-8699.

CIVIL RIGHTS, OFFICE OF
Dept. of Social Services, Blair Bldg., 8007 Discovery Dr., Richmond, VA 23288.

CLERK OF THE HOUSE
House of Delegates, State Capitol, Capitol Square, Richmond, VA 23219.

CLERK OF THE SENATE
State Capitol, Capitol Square, P.O. Box 396, Richmond, VA 23203.

COMMERCE, DEPARTMENT OF
Washington Bldg., Rm. 1000, Capitol Sq., 1100 Bank St., Richmond, VA 23219.

COMMUNITY AFFAIRS, DEPARTMENT OF
4th Street Office Bldg., 205 N. 4th St., Richmond, VA 23219-1747.

COMPTROLLER, OFFICE OF
James Monroe Bldg., 101 N. 14th St., P.O. Box 6-N, Richmond, VA 23215.

CONSERVATION & HISTORIC RESOURCES, DEPARTMENT OF
221 Governor St., Richmond, VA 23219.

CONSUMER AFFAIRS, OF
Washington Bldg., Capitol Sq., 1100 Bank St., P.O. Box 1163, Richmond, VA 23209.

CORPORATION COMMISSION
Jefferson Bldg., 122 Bank St., P.O. Box 1157, Richmond, VA 23219.

CORRECTIONS, DEPARTMENT OF
4615 W. Broad Street, Rm. 314, P.O. Box 26963, Richmond, VA 23261.

DATA PROCESSING
Computer Services Department, 110 S.7th St., 3rd Fl., Richmond, VA 23219.

DEVELOPMENTAL DISABILITIES, DIVISION OF
Department of Mental Health, James Madison Bldg., 109 Governor Street, P.O. Box 1797, Richmond, VA 23214.

ECONOMIC DEVELOPMENT DEPARTMENT
Washington Bldg., Rm. 1000, 1100 Bank St., Richmond, VA 23219.

Directory of State Services

ECONOMIC OPPORTUNITY, DIVISION OF
Department of Human Services, 8007 Discovery Drive, Richmond, VA 23219.

EDUCATION, DEPARTMENT OF
James Monroe Bldg., 101 N. 14th Street, P.O. Box 6Q, Richmond, VA 23216-2060.

ELECTIONS DIVISION
Office of the Secretary of State, 9th Street Office Bldg., Rm. 101, 9th & Grace Streets, Richmond, VA 23219.

EMPLOYMENT SECURITY DEPARTMENT
703 E. Main Street, P.O. Box 1358, Richmond, VA 23211.

ENERGY RESOURCES
2201 W. Broad Street, Richmond, VA 23220.

ENVIRONMENT CONCERNS
Ninth Street Office Bldg, Rm. 903, 202 N. 9th Street, Richmond, VA 23219.

FEDERAL-STATE RELATIONS
Hall of the States, Rm. 322, 444 N. Capitol St., Washington DC 20001.

FINANCE, DEPARTMENT OF
P.O. Box 1475, Richmond, VA 23212.

FISH & GAME, DIVISION OF
Department of Natural Resources, P.O. Box 11104, Richmond, VA 23230.

FOOD & DRUGS DIVISION
Department of Agriculture, P.O. Box 1163, Richmond, VA 23209.

FORESTRY, DIVISION OF
Department of Conservation, P.O. Box 3758, Charlottesville, VA 22903.

GENERAL SERVICES DIVISION
Department of General Services, Ninth Street Office Bldg., Rm. 209, 9th & Grace Sts., Richmond, VA 23219.

GEOLOGY DIVISION
Department of Natural Resources, P.O. Box 3667, Charlottesville, VA 22903.

HANDICAPPED, COUNCIL ON
Department of Human Services, P.O. Box 11045, Richmond, VA 23230.

HEALTH, DEPARTMENT OF
James Madison Bldg., Rm. 400, 109 Governor St., Richmond, VA 23219.

HIGHWAYS SAFETY, OFFICE OF
P.O. Box 27412, Richmond, VA 23219.

Encyclopedia of Virginia

HIGHWAYS
Department of Transportation, 1401 E. Broad St., Rm. 311, Richmond, VA 23219.

HISTORIC PRESERVATION
Department of Conservation, 221 Governor St, Richmond, VA 23219.

HOUSING, DEPARTMENT OF
4th Street Office Bldg, 205 N. 4th St, Richmond 23219.

HUMAN RIGHTS, DEPARTMENT OF
Office of Civil Rights, Blair Bldg., 8007 Discovery Drive., Richmond, VA 23288.

INSURANCE, BUREAU OF
P.O. Box 1157, Richmond, VA 23219.

JUVENILE DELINQUENCY
Department of Youth Services, Commonwealth Bldg., 4615 W. Broad St., Richmond, VA 23261.

LABOR & INDUSTRY, DEPARTMENT OF
4th Street Office Bldg, 205 N. 4th Street, Richmond, VA 23241.

LEGISLATIVE RESEARCH, DEPARTMENT OF
P.O. Box 3-AG, Richmond, VA 23208.

LIBRARY SERVICES, OFFICE OF
11th & Capitol Streets, Richmond, VA 23219.

LICENSING CORPORATE DIVISION
P.O. Box 1197, Richmond, VA 23219.

LICENSING COMMERCIAL DIVISION
Department of Commerce, Travelers Bldg., 3600 W. Broad St., Richmond, VA 23230-4917.

LIQUOR CONTROL, DEPARTMENT OF
2901 Hermitage Rd., Richmond, VA 23261.

MASS TRANSIT DIVISION
Department of Transportation, 1221 E. Broad St., Richmond, VA 23219.

MENTAL HEALTH DIVISION
Department of Human Services, James Madison Bldg., Rm. 1301, 109 Governor St., Richmond, VA 23005.

MINING & MINERALS, DIVISION OF
Department of Natural Resources, 219 Wood Ave., Big Stone Gap, VA 24219.

MOTOR VEHICLES, DEPARTMENT OF
P.O. Box 27412, Richmond, VA 23269.

Directory of State Services

NATURAL RESOURCES, DEPARTMENT OF
Washington Bldg., Capitol Sq., 1100 Bank St., Richmond, VA 23219.

OCCUPATIONAL SAFETY & HEALTH DIVISION
Department of Human Services, P.O. Box 12064, Richmond, VA 23241.

OMBUDSMAN
P.O. Box 1475, Richmond, VA 23212.

PARKS & RECREATION, DEPARTMENT OF
Washington Bldg-Capitol Sq., Rm. 1201, 1100 Bank St, Richmond, VA 23219.

PLANNING DIVISION
Office of Planning & Budget, P.O. Box 1422, Richmond, VA 23211.

POLICE DEPARTMENT
Department of Public Safety, 7700 Midlothian Turnpike, Richmond, VA 23261-7472.

PROBATION & PAROLE, STATE BOARD OF
Koger Center, Culpeper Bldg., 1606 Santa Rosa Road, Richmond, VA 23288.

PUBLIC DEFENDER, OFFICE OF
8550 Mayland Dr., Rm. 201, Richmond, VA 23229-2697.

PUBLIC SERVICE, DEPARTMENT OF
P.O. Box 1197, Richmond, VA 23209.

PUBLIC WORKS DEPARTMENT
Department of Administration, 805 E. Broad St., Richmond, VA 23219.

PURCHASING, DIVISION OF
Department of Administrative Services, 805 E. Broad St, Richmond, VA 23209.

RAILROADS OFFICE OF
Department of Transporation, 1220 Bank St, Richmond, VA 23209.

REAL ESTATE, COMMISSION ON
Department of Commerce, 3600 W. Broad St, Richmond, VA 23230.

REFUGEE RESETTLEMENT, OFFICE OF
Department of Human Services, Koger Center, 219 Lee Bldg., 8004 Franklin Farms Dr., Richmond, VA 23229-8699.

SECRETARY OF STATE
9th Street Office Bldg, 9th & Grace Streets, Richmond, VA 23201.

SECRETARY OF THE SENATE
P.O. Box 396, Richmond, VA 23203.

SECURITIES REGISTRATION, DIVISION OF
Department of Commerce, P.O. Box 396, Richmond, VA 23203.

Encyclopedia of Virginia

SOCIAL SERVICES DIVISION OF
Department of Human Services, Koger Center, 8004 Franklin Farms Dr, Richmond, VA 23229-8699.

SOLID WASTE, DIVISION OF
Department of Natural Resources, James Monroe Bldg., 11th Fl., 101 N. 14th St., Richmond, VA 23219.

SURPLUS PROPERTY DIVISION
Department of General Services, P.O. Box 1199, Richmond, VA 23209.

TAXATION
Department of Tax & Revenue, 2220 W. Broad Street, Richmond, VA 23282.

TEXTBOOKS
Department of Education, P.O. Box 6-Q, Richmond, VA 23216.

TOURISM, OFFICE OF
202 N. 9th St, Richmond, VA 23219.

TRANSPORTATION, DEPARTMENT OF
1221 E. Broad Street, Richmond, VA 23219.

TREASURER
Department of the Treasury, 101 N. 14th Street, Richmond, VA 23215.

UNCLAIMED PROPERTY DIVISION
Department of the Treasury, 101 N. 14th Street, Richmond, VA 23207.

UNEMPLOYMENT
Department of Labor, 703 E. Main Street, Richmond, VA 23211.

VETERANS' AFFAIRS, DEPARTMENT OF 210 Franklin Road, S.W., Roanoke, VA 24004.

VITAL RECORDS & STATISTICS BUREAU
Department of Health, 109 Governor St, Richmond, VA 23208-1000.

WATER POLLUTION CONTROL
Department of Natural Resources, 2111 N. Hamilton Street, Richmond, VA 23230.

WEIGHTS AND MEASURES DIVISION
Department of Agriculture, 402 Washington Bldg., 1100 Bank St, Richmond, VA 23209.

WELFARE DIVISION
Department of Human Services, Blair Bldg., Ste. G., 8007 Discovery Dr., Richmond, VA 23229-8699.

WORKERS' COMPENSATION
Department of Labor, Industrial Commission, 1000 DMV Dr., Richmond, VA 23214.

COLONIAL GOVERNORS OF VIRGINIA

WINGFIELD, EDWARD MARIA (ca.1560-?), first colonial Governor of Virginia (1607), was born in England about 1560, son of Thomas Maria Wingfield of Stoneley, Huntingdonshire, whose wife was a member of the Yorkshire family named Kerrye. He began life as a soldier, serving in Ireland and in the Low countries, and was a prisoner of war at Lisle with Ferdinando Gorges. He was one of those to whom the original patent of Virginia was granted on April 10, 1606, and was the only patentee who sailed with the first planters for Virginia, December 19, 1606. The list of the intended colonial council was sealed up, together with the royal instructions, to be opened after landing. Wingfield was among its members, and when the colonists took possession of the peninsula on the north side of the River Powhatan (James River), on May 13, 1607, he was elected the first president of the initial council of the first permanent English colony in America. In honor of King James, the new settlement was called Jamestown, and the code of laws, which had been cautiously concealed, was at length promulgated. Affairs of the moment were to be examined by a jury, but determined by the major part of the council, in which the president was to have two votes, and thus "commenced the rule of the most ancient administration of Virginia, consisting of seven persons and forming a pure aristocracy."

Wingfield did not remain long at the head of the government. The colonists suffered illness, famine, and other misfortunes, and he was blamed for what he could not prevent, and was made a scapegoat by the other members of the council. In addition to all this, serious charges were brought against him by his opponents, among others, that he conspired with the Spaniards to destroy Virginia, with the fact that he was of a prominent Catholic family naturally lending color to this accusation. He was finally deposed, not only from the presidency, but from the council as well, on September 10, 1607, and returned to England the following April. No further details of his life are known, except that he lived, unmarried at Stoneley in Huntingdonshire in 1613. Wingfield wrote "A Discourse of Virginia," which was first printed in 1860 by the American Antiquarian Society.

RATCLIFFE, JOHN (?- ca.1616), colonial Governor of Virginia (1607-08), was born in England. It is believed that he was connected with the Suffolk family of Sicklemore which was originally settled at Bramford, near Ipswich, England, and to have changed his name in early life to Ratcliffe. On December 20,

1606, he sailed from London in command of the "Discovery," in company with Captain Newport of the "Susan Constant" and Captain Gosnold of the "God-Speed," and after the settlement of Jamestown, Virginia, became a member of the first council presided over by E. M. Wingfield as Governor. But the early fortunes of the colony were disastrous, and this being imputed to the Governor's shortcomings, a party in the council, headed by Ratcliffe and the famous John Smith, deposed Wingfield and chose Ratcliffe in his stead. Although the sufferings of the new settlers were scarcely lessened by the change, and difficulties with the natives were added to the continuous internal dissensions, Ratcliffe seems to have held office for his full term, until September 10, 1608. The misfortunes of his year of rule do not appear to have been due to any misgovernment on his part, but rather to the colonists' incapacity for organization.

About December, 1608, he went to England, but in 1609, sailed again for Jamestown in the "Diamond," in company with Newport in the "Sea Adventure," and with Captain Martin in the "Falcon." The "Sea Adventure" was driven out of her course and wrecked on the Bermudas, and Ratcliffe on his arrival at Jamestown, being senior officer of the remaining vessels, took it upon himself to arrest Smith, who had concentrated all the authority of Governor and council in his own person, and to send him home to answer for his conduct. It is said that Ratcliffe was betrayed and murdered by Powhatan in the winter of 1609-10.

SMITH, JOHN (1579-1631), colonial Governor of Virginia, (1608-09), was born in Willoughby, Lincolnshire, England, in January of 1579. He was the eldest son of George and Alice Smith, poor tenants of Peregrine Bertie, Lord Willoughby. Many biographies have been written of him, but they are generally based on the accounts furnished by himself which are not trustworthy and have been gross inaccuracies. But as few data regarding him have been found beside what he tells of his life in his own works, these latter still remain the chief source of all his biographies. It is said of his early life that, while he could have acquired a good education at the free schools in England which existed at this period, he was of so daring and adventurous a nature that he cared little for study, and having decided to become a sailor, had even sold his schoolbooks and satchel to obtain the means to go to sea. He already had the misfortune to lose his mother, and at this time his father died suddenly, which temporarily delayed his intention. He was in charge of guardians who proved, however, to be false to their trust, and who encouraged him to follow his own wishes with the hope of profiting by his running away, by obtaining the little property which his father had left him. He was apprenticed to a merchant, but, as we anticipated, he ran away when he was fifteen years old and visited France and the Low Countries, traveling for a part of the time as a servant to the young sons of the noblemen who were make a tour of the continent. He soon left this party, receiving on his departure, a sum of money.

Colonial Governors

At this time, France was in the throes of war, which at length, ended with the assassination of Henry IV. Young Smith enlisted as a soldier and fought on the side of the Protestants, and when there was no more fighting in France, he offered his services to the insurgents in the Low Countries, with whom he remained for three or four years, when he became restless and took ship for Scotland. The series of extraordinary adventures which he describes as having occurred at different periods during his life, began with this voyage. These adventures, beyond doubt were tinged with romance, including an encounter with thieves, a shipwreck, casting into the sea, Jonah-like, capture by pirates, fighting the Turks both in the Austrian army and in single combat, commanding a cavalry, being sold for a slave, being involved in a fight for his life, a miraculous escape, and finally his return home on an English man-of-war.

On his arrival he found that a deep interest had become prevalent in regard to the settlement of North America. The dazzling stories told of Cortez, in Mexico, and of Pizarro, in Peru, with the account given of parts of Florida and the shores of the Mississippi that had been visited, had awakened an intense desire among Englishmen of an adventurous character to cross the ocean themselves, and seek their fortunes in these new and strange lands. Already Frobisher was exploring the coast of Labrador; Raleigh had successfully reached the southern shore which he named Virginia, after the virgin queen. So Smith, after a long delay, succeeded in forming a company, and obtaining a patent, set sail on December 19, 1606, with an expedition, comprising 105 men and three vessels. During the voyage, Smith, owing to his excitable disposition and determination to command, got into trouble with others of the party, and was put in irons, in which condition he remained thirteen weeks.

They stopped at the West India islands for water, and then sailed north, but grew disheartened at not reaching land, and were about to return to England when a terrible storm drove the little fleet straight into Chesapeake Bay. They landed April 26, 1607, at what is now Jamestown. Smith immediately began explorations to discover the source of the James River, and by his kind treatment of the Indians, insinuated himself into their good graces, making a league of friendship with Powhatan and others of the great chiefs. He soon acquired the real leadership of the colony, through his shrewdness and foresight. He was respected and feared by the Indians, and protected the colony from their depredations by his kind treatment and strong personality, even when they were provoked beyond endurance by the inhumanity of the settlers. He fortified Jamestown, and explored the Chickahominy River, and procured supplies of provisions by trading with Indians.

At one time, according to his account, the settlers would have starved to death if not for the exertions of Smith, who alone was able to procure corn from the Indians. While on a mission of this kind, he was captured by the Indians and carried before Powhatan, their chief, who, angered by the constant aggressions of the settlers, ordered him to be put to death. As he was about to be dispatched with war clubs, his life, according to the well-known story, was saved by the intervention of Pocahontas, the king's favorite daughter. Smith made no allusion to this story of his rescue until Pocahontas' arrival in England as the wife of John Rolfe, when he wrote an account of it in a letter to Queen Anne. He was sent back to Jamestown, where he found the colony reduced to forty men who were so disheartened that many of them were preparing to return to England, but after a good deal of entreaty with the other leaders, he succeeded in preventing the abandonment of the plantation.

During the next year, Smith explored the whole country, from Cape Henry to the Susquehanna River, and drew a map of the bay and rivers, sailing about 3,000 miles. On September 10, 1608, he became president of the council, and retained this post until August of the following year. The settlers, who were more bent on gaining riches than in founding a colony, conspired to depose Smith, sending bad reports of his administration to England. Lord Delaware was made Governor under a new charter, and three commissioners, Captain Newport, Sir Thomas Gates, and Sir George Somers, were given power to rule the colony until his arrival. The vessel containing this commission was wrecked, however, and Smith remained in authority, and enforced it to preserve the colony from anarchy until superseded by Captain George Percy.

In September of 1609, he was so injured by an explosion of gunpowder that he was obligated to return to England for medical treatment. Here, for a long time, his life was in danger, and it was evident that it might take years for his health to be fully restored. As a matter of fact, he disappeared from sight for five years. It is said that he devoted this period to study and reading, trying to make up the time he had lost in his youth when he had thrown away his opportunities for early education.

In 1614, Captain Smith again sailed from London for North America, keeping well to the northward, and landing in a new country, which he called New England. He remained for six months on this coast, devoted his time to catching codfish, of which he obtained about 60,000, while from the Indians, he bought about 10,000 beaver skins, besides a large number of other pelts. He subsequently made other voyages back and forth, had some adventures with pirates, awakened the first interest in the New England cod fisheries, and wrote and published a number of volumes describing the voyages which had been made to America, and relating the history of the Jamestown settlement, which was published under the title of "The True Travels, Adventures, and Observations of Captain John Smith, in Europe, Asia, Africa, and American, from 1593 to 1629, together with a continuation of his General History" (1630).

His pen was very active in these later years, while his memory was clear and full with regard to his adventures. His other works are: "A True Relation" (1608); "A Map of Virginia" (1612); "A Description of New England" (1616); "New England's Trials" (1620); "The General Historie of Virginia, New

England, and the Summer Isles" (1622); "An Accidence for Young Seamen" (1626); "Advertisements for the Inexperienced Planters of New England" (1631). Nothing definite is known as to the circumstances surrounding his death, but it is certain that it occurred in London on June 21, 1631.

PERCY, GEORGE (1580-1632), colonial Governor of Virginia (1609-10); 1611), was born in Lyon House, Northumberland County, England on September 4, 1580, eighth son of Henry Percy, eighth Earl of Northumberland, by his wife Catherine, eldest daughter of John Neville, Lord Latimer. He served for a time in the Low Countries, sailed for Virginia in the first expedition in December of 1606, and became one of "the respected gentlemen" of that colony. On May 23, 1609, his name appeared among the incorporators of the Second Company of Virginia, and in August following, he succeeded Captain John Smith in the administration of the colony. He held office during a critical period until the arrival of Sir Thomas Gates on May 24, 1610. The provisions having been used up soon after the departure of Captain Smith, a famine ensued, and prevailed to such that this period ws afterward "the starving time," and of nearly five hundred persons left in the colony by the late President, only sixty remained at the end of six months.

George Percy was subsequently a member of Lord De la Warr's council, and when the latter sailed for England on March 28, 1611, he was reappointed Deupty Governor "in recognition of former services," and he conducted the affairs of the colony until the arrival of Thomas Dale on May 19th of that year. He left Virginia for England on April 22, 1612, and war having broken out again in the Low Countries, returned for a time, probably in 1625, to his old occupation of volunteering against Spain in the service of the United Netherlands. Here he distinguished himself, and was captain of a company in 1629.

Percy wrote "A Discourse or Observations of the Plantation of the Southern Colony in Virginia," which is chiefly devoted to accounts of native customs and of the hardships and suffering of the first colonists; and "A True Relation of the Proceedings and Occurrents of Moments which have Happened in Virginia from the Time Sir Thomas Gates was Shipwrecked upon the Bermudas, 1609, until my Departure out of the Country, 1612," which is a defense against the aspersions cast on his administration in Virginia by the unjust account in Smith's "General History." Percy died in England in March of 1632.

WEST, THOMAS (LORD DE LA WARR) (1577-1618), colonial Governor of Virginia (1610-11), was born in England on July 9, 1577, probably at Wherwell, Hampshire, the family seat, where he was baptized. He was the grandson of William West, first Baron De la Warr, and second but eldest surviving son of Thomas and Ann (Knollys) West, his father being the second baron. Thomas entered Queen's College, Oxford, in 1592, but did not remain long enough to take his degree, and in 1595, traveled to Italy. In October of 1597, he returned to Parliament from Lymington Hants; in 1598, he served with distinction in the Netherlands. In 1599, he went to Ireland, under the Earl of Essex, to aid in putting down a rebellion, and was knighted for bravery by the lord deputy. In 1601, he barely escaped death for supposed complicity in the insurrection fomented by Essex.

On March 24, 1602, West succeeded to the title, and not long after, was made a member of the privy council of Elizabeth, in which office he continued under James I. In 1605, the Univeristy of Oxford conferred upon him the degree of M.A. Lord De la Warr became deeply interested in the founding of the Protestant colonies in the New World; joined the Virginia Company of London when it was reorganized under the charter of May 23, 1609, and on February 28th, was appointed Governor of Virginia and Captain-General for life. He remained in England however, Sir Thomas Gates and Sir George Somers having been sent with a band of colonists in May. The vessels were scattered by a storm off the Bermudas, on one of whose islands the ship bearing Gates and Somers was wrecked, and as those men and their companies were forced to winter there and to build new boats, they did not reach Jamestown until the following May.

Meanwhile, De la Warr had heard that anarchy and destitution threatened the plantation in Virginia, and had set sail with 150 colonists and supplies. Gates, on his arrival, found the population of Jamestown reduced to sixty people, through disease, misfortune and mismanagement, and decided that the plantation must be abandoned. On June 7th, the company embarked to return to England; on the 8th, they reached the lower part of the river, and there, while waiting for the ebb-tide, were approached by a long boat, the forerunner of De la Warr's vessels. Thus intercepted, because the Governor had heard at Point Comfort of their intentions, the would-be emigrants returned to Jamestown, and on June 10th, Lord De la Warr arrived. He at once restored order, appointing a council of six to aid him, revived industries, repaired the church, and by establishing forts at different points along the James, induced the Indians to keep the peace. He was more successful as an administrator than any of his predecessors, but his government was brief. He suffered from such poor health the ensuing winter, that on March 28, 1611, he sailed for the island of Nevis for the benefit of the warm baths, leaving the colony in the charge of Captain George Percy.

His health improved somewhat, he wanted to return to Virginia, but was persuaded to go to England, where he remained seven years, during which period Pocahontas was presented at court by Lady De la Warr. On his way, being driven out of his course by winds, he entered a river, called by the natives Chickohocki, and later this was named in his honor, though the real discoverer was Henry Hudson.

On March 16, 1618, he again sailed for Virginia, with 200 colonists, going by way of the Aores, and touching at St. Michael. "There," says the historian Fiske, "he and thirty others fell sick and died in such a way as to raise suspicion that their Spanish hosts had poisoned them." Other historians state that he died off the coast of Virginia or New England, assigning June 7th as the date. He spent his wealth generously to promote the colony, and although his connection with it was comparatively brief, he undoubtedly saved it from ruin at a critical moment. It is not strange, therefore, that his services were universally recognized, and Alexander Brown went so far as to say that "if any one man can be called the founder of Virginia...he is that man."

Lord De la Warr was married on November 25, 1596 to Cecilia Shirley, who bore him seven children, the eldest of whom was Henry, successor to the title. One of his descendants, John West, first Earl De la Warr, Speaker of the House of Peers in 1733, was appointed Captain-General and Governor of New York and New Jersey in 1737, but did not leave England. Penelope West, sister of Lord De la Warr, was the mother of Herbert Pelham, a promoter of emigration to New England and the first treasurer of Harvard College.

GATES, THOMAS (ca.1560-1621), colonial Governor of Virginia (1610; 1611-14), was born at Colyford, Devonshire, England, about 1560. He was lieutenant of Captain Christopher Carleill's company in the celebrated Drake-Sidney voyage to America, 1586-86, served in the expedition against Cadiz in 1596, and took part in the island voyage from August through October, 1597. He entered Gray's Inn on March 14, 1598, and the following year, was in public service at Plymouth. About 1604, he enlisted in the service of the Netherlands, was in the garrison at Ondewater in South Holland with Thomas Dale in November of 1606, but meanwhile having become an incorporator of the first charter on April 10, 1606, he obtained from the States-General, a leave of absence to go to Virginia in April of 1608.

About that time, the movement for the colonization of Virginia culminated in the formation of a new company, to which James I granted another charter, dated May 23, 1609, with larger powers and privileges. Under this charter, the company was empowered to choose the supreme council in England and by its instruction and regulation, a Governor was provided, invested with absolute civil and military authority, with the title of "Governor and Captain-General of Virginia." Thus although the resident council was still retained, the orginal aristocracy was converted into a rule of one, over whose deliberations the people had no control.

Among the new incorporators were Robert Cecil, Earl of Salisbury, Sir Francis Bacon, Captain John Smith, Sir Oliver Cromwell, uncle to the protector, together with a number of public companies of London. The chief officers of the company were Sir Thomas West, Lord De la Warr, Captain General, Sir Thomas Gates, Lieutenant-General, Sir George Somers, Admiral, and Sir Thomas Dale, High Marshal. The project caused great enthusiasm, large sums of money were contributed, and so many people wanted to go that nine ships, with more than five hundred emigrants, were dispatched in charge of Gates, Somers, and Captain Newport. They sailed from England at the end of May,

1609, but only seven vessels arrived in Virginia. The ship of the three commissioners, the Sea Venture, was separated from the rest of the fleet by a storm and stranded on the rocks of Bermuda on July 28, 1609. Gates and his fellow voyagers managed a landing and remained nine months in Bermuda when they sailed for Virginia, arriving there on May 24, 1610.

The colony was found in a desolate and miserable condition, and the desperate settlers resolved to burn the town in which they had been so wretched, but Gates, who in the absence of Lord De la Warr superceded Percy as Governor under the new charter, prevented this, but intended to sail for Newfoundland with the survivors, in order to seek a passage for England. Lord De la Warr, however, arrived on June 9, 1610, to assume the reins of government, and Gates returned with him to Jamestown. The following July, Gates left Virginia for England where he aided in preparing a confutation of the scandalous report, and succeeded in reviving faith in the permanence of the colony. He returned to Jamestown in August of 1611 with 300 men and ample supplies, and assumed the office of Governor in succession to Sir Thomas Dale.

From that time, the colony began to gather strength and to prosper, the most salutary change resulting from the establishment of private property. To each settler a few acres of ground were assigned for his orchard and garden, and from then on, the stability of the colony, based on agriculture, was no longer a matter of doubt. Gates wanted to make religion the foundation of law and order, and in the words of Sir Edwin Sandys, "was the first that, by his wisdom, industry, and valor, accompanied with exceeding pains and patience, in the midst of many difficulties, had laid the foundation of the prosperous state of the colony." He effected a new settlement; built a new town called Henrico, in honor of Prince Henry, and during his administration, a third patent for Virginia, signed on March 12, 1612, was granted to the stockholders. This charter not only confirmed all the former privileges and prolonged the term of exemption from payment of duties on the commodities exported by the company, but granted them the Bermudas and all islands within three hundred leagues of Virginia. This acquistion, however, was subsequently transferred to a separate company.

Sir Thomas Gates sailed for England in April of 1814, and employed himself in advancing the interest of the colony. Little is known of his later career, and his death is said to have taken place in 1621.

THOMAS, DALE (?-1619), colonial Governor of Virginia (1611; 1614-16), was born in England at an unknown date. He served with honor in the Netherlands, was knighted by James I, in June of 1606. In 1611, on obtaining a long leave of absence from the Dutch States-General, he entered the service of the Virginia Company of London, which appointed him High Marshal, and sent him with supplies for the relief of the settlers. Having arrived in Virginia on May 19, 1611, in the absence of Lord De la Warr, he took control of the infant colony, which then contained some 200 English settlers. He found the old anarchy threatening to break out again, but quickly restored order by adopting and applying a severe, almost military code, which had been sent to Virginia without the company's authority by its treasurer, Sir Thomas Smith. Despite his merciless severity, he received praise for his vigor and hard work, and easily reconciled the settlers to his rule by his energetic measures for their relief.

He at once wrote to England for aid and in August of 1611, a new fleet reached Jamestown under Sir Thomas Gates, who relieved Dale of the government. The latter remained in the province, assisted in planting a new settlement called Henrico, with brick houses, a church and a hospital. He overcame the Appomattox Indians and took their town. In March of 1614, Gates sailed for England and Dale, again succeeding to the governorship, ruled the colony for two years "with firmness and ability." He brought in changes in the laws regarding the land, which were in the interest of progress and democracy by giving each man an opportunity to acquire property of his own.

During his administration, Rolfe married Pocahontas, and Dale returned with them in 1616. This union brought peace with the Indians. In November, 1617, Dale was appointed commander of the East Indian fleet, and upon arriving in Bantam a year later, engaged the Dutch fleet off Jacatra, on December 23, and put it to flight. But the climate proved fatal, and he died in Masulipitam on August 9, 1619.

YEARDLEY, GEORGE (1588-1627), colonial Governor of Virginia (1616-17; 1619-21; 1626-27), was born in Southwark, England in 1588, son of Ralph Yeardley, a merchant-tailor of London. After a brief service in the Low Countries, he sailed with Sir Thomas Gates for Virginia in 1609, was shipwrecked in the Bermudas, but eventually reached his destination in May of 1610. When Sir Thomas Dale, the Governor, returned to England in 1616, he appointed Yeardley his deputy, and under him, the colony appears to have prospered. He encouraged the people to plant tobacco instead of corn, which he compelled the natives to furnish by way of tribute, and showed both ability and firmness in the administration of affairs, but in spite of that, he was, through Sir Thomas Smith's influence, superseded by Captain Samuel Argall, who arrived in Virginia on May 15, 1617.

The following year, Yeardley visited England, and Argall having been displaced in the meantime, he was again appointed Governor of Virginia on November 18, 1618 for a term of three years, and six days later, was knighted by James I, who had a long conversation with him about the religion of the Indians. He arrived in Virginia on April 19, 1619, and in accordance with "commissions and instructions from the Company for the better establishing of a commonwealth," he relaxed the exceedingly severe system of government adopted by Dale, and convened a legislature which was the first representative assembly in the Western Hemisphere, and which met on July 30, 1619, at Jamestown.

Yeardley was succeeded by Sir Francis Wyatt on November 8, 1621, and after the latter's retirement in May of 1626, he was again appointed Governor by Charles I, holding the post until his death. During his three administrations, important events in the life of the colony had taken place. Following the convening of the first legislature in America, a written constitution was established for the colony by the London Company on July 24, 1621. In 1620, a Dutch man-of-war landed twenty black slaves for sale, the first brought into the English colonies. While in the last year of his governorship, a thousand new emigrants from England arrived. As an evidence of the increased prosperity of the colony, it may also be stated that in 1619, 20,000 pounds of tobacco were exported to England from Virginia. Yeardley died in Jamestown, Virginia on November 10, 1627.

ARGALL, SAMUEL (ca.1580-1626), colonial Governor of Virginia (1617-19), was born in England about 1580. He gained renown as a mariner at an early age, and in 1609, was selected to discover a shorter way to Virginia, a mission he successfully accomplished. His next task was to bring Lord De la Warr to Virginia, and the two men arrived just in time to prevent the abandonment of Jamestown by the exasperated colonists. He was then dispatched to Bermuda with Sir George Somers for further relief of the colony, but becoming separated from Somers, he was driven northward to Cape Cod. Here he found good fishing, and after surveying the coast of New England, he explored Chesapeake Bay, and returned to Jamestown. He sailed for England with Lord De la Warr, March 28, 1611.

In September of 1612, he returned to Jamestown, "after a quick passage of fifty-one days," and the following December, set out for his firt voyage up the Potomac to procure corn from the Indians. It was while on this business that he devised and carried out the plan of abducting Pocahontas. She had been entrusted by Powhatan, to the care of another chief, but was surrendered for the bribe of a copper kettle. Argall took her as captive to Jamestown and handed her over to Sir Thomas Gates.

About July of 1613, acting under orders, he sailed from Virginia in a well-armed English man-of-war, and attacked the newly established French settlements of Mount Desert, off the coast of Maine, St. Croix, on an island in the river of the same name, and Port Royal, Nova Scotia, all of which were regarded by the Virginia authorities as infringements of their character. While on this expedition, Argall is said to have visited the Dutch settlement on the Hudson, and to have compelled it to submit to the crown of Great Britain. He was variously employed in Virginia from December of 1613 to June 18, 1614, when he sailed for England.

He was again sent by the London Company to Virginia in February of 1615, returning with Dale in May of 1616. In May of the following year, he arrived once more in Virginia, this time as Deputy-Governor and Admiral, and having superseded Yeardley, retained control of the colony until April 1619. Governor Argall incurred the displeasure of the people and the proprietors by his arbitrary course. He was arrogant and greedy, and by his highhanded rule, he "imported more hazard to the plantation than ever did any other thing that befell that action from the beginning." He imposed martial law, which had been proclaimed and executed during the turbulence of former times, the common law of the land, and under this regime, the colony languished, for no emigrants could be found for a settlement where life itself was insecure against the whims of so tyrannical a Governor.

When at last an account of his despotic sway reached London, he was displaced and ordered home "to answer everything that should be laid to his charge," and the popular Yeardley was appointed to succeed him. Argall, however, appears to have escaped punishment, largely owing to the protection of his partner in trade, the Earl of Warwick. Upon leaving the colony, he continued to lead an adventurous life, taking part in expeditions against Algiers in 1620, and against Cadiz, Spain, in 1625, and occupied important positions in the English Navy. Argall died in March of 1626.

WYATT, FRANCIS (1588-1644), colonial Governor of Virginia (1621-26; 1639-42), was born in England in 1588. For some time, he was active in the affairs of the Virginia Company, and when the commission of Sir George Yeardley was about to expire, he was proposed and elected as his successor, in early 1621. He arrived in Jamestown at the end of October of 1621, and entered office on November 8th. He was accompanied by his brother, Hawte Wyatt, as chaplain, by William Clairborne as surveyor, John Pott as physician, and George Sandys, the translator of Ovid, as treasurer. Wyatt brought with him the newly written constitution, established July 24, 1621, under which all former immunities and franchises were confirmed. Trial by jury was secured, and the assembly was privileged to meet annually upon the call of the Governor, who was vested with the right of veto. No act of the assembly was to be valid unless it was ratified by the Virginia company, and, on the other hand, no order of the company was to be obligatory without the concurrence of the assembly. This celebrated ordinance, on which Virginia erected the superstructure of its independence, furnished the model of every subsequent form of government in the Anglo-American colonies.

During the first year of Wyatt's administration, twenty-one vessels arrived in Virginia, bringing more than 1,300 settlers, and for a brief time, new life was given to the community. Jabez Whitaker set up a large guest-house for the accommodation of immigrants. Captain William Norton erected glass works near Jamestown, and great attention was paid to the manufacture of iron and the importation of metal and skilled ironworkers. Unfortunately, the prosperity of Wyatt's governorship received a severe check by a great Indian uprising, which on March 22, 1622, ended in the massacre of 347 colonists.

This and other disasters, together with the internal dissensions which had agitated the company, subsequently induced the King to institute an inquiry, which resulted in the annullment of the old Virginia Company's charter on June 16, 1624. Sir Francis, however, continued to serve as Governor by royal commission, which empowered him, and his council of eleven, to govern "as fully and amply as any Governor and council resident there, at any time within the space of five years now last past." Upon King James' death in March of 1625, he was continued in office by Charles I, but after learning of the death of his father in Ireland, he resigned on May 17, 1626, and was succeeded by Sir George Yeardley. Thirteen years later, Wyatt returned again to Virginia, and superseding Sir John Harvey as Governor, ruled from November 1639, until the arrival of Sir William Berkeley, in February of 1642. Wyatt returned to England in 1643, and died there in August of 1644.

WEST, FRANCIS (1586-?), colonial Governor of Virginia (1627-29), was born at Wherwell, Hampshire, England, October 28, 1586, fourth, but second surviving son of Thomas West, second Baron De la Warr, and Ann Knollys, and younger brother of Thomas West, third Baron De la Warr, who was Governor of Virginia from 1610-11. Francis West became a resident of Jamestown about July 1608. He was a member of the council in 1609, and subsequently had a quarrel with Captain John Smith who was accused of conspiring with Powhatan to put West out of the way. He visited England in 1610, returning the same year. In 1612, he succeeded George Percy as commander of Jamestown, and probably sat in the Council.

In 1622, the New England Co. appointed West admiral of New England, and after that date, he spent much of his time out of Virginia. He was authorized to restrain vessels from fishing or trading on the coast without a license from the New England Council, but, meeting with difficulty in executing this part of his commission, he sailed for Virginia. He was elected by the Council Governor of Virginia on November 14, 1627, and held office until March 5, 1629, when he was succeeded by John Pott.

During his control of affairs, the colony received large numbers of emigrants from Europe. West visited England in 1629, and while there, opposed Lord Baltimore's project of founding a colony within the limits of Virginia. Returning to Virginia before December, 1631, he was a member of the Governor's Council until 1633, the date of the last undoubted reference to him. He had estates at Westover and Shirley on the James, and he left children. According to family reports, he died from drowning.

POTT (or POTTS), JOHN (?-ca.1642), colonial Governor of Virginia (1629-30), was born in England. He was a physician by profession and accompanying Sir Francis Wyatt to Virginia in October of 1621, was a member of the Council under the Provisional Government constituted by the King in 1624. On March 5, 1629, he was elected by the Council to succeed Captain Francis West as Governor of the colony, and continued in office until the arrival of Sir John Harvey in March of 1630. During this period, the Assembly convened twice, and many regulations were adopted for the defense of the colony.

Soon after his retirement, he was charged by his enemies with pardoning Edward Wallis, a convicted murderer, and also with keeping cattle that did not belong to him. Harvey confined him at Harrope, which was his plantation, seven miles from Jamestown, and confiscated his property. The jury declared him guilty, but the Governor declined to pronounce judgment until he had consulted the King. The case was finally referred to commissioners who reported that the condemnation of Dr. Pott, upon a superficial hearing, for felony, was very rigorous, if not erroneous. The King, on July 25, 1631, pardoned him, especially as he was "the only physician in the colony skilled in epidemical diseases."

Dr. Pott was esteemed as an excellent and well-educated surgeon, but was careless in business, and fond of good living. It is assumed he died in Virginia, around 1642.

HARVEY, JOHN, (?-ca. 1650), colonial Governor of Virginia (1630-35; 1636-39), was born in England. He was named in Governor Yeardley's commission as his eventual successor. He was appointed Governor of the colony on March 26, 1628, and was knighted soon afterwards by Charles I. He arrived in Virginia in March, 1630, and on the 24th of that month, he attended his first meeting in the Assembly of Burgesses. His arbitrary methods at once aroused opposition, and his abuse of power finally led to a clash with the representatives of the colonists. Having a warrant to appropriate all fines arising from any sentence in the judicial courts, the number and amounts of these were greatly increased. He also incurred their enmity by betraying their territorial interests, as he courted the favor of Lord Baltimore, and when, on June 20, 1632, Charles I granted to the latter a patent for a portion of Virginia, he openly sided with Maryland in the dispute over Kent Island and trade in the Chesapeake. The formation of Maryland as a new province, with separate and equal rights, distressed the planters of Virginia, and offers the first example in colonial history of the dismemberment of an ancient colony. Virginia regarded the severing of its territory with apprehension, and spoke out against the grant "as an invasion of her commercial rights, an infringement on her domain, and a discouragement to her planters."

Exasperated at last by the Governor's conduct in this controversy, the Assembly suspended and impeached him, and after arresting him "for treason," drove him out of the country on April 28, 1635. He went to England, but after an investigation of his cause by the Privy Council, he was restored by the King and returned to Virginia, April 2, 1636. Without delay he met the Council at Elizabeth City, and published the King's proclamation pardoning, with a few exceptions, all persons who had given aid in the late uprising against him. He continued in office until November of 1639. During his administration, the accustomed

Encyclopedia of Virginia

legislative rights of the colony were unimpaired, despite his rapacity, partial judgments and cruel abuse of power. He is believed to have died in Virginia around 1650.

WEST, JOHN (1590-ca. 1660), colonial Governor of Virginia (1635-36), was born in England on December 14, 1590, fifth son of Thomas West, second baron De la Warr, and Ann Knollys, and younger brother of Thomas West, third baron De la Warr, who was Governor of Virginia in 1610-11. He came to Virginia early, and became prominently identified with the history of the colony. He owned a plantation at Westover, which suffered from Indian depredations at the time of the massacre, in March of 1621. During 1629-30, he was a Burgess of the Assembly, and after 1630, a member of the Council. When Sir John Harvey was "thrust out of his government," on April 28, 1635. John West was selected to succeed him, and served as chief executive until Harvey's reinstatement, April 2, 1636. He was Marshal and Muster-Master General in 1641. In March, 1659, the House of Burgesses passed an act remitting the levies of himself and his family, and exempting them from payment for the rest of their lives in recognition of the important services rendered to Virginia by "the noble family of the Wests, predecessors to Mr. John West, their now only survivor." He died in Virginia shortly afterwards. By his wife, Anne, he had one son, John, many of whose descendants have been distinguished in that annals of the country.

BERKELEY, WILLIAM, (1608-1677), colonial Governor of Virginia, (1642-44; 1645-52; 1660-61; 1662-77), was born near London, England in July of 1608. After graduating from Merton College, Oxford, in 1629, he made the tour of Europe, and in 1632, was sent out as a commissioner to Canada. On his return, he was attached to the privy chamber of Charles I. On August 9, 1641, he was appointed to succeed Sir Francis Wyatt as Governor of the colony of Virginia, but he did not arrive until February of 1642. Harmony prevailed, and for two years, the colony enjoyed peace; but in April, 1644, an Indian outbreak occurred in which several hundred of the colonists were killed. The war dragged on for two years until Berkeley headed a company of horses in an attack on the Indians and captured the aged chief Oppecancanough, who was afterward brutally shot by a soldier while in captivity. The Indians fled to the woods, and so little was gained from them after this that the following June, Governor Berkeley embarked for England and left as his substitute, Richard Kemp, president of the Council, who remained in control of affairs until Berkeley's return in June, 1645, and continued to serve as a member of the Council and as secretary until his death in 1656.

During the Civil War in England, Governor Berkeley was on the side of the cavaliers, and his colony was the last of all the possessions of England to submit to the authority of Oliver Cromwell. In fact, severe laws were enacted against the Puritans, although there were few of them in Virginia. Parliament had sent a fleet to reduce Barbadoes, and from there, a small squadron under command of Captain Dennis was detached in 1651 and sent to the James River. The Virginians received aid, however, from certain Dutch vessels in port, and it was found necessary to make some terms with Berkeley and his adherents. The result was that Sir William was pardoned and the Virginians were not persecuted for their resistance.

Berkeley was superseded by an appointee of the newly-constituted Commonwealth of England, on April 30, 1652, but he continued to live on his plantation in the colony as a private person. On the death of Governor Matthews, in January of 1660, Berkeley was requested by the colonists to resume the government, but would do so only on the condition that they submitted to the authority of the King. They did this, and on March 13, 1660, the Assembly elected him Governor. On April 30 of the following year, Berkeley sailed for England, to protest on behalf of the colonists against the enforcement of the Navigation Act, and while he was absent on this mission, Col. Francis Moryson was elected by the Council to be Governor and Captain General of Virginia. Berkeley resumed the administration on his return, December 23, 1662, thus entering his fourth term in office, which proved to be the most turbulent and eventful in his career. He got into trouble with the colonists because of his arbitrary mode of government, and although he was ordered to return to England in 1665, he continued to administer the affairs of the colony for the next eleven years. The local outbreak known as "Bacon's Rebellion" occurred in 1676, instigated by Nathaniel Bacon, the "Virginia rebel," as he was called. When Bacon died, Ingram, who succeeded him in command of the rebels, was won over by Berkeley and several of Bacon's principal adherents having been put to death, the rebellion was put down.

Shortly afterwards, a board of commissioners was sent out by royal mandate to examine into the condition of the colony, and Berkeley was compelled to resign the governorship and return to England on April 27, 1677. He died in Twickenham, July 13, 1677.

BENNETT, RICHARD, (ca. 1607-ca. 1675), colonial Governor of Maryland and Virginia (1652-57) by appointment of Oliver Cromwell, was born in England around 1607. Being a prominent Puritan and one of the colony in Virginia, he was, upon the arrival of the frigate Guinea, and the army which established Cromwell's power in America, appointed a parliamentary commissioner. Shortly after he was chosen Governor of both colonies by the Puritan element, with Captain William Claiborne, "the evil genius of Maryland," as his Secretary of State. In their capacity as commissioners, they arrived in St. Mary's, Maryland, toward the end of March, 1652, and having deposed Governor Stone on the 29th, issued a proclamation divesting him and Lord Baltimore of all authority and power in the province. They then returned to Virginia, but in June, established their government more fairly in Maryland, appointing Captain Stone and a special council to direct the affairs of the province under their control.

Encyclopedia of Virginia

By act of Parliament practical liberty was granted to Virginia under the protectorate, and laws were formulated by the people for the "general good and prosperity," in perfect accord with the new regime. With Maryland it was different--that colony submitted only after a formidable display of military power. The Lord Proprietor did not rest quietly under the flagrant wrong and injustice which had been done him. He directed Governor Stone, in 1654, to reestablish the proprietary government, and the loyal element was not slow to engage in armed resistance to Governor Bennett. They were, however, ultimately unsuccessful, and the parliamentarians continued in power until the close of 1657, when Governor Bennett retired into private life.

Governor Bennett was married to Henrietta Maria, formerly of Spain. With his four daughters, all natives of Spain, he had been naturalized by the Assembly of Maryland. After Bennett's death, his widow was married to Philemon Lloyd, by whom she was the mother of many children. Prominent among Bennett's descendants was his grandson Richard Bennett (1667-1749), a wealthy planter of Queen Anne County, Maryland. Richard Bennett died about 1675.

DIGGES, EDWARD, (1620-1675), colonial Governor of Virginia (1655-56), was born in England in 1620, son of Sir Dudley Digges, the English politician, and grandson of Sir Thomas Digges, the famous English geometer. In November, 1644, he was chosen a member of the Council of Virginia in recognition of his "fidelity to this colony and commonwealth of England," and on the retirement from office of Richard Bennett in March, 1655, he was made Governor by the Assembly, which voted him a salary of 25,000 pounds of tobacco in addition to the duties levied on vessels and marriage-license fees. He filled the office of Governor until 1657, and during his rule, an act was passed allowing all free men the right of voting for Burgesses, on the grounds that "it is something hard and unagreeable to reason that any person shall pay equal taxes, and yet have no votes in elections."

After retiring from the administration, Digges went as the colony's agent to England to negotiate with merchants about the price of tobacco. While in England, he was instrumental in settling the colony's dispute with Lord Baltimore, and through his social position and influence, succeeded in securing redress for many of the colonists' grievances. He was the pioneer of silkworm culture in Virginia, in which he was engaged at Denbigh, on James River, and at Bellfield, eight miles from Williamsburgh, and during his term as Governor, an act was passed for "ten mulberry trees to be planted for every hundred acres of land held in fee-simple, and sufficiently fenced and tended," as well as other measures that were taken to encourage the silk culture. Digges died in Virginia on March 15, 1675.

MATTHEWS, SAMUEL, (ca. 1600-1660), colonial Governor of Virginia (1657-60), was born in England about 1600. Having emigrated to Virginia in 1622, he became a wealthy planter and at once began to take an active part in public affairs. A year after his arrival, he was made leader of an expedition against the Tanx Powhatan Indians, was appointed by the Privy Council, a commissioner to report on the government of the colony, and in 1624, acted in a similar capacity under a mandate from King James. He was variously a member of the Council from 1625-57; was appointed justice of the monthly court for Warwick in March of 1632, and as one of the leaders of the opposition to Governor Harvey during the territorial dispute between Virginia and Lord Baltimore, was ordered, Dec. 22, 1635, to be sent to England with John West and William Pierce, to answer for their conduct.

In 1652, he was again sent to England, this time to obtain the ratification of the articles of an agreement between Virginia and the parliamentary commission, and remained there until 1657, when he was chosen by the House of Burgesses' successor to Governor Digges. Before his return to Virginia, however he signed, as Commissioner for the colony, the articles of an agreement with Lord Baltimore that was to settle the differences between the two colonies.

Governor Matthews filled his position with honesty and ability, and under him the colony made rapid progress in both population and industrial development. On account of the Governor's exalted ideas of his station, however, he and the council became involved in a disagreement with the Assembly, which served to further strengthen the sentiment for popular liberty in the colony. Before 1658, the Governor and Council had been admitted to seats with the Burgesses, but in that year, the Burgesses excluded them by formal vote. Governor Matthews then dissolved the Assembly in April of 1658, but the Assembly refused to disperse, declared itself still a House, and pledged its members to secrecy. The following day, the Governor made the concession of an offer to submit to Cromwell the question in dispute on condition that the public business before the Assemly be expeditiously disposed of. This offer was also flatly refused by the Assembly, which declared that full power of election of all officers rested with it alone, and deposing the Governor, reelected him as responsible to it alone. Governor Matthews at first resisted, but the next day, he took the oath as required by the representatives of the people. The remainder of his administration was uneventful, and he died in office, in January of 1660.

MORYSON, FRANCIS, (?-ca. 1678), colonial Governor of Virginia (1661-62), was born in England. In 1649, he arrived in Virginia, and as a loyalist, received a warm welcome from Sir William Berkeley, who gave him command of the fort at Point Comfort. He subsequently became a member of the Council, was Speaker of the House of Burgesses in 1656, and on Governor Berkeley's departure for England on April 30, 1661, was selected to administer the affairs of the colony. He held the governorship until Berkeley's return on Dec. 23, 1662. During his term of office, at a grand assembly, held in James City, March 23, 1662, the whole body of the laws of the colony was reviewed under the Governor's supervision, and a copy sent to England to Sir William Berkeley, "to procure his Majesty's royal confirmation." Upon his retirement from office, Moryson was sent to England as the colony's agent, and in 1676, he was one of the commissioners appointed to inquire into Berkeley's conduct and to report on Bacon's rebellion. He is thought to have died in England about 1678.

JEFFREYS, HERBERT, (?-1678), colonial Governor of Virginia (1677-78), was born in England. In September of 1676, with Sir John Berry and Colonel Francis Moryson, he was appointed on a commission to examine and report on the condition of the colony of Virginia. On November 11th of that year, he was also commissioned to succeed Governor Berkeley, who had resigned in the meantime. He worked to restore peace to the distracted country. In May of 1677, a conference was held with the representatives of the Indian tribes, and a peace concluded. The Indians agreed to acknowledge the King by an annual tribute of three arrows and twenty beaver skins from each town, and in return, no Indian was to be imprisoned except by a legal warrant, their reservations of land were to be inalienable, and they were to be permitted to catch fish and dig oysters within the ceded territory. Arrangements were also made for the establishment of fairs, where friendly Indians could assemble and trade.

In October of 1677, Governor Jeffreys convened an assembly which met at Middle Plantation (afterwards Williamsburg), Jamestown having been burned during Bacon's Rebellion. The session lasted for one month, although the new instructions, which were issued by the King in November, 1676, but did not arrive before 1677, limited the session to fourteen days, unless the Governor should see good cause to continue it beyond that time. These instructions also required the assembly to meet once every two years, and that the members be elected "only by free-holders, as being more agreeable to the custom of England." Governor Jeffreys died in office on Dec. 30, 1678.

CHICHELEY, HENRY, (1615-1683), colonial Governor of Virginia (1678-80), was born in England in 1615. He emigrated to Virginia about 1650. He was a Burgess from Lancaster County in 1656, and in 1674, was a member of the Council. In March, 1676, he was made commander of the forces to be sent against the Indians, but Sir William Berkeley disbanded them before they served on any missions. Upon the death of Governor Jeffreys on December 30, 1678, he became Deputy Governor under a commission dated February 28, 1674, and exercised executive authority until the arrival of Lord Culpepper, May 10, 1680. He continued to hold the title of Deputy Governor until his death, and conducted the affairs of the colony when Lord Culpepper was absent in England. Sir Henry Chicheley took energetic measures for the protection of the colonists against the encroachments of the Indians, causing that "fewer houses for stores or garrisons be erected and built at the

Colonial Governors

heads of the great rivers," namely, the Potomac, Rappahannock, Mattapony and James. He had a kind disposition and by his measures for the public good, greatly ingratiated himself with the people. He died in Middlesex County, Virginia, February 5, 1683.

COLEPEPER (or CULPEPPER), (1635-1689), colonial Governor of Virginia (1680-83), was born in England in 1635, the son of John, the first Lord Colepepper, by his second wife, Judith. He succeeded his father in the title upon the latter's death in 1660, and in July of 1661, was appointed Governor of the Isle of Wight. In this office, he was disliked for his arbitrary measures, and in 1666, the inhabitants of the island presented to the King a petition, stating their grievances. He was one of the royal favorites, to whom, in 1673, King Charles II granted the entire Territory of Virginia for a period of thirty-one years, and in 1675, he purchased from the Earl of Arlington, his co-grantee, the latter's rights between the Rappahannock and Potomac Rivers.

In July of the same year, he was proclaimed Governor of Virginia for life. He was disposed to look on his office as a sinecure, but being reproved by the King for remaining so long in England, he went to the colony in 1680, and was sworn into office on the 10th of May. In August of the same year, he returned to England, entrusting affairs to Sir Henry Chicheley, then Lieutenant-Governor, but when news of the riotous proceedings relative of tobacco planting reached England, Colepeper was ordered back. This so-called "Tobacco Rebellion" was the result of a law that had been passed, requiring planters to load their tobacco at certain specified places along the river banks. For many years Jamestown was the only town in the colony, and after it was burned, there was a great need for some fixed places of trade. It was in order to secure the building of towns that this act was passed. But the planters, accustomed to loading the vessels at their own plantations, resisted the measure, and some of them actually destroyed their entire crop, rather than comply with the law. Colepeper determined to make short work of the difficulty. He filled the jails with prisoners, hanged some of them, and proclaimed the penalty of death against all "plant cutters."

On September 17, 1683, he again returned to England without permission, on the grounds that it was necessary to report in person to the crown. The plea, however, was not accepted, and as he had corruptly received presents from the Assembly, his commission was declared forfeited by a jury. After that, now more governors were appointed for life. Governor Colepeper was described as an able but devious man, who had enriched himself by bribery and extortion. In spite of the impoverished condition of the colony, he contrived to increase his salary by buying up Spanish piasters at the rate of five shillings each, and then by proclamation declaring it a legal tender to the amount of six shillings. He procured the enactment of several popular acts, including one of indemnity and oblivion for offenses committed during Bacon's Rebellion and one forbidding the frequent meetings of slaves to prevent their insurrection. He also passed an act enabling the Governor to grant naturalization and several other measures drafted in England and designed to strengthen the authority of the crown. He died in England on January 27, 1689.

SPENCER, NICHOLAS, (?-1689), colonial Governor of Virginia (1683-84), was born in England. He was said to have been a kinsman of Lord Culpepper, and is known to have exerted considerable influence on political events in Virginia, but definite data concerning his life is scarce. In June, 1666, he was a member of the House of Burgesses, and from 1679 until his death, he held the post of Secretary of the colony. At the time of Lord Culpepper's departure for England on Sept. 17, 1683, Spencer was President of the Council, and as such, administered the government until April 16, 1684. On that day a commission to Francis Howard, Baron of Effingham, was read. He died in Virginia, Sept. 23, 1689.

HOWARD, FRANCIS, LORD EFFINGHAM, (1643-1694), colonial Governor of Virginia (1684-88), was born in England in September of 1643, son of Sir Charles Howard, to whose title he succeeded in 1681. On September 28, 1683, he was commissioned Governor of Virginia, but did not arrive in the colony until the following February, entering office on April 16, 1684. He opened his career in Virginia with instructions from England to forbid the use of printing presses, which course had also been followed by his predecessors, Berkeley and Culpepper. During his administration, acts were passed to prevent plant cutting, to provide for the better defense of the colony, and establishing for the first time, a tax on liquors imported from other English plantations.

Trouble with the Indians again disturbed the tranquility of the colony and the Governor went to Albany, and there, with the Governor of New York, met the Chiefs of the Five Nations and signed a peace treaty with them. Lord Effingham was as unscrupulous and avaricious as Lord Culpepper, and by his extortion and mismanagement, aroused a general spirit of indignation. He was at length recalled at the request of the colonists, and sailed for England on October 20, 1688. He died in England on March 30, 1694.

BACON, NATHANIEL, (1620-1629), colonial Governor of Virginia (1688-90), was born in England on August 29, 1620, son of Reverend James Bacon, and grandson of Sir James Bacon, of Triston Hall, Suffolk. In 1647, he lived in France, but about three years later, he went to Virginia, where he soon became prominently identified with public affairs. He was a member of the Council for over forty years, and as such, took an active part in the turbulent events during the rebellion led by his namesake and kinsman, Nathaniel Bacon, Jr. It was by his pressing requests, that the "rebel" was reluctantly prevailed on to repeat at the bar of the House, the recantation written by him, and he was also supposed to have given a timely warning to young Bacon to run for his life when secret warrants to seize him were issued by Governor Berkeley.

Colonial Governors

In 1677, Colonel Nathaniel Bacon, Sr. was appointed auditor of the public accounts, and as President of the Council, he became the Acting Governor of Virginia, after the departure of Lord Effingham for England on October 20, 1688. He served until the arrival of Sir Francis Nicholson, October 16, 1690. It was during his short administration that the project for a college was first formed and approved by the president and council of Virginia, thus marking the beginning of William and Mary College. Bacon died in Virginia on March 16, 1692.

NICHOLSON, SIR FRANCIS, (1655-1728), colonial Governor of Virginia (1690-93; 1698-1705), was born on November 12, 1655, near Richmond. When Lord Effingham was recalled to England on October 20, 1688, Nicholson was appointed Lieutenant-Governor under him, and in such capacity arrived in the colony, October 16, 1690. He relieved Governor Nathaniel Bacon, and held the reins of government until October 16, 1693, when he, in his turn, was relieved by Sir Edmund Andros, Governor-in-Chief. During the early part of his administration in Virginia he was very popular, and this period formed perhaps the most creditable part of his colonial career. He instituted athletic games, and offered prizes in riding, running, shooting, wrestling and fencing. He also proposed the establishment of a post office, and devoted his energy to the founding of schools, and the improvement of the condition of the clergy. To the establishment of the first college in the oldest colony in the New World, he personally contributed 300 pounds, secured the charter, and, together with seventeen other persons, was appointed by the Assembly, trustee of the institution, which was named the College of William and Mary in honor of the sovereigns.

On December 9, 1698, for a second time, he was appointed to the administration of affairs in Virginia. One of his earliest measures was to move the seat of government from Jamestown to "Middle Plantation," afterwards called Williamsburg. He encouraged the immigration of settlers, who, under him, had a certain quantity of land allotted to them, who were to be exempt from taxes or levies for twenty years, and from military service except in their own defense. But in the midst of his plans for the benefit of the colony, he became involved in conflicts with the Assembly and with the clergy, upon whose complaints he was recalled to England on August 15, 1705. He died on March 5, 1728, in London.

ANDROS, SIR EDMUND, (1637-1714), colonial Governor of New England, Royal Governor of Virginia, was born on the Island of Guernsey on December 6, 1637. He was brought up as a page in the English royal family, served during its exile in the army of Prince Henry of Nassau, and was attached to the household of the Princess Palatine, grandmother of George I. After the Restoration, he gained some distinction in the war against the Dutch, and in 1672, having meanwhile married an heiress, was made major of a regiment of dragoons. This was the highest promotion he had reached before he came to New York, as the Duke of York's lieute-

Encyclopedia of Virginia

nant in 1674, except that the proprietors of Carolina had made him a land-grave with an endowment of four baronies of 12,000 acres of land each, with four castles in Spain.

Andros took possession of New York when it finally fell into the hands of the English after its short reoccupation by the Dutch. He began his administration by laying claim to a part of the territory of Connecticut, on behalf of the Duke of York, but it was not allowed. In the King Philip's War, he was charged by the New England colonists with indifference to their danger, and it was even alleged that he allowed the Indians to obtain their ammunition from Albany.

In August, 1676, he sent a force to Pemaquid (Maine) to build and occupy a fort, and the officer in command began talks with the neighboring Indians and procured the release of fifteen English captives. In 1680, he was found laying claim for the Duke of York, to Fisher's Island, off New London Harbor, which claim was also resisted by the Connecticut authorities. In January, 1681, Andros went back to England, and was succeeded by Thomas Dongan, in August of 1683. But Andros returned to America, landing at Boston on December 20, 1686, and bearing with him a royal commission for the government of all New England. He was now "Governor-in-Chief," to put in practice, as opportunity should serve, the theory of rules by which King James II of England became owner of all the land in New England, and might, if it pleased him, oust all the holders from property which their families had acquired at great cost and hardship, and had peaceably possessed for nearly sixty years.

Andros had gotten the honor of knighthood in England, and had risen to the command of a regiment in the royal army. He forthwith demanded the surrender of the Rhode Island charter, which had been given him. He also instituted at Boston the worship of the Church of England, frightening the sexton of the "Old South Meeting House" into opening the doors and ringing the bell, so that Episcopal worship was afterwards held there on Sundays and other holidays of the church, at hours when the building was not occupied by the regular congregation. It was moreover charged against him that he or his officials corrupted juries; taxes were arbitrarily imposed on the people, and the demand was made on the landholders that they take out new patents for the ownership of their lands. Quit rents were insisted on for the conformation of land titles. Portions of the common lands of towns were also enclosed, and given to friends of the Governor.

Andros browbeat his council. He also exercised the same despotic government in the district of Maine, which was included in his commission as in that of Massachusetts. The New Hampshire and Rhode Island colonies submitted with little or no resistance. He next assumed the government of Connecticut, and the story of the non-surrender of its charter, and of its being hidden in the Charter-Oak at Hartford, which was long current, is now regarded as apocryphal by the best historians. This assumption consolidated New England under one despotism. The Governor resumed his attacks on ancient laws and vested rights in

Colonial Governors

Massachusetts, and when he returned to Boston, began to vacate the prior land bills. Writs of intrusion were served on some of the most considerable of those persons who did not come forward to buy new land patents.

The Governor built a fort on Fort Hill, commanding the harbor, and felt that the great features of his administration were satisfactorily settled. It was at this time (June, 1688), that he received from James II another commission, which made him Governor of all the English possessions on the mainland of America, except Pennsylvania, Delaware, Maryland and Niagara, and extended the territory and dominion of New England southward to latitude 14 degrees, this taking in New York and the Jerseys. The Governor at once went south to take possession. Meanwhile the Reverend Increase Mather, minister of the Second Church at Boston, and president of Harvard College, having gotten away from America in disguise, was in England presenting colonial complaints against Andros to the King, and had been well received by James, who was then courting Dissenters, although no decided measures of relief were promised him.

Meanwhile, Governor Andros led an abortive military expedition into Maine in 1688, to chastise recalcitrant Indians, and by its poor success, increased his unpopularity. When the news of the Prince of Orange's arrival in England to overthrow King James reached Boston, in April of 1689, Andros saw such threatening signs in the local political atmosphere that he at once withdrew inside the walls of Fort Hill. On April 18th, the townspeople assembled, deposed him from his governorship, and imprisoned him with fifty of his followers. On June 27th, Andros, along with several others, was impeached before a colonial counsel by the newly formed house of deputies, and was denied admission to bail. The folowing November, the new ministry in England sent an order to Boston for the forwarding of Andros to Great Britain. There the colonists made their charges against him, but he was not tried because the American agents declined to sign the statement of grievances which was prepared for them by their legal counsel. Andros and his fellow culprits were therefore set free.

In 1692, he was again in America, this time as Royal Governor of Virginia, where for six years, he had a remarkably prosperous administration, encouraging manufactures and cotton culture, and with others, laying the foundation of William and Mary College, which next to Harvard University, is the oldest seat of learning in the United States. Commissary James Blair (1656-1743), its first president and the highest ecclesiastical officer in Virginia, became involved in controversy with Andros, whom he called an enemy to religion, the church, and the college. Charges were made against Andros, and he was finally removed, but was made Governor of the Island of Guernsey in 1704.
He occupied this position for two years, and the took up his residence in London, England, where he died on February 24, 1714.

NOTT, EDWARD, (1657-1706), colonial Governor of Virginia (1705-06), was born in England in 1657. On August 15, 1705, he succeeded Sir Francis Nicholson as Governor of Virginia. In that capacity, he was in some measure subordinate to George Hamilton, Earl of Orkney, who had been appointed Governor-in-Chief, and enjoyed his sinecure for forty years. Governor Nott was a mild, benevolent man, winning affection of the people, and his official acts were always for the benefit of the colony. But he was in office only one year, not surviving long enough to realize what the people hoped from his administration.

In the fall after his arrival, he called an Assembly, which concluded a general revision of the laws that had been long in hand. Some other acts went into operation, among them, one providing funds to build a palace for the Governor, and another, continuing the act directing the building of the capital and city of Williamsburg at Middle Plantation. Special provision was also made under him for the French refugees, whose settlement was above the falls of the James River at "King William Parish in the County of Henrico." During the first year of his government, William and Mary College was burned to the ground. The building, in which the assembly had held their sessions for several years, was first modeled by Sir Christopher Wren and it was afterwards rebuilt under the direction of Governor Spotswood. Governor Nott died in Virginia on August 23, 1706.

JENINGS, EDMUND, (1659-1727), colonial Governor of Virginia (1706-10), was born in Rippon, Yorkshire, England in 1659, son of Sir Edmund and Margaret (Barkham) Jenings. After settling in Virginia, he was prominent in the affairs of the colony for many years, first as Attorney-General during 1680-91, and afterwards as a member of the Council, and succeeded to the administration of the government. He remained in office until the accession of Lieutenant-Governor Spotswood on June 23, 1710.

His administration was not marked by any events of great importance, but the colony at this period enjoyed tranquility and increasing prosperity. Governor Jenings was married to Frances Corbin, and his descendants were among some of the most distinguished families in Virginia. He died in Virginia on December 5, 1727.

SPOTSWOOD, ALEXANDER, (1676-1740), colonial Governor of Virginia (1710-22), was born in Tangier, Africa in 1676, the only son of Robert and Catherine (Elliott) Spotswood. His father was physician to the Governor and Garrison of Tangier. The son was educated for a military life, became aide to the Duke of Marlborough, and was severely wounded at the Battle of Blenheim. In 1710, he was appointed Lieutenant-Governor of Virginia under George Hamilton, the nominal Governor and Commander-in-Chief, and his accession to the adminstration on June 23, 1710, marked a new era in the history of Virginia. He at once ingratiated himself with the people by bringing with him the Writ of Habeas Corpus, which previously had been withheld from the province, and by introducing reforms in the Constitution, in the administration of justice, and in the character of the revenue laws and the collecton of taxes. He showed himself from the outset as a conspicuously energetic administrator, and as early as 1710, sought to extend the line of the Virginia settlements to interrupt the chain of communication between Canada and the Gulf of Mexico, with the object of checking the further extension of French claims on the continent.

About the same time a number of German Protestants having settled above the falls of Rappahanock River at a place afterwards named Germanna, the Assembly passed an act to exempt them from levies for seven years, and for erecting Germanna into a distinct parish by the name of "St. George." Here, in the county of Spotsylvania, Governor Spotswood acquired a landed estate of 40,000 acres, where he cultivated vines, and having found beds of iron ore, established a furnace, thus giving to Virginia a new industry.

In 1716, with a company of his friends, he led an expedition to search for a passage through the Appalachian Mountains. The highest summit of this range he named Mount George, for the King, while the men of the party called the peak next to it, in honor of the Governor, Mount Spotswood. This was the first time "the great mountains" were explored, and to commemorate the event, the Governor on his return presented each of his companions with a golden horseshoe, bearing the inscription, "Sic juvat transcendere Montes," and instituted the "Tramontaine Order" to stimulate them to return to this wild region and open the country to future settlers. When King George heard of the expedition, he bestowed on Spotswood the honors of knighthood, and sent him a golden horseshoe set with jewels, and each one who took part in the memorable trip was recognized by the title of "The Knight of the Golden Horseshoe."

Governor Spotswood is regarded as one of Virginia's wisest Governors. He pressed the passage of an act for improving the staple of tobacco and making tobacco-notes the medium of circulation, built an octagon magazine at Williamsburg, rebuilt the College of William and Mary, which had burned down several years before his arrival, and at his request, a grant of 1,000 pounds was made to the college in 1718. A fund was also created for instructing Indian children in Christianity, for which purpose a school was established at Fort Christiana. Being a thorough soldier, he kept the militia in excellent discipline, and dealt resolutely with the enemies of the colony, capturing and putting death the famous pirate Edward Teach, and holding in check the Indians on the frontier. He urged England to approve the policy of establishing a chain of posts beyond the mountains, from the lakes to the Mississippi, to restrain the encroachment of the French, but his voice fell upon deaf ears, although his plan was carried out years afterwards.

In 1722, he held a conference with the Six Nations, and by his diplomacy, the Tuscaroras, who were threatening the Carolinas, lost support. But, as was usual with the colonial assemblies, the legislature of Virginia was slow in finding funds for the Governor's undertakings against the Indians, and disputes resulted. Spotswood also, in 1719, entangled himself in a disagreement with the crown as to the right of presentation to benefices in Virginia, and these controversies finallly led to his removal from office on September 27, 1722.

He continued to live in Virginia, and from 1730-39, was Deputy Postmaster-General for the American colonies, in which capacity he arranged the transfer of mails with much energy, bringing Philadelphia and Williamsburg within eight or ten days of each other. It was also he who made Benjamin Franklin Postmaster for the province of Pennsylvania. In 1740, he received his commission as Major-General, and was engaged in collecting forces for the expedition against Cartagena. He was a master of mathematics, and bequeathed his books, maps and mathematical instruments to William and Mary College. He was married in 1724 to Ann Butler, and the couple had two sons and two daughters. He died in Annapolis, Maryland, June 7, 1740.

DRYSDALE, HUGH, (?-1726), colonial Governor of Virginia (1722-26), succeeded Governor Spotswood in the administration of the colony on Sept. 27, 1722, and remained in office until his death. He was described as a "man of mediocre calibre," who "yielded to the current of the day, solicitous only to retain his place." He was strongly opposed to bringing slaves into Virginia, and to relieve the people from a poll tax, a duty was imposed by the Assembly on the importation of liquor and slaves, but owing to the opposition of the African Company and interested traders, the act was annulled by the British Board of Trade. Governor Drysdale announced to the House of Burgesses that "the interfering interest of the African Company had obtained the repeal of that law." The planters were alarmed by the increase of slaves, but the slave trade being advantageous to Great Britain, the British government constantly checked the attempts of Virginia and the other colonies to put a stop to it. An act regulating the importation of convicts was also rejected by the Board of Trade. Governor Drysdale died in Virginia on July 22, 1726.

CARTER, ROBERT, (1663-1732), colonial Governor of Virginia (1726-27), was born in Virginia in 1663, son of Colonel John and Sarah (Ludlow) Carter. His father came to this country in early life, was a member of the Virginia House of Burgesses, and held many other important positions. Robert Carter was for many years the agent of Lord Fairfax, the proprietor of the Northern Neck grant. He was Treasurer of the colony Speaker of the House of Burgesses, 1694-99, and member of the Council for twenty-seven years, 1699-1726. As President of the Council, he undertook the administration of the government after the death of Hugh Drysdale, and continued in the office of Governor until the appointment of William Gooch, in October 1727.

He was a man of great wealth, and owing to the extent of his landed possessions, acquired the sobriquet of "King Carter." He lived at Corotoman, on the Rappahannock, in Lancaster County, where the old Christ Church was built by him shortly before his death. He was married twice: first, to Judith, Armistead, and then to a widow named Willis, whose maiden name was Elizabeth Landon, of an ancient family of Hereford County, England. He died in Lancaster County, Virginia on August 4, 1732.

GOOCH, WILLIAM, (1681-1751), colonial Governor of Virginia (1727-40; 1741-49), was born in Yarmouth, England, October 21, 1681. He was educated for the army, served under Marlborough, and was an officer of superior military ability. On or about October 13, 1727, he superseded Robert Carter in the administration of Virginia, and for upwards of twenty years, conducted the affairs of the colony, which under him, enjoyed prosperity. His rule was so commendable that he is said to have been the only colonial Governor in America against whom, at home or abroad, there was never a shadow of complaint.

In 1728, the boundary line between Virginia and North Carolina was satisfactorily settled, an act of great importance to the inhabitants of these colonies who lived on their respective borders. In 1740, troops were transported from the colonies for the first time, to assist the soldiers of the mother country, with Major-General Alexander Spotswood having been appointed to the command of the four colonial battalions raised to join in an attack on Cartagena, New Grenada. On account of Spotswood's unexpected death on the eve of the battle, Governor Gooch assumed command of the expedition in June of 1740, the administration devolving during his absence upon Commissary James Blair, then president of the council. Gooch was severely wounded in the campaign, and contracted the fever from which many of the English squadron died.

Upon his return to Virginia in July, 1741, he resumed the government of the colony. During this part of his administration (1734), the settlement of the beautiful valley of Virginia was effected. On June 20, 1749, he embarked for England "amid the blessings and tears of his people, among whom he had lived as a wise and beneficent father." He had been previously named a baronet, and in 1747, was made a Major-General. He died in London on December 17, 1751.

ROBINSON, JOHN, (1683-1749), colonial Governor of Virginia (1749), was born in Virginia in 1683, son of Christopher Robinson, who prior to 1664 had settled on the Rappahannock River. Christopher's brother, Dr. John Robinson, Bishop of Bristol and subsequently of London, was for some years British envoy at the court of Sweden, and also served as the British plenipotentiary at the Treaty of Utrecht. John Robinson occupied many important positions in the colony. He was Speaker of the House of Burgesses under Sir William Gooch, and was the first on the list of men named by the Governor to disburse the 4,000 pounds appropriated by the General Assembly for an expedition against Canada. On his departure for England, June 20, 1749, Gooch left John Robinson, then President of the Council, as Acting Governor of Virginia, in which capacity he served until his death of September 5, 1749.

Encyclopedia of Virginia

The most important feature of his brief administration was the passage of several acts by the Assembly, touching the government of the colony, which, according to Hening, made a very important change in the Virginia system of jurisprudence, and necessitated the publication of a new edition of laws. These acts, however, were afterwards repealed by the King (1752). Governor Robinson was married to Catherine Beverley and their son John was Speaker of the House of Burgesses and Treasurer of the colony.

LEE, THOMAS, (ca. 1690-1750), colonial Governor of Virginia (1749-50), was born in Stratford, Virginia, about 1690, son of Richard and Lettice (Corbin) Lee. He was a grandson of Richard Lee, of the Privy Council of Charles I, who emigrated from Shropshire, England in 1641, and settled in Westmoreland County, Virginia. Thomas Lee received a common education, "yet having strong natural parts, long after he was a man, he learned the languages without any assistance but his own genius, and became a tolerable adept in the Greek and Latin."

He was long a member of the House of Burgesses and of the Council, was Commander-in-Chief of the colony of Virginia, and in 1744, was appointed by Governor William Gooch to serve with William Beverly, as commissioner to negotiate with the Iroquois Indians. They journeyed to Philadelphia in a yacht, and at a conference with the Indians in Lancaster, secured the right to the lands west of the mountains as far as the Ohio River. He organized a company for the exploration and settlement of lands in the Ohio Valley, but the plan failed. He is said to have predicted the separation of the American colonies from Great Britain.

He was President of the Virginia Council at the time of John Robinson's death on September 5, 1749, and as such, succeeded to the administration of the government of the colony. In this station he continued until his death. The King appointed him as Governor in 1750, but he died before the commission reached him. Governor Lee built the second manor-house, with nearly one hundred rooms, the original house built by Richard Lee having been burned about 1735. The necessary funds were furnished by private subscriptions, headed by the Governor, as well as by Queen Caroline who contributed "a bountiful present out of her own privy purse."

He was married in 1721 to Hannah Ludwell, and the couple had six sons, and two daughters. He died at Stafford House, Virginia on November 14, 1750.

BURWELL, LEWIS, (1710-1752), colonial Governor of Virginia (1750-51), was born in Virginia in 1710, son of Major Nathaniel and Elizabeth (Carter) Burwell. Lewis Burwell was educated at Cambridge, England and became distinguished as a scholar. He is said to have embraced within the circle of his studies almost every branch of knowledge. On his return to the colony, he was called to fill many important offices in Virginia; was a burgess from Gloucester County in 1736, became a member of the Council in 1743,

Colonial Governors

and as President of that body, succeeded Thomas Lee in the administration of affairs, holding the office from November 14, 1750, until November 20, 1751.

During this brief period some Cherokee chiefs, with a party of warriors, visited Williamsburg professedly to open a direct trade with Virginia. While on this mission, a clash occurred between them and a party of the Nottoways, which if not for the tact of Governor Burwell, who effected a reconciliation, might have resulted disastrously for the settlers. During his term, a New York company of actors was permitted to erect a theatre in Williamsburg. Governor Burwell was married in 1736 to Mary Willis, and had one son and three daughters, the youngest of whom, Rebecca, was the "Belinda" of Jefferson's college days. Burwell died in Virginia in 1752.

DINWIDDIE, ROBERT, (1693-1770), colonial Governor of Virginia (1751-58), was born near Glasgow, Scotland in 1693, son of Robert and Sarah (Cumming) Dinwiddie. In December of 1727, he was appointed collector of the customs on the Island of Bermuda, a position he filled until 1738, when, in acknowledgment of his services in exposing a long practiced system of fraud in the collection of the customs of the West Indian Islands, he was made "Surveyor General of the Customs of the southern ports of the continent of America." In August, 1743, he was specially commissioned to examine the duties of the Collector of Customs of the Island of Barbadoes, and here he also exposed enormous frauds.

In July of 1751, he was appointed Lieutenant-Governor of Virginia. Upon his arrival in the colony on November 20th, Governor Dinwiddie directed his first efforts towards checking the encroachments of the French on British territory. Learning that the French had made treaties with all the western tribes of Indians and were building forts on the Ohio River, he decided to send a messenger to remonstrate St. Pierre, the French commander of the Ohio, and George Washington, whose military capacity he was quick to recognize, was selected for the difficult enterprise. In 1753, he appointed Washington Adjutant-General of one of the four military districts of Virginia, with the rank of major. The French, having refused to accede to the governor's demand for the withdrawal of troops, made through Major Washington, Dinwiddie determined to expel them by force. Washington's expedition, and the capture of Fort Trent by the French followed, and in 1755, a fleet and two regiments of the regular army under Braddock was sent into the North American waters.

Meanwhile, the Governor met five of the other colonial Governors in Annapolis and Alexandria, and planned various expeditions against the French, but was continually hampered in his military operations by the reluctance of the Legislature to vote money for the public defense. He and the other Governors therefore recommended the imposition of a general poll-tax by the British Parliament and a general land-tax on the American colonies, for the purpose of raising funds to carry on the war, urging that it was impossible to obtain joint efforts by appealing to their Assemblies. The defeat of Braddock, however, alarmed colonists so much that they began to organize local companies. The Assembly voted 40,000 pounds for the service, the Virginia regiment was enlarged to sixteen companies, and the command of the same given to George Washington.

Governor Dinwiddie remained at the head of affairs in Virginia until January, 1758, when he left for England. He passed the remainder of his life at Clifton, where he had gone in search of health, and died there on July 27, 1770.

BLAIR, JOHN, (1689-1771), colonial Governor of Virginia (1758; 1768), was born in Williamsburg, Virginia in 1689, son of Dr. Archibald Blair, and a nephew of Reverend James Blair, president of William and Mary College. He occupied many important positions in the government, was a burgess from James City County in 1736, and later a member of the Council. As President of that body, he succeeded to the direction of affairs on the departure of Governor Dinwiddie for England in January of 1758, and held the position until the arrival of Francis Fauquier on June 7, 1758.

The most important event of this period was the "passage of an act augumenting the forces in the pay of this colony to two thousand men," and authorizing the issuance of treasury notes to the sum of 32,000 pounds for defraying the expenses of the increased defense of the colony. John Blair subsequently served for several years as Deputy Auditor of the colony, and was a visitor of William and Mary College. As President of the Council, he was again Acting Governor from the time of Governor Fauquier's death on March 3, 1768, until the arrival of Lord Botetourt on October 24th. During this trying period of dissensions with England, he displayed conspicuous ability and fidelity to the colony's interests. Blair died in Williamsburg, Virginia on November 5, 1771.

FAUQUIER, FRANCIS, (1703-1768), colonial Governor of Virginia (1758-68), was born in England in 1703, son of Dr. John Francis Fauquier, a director of the Bank of England, and Elizabeth Chamberlayne, his wife. He was a director of the South Sea Company in 1751, and was elected fellow of the Royal Society on February 15, 1753. On February 10, 1758, he was appointed Lieutenant-Governor of Virginia, and arriving in the colony on June 7th, assumed the duties of government, which he conducted until his death. In the first year of his administration, Fort Du Quesne fell into the hands of the English, and this event marked the end of the war between the French and English on the frontiers of Virginia. Governor Fauquier sympathized with the colonists in their struggle against the British encroachments on their rights, but in his official position, opposed everything looking towards disloyalty.

In 1764, he dissolved the Assembly for having adopted Patrick Henry's resolutions, which declared that the sole right of taxation existed in the colonial legislature, and when, the following year, Massachusetts invited the other colonies to join the

Colonial Governors

General Congress, he refused to summon the House of Burgesses to the end that it might appoint delegates to such a Congress. Nevertheless, he was one of the most popular, as well as one of the wisest of the royal Governors. In the progress of the stirring events which preceded the Revolution, he preserved the respect of the people over whom he presided. In his private character, he stood among the highest in the colony, and Thomas Jefferson, who was his personal friend, called him "the ablest man who had ever filled the governor's office."

Francis Fauquier was the author of "An Essay on Ways and Means of Raising Money for the Support of the Present War without Increasing the Public Debts" (1756), in which he strongly contended that by no means could any taxation be made on the poor. He was married to Catharine Dalston, and died at Williamsburg, Virginia on March 3, 1768.

BERKELEY, NORBORNE, (1718-1770), baron Botetourt, colonial Governor of Virginia (1768-70), was born in England in 1718. He was colonel of the North Gloucestershire Militia in 1761, was a member of Parliament until he was named a peer in 1764, and in July of 1768, was appointed Governor-in-Chief of Virginia. He arrived in the colony on October 28, 1768, and owing to his courtesy and patience in public life, was soon on friendly terms with the Virginians.

However when in May of 1769, the Assembly passed two resolutions--first that Virginia should no longer submit to taxation by England; and second, that it would not send its criminals to England to be tried. Lord Botetourt, although sympathizing with the colonists, would not tolerate what seemed to be open rebellion, and dissolved the Legislature. The Burgesses, instead of returning quietly to their homes, met on the next day at a private house in Williamsburg, and adopted resolutions, "which formed a well-digested, stringent, and practicable scheme of non-importation, until all the unconstitutional revenue acts should be repealed." They also made a special covenant with one another not to import any slaves, nor purchase any imported, and these compacts, signed by Peyton Randolph, Richard Bland, Archibald Cary, Robert Carter Nicholas, Richard Henry Lee, George Washington, Thomas Jefferson, Patrick Henry, and all the burgesses there assembled, were then sent throughout the colony for every man to sign.

In spite of this conflict between the Lesiglature and the representative of the crown, Lord Botetourt did not forfeit the esteem of the people, and having been assured, in answer to his requests to the Earl of Hillsborough, Secretary of State for the colonies, that the ministry would advocate a repeal of the obnoxious taxes, the relations between the Governor and the colonial legislative bodies were fully restored. On finding, soon after, that he had been misled, he indignantly demanded the Earl of Hillsborough's recall.

His death, it is said, was hastened by chagrin at the failure of his efforts to effect a reconciliation between the colonists and England. Governor Botetourt was admired and respected by the

Virginians, who showed their appreciation by erecting a monument to his memory in Williamsburg, and naming a county after him. He died in Williamsburg, Virginia on October 15, 1770.

NELSON, WILLIAM, (1711-1772), colonial Governor of Virginia (1770-71), was born in Yorktown, Virginia, in 1711, son of Thomas Nelson (1677-1745), who came to America from Penrith, Scotland, about 1690. He settled in Virginia, and in 1705, laid out the town of York, where he built the first custom-house in the colonies, and erected the famous Nelson house. William Nelson inherited a considerable fortune from his father, and having himself been a successful merchant, became a great proprietor. He was President of the general or Supreme Court of law and equity for the province; served for many years in the Governor's Council; and as President of that body, acted as Chief Executive of Virginia between the death of Lord Botetourt on October 15, 1770, and the coming of the Earl of Dunmore, in August of 1771. He was widely known for his liberal hospitality and his extensive charities. His wife was Miss Burwell of Virginia, by whom he had a son, Thomas Nelson, signer of the Declaration of Independence. He died in Yorktown, Virginia on Nov. 19, 1772.

MURRAY, JOHN, (1732-1809), fourth Earl of Dunmore, and colonial Governor of Virginia (1771-75), was born in 1732, eldest son of William Murray, third Earl of Dunmore, and Catherine Nairn, his wife. He succeeded to the peerage in 1756, and from 1761-69, sat in the House of Lords. In 1770, he was appointed Governor of the colony of New York, which was added that of Virginia, July, 1771.

He arrived in New York in October, 1770, and in Williamsburg the following August, and having met the Virginia Assembly in the spring of 1772, adjourned it after a brief session. He did not again convene it until March of 1773, when he dissolved it upon its adoption of resolutions for the appointment of a committee of correspondence to coordinate common action on the part of the colonies in the struggle with England. A vote for a public fast to be observed on June 1st, the day for closing the port of Boston, led to another dissolution, on May 26, 1774. The burgesses then immediately repaired to the Raleigh tavern, where they adopted resolutions against the use of tea and other imported commodities, and recommended an annual congress of representatives of the colonies. On May 29th, the burgesses again held a meeting, at which a circular was issued, calling an assembly of deputies to meet in convention in Williamsburg on August 1st of that year. This was the first public revolutionary assemblage.

Meanwhile, an Indian outbreak occurred on the colony's frontier which resulted in the bloody expedition to Point Pleasant, and Governor Dunmore further aggravated the colonists' by concluding a disadvantageous peace with the Indians. Early in 1775, the people of Virginia called another convention, which met in Richmond on March 20th, in spite of the Governor's proclamation prohibiting it. Alarmed at the threatening aspect of affairs, Lord Dunmore moved part of the powder from the Williamsburg magazine to an English man-of-war in James River. The people then armed themselves under the command of Patrick Henry, volunteers by thousands flocked into the town, and peace was only preserved by payment of the value of the powder.

One June 1st, Dunmore convened the Assembly to consider Lord North's conciliatory proposition, and while they were under discussion, he took refuge on board the "Fowly," a British man-of-war lying off Yorktown, and declared it to be the seat of government. This was on June 6th, and the Assembly continuing its deliberations, forwarded to him various bills to which he refused to give his assent without the attendance of the burgesses on board the vessel. The burgesses voted this to be a high breach of their privileges and resolved that the Governor had abdicated, and constituted themselves a convention, vesting the executive in a committee of safety.

Meanwhile, Dunmore collected and manned a small flotilla, and began a series of desultory operations on the river banks. He attacked Hampton, but was driven back with loss on October 25, 1775; proclaimed freedom to all blacks who would join his ranks; was severely beaten by the colonists at Great Bridge on December 9th; and burned Norfolk, then the most populous and flourishing town in Virginia on January 1, 1776. He occupied Gwynn's Island in the Chesapeake on June of 1776, from where he was dislodged by the Virginians on July 8. Shortly afterwards, he disbanded his forces and returned to England, where he was twice chosen to the House of Lords. He was Governor of the Bahama Islands from 1787-96. He died at Ramsgate, England in May of 1809.

GOVERNORS OF VIRGINIA

HENRY, PATRICK, (1736-1799), statesman, orator, and Governor of Virginia, (1776-1779) and (1784-1786), was born at Studley, Hanover Co., Virginia on May 29, 1736. His father, John Henry, was from Aberdeen, Scotland. Among the country gentlemen in Virginia, John Henry was held in high esteem for superior intelligence and character. On his mother's side, Patrick Henry was of Welsh stock. Her family were the Winstons, noted in Virginia for "vivacity of spirit, conversational talent, with a lyric and dramatic turn, a gift for music and for eloquent speech, and as well for their fondness for country life." For the first ten years of his life, young Henry appears to have been educated at a small school near his home, but around the end of that time, his father took it upon himself to provide his son with an education, assisted by Patrick's uncle who was rector of St. Paul's parish in Hanover, and a good classical scholar. When he was fifteen years old, Patrick began working in the shop of a country tradesman, but remained with him only a year. Then his father set him up with his older brother William to run a store, but they were unsuccessful.

At the end of a year there, Patrick married Mary Shelton, daughter of a farmer, and the parents of the young couple established them on a farm close by from which, by their own work with that of a half dozen slaves, they were to earn a living. This, however, they did not do, and at the end of two years, making a forced sale of the slaves, Patrick invested the proceeds in another country store only to find himself insolvent at the age of twenty-three. He then decided to become a lawyer. His mental equipment for the profession at this time is summarized by a biographer: "Not a scholar surely, nor even a considerable miscellaneous reader, he yet had the basis of a good education; he had the habit of reading over and over again, a few of the best books; he had a good memory; he had an intellect strong enough to grasp the great commanding features of any subject; he had a fondness for the study of human nature, and singular proficiency in that branch of science; he had quick and warm sympathies, particularly with persons in trouble; an amiable propensity to take sides with the underdog in any fight."

Presenting himself before the examiners in Richmond for admission to the bar in the early spring of 1760, two out of four signed his license with reluctance--one absolutely refused to affix his signature, and the fourth signed only on repeated importunities and promises of future reading. It has been alleged that Patrick Henry "was originally a barkeeper," and that "for three years after getting his license to practice law, he tended travelers and drew corks." With regard to these allegations it may be said that for the period referred to, he made the tavern of his father-in-law his home where his service probably consisted in sometimes lending hand in case of need in the business of the house. His fee-books indubitably settle the fact that in the first three and a half years of his actual practice, he charged fees in 1,185 suits, and of course prepared, in addition, many legal papers out of court, while the same fee-books show that during the early period he was able to assist his father-in-law by an important advance of money.

In December of 1763, he appeared for the province of Virginia in what is known as "The Parson's Cause," and although the side on which he was retained happened to be the wrong side, wrong both in law and equity, "there were enlisted in its favor passions of the multitude the most selfish, the most blinding, and at the same time, most energetic." "And Patrick Henry," said Prof. M.C. Tyler, "proved to be the advocate skillful enough to play, effectively upon those passions and raise a storm before which mere considerations of law and equity were swept out of sight." The effect on his auditors, of Henry's plea against the clergy was described in terms which leave no doubt that this was the first of those not infrequent and marvelous occasions in his career when his great prowess as an orator was apparent. The jury came in with a verdict of one penny damages for the clergyman who had brought the suit to recover his salary, and from that day, the repute of Patrick Henry, both as lawyer, and as orator, was established throughout his native state. His legal practice increased greatly.

In May of 1765, he was chosen as a member of the Virginia Legislature from the county of Louisa to fill an unexpired term. He at once distinguished himself in a way that made it plain to the people of Virginia that a new political leader of unique and unrivaled force had come upon the stage. He absolutely opposed and defeated the proposal for a "public loan office" by which the profligate practices of an official who had been Speaker of the House of Burgesses and Treasurer of the colony for many years would have been covered and then carried through the House after hot debate and against the opposition of the older leaders and members five out of seven resolutions which he offered, affirming the rights of the colony, and declaring in face of the British Stamp Act, which had just been passed on March 8, 1765, "that the General Assembly of this colony have the only and sole exclusive right and power to lay taxes and impositions upon the inhabitants of this colony, and every attempt to vest such power in any person or persons whatever other than the General Assembly aforesaid has a manifest tendency to destroy British as well as American freedom." It was in one of his speeches in the debate which preceded the passage of these resolutions that he said in a tone of thrilling solemnity: "Caesar had his Brutus; Charles the First his Cromwell; and George the Third ('Treason!' shouted the speaker. 'Treason! Treason!' rose from all the sides of the room. The orator paused, and then raising himself with a look and bearing of still prouder and fiercer determination, so closed the sentence as to baf-

Governors

fle his accusers without in the least flinching from his own position)--"and George the Third may profit by their example. If this be treason, make the most of it."

The effect of the debate and the resolutions could not easily be misstated. Manuscript copies of the resolutions were dispatched immediately to the northern states, and were powerful in awakening resistance to the "Stamp Act," where that had not begun, and in stimulating resistance to new life where the disposition towards resistance had begun to cool. "The publishing of the Virginia Resolves proved an alarm bell to the disaffected," wrote the royalist Bernard, Governor of Massachusetts. Gage, commander of the British forces in America, wrote from New York that the Virginia Resolves had "given the signal for a general outcry over the continent." In 1774, an able loyalist writer singled them out as the cause of all the troubles that had come on the land. The author of the resolutions from then on had an assured position among the foremost of the influential statesmen of his commonwealth, and it is even doubtful if he ever parted in any marked degree with the primacy among contemporary public men in Virginia, which he had by this time acquired. He was sent to every session of the Virginia House of Burgesses from 1765 to 1774. He was at the front in all local committees and conventions, and was a member of the first committee of correspondence.

Meanwhile, he continued his law practice and his legal reputation grew. When the members of the House which had been dissolved by Lord Drummond, the Provincial Governor, met at Williamsburg in August, 1774, to appoint deputies to the proposed Colonial Congress to convene in Philadelphia, on September 5, 1774, he was one of the seven elected. His first two speeches in this Congress were on a motion to prepare regulations for its government made by Mr. Duane of New York. In the second, going broadly into the subject of public affairs, he said: "Government is dissolved, fleets and armies and the present state of things show that government is dissolved...The distinctions between Virginians, Pennsylvanians, New Yorkers and New Englanders are no more." To this he added the notable exclamation--"I am not a Virginian, but an American."

In his assault on the plan for a permanent reconciliation between Great Britain and the colonies submitted by Joseph Galloway of Pennsylvania, he declared: "I am inclined to think the present (British) measures lead to war." He was placed on the committee of the Congress to prepare and address to the King of England, also "on the committee appointed to state the rights of the colonies." After the adjournment of Congress, the sentiment for war began to take more definite shape throughout the country, and when in the spring of 1775, the Second Revolutionary Convention of Virginia met in Richmond, he was ready on March 23rd with resolutions providing for putting the colony into a state of defense. His speech in support of these resolutions was perhaps the speech of his life. Beginning (after preliminary sentences) "Mr. President! It is natural for man to indulge in the illusions of hope," and ending "I know not what course others may take, but as for me, give me liberty or give me death!" It has been said that "for true eloquence it has never been surpassed." This speech is well known. Among the questions concerning it, none has excited more profound interest than that which relates to the faithfulness of its record and preservation. This and other pertinent topics in connection with the speech are amply treated in Tyler's "Life of Patrick Henry" (1890). The resolutions it advocated were passed as offered by Henry, and the committee which they called for to prepare a plan for "embodying, arming and disciplining" the militia was at once appointed. Patrick Henry was its chairman and with him were Richard Henry Lee, Nicholas Harrison, Reddick, Washington, Stephens, Lewis, Christian, Pendleton, Jefferson and Zane.

It is little known to the world at large that "the first overt act of war" in Virginia and the first act of physical resistance to a Royal Governor in the colonies was made in that province almost as early as the engagements in Massachusetts at Lexington and Concord. This occurred on May 4, 1775, when with the independent company of his own county of Hanover, Henry compelled His Majesty George the Third's Receiver-General to pay over to him 330 pounds "as a compensation for gunpowder lately taken out of the public magazine by the Governor's (Lord Dunmore) order," the money to be conveyed to "the Virginia delegates at the General Congress." To this second Continental Congress, Henry at once proceeded. He left it near the end of July to become colonel of the 1st Virginia regiment. He was next made Commander-in-Chief of the forces of Virginia by the Provincial Convention, but this was the sum of his military service, all connection with the army being ended by his own action in February of 1776, when he resigned. Joseph Reed of Philadelphia probably touched the core of fact as to this matter when he wrote to George Washington (March, 1776): "His resignation rather gives satisfaction than otherwise, as his abilities seem better calculated for the Senate than for the field."

It was just before this (1775) that his wife, Sarah, mother of his six children, had died. On October 9, 1777, he was married to Dorothea Dandridge, a granddaughter of the old Royal Governor, Alexander Spotswood. In May 1776, he was again a delegate to the Virginia Convention in attendance at Williamsburg for its first meeting. Besides serving on perhaps a majority of its committees, he advocated the motion unanimously adopted to instruct the Virginia delegates to the Continental Congress to propose to that body to declare the united colonies free and independent states; was a member of the committee to prepare a declaration of rights and plan of government, and on the adoption of the state constitution by the convention (June 29, 1776) was at once elected its first Governor by a clear majority of all votes cast. To this post, he was reelected in 1777 and in 1778. The office then passed to others under the constitutional provision whch rendered him ineligible for four years.

In 1784 and in 1785, he was again chosen Governor, but in 1786, he declined further reelection. Elected in 1779 as one of the Virginia delegates to Congress, he also declined that office, and

Governors

from then on, served in no public capacity outside of Virginia. He at once retired because of delicate health and the impairment of his fortune, to Heatherwood, an estate of 10,000 acres in the county of Henry (which had been named in his honor) some two hundred miles southeast of Richmond, where he remained until November, 1784. He served in the Virginia House of Delegates during this period.

From 1786 to 1794, Henry resumed his law practice and was successful in recovering his financial standing. In 1791 and in 1793, he appeared before the Circuit Court of the United States in what was probably the most difficult and important, in a legal aspect, of all cases which he ever tried--that known as the case of "The British Debts." He finally established himself in the county of Charlotte, at an estate called Red Hill, and the picture of his declining years there spent is idyllic. General Henry Lee, then Governor of Virginia had appointed him as a U.S. Senator in 1794 to fill an unexpired term. President Washington offered him the post of U.S. Secretary of State and of Chief Justice of the United States Supreme Court in 1795 and 1796. President John Adams had sent his name to the U.S. Senate as one of three envoys extraordinary and ministers plenipotentiary to the French Republic, but each of these offices he had declined.

In 1799, however, at the special request of George Washington, he stood for a seat in the Virginia legislature and was of course elected, but his death prevented his taking the position. The occasion of Washington's plea to the old statesman that he should once more enter into public life was the passage of resolutions by the Virginia Legislature claiming the right of a state to resist the execution of an obnoxious act of Congress.

Many of Henry's contemporaries left on record their admiration for his gifts as an orator. According to Randolph of Roanoke, he was "Shakespeare and Garrick combined." Thomas Jefferson said of his speech, on moving the resolutions against the Stamp Act: "I heard the splendid display of Mr. Henry's talents as a popular orator. They were great, indeed--such as I have never heard from any other man. He appeared to me to speak as Homer wrote." Dr. Archibald Alexander said: "The power of his eloquence was felt equally by the learned and the unlearned. No man who ever heard him speak on any important occasion could fail to admit his uncommon power over the minds of his hearers."

A statue of Patrick Henry in bronze is on the Washington monument in Richmond, Virginia. His life story was written by William Wirt (1817); and one, the best, by William Wirt Henry (1891). Henry died on his estate, June 6, 1799, and was buried there. The slab above his grave bears the inscription: "His Fame--his Best Epitaph."

JEFFERSON, THOMAS, (1743-1826), third President of the United States, and Governor of Virginia (1779-1781), was born in Shadwell, Albemarle Co., Virginia on April 2, 1743. Thomas Jefferson was the third son of Peter and Jane (Randolph) Jefferson, and his education, which was designed to be of the best quality attainable, had been well advanced when he was fourteen years of age, at which time (in 1757), his father died at the age of fifty.

In 1760, he entered the College of William and Mary in Williamsburg, Virginia. Being endowed with an ardent thirst for knowledge and great industry and determination, he devoted himself to study with such earnestness as to even threaten his health. He was, at that time, a tall, raw-boned, freckled, sandy-haired youth, as well as being very shy. Like nearly all the members of his family, he was an excellent musician, and a very capable performer on the violin. He had already made up his mind as to his profession in life, and choosing the law, and, although deeply interested in science, he pursued his studies in college mainly with a view to the legal profession as their practical outcome.

After completing his course of study at William and Mary, Jefferson began to devote himself to law, and around his twenty-fourth birthday, he was admitted to the bar. He began to practice law at once, and business rapidly came to him. He had good connections through both sides of his family, and there was no difficulty in obtaining business. He was said to be always on the right side, and, that being the case, the fact that he was not eloquent did not so much matter in regard to his success.

Two years after he began to practice law, in 1769, Jefferson was elected a member of the House of Burgesses, of which Washington was also a member. It was this session of the Burgesses which introduced four resolutions practically revolutionary: that the colonies could not legally or in right be taxed by a body in which they were not represented, and that they might in such case unite in order to obtain a redress of their grievances. These resolutions, in fact, were embodied in the Declaration of Independence.

It is evident from all that is known of Jefferson's early life that he had entered a public career deliberately and with the intention of following it as a pursuit. In fact, he said at one time: "When I first entered upon the stage of public life, I came to a resolution never to engage, while in public office, in any kind of enterprise for the improvement of my fortune, nor to wear any other character than that of a farmer. I have never departed from it in a single instance, and I have in multiplied instances found myself happy in being able to decide and to act as a public servant clear of all interests in the multiform questions that have arisen, wherein I have seen others embarrassed and biased by having got themselves in a more interested situation. Thus I have thought myself richer in contentment than I should have been with any increase of fortune. Certainly I should have been much wealther had I remained in that private condition which rendered it lawful, and even laudable, to use proper efforts to better it." Meanwhile, Jefferson admitted candidly that he wanted the respect and consideration of his colleagues, and, long after, said to Madison, that in the earlier years of his public service, the esteem of the world was perhaps of higher value in his eyes than everything in it.

Governors

Jefferson married on January 1, 1772 to Mrs. Martha Skelton, a childless young widow, said to have been a very beautiful woman. She was the daughter of John Wayles, who was practicing at the Williamsburg bar. Jefferson had just then finished the new house he had been building at Monticello, on his estate, and the couple went to it to live shortly after their marriage. Jefferson's estate nearly doubled the year after his marriage through the death of his wife's father, by which she received nearly 50,000 acres of land and 135 slaves. Here Jefferson began to lead the actual life of a farmer, which he had said was the one which he would pursue, still continuing, however, his practice, which in 1774, although lucrative, had not extended his name beyond his own immediate neighborhood.

By the close of that year, however, the name of Jefferson was among the first of the patriotic leaders in the colonies. The Continental Congress was about to assemble in Philadelphia, and Jefferson, before leaving to attend the meeting of Burgesses in Williamsburg, which would elect the deputies of Virginia, prepared a draft of such instructions as he deemed should be given to the representatives of Virginia in the Continental Congress. These instructions amounted to a small pamphlet, the substance of which became practically the Declaration of Independence. Jefferson now put his law business into the hands of this friend, Edmund Randolph, and withdrew from practice, as it afterward proved, forever.

The Williamsburg Convention of 1774 appointed Thomas Jefferson as an alternate with John Randolph, in case the latter should be obliged to leave the Congress before its adjournment. The affair at Lexington precipitated events, and the convention becoming convinced of the gravity of the situation, began to arm for the conflict. A committee of thirteen, appointed to arrange a plan of defense, included such men as George Washington, Patrick Henry, Richard Henry Lee and Thomas Jefferson. On June 20, 1775, Randolph's seat became vacant and Jefferson took his seat in the Congress in Philadelphia, and that same day he learned and apprised the Congress of the news of the Battle of Bunker Hill, having obtained it from the same messenger who gave the information to General Washington, then on his way to join the army at Cambridge.

On May 13, 1776, Jefferson resumed his seat in Congress, after an absence of four and a half months, during which period he had been obliged to look after matters connected with his estate. He was at once appointed one of a committee to draft a declaration. The committee included, besides himself, Benjamin Franklin, John Adams, Roger Sherman and R. R. Livingston. Already Jefferson had become noted for his skill at writing and he was therefore urged to prepare the rough draft of what was to be an immortal document. It is stated that the paper was written in a house where Jefferson lived, at the corner of Market and Seventh Streets, Philadelphia, in a room on the second story, and a writing desk which he made himself, and which is still in existence.

While the document was under consideration by Congress, the weather, it is said, was extremely hot. This discussion lasted through the 2nd, 3rd, and 4th of July, and on the last day the session was a prolonged one, and everybody was tired and anxious to complete their task and get away. Moreover, it is said that swarms of flies from a neighboring stable annoyed the delegates and increased their anxiety to be through with the business at hand. It was late on the afternoon of Thursday, July 4, 1776, when the Declaration was signed. One or two of the delegates indulged in humorous remarks on the occasion, with John Hancock saying, as he wrote his superb signature: "There, John Bull may read my name without spectacles!" and when the president of the Congress told the members that they must now all hang together, Dr. Franklin said: "Yes, we must indeed all hang together, or else we shall all hang separately!"

Meanwhile, Jefferson had been reelected a member of the Virginia Legislature, and anxious to return home, the health of his wife being precarious and his estate continually needing his care, he resigned from Congress and went back to Monticello, and afterward to Williamsburg, where he devoted himself to a careful examination of the Virginia statutes, with a view of improving them on the basis of knowledge he had acquired with regard to such institutions during his residence in the North. In October, he was appointed, with Benjamin Franklin and Silas Deane, a commissioner to represent the new United States in Paris, but his wife's condition was still unsatisfactory, and he decided to decline the appointment.

In January of 1779, Jefferson was elected by the Legislature as successor to Patrick Henry as Governor of Virginia, and he was reelected in 1780. He had now become a power in the state. He succeeded moving the capital to Richmond, and obtained the passage of many important legislative acts. As Governor of the state of Virginia, it fell to Jefferson to keep up Virginia's quota in the ragged army of Washington, while sending supplies to Gates, who was making his southern campaign. At the end of December, 1780, a British fleet, having on board Benedict Arnold, the traitor, went up Chesapeake Bay, and Arnold, with something under a thousand men, reached and captured Richmond, which, however, they were able to hold less than a day, since a large mass of militia was at once sent against Arnold, and his pursuit was so close as nearly to result in his capture.

The following Spring, the enemy came so close and were so formidable that the Legislature of Virginia had to adjourn while Monticello was captured by cavalry and Jefferson narrowly escaped. Indeed, for ten days, Lord Cornwallis lived at the residence of the Governor at Elk Hill, on the James River. Though there had been some feeling in regard to the administration of the state government, an application by Jefferson for examination showed that there was no one to make any charge against him, and a resolution of thanks for his conduct while occupying the gubernatorial chair was introduced and passed both Council and Assembly unanimously.

Governors

When the French government instructed its minister at Philadelphia to collect and send to Paris all information that could be obtained respecting the American states, the secretary of the French legation forwarded to Jefferson a list of questions to answer concerning Virginia in this connection. From this resulted his "Notes on Virginia," a work still held in the highest esteem for its structure and its completeness, both as to thought and detail. In this work, there is a chapter which was afterward used by the northern abolitonists during their many years of warfare with the institution of slavery. One passage runs: "The whole commerce between master and slave is a perpetual exercise of the most boisterous passions, the most unremitting despotism on the one part and degraded submission on the other. Our children see this and learn to imitate it, for man is an imitative animal. This quality is the germ of all educations in him. From his cradle to his grave, he is learning to do what he sees others doing. The parent storms, the child looks on, catches the lineaments of wrath, puts on the same airs in the circle of smaller slaves, gives loose rein to the worst of passions, and this education in the daily exercise of tyranny cannot but be stamped by it with the most odious peculiarities that man must be a prodigy who can restrain his manners and morals undepraved by such circumstances. I tremble for my country when I reflect that God is just, that His justice cannot sleep forever; but considering numbers, nature and natural means only, a revolution of the wheel of fortune, an exchange of the situations, is among possible events. That it may become probable by the supernatural interference, the Almighty has no attribute which can take sides with us in such a contest."

Jefferson's wife died on September 6, 1782, and it was a great loss for him. In the meantime, through the Virginia members of Congress, his name was suggested as a plenipotentiary to treat for peace, it being believed that he might by this means be recalled to the public service, which he had seemingly left forever--having, in fact, announced that his public life had ended. But the death of his wife had changed his views, and he accepted the appointment. Peace, however, was concluded before he sailed, and in 1783, he was elected to Congress, and took his seat in November of that year in Annapolis, Maryland. On May 7, 1784, Congress again elected him Plenipotentiary to France, where Franklin and Adams were engaged in negotiating commercial treaties with the different foreign powers. He accepted, and sailed from Boston on July 5th, and after a voyage of a month, settled in Paris.

On May 2, 1758, Jefferson was appointed Minister Plenipotentiary to the King of France for three years, in place of Benjamin Franklin. The years that Jefferson spent as minister to the French court, although he had important official duties, gave him more time than he had had before for the study of science, which had so much interested him when he was younger. He became acquainted personally with the ablest men in science, among whom was Buffon, the great naturalist, who had a theory that animals degenerated in America. In order to remove this prejudice, Jefferson succeeded in obtaining the bones, skin and horns of some of the larger American animals, such as the moose, the caribou, the elk, etc., and presented them to Buffon, who, on examining them, admitted that he would have to reconstruct his theory on the subject of American animals.

Among other duties which Jefferson successfully carried out while in Europe, was that of negotiating and arranging a satisfactory consular system between France and the United States. Meanwhile, his "Notes on Virginia" had been published in England, and translated into French, and printed in Paris, being universally admired. He traveled to different parts of Europe, and supplied the American colleges and other institutions with books, accounts of new discoveries, inventions and seeds, roots and nuts indigenous in the different countries he visited, and which he thought might possibly be introduced into America. Meanwhile, his acquaintance with European courts had only confirmed for him his sense of democracy. His investigation into the way of life and the inequalities existing abroad filled his mind and heart with deep compassion, especially for the people of France, who seemed to be suffering the most.

In November of 1789, Jefferson received a six months' leave of absence, and returned with his two daughters, to find that he had been appointed by President Washington to the office of Secretary of State. After some consideration, Jefferson accepted the appointment, and after attending at Monticello on February 23, 1790, his eldest daughter's marriage to Thomas Mann Randolph, he went to New York and entered the cabinet. It was a cabinet which soon displayed considerable personal animosity and opposition, particularly between Hamilton and Jefferson, who, in fact, represented the two extremes of the different parties. This feeling reached serious proportions. On January 1, 1794, Jefferson withdrew, although it was with difficulty that Washington was induced to accept his resignation. He returned to his home at Monticello, and now once more believed that he was completely done with public life.

At this time, the Republican Party accepted the views of Jefferson, and as he openly accepted Tom Paine's "Rights of Man," it followed that the advanced views contained in that book grew to be held measurably as the party tenets of his followers. At the end of the year 1794, Jefferson was requested by Washington to resume the office of Secretary of State, but he declined and said emphatically that nothing could ever tempt him to again engage in any public service. Yet, within six months, he was the candidate of his party for the Presidency. This was in 1796, and he fell behind John Adams, who was elected, by only a few votes, and, according to the Constitution, became Vice-President. This office pleased Jefferson, as he had no practical part in the administration of the government, not being consulted by Adams on political matters, and was able to follow out his tastes in study and research. It was at this time that he prepared his celebrated "Manual of Parliamentary Practice."

The election of 1800 brought Jefferson again before the country as the candidate of his party for the Presidency, and he received seventy-three votes, the precise number given for Aaron Burr, which threw it into the House, where, after seven days of

Governors

balloting, Jefferson was elected President and Burr, Vice-President. The election of Jefferson was hailed by both parties as certain to bring about a peaceful condition such as had not been known during the previous administration. Party politics had run so high, and the divergence of opinion was so wide between the Federalists and Republicans, that probably no other man could have reconciled the existing conditions. Contrary to the general expectation, Jefferson resisted the powerful appeals that were made to him to remove from office those who had been inimical to him, holding that a difference of politics was not a reason to removed one who had proved himself competent and efficient in office.

Jefferson introduced simplicity into the White House and the abolition of the formal plan which had been copied from European court etiquette, abolishing the weekly levees and the system of precedence at once. He also introduced the message to Congress, in place of the speech which had been formally delivered, in imitation of foreign potentates. He would not accept any special attentions while traveling or sojourning anywhere, different from what would be paid him as a private citizen. Indeed, in his whole course, and throughout his first administration, Jefferson was consistent in conducting himself and conducting the government on what he believed to be true democratic principles. Jefferson owed his democracy mainly to what he had seen while living in France, an experience which had entirely changed his own views on political subjects, and on the rights of citizenship.

Jefferson continued to administer the government for eight years, during which period, he showed himself a thoroughly qualified statesman and a man of unusual ability, tact and decision. One instance of the possession of these qualities was his purchase from Napoleon of the territory of Louisiana. Another was the skill with which he kept the country from becoming involved in the long and bitter European war. The benefits which he conferred on his country were not only immediate but lasting, yet on the 4th of March, 1809, when he retired finally to private life, after the most valuable public service, extending over more than four decades, it was to find himself impoverished--practically bankrupt. He was forced to borrow money, and was in difficult straits up to the end of his life.

Jefferson spent the remainder of his days establishing a complete system of education in Virginia. It was to include a series of common schools of different grades crowned with the highest collegiate institution which could be organized and established. The latter (the University of Virginia), he lived long enough to see in working order, having personally superintended even the smallest details of its construction, and being present at its opening in March of 1825.

In the meantime, he had sold his library to Congress for about a quarter of its value, and was at length, through the kindness which induced him to endorse largely for a friend, in danger of losing Monticello, but this misfortune was averted through public subscriptions in New York and Philadelphia, which raised money enough to spare him this crowning indignity. Jefferson died a few hours before John Adams, a half-century after the signing of the Declaration of Independence, which he himself composed, and which is still considered to be one of the most highly-respected writings in the world. The sale of his estate after his death, and the application of the proceeds toward the payment of his debts, left his daughter and her children without their home, and without support. The Legislatures of South Carolina and Virginia voted to his daughter, Mrs. Randolph, the sum of $10,000, which enabled her to spend the rest of her life in comfort and security.

Monticello was later the property of Jefferson's grandson, Jefferson M. Levy, a prominent citizen and lawyer of New York. It was purchased by his uncle, Com. Uriah P. Levy, of the United States Navy, and from him descended to its present owner. The mansion was built somewhat after the style of the Petitie Trianon, at Versialles. Its public rooms included a grand salon, dining-hall, library, Jefferson, Madison, and Monroe rooms, ballroom and grand hall. It stands in a commanding position on a small plateau, elevated some 300 feet above the surrounding country, and 538 feet above sea level. The estate embraces 500 acres of park land, gardens and lawns.

Of Monticello, Jefferson himself said: "After much roaming in many lands, I have found and pitched my tent in what I believe to be one of the fairest spots of earth. This tent, which is strong enough to keep out wind and water, is set in the midst of a lofty mountain plateau. Looking around, I find myself, to all seeming, in a world of my own. All around, in the far, shining silvery distances, are cloud-capped mountain ranges of surpassing grandeur, rising one above another until, apparently the limits of the world are reached." Despite the spirit of romance in Jefferson's character, shown in this description of his Virginia home, he possessed a vein of practical common sense unequaled, perhaps, by anybody of his time, except perhaps, Benjamin Franklin.

The following ten bits of proverbial philosophy have surfaced under the name of "Jefferson's Ten Rules": "1. Never put off till tomorrow what you can do today. 2. Never trouble another for what you can do yourself. 3. Never spend your money before you have it. 4. Never buy what you do not want because it is cheap; it will be dear to you. 5. Pride costs us more than hunger, thirst and cold. 6. We never repent of having eaten too little. 7. Nothing is troublesome that we do willingly. 8. How much pain have cost us the evils which have never happened. 9. Take things always by the smooth handle. 10. When angry, count ten before you speak; if very angry, a hundred."

Jefferson died at Monticello, Albemarle County, Virginia on July 4, 1826. He was buried in his own graveyard at Monticello, and over him a stone was placed with the inscription by himself: "Here was buried Thomas Jefferson, author of the Declaration of American Independence, of the Statutes of Virginia for Religious Freedom, and Father of the University of Virginia." This was later replaced by a monument provided by the government, a square, massive pillar of granite, and containing the same inscription from the original stone.

Governors

NELSON, THOMAS, JR. (1738-1789), signer of the Declaration of Independence, governor of Virginia (1781), was born in York, Virginia on December 26, 1738. His father was William Nelson (1711-72), son of Thomas Nelson (1677-1745), an Englishman, who settled in Virginia early in the eighteenth century, and acquiring a large fortune in mercantile business, invested it in landed estates. William Nelson was Governor of Virginia between the administrations of Lords Botetourt and Dunmore (1770-71), and also presided over the Supreme Court of the province. He left five sons, of whom the eldest, Thomas, was sent to England to be educated in the summer of 1753; and after attending private school, he entered Trinity College at Cambridge University, and graduated in 1761. He returned to America in the following winter, and in 1762, was married to Lucy Grymes of Middlesex County, Virginia, and settled in York, where they lived in great elegance.

His public career began in 1774, when he was elected as a member of the House of Burgesses, dissolved by Lord Dunmore on account of its resolutions censuring and condemning the Boston port bill. He was one of the eighty-nine delegates who assembled at a friendly tavern the day following this act, and formed themselves into the celebrated association which resolved at all to defend their rights and maintain their liberties. He was elected from York County to the first Virginia Convention, which met at Williamsburg on August 1, 1774, and by March 1775, was again a representative, and prominent in the debate on the advisability of a military force. He took the stand that such a force was necessary to the interests of the colonists. When the third Virginia Convention assembled in Richmond on July 17, 1776, he was again a delegate from York. The raising of colonial troops was now actively pursued, and he was made colonel of the second regiment raised, the command of the first being given to the celebrated orator, Patrick Henry.

On August 11, 1775, he was appointed a delegate to the Continental Congress in Philadelphia, and believing that the post of danger and duty was there, resigned his military command and took his seat on September 13, 1775. He was one of the first advocates of absolute separation from the domination of the British crown. In a letter to a friend, dated February 13, 1776, Colonel Nelson wrote: "Independence, confederation, and foreign alliances are as formidable to some of the Congress (I fear a majority), as an apparition to a weak, enervated woman. Would you think we have still some among us who expect honorable proposals from the administration! By heavens! I am an infidel in politics; for I do not believe, were you to bid one thousand pounds per scruple for honor at the court of Britain, that you would get as many as would amount to an ounce! If terms should be proposed, they will savor so much of despotism that America cannot accept them...What think you on the right reverend fathers in God, the bishops? One of them *refused* to ordain a young gentleman who went from this country, because he was a 'rebellious American,' and so that, unless we submit to parliamentary oppression, we shall not have the Gospel of Christ preached among us!"

Through the opening of the session of 1776, he maintained this advanced position on the question of independence, and in that spirit signed his name to the Declaration. During the remainder of the term, and the beginning of that of 1777, he served on many important committees, and took an active part in all measures that advanced the general welfare of the new states. A severe illness seized him while in his seat in Congress, May 2, 1777, and a recurring trouble of the head warned him, for a time at least, to stop work. He therefore returned home, allowing his term to be filled by another.

The following August, the British fleet appeared off the coast of Virginia a second time, and Colonel Nelson was again called to the field, and appointed by the Governor, Brigadier-General and Commander of the forces of the Commonwealth of Virginia. He at once entered on the discharge of this duties, refusing pay for his services. General Nelson continued in active service with the army until his health was restored. On February 18, 1779, he took his seat in the State Assembly, but again his same illness attacked him, and yielding to the advice of his physician and his friends, he returned home to rest.

The following month, he again took the field, and during the gloomy days of financial depression and disastrous defeats that followed, no man's influence was more widely felt or more generously given to the American cause than was his. While a member of the House of Burgesses, an incident occurred which shows the high sense of honor he had regarding financial obligations, both private and public. An act was introduced and passed by the Assembly for the sequestration of British property. Such an act could, and would, of course, be construed so that all debts owed those who were known to be loyal to England, should be considered outlawed. General Nelson vehemently opposed the passage of the bill, and in closing a speech denunciatory of it, said: "I hope the bill will be rejected; but whatever its fate, by God! I will pay my debts like an honest man!" The breach of order into which his feelings had betrayed him was overlooked. The bill became a law.

In the spring of 1781, he was elected Governor; but after performing the duties of the office until the following November, he was forced, by constant and increasing illness, to resign. His last days were those of severe austerity--he having been reduced from affluence to a state bordering on poverty by his sense of honor, his honesty and self-denial and his patriotic efforts in the cause of his country's independence during the Revolutionary War. When he was laid to rest in the old church yard at York, without a headstone or slab to mark the spot, his property--save the old house in deserted York, and some broom-straw fields in Hanover County--was put up for public sale, to pay the debts contracted in his country's cause. Even the old family Bible, with the births and baptisms of the family, was sold. The state of Virginia honored his patriotic memory with a heroic life-size bronze statue in Capital Park, Richmond. He died on January 4, 1789.

Governors

HARRISON, BENJAMIN (1726-1791), signer of the Declaration of Independence and Governor of Virginia (1781-84), was born in Berkeley, Virginia in 1726, son of Benjamin and Anne (Carter) Harrison. His father was a sheriff and a member of the House of Burgesses of Virginia. The son was a student of William and Mary College, though he left that institution before the usual period, due to a quarrel with one of the professors. He displayed such firmness and decision of character that the management of his estate was committed to his care soon after his return home. As a descendant of the political leaders of the colony, he was elected early to the House of Burgesses, where he took a conspicuous part, serving on the committee which drew up the address to the King and the remonstrance to Parliament, on the passage of the Declaratory Act in 1764. He opposed the Stamp Act resolutions of Henry as impolitic. In 1774, he was one of the delegates from Virginia to the first Continental Congress, and continued in that body until 1777, longer than any of the others appointed with him.

In 1775, he lived in Philadelphia in the same house with Washington and Peyton Randolph, and, on the resignation of the office of president of Congress by the latter, and the election of John Hancock, he lifted Hancock bodily to the chair, exclaiming "We will show mother Britain how little we care for her by making a Massachusetts man our president, whom she has excluded from pardon by a public proclamation." In June of the same year, he was a member of the committee which framed the militia system adopted and carried through the war, and in September, with two others, he visited the camp at Cambridge to arrange for the continuance, support and regulation of the army, a service he afterwards performed for the troops in South Carolina and New York. He was also chairman of the committee which until the creation of the department of foreign affairs, conducted the foreign affairs of the United Colonies, and from June of 1776, until his retirement from Congress, he was at the head of the Board of War.

Sent on a mission to Maryland, he put an end to aggressions of the enemy along the coast by fitting out a number of small vessels, and in March of 1776, he was chairman of the committee for fortification of ports and protection of American privateers. As chairman of the committee of the whole, he presided in Congress over the debates on the Declaration of Independence, brought up the resolution for the same on June 10th, and reported the document as having received approval on July 4th. At the solemn moment of affixing his name, he broke out with a humorous remark about "the hanging scene" to come. Later, he again presided over the discussions relative to the admission of Vermont and on the Articles of Confederation, as well as other questions of vital importance, but his favorite department, and one in which he was peculiarly efficient, was that which provided for the support and increase of the army.

In the most trying times of Congress, he remained with that body, on the flights both to Baltimore and Yorktown, and he was continually engaged until his voluntary retirement at the end of 1777. From that year until 1782, he was Speaker of the House of

Burgesses of Virginia, when that body was driven from place to place by the invasion of Arnold and Cornwallis. He went in person to ask the assistance of Washington, which that commander was forced to refuse. In 1782-84, he held the office of Governor, with a popularity that never waned, and being then ineligible for four years for reelection, returned to the Legislature and to the speakership. In 1788, he was a member of the convention that ratified the Federal Constitution, the amendments to which he considered essential. In 1790, he declined the nomination for Governor tendered him at the expense of his friend, Beverly Randolph, then in office.

He was married to Elizabeth, daughter of William and Elizabeth (Churchill) Bassett, and niece of a sister of Martha Washington. He and Elizabeth had seven children. His eldest son, Benjamin, educated in the counting-room of Willing & Morris, Philadelphia, was paymaster-general of the southern department during the Revolution, and later a merchant of Richmond, Virginia, where he acquired a large fortune. This he used to assist Robert Morris in the distresses of the famous financier. His youngest son was William Henry Harrison, ninth president of the United States. Benjamin Harrison died suddenly on April 24, 1791, from a fit of the gout, the day after his unanimous election to the Legislature.

RANDOLPH, EDMUND (1753-1813), Secretary of State, Attorney-General, and Governor of Virginia (1786-1788), was born in Williamsburg, Virginia on August 10, 1753, the son of John Randolph, King's attorney for Virginia. He attended William and Mary College, studied law, and had just begun its practice when the Revolution broke out. Upon the departure of his father for England in August of 1775, the son became an aide-de-camp to Washington, but after a brief taste of military life, he returned to Virginia to take, so far as his youth might permit, the place his family had long filled in public affairs, now left vacant by the death of his uncle Peyton.

He became mayor of Williamsburg in 1776, took part in framing the Virginia constitution, was first Attorney-General of the state, a member of Congress from 1779 to 1782, and Governor 1786-88. He married a daughter of R. C. Nicholas, and refused to sell his slaves, though his property came to him heavily burdened. No man was more prominent in the convention which framed the federal constitution. He took a peculiar course, objecting to many of the provisions adopted in the way of compromise, and to some which met general approval, favoring a second convention to revise the document after discussion and a brief trial. His own scheme was found in G. Mason's papers a hundred years later. He secured the omission of the word slavery. He did not sign or approve the constitution as adopted, but urged its acceptance by his state on the grounds that the Union was a necessity at almost any terms, and that amendments could be worked for within the Union better than without.

An independent and philosophic Democrat, never able to follow entirely the lines of any party, his influence at home was great, and his services in securing ratification against strong

Governors

opposition very memorable. In 1788, he entered the Assembly, serving on the committee to codify the Virginia laws. He was the leader of this work, which was finished in 1794. In September of 1789, President Washington appointed him Attorney-General in which position he made a report on the judiciary system, defending the right of foreigners to bring action against a state.

In January of 1794, he became Secretary of State, succeeding Jefferson, who urged his appointment. That office then involved a burden of personal and financial responsibility for official acts which was probably the cause of Jefferson's withdrawal from the post, and proved ruinous to his successor. The times were trying and dangerous; the relations of the administration with France and England, with public opinion at home, violently divided and bitterly excited on many subjects, gave rise to the greatest anxiety; the continued existence of the nation seemed at stake. In pursuing Washington's policy, the secretary was inevitably involved in secret and tortuous negotiations with Fauchet, the French minister, a needy and adroit intriguer. A dispatch from this man to his government, reflecting on Randolph's honor, was taken at sea and sent to the British minister, Hammond. He handed it to the president who kept it secret for ten days, and during this interval, took every means of showing his regard for his Secretary of State. The public situation was desperate, involving the near prospect of civil as well as foreign war. Washington might have sacrificed himself and the interest committed to him in a vain effort to save a faithful servant as he was strongly tempted to do. But public duty triumphed over personal feeling. He saw no better way than to sign Jay's treaty with England, which, under the Secretary's advice, he had agreed not to sign until the obnoxious clause continuing the British right of search of neutral vessels was removed. Randolph now stood alone, with all the cabinet against him. On the production of Fauchet's dispatch he denied the guilt imputed to him, and resigned under a cloud of abuse which covered the fame of one of the ablest and most distinguished public servants of his time.

His "Vindication" in 1795 was disregarded, and his estate was swept away by an unjust decision of the Comptroller of the Treasury. But his memory was rehabilitated by Mr. M. D. Conway, whose research brought to light the main facts of the incident in an article, "A Suppressed Statesman" in *Lippincott's Magazine*, September 1887, and in a "Life of Randolph," 1888. Randolph returned to Virginia where he was still held in honor, and spent his later years in legal practice. He wrote pamphlets on "Democratic Societies," 1795, and "Political Truth," 1796, besides a history of Virginia which was never published. He died in Clarke County, Virginia on September 13, 1813.

RANDOLPH, BEVERLEY (1754-1797), Governor of Virginia (1788-1791), was born in Chatsworth, Virginia in 1754, son of Colonel Peter and Lucy Bolling Randolph. His father was surveyor of customs of North America in 1749, and a member of the House of Burgesses. The son graduated from William and Mary College in 1771, was visitor in 1784, a member of the General Assembly of

Virginia during the Revolutionary War, and an active supporter of all measures for securing American independence. In 1787, he was chosen president of the executive council of Virginia, and on December 3, 1788, succeeded his relative, Edmund Randolph, as Governor of the state for one year. Every governor was eligible for three years, but in 1790, Benjamin Harrison was announced as a candidate for governor against Randolph, although the latter had served only two years. Harrison, however, refused to countenance such a movement, and Randolph was again reelected. His administration is especially interesting, with respect to Indian depredations on the frontier and the relations of Virginia with the state of Pennsylvania. Governor Randolph died in 1797 at "Green Creek," his home, in Cumberland County, Virginia.

LEE, HENRY (1756-1818), soldier and Governor of Virginia (1791-1794), was born in Westmoreland County, Virginia on January 29, 1756. He was educated at Princeton College, New Jersey where he graduated in 1774. On his return to Virginia, the young man was entrusted with the management of the private affairs of the family, as his father, who was a member of the House of Burgesses was engaged at the time in negotiating a treaty with the Indian tribes. In 1776, Henry Lee received an appointment as Captain of the cavalry under Colonel Theodoric Bland, but it was not until September of the following year that he joined the main army. There his skill, his discipline, and his soldier-like bearing attracted the notice of the Commander-in-Chief, and he was soon promoted to the rank of Major and given the command of a separate cavalry corps, which included three companies of horse and was known as "Lee's Legion." It was from this command the young officer received the name of "Lighthorse Harry." One of his most daring expeditions was a successful attempt to surprise the British garrison at Pawlus Hook, where, with the loss of only five men, he captured more than 150 prisoners, Congress recognizing this feat by the gift of a gold medal.

From 1780 to the end of the Revolutionary War, Lee served under General Greene, for whom he did very important work in a number of actions, especially distinguishing himself at the battle of Guilford and capturing, among other forts, Fort Cornwallis. At Guilford, Lee's Legion is said to have actually routed Tarleton's dragoons. In June of 1781, Lee besieged the city of Augusta for sixteen days, at the end of which it was surrendered to him. He was conspicuous also in the siege of Ninety-six and at the battle of Eutaw Springs. He was one of the best-known officers on the American side in the Revolution and was greatly admired and highly esteemed by Washington.

After the war, Lee married a cousin, Matilda Lee, who owned Stratford House, where he thereafter resided. In 1786, he was appointed a delegate to Congress from Virginia, and remained in that body until the constitution was adopted. He was a member of the Virginia Legislature from 1789-91, succeeding, in the latter year, Beverly Randolph as Governor of the state of Virginia, an office he held three years. In 1794, Washington appointed him to com-

Governors

mand the forces sent to suppress the whiskey insurrection in Pennsylvania. Five years later, he was a member of Congress, where he was chosen to pronounce a funeral oration on Washington, and it was in this oration that Lee used the words that later became celebrated: "First in war, first in peace, first in the hearts of his countrymen."

In 1801, Colonel Lee retired to private life, and unfortunately his final years were distressed by financial troubles. About the year 1809, when he is said to have been imprisoned for debt, he wrote his "Memoirs of the War in the Southern Department of the United States." In 1814, he happened to be in Baltimore at the time when a riot occurred in which the mob attacked the printing office. He was carried for safety to the jail, which was attacked, with Lee himself being severely wounded. He then went to the West Indies for his health. He found no relief in a change of climate and remained only a short time, soon turning his face toward his old home, which, unfortunately, he never reached alive. Being in poor health, he made the journey by easy stages. In the spring of 1818, he reached the house of Mrs. Shaw, a daughter of his old friend and compatriot, Nathaniel Greene, where he died. He was the father of General Robert E. Lee, by his second wife, Anne Carter. He had three sons and two daughters by this wife, and one son and one daughter by his first wife. He died on Cumberland Island, near St. Mary's, Georgia on March 25, 1818.

BROOKE, ROBERT (1751-1799), Governor of Virginia (1794-1796), was born in that state in 1751, son of Richard Brooke. He was educated at the University of Edinburgh. Upon his return voyage to America at the beginning of the Revolution, he was captured by Lord Howe, the British admiral, and sent back to England. From England, Brooke went to Scotland and then again over to France, and finally reached Virginia in a French frigate that carried the arms supplied to the continentals by the French government. He joined at once a volunteer troop of cavalry commanded by Captain Larkin Smith, was captured by Simcoe in 1781, at Westham near Richmond, but was soon exchanged and returned to the service. After the war, he practiced his profession and in 1794, represented the County of Spottsylvania in the House of Delegates, and in the same year, he was elected Governor of the state by the Legislature over James Wood by ninety-odd votes, against sixty-odd given to his competitor. He supported the principles advocated by the Republican Party, and in 1798, he was elected Attorney-General of Virginia over Bushrod Washington, the nephew of George Washington. The County of Brooke, formed in 1797 from Ohio County, commemorates the name of the Governor. In 1795, he was elected grand master of the grand lodge of Masons of Virginia and served until 1797. Robert Brooke died in 1799, while holding the office of Attorney-General of Virginia.

WOOD, JAMES (1747-1813), Governor of Virginia (1796-1799), was born in Frederick County, Virginia in 1747, son of Colonel James Wood. From the very beginning to its termination, the son's life was unremittingly applied to public service. At the age of sixteen years, during the war which began with the Indians in 1763, he entered the service as a private. In 1764, he was made captain, raised a company and continued in service until the end of the war. In 1774, he again commanded a company against the Indians, and took a conspicuous part in the expeditions which were sent out against the Shawanese tribes.

In 1775, he was elected to the House of Burgesses from Frederick County. The Convention of Virginia, of which he was a member in 1776, appointed him colonel of the Virginia line, commanding the 8th regiment. In 1777, he behaved gallantly at the battle of Brandywine. When Burgoyne surrendered, he was put in charge of the prisoners in Charlottesville.

In 1781, Wood was made superintendent of all prisoners of war in Virginia. He was president of the last board of officers that made an arrangement for the Virginia line. In 1783, the Governor commissioned him Brigadier-General of state troops, in which capacity he rendered essential service in connection with the troubles with the Indians that continued to harass the state.

In 1784, he was elected a member of the executive council, and became, by seniority in that body, Lieutenant-Governor of the state. In 1789, he was a presidential elector. On December 1, 1796, he was elected Governor of Virginia, and served until December 1, 1799, when he was succeeded by Governor James Monroe. During his administration, the armory was erected in Richmond. Governor Wood was president of the Society of the Cincinnati from October 9, 1784, until his death. He was also vice-president in 1797, and president in 1801 of the Society for promoting the abolition of slavery in Virginia. He was twelve years a member of the Legislature and twenty years a member of the Executive Council. He was still a member of the latter branch of the government when he died on June 16, 1813, at the age of sixty-six. He was interred in St. John's churchyard in Richmond, with military honors.

MONROE, JAMES (1758-1831), fifth President of the United States and Governor of Virginia (1799-1802), (1811), was born in West Walden County, Virginia on April 28, 1758, son of Spence and Elizabeth (Jones) Monroe. He was educated at William and Mary College. He left in 1776 to enter the army, and soon afterward, was commissioned lieutenant. A large part of his active service was in the campaigns on the Hudson River. Later he was engaged in the affair at Trenton, New Jersey, where, with a small detachment, he captured one of the British batteries. He was wounded in the shoulder in this action, and for his conduct, was promoted to a captaincy. In 1777, he was appointed aide-de-camp to Lord Stirling, with the rank of major, and during that and the following year, participated in the battles of Brandywine, Germantown and Monmouth, but by having accepted a staff position, he forfeited his rank as a commissioned officer in the regular army.

Governors

Returning to Virginia, he began to study law under the supervision of Thomas Jefferson, at that time, Governor of the state, but the British soon appeared in Virginia, and Monroe organized the militia of the lower counties. When the army proceeded southward, Jefferson sent him as military commissioner of the state to South Carolina from the county of King George. Monroe was elected to the Virginia Assembly, and although only twenty-three years old, he was appointed by that body as a member of the Executive Council.

In 1783, he was sent to Congress as a delegate for three years. He advocated an extension of the powers of Congress, and in 1785, moved to invest that body with authority to regulate trade between the states. It was this resolution which was referred to a committee and favorably reported, that led to the convention in Annapolis and the subsequent adoption of the Federal Constitution. Later, Monroe was appointed a member of the commission to decide the boundary between Massachusetts and New York. He also helped devise a system for the settlement of the public lands.

In May of 1794, Monroe was appointed Minister Plenipotentiary to France, where he was received with respect and enthusiasm. However, his marked sympathy with the French Republic was displeasing to the administration. John Jay had been sent to negotiate a treaty with England, and the course pursued by Monroe was considered injudicious, as tending to throw serious obstacles in the way of the proposed negotiations. On the conclusion of the treaty, Monroe's alleged failure was presented in its true character to the French government, and in August, 1796, he was recalled under an informal censure.

Soon after his return to America, Monroe published a review of the conduct of the foreign affairs of the United States, which served to widen the breach between himself and the administration. He remained on good terms with Washington and Jay, however. From 1799 to 1802, Monroe was Governor of Virginia, and at the end of his term, was appointed Envoy Extraordinary to the French government to negotiate, in conjunction with the resident minister, Mr. Livingston, for the purchase of Louisiana. The result was that within a fortnight after his arrival in Paris, the entire territory of Orleans and district of Louisiana was secured for $15,000,000, an acquisition of territory whose worth was almost inestimable.

That same year, Monroe was commissioned Minister Plenipotentiary to England, but was soon sent to Madrid as Minister Extraordinary and Plenipotentiary to mediate the controversy between the United States and Spain in relation to the boundaries of the new purchase of Louisiana. He failed in this, and in 1806, he was recalled to England where a treaty was concluded for the protection of neutral rights, but which was deemed ambiguous in relation to certain important points, and as a consequence, the President sent it back for revision, pending which Monroe returned to America.

In 1810, Monroe was appointed to the General Assembly of Virginia, and in 1811, was again Governor of the Commonwealth, but in the same year, assumed the position of Secretary of State, to which he was appointed by President Madison. After the capture of Washington in 1814, Monroe was appointed to the War Department which he took without relinquishing his former post. He improved the condition of the army greatly by his judicious administration and even pledged his private means to sustain the public credit, which was completely wiped out. It was this latter act which enabled the city of New Orleans to successfully oppose the attack of the enemy.

Monroe continued to serve as Secretary of State to the end of Madison's administration in 1817 when he succeeded to the presidency as a candidate of the party, then generally known as Democratic-Republicans, by an electoral vote of 183 out of 217. During a tour which Monroe made through the Middle and Eastern states for the inspection of arsenals, naval depots, fortifications and garrisons, he found that the party spirit, which had been lately so rampant, was greatly allayed. He was careful, however, in making appointments to the office within his gift, to select none but his most devoted adherents. John Quincy Adams was recalled from the Court of St. James to become his Secretary of State. The other members of his cabinet were William H. Crawford of Georgia, Secretary of the Treasury; John C. Calhoun of South Carolina, Secretary of War; Benjamin W. Crowninshield of Massachusetts, Secretary of the Navy; and William Wirt of Virginia, Attorney-General.

In the meantime, the influence of the Revolution had affected other nations. The Spanish colonies in South America threw off their allegiance to Spain and declared themselves independent. Under pretext of having commissions from these new republics, adventurers seized Amelia Island off the harbor of St. Augustine. A similar haunt for buccaneers--for many had begun to smuggle merchandise and slaves into the United States--had existed for some time in Galveston, Texas. Both of these establishments were now broken up by order of the United States government. The condition of the South American republics excited great sympathy among the people. Some advocated giving them aid, while others were anxious that Congress should at least acknowledge their independence. Cruisers bearing the flags of these republics were fitted out in some of the ports of the United States to prey on Spanish commerce.

In regard to the Florida trouble, it was somewhat serious. It originated in the conflict between the South American republics and Spain, and because privateers bearing the flags of these republics were fitted out in some of the southern ports of the United States to prey upon Spanish commerce. All of this led to a lingering war, and the Georgia settlements were attacked by bands of Seminoles, refugee Creeks, and others, and, finally, a boat ascending the Appalachicola was attacked, and more than fifty persons, men, women and children were massacred. This brought orders from Washington to General Jackson to invade the Indian territory, which he did with small ceremony, hanging some of the hostile chiefs whom he captured, and seizing the only Spanish fort in the disturbed part of Florida, on the grounds that its officers were aiding the Indians in their hostility to the United

Governors

States. He also captured Pensacola. These arbitrary proceedings were brought to the consideration of the government in Washinton by the Spanish Minister, with the result that Florida was ceded to the United States for the consideration that the United States assumed a debt of about $5,000,000, which American citizens had claims against the Spanish government.

In March of 1822, new interest was awakened in behalf of the South American republics. Great efforts had been made by Henry Clay during their struggle to induce Congress to acknowledge their independence, but it was then thought premature. Now the bill was passed. The next year the President declared in his message to Congress that "As a principle, the American continents by the free and independent position which they have assumed and maintained are henceforth not to be considered as subjects for future colonization by any European power." This has since been known as the "Monroe Doctrine," though its authorship, it would seem, belonged rather to Monroe's Secretary of State, John Quincy Adams.

The last year of Monroe's administration was noted for the visit of the Marquis de Lafayette to the United States as the invited guest of the nation. On March 4, 1825, Monroe retired from office and returned to his home at Oak Hill in Virginia. He was chosen a justice of the peace and as such, sat in the county court. In 1829, he became a member of the Virginia Convention to revise the old constitution, and was chosen to preside over the deliberations of that body but he was compelled by ill health to resign his post in the convention and to return to Oak Hill. In addition to his physical infirmities, Monroe suffered under the misfortune of financial embarrassment, and although he had received $350,000 for his public services, in his old age, he was harassed by debt.

Monroe's wife died in 1830 and in the summer of that year, he moved to the house of his son-in-law, Samuel L. Gouverneur in New York where he died. In 1858 his remains were removed with great pomp to Richmond, Virginia, and reinterred on July 5th in the Hollywood Cemetery. It is said of Monroe that he held the reins of government at an important period and administered it with prudence, discretion and a single eye to the general welfare. He went further than any of his predecessors in developing the resources of the country. He encouraged the army, increased the navy, augmented the national defenses, protected commerce and infused life and efficiency into every department of the public service. His honesty, good faith and simplicity were generally acknowledged and disarmed the political rancor of his strongest opponents. In person, Monroe was tall and well-formed, with a light complexion and blue eyes. He died in New York City on July 4, 1831.

PAGE, JOHN (1744-1808), Governor of Virginia (1802-1805), was born at Rosewell, Gloucester County, Virginia on April 17, 1744. He studied at William and Mary College where he graduated in 1763. He was an intimate friend and follower of Thomas Jefferson. He was with Washington in one of his expeditions against the

French and Indians. He was also a member of the Virginia House of Burgesses and of the Colonial Council, and in 1776, was a visitor of the College of William and Mary.

He was a delegate to the convention which framed the Virginia state constitution, and a member of the committee of public safety during the Revolutionary War. He was Lieutenant-Governor of the commonwealth at the time, and not only used his own influence to forward the cause of the patriots, but devoted to it large sums of money. He raised a regiment of militia in the Gloucester county, and was one of the first representatives in Congress from Virginia, and was reelected three times, serving from 1789 to 1797. In 1800, he was a presidential elector, and in 1802, he succeeded James Monroe as Governor of Virginia, holding the office for three years. At the end of that time, he was appointed by President Jefferson as U.S. Commissioner of Loans for Virginia, and continued to hold that office until his death. Governor Page is described as a man of learning, a statesman, an admirable soldier, and was also noted for his theological learning. He published "Addresses to the People" in 1796 and 1799. Page died in Richmond, Virginia on October 11, 1808.

CABELL, WILLIAM H. (1772-1853), Governor of Virginia (1805-1808), was born at Boston Hill, Cumberland County, Virginia on December 16, 1772. He was the son of Colonel Nicholas and Hannah (Carrington) Cabell. He attended a private school, and in February of 1785, entered the Hampden Sidney College, where he stayed until September, 1785. In February of 1790, he entered William and Mary College, where he continued until July of 1793, as a student of law. He was a member of the Assembly in 1795, and again in 1798, when he voted for the celebrated Virginia Resolutions construing the meaning of the constitution. He belonged to the Republican Party, and was presidential elector in 1800 and in 1804.

In 1804, he also became a member of the General Assembly once again, but within a few days after the commencement of the session, on December 7, 1805, he was elected Governor, and held that office for the next three years, then was succeeded by John Tyler. The trial of Aaron Burr for high treason against the United States, and the attack on the frigate Chesapeake, by the British sloop-of-war Leopard, occurred during his administration. In 1808, he was elected by the General Assembly a judge of the General Court, and in 1811, he became a judge of the Court of Appeals. After the adoption of the new constitution for the state in 1830, Judge Cabell was again elected a member of the bench of the court of appeals, and on January 18, 1842, he was elected president of the court. He continued to serve until 1851, when he retired from the bench. He died in Richmond on January 12, 1853, and was interred in Shockhoe Hill Cemetery. The resolutions adopted by the Court of Appeals and Bar ascribed to him much of the credit which may be claimed for the judiciary system of Virginia and its literature.

Governors

TYLER, JOHN (1747-1813), Governor of Virginia (1808-1811), was born in James City County, February 28, 1747, son of John Tyler, marshal of the colonial vice-admiralty court. He attended the College of William and Mary, with Thomas Jefferson being among his fellow-students. Bred in the surroundings of the old vice-admiralty court, he chose the law as his vocation. In company with Jefferson, he listened to Henry's speech on the stamp act. He became so bitter an opponent of the British government that his father often predicted that he would be hanged as a rebel.

About 1770, he moved into the county of Charles City, and was appointed on the committee of safety. When the first shots were fired at Williamsburg in 1775, by Lord Dunmore, John Tyler, then captain of a military company in Charles City, hastened to join his troops with those already on the march under Patrick Henry. By the convention which met in 1776, he was made a judge of admiralty, but in 1778, took his seat in the Legislature, where his bold, uncompromising patriotism put him at once among the leaders of the revolution. He held successfully all the responsible offices of the House of Delegates, being chairman of the committee of justice, of the committee of the whole, and eventually, in 1781, speaker, succeeding Richard Henry Lee, whom he defeated in 1783 for the chair. During the whole revolution, his courage was unfaltering. Schools for the people, funds for the army, and taxes for the just creditors of the state were the themes of his oratory on every occasion.

In February of 1781, the rapid depreciation of paper money forced Congress to request of the states, power to levy an impost of five percent. Tyler was one of the committee of the House of Delegates which drafted the bill, and acted as a messenger of the House to the Senate to convey the request for its concurrence. The law was, however, reversed the next year by the activity of Dr. Arthur and Richard Henry Lee, who opposed the increase of federal power. Under the lead of James Madison, Congress, in 1783, urgently repeated the former request. Peace ensued, and there was a general relaxation of the policy. Despite Tyler's opposition, the Legislature voted to take off the restriction imposed on British trade, and to invite the Tories back. But when they found their calculations of a liberal, definitive treaty defeated, the Legislature voted to allow Congress the five percent impost, and to retaliate by decisive measures on British trade. Edmund Randolph explained that at this time (1784) there were three parties in the Legislature. Patrick Henry had one corps, R. H. Lee a second, and the speaker (Tyler), a third, "founded on a riveted opposition to our late enemies, and everything that concerned them." Henry and Tyler had generally acted together in opposition to the Lees; but Henry's advocacy of the return of the Tories, and his policy of postponing taxation led to his temporary separation from Tyler, though it pacified the old antagonisms with the Lees, and procured, Tyler said, Henry's unanimous reelection to the governorship in 1784.

Tyler and Henry agreed, however, on the construction of the treaty of peace, which, they maintained, had been violated by the British in two instances--by the retention of the western posts and the failure to return the slaves and records carried off during the war. They, therefore, were opposed to permitting the operation of the provision of the treaty forbidding any impediments in the way of the collection of debts due British subjects before the war. In this they had the support of the Virginia people. The feeling of hostility to the British dominated the masses, who felt the severe effects of the new British duties on American imports, and the impulse now given to the question of revenue and trade was due to this. In the House, in the fall of 1784, Tyler moved that the Congress should be allowed to collect the five percent duty without waiting for the consent of Rhode Island, which obstinately held out against the measure. In 1785, being narrowly defeated by Benjamin Harrison for the speakership, after having defeated him for the House in Charles City County, Tyler was one of the committee in the House of Delegates to whom the question about revenue and commerce was referred.

In the last moments of the session in January of 1786, he forced through the House a measure for a convention of all the states to be called at Annapolis, which should have full power to amend the constitution. The Annapolis Convention led the next year (1787) to the federal convention in Philadelphia. Tyler, who by virtue of a reelection to the Court of Admiralty in 1786, was also judge of the Supreme Court, was vice-president of the Virginia Convention of 1788, called to accept or reject the constitution proposed. But he vehemently denounced the article in it permitting the slave trade, and with most of the lawyers of Virginia, he feared the opportunity for construction, which its ambiguous provisions afforded, and was in favor of a new convention to correct its flaws. He was defeated in this hope, though the amendments which were offered in the state convention, and afterward in part adopted by Congress, removed much of his objections.

Tyler, on the abolition of the state Admiralty Court by the operation of the new constitution, was elected in 1788 a judge of the General Court of Virginia, in which office he remained for twenty years. He celebrated his stay on the bench by an opinion, in the case of Kamper vs. Hawkins, on the authority of the constitution over mere legislative enactment, and contributed to making the overruling power of the judiciary an accepted principle of American jurisprudence. Numerous offices were tendered to him. In 1781, Jefferson, then Governor of the state, invited him into his council, but he preferred service in the legislature. In 1803, he was appointed by the council to succeed William Wirt as Chancellor of the Williamsburg district, but declined the appointment. In 1808, he was elected Chief Magistrate of the commonwealth, and in that office, which he filled for three years, he urgently pressed the importance of schools, and became the founder of the literary fund devoted to the purposes of education. In 1811, he was appointed by Madison, judge of the district court of the United States for the state of Virginia, to fill the vacancy caused by the death of Judge Cyrus Griffin. Jefferson did him the honor to make his nomination the single exception to the rule that he had laid down for his government, "never to solicit an appointment from the president."

Governors

As federal judge, Tyler in the Circuit Court of the United States sat with John Marshall, the chief justice, to whom he was politically opposed, and contended successfully against the principle of a universal common law jurisdiction for the federal courts, favored by his colleague. He supported the war with Great Britain in 1812, and decided the first prize case that came up for adjudication in that war. He died on January 6, 1813, and his only regret was that he "could not live long enough to see that proud British nation once more humbled by American arms."

SMITH, GEORGE WILLIAM (1762-1811), Governor of Virginia (1811), was born in that state about 1762, son of an eminent member of the Continental Congress, Meriwether Smith, and Elizabeth, his wife, daughter of Colonel William Daingerfield, member of the House of Burgesses in 1758. He was married on February 7, 1793, to Sarah Adams of Richmond. In 1794, he represented the town of Essex in the House of Delegates. Soon thereafter, he made his home in Richmond, where he took a leading position at the bar. He represented the city in the Legislature from 1802 to 1808 inclusive. In 1805, he was captain of the "Richmond Republican blues." On December 15, 1807, he qualified as member of the privy council, and as senior member of that body, became chief executive of the state on December 5, 1811, succeeding Governor James Monroe, who resigned to accept the position of Secretary of State in the cabinet of President Madison. Three weeks later, while attending a performance at the Richmond Theatre, Governor Smith, with many others, died in a fire that consumed that building. The calamity was felt as a national one, since both the Senate and the House of Representatives adopted resolutions that their members should wear crape on the left arm for one month. The Monumental Church, a handsome octagonal building was erected in 1812 on the site of the ill-fated theatre. The remains of the victims were buried in the portico of the church, beneath a marble monument inscribed with their names.

BARBOUR, JAMES (1775-1842), Governor of Virginia (1812-1814), was born in Orange County, Virginia on June 10, 1775, a son of Colonel Thomas Barbour. Having received an appointment as deputy sheriff, he became so interested in the study of the law, and his proficiency was such that he was admitted to the bar at the age of nineteen. He entered a successful practice, and when he was only twenty-one years old was elected to a seat in the Virginia House of Delegates, and kept it for sixteen years. In 1812, he was elected Governor of Virginia. During his sitting in the House of Delegates, he bore a prominent part in all important legislation, was the author of the anti-dueling act, and frequently occupied the speaker's chair. At the end of his term as Governor, he was in 1815, elected to the U.S. Senate, where he was repeatedly appointed chairman of the Committee on Foreign Relations. In 1825, he became Secretary of War under President John Q. Adams, and was appointed Minister to England in 1828, to be recalled by President Jackson the following year, whom he had vigorously opposed. In 1839, he presided over the Whig Convention in Harrisburg, Pennsylvania, which nominated General Harrison for president. He died at his home in Orange County, Virginia on June 8, 1842.

NICHOLAS, WILSON CARY (1761-1820), Governor of Virginia (1814-1816), was born in Hanover, Virginia on January 31, 1761, son of Robert Carter Nicholas, jurist. He graduated from William and Mary in 1774 and entered the army, in which he became an officer and commanded Washington's life guard until it was disbanded in 1783. He was a member of the state convention to ratify the constitution of the United States. He succeeded Henry Tazewell as U.S. Senator, serving in the sixth, seventh, and eighth Congresses until December 13, 1804, when he resigned to accept the office of collector of the ports of Norfolk and Portsmouth. He held the position three years when he was elected to represent his district in the tenth and eleventh Congresses. In 1814, he was elected Governor, serving until 1817. Nicholas was a powerful friend of Thomas Jefferson in the state of Virginia. He died in Milton, Virginia, October 10, 1820.

PRESTON, JAMES P. (1774-1843), Governor of Virginia (1816-1819), was born in Smithfield, Virginia on June 21, 1774, son of Colonel William and Susanna (Smith) Preston. He was a student at William and Mary College from 1790 to 1795. In 1799, he organized a company of artillery. He was elected to the state Senate in 1802, was appointed lieutenant-colonel of the 12th U.S. infantry on March 19, 1812, and for gallantry during the war with Great Britain, was promoted on August 15, 1813, to the rank of colonel, and assigned to the command of the 23rd regiment of infantry. He participated in the Battle of Chrystler's Field, November 11, 1813, and was so severely wounded in the thigh, that he was crippled for life. In recognition of his military services, he was elected by the General Assembly to succeed Wilson Cary Nicholas as Governor on December 1, 1816. During the last year of his incumbency, on the 25th of January, 1819, the law was passed establishing the University of Virginia in Albemarle County, on a site near Charlottesville, which was purchased from Centre College, to which it had previously belonged. Subsequently to his gubernatorial service, Preston was for several years, postmaster of Richmond. He finally retired to his homestead, "Smithfield," in Montgomery County, where he died on May 4, 1843. The county of Preston was named in his honor. He left three sons: William Ballard Preston, Secretary of the Navy in the cabinet of President Taylor, and Confederate states who were colonels in the Confederate Army during the Civil War.

RANDOLPH, THOMAS MANN (1768-1828), Governor of Virginia (1819-1822), was born in Tuckahoe, Virginia on October 1, 1768. He showed an early aptitude for study, and with a younger brother, enrolled in Edinburgh University in 1785. Upon their return home, they were accompanied by Sir John Leslie, who remained

Governors

with them for two years as tutor. On February 23, 1799, young Randolph was married to Martha, daughter of Thomas Jefferson, the life-long friend of his own father, and whose friendship he had early gained for himself. After his marriage, Randolph made his home with the Jeffersons, both at Monticello and at the White House. He served in Congress from 1803 to 1807, during which period, he became involved in so serious an altercation with John Randolph of Roanoke, that a duel was only averted with much difficulty. During the War of 1812, he entered the military service and became an officer of the 20th infantry. In 1819, he was elected Governor of Virginia, serving until 1821. His death at Monticello on June 20, 1828, was the result of exposure from riding, his generosity having prompted him to take off his coat and give it to a beggar on the highway. He kept up his studious habits throughout life, and was the valued friend of many schools and men of learning. Jefferson epitomized him as "a man of science, sense, virtue, and competence."

PLEASANTS, JAMES, JR. (1769-1836), Governor of Virginia (1822-1825), was born in Goochland County, Virginia on October 24, 1769, son of James Pleasants. He was a descendant of John Pleasants who emigrated from England in 1665. After a thorough school education, he studied law with the distinguished Judge Fleming and began practice with considerable success. In 1796, he was elected to represent Goochland County in the House of Delegates, and as a Republican, supported the resolutions of 1798-99. In 1803, he was chosen clerk of that body, a position he filled most acceptably until 1811. In that year, he was elected a member of the House of Representatives. He supported Madison's administrative policy during the War of 1812, and after a service in the House, was elected by the General Assembly in 1819, as a Senator of the United States. He resigned, however, in 1822, and was then elected Governor of Virginia, an office he held by annual elections until 1825. He was next a member of the convention of 1829-30, his last public service, for though twice appointed to judicial position, he declined acceptance from a distrust of his qualifications. He died on November 9, 1836, in Goochland County, universally esteemed for his many virtues. He left a son, John Hampden Pleasants, who attained almost unrivaled success as editor of the Richmond "Whig."

TYLER, JOHN (1790-1862), tenth President of the United States and Governor of Virginia (1825-1827), was born in Greenway, Charles City County, Virginia on March 29, 1790, son of John and Mary Marot (Armistead) Tyler. His father was a man of great distinction in the early days of national history in Virginia, having been judge of the admiralty court of the state in 1776; a member of the House of Delegates (1778-86), and Speaker during the last six years of his service; a member of the State Council (1780-81); judge of the Admiralty and Supreme Courts (1786-88); judge of the General Court (1788-1808), Governor of Virginia (1808-11); and judge of the U.S. District Court for Virginia (1811-13).

Encyclopedia of Virginia

John Tyler, the fourth of the name, received his education in an "old-field" school, and graduated from William and Mary College in July of 1807. James Madison, the president of the college, and Judge Tyler had been college-mates of Thomas Jefferson and the political principles of the rising statesman came naturally to favor "states-rights." At college, Tyler showed a strong interest in ancient history. He was also fond of poetry and music and was a skillful performer on the violin. In 1809, before attaining his majority, he was admitted to the bar. He was elected to the Legislature and took his seat in that body in December of 1811. He was a firm supporter of Madison's election; and the war with Great Britain, which soon followed, afforded him an opportunity to gain reputation as a forcible and persuasive orator. The bank as an institution had always been unpopular in Virginia, but the Virginia senators in Washington ignored the instructions to the Legislature and favored its recharter in 1811. On Janaury 14, 1812, Mr. Tyler introduced resolutions in which the Senators were taken to task, and the binding force of their instructions was formally asserted.

He was married on March 20, 1813, to Letitia Christian, and a few weeks afterward, he was called to military duty at the head of a company of militia to take part in defense of Richmond, now threatened by the British. His service lasted only a month. He was reelected to the Legislature annually until, in November, 1816, he was chosen to fill a vacancy in the House of Representatives, caused by the death of John Clopton.

As a member of the House, during the fourteenth and fifteenth Congresses, he soon made himself conspicuous as a strict constructionist. He voted against the bill introduced by Calhoun in favor of internal improvements on the ground of its unconstitutionality and its lack of a principle of uniform application among the states. He voted against changing the per diem allowance of $6 a day to members of Congress to an annual salary of $1,500. He also opposed the passage of the national bankrupt law, and condemned the course of General Jackson in Florida. He was a member of the committee for inquiring into the affairs of the national bank.

After being reelected to the Congress a second time, Tyler declined a third bid in 1821 and returned to private life because of poor health. However, in 1823, he was again elected to the House of Delegates of Virginia. The next year he was nominated to fill the vacancy created in the U.S. Senate by the death of John Taylor, but his friend, Littleton Tazewell, a much older man in politics, was elected. In the Legislature in 1824, he opposed the attempt to move William and Mary College to Richmond, and received his reward in being afterwards made successively rector and chancellor of the college, which prospered significantly under his auspices. In December of 1825, he was chosen by the Legislature to the governorship of Virginia, and the following year, he was reelected by a unanimous vote.

Before the presidential election in 1824, William H. Crawford was the only candidate of the Republican Party whose opinions were unequivocal against the American system of high tariffs, national bank, and internal improvements. He accordingly received the support of Jefferson and all the Virginia leaders, including John Tyler. When Crawford, by reason of a stroke, was deemed out of the contest, Tyler and the rest of the strict-constructionists preferred John Quincy Adams to either Henry Clay or Andrew Jackson. When Adams came out in the same colors, the strict constructionists who had adhered to Crawford, remained neutral for a time, but were finally forced into cooperation with the followers of Andrew Jackson--the majority of whom were members of the old Federal Party. Tyler went along with the rest of the Crawford men, but from the first, his support of Jackson was coupled with the condition of Jackson's sustaining the Republican doctrines as maintained in Virginia. Parties now assumed new names. The friends of Adams and Clay took that of National Republicans, while the friends of Jackson and Crawford assumed that of Democrats. But each party claimed to be the true representative of the old Republican party of Jefferson.

Firmly devoted to his principles, Tyler would not be partisan. He never attached any importance to the widely prevalent story of a corrupt bargain between Adams and Clay. When the Clay and Adams men in the Legislature momentarily united in 1827 with a majority of the Crawford men and elected Tyler as Senator over John Randolph, some zealous friends of Jackson attempted to show that there must have been some secret and reprehensible understanding between Tyler and Clay. Tyler subsequently supported Jackson for President in the fall of 1828, deciding he was the lesser of two evils. He strongly condemned Jackson's policy in his first administration; still, in the Presidential election of 1832, he supported him again as a less objectionable candidate than either Clay or Wirt. Tyler disapproved of nullification and condemned the course of South Carolina as both "impolitic and unconstitutional." But he condemned the tariff measures of the administration for the same reasons, and for the additional one that they were the cause of the errors of South Carolina. Jackson's famous proclamation of December 10, 1832, was denounced by him as "sweeping away all the barriers of the constitution," and as establishing in principle "a consolidated, military despotism."

Under the influence of these feelings he undertook to play the part of mediator between Clay and Calhoun, and suggested to them the idea of the Compromise Tariff of 1833. On the so-called "force bill," clothing the President with extraordinary powers for the purpose of enforcing the tariff which had caused all the trouble, Tyler showed the courage of his convictions. The vote stood at 32 yeas and one nay (John Tyler). The tendency of successive defections was to bring Tyler and his friends into closer and closer association with Clay and the National Republicans. Tyler opposed the removal of the deposits from the United States Bank. He voted in favor of Clay's proposition to censure the President, but his entire opposition was founded on a theory of states-rights, which was really repugnant in principle to all the views expressed by Clay and the National Republicans in 1828.

In 1836, no common candidate could be agreed upon. The states-rights men nominated Hugh White of Tennessee for President, and John Tyler for Vice-President. The National Republicans, wishing to gather votes from the other parties, nominated for President, General William Henry Harrison, who, as a soldier, was not identified with any political party. The Democratic friends of Jackson nominated Van Buren, who received many National Republican votes in the election. There was a great deal of bolting among the states. Massachussetts threw its votes for Webster for President, and South Carolina for Willie Mangum. Virginia, which voted for Van Buren, rejected his colleague, Richard Johnson, and cast its electoral vote for Vice-President on William Smith of Alabama. White obtained the electoral votes of Tennessee and Georgia, twenty-six in all, but Tyler made a better showing--he carried, besides those two states, Maryland and North Carolina, making forty-seven in all. No one of the candidates for the Vice-Presidency having received a majority of the electoral college, the choice devolved on the Democratic Senate, who chose R.M. Johnson.

On the seventh anniversary of the Virginia Colonization Society, Tyler was chosen its president. While maintaining the sovereignty of the states over the subject of slavery, he had always supported projects to put a stop to the slave-trade and to improve the condition of the slaves. And, as early as 1832, he had, as chairman of the Senate Committee, proposed a code for the District of Columbia, one section of which prohibited the slave-trade in the District.

In the spring elections of 1838, Tyler was again returned to the Virginia Legislature. On the advice of Clay, the majority of the Whigs decided to go for William Rives in preference to Tyler. Naturally indignant at this treatment, the personal friends of Tyler would not yield, and no election ensued at this Legislature because of the deadlock. Before the Whig convention in Harrisburg, the old issues of bank, tariff, and internal improvements were distinctly surrendered by Clay, Webster, Adams, and all the leaders of the old National Republican Party. Clay especially, had gone so far in conciliating Southern sentiment as to be considered the Southern candidate. The Northern representatives sought to defeat his election by again putting up General Harrison, a Southerner, who was preferable to Clay in the eyes of the manufacturers, since, although approving the Compromise Tariff of 1833, he had not been the mover of it. They succeeded in defeating Clay, and General Harrison became the candidate of the Whig Party for the Presidency. Tyler was the choice for the Vice-Presidency. Borne on a great wave of popular excitement, "Tippecanoe and Tyler too" were carried to the White House. A deep-seated conviction of the necessity of reform prevailed, and this conviction swept the Democrats from power.

The triumph of the Whigs was followed by the startling results. A collision between their varying factions was unavoidable. Clay speeded up the argument. Without waiting for Harrison's inauguration, he at once assumed the dictatorship of the Whig Party and revived the old National Republican measures

Governors

which in his letters and public speeches he had declared "obsolete." Matters had already come to a head between Clay and Harrison when the latter died one month after his inauguration. The Presidency, then devolved on the Vice-President, whose views were even more fixed against the policy proposed than Harrison's. The national bank was announced by Clay as the great cardinal object of the new Whig administration. But neither in his inaugural address, nor in his message calling the Congress in extra-session on May 31, 1841, had Harrison indicated that the bank would be agreeable to him.

Tyler privately submitted several financial projects to his cabinet, which while they avoided recognizing the power of Congress to create corporations in the states, really accomplished all that a national bank could have effected, respecting the finances and business of the country. A measure similar in all respects to the plan which Harrison favored was finally adopted by the Whig cabinet and recommended to Congress by Thomas Ewing, the Secretary of the Treasury. Clay forced a fight on the constitutional question by substituting a bill differing from the cabinet bill in allowing the bank to establish its branches at will in the states. Despite the opposition of the Senators from Virginia and Massachusetts, the bill in this form passed both houses of Congress. The President was not only committed against the principle of Clay's bill, but he had, in an interview with Clay himself, at the beginning of the extra-session of Congress, assembled in obedience to a proclamation of the late President, clearly forewarned him of the folly of his course. He therefore vetoed the bill, but by withholding the veto until the ten days allowed by the Constitution had nearly expired, he afforded another signal proof of his wish to harmonize with the Whigs.

He could not yet fully believe that the Whigs would be so blind as to deliberately sacrifice the result of the recent election by a conflict with their own President. As Clay's objection was against requiring the assent of the states to the establishment of the bank, or its branches within them, the President thought that the Whigs might be satisfied with a proposition which by limiting the bank to dealings in exchanges would, under a recent decision of the Supreme Court of the United States, avert the necessity of obtaining the expressed consent of the states for branches. In accepting this distinction, Tyler made no surrender of his consistency, for it was a distinction made by the law of nations, which was itself founded on the voluntary consent of states. But as the will of a free state or nation is not subject to a coercive code, Tyler made provision for the possible interdiction by a state of branches of the bank within it. He wrote a suitable reservation in the margin of the paper that had been made the basis of the bill, which with this reservation, was carried to the Whig caucus.

Now the bill, as adopted by Congress, did not contain the marginal words, and a second veto followed. Some of the Whigs hoped to frighten the President into signing the bill, or resigning his office. Threats were fulminated against him on all sides. Private letters warned him of plots to assassinate him, and Clay, in the Senate, referred to his resignation in 1836, and asked why he should not follow that example now. The adjournment of Congress was fixed for Monday, September 13, 1841. The second veto was sent to Congress on September 9th. On the 11th all the cabinet except Webster resigned. The members were fully aware that according to the president's view, all vacancies happening during the session had to be filled and sanctioned by the Senate during the session. The President would make no bargain of any kind, but before sending in his veto message, he had submitted it to his cabinet and expressed his willingness to incorporate in the paper, a declaration against a second term which the Whig papers were continually charging as the object of his conduct. The cabinet members opposed his insertion of such a paragraph. Some of the leading Whig members of Congress now issued addresses to the people, declaring "all political connection between them and John Tyler at the end from that day." Daniel Webster, who warmly condemned the course of Clay, adhered to the President.

For the next two years, while the Whigs controlled Congress, Tyler received little support from that party, and the case was not changed much for the better when the Democrats, controlled by the Van Buren wing of the party, succeeded to the seats which the Whigs had vacated. Tyler's reliance was on the wing of either party, known as the "states-rights" men in contradistinction to the Clay Whigs and Van Buren Democrats.

After the resignation in 1841, he filled his cabinet with states-rights Whigs, who, like himself, had voted for Harrison, and in 1843, he added several states-rights Democrats who were opposed to Van Buren, whose principles he had always distrusted. The domestic history of the rest of Tyler's administration must be briefly told. The leading facts were the exchequer system rejected by the Whigs, made afterwards by Lincoln, the basis of the system of finance, the tariff which Tyler procured after two vetoes, the adjustment of the Rhode Island difficulties, the settlement of the war with the Florida Indians, the renovation of all the departments of the government, and the reform of the civil service by the enforcement of the merit system and the supervision of subordinates. The success that marked the administration in these matters was chiefly due to Tyler, who drafted the Exchequer Bill, wrote the correspondence with the Rhode Island authorities, saved the Treasury by his vetoes and exerted the most rigid personal surveillance over every officer in the departments. And no less marked was his personality in this management of the foreign policy of the administration whose negotiations resulted in securing peace by the settlement of questions of fifty years standing and enormously advancing the authority and power of the Union.

Tyler, as early as 1841, pointed out to Webster the importance to all our interests of the acquisition of Texas. In 1842, he suggested to him, with the concurrence of Lord Ashburton, the negotiation of a tripartite treaty by which to end the Texas War with Mexico, and to add California and the West to the Union in return for the concession to Great Britain of the line of the Columbia River, as her boundary on the Northwest, and the release to Mexico of the spoliation claims.

Governors

To Tyler also belongs the credit of encouraging the missionary Whitman in his plan of transporting caravans of emigrants to the West to counteract the work of the Hudson Bay Fur Co. After Upshur's death in 1844, it was Tyler, and not Calhoun who secured the mastery of the Texas question. Calhoun was unaware of the efforts of the President to get Texas until he was nominated secretary. Then he thought it was an "unpropitious time" to carry through so important a measure, and he declared that he had hesitated to accept office under Tyler. He delayed nearly three weeks before he reached Washington, after his nomination as Secretary of State. And when the Treaty of Annexation was defeated in the Senate, Calhoun advised Tyler to abandon the project. The final annexation of Texas was distinctly a crowning victory for President Tyler's policy.

Tyler left the government on March 4, 1845, but before he departed, he had the happiness to announce to Congress the successful negotiation of the first treaty with China by Caleb Cushing. When his term expired, the condition of the govenment was good. A balance of $8,000,000 was found in the Treasury. Tyler, during his administration, was a strong advocate of civil service reform and the chief missions were for years filled with persons politicaly opposed to him. After leaving the White House, Tyler took up his residence on an estate three miles from Greenway, where his father had lived in Charles City County, Virginia. He gave the name of "Sherwood Forest" to this estate, and he lived there for the rest of his life. He no longer took an active part in politics, but even in his retirement, he exerted a great influence on public opinion in Virginia. He made a number of addresses, which rank high as literary productions. He had borne great and undeserved misrepresentation, which by his sensitive nature was keenly felt. He was, therefore, greatly gratified to find his popularity in Virginia and the South return after a few years.

When Lincoln was elected, and South Carolina seceded, the Virginia people elected him to the state convention in January of 1861. In order to preserve the Union, he suggested a peace conference of the states, which met in Washington in February. Of this distinguished body Tyler was the president, but his best efforts could not avert the impending clash. When war was certain, he voted in the state convention to repeal the ordinance of the Convention of 1788, which expressly provided that he powers granted by the people of Virginia to the Federal government might be resumed "whensoever the same should be perverted to their injury or oppression." Tyler was a delegate to the Provisional Congress, and was member-elect of the Confederate House of Representatives, but died before he could take his seat in the latter body on January 18, 1862.

GILES, WILLIAM BRANCH (1762-1830), Governor of Virginia (1827-1830), was born in Amelia County, Virginia on August 12, 1762. He studied at Hampden Sidney College and at Princeton, then devoted himself to the study of law, at first in the office of Chancellor George Wythe. Upon his admission to the bar, he began his practice in Petersburg, Virginia where he remained for a number of years. In 1791, he was elected a member of Congress and continued to serve in that capacity, excepting one session until March, 1803. At first he was a member of the Federal Party, but the proposition to create the U.S. Bank led to his joining with the Democrats. While Alexander Hamilton was Secretary of the Treasury, Giles attacked him sharply from his seat in the House, accusing him of corruption, and afterward moved resolutions censuring Hamilton for arbitrary assumption of authority and for lack of proper respect for the legislative body. Giles was opposed to John Jay's treaty with Great Britain, and took an active part in opposition to it. He was equally against the proposed war with France on account of outrages which, it was alleged, that country had committed on American commerce.

In 1798, Giles was a member of the Virginia Legislature, and in 1801, was a presidential elector. In 1804, he succeeded Wilson Cary Nicholas in the U.S. Senate, and being reelected, continued to serve in that body until March 3, 1815, when he resigned. His position in the Senate was prominent, being that of a Democratic leader. He was particularly noticeable for his opposition to the Madison administration. Giles returned to private life from 1811 until 1825, then ran as a candidate for the U.S. senatorship, but was defeated by John Randolph. The next year he was elected a member of the Legislature of Virginia, and in the same year, Governor of Virginia, an office he held until 1829.

Giles was considered to be one of the ablest parliamentarians of his time. He was an accomplished debator, and, not in the least to his detriment, was generally compared with Charles James Fox. It was alleged in the comparison that, while Fox was thoroughly educated and a scholar, Giles possessed no such advantages, and still it was claimed by no less an authority than John Randolph that in the House of Representatives, Giles held the same position in the judgment of the members that Fox held in the British House of Commons.

Giles published a number of writings, among which were "A Speech on the Embargo Laws" (1808); "Political Letters to the People of Virginia" (1813); a series of letters signed "A Constituent," which were printed in the "Richmond Inquirer," and which were in opposition to a plan for general public education (1818). He also published, in 1824, a sharp letter antagonizing President James Monroe and Henry Clay on account of their interest in the South American case and that of the Greek revolution, as also the question of the tariff. Giles died in Albemarle County, Virginia on December 4, 1830.

FLOYD, JOHN (1783-1837), Governor of Virginia (1830-1834), was born in Jefferson County, Virginia on April 24, 1783, son of Colonel John Floyd, and the descendant of a family early established in Virginia. For a time, he attended Dickinson College, Carlisle, but in October, 1804, entered the University of Pennsylvania as a student of medicine. Upon graduation in April, 1806, he settled in Montgomery County, Virginia. He was appointed a Justice of the Peace in June of 1807, commissioned as ma-

Governors

jor of militia in 1808, served as surgeon in the Virginia line in 1812, and in the same year, was elected a member of the House of Delegates. He subsequently became Brigadier-General of militia, and in 1817, was elected to the U.S. House of Representatives, where he served ably until 1829. During much of the time, he was a leader of that body, exerting an immense influence on public opinion. He opposed the administration of John Quincy Adams, and contributed largely to the election of Andrew Jackson in 1828. In 1820, he introduced the first bills for the occupation and settlement of Oregon, and in a speech, demonstrated the importance and value of that territory, which was then and for many years afterward, so little appreciated, that Benton, in 1825, named the ridge of the Rocky Mountains as "the convenient, natural and everlasting boundary" of the Union.

In 1830, Dr. Floyd was elected Governor of Virginia to succeed William B. Giles. The tariff question was creating great interest at the time, and Floyd was still Governor when South Carolina, in 1832, announced its intention to nullify the federal tariff law. In his several messages to the Legislature, Floyd severely condemned the proclamation of President Jackson and recommended a convention of the states. He did not, however, believe in the doctrine of nullification. South Carolina voted for him for President in 1832. The same year, Nat Turner's insurrection occurred among the slaves of Southampton County, resulting in the destruction of fifty-five white persons. Gabriel Turner, the slave leader, was taken and executed for treason. Floyd served until March 31, 1834, when he was succeeded as chief magistrate by Littleton W. Tazewell.

Governor Floyd had been in poor health previous to his gubernatorial term, and his disease finally exhibited itself in paralysis. Excitement induced by the visit of a son caused a return of the paralysis, and on August 15, 1837, he died at Sweet Springs, Montgomery County, Virginia. John Hampden Pleasants said that "Nature had endowed Floyd with the qualities of a hero, and the stage and opportunity were only wanting to have enabled him to shine among those who have dazzled mankind with deeds of chivalry and prowess." As a member of Congress, he easily held a position among the first. And this recognition of worth was due not to superficial effects of oratory or personal popularity, but to the commanding influence of his moral character and real worth.

TAZEWELL, LITTLETON WALLER (1774-1860), Governor of Virginia (1834-1836), was born in Williamsburg, Virginia on December 17, 1774. He graduated from William and Mary College in 1791, studied law under John Wickham of Richmond, and in 1796, was admitted to the bar. During the latter year, he was also elected to the House of Delegates where he remained until 1800, suppporting the resolutions of 1798 and Madison's report of 1799. As representative to Congress, he, in 1800, succeeded John Marshall, who had left to become Secretary of State. While in his Congressional capacity, Tazewell supported Jefferson in the presidential election which fell to the House, thus opposing the claims of Aaron Burr. He declined a subsequent reelection to Congress, and on moving to Norfolk in 1802, soon established himself as one of the ablest lawyers in that area. He was especially prominent as an admiralty or criminal advocate. Roman Catholic priests consulted him about canon law, and London merchants did the same regarding points affecting their trade. He took an active interest in all public questions and their underlying principles, his wide reading and unquestioned capability giving him much influence. He was an independent thinker, and the reverse of an opportunist. He was an ardent supporter of the general views and constitutional opinions of Jefferson, although dissenting with equal ardor from various special policies of the administration.

He was strenuously outspoken against both France and England, and urged hostilities with each, even going so far as to offer his immediate services in the field. When public sentiment began to tend toward war, however, he reversed his position, declaring the administration to be incapable at all points, his opposition being equally fierce against Madison during the latter's presidential campaign. Tazewell continued to decry the policy that was bringing about the impending struggle with Great Britain until the formal declaration of war in 1812, when he again wheeled around and gave the government his loyal support. In 1816, he became a member of the Virginia Legislature, where his profound knowledge of economical and fiscal questions gave him an active part in the deliberations of that body. Under Monroe, he was one of the U.S. commissioners instrumental in the purchase of Florida from Spain.

From 1824 to 1830 Tazewell was once more a member of the U.S. Senate. During this second senatorial career, he was most conspicuous as chairman of the committee on foreign relations. His report on the Panama mission was widely known, as were also his addresses on the tariff, the piracy act, the bankrupt act, and the prerogatives of the President in the appointment of foreign ministers. He opposed the respective administrations of both John Quincy Adams and Andrew Jackson. In 1833, he resigned from the Senate, after refusing the office of chairman of that body, and after having made himself particularly antagonistic to the presidential action in removing deposits from the Bank of the United States. He was, in fact, generally in the opposition, denouncing the proclamation against the South Carolina movement, though he had little sympathy with the nullifiers. He was elected Governor of his state in 1834, after which service he relinquished all active participation in politics. He died in Norfolk, Virginia on May 6, 1860.

ROBERTSON, WYNDHAM (1803-1888), Governor of Virginia (1834-1836), was born near Manchester, Virginia on January 26, 1803. He was a brother of Judge John and Thomas Bolling Robertson, the latter having been Governor of Louisiana. Upon his graduation from William and Mary College, he studied law, and

Governors

in 1824, established himself in Richmond, where he soon won an enviable position in his profession. He also took an active part in public affairs, was a member of the Council of State in 1830, and again in 1833. On March 31, 1836, he was made Lieutenant-Governor, and on the same day, through the resignation of Littleton W. Tazewell, succeeded to the gubernatorial chair, where he remained for one year. He served in the Legislature from 1838 to 1841, and again from 1858 to 1865. As a state-rights unionist, he opposed both secession and coercion, and was the author of a legislative paper defining the position of Virginia in view of the impending troubles. He also wrote "A Vindication of the Course of Virginia throughout the Slave Controversy." In 1863, he spoke out against the attempt to fix food prices, and upon the legislature seriously considering such a measure in 1864, he was, with difficulty, dissuaded from withdrawing from that body. He published in 1887, "Pocahontas *alias* Matoaka and her Descendants through her Marriage with John Rolfe." Governor Robertson died at his home in Washington County, Virginia on February 11, 1888.

CAMPBELL, DAVID (1779-1859), Governor of Virginia (1837-1840), was born at Royal Oaks, Botetourt County, Virginia on August 2, 1779, son of John Campbell and Elizabeth McDonald. He received such education as the frontier settlements could provide, and in 1794, at age fifteen, was appointed an ensign in Captain John Davis' company of militia in the 2nd battalion of the 70th regiment, which position he held until he moved to Abingdon as an assistant in the clerk's office there. In 1799, the 105th regiment formed in the 29th battalion of which David Campbell was commissioned as captain of a company of light infantry assigned to it, and which he raised and organized. In the fall of the same year, Captain Campbell married his cousin Mary Hamilton. He now studied law and obtained a license, although never practicing his profession. He was fond of reading history and thus acquired his style of written composition.

In 1802, he was appointed deputy clerk of the county of Washington, and chiefly discharged the duties of the office on the 6th of July, 1812 when he was commissioned a major of the 12th infantry, U.S. Army. On March 12, 1813, he was promoted to the rank of Lieutenant-Colonel of the 20th U.S. regiment, and participated in campaigns on the St. Lawrence and toward Lake Champlain. In these campaigns he was so severly attacked with rheumatism that he had to resign his commission on January 28, 1814. On returning home, he served as aide-de-camp to Governor Barbour, and soon after, was elected general of the 3rd brigade of Virginia. On January 25, 1815, he was appointed colonel of the 3rd Virginia cavalry.

After this, he again served as clerk of his county until 1820, when he was elected to the State Senate. In 1824 he was elected clerk of the county court of Washington County and continued to hold the office until he was elected Governor of Virginia in 1836, and entered the office on March 31, 1837. Governor Campbell had supported Andrew Jackson for the Presidency, but, in common with most of the states'-rights men of the South, he withdrew his support from the Democratic Party when it brought forward the subtreasury scheme and the standing Army bill.

He was a member of the new Whig Party, formed about this time, and warmly supported the nominations of General Harrison and John Tyler for the Presidency and Vice-Presidency. In his messages he earnestly urged the establishment of the common-school system. He retired from the governorship on March 31, 1840. He afterward accepted the office of Justice of the Peace for his county. He died on March 19, 1859.

GILMER, THOMAS WALKER (1802-1844), Governor of Virginia (1840-1841), was born at Gilmerton, Albemarle County, Virginia on April 6, 1802, the son of George and Eliza Gilmer. He received his early education from Dr. Frank Carr, an excellent classical scholar, and later from John Robertson, a Scotchman. He studied law under his uncle, Pendey R. Gilmer in Liberty, Virginia and was aided in his studies by correspondence with another uncle, Francis W. Gilmer, one of the literary lights of the Old Dominion. At the bar of Albemarle, Gilmer soon won a first place. He was among the delegates to the Staunton convention, summoned to bring about a change in the state constitution. During the political canvass which resulted in the election of Andrew Jackson to the presidency. Gilmer edited "The Virginia Advocate." From 1829 to 1837, Gilmer represented Albemarle County in the House of Delegates, where he served on many committees including that on revolutionary claims. Later, he was appointed by Governor John Floyd, commissioner of the state to prosecute the revolutionary claims of Virginia.

He supported General Jackson for the Presidency in 1832, but when the President issued his proclamation in 1833 against South Carolina, Gilmer, in common with most of the leading Virginia Democrats, withdrew his support and aided in forming the Whig Party. In 1837, Gilmer spent the latter part of the winter in Texas as an agent for capitalists in Virginia. This trip made him cognizant of the resources of the infant Republic of Texas, and he became an ardent advocate of its annexation to the Union.

When the Legislature met in 1838, Gilmer was, without opposition, elected Speaker of the House of Delegates. He was reelected Speaker in December of 1839 and on February 4, 1840, he was elected Governor of Virginia to succeed David Campbell on the expiration of his term of office on March 31, 1840. He entered zealously upon his duties, and at his own expense toured the state for the purpose of carefully examining all the public works.

A noteworthy event of his administration was his dispute with Governor Seward of New York concerning fugitive slaves. Seward had, on several occasions, refused to surrender slaves, and also those persons who had incited them to escape, whereupon Gilmer subsequently refused to give up certain New York criminals who had taken refuge in Virginia. In this latter action, he was, however, not supported by the Legislature, and after an able message to that body vindicating his course, he resigned from the gubernatorial chair on March 1, 1841.

Governors

Despite the expectations of the Southern Whigs, Henry Clay forced upon the party the measure of a Bank of the United States. Gilmer sustained President Tyler in his vetoes of the bill to charter such an institution. He was chairman of a special committee of retrenchment and reform, and in 1842 made a report upon the veto by the president of the tariff bill. He aided Tyler in his move to annex Texas to the Union. In 1843, he defeated W. L. Goggin for Congress, and on February 15, 1844, he was nominated by President Tyler as Secretary of the Navy. The nomination was unanimously confirmed, but in less than two weeks after his nomination, he died during the catastrophe on the steamer Princeton, which also took the lives of many others including the Secretary of State.

RUTHERFORD, JOHN (1792-1865), Governor of Virginia (1841-1842), was born in Richmond, Virginia on December 6, 1792, son of Thomas Rutherfoord, a talented merchant of Richmond, Virginia, distinguished for his political writings. The son received his education at Princeton College, and subsequently studied law, a profession he practiced for a short time. He was, for many years, president of the Virginia Mutual Assurance Society, the first institution of the kind in the state. He was first captain of the Richmond Fayette Artillery, and became colonel of the regiment. In the division of parties, Rutherford was a states-rights man, and was a Whig until, in 1837, he returned to an association with the Democrats. He was a member of the Legislature, and in 1840, was Lieutenant-Governor, and, upon the death of Governor Thomas Gilmer in 1841, succeeded him as Acting Governor, which place he filled for more than a year. During this period, he conducted a correspondence with Governor William H. Seward of New York, which had been pressed by his predecessor concerning a demand for the surrender of certain fugitives.

For years he was associated in intimate correspondence with the first public men of the day, among them, John Tyler, William C. Rives and President Madison. Rutherford died in July of 1865, leaving an only son, John Coles Rutherford, who served in the State Legislature, and was favorably known as a debater and writer.

GREGORY, JOHN MUNFORD (1804-1887), Governor of Virginia (1842-1843), was born in Charles City County, Virginia on July 8, 1804, son of John M. Gregory and Letitia Power Graves. He attended the old-field school in his county until he reached the age of sixteen, after which he alternately taught school himself, and was employed in farm labor. Moving to James City County, he taught there for a time, and having begun the study of law, entered William and Mary College, from which he was graduated with the degree of Bachelor of Law in 1830. In the same year, he was elected as a delegate from James City County in the State Assembly, an office he was reelected to several times until 1841, when he was elected a member of the council of state, and after the resignation of Mr. Gilmer on March 1, 1841, succeeded John

Rutherfoord as Acting-Governor of the state. He continued the state executive until Janaury 1, 1843 when he was succeeded by Governor James McDowell.

During his service in the Legislature and executive branch, Gregory was a states-rights Whig, opposed to a bank and the other measures popular with the Whigs of the North. In 1853, Governor Gregory was appointed U.S. Attorney for the eastern district of Virginia, a position he held until the year 1860, when he was elected judge of the sixth judicial circuit of Virginia, and continued to serve in this capacity until displaced by the Federal authorities in 1866. He then resumed his law practice in Charles City County, but was soon elected commonwealth's attorney for the county, and served until the year 1880, when poor health forced his retirement. He spent his last days in Williamsburgh, and was buried in Shockoe Hill cemetery, Richmond, in 1887.

MCDOWELL, JAMES (1795-1851), Governor of Virginia (1843-1846), was born at Cherry Grove, Rockbridge County, Virginia on October 11, 1795. He was a descendant of John McDowell who emigrated from Ireland to America in the year 1735, and settled in Rockbridge County, Virginia where he was killed by the Indians on December 25, 1742. Among his children was Colonel James McDowell who served in the War of 1812, and married Sarah Preston.

James McDowell was their third child. He attended several private schools, entered Yale College and later completed his education in Princeton, New Jersey where he graduated in 1810. He next studied law under Chapman Johnson in Staunton, Virginia, but never practiced it. In 1831, he entered the Legislature, and after the Nat Turner insurrection broke out, he advocated gradual abolition of slavery. From this time, McDowell was continuously in public life, and in the service of the state. McDowell supported President Jackson's proclamation against South Carolina. His speech on foreign relations brought him to the front in 1833 as a rival of John Tyler for the senatorship, but he was defeated.

In December of 1842, McDowell was elected Governor, and on January 1, 1843, entered on the discharge of his duties. Before the close of his term of three years, Governor McDowell was elected to a seat in the U.S. House of Representatives, made vacant by the death of his brother-in-law, William Taylor. He served in Congress until 1851. His most memorable effort in Congress was his speech on the admission of California as one of the United States. He died in Lexington on August 24, 1851, at the age of fifty-six, leaving nine children.

SMITH, WILLIAM (1796-1887), Governor of Virginia (1846-1849), was born in King George County, Virginia on September 6, 1796. He received a good education in the schools of his county, and attended several academies. After some years of law study, he was qualified in the county court of Culpeper County in August of 1829.

Governors

He was an ardent Democrat and at the age of thirty-nine, was elected a member of the State Senate. He was reelected to this body, but resigned after serving one session.

In 1827, he obtained a contract for carrying the mails, and as his route was one of rapid development, he was repeatedly ordered by the government to perform extra duties, for which he was entitled to extra compensation. The circumstance was noticed in Congress by a Whig Senator, B.W. Leigh of Virginia, who, without calling the name of Mr. Smith, yet fixed on him the sobriquet of "Extra Billy," stayed with him through life.

In 1840, Smith was elected to Congress over Lynn Banks, and was in Congress until 1843. In December of 1845, he was elected Governor of Virginia for the term of three years, succeeding James McDowell on January 1, 1846. In 1850, Governor Smith moved to California, where two of his sons were living. He was a member of the constitutional convention, which met at Bernica in the autumn of that year, and was unanimously elected permanent president of the body. After acquiring much property by the practice of the law, he returned to Virginia in December of 1852, and in May of 1853, was elected to Congress where he served until 1861.

Though sixty-five years old, Governor Smith offered his services to Governor Letcher for command in the Confederate Army, and was appointed colonel of the 49th regiment of Virginia infantry. He performed with bravery in many bloody engagements, and received the commission of Brigadier-General. He served a brief interval in the Confederate Congress, and in May of 1863, was elected a second time as Governor of Virginia, assuming the duties of the office in Janaury of 1864. Early in August, 1863, he was made Major-General. As Governor, he aided the sinking fortunes of the Confederacy by supplies of food and money. Upon the evacuation of Richmond on April 3, 1865, Governor Smith moved the seat of government to Lynchburg. Soon after, the Confederacy collapsed, and Governor Smith returned to Warrenton, Virginia and devoted himself to agricultural pursuits.

He came to the front again in the election between Walker and Wells, upon the issues involved in reconstruction. In 1877, though eighty-one years old, he was reelected to the State Senate, and in 1878, came within a few votes of an election to the U.S. Senate. After this, he returned finally to private life. Smith was an advocate of temperance all his life, and was opposed to the use of liquor in elections. His marvelous activity, fearless character, and powerful talents place him among the remarkable men of the age. He died on May 18, 1887 at the age of ninety.

FLOYD, JOHN BUCHANAN (1806-1863), Secretary of War and Governor of Virginia (1849-52), was born in Blacksburg, Virginia on June 1, 1806. He was the son of John Floyd, also a Governor of Virginia, and a candidate for the Presidency in 1832. John B. Floyd received a liberal education, graduating in 1826 from the College of South Carolina, and afterward, studying law and being admitted to practice. From 1836 to 1839, Floyd lived in Arkansas, but in the latter year, he settled in Washington County, Virginia to practice law, at the same time interesting himself in politics, and serving in the State Legislature for several years.

In 1850, Floyd was elected Governor of Virginia, and on retiring from that office in 1853, was again elected a member of the Legislature. During the campaign of 1856, he supported Buchanan, who, while making up his cabinet after his inauguration on March 4, 1857, appointed Floyd as Secretary of War. He continued in this office until the end of 1860, when, having decided to follow his state into secession, he resigned and was succeeded by Simon Cameron. During the following winter, Floyd was generally accused of having secretly aided the secession cause by purposely sending the army to extreme ends of the country, and at the same time, forwarding large quantities of ammunition and arms to the South where they were deposited in the arsenals, ready to be captured whenever the Southerners wanted them. These and other serious charges against Secretary Floyd's integrity having been very generally put in circulation, he went to Washington and presented himself in court where he was placed under bail while awaiting a trial. Accordingly, the House of Representatives ordered the appointment of a special committee, and the charges against Floyd were thoroughly investigated, with the result that he was found completely innocent.

Returning to Virginia, Floyd was appointed Brigadier-General in the Confederate Army, and saw his first service in September of 1861. In February of 1862, General Floyd was in command at Fort Donelson, and so managed that by hard fighting, he succeeded in getting his troops out of the fort, leaving General Pillow with his force and General Buckner to bear the brunt of Grant's attack, while Floyd managed to save most of his men. General Floyd fell under the displeasure of Jefferson Davis for having taken to flight with his army, and was relieved of his command.

Floyd married Sally Buchanan Preston, his cousin, who was a niece of Patrick Henry, and sister of William C. Preston of South Carolina. Floyd died near Abington, Virginia on August 26, 1863.

JOHNSON, JOSEPH (1785-1877), Governor of Virginia (1852-1856), was born in Orange County, New York on December 10, 1785. When he was five years old, his father, who had been a soldier during the Revolutionary War, died, and the family moved, first to Sussex County, New Jersey, and in 1801 to Bridgeport, Harrison County, Virginia. Harrison County, was at that time "the forest primeval," and educational facilities were limited. Young Johnson was therefore only able to acquire a rudimentary English education by studying at night and at odd intervals. Soon after settling in Bridgeport, he engaged to live with an old farmer. When Johnson attained his majority, he married the daughter of his employer, and, upon the death of the latter four years later, purchased the interests of the other heirs in the farm where he made his home for over seventy years.

Governors

His first public service was as captain of a military company in the War of 1812. In 1815, he was elected to the State Legislature, and after serving four years, declined reelection. In 1823, he was nominated for Congress by the Democratic Party, and, after an exciting campaign, succeeded in defeating the eminent Philip Doddridge of Brooke County, whom he again defeated in 1825. In 1835, he once more consented to become his party's candidate, and remained in Congress for six years, when he retired, declining a renomination. In 1843, he was again forced by his party to become a candidate, and in 1847, once more declined reelection.

In 1850, he was elected to the Constitutional Convention of Virginia, and while a member of the Convention, was elected Governor of Virginia by the Legislature, and was subsequently made the nominee of the Democratic Party for the office he was filling. His opponent, Judge George W. Summers of Kanawha, was one of the greatest orators Virginia ever produced, and, like Johnson, had never yet suffered defeat in an election by the people. In this event, however, Johnson came off the victor by a plurality of 9,000 votes. This was his last public office, with the exception of that of presidential elector in 1860. For more than half a century he was a consistent member of the Baptist church. He was, perhaps, the only man in Virginia who had served the people almost continuously for forty years. He died on February 27, 1877.

WISE, HENRY ALEXANDER (1806-1876), Governor of Virginia (1856-1860), was born in Drummondtown, the county seat of Accomac County, Virginia on December 3, 1806, son of Major John Wise and his wife, Sarah Corbin Cropper--both the Wises and the Croppers being among the oldest families in Virginia. Henry Alexander Wise was left an orphan at the age of six. His earlier training was committed to an aunt, and to his guardian and uncle, by marriage, Major John Custis. At sixteen, he was sent to Washington College, Pennsylvania, and afterward, he attended the law lectures of Judge Tucker at Winchester, Virginia.

Upon his return home, he qualified himself for the practice of law, and his first vote for president was cast for Andrew Jackson. He then moved to Nashville, Tennessee, where he was married to Ann Jennings, daughter of a Presbyterian divine, Rev. Obadiah Jennings. After a brief residence in Nashville, Wise returned to Virginia and entered politics, being elected to Congress over Richard Coke. Coke was suspected of nullification tendencies, while Wise opposed nullification and the campaign resulted in a duel, in which Wise slightly wounded Coke in the arm.

Following this election, Wise returned to Congress for six successive terms. In this capacity he rose to the highest prominence as a debater, and crossed swords with the most celebrated men of his day. In the famous controversy between President Tyler and Congress, Wise was one of the few who adhered to the President, and, with Bailie Peyton and others, belonged to what was known as the "Corporal's Guard." In 1844, he was nominated as minister to France, but was rejected by the Senate. Afterward he was nominated as minister to Brazil and went to that post in 1844.

Prior to this, his first wife, Ann Jennings had died and he married Sarah Sergeant, daughter of John Sergeant of Pennsylvania. He remained in Brazil until 1847 when he returned to the United States, and in 1850, was elected a member of the State Convention of Virginia. While he was engaged in the duties of that body, his second wife died, and he was married a third time on November 1, 1853 to Mary Lyons of Richmond, Virginia. In 1855, Wise was nominated by the Democrats for Governor of Virginia at a time when the American (or Know-Nothing) Party seemed to be sweeping everything before it. Wise's campaign attracted the attention of the whole country. The result was his election by a large majority, and the Know-Nothing Party never recovered from the blow.

During his gubernatorial term of office, the John Brown outbreak occurred, which he promptly suppressed by the capture and execution of Brown. Upon the expiration of his official term on January 1, 1860, Governor Wise established himself at a farm near Norfolk. In the Democratic Conventions of 1860, he was prominently mentioned as a candidate for the presidency, and in 1861, was elected a member of the Secession Convention, where he strenuously opposed secession and advocated "fighting in the Union." While most indignant against what he believed to be the unwarranted aggressions of the North, he dearly loved the Federal Union, and had no sympathy with the ultra secessionists. His attitude won him few adherents, although, when a decision was forced upon Virginia, Governor Wise voted for secession.

At the outbreak of the Civil War, he was appointed Brigadier-General and sent to Western Virginia, where he fought and won the Battle of Scary Creek, and from where he was ultimately recalled, owing to misunderstandings between himself and General Floyd. He was then ordered to Roanoke Island where he remained until the capture of that place by General Burnside in February of 1862. In the assault, Captain O. Jennings Wise, the Governor's eldest son was killed. The Governor himself was ill at Nag's Head at the time of the attack, and so escaped. Later he was stationed on the defenses at Chaffin's farm and then transferred to South Carolina. In May of 1864, he was recalled to Virginia, reaching Petersburg with his command just in time to resist the first attack on that city by General W. F. (Baldy) Smith, and at great odds, held the place, receiving the highest endorsements for his brilliant defense. His command remained in the trenches at Petersburg from then on, and was the last engaged at Appomattox.

After the close of the war, Wise resumed the practice of law, making his home in Richmond. He had a large and lucrative clientele and beyond a brief term as commissioner for Virginia to run the boundary line between that state and Maryland, he took no part in politics. Wise was the author of "Seven Decades of the Union," a valuable contribution to the political history of his day. He possessed a remarkable intellect and marked individuality, being one of the most eloquent public speakers of a period in American history when oratory was a most common weapon.

Governors

Wise had four children by his first marriage and three children from his second. He died in Richmond, Virginia on September 12, 1876.

LETCHER, JOHN (1813-1884), Governor of Virginia (1860-1864), was born in Lexington, Virginia on March 28, 1813. He was educated at local schools, and then took a course at Washington College. He subsequently attended Randoph Macon College where he graduated in 1833. He also studied law at the latter institution, and was admitted to the Virginia bar in 1839, establishimg himself in Lexington. During his early years of practice, he entered into journalism, and for some time, edited a newspaper known as the "Valley Star." In 1850, he was a member of the convention for reforming the constitution of Virginia, and from 1852-59, served in Congress as a Democrat. In the latter capacity, he was active in the Committee of Ways and Means.

He was elected Governor of Virginia in 1859, serving until 1864. He was thus in possession of this office when his state adopted the ordinance of secession in 1861, which although he had previously opposed, he now gave his full support. It was at his instigation that all the state forces were immediately placed at the disposal of the Confederate government, without waiting for the vote of the people of Virginia. At the close of the Civil War, Governor Letcher resumed the practice of his profession in Lexington, where he died on January 26, 1884.

PIERPONT, FRANCIS H. (1814-1899), Governor of Virginia (1865-1868), was born in Monongahela County, Virginia on January 25, 1814. He worked on his father's farm and in the tan-yard until he attained his majority, meanwhile attending a local school. At the age of twenty-one, he entered Allegheny College in Pennsylvania, from which he graduated in 1839. Afterward he went South where he taught school in Mississippi. He studied law, and having returned to Virginia, was admitted to the bar in Fairmont, Marion County.

He was a pronounced anti-slavery man, and at the convention held at Wheeling in 1861, for the purpose of reorganizing the government of Virginia, after the state had seceded from the Union, he was unanimously elected Governor by the representatives of the forty counties that had sent delegates to the convention. He held office under this election for twelve months, and meanwhile was elected by the people to fill an unexpired term of two years, and was afterward reelected for the full term of four years.

After the division of Virginia into two separate states, he moved the state archives to Alexandria, convened the Legislature, and remained there two years, and called the convention in 1864, which assembled and abolished slavery in the state. At the fall of Richmond, he moved the seat of government from Alexandria to that city, and in a few months, had the state property reorganized. At the conclusion of his term as Governor in 1868, he returned to Fairmont and resumed the practice of law, and in 1870, was elected a delegate from Marion County to the West Virginia Legislature. He was appointed collector of internal revenue by President Garfield. Pierpont died in Pittsburgh on March 24, 1899.

WELLS, HENRY HORATIO (1823-1900), Governor of Virginia (1868-1869), was born in Rochester, New York on September 17, 1823. He was educated at Romeo Academy, Michigan, studied law in Detroit with Theodore Romeyn, was admitted to the bar in 1846, and in 1854-56, was a member of the Legislature of Michigan. He entered the Federal army in September of 1862 as colonel of the 26th Michigan infantry in which he served with distinction, attaining the brevet rank of Brigadier-General.

In 1865, he settled in Richmond, Virginia and resumed his law practice. General John M. Schofield, who was commanding the first military district of Virginia, appointed him on April 16, 1868, Provisional Governor of Virginia, superseding Governor Francis H. Pierpont. In 1869, he was the Republican candidate for Governor of the state under the new constitution, but was defeated by Gilbert C. Walker. Governor Wells was soon after appointed as U.S. District Attorney for the eastern district of Virginia, which position he held until 1872, when he resigned and resumed his law practice once again.

In 1875, he moved to Washington, and in September of that year, was appointed and entered upon the duties of U.S. Attorney for the District of Columbia. His son, H. H. Wells, Jr. received the appointment of assistant attorney for the district. The two held office until 1879 when they were succeeded respectively by George B. Corkhill and R. Ross Perry. Wells died in Washington, D.C. of February 13, 1900.

WALKER, GILBERT CARLTON (1832-1885), Governor of Virginia (1869-1874), was born in Binghamton, New York on August 1, 1832. He prepared himself for college at the Delaware and Binghamton Academy and entered Williams College, Massachusetts, in 1851. Here he acquired the reputation of a thorough student, and in particular, developed his abilities as a debater and public speaker. He left Williams College a year after his entrance on account of having been treated, as he thought, unjustly, in connection with the annual commencement exercises, and entered the junior class of Hamilton College. He was appointed prize speaker, and at the exhibition in July of 1852, was awarded the first prize. He graduated in July of 1854, and began to study law in the office of Judge Horace S. Griswold in Binghamton. The following year, he formed a co-partnership with Col. N. W. Davis in Oswego, New York, and in the autumn of the same year, was admitted to the bar and soon became the recognized leader of the young democracy of Tioga County.

In 1856, he was nominated for the office of the District Attorney of the county, but was defeated. His successful opponent, who soon after became his law partner, was General B.S. Tracy, later the Associate Justice of the New York Court of Appeals and Secretary of the Navy. On April 15, 1857, Walker married Miss

Governors

Evans, daughter of Alfred J. Evans, a merchant. In 1859, Walker moved to Chicago, Illinois where he soon became a prominent lawyer and businessman and took a leading part in politics. In 1860, he supported Senator Douglass for the Presidency, but immediately after the outbreak of the Civil War, became an active and uncompromising Federalist.

In 1863, Walker became the head of the firm of Walker, Thomas & Hart, one of the prominent law firms of Chicago. The following year he went to Fortress Monroe in Norfolk on business, and, his health having been greatly improved from the serious condition which had overtaken it in Chicago, and which returned as soon as he left Virginia, he determined to settle in the latter state, and accordingly moved to Norfolk where, in the early part of 1865, he organized the Exchange National Bank which soon became one of the most successful and prosperous institutions in the South, and of which he was elected first president.

He was also largely interested in other business enterprises, including the American Fire Insurance Company and the Atlantic Iron Works and Dock Company, of which in 1866, he became president, and was reelected every year thereafter until he became Governor. On July 6, 1869, by virtue of an Act of Congress, the President ordered an election to be held in Virginia, and Walker was solicited to become a candidate for Governor in opposition to the Republican nominee. He at length consented, and the contest was made between Walker and General H. H. Wells. During six weeks of the campaign, Walker made over forty public speeches in different parts of the state, and was eventually elected by a majority of over 18,000, the largest that had ever been given at a gubernatorial election in Virginia.

His administration was marked by a rigid enforcement of law and order, which were constantly maintained throughout the state, earning him the title of "The Political Saviour of Virginia." Governor Walker took great interest in the cause of education, and exerted a powerful influence in the establishment of a well-organized system of free schools. He took strong ground in favor of rigid economy in the state administration, the reorganization of the state debt and the inauguration of such measures as would reestablish the public credit.

When he retired from the governorship on January 1, 1874, he was unquestionably the most popular man in Virginia. The one-term principle, incorporated in the state constitution when it was framed, prevented his reelection. The same year he was sent to Congress by the Richmond or Metropolitan district and two years later was reelected. During his four years of Congressional service, he worked in behalf of four committees: Pacific railroads, revision of the laws, expenditures of the state department and education and labor. In 1881, Walker established himself in New York City where he secured a large and lucrative law practice, also becoming recognized as a most popular and effective orator. He died in May, 1885, and was survived by his wife.

Encyclopedia of Virginia

KEMPER, JAMES LAWSON (1823-1895), Governor of Virginia (1874-1878), was born in Madison County, Virginia on June 11, 1823, son of William Kemper, a planter, and a descendant of John Kemper, who arrived in Virginia in 1714 as a member of one of the twelve families from Oldenburg, seated by Governor Alexander Spotswood on his lands at Germania in Virginia. His mother's grandfather was John Jasper Stadler, a colonel of engineers on the staff of Washington. Young Kemper studied in local schools and graduated from Washington College with the degree of A.M. He then studied law under George W. Summers of Charleston.

In 1847, he was commissioned by President Polk, a captain in the volunteer service of the United States. Afterward, he served ten years in the Legislature of Virginia, where he was the speaker for two years, and was, for a number of years, chairman of the committee on military affairs. He also served as president of the Board of visitors of the Virginia Military Institution.

On May 2, 1861, the Virginia Secession Convention appointed him colonel of the 7th Virginia regiment. He was commissioned Brigadier-General in May of 1862, and during the war, was engaged in many battles, being badly wounded while leading his brigade in the charge at Gettysburg. From the effects of this wound, he recovered sufficiently to be entrusted with the command of the local forces in and around Richmond, and on March 1, 1864, he was commissioned Major-General. He held command in Richmond until the evacuation, and after the close of the war, retired to Madison County, where he resumed the practice of law.

He took an active part against the Republican Party, and in 1873, was elected Governor of Virginia, the duties of which office he discharged with that stern conviction of right which had marked his career throughout. During his gubernatorial term, he was waited on by a committee from the legislative caucus of the Democratic Party, who assured him of his unanimous election as U.S. Senator if he would signify his willingness to accept the honor. This, however, Governor Kemper declined to do, declaring that the state had already bestowed upon him the highest position in its power--that of Governor.

On July 4, 1853, he married Miss C. Conway Cave, and after the close of his term as Governor, his health having become impaired, he engaged in farming in Orange County, Virginia. He died in Gordonsville, Virginia on April 7, 1895.

HOLLIDAY, FREDERICK WILLIAM MACKEY (1828-1899), Governor of Virginia (1878-1882), was born in Winchester, Virginia on February 22, 1828, son of William Holliday. He graduated from Yale College in 1847. After a preparatory study of the law with the firm of Barton & Williams, he entered the University of Virginia where, after one session, he was graduated in law, political economy and moral and mental philosophy, and was selected as final orator of the Jefferson Literary Society of the institution. Within a year after coming to the bar, he was elected commonwealth's attorney for Winchester and the county of Frederick, a position he held until the outbreak of the Civil War in 1861.

180

Governors

He then entered the southern army under General Jackson and rose rapidly by successive promotions to the rank of colonel, with command of the 33rd regiment of infantry, a part of the "Stonewall Brigade." He engaged in numerous battles until, at the battle of Cedar Run or Slaughter's Mountain, he lost his right arm. This injury, which caused him long suffering, prevented him from future active service in the field. He then accepted a nomination for the confederate Congress and served as a member until the close of the war. Colonel Holliday resumed the practice of the law and was recognized as one of the first lawyers of the Winchester bar. He was the commissioner for Virginia at the United States Centennial Exposition held in Philadelphia in 1876, and was appointed elector-at-large for the state in the presidential campaign of the same year.

In 1877, he was, without opposition, elected Governor, and entered on the duties of that office on January 1, 1878. His administration was principally concerned with the question of the state debt and in the veto of schemes for repudiation. As Governor, he delivered the address of welcome at the Yorktown centennial by appointment of Congress, and many addresses to public bodies. After his retirement from office, Holliday spent much of his time in literary pursuits and in the cultivation of his farm. The rest he devoted to travel, and he has visited nearly all the countries of the world. During these tours, he was often the recipient of marked attention, private and official. Governor Holliday was married twice. He died in Winchester, Virginia on May 29, 1899.

CAMERON, WILLIAM EVELYN (1842-1927), governor (1882-1886), was born in Petersburg, Virginia on November 29, 1842, the son of Walker and Elizabeth (Walker) Cameron. He studied in local schools and at the classical school of Charles Campbell before entering West Point. During the Civil War, he served on the Confederate side and participated in every battle with Robert E. Lee's army except the engagement at Sharpsburg. He was wounded at the Second Battle of Manassas. Between 1861 and 1864, he was promoted various times: second lieutenant (1861); regimental adjutant (1862); brigade staff (1863); inspector of Davis' Mississippi Brigade (1864); and adjutant-general of Weisiger's Virginia Brigade (1864)

At the end of the war, in 1865, he returned to Petersburg and found work as a newspaper editor, serving the Petersburg *Index*, and later the *Norfolk Virginian*. He purchased the *Index* in 1867, and remained its editor until 1872, when he became an editor for the *Richmond Enquirer*. Meanwhile, in 1868, he married Louisa Egerton. They had three children.

Cameron entered politics in 1876, when he was elected Mayor of Petersburg. He served until 1879. In 1881, he was a Democratic Presidential Elector, and that same year ran for governor on the Readjuster Party ticket. He was elected, and entered office in January, 1882. As governor, he carried through on the Readjuster platform, pushing the enactment of legislation to readjust the state debt. Also during his administration, appropriations were made to the Literary Fund, the state school system, the Virginia Agricultural and Mechanical College in Blacksburg, the Normal and Collegiate Institute for Negroes in Petersburg, and the Central Hospital in Petersburg for mentally ill blacks. Use of the whipping post was abolished during his term, as were poll taxes; however taxation of corporations was increased.

Constitutionally unable to succeed himself, Cameron left office in 1886 and went to Petersburg to practice law. Between 1892 and 1894, he served as an official at the Columbian Exposition in Chicago. He was a member of the Virginia Constitutional Convention in 1901. In 1908, he moved to Norfolk where he became editor of the *Norfolk-Virginian* until 1915. He became editor-in-chief of the *Virginian-Pilot* in 1915, and remained until 1919, when he was forced to retire because of poor health. Cameron was the author of two books: *History of the World's Columbian Exposition* (1893) and *The Life and Character of Robert E. Lee* (1901). He also wrote biographical sketches of various well-known Virginians. He died on January 1, 1927.

LEE, FITZHUGH (1835-1905), Governor of Virginia (1886-1890), was the son of Robert Carter and Elizabeth Mason Lee. He was born November 19, 1835 in Clermont, Fairfax County, Virginia. He graduated from West Point in 1856 and served as a cavalry instructor at Carlile Barracks, Pennsylvania until January 1, 1858. At that time he was ordered to serve as a Second Lieutenant in the Second Cavalry in Texas.

He was assigned as assistant instructor in the Department of Tactics at West Point starting December 29, 1860 until May 3, 1861.

After resigning this post he was assigned as First Lieutenant in the Regular Confederate Army in Virginia. He was promoted to Lieutenant Colonel of the First Virginia Cavalry in August, 1861. On July 15, 1862 he was made Brigadier General, then Major General on August 3, 1863.

He was given the command of Cavalry Troops Army of Northern Virginia, March, 1865. After surrendering his troops on April 11, 1865 he retired for several years before running as a Democrat for Governor, being elected to that position November 3, 1885, defeating Republican John Sargent Wise. Lee left office January 1, 1890 and retired to his estate in Stafford County.

He was married to Ellen Bernard Fowle on April 19, 1871 and they had three daughters and two sons.

MCKINNEY, PHILIP WATKINS (1832-1899), Governor of Virginia (1890-94), was born in Buckingham County, Virginia on May 1, 1832, son of Charles and Martha (Guerraut) McKinney. His father was an influential farmer. Philip entered Hampden-Sidney College at the age of seventeen, and graduated in 1851, making a

Governors

mark there as a speaker, and receiving a gold medal from the Philanthropic Society in recognition of his abilities. Immediately after his graduation, he studied law at the school of Judge Brockenborough, Lexington. He also renewed his law studies at Washington and Lee University, and came to the profession well-equipped with a knowledge of law. In 1858, he was admitted to practice, and the same year, was elected to the General Assembly, where he served with distinction for four consecutive terms until the close of the Civil War. He was a strong Union man, but on the secession of Virginia, felt it his duty to side with his state, and entered the Confederate service as captain of a company of cavalry formed from the youth of Buckingham and the adjoining counties, which was assigned as Company K to the 4th regiment. He continued at its head until severely wounded at Brandy Station on June 9, 1863. His wound incapacitated him for further field service, but he was on post duty in Danville, Virginia for one year, at the end of which period, he was relieved from military duty by Colonel George C. Cabell, and took his seat as a member of the General Assembly of Virginia, to which post he had previously been elected three times, 1858 through 1862.

Having lost his fortune through the war, when hostilities ended, he resumed the practice of the law in Farmville. He took leading rank almost immediately among the eminent members of the Virginia Bar, and at the same time, took an active interest in state politics. He was a Democratic candidate for Congress in 1872, twice a Presidential elector, several times Commonwealth's Attorney, a delegate to the National Democratic Convention of 1884, which nominated Cleveland for the Presidency, and again a delegate to the St. Louis Democratic Convention of 1888. In 1881, he was the Democratic candidate for Attorney-General on the ticket headed by Senator Daniel for Governor, but was defeated. He was also defeated in the Virginia Democratic State Convention in 1885 as candidate for Governor, by Fitzhugh Lee.

In August, 1889, he was nominated as the Democratic candidate for Governor of Virginia, to oppose the well-known Republican, William Mahone, and was elected by about 45,000 majority, receiving the largest vote ever cast for a candidate in his state up to that time. Governor McKinney's administration was a very popular one, at home and abroad, because of its rehabilitation of the state's credit by a settlement with the English bond holders. In addition, he instigated a thorough investigation of the oyster industry of the state, including a survey of the oyster beds by Captain James Baylor of the U.S. Coast Survey, and also established a state farm to utilize the state's convict labor.

At the end of his term, he resumed the practice of law in Farmville. He was twice married, first about 1855 to Nannie Christian of New Kent County, Virginia, by whom he had one son, Robert Christian McKinney. She died in 1859 and he was married on December 23, 1884 to Annie Clay Lyle of Farmville, Virginia, by whom he had one daughter. McKinney died on March 1, 1899.

Encyclopedia of Virginia

O'FERRALL, CHARLES TRIPLETT (1840-1905), Governor of Virginia (1894-1898), was born on a farm near Brucetown, Virginia on October 21, 1840, of Irish ancestry, his family being well-known and influential. His father, John O'Ferrall, was a prominent man of his day, having been for a number of terms, a member of the Virginia House of Delegates, and at the time of his death, clerk of the county and circuit courts. The son gave early evidence of his ambition and energy. He was, as a child, conspicuous for his love for business, and his fondness for history. At the age of fifteen, he was appointed clerk *pro tempore* of the circuit court to fill the vacancy occasioned by the death of his father, and, at the age of seventeen, by reason of his marked ability for the position, he was elected clerk of the county court, for the full term of six years, but by the time he had served half the term, the Civil War broke out.

He at once enlisted as a private in the cavalry service, became sergeant, and rapidly rose to a colonelcy. At the surrender of Lee, he was in command of all the Confederate cavalry in the Shenandoah valley. His regiment, in fact, held the last line, had the last fight and captured the last prisoner on Virginia soil. During his military career, he was several times wounded, once through the lungs. Soon after the close of the war, he studied law at Washington College, Lexington, Virginia, and, on admission to the bar, began to practice law in Harrisonburg.

In 1871, he was elected a member of the Legislature from Rockingham County. Subsequently he was chosen as Judge of the county, and later he secured six nominations for Congress, virtually by acclamation. During the forty-eighth Congress, he was assigned to the Committee on Commerce. In the forty-ninth, he was chairman of the committee on Mines and Mining, and through three Congresses, was on the Elections Committee, of which he was chairman when his resignation took effect. Speaker Crisp was on this committee for four years with O'Ferrall, and it was this association that caused such a warm and lasting friendship between them.

On August 17, 1893, he was nominated for Governor of Virginia, and after a victorious campaign, took his seat on January 1, 1894. His administration was a most successful one, all acts of the executive having been marked by that determination, decision and energy which characterized the man. Governor O'Ferrall was a handsome man and was known as a superb rider. He had a large family and was a most affectionate father and husband. He died in Richmond, Virginia on September 22, 1905.

TYLER, JAMES HOGE (1846-1925), governor (1898-1902), was born at Blenheim, Caroline County, Virginia on August 11, 1846, the son of George and Elva (Hoge) Tyler. His mother died giving birth, and James was brought up by his maternal grandparents. When his grandfather died in 1861, he returned to live with his father in Caroline County. He received private education during his early years, and later attended a school run by Franklin Minor in Albemarle County. He served in the Confederate Army as a private towards the end of the Civil War. After the war, he took up farming. He was married to Sue Montgomery Hammet in 1868. They had seven children.

Tyler served in the Virginia State Senate from 1877 to 1879. In 1889, he was elected Lieutenant Governor, and served from January, 1890 to January 1894. He ran for governor in 1893, but was defeated for the Democratic nomination. However in 1897, he gained the nomination, and went on to win the governorship from Republican opponent, Patrick H. McCaull. During his administration, funding for public schools was increased, and the state debt was reduced by more than one million dollars. Other accomplishments included: establishment of the State Labor Bureau, creation of a conditional parole system, settlement of the dispute of the state's oyster beds, and settlement of the boundary dispute with Tennessee.

Tyler left office in 1902 and moved to East Radford, Virginia where he resumed farming and other business interests. He was president of the Virginia State Farmers' Institute and the Southwest Virginia Livestock Association, and served as a trustee for the Union Theological Seminary. In 1896, he went to Scotland as a delegate to the Pan-Presbyterian Alliance Convention. He also served as a member of the boards of the Synodical Orphans' Home, and Hampden-Sydney College. He died in East Radford on January 3, 1925.

MONTAGUE, ANDREW JACKSON (1862-1937), governor (1902-1906), was born near Lynchburg, Virginia on October 3, 1862, the son of Robert and Gay (Eubank) Montague. He attended Richmond College, and after graduation in 1882, worked as a private tutor in Orange County, Virginia. He returned to school in 1884, to study law at the University of Virginia, and received his LL.B. in 1885. Admitted to the bar that same year, he moved to Danville and began to practice law. In 1889, he married Elizabeth Lynn Hoskins. They had three children.

Montague was appointed U.S. Attorney for the Western District of Virginia in 1893. He remained in that position five years, then served as Attorney General of Virginia from 1898 to 1902. In 1901, he was elected governor on the Democratic ticket. His term as governor was marked by the passage of the Mann Act, which outlined strict licensing regulations for saloons. Other legislation included: a law which made employers liable for job-related injuries, and a primary plan for the nomination of U.S. senators.

After Montague's term expired in 1906, he served as a delegate to the Third Conference of American Republics in Rio de Janeiro. In 1910, he went to Brussels as a delegate to the Third International Conference on Maritime Law. He was also in 1910, a trustee of the Carnegie Institute, and the Carnegie Endowment for International Peace. He later served as vice president of the Endowment, as a member of its executive committee (1911-1935), assistant treasurer (1917-1923), and treasurer (1923-1929.) Among his other posts, he was president of the American Society for

Judicial Settlement of International Disputes in 1917, president of the American group of the Interparliamentary Union from 1930 to 1935, and a member of the council and executive committee of the American Institute of Law. Montague was elected to the U.S. House of Representatives in 1913, and served in that position until his death on January 24, 1937.

SWANSON, CLAUDE AUGUSTUS (1862-1933), governor (1906-1910), was born in Swansonville, Virginia on March 31, 1862, the son of John and Catherine (Prichett) Swanson. He attended public schools, and worked on his father's farm. From 1878 to 1880, he taught school. Then he enrolled in the Virginia Agricultural and Mechanical College in Blacksburg for a short time. He worked as a clerk in a grocery store for two years, and continued his studies, receiving his A.B. degree in 1885 from Randolph-Macon College, and an LL.B. degree in 1886 from the University of Virginia. He was admitted to the Virginia Bar, and began a law practice in Chatham. In 1894, he married Lizzie Deane Lyons.

Swanson entered politics in 1893 when he was elected as a Democrat to the U.S. House of Representatives. He served for seven consecutive terms, resigning in 1906. He ran for governor of Virginia in 1901, but was defeated. Four years later he ran again, and this time was elected by a vote of 84,235 to Republican challenger, Lunsford L. Lewis' 45,815 votes. During Swanson's term, strides were made in the area of education: funding for primary schools was increased; two teachers' colleges were created; and low interest loans were made available for the construction of high schools. Other developments included a street ban on cocaine, and the first use of electrocution instead of hanging as a means of capital punishment.

Swanson left office in 1910, and entered the U.S. Senate to fill a position left vacant by the death of John W. Daniel. He was elected to the position in his own right a short time later, and continued to serve until 1933, when he resigned to accept the post of Secretary of the Navy under President Franklin Roosevelt. He remained in that office until July 7, 1939, when he died while on a visit to a camp in the Blue Ridge Mountains, Madison County, Virginia. Swanson was married for a second time in 1923, to Lulie Lyons Hall. He had no children.

MANN, WILLIAM HODGES (1843-1927), governor (1910-1914), was born in Williamsburg, Virginia on July 30, 1843, the son of John and Mary (Bowers) Mann. He attended Brownsburg Academy until 1857, then served as deputy clerk for Nottoway County for three years. In 1861, at the beginning of the Civil War, he joined the Virginia Volunteers. He was wounded two years later at the Battle of Seven Pines, and left service and returned to his position as deputy clerk in Nottoway County. He studied law, and was admitted to the Virginia Bar in 1867. In 1869 he married Sallie Fitzgerald.

Mann was elected to serve as the first County Judge of Nottoway County. He held that post from 1870 to 1892. In 1885, after the death of his first wife, he married Etta Donnan. He had two

Governors

sons. Mann was elected to the Virginia Senate in 1899, and served until 1910. During that time, he authored the Mann Act, which put strict licensing regulations on bars, and closed about eight hundred saloons in areas where there was no police protection. He was elected Governor of Virginia in 1909. During his administration, he supported Prohibition, but saw a state-wide prohibition bill defeated in the State Senate. He also supported aid for public schools. In 1914, at the end of his term, he left office and returned to private life. He served as president of the Bank of Crewe, and president of the Citizens' Bank in Blackstone, Virginia. He died on December 12, 1927.

STUART, HENRY CARTER (1855-1933), governor of Virginia (1914-1918), was born in Wytheville, Virginia on January 18, 1855, the son of William and Mary (Carter) Stuart. He attended Emory and Henry College where he received his A.B. degree in 1874, then studied law for a year at the University of Virginia. After leaving the university, he managed his father's business concerns, and began to farm and to raise livestock. In time, he became well-known as the largest livestock breeder east of the Mississippi River. He was married in 1896 to Margaret Bruce Carter. They had one daughter.

In the years that followed, Stuart headed various businesses. He was president of the Stuart Land & Cattle Company of Virginia; president of the Buckhorn Coal Company; president of the First National Bank of Lebanon, Virginia; director of the State Planters' Bank & Trust company. He became involved in politics in 1901, when he served as a member of the State Constitutional Convention. The following year, he was appointed to the State Corporation Commission, a position he held from 1902 to 1908. In 1913, he ran for governor on the Democratic ticket, and was elected. He entered office in February, 1914. Serving during World War I, he gave priority to preparing the state's war machinery. He was a member of the price-fixing committee of the War Industries Board. In 1917, President Wilson appointed him chairman of the National Agricultural Advisory Commission.

He left office in 1918 at the end of his term. He and subsequently served as a representative to the National Industrial Conference, and was president of the Virginia Pay-as-you-go Association. He was offered a position on the Interstate Commerce Commission in 1920, but declined the appointment. He did, however, serve as chairman of the Emory and Henry College Board of Trustees. He died in Elk Garden, Virginia on July 24, 1933.

DAVIS, WESTMORELAND (1859-1942), governor (1918-1922), was born on August 21, 1859, the son of Thomas and Annie (Morris) Davis, on board a ship traveling to England. He attended the Virginia Military Institute, graduating in 1877. From there, he went on to study at the University of Virginia, and then Columbia University, where he received his LL.B. degree in 1886. He was admitted to the New York Bar that same year, and began to practice law in New York City. In 1892, he married Marguerite Inman.

As a practicing attorney in New York for fifteen years, he served as general counsel for the National Standard Insurance Company, the Lafayette Fire Insurance Company, Watson Elevator Company, and the Assurance Company of America. In 1901, he moved to Virginia and took up farming at a large estate in Leesburg. He became interested in studying scientific methods of farming, and in improving agriculural practices throughout the state. From 1908 to 1915, he was president of the Virginia State Farmers' Institute. In 1912, he served as Democratic presidential elector from Virginia's eighth district. He ran for governor in 1917 on the Democratic ticket and was elected. His administration was marked by widespread reforms: he created the executive budget system; overhauled the state prison system; and established the State Industrial Commission to administer worker's compensation. Also during his term, prohibition took effect in the state, and women were given the right to vote.

Davis left office in 1922 and became the editor and publisher of the *Southern Planter*. He remained in that position until his death in 1942. In addition, he was president of the Virginia State Farmers' Institute between 1923-24 and 1941-42, a member of the Virginia Polytechnic Institute Board of Visitors, and president of the Virginia State Fair Association. He died in Baltimore, Maryland on September 2, 1942.

TRINKLE, ELBERT LEE (1876-1939), governor (1922-1926), was born in Wytheville, Virginia on March 12, 1876, the son of Elbert and Letitia (Sexton) Trinkle. He attended Wytheville Military Academy, and then Hampden-Sydney College, where he received his A.B., and his B.S. degree in 1896. He went on to the University of Virginia Law School, and received his LL.B. degree in 1898. He was admitted to the Virginia Bar that same year, and began to practice law in Wytheville. In 1910, he married Helen Ball Sexton. They had four children.

Trinkle continued to practice in Wytheville until 1921. He was also served for various years as a partner in the Trinkle Brothers farming company, vice-president of the Shenandoah Life Insurance Company, director of the United Life & Accident Insurance Company, and vice-president of the American Life Insurance Convention. Trinkle became involved in politics in 1916 when he served as a Democratic Presidential Elector-at-Large. He ran for governor of Virginia in 1921, and was elected over Republican Henry Anderson. During his administration, Trinkle supported fiscal conservatism and required state institutions to operate on a pay-as-you-go basis. The Legislature instituted worker's compensation for state and city employees, raised teaching standards for public schools, and amended the Compulsory Education Act to apply to children up to fourteen years old. Trinkle was active as chairman of the Executive Committee of the Conference of Governors, and was recognized with a medal from

Governors

the National Committee on Prisons and Prison Labor for his work in establishing an exchange of prisonmade goods between states.
Trinkle left office in 1926 and served in various capacities both public and private over the next thirteen years. He was president of the Virginia State Boards of Education (1930-39); president of the Children's Home Society of Southwestern Virginia (1935-38); director of Southwestern Virginia, Inc.; and a trustee of Hampden-Sydney College. He died in Richmond, Virginia on November 25, 1939.

BYRD, HARRY FLOOD (1887-1966), governor (1926-1930), was born in Martinsburg, West Virginia on June 10, 1887, the son of Richard Evelyn and Elinor (Flood) Byrd. He attended Shenandoah Valley Academy in Winchester, Virginia. In 1902, he became manager of the *Winchester Star*. He became owner and publisher of the paper, and in 1907, established his own paper, the *Martinsburg Evening Journal*. He also founded the Winchester Storage Company. From 1908 to 1918, he was president of the Valley Turnpike Company. He was married in October, 1913, to Annie Douglas Beverly. They had four children.
Byrd was elected to the Virginia State Senate and served from 1915 to 1925. He was also the Virginia Fuel Commissioner in 1918, and was chairman of the Democratic State Committee in 1922. In 1923, he became publisher of the *Harrisonburg Daily News-Record*. He ran for governor in 1925, and won by a wide margin against Republican opponent, S. Harris Hoge. During Byrd's term, the Legislature trimmed government by abolishing over thirty boards, commissions and bureaus, and brought government activities under the control of twelve departments. The Legislature also approved the reform measure known as the "short ballot," which limited the number of elected state officials to three: the governor, lieutenant governor, and attorney general. Also during Byrd's administration: lynching was made an offense against the state, and tax laws were revised.
Since he was constitutionally ineligible to succeed himself, Byrd left the governorship at the end of his term in 1930. In 1933, he was appointed to the U.S. Senate, to fill the vacancy left by the resignation of Claude Swanson. Byrd was elected in his own right in the subsequent election, and maintained his Senate seat until 1965. He died on October 20 of the following year in Berryville, Virginia.

POLLARD, JOHN GARLAND (1871-1937), governor (1930-1934), was born in King and Queen County, Virginia on August 4, 1871, the son of John and Virginia (Bagby) Pollard. He attended Richmond College and graduated in 1891, then went on to Columbian (later George Washington) University Law School where he received his LL.B. degree in 1893. He was admitted to the Virginia Bar that same year, and began to practice law in Richmond. In 1898, he married Grace Phillips. They had three children.
Pollard continued his law practice in Richmond for twenty-five years. During that period, he also was president of the Capitol Savings Bank; director of the Bank of Commerce & Trusts, the Peninsula Bank & Trust Company, the National Bank of

Virginia, Central National Bank, and Old Dominion Trust Company; and vice-president and managing director of the American Terminal Warehouse Corporation. Pollard was a member of the Virginia Constitutional Convention in 1901. From 1902 to 1907, he served as chairman of the Virginia Commission on Uniform State Laws. He was a Democratic Elector in 1904. From 1913 to 1917, he served as Attorney General of Virginia, and at the same time, as a member of the State Board of Education. He ran for governor, but failing in this effort, decided to go to France and Germany where he did World War I assistance work from 1918 to 1919. Upon his return, he was chosen as a member of the War Department's Board of Contract Adjustment. From 1920 to 1921 he was a member of the Federal Trade Commission. In 1922, he taught constitutional law and history, and in 1923, he was a professor of government and citizenship at the College of William and Mary. He was made dean of the Marshall Wythe School of Government and Citizenship from 1924 to 1929.

In 1929, running as a Democratic candidate, he was elected Governor of Virginia. His administration was marked by the implementation of economic measures designed to offset the effects of the Great Depression. The measures included reducing his own salary by ten percent and establishing a pay-as-you-go program to improve state resources without a tax increase. When violence broke out during a strike of four thousand workers at the Riverside and Dan River textile mills in Danville, Governor Pollard sent in state troops to restore order.

Pollard married Violet McDougall in 1933, his second wife. He left office the following year. During the next three years, he served as chairman of the U.S. Board of Veteran's Appeals. He was the author of several works, including: *The Pamunkey Indians of Virginia* (1894); *Virginia Code, Annotated* (1904); *Virginia Law Register* (1904 and 1906); and *A Connotary* (1935). Pollard died in Washington, D.C. on April 28, 1937.

PEERY, GEORGE CAMPBELL (1873-1952), governor (1934-1938), was born in Cedar Bluff, Virginia on October 28, 1873, the son of James and Mary (Spotts) Peery. He graduated from Emory and Henry College in 1894 with a B.S. degree. From 1894 to 1896, he was principal of Tazewell High School. He then returned to college, attending Washington and Lee University, and received his LL.B. degree in 1897. He was admitted to the Virginia Bar and began to practice law in Tazewell. In 1899, he went to work for the legal department of the Virginia Iron, Coal & Coke Company. He moved to Wise, Virginia in 1902, and from 1904 to 1915 was a member of the law firm of Vicars & Peery. In 1907, he married Nanie Bane Pendleton. They had three children.

Peery moved back to Tazewell in 1915, and joined the firm of Chapman, Peery & Buchanan, remaining with that practice until 1930. During that time he also served in various other business capacities, including: vice-president and director of Norton Hardware Company; director of Coeburn Home Company, Inc.; secretary and director of Banner Raven Coal Corporation; director of the Buckhorn Coal Company; director of Hazard Coal Cor-

Governors

poration; and director of the Richmond, Fredericksburg & Potomac Railroad Company. He became involved in politics in 1916 when he was a Democratic Presidential Elector-at-Large. In 1920 and 1924, he was a delegate to the Democratic National Convention. He was elected to the U.S. House of Representatives in 1923, and served until 1929. In 1928, he was made temporary chairman of the Democratic State Convention. He was a member of the Virginia State Corporation Commission from 1929 to 1933. In the latter year, he ran for governor, and was elected in an easy victory over Republican, Fred McWane.

As governor, Peery supported increased funding for public schools. He also appointed the first members of the State Alcoholic Beverage Control Board, the State Milk Commission, and the Unemployment Compensation Commission. Other accomplishments during his term included reorganization of the Conservation Commission, and the establishment of the trial justice system in Virginia. Peery left office in 1938 and retired to his livestock farm near Tazewell. He died in Richlands, Virginia on October 14, 1952.

PRICE, JAMES HUBERT (1878-1943), governor (1938-1942), was born in Greenbriar County, West Virginia on September 7, 1878, the son of Charles and Nancy (Boone) Price. His family moved to Staunton, Virginia, and he attended Dunsmore Business College there, and later taught at the College for a short time. He was secretary-treasurer and director of the insurance firm, W. J. Perry Corporation, before attending law school at Washington and Lee University. He graduated with his LL.B. degree in 1909, was admitted to the Virginia Bar that same year, and began to practice law in Richmond. Shortly thereafter, he became a member of the Richmond Democratic Committee, and served as its chairman for three years. From 1904 to 1913, he served in the Virginia National Guard, where he rose to the rank of captain and commissary of the First Infantry. He was a legal advisor to the Richmond local draft boards during World War I. Also, about that time, in October, 1918, he married Lillian Martin. They had two children.

Price was elected to the Virginia House of Delegates in 1915, and served until 1928. He was Lieutenant Governor of Virginia from 1930 to 1938, and then went on to the governorship, elected on November 2, 1937, as a Democrat to fill that post. During his administration, the state Social Security Act was adopted and a judicial retirement act was passed. A merit system was also set up for public service work. Other accomplishments included the construction of the Supreme Court building, the state library, and a new building for the Medical College of Virginia. Price ended his term in 1942 with a surplus of about fourteen million dollars in the state treasury.

After leaving office, he became a director of the Central National Bank of Richmond and of the Jefferson Realty Company. He died in Richmond on November 22, 1943.

DARDEN, COLGATE WHITEHEAD (1897-), governor (1942-1946), was born near Franklin, Virginia on February 11, 1897, the son of Colgate Whitehead and Katherine (Pretlow) Darden. He was educated at the University of Virginia where he received his B.A. in 1922, and Columbia University, where he received his M.A. and LL.B. degrees in 1923. During World War I, he served as an ambulance driver with the French Army, as a member of the American Ambulance Corps, in the aviation branch of the U.S. Navy, and finally as a fighter pilot with the U.S. Marine Corps. Returning after the war, he was admitted to the Virginia Bar in 1922, and began to practice law in Norfolk. In 1923, he received a Carnegie Fellowship to study international law at Oxford University for a year. He was married in 1927 to Constance duPont. They had three children.

Darden was elected to the Virginia House of Delegates, and served from 1930 to 1933. He also served in the U.S. House of Representatives, from 1933 to 1937, and once again, from 1939 to 1941. In the latter year, he ran for governor of Virginia, and was elected by a wide margin over Republican opponent B. Muse. During his term, strides were made in the area of education as the state made appropriations to purchase visual aids for public schools, and to assist blacks who wanted to study medicine at Meharry Medical College in Tennessee. Ineligible constitutionally to succeed himself as governor, Darden left office in 1946 and became chancellor of the College of William and Mary. In addition, he was vice-chairman, and later chairman, of the Navy's Civilian Advisory Committee. He became president of the University of Virginia in 1947, remaining until 1959, when he retired into private life.

TUCK, WILLIAM MUNFORD (1896-), governor (1946-1950), was born in Halifax County, Virginia on September 28, 1896, the son of Robert and Virginia (Fitts) Tuck. He attended the College of William and Mary from 1915 to 1917, then entered the U.S. Marines as a private during World War I. On his return after the war, he studied law at Washington and Lee University, and graduated with an LL.B. degree in 1921. He was admitted to the Virginia Bar that same year, and began to practice law in South Boston, Virginia. In 1928, he married Eva (Lovelace) Dillard.

Tuck became involved in politics about 1920, when he was a delegate to the Democratic Convention. He was a delegate to numerous subsequent conventions. In 1923 he was elected to the Virginia House of Delegates. He served from 1924 to 1932, then held a seat in the State Senate for ten years. He was a Democratic elector-at-large in 1936. In 1941, he was elected Lieutenant Governor of Virginia, a post he retained from 1942 to 1946. Tuck ran for governor on the Democratic ticket in 1945, and defeated his Republican opponent, S. Lloyd Landreth by a vote of more than two to one. During his administration, Tuck sought to limit the power of unions, and secured the passage of legislation which outlawed the reemployment of any public worker for one year after that employee had gone on strike, made it "against public policy" for a public official to bargain with a labor union, and made it illegal to require union membership as a condition of employment. As a means of avoiding a strike at the Virginia Electric and Power Company, Governor Tuck declared 1,600 essential workers from the plant to be part of the state's "unorganized militia." Also during his term, Tuck came out against grants from Congress for most highways, and supported the elimination of the federal gasoline tax in favor of a state gasoline tax.

At the end of his term, in 1950, Tuck returned to his law practice. He was a delegate-at-large to the 1948 and 1952 Democratic National Conventions. He was elected to the U.S. House of Representatives in 1953, and remained in Congress until 1969, when he returned to his law practice in South Boston, Virginia.

BATTLE, JOHN STEWART (1890-1972), governor (1950-1954), was born in New Bern, North Carolina on July 11, 1890, the son of Rev. Dr. Henry and Margaret (Stewart) Battle. He received his education at Wake Forest College and the University of Virginia, where he graduated with an LL.B. degree in 1913. He was admitted to the Virginia Bar that same year, and began to practice law in Charlottesville. During World War I, he was a private in the U.S. Army. In 1918, he married Mary Jane Lipscomb. They had two children.

Battle was elected to the Virginia House of Delegates and served from 1930 to 1934. In the latter year, he became a member of the State Senate, where he remained until 1950. In 1949, he ran for governor as a Democrat and won easily over Republican Walter Johnson. During his administration, Battle supported expansion of local health care programs; funding for mental hospitals; and higher salaries for teachers. At the outbreak of the Korean War, he reinstated the State Council of Defense. Other developments during his term included new legislation which provided funding for school construction, and gave power to the governor to seize coal mines for state operation in the event it became necessary.

Battle left office at the end of his term in 1954, and joined the law firm of Perkins, Battle and Minor. He was a member of the Civil Rights Commission in 1959. He died in Albemarle County, Virginia on April 9, 1972.

STANLEY, THOMAS BAHNSON (1890-1970), governor (1954-1958), was born near Spencer, Virginia on July 16, 1890, the son of Crockett and Susan (Walker) Stanley. He attended public schools in Spencer, then went to work in the coal mines in Maybeury, West Virginia. After a short time, he moved to Poughkeepsie, New York and attended the Eastman National Business College. After his graduation in 1912, he became a bookkeeper for the R.J. Reynolds Tobacco Company in Winston-Salem, North Carolina for a year. He worked as a clerk for the Bank of Ridgeway, Virginia in 1913; a clerk-bookkeeper for the First National Bank in Martinsville, Virginia from 1914 to 1916; and a cashier for the First National Bank in Rural Retreat, Virginia from 1916 to 1920. In 1918, he married Anne Pocahontas Bassett. They had three children.

Stanley moved to Galax, Virginia and became vice-president of the Vaughan-Bassett Furniture Company from 1921 to 1922. He was vice-president of the Bassett Furniture Company, Inc. from 1922 to 1924, and then established his own business, the Stanley Furniture Company, Inc. in 1924. He was also president of the Ferrum Veneer Corporation, and director of Virginia & Forests, Inc. for a time. In 1929 he was elected to the Virginia House of Delegates where he served from 1930 to 1946, acting as speaker from 1942 to 1946. He was subsequently elected to the U.S. House of Representatives, and held that position from 1946 to 1953. In the latter year, he was elected Governor of Virginia, defeating Republican candidate Ted Dalton.

During his administration, Stanley supported an increased gasoline tax to raise funds for state highways, and advocated higher salaries for teachers. He spoke out in favor of federal funding to maintain interstate highways, and signed legislation to restrict billboards along state roads. He also joined with eight governors from coal-producing states to ask Congress to limit imports of oil and natural gas. He left office in 1958, and returned to his business interests. In the years that followed, he became president and director of the First National Bank in Bassett, Virginia, and chairman of the Commission on State and Local Revenues and Expenditures. He was also a trustee of Randolph-Macon College. He died in Martinsville, Virginia on July 10, 1970.

ALMOND, JAMES LINDSAY (1898-), governor (1958-1962), was born in Charlottesville, Virginia on June 15, 1898, the son of James and Edmonia (Burgess) Almond. He attended the University of Virginia during World War I and served in the Students' Army Training Corps as a private. In 1923, he received his LL.B. degree from the University of Virginia. Meanwhile, in 1919, he worked as a school teacher in Locust Grove, Virginia, and from 1921 to 1922, he was principal of Zoar High School. He was admitted to the Virginia Bar in 1921, and began to practice law in Roanoke. In 1925, he married Josephine Katherine Minter.

Almond continued with his Roanoke law practice until 1930 when he became assistant commonweath's attorney of Virginia. He remained at that post until 1933 when he was made judge of the Hustings Court of Roanoke City. In 1945, he was elected to the U.S. House of Representatives and served from 1946 to 1948. He resigned the House in order to become Attorney General of Virginia, an office he held from 1948 to 1957. In November of the latter year, he ran for governor of Virginia on the Democratic ticket and won easily over Republican contender, Ted Dalton.

Almond's administration was marked by the controversy over racial integration. The Virginia Legislature attempted to diffuse the federal order for integration of public schools by repealing the compulsory school attendance law. It also offered tuition grants of $250 per year for students who attended private nonsectarian schools. At the same time, it attempted to keep the peace by imposing stiff penalties for bomb threats to houses, schools and other buildings. Other developments during Almond's term included increases to unemployment benefits and worker's compensation, and pay raises for teachers.

Governors

Almond left office in 1962 and soon afterward was appointed interim judge of the U.S. Court of Customs and Patent Appeals. He served as associate judge of that court from 1963 to 1973 when he retired into private life.

HARRISON, ALBERTIS SYDNEY (1907-), governor (1962-1966), was born in Alberta, Virginia on January 11, 1907, the son of Albertis Sydney and Lizzie (Goodrich) Harrison. He attended the University of Virginia and graduated with an LL.B. degree in 1928. That same year, he was admitted to the Virginia Bar. In 1930, he was the city attorney for Lawrenceville, Virginia. Also, in May of that year, he married Lacey Barkley. They had two children.

Harrison was the commonwealth's attorney for Brunswick County, Virginia from 1932 to 1948, taking time out during World War II to serve as a lieutenant in the U.S. Navy. In 1947, he was elected to the Virginia State Senate and served from 1948 to 1957, when he was elected State Attorney General. In 1961, he ran for governor on the Democratic ticket, and was elected over Republican H. Clyde Pearson. During his administration, funding for public schools was increased, and the daylight savings time bill was enacted. The governor's office took over responsibility for industrial development from the Department of Conservation and Economic Development. Also, the Kerr-Mills hospitalization program for the elderly was established.

Since he was ineligible constitutionally to run for a second term, Harrison left office in 1966. The following year, he was appointed Justice of the Virginia Supreme Court. In 1968, he was a member of the Commission to Revise the Constitution of Virginia. He was also a member of the Board of Visitors of the University of Virginia, and a fellow of the American College of Trial Lawyers.

GODWIN, MILLS EDWIN (1914-), governor (1966-1970), (1974-1978) was born in Chuckatuck, Virginia on November 19, 1914, the son of Mills Edwin and Otelia (Darden) Godwin. He attended the College of William and Mary division in Norfolk and later in Williamsburg, then went on to the University of Virginia where he received his LL.B. degree in 1938. He was admitted to the Virginia Bar, and began to practice law in Suffolk, Virginia. In 1940, he married Katherine Beale. They had one child.

Godwin maintained his Suffolk law practice from 1938 to 1960. During that time he was also a special agent for the Federal Bureau of Investigation from 1942 to 1946; a member of the Virginia House of Delegates from 1947 to 1952; and a member of the State Senate from 1952 to 1961. He was elected Lieutenant Governor of Virginia in the latter year, and served from 1962 to 1966. In the November 1965 election, he ran for governor on the Democratic ticket and defeated Republican, Linwood Holton and Conservative candidate, William J. Story, Jr. During his administration, Godwin was a strong supporter of education. He became known as "Virginia's Education Governor" for his work to establish a community college system, increase salaries and other benefits for teachers, provide schooling for the handicapped, and fund kindergartens. He also, following programs set down by Gov. Albertis Harrison, promoted industrial development and attempted to attract new businesses to Virginia.

Since he was ineligible to succeed himself in office, he returned to his business interests in 1970. He was director of the Western Railway Company; director of Standard Brands, Inc. of Norfolk; director of the Union Camp Corporation; director of the Virginia Real Estate Investment Trust; director of Dan River, Inc.; and a member of the Executive Committee and Board of Directors of the Virginia National Bank. He ran for a second term as governor in 1973, this time on the Republican ticket, and was elected in a narrow victory over Independent, Henry Howell. During his second term, the Equal Rights Amendment was defeated in committee, and legislation to permit collective bargaining by public employees, and to allow "death with dignity" was defeated.

Godwin completed his second term in 1978. During his career he has received numerous awards, including the First Citizen's Award of Suffolk and Nansemond County; the Virginia State Chamber of Commerce's Distinguished Service Award; the Virginia National Guard's Distinguished Citizen's Medal; the Thomas Jefferson Award for Public Service, and honorary degrees from Elon College, the College of William and Mary, Roanoke College, Washington and Lee University, Elmira College, Hampden-Sydney College, the University of Richmond, and Bridgewater College.

HOLTON, ABNER LINWOOD (1923-), governor (1970-1974), was born in Big Stone Gap, Virginia on September 21, 1923, the son of Abner Linwood and Edith (Van Gorder) Holton. He attended Washington and Lee University and received his B.A. degree in 1944. During World War II, he served as an apprentice seaman in the submarine force of the U.S. Navy. After the war, he entered Harvard University Law School and graduated with an LL.B. degree in 1949. He was admitted to the Virginia Bar, and began to practice law in Roanoke with the firm of Hunter and Fox. He later formed the new firm of Eggleston, Holton, Butler and Glenn with three partners. In 1953, he married Virginia Harrison Rogers. They had four children.

Holton became involved in politics, and during the 1950's was chairman of the Roanoke City Republican Committee. He ran for the House of Delegates in 1955 and 1957, but was defeated in both campaigns. In 1960, he was elected vice-chairman of the Virginia Republican Central Committee. He was also a delegate to the Republican National Conventions of 1960 and 1968, and was a regional coordinator for Richard Nixon's presidential campaign. Holton ran for governor in 1965, but was defeated by Democratic candidate, Mills Godwin. He ran again in 1969, and this time won the election, and was inaugurated on January 17, 1970. During his administration, Holton established the Judicial Inquiry and Review Commission. The Legislature increased corporate, gasoline, and income taxes; provided funding for low-

Governors

cost housing; made appropriations for higher education; lowered the age of majority to eighteen except for liquor purchases and jury duty; reduced penalties for possession of marijuana; and rejected ratification of the Equal Rights Amendment. Also during Holton's term, the State Constitution was revised and amendments were added to: limit the appointive powers of judges, establish yearly legislative sessions, decrease the residency requirement for voting, and to bar govermental discrimination based on race, sex, religion or national origin.

Holton left office in 1974, and was soon after named Assistant Secretary of State for Congressional Relations. He served in that position for ten months, then went back to practicing law.

DALTON, JOHN NICHOLAS (1931-), governor (1978-1982), was born in Emporia, Virginia on July 11, 1931, the son of Ted and Mary (Turner) Dalton. He attended William and Mary College and received his A.B. degree in 1953. He subsequently served in the U.S. Army from 1954 to 1956, where he attained the rank of first lieutenant. He returned to school, attending the University of Virginia, and in 1957, graduated with a J.D. degree. He was admitted to the Virginia Bar, and became a partner in the law firm of Dalton and Jebo in Radford, Virginia. In 1956, he married Edwina Panzer. They had four children.

Dalton continued with the law firm of Dalton and Jebo until 1974. Meanwhile, he was also active in various businesses. He was vice-president and director of Meredith and Tate in Pulaski; director of Sutton Development Corporation in Radford; and director of the First Merchant Bank in Radford. He entered politics around 1960 when he served as president of the Young Republican Federation of Virginia. He was treasurer of the Virginia Republican Committee that same year, and from 1961 to 1972, was general counsel for the Virginia Republican Committee. In 1965, he was elected to the Virginia House of Delegates. He remained at that post until 1972, then served a year in the Virginia Senate. From 1974 to 1978, he was Lieutenant Governor of Virginia, and in the following gubernatorial election, he ran as a Republican, and won over Democrat, Henry Howell.

Dalton entered office in January, 1978. As governor, he cut federally funded programs for the mentally handicapped, made general reductions to Medicaid payments, and vetoed the use of Medicaid in abortions for rape and incest. Later however, in 1981, when the Virginia State Treasury was showing a surplus, he supported restoration of some funding to Medicaid, and salary increases for state employees. He also secured a higher gasoline sales tax to finance highway construction and the Washington, D.C. area subway system, and he created a program to help needy people pay their heating bills. Dalton left office in 1982, and returned to private life.

ROBB, CHARLES SPITTAL (1939-), governor (1982-1986), was born in Phoenix, Arizona on June 26, 1939, the son of James and Frances (Woolley) Robb. He was educated at Cornell University, and at the University of Wisconsin where he received his B.A.A.

degree in 1961. He served in the U.S. Marine Corp during the Vietnam War, and in 1967, married Lynda Bird Johnson, daughter of President Lyndon B. Johnson. They have three children.

After his return from Vietnam in 1970, Robb attended the University of Virginia Law School. While still at law school, he became director of the LBJ Company. He graduated from the University of Virginia in 1973, and was admitted to the Virginia Bar. He served as a law clerk for a short time, then joined the Washington, D.C. law firm of Williams, Connally and Califano in 1974. He also became deputy general counsel and assistant parliamentarian for the Democratic National Committee's Platform Committee. In 1977, he was elected as a Democrat to serve as Lieutenant Governor of Virginia under Republican Governor Dalton. Robb ran for the governorship in 1981 and was elected over J. Marshall Coleman. As governor, Robb came out in favor of budget cuts to alleviate the national deficit, and sought to make Virginia a leader in racial progress. The interest ceiling on credit card transactions was raised during his term, and approval was given for "no-fault" divorces after a waiting period of six months. Ineligible constitutionally to succeed himself, Robb left office in 1986. In 1985, he helped found the Democratic Leadership Council. He currently serves as chairman of its board of directors.

BALILES, GERALD L. (1940-), governor (1986-1989) , was born in Patrick County, Virginia on July 8, 1940. He grew up on his grandparents' farm and attended local public schools. At age fifteen, he left Patrick County to attend Fishburne Military School in Waynesboro, Virginia. He went on to Wesleyan University in Connecticut, where he earned his undergraduate degree in 1963, and then to the University of Virginia, where he received his law degree in 1967. About that time, he was married to Jeannie Patterson. They have two children.

Between 1967 and 1975, Baliles worked in the Virginia Attorney General's Office as an Assistant Attorney General and then Deputy Attorney General. In 1975 he was elected to the Virginia House of Delegates, and served until 1982. He became Virginia Attorney General in the latter year, and while in office served as chairman of the Southern Association of Attorneys General. In 1985, he ran for governor, and won in a historic Democratic victory that included the election of the first black Lieutenant Governor of Virginia, and the first woman Attorney General. As governor, Baliles has been a strong proponent of environmental issues, and has made efforts to end pollution of Chesapeake Bay. Other of his initiatives include a major transportation program to improve roads, seaports, airports and mass transit; projects to fight illiteracy; and an emphasis on international trade and educational reforms to promote competition in world markets.

WILDER, LAWRENCE DOUGLAS (1931-), Governor of Virginia (1990-) was born in Richmond, Virginia on January 17, 1931. He is the grandson of slaves and was named after Frederick Douglass and poet Paul Lawrence Dunbar. He attended Virginia Union

Governors

University, earning a B.S. degree in chemistry in 1951, then continued his studies at Howard University School of Law where he received a J.D. degree in 1959. That same year, he became a founder of the law firm of Wilder, Gregory and Martin, where he remained a partner until his victory for the governorship.

His first foray into politics was his successful bid for a Senate seat in 1969, on the Democratic ticket. Wilder was then elected to his post for an additional four terms. During his years in the Senate, he served as chairman on such committees as: Senate Committee on Transportation; Senate Committee on Rehabilitation and Social Services; Senate Committee on Privileges and Elections; Virginia Advisory Legislative Council; and Democratic Steering Committee. A popular political figure, he was consistently named as one of the most effective government officials in an annual survey conducted by the Norfolk *Virginian-Pilot*.

Some of the major legislation he was directly involved in during his senatorial tenure included: prohibiting or regulating the possession, sale or distribution of drug paraphernalia; requiring that the disease of sickle cell anemia be placed under the jurisdiction of the State Health Department; establishing a state holiday in honor of the late Dr. Martin Luther King, Jr. on January 15; requiring detailed investigations concerning discriminatory housing practices; and establishing severe penalties, including additional time, for prisoners that escape, or who have committed capital crimes.

In 1985, Wilder was elected Lieutenant Governor of Virginia. While in that office, he served as chairman of both the National Democratic Lieutenant Governors' Association, and of the National Conference of Lieutenant Governors' Drug Interdiction Task Force.

Wilder was elected Governor of the State of Virginia in the November, 1989 race. Right before the general election, he was lauded by several newspapers, including the Washington *Post*, whose editor stated: "Mr. Wilder is an uncommon figure in contemporary politics in that he has not ridden the media to his present position but has worked his way up, has served a long, and we believe valuable, apprenticeship." The Charlottesville *Daily Progress* concurred, saying: "Mr. Wilder comes to us after more than 19 years in public office, where he has proven his mettle and shown, if anything, he is his own man. Wilder's famous eyeball-to-eyeball confrontations with his own party's power structure have inspired respect among friends and political opponents. Like his two predecessors, he has a reputation among colleagues as a consensus builder and strong inside player."

Some of the professional organizations he is a member of include: the American Bar Association; the Virginia State Bar; the American Trial Lawyers Association; and the National Association of Criminal Defense Lawyers. He is also a Permanent Member of the Judicial Conference of the Fourth Circuit (federal), and a Life Member of the National Bar Association.

Governor Wilder served in the United States Army, and was awarded the Bronze Star for heroism in ground combat in Korea. He has three children: Lynn, Lawrence, Jr., and Loren.

UNITED STATES SENATORS from VIRGINIA

ARCHER, WILLIAM SEGAR (1789-1855), a U.S. Senator and Representative from Virginia; born at "The Lodge," Amelia County, Va., March 5, 1789; (nephew of Joseph Eggleston), received private instruction; was graduated from William and Mary College, Williamsburg, Va., in 1806; studied law; was admitted to the bar in 1810 and practiced in Amelia and Powhatan Counties; served four terms in the State house of delegates between 1812 and 1819; elected to the Sixteenth Congress to fill the vacancy caused by the resignation of James Pleasants; reelected to the Seventeenth and to the six succeeding Congresses (January 3, 1820-March 3, 1835); unsuccessful candidate for reelection in 1834 to the Twenty-fourth Congress; chairman, Committee on Foreign Affairs (Twenty-first through Twenty-third Congresses); elected as a Whig to the United States Senate and served from March 4, 1841, to March 3, 1847; unsuccessful candidate for reelection in 1846; chairman, Committee on Foreign Affairs (Twenty-seventh Congress); resumed the practice of law; died at "The Lodge," in Amelia County, Va., March 28, 1855; interment in a private cemetary at "The Lodge."

BARBOUR, JAMES (1775-1842), a U.S. Senator from Virginia; born at "Frascati," near Gordonsville, Orange County, Va., June 10, 1775; (brother of Philip Pendleton Barbour and cousin of John Strode Barbour), attended the common schools; deputy sheriff of Orange County; studied law; was admitted to the bar in 1794 at Orange Court House; served several terms in the Virginia house of delegates between 1796 and 1812, serving as speaker from 1809 to 1812; Governor of Virginia 1812-1814; elected as an Anti-Democrat and State Rights candidate to the United States Senate in 1814 for the term commencing March 4, 1815; subsequently elected to fill the vacancy in the term ending March 3, 1815, caused by the death of Richard Brent; reelected in 1821 and served from January 2, 1815, to March 7, 1825, when he resigned to accept a Cabinet portfolio; served as President pro tempore of the Senate during the Fifteenth and Sixteenth Congresses; chairman, Committee on Foreign Relations (Fifteenth, Sixteenth, and Eighteenth Congresses), Committee on the District of Columbia (Seventeenth Congress); appointed Secretary of War by President John Quincy Adams and served from March 7, 1825, to May 26, 1828, when he resigned to accept a diplomatic position; United States Minister to England from May 26, 1828, to September 23, 1829; chairman of the Whig National Convention in 1839; founder of the Orange County Humane Society, established for the advancement of education; died in Barboursville, Orange County, Va., June 7, 1842; interment in the family cemetary.

BARBOUR, JOHN STRODE, JR. (1820-1892); a U.S. Senator from Virginia; born at "Catalpa," near Culpeper, Culpeper County, Va., December 29, 1821; (son of John Strode Barbour) attended the common schools and was graduated from the law department of the University of Virginia at Charlottesville; was admitted to the bar in 1841 and commenced practice in Culpeper; member of the State house of delegates 1847-1851; president of the Orange & Alexandria Railroad Co. 1852-1881; elected as a Democrat to the Forty-seventh, and the two succeeding Congresses (March 4, 1881-March 3, 1887); chairman, Committee on the District of Columbia (Forty-eighth and Forty-ninth Congresses); declined to be a candidate for renomination in 1886; elected as a Democrat to the United States Senate and served from March 4, 1889, until his death in Washington, D.C., May 14, 1892; interment in the burial ground at "Popular Hill," Prince Georges County, Md.

BOWDEN, LEMUEL JACKSON (1815-1864), a U.S. Senator from Virginia; born in Williamsburg, James City County, Va., January 16, 1815; (uncle of George Edwin Bowden), graduated from William and Mary College, Williamsburg, Va.; studied law;; was admitted to the bar in 1838 and commenced practice in Williamsburg; member, State house of delegates 1841-1846; delegate to the Virginia constitutional conventions in 1849 and 1851; elected as a Republican to the United States Senate and served from March 4, 1863, until his death in Washington, D.C., on January 2, 1864; interment in Congressional Cemetery.

BRENT, RICHARD (1757-1814), a U.S. Senator from Virginia; born at "Richland," on the Potomac River, at Aquia Creek, Stafford County, Va., in 1757; studied law; (uncle of William Leigh Brent and nephew of Daniel Carroll), was admitted to the bar and practiced; member of the Virginia house of delegates from Stafford County in 1788 and from Prince William County in 1793, 1794, 1800, and 1801; elected to the Fourth and Fifth Congresses (March 4, 1795-March 3, 1799); elected again to the Seventh Congress (March 4, 1801-March 3, 1803); member, State senate 1808-1810; elected to the United States Senate and served from March 4, 1809, until his death in Washington, D.C., on December 30, 1814; interment in the family burial ground at "Richland," on the Potomac River, at Aquia Creek.

BURCH, THOMAS GRANVILLE (1869-1951), a U.S. Senator and Representative from Virginia; born on a farm near Dyer's Store, in Henry County, Va., July 3, 1869; attended the public schools; engaged in agricultural pursuits and in the tobacco manufacturing

U. S. Senators

business; move to Martinsville, Va., in 1886 and engaged in the banking business; also interested in the insurance real estate businesses; member of the State board of agriculture 1910-1913; mayor of Martinsville, Va., 1912-1914; United States marshal for the western district of Virginia 1914-1921; member of the commission in 1927 to simplify and reorganize the State government; served with the State transportation and public utility advisory commission in 1929; member of the State board of education in 1930 and 1931; elected as a Democrat to the Seventy-second Congress and to the seven succeeding Congresses and served from March 4, 1931, to May 31, 1946, when he resigned; chairman, Committee on Post Office and Post Roads (Seventy-eighth and Seventy-ninth Congresses); appointed to the United States Senate to fill the vacancy caused by the death of Carter Glass and served from May 31, 1946, until November 5, 1946, when a duly elected successor qualified; was not a candidate for election to the vacancy in 1946; chairman of Governor's Commission on Reorganization of the State Government in 1947; resumed his business pursuits; died in Martinsville, Va., March 20, 1951; interment in Oakwood Cemetery.

BYRD, HARRY FLOOD (1887-1966), a U.S. Senator from Virginia; born in Martinsburg, Berkeley County, W. Va., June 10, 1887; (father of Harry Flood Byrd, Jr., and nephew of Henry De La Warr Flood and Joel West Flood), moved with his parents to Winchester, Va., in 1887; attended the public schools and Shenandoah Valley Academy at Winchester, Va.; entered the newspaper publishing business in 1903 and became publisher of the Winchester (Va.) Star; also engaged extensively in agricultural pursuits near Berryville, Va., in 1906, specializing in growing and storing apples and peaches; president of the Valley Turnpike Co. 1908-1918; member, State senate 1915-1925; State fuel commissioner in 1918; was elected chairman of the Democratic State Committee in 1922; Governor of Virginia 1926-1930; Democratic National committeeman 1928-1940; was appointed March 4, 1933, and subsequently elected as a Democrat to the United States Senate to fill the vacancy caused by the resignation of Claude A. Swanson; was reelected in 1934, 1940, 1946, 1952, 1958, and 1964, and served from March 4, 1933, until his resignation November 10, 1965; chairman, Committee on Rules (Seventy-seventh through Seventy-ninth Congresses), Committee on Finance (Eighty-fourth through Eighty-ninth Congresses), Joint Committee on the Reduction of Nonessential Federal Expenditures (Eightieth through Eighty-ninth Congresses), Joint Committee on Internal Revenue Taxation (Eighty-fourth through Eighty-ninth Congresses); died in Berryville, Va., October 20, 1966; interment in Mount Hebron Cemetery, Winchester, Va.

BYRD, HARRY FLOOD, JR. (1914 -), a U.S. Senator from Virginia; born in Winchester, Va., December 20, 1914; (son of Harry Flood Bryd, Sr.) educated at Virginia Military Institute and the University of Virginia; newspaper editor and fruit grower; member of Democratic State central committee

1940-1965; during the Second World War, served in the United States Naval Reserve as a lieutenant commander; member, State senate 1948-1965; appointed as a Democrat to the United States Senate November 12, 1965, to fill the vacancy caused by the resignation of his father, Harry Flood Byrd, and was subsequently elected on November 8, 1966, to fill the unexpired term ending January 3, 1971; reelected as an Independent in 1970 and in 1976 and served from November 12, 1965, to January 2, 1983; was not a candidate for reelection in 1982; is a resident of Winchester, Va.

CARLILE, JOHN SNYDER (1817-1861), a U.S. Senator and Representative from Virginia; born in Winchester, Va., on December 16, 1817; educated by his mother; clerked in a store and commenced business for himself in 1834; studied law; was admitted to the bar in 1840 and commenced practice in Beverly, Va. (now West Virginia) in 1842; moved to Philippi and later to Clarksburg and continued the practice of law; member, State senate 1847-1851; delegate to the State constitutional convention in 1850; elected as the candidate of the American Party to the Thirty-fourth Congress (March 4, 1855-March 3, 1857); delegate to the State secession convention in February 1861; elected as a Unionist to the Thirty-seventh Congress and served from March 4, 1861, until July 9, 1861, when he resigned to become Senator; elected as a Unionist to the United States Senate to fill the vacancy caused by the retirement of Robert M. T. Hunter and served from July 9, 1861, to March 3, 1865; member of the convention that submitted the new State ordinance in August 1861; died in Clarksburg, Harrison County, W. Va., October 24, 1878; interment in Odd Fellows Cemetary.

DANIEL, JOHN WARWICK (1842-1910), a U.S. Senator and Representative from Virginia; born in Lynchburg, Va., September 5, 1842; attended private schools, Lynchburg College, and Dr. Gessner Harrison's University School; during the Civil War served in the Confederate Army 1861-1864, attained the rank of major; permanently crippled in the Battle of the Wilderness in May 1864; studied law at the University of Virginia at Charlottesville; was admitted to the bar in 1866 and commenced practice at Lynchburg, Va.; member, State house of delegates 1869-1872; member, State senate 1875-1881; unsuccessful candidate for Governor in 1881; elected as a Democrat to the Forty-ninth Congress (March 4, 1885-March 3, 1887); did not seek renomination in 1886, having been elected Senator; elected in 1885 as a Democrat to the United States Senate; reelected in 1891, 1897, 1904, and 1910, and served from March 4, 1887, until his death on June 29, 1910; died before his credentials for the last election could be presented; chairman, Committee on Revision of the Laws of the United States (Fifty-third Congress), Committee on Corporations Organized in the District of Columbia (Fifty-fifth Congress), Committee on Public Health and National Quarantine (Sixtieth Congress); died in Lynchburg, Va.; interment in Spring Hill Cemetery.

U. S. Senators

EPPES, JOHN WAYLES (1773-1823), a U.S. Senator and Representative from Virginia; born at Eppington, Chesterfield County, Va., April 19, 1773; attended the University of Pennsylvania at Philadelphia; was graduated from Hampden-Sydney College in Virginia in 1786; studied law; was admitted to the bar in 1794 and commenced practice in Richmond, Va.; member, State house of delegates 1801-1803; elected as a Republican to the Eighth and the three succeeding Congresses (March 4, 1803-March 3, 1811); unsuccessful candidate for reelection to the Twelfth Congress; chairman, Committee on Ways and Means (Eleventh Congress); engaged in agricultural pursuits; elected to the Thirteenth Congress); (March 4, 1813-March 3, 1815); unsuccessful candidate for reelection to the Fourteenth Congress; chairman, Committee on Ways and Means (Thirteenth Congress); elected to the United States Senate and served from March 4, 1817, until December 4, 1819, when he resigned because of ill health; chairman, Committee on Finance (Fifteenth Congress); retired to his estate, "Millbrooke," in Buckingham County, Va., where he died September 13, 1823; interment in the private cemetery of the Eppes family at Millbrook, near Curdsville, Va.

GILES, WILLIAM BRANCH (1762-1830), a U.S. Senator and Representative from Virginia; born near Amelia Court House, Amelia County, Va., August 12, 1762; pursued classical studies and graduated from the College of New Jersey (now Princeton University) in 1781; studied law; was admitted to the bar and practiced in Petersburg, Va., 1784-1789; elected to the First Congress to fill the vacancy caused by the death of Theodorick Bland; reelected to the Second and to the three succeeding Congresses and served from December 7, 1790, to October 2, 1798, when he resigned; member, State house of delegates 1798-1800; elected as a Republican to the Seventh Congress (March 4, 1801-March 3, 1803); appointed to the United States Senate as a Republican to fill the vacancy in the term beginning March 4, 1803; caused by the resignation of Abraham B. Venable; while holding the office of Senator-designate was elected on December 4, 1804, to fill the vacancy in the term beginning March 4, 1799, caused by the resignation of Wilson C. Nicholas; was reelected in 1804 and 1811 and served from August 11, 1804, to March 3, 1815, when he resigned; member, State house of delegates 1816-1817, 1826-1827; unsuccessful candidate for election to the United States Senate in 1825; Governor of Virginia 1827-1830; was a member of the State constitutional convention in 1829 and 1830; again elected Governor in 1830, but declined; died on his estate, "Wigwam, " near Amelia Court House, Amelia County, Va., December 4, 1830; interment in a private cemetery on his estate.

GLASS, CARTER (1858-1946) a Representative and a Senator from Virginia; born in Lynchburg, Cambell County, Va., January 4, 1858; attended private and public schools; newspaper reporter, editor and owner; member, State senate 1899-1903, when he resigned; delegate to the State constitutional convention in 1901; elected as a Democrat to the Fifty-seventh Congress to fill the vacancy caused by the death of Peter J. Otey; reelected to the Fifty-eighth and to the eight succeeding Congresses and served from November 4, 1902, until December 16, 1918, when he resigned to accept a cabinet position; chairman, Congress on Banking and Currency (Sixty-third through Sixty-fifth Congresses); member of the Democratic National Committee 1916-1928; appointed Secretary of the Treasury by President Woodrow Wilson and served from 1918 to 1920 when he resigned, having been appointed a Senator; appointed as a Democrat to the United States Senate on December 18, 1919, and subsequently elected to fill the vacancy caused by the death of Thomas S. Martin in the term ending March 3, 1925, but did not qualify until February 2, 1920, preferring to retain his Cabinet portfolio; reelected in 1924, 1930, 1936, and again in 1942, and served from February 2, 1920, until his death on May 28, 1946; served as President pro tempore during the Seventy-seventh and Seventy-eighth Congresses; chairman, Committee on Expenditures in the Interior Department (Sixty-sixth Congress), Committee on Appropriations (Seventy-third through Seventy-ninth Congresses); declined an appointment as Secretary of the Treasury in the Cabinet of President Franklin D. Roosevelt; died in Washington, D. C., May 28, 1946; interment in Spring Hill Cemetery, Lynchburg, Va.

GRAYSON, WILLIAM (1740-1790), a U.S. Senator and Delegate from Virginia; born in Prince William County, Va., around 1740; attended the College of Philadelphia, now the University of Pennsylvania; pursued classical studies in England at the University of Oxford and studied law in London; returned to Virginia and practiced law in Dumfries; during the Revolutionary War was commissioned lieutenant-colonel and aide-de-camp to General George Washington and promoted to colonel January 1777; commissioner of the Board of War 1780-1781; resumed the practice of law; member, Virginia house of delegates 1784-1785, 1788; member of the Continental Congress 1785-1787; delegate to the Virginia convention of 1788 for the adoption of the Federal Constitution, which he opposed; elected to the United States Senate and served from March 4, 1789, until his death in Dumfries, Va., March 12, 1790; interment on the old family estate at Belle Air, near Dumfries, Va.

HUNTER, ROBERT MERCER (1809-1887), a U.S. Senator and Representative from Virginia; born at "Mount Pleasant," near Loretto, Essex County, Va., April 21, 1809; tutored at home; graduated from the University of Virginia at Charlottesville in 1828; studied law; was admitted to the bar in 1830 and commenced practice at Lloyds; member, State general assembly 1834-1837; elected as a States-Rights Whig to the Twenty-fifth, Twenty-sixth, and Twenty-seventh Congresses (March 4, 1837-March 3, 1843); Speaker of the House of Representatives in the Twenty-sixth Congress; unsuccessful candidate for reelection to the Twenty-eighth Congress elected to the Twenty-ninth Congress (March 4, 1845-March 3, 1847); chairman, Committee on the District of Columbia (Twenty-ninth Congress); elected to the

U. S. Senators

United States Senate in 1846; reelected in 1852 and 1858 and served from March 4, 1847, to March 28, 1861, when he withdrew; expelled from the Senate in 1861 for support of the rebellion; chairman, Committee on Public Buildings (Thirtieth through Thirty-second Congresses), Committee on Finance (Thirty-first through Thirty-sixth Congresses); delegate from Virginia to the Confederate Provincial Congress at Richmond; Confederate Secretary of State 1861-1862; served in the Confederate Senate from Virginia in the First and Second Congresses 1862-1865 and was President pro tempore on various occasions; was one of the peace commissioners that met with President Abraham Lincoln in Hampton Roads in February 1865; briefly imprisoned at the end of the Civil War; State treasurer of Virginia 1874-1880; collector for the port of Tappahannock, Va. 1885; died on his estate "Fonthill," near Lloyds, Va., on July 18, 1887; interment in "Elmwood, " the family burial ground, near Loretto, Va.

HUNTON, EPPA (1822-1908), a U.S. Senator and Representative from Virginia; born near Warrenton, Fauquier Conty, Va., September 22, 1822; attended New Baltimore Academy; taught school three years; studied law; was admitted to the bar in 1843 and commenced practice in Brentsville, Va.; served as colonel, and later general, in the Virginia militia; Commonwealth attorney for Prince William County 1849-1861; member of the Virginia convention at Richmond in February 1861 and advocated secession; entered the Confederate Army as colonel of the Eighth Regiment, Virginia Infantry; promoted to brigadier general after the Battle of Gettysburg and served through the remainder of the Civil War; resumed the practice of law; elected as a Democrat to the Forty-third and to the three succeeding Congresses (March 4, 1873-March 3, 1881); was not a candidate for renomination in 1880; chairman, Committee on Revolutionary Pensions (Forty-fourth Congress), Committee on the District of Columbia (Forty-sixth Congress); appointed a member of the Electoral Commission created by an act of Congress in 1877 to decide the contests in various States in the presidential election of 1876; resumed the practice of law; appointed and subsequently elected as a Democrat to the United States Senate to fill the vacancy caused by the death of John S. Barbour and served from May 28, 1892, to March 3, 1895; was not a candidate for renomination in 1894; resumed the practice of law in Warrenton, Va.; died in Richmond, Va., October 11, 1908; interment in Hollywood Cemetery.

JOHNSTON, JOHN WARFIELD (1818-1889), a U.S. Senator from Virginia; born in Panicello, near Abingdon, Va., September 9, 1818; (uncle of Henry Bowen and nephew of Charles Clement Johnston and Joseph Eggleston Johnston) attended Abingdon Academy, South Carolina College at Columbia, and the law department of the University of Virginia at Charlottesville; was admitted to the bar in 1839 and commenced practice in Tazewell, Tazewell County, Va.; Commonwealth attorney for Tazewell County 1844-1846; State senator 1846-1848; during the Civil War, held the position of Confederate States Receiver; judge of the circuit court of Virginia 1866-1870; upon the readmission of the State of Virginia to representation was elected as a Democrat to the United States Senate and served from January 26, 1870, to March 3, 1871; reelected on March 15, 1871, for the term beginning March 4, 1871; reelected in 1877 and served from March 15, 1871, until March 3, 1883; unsuccessful candidate for reelection; chairman Committee on Revolutionary Claims (Forty-fifth and Forty-seventh Congress); resumed the practice of his profession; died in Richmond, Va., February 27, 1889; interment in St. Mary's Cemetery, Wytheville, Va.

LEE, RICHARD HENRY (1732-1794), a U.S. Senator and Delegate from Virginia; born at "Stratford," in Westermoreland County, Va., January 20, 1732; after a course of private instruction attended Wakefield Academy, England; returned in 1751; justice of the peace for Westmoreland County 1757; member, house of burgessess 1758-1775; Member of the Continental Congress 1774-1779; a signer of the Declaration of Independence; author of the first national Thanksgiving Day proclamation issued by Congress at York, Pa., October 31, 1777; member, state house of delegates 1777, 1780, 1785; served as colonel of the Westmoreland Militia; again a Member of the Continental Congress 1784-1785 and 1787 and served as President of the Congress in 1784; member of the Virginia convention which ratified the Federal Constitution in 1788; elected to the United States senate and served from March 4, 1789, until his resignation October 8, 1792; served as President pro tempore during the Second Congress; retired from public life; died at his home, "Chantilly," Westmoreland County, Va., June 19, 1794; interment in the old family burying ground "Mount Pleasant," near Hague, Westmoreland County, Va.

LEIGH, BENJAMIN WATKINS (1781-1849), a U.S. Senator from Virginia; born in Chesterfield County, Va., on June 18, 1781; studied under private tutors; graduated from William and Mary College, Williamsburg, Va., in 1802; studied law; was admitted to the bar and commenced practice in Petersburg, Va.; served in the War of 1812; member, State house of delegates 1811-1813; moved to Richmond, Va., in 1813; prepared the revised code of 1810; delegate to the State constitutional convention of 1829 and 1830; member, State house of delegates 1830-1831; official reporter of the State court of appeals 1829-1841; elected as a Whig to the United States Senate to fill the vacancy in the term ending March 3, 1835, caused by the resignation of William C. Rives; reelected in 1835 and served from February 26, 1834, to July 4, 1836, when he resigned; resumed the practice of law; died in Richmond, Va., February 2, 1849; interment in Shockoe Cemetery.

LEWIS, JOHN FRANCIS (1818-1895), a U.S. Senator from Virginia; born in Lynnwood, Rockingham County, Va., March 1, 1818; attended an old field school; engaged in agricultural pursuits; delegate to the State secession convention in 1861 and refused to sign the ordinance of secession; elected lieutenant governor in 1869; upon the readmission of the State of Virginia to representa-

U. S. Senators

tion was elected as a Republican to the United States Senate and served from January 26, 1870, to March 3, 1875; was not a candidate for reelection; chairman, Committee on the District of Columbia (Forty-thirty Congress); appointed by Presidents Ulysses Grant and Rutherford Hayes United States Marshal for the western district of Virginia 1875-1882, when he resigned; again elected lieutenant governor in 1881; resumed agricultural pursuits; died at "Lynnwood," Rockingham County, Va., September 2, 1895; interment in the family burial ground.

MAHONE, WILLIAM (1826-1895), a U.S. Senator from Virginia; born in Southampton County, Va., December 1, 1826; was graduated from the Virginia Military Institute at Lexington in 1847; taught two years at the Rappahannock Military Academy; became a civil engineer with the Norfolk & Petersburg Railroad and rose to president, chief engineer, and superintendent; joined the Confederate Army and took part in the capture of Norfolk Navy Yard; was commissioned brigadier general and major general in 1864; at the close of the Civil War returned to railroad engineering, and became president of the Norfolk and Western; elected to the United States Senate as a Readjuster and served from March 4, 1881, until March 3, 1887; unsuccessful candidate for reelection in 1887; chairman, Committee on Agriculture (Forty-seventh Congress), Committee on Public Buildings and Grounds (Fortheighth and Forty-ninth Congresses); died in Washington, D. C., October 8, 1895; interment in Blandford Cemetery, Petersburg, Dinwiddie County, Va.

MARTIN, THOMAS STAPLES (1847-1919), a U.S. Senator from Virginia; born in Scottsville, Albemarle County, Va., July 29, 1847; attended the Virginia Military Institute at Lexington 1864-1865, and the University of Virginia at Charlottesville 1865-1867; served in the Confederate army; studied law was admitted to the bar in 1869 and practiced in Albemarle County; member of the board of visitors of the Miller Manual Labor School of Albemarle County; member of the board of visitors of the University of Virginia; elected as a Democrat to the United States Senate in 1893; reelected in 1899, 1905, 1911, and 1918, and served from March 4, 1895, until his death in Charlottesville, Va., November 12, 1919; Democratic caucus chairman, Committee on Corporations Organized in the District of Columbia Fifty-seventh through Fifty-ninth Congresses), Committee on Public Health and National Quarantine (Sixty-first Congress), Committee on Appropriations (Sixty-third through Sixty-fifth Congresses); interment in the University of Virginia Cemetery.

MASON, ARMISTEAD THOMSON (1787-1819), a U.S. Senator from Virginia; born at the "Armisteads," in Louisa County, Va., August 4, 1787; (son of Stevens Thomson Mason) graduated from William and Mary College, Williamsburg, Va., in 1807; engaged in agricultural pursuits; colonel of Virginia Volunteers in the War of 1812 and subsequently brigadier general of Virginia Militia; elected as a Republican to the United States Senate to fill the

Encyclopedia of Virginia

vacancy caused by the resignation of William B. Giles and served from January 3, 1816, to March 3, 1817; chairman, Committee on the District of Columbia (Fourteenth Congress); moved to Loudoun County, Va.; unsuccessful candidate for election in 1816 to the Fifteenth Congress in a campaign of much bitterness, which gave rise to several duels, and later resulted in his being killed in a duel with his brother-in-law, John Mason McCarty, at Bladensburg, Md., near Washington, D.C., February 6, 1819; interment in the churchyard of the Episcopal Church at Leesburg, Loudoun County, Va.

MASON, JAMES MURRAY (1798-1871), a U.S. Senator and Representative from Virginia; born on Analostan Island, Fairfax County, Va. (now Theodore Roosevelt Island, Washington, D. C.), November 3, 1798; studied under a private tutor and at an academy at Georgetown, D. C.; graduated from the University of Pennsylvania at Philadelphia in 1818 and from the law department of William and Mary College at Williamsburg in 1820; was admitted to the bar and practiced in Winchester, Va., in 1820 and 1821; delegate to the Virginia constitutional convention 1829; member, State house of delegates 1826-1832, with the exception of 1827-1828; presidential elector on the Democratic ticket in 1832; elected as a Jackson Democrat to the Twenty-fifty Congress (March 4, 1837-March 3, 1839); elected as a Democrat to the United States Senate in 1847 to fill the vacancy caused by the death of Isaac S. Pennybacker; reelected in 1850 and 1856 and served from January 21, 1847, until March 28, 1861, when he withdrew; served as President pro tempore of the Senate during the thirty-fourth and thirty-fifth Congresses; expelled from the Senate in 1861 for support of the rebellion; chairman, Committee on Claims (Thirtieth Congress), Committee on the District of Columbia ((Thirty-first Congress), Committee on Foreign Relations (Thirty-second through Thirty-sixth Congresses), Committee on Naval Affairs (Thirty-second Congress), delegate from Virginia to the Provisional Congress of the Confederacy; appointed commissioner of the Confederacy to Great Britain and France and while on his way to his post was taken from the British mail steamer *Trent* November 8, 1861, and confined in Fort Warren, Boston Harbor; released in January 1862; proceeded to London and represented the Confederacy until its downfall in April 1865; resided in Canada after after the close of the war until 1868, when he returned to Virginia; died near the city of Alexandria, Va., April 28, 1871; interment in St. Paul's Cemetery, Alexandria, Va.

MASON, STEVENS THOMSON (1760-1803), a U.S. Senator from Virginia; born in "Chappawamsic," Stafford County, Va., December 29, 1760; (father of Armistead Thomson Mason) attended William and Mary College, Williamsburg, Va.; studied law; was admitted to the bar and commenced practice in Dumfries, Prince William County, Va.; served in the Revolutionary Army as an aide to General George Washington at Yorktown; brigadier general in the Virginia Militia; member, State house of delegates 1783, 1794; member, State senate 1787-1790; delegate to the State

U. S. Senators

constitutional convention in 1788; elected to the United States Senate to fill the vacancy caused by the resignation of James Monroe; reelected in 1797 and again in 1803 as a Republican, and served from November 18, 1794, until his death in Philadelphia, Pa., May 10, 1803; interment in the family burying ground at "Raspberry Plain" in Loudoun County, Va.

MONROE, JAMES (1758-1831), a U.S. Senator, Delegate and 5th President of the United States; from Virginia; born in Westmoreland County, Va., April 28, 1758; (nephew of Joseph Jones and uncle of James Monroe *1799-1870*) pursued classical studies; attended William and Mary College, Williamsburg, Va., in 1776 and left to enter the Continental Army in the Revolutionary War; appointed a lieutenant in the Third Virginia Regiment, participated in numerous engagements, and was severly wounded in the Battle of Harlem Heights; rose to the rank of lieutenant colonel; member, State assembly 1782; Member of the Continental Congress 1783-1786; resumed the study of law; was admitted to the bar and engaged in practice in Fredericksburg, Va.; member, state assembly 1786; delegate to the State convention to consider the Federal Constitution in 1788; unsuccessful candidate for election to the First Congress; elected to the United States Senate to fill the vacancy caused by the death of William Grayson; reelected in 1791 and served from November 9, 1790, until his resignation May 27, 1794; appointed by President George Washington as Minister Plenipotentiary to France 1794-1796; Governor of Virginia 1799-1802; appointed by President Thomas Jefferson as Minister Plenipotentiary to France in 1803, and Minister Plenipotentiary to England 1803-1807, and during this period headed a diplomatic mission to Spain; returned home in 1808; member, State assembly 1810-1811; Governor of Virginia 1811; appointed Secretary of State in the Cabinet of President James Madison and served from 1811 to 1817; also served as Secretary of War 1814-1815; elected and reelected President of the United States and served from March 4, 1817, to March 3, 1825; retired to his farm in Loudoun County, Va.; member and president of the Virginia constitutional convention of 1829; moved to New York City in 1831, and died there July 4, 1831; interment in Marble Cemetery on Second Street, New York City; reinterred in Hollywood Cemetery, Richmond, Va., July 4, 1858.

MOORE, ANDREW (1752-1821), a U.S. Senator and Representative from Virginia; born at "Cannicello," near Fairfield, Rockbridge (formerly Augusta) County, Va., in 1752; (father of Samuel McDowell Moore) attended Augusta Academy (now Washington and Lee University), Lexington, Va.; studied law; was admitted to the bar in 1774 and practiced; served in the Revolutionary War as a captain until 1779; commissioned brigadier general, then major general of Virginia Militia; member, State house of delegates 1780-1783, 1785-1788; delegate to the Virginia convention that ratified the Federal Constitution in 1788; elected to the First and to the three succeeding Congresses (March 4, 1789-March 3, 1797); member, State house of delegates 1799-1800, and State senate 1800-1801; successfully contested the election of Thomas Lewis to the Eighth Congress and served from March 5 to August 11, 1804, when he was appointed as a Republican to the United States Senate to fill the vacancy in the term beginning March 4, 1799, caused by the resignation of Wilson C. Nicholas; while holding the office of Senator designate was elected on December 4, 1804, to fill the vacancy in the term beginning March 4, 1803, caused by the resignation of Abraham B. Venable and served successively in the two classes from August 11, 1804, until March 3, 1809; appointed United States marshall for the State of Virginia in 1810 and served until his death in Lexington, Va., April 14, 1821; interment in Lexington Cemetery.

NICHOLAS, WILSON CARY (1761-1820), a U.S. Senator and Representative from Virginia; born in Williamsburg, Va., January 31, 1761; (brother of John Nicholas and uncle of Robert Carter Nicholas), attended the College of William and Mary, Williamsburg, Va.; served in the Revolutionary Army and commanded George Washington's Life Guard until it disbanded in 1783; member, State house of delegates 1784-1789; delegate to the State constitutional convention which ratified the Federal Constitution in 1788; member, State house of delegates 1794-1800; elected as a Republican to the United States Senate to fill the vacancy caused by the death of Henry Tazewell and served from December 5, 1799, until May 22, 1804, when he resigned to become collector of the port of Norfolk 1804-1807; elected to the Tenth and Eleventh Congresses and served from March 4, 1807, until his resignation November 27, 1809; Governor of Virginia 1814-1817; died at "Tufton," near Charlottesville, Va., October 10, 1820; interment in the Jefferson burying ground at "Monticello," near Charlottesville.

PARKER, RICHARD ELLIOTT (1783-1840), a U.S. Senator from Virginia; born at "Rock Spring," Westmoreland County, Va., December 27, 1783; attended the public schools and graduated from Washington College (now Washington and Lee University), Lexington, Va., in 1803; studied law; was admitted to the bar in 1804 and practiced in Westmoreland County; member, State house of delegates 1807-1809; served as a lieutenant-colonel with the 111th Regiment during the War of 1812; returned to practice in Westmoreland County; judge of the general court of Virginia 1817-1836; judge of the Virginia court of law and chancery 1831-1836; elected as a Jacksonian to the United States Senate to fill the vacancy caused by the resignation of Benjamin W. Leigh and served from December 12, 1836, to March 13, 1837, when he resigned; judge of the State supreme court of appeals 1837-1840; died on his estate, "Soldier's Retreat," near Snickersville (now Bluemont, Loudoun County), Va., September 10, 1840; interment in the family cemetery near Warsaw, Richmond County, Va.

PLEASANTS, JAMES (1769-1836), a U.S. Senator and Representative from Virginia; born at "Cold Comfort," in Powhatan County, Va., October 24, 1769; pursued classical studies and graduated from the College of William and Mary, Williamsburg,

U. S. Senators

Va.; studied law; was admitted to the bar and commenced practice in Amelia County in 1791; member, State house of delegates 1797-1802; clerk of the Virginia house of delegates 1803-1811; elected as a Republican to the Twelfth and to the four succeeding Congresses and served from March 4, 1811, to December 14, 1819, when he resigned, having been elected a United States Senator December 10, 1819; chairman, Committee on Public Expenditures in the Department of the Navy (Fifteenth Congress); elected as a Republican to the United States Senate to fill the vacancy caused by the resignation of John W. Eppes and served from December 14, 1819, to December 15, 1822, when he resigned; chairman, Committee on Naval Affairs (Sixteenth and Seventeeth and Congresses); Governor of Virginia 1822-1825; delegate to the State constitutional conventions in 1829 and 1830; retired and lived on his estate, "Contention," near Goochland, Goochland County, Va., where he died on November 9, 1836; interment on his estate.

RANDOLPH, JOHN (1773-1833), a U.S. Senator and Representative from Virginia; born in Cawsons, Prince George County, Va., June 2, 1773; known as John Randolph of Roanoke to distinguish him from kinsmen; studied under private tutors, at private schools, the College of New Jersey (now Princeton University), and Columbia College, New York City; studied law in Philadelphia, Pa., but never practiced; engaged in several duels; elected to the Sixth and to the six succeeding Congresses (March 4, 1799-March 3, 1813); one of the managers appointed by the House of Representatives in January 1804 to conduct the impeachment proceedings against John Pickering, judge of the United States District Court for New Hampshire, and in December of the same year against Samuel Chase, Associate Justice of the Supreme Court of the United States; unsuccessful candidate for election in 1812 to the Thirteenth Congress; chairman, Committee on Ways and Means (Seventh through Ninth Congresses); elected to the Fourteenth Congress (March 4, 1815-March 3, 1817); not a candidate for reelection in 1816 to the Fifteenth Congress; elected to the Sixteenth and to the three succeeding Congresses and served from March 4, 1819, until his resignation, effective December 26, 1825; appointed to the United States Senate December 8, 1825, to fill the vacancy in the term beginning March 4, 1821, caused by the resignation of James Barbour and served from December 26, 1825, to March 3, 1827; unsuccessful candidate for reelection to the Senate in 1827; elected to the Twentieth Congress (March 4, 1827-March 3, 1829); was not a candidate for reelection to the Twenty-first Congress; chairman, Committee on Ways and Means (Twentieth Congress); member of the Virginia constitutional convention at Richmond in 1829; appointed United States Minister to Russia by President Andrew Jackson and served from May to September, 1830, when he resigned; elected to the Twenty-third Congress and served from March 4, 1833, until his death in Philadelphia, Pa., May 24, 1833; interment at his residence, "Roanoke," in Charlotte County, Va.; reinterment at "Hollywood," Richmond, Va.

Encyclopedia of Virginia

RIDDLEBERGER, HARRISON HOLT (1844-1890), a U.S. Senator from Virginia; born in Edinburg; Shenandoah County, Va., October 4, 1844; attended the common schools; served three years during the Civil War in the Confederate Army as second and first lieutenant of Infantry and as captain of Cavalry; returned to Edinburg and became editor of the Tenth Legion Banner; studied law; was admitted to the bar and commenced practice in Woodstock, Va.; member, State house of delegates 1871-1875; Commonwealth attorney of Shenandoah County 1876-1880; member, State senate 1879-1882; editor of the Shenandoah Democrat and later of the Virginian at Woodstock; presidential elector on the Democratic ticket in 1876 and the Readjuster ticket in 1880; elected as a Readjuster to the United States Senate in 1881 and served from March 4, 1883, to March 3, 1889; chairman, Committee on Manufacturers (Forty-eighth through Fiftieth Congresses); died in Woodstock, Va.; January 24, 1890; interment in Cedarwood Cemetery, Edinburg, Shenandoah County, Va.

RIVES, WILLIAM CABELL (1793-1868), a U.S. Senator and Representative from Virginia; born at "Union Hill," Amherst County, Va., May 4, 1793; attended Hampden-Sidney College in Virginia and graduated from the College of William and Mary, Williamsburg, Va., in 1809; studied law; was admitted to the bar about 1814 and commenced practice in Charlottesville, Albemarle County; delegate to the State constitutional convention in 1816; member, State house of delegates 1817-1820, 1822-1823; moved to "Castle Hill," Albemarle County, in 1821; elected to the Eighteenth and to the three succeeding Congresses and served from March 4, 1823, until his resignation in 1829; Minister to France 1829-1832 elected as a Jacksonian to the United States Senate to fill the vacancy caused by the resignation of Littleton W. Tazewell and served from December 10, 1832, February 22, 1834, when he resigned; again elected to the United States Senate to fill the vacancy caused by the resignation of John Tyler and served from March 4, 1836, to March 3, 1839, chairman, Committee on Naval Affairs (Twenty-fourth and Twenty-fifth Congresses); subsequently reelected as a Whig on January 18, 1841, for the term beginning March 4, 1839, and served until March 3, 1845; chairman, Committee on Foreign Relations (Twenty-seventh Congress); again Minister to France 1849-1853; member of the peach convention of 1861 held in Washington, D. C., in an effort to devise means to prevent the impending war; delegate from Virginia to Confederate Provisional Congress in Montgomery, Ala., and Richmond, Va., in 1861; member of the house of representatives from Virginia in the Second Confederate Congress; died on his plantation, "Castle Hill," near Charlottesville, Va., April 25, 1868; interment in the private burial ground on the family estate.

ROANE, WILLIAM HENRY (1787-1845), a U.S. Senator and Representative from Virginia; born in Virginia, September 17, 1787; (grandson of Patrick Henry) completed preparatory studies; member, State house of delegates 1812-1815; elected as a Republican to the Fourteenth Congress (March 4, 1815-March 3,

U. S. Senators

1817); was not a candidate for renomination; member of the executive council of Virginia; elected as Democrat to the United States Senate to fill the vacancy caused by the resignation of Richard E. Parker and served from March 14, 1837, to March 3, 1841; chairman, Committee on the District of Columbia (Twenty-fifth Congress); unsuccessful candidate for reelection in 1841; engaged in agricultural pursuits; died in Tree Hill, near Richmond, Va., May 11, 1845; interment in the private cemetery of the Lyons family in Hanover County, Va.

ROBERTSON, ABSALOM WILLIS (1887-1971), a U.S. Senator and Representative from Virginia; born in Martinsburg, Berkeley County, W. Va., May 27, 1887; moved to Lynchburg, Va., with his parents in 1891; attended the public schools of Lynchburg and Rocky Mount, Va., graduated from the University of Richmond, Richmond, Va., in 1907, and from its law department in 1908; was admitted to the bar in 1908 and commenced practice in Buena Vista, Rockbridge County, Va.; moved to Lexington, Rockbridge County, Va., in 1919 and continued the practice of law; member, State senate 1916-1922; during the First World War served in the United States Army as assistant camp adjutant at camp Lee, Va., and in the Adjutant General's Office, Washington, D. C., with the rank of major 1917-1919; served as Commonwealth's attorney for Rockbridge County 1922-1928; chairman of the State Commission of Game and Inland Fisheries 1926-1932; elected as a Democrat to the Seventy-third Congress reelected to the six succeeding Congresses and served from March 4, 1933, until November 5, 1946, when he resigned; was nominated to the Eightieth Congress in 1946 but withdrew, having received the nomination for United States Senator; elected in 1946 as a Democrat to the United States Senate to fill the vacancy in the term ending January 3, 1949, caused by the death of Carter Glass; reelected in 1948, 1954, and 1960, and served from November 6, 1946, until his resignation December 30, 1966; unsuccessful candidate for renomination in 1966; co-chairman, Joint Committee on Defense Production (Eighty-fifth, Eighty-seventh, and Eighty-ninth Congresses); served as consultant to the International Bank for Reconstruction and Development 1966-1968; retired and resided in Lexington, Va., until his death there November 1, 1971; interment in Stonewall Jackson Memorial Cemetery.

SPONG, WILLIAM BELSER, JR. (1920-), a U.S. Senator from Virginia; born in Portsmouth, Va., September 29, 1920; attended the public schools of Portsmouth, Va.; attended Hampden-Sydney College, University of Virginia, and the University of Edinburgh, Scotland; studied law; served in the Army Air Corps, Eighth Air Force, 1942-1945; admitted to the bar in 1947 and commenced the practice of law in Portsmouth, Va.; lecturer in law and government, College of William and Mary, 1948-1949; member, State house of delegates 1954-1955; member, State senate 1956-1966; chairman of the Virginia Commission on Public Education 1958-1962; elected as a Democrat to the United States Senate in 1966, for the six-year term commencing January 3, 1967; subsequently appointed by the Governor, December 31, 1966, to fill the vacancy caused by the resignation of A. Willis Robertson for the term ending January 3, 1967; served from December 31, 1966, to January 3, 1973; unsuccessful candidate for reelection in 1972; lawyer; law professor and dean, Marshall-Whyte School of Law, College of William and Mary 1976-1985; is a resident of Williamsburg, Va.

SWANSON, CLAUDE AUGUSTUS (1862-1939), a U.S. Senator and Representative from Virginia; born in Swansonville, Va., March 31, 1862; attended the public schools; taught school; attended the Virginia Agricultural and Mechanical College (now the Virginia Polytechnic Institute) at Blacksburg; graduated from Randolph-Macon College, Ashland, Va., in 1885 and from the law department of the University of Virginia at Charlottesville in 1886; was admitted to the bar in 1886 and commenced practice in Chatham, Pittsylvania County, Va.; elected as a Democrat to the Fifty-third and to the six succeeding Congresses and served from March 4, 1893, until his resignation, effective January 30, 1906; unsuccessful candidate for nomination as governor in 1901; Governor of Virginia in 1906-1910; appointed as a Democrat to the United States Senate in August 1910, to fill the vacancy in the term ending March 3, 1911, cuased by the death of John W. Daniel; again appointed, on February 28, 1911, and subsequently elected to fill the vacancy caused by the death of John W. Daniel, who had been reelected for the term commencing March 4, 1911; reelected in 1916, 1922, and in 1928, and served from August 1, 1910, until March 3, 1933, when he resigned to accept a Cabinet portfolio; chairman, Committee on Public Buildings and Grounds (Sixty-third through Sixty-fifth Congresses), Committee on Naval Affairs (Sixty-fifth Congress), Committee on Expenditures in the Department of the Navy (Sixty-sixth Congress); Secretary of the Navy in the Cabinet of President Franklin D. Roosevelt from 1933 until his death at Rapidan Camp in the Blue Ridge Mountains, near Criglersville, Madison County, Va., July 7, 1939; funeral services were held in the Chamber of the United States Senate; interment in Hollywood Cemetery, Richmond, Va.

TAZEWELL, HENRY (1753-1799), a U.S. Senator from Virginia; born in Brunswick County, Va., November 27, 1753; (father of Littleton Waller Tazewell) attended the rural schools; graduated from the College of William and Mary at Williamsburg in 1770; studied law; was admitted to the bar and commenced practice in 1773; member, provincial house of burgesses 1775; raised and was commissioned captain of a troop of cavalry in the Revolutionary War; delegate to the State Assembly 1778-1785; judge of the State supreme court 1785-1793, chief justice 1789-1793; judge of the high court of appeals 1793; elected in 1794 to the United States Senate to fill the vacancy caused by the resignation of John Taylor, reelected in 1798, and served from December 29, 1794, until his death; served as President pro tempore of the Senate during the Third and Fourth Congresses; died in Philadelphia, Pa., January 24, 1799; interment in Christ Church Cemetery.

U. S. Senators

TRIBLE, PAUL SEWARD, JR. (1946 -), a U.S. Senator and Representative from Virginia; born in Baltimore, Baltimore County, Md., December 29, 1946; attended public and private schools in New Orleans, La., and Clark's Summit, Pa.; graduated, Hampden-Sydney College 1968; graduated, Washington and Lee Law School, Lexington, Va., 1971; admitted to the Virginia bar in 1971 and commenced practice in Alexandria; served as law clerk in the United States District Court for Eastern Virginia 1971-1972; assistant United States attorney for the Eastern District of Virginia 1972-1974; Commonwealth's attorney, Essex County, Va., 1974-1976; appointed to Virginia Law Enforcement Officers Training and Standards Commission 1976; elected as a Republican to the Ninety-fifth Congress in 1976; reelected to the Ninety-sixth and Ninety-seventh Congresses (January 3, 1977-January 3, 1983); was not a candidate for reelection to the House of Representatives in 1982, but was elected to the United States Senate for the term ending January 3, 1989.

TYLER, JOHN (1790-1862), a U.S. Senator and Representative from Virginia; born in Charles City County, Va., March 29, 1790; (father of David Gardiner Tyler) attended private schools and graduated from the College of William and Mary, Williamsburg, Va., in 1807; studied law; was admitted to the bar in 1809 and commenced practice in Charles City County; captain of a military company in 1813; member, State house of delegates 1811-1816; member of the council of state in 1816; elected as a Republican to the Fourteenth Congress to fill the vacancy caused by the death of John Clopton; reelected to the fifteenth and Sixteenth Congresses and served from December 16, 1817, to March 3, 1821; declined to be a candidate for renomination in 1820 because of impaired health; member, State house of delegates 1823-1825; Governor of Virginia 1825-1827; elected to the United States Senate in 1827; reelected in 1833 and served from March 4, 1827, to February 29, 1836, when he resigned; served as President pro tempore of the Senate during the twenty-third Congress; chairman, Committee on the District of Columbia (Twenty-third and Twenty-fourth Congresses), Committee on Manufactures (Twenty-third Congress); member of the State constitutional convention in 1829 and 1830; member, State house of delegates 1839; elected Vice Presient of the United States on the Whig ticket with William Henry Harrison in 1840; was inaugurated March 4, 1841, and served until the death of President Harrison April 4, 1841; took the oath of office as President of the United States April 6, 1841, and served until March 3, 1845; did not seek reelection; delegate to and president of the peach convention held in Washington, D.C., in 1861 in an effort to devise means to prevent the impending war; delegate to the Confederate Provisional Congress in 1861; elected to the House of Representatives of the Confederate Congress, but died in Richmond, Va., January 18, 1862, before the assembling of the Congress; interment in Hollywood Cemetery.

Encyclopedia of Virginia

VENABLE, ABRAHAM BEDFORD (1758-1811), a U.S. Senator and Representative from Virginia; born on "State Hill" farm, near Prince Edward Court House (now Worsham), Prince Edward County, Va., November 20, 1758; (uncle of Abraham Watkins Venable), attended Hampden-Sidney (Va.) College and graduated from the College of New Jersey (now Princeton University) in 1780; engaged as a planter in his native county; studied law; was admitted to the bar in 1784 and commenced practice at Prince Edward Court House; elected to the Second and to the three succeeding Congresses (March 4, 1791-March 3, 1799); was not a candidate for renomination in 1798; chairman, Committee on Elections (Fourth Congress); elected as Republican to the United States Senate to fill the vacancy cuased by the death of Stevens T. Mason and served from December 7, 1803, to June 7, 1804, when he resigned to become president of the first national bank organized in Virginia; perished at the burning of a theater in Richmond, Va., December 26, 1811; interment of ashes, with those of other fire victims, under a stone in front of the altar in Monumental Church, Richmond, Va.

WALKER, JOHN (1744-1809), a U.S. Senator and Delegate from Virginia; born at "Castle Hill," near Cobham, Albemarle County, Va., February 13, 1744; received private schooling and graduated from the College of William and Mary, Williamsburg, Va., in 1764; moved to "Belvoir," Albemarle County, and engaged in planting; commissioned with his father to make special terms with the Indians at Fort Pitt, Pa., so as to retain their friendship during the Revolutionary War; served as an aide to General George Washington in 1777 with the rank of colonel; Delegate to the Continental Congress 1780; studied law; was admitted to the bar and commenced the practice of law; appointed to the United States Senate to fill the vacancy caused by the death of William Grayson and served from March 31 to November 9, 1790, when a successor was elected; was not a candidate for reelection; resumed his agricultural pursuits; died near Madison Mills, Orange County, Va., December 2, 1809; interment in the family cemetery on the Belvoir estate near Cismont, Va.

WARNER, JOHN WILLIAMS (1927 -), a U.S. Senator from Virginia; born in Washington, D.C., February 18, 1927; attended schools in Washington, D.C., and Virginia; served in the United States Navy 1944-1946; graduated, Washington and Lee University, Lexington, Va., 1949; served in the United States Marine Corps during the Korean conflict 1950-1952; United States Marine Corps Reserve 1952-1956; graduated, University of Virginia Law School 1953; cattle farmer, admitted to the Washington, D.C. bar in 1953 and commenced practice the same year; law clerk, United States Court of Appeals for District of Columbia Circuit 1953-1954; Assistant United States Attorney 1956-1960; Under Secretary; United States Navy 1969-1972; Secretary, United States Navy 1972-1974; administrator, American Revolution Bicentennial Administration 1974-1976; elected as a Republican to the United States Senate, November 7, 1978, for the six-year term commencing January 3,

U. S. Senators

1979; subsequently appointed by the Governor, January 2, 1979, to fill the vacancy caused by the resignation of William Scott for the term ending January 3, 1979; reelected in 1984 for the term ending January 3, 1991.

WILLEY, WAITMAN THOMAS (1811-1900), a U.S. Senator from Virginia; born in Monongalia County, Va., in what is now a part of Marion County, W. Va., October 18, 1811; graduated from Madison (Pa.) College in 1831; studied law; was admitted to the bar in 1833 and commenced practice in Morgantown, Va. (now West Virginia); appointed clerk of the county court of Monongalia County in 1841 and later clerk of the circuit superior court, and held both positions until 1852; delegate to the Virginia constitutional convention in 1850 and 1851; elected as a Unionist to the United States Senate from Virginia to fill the vacancy caused by the retirement of James M. Mason and served from July 9, 1861, to March 3, 1863; chairman, Committee on Enrolled Bills (Thirty-seventh Congress); delegate to the State constitutional convention of West Virginia; upon the admission of West Virginia as a State into the Union was elected as a Unionist to the United States Senate; reelected in 1865 as a Republican and served from August 4, 1863, to March 3, 1871; chairman, Committee on Engrossed Bills (Thirty-ninth Congress), Committee on Patents and the Patent Office (Thirty-ninth and Fortieth Congresses); again served as clerk of the county court of Monongalia County 1882-1896; retired from public life; died in Morgantown, W. Va., May 2, 1900; interment in Oak Grove Cemetery.

WITHERS, ROBERT ENOCH (1821-1907), a U.S. Senator from Virginia; born near Lynchburg, Campbell County, Va., September 18, 1821; (cousin of Thomas Withers Chinn) attended private schools; graduated from the medical department of the University of Virginia at Charlottesville in 1841 and commenced practice in Campbell County; moved to Danville, Pittsylvania County, Va., in 1858; during the Civil War entered the Confederate Army as major of Infantry in 1861 and was promoted to colonel of the Eighteenth Virginia Infantry, which he commanded until retired in consequence of numerous disabling wounds; appointed to command the post at Danville, Va., which position he held until the close of the war; moved to Lynchburg, Va., in 1866 and established the Lynchburg News, a daily paper devoted to the interests of the Conservative Party; nominated for governor by that party, but withdrew; presidential elector on the Democratic ticket in 1872; elected lieutenant governor in 1873; elected as a Democrat to the United States Senate and served from March 4, 1875, to March 3, 1881; unsuccessful candidate for reelection in 1881; chairman, Committee on Pensions (Forty-sixth Congress); appointed by President Grover Cleveland as United States consul at Hong Kong, China, 1885-1889, when he resigned; returned to Wytheville, Wythe County, Va.; died at "Ingleside," Wytheville, Va., September 21, 1907; interment in the East End Cemetery.

DICTIONARY OF PLACES

This is a gazetteer of geographical places in the State.

It contains listings of all of the *incorporated* populated places (1990 census figures); prominent physical features and cultural locations. Many points of interest are included as well as the names of Nationally recognized Historical Sites. Details on the Historical Places can be found in the section of the book titled Historical Places. They are arranged in that section by County, so it will be necessary to note the name of the County when cross-referencing.

It is anticipated that additional populated places and other geographical entities not included in this first edition will appear in subsequent editions, along with updating, correcting and expanding entries presented here.

•ABINGDON, Town; Washington County Seat; Pop. 7,003; Zip Code 24210; Elev. 2069; 15 mi. NE of Bristol; Lat. 36-42-57 N long. 081-58-07 W; Settled in the 1760's and named either for Lord Abingdon or Mary Washington's home town. Wolf Hills was the name originally given to the settlement made between 1765 and 1770 on land granted to Dr. Thomas Walker in 1752. The small fort built here was enlarged in 1776 to afford refuge for settlers terrified by the Cherokee uprising. Blacks' Fort was attacked several times during the year but survived and became the center of 120 acres of land donated for a county seat. In 1778 the village was established as Abingdon, and by 1793, it had become distributing center for all the mail sent to southwest Virginia.

On December 14, 1864, some 10,000 Federal troops, under General George Stoneman, burned the depot, jail, barracks, and wagon-shops-all storehouses for Confederate supplies. The following day, a straggler from the Federal army-a former resident of Abingdon-set fire to the remaining buildings on Main Street.

Abingdon was the home of John Campbell, Secretary of the Treasury (1829-39); the Confederate general, Joseph E. Johnston;

Encyclopedia of Virginia

George W. Hopkins (1804-61), congressman and charge d'affaires to Portugal; and three Virginia governors. Wyndham Robertson (1836-37), David Campbell (1837-41), and John Buchanan Floyd (1849-52).

POINTS OF INTEREST:
•Grayson Highland State Park

HISTORICAL PLACES... (See Historical Places Section for details).
Abington Bank; Abington Historic District; Mont Calm; White's Mill

•**ACCOMAC**, Town; Accomack County Seat; Pop. 466; Zip Code 23301; on Northern part of the Delaware Peninsula; Lat. 37-43-15 N long. 075-40-06 W; The town is named after the Accomac Indians. The name means "other side of water place."

In 1786 the general assembly voted that 'ten acres of land, the property of Richard Drummond, adjoining to Accomack courthouse, shall be ... laid out into lots of half and acre each, with convenient streets,' as 'a town by the name of Drummond.'

Henry Alexander Wise (1806-76), a native of Accomac, was governor of Virginia from 1856 to 1860. During the trial of John Brown and his associates, Governor Wise went himself to Harpers Ferry to see that the laws of Virginia were properly carried out; and, after the prisoners were condemned, he ordered troops to Charles Town to guard them. In the army of the Confederacy he served with distinction as brigadier general.

HISTORICAL PLACES... (See Historical Places Section for details).
Bank Building; St. James Church

•**ACCOMACK COUNTY**, E Virginia; 470 sq. mi.; Pop. 31,703; Named after Accomack Indian tribe; word means "land on the other side."

•**ALBEMARLE COUNTY**, N central Virginia; 739 sq. mi.; Pop. 68,040; Named after the Earle of Albemarle, Aide-de-camp to George I, 1927; governor of Virginia (1737-1754) but never came to Virginia.

•**ALBERTA**, Town; Brunswick County; Pop. 337; Zip Code 23821; 35 mi. SW of Petersburg; Lat. 36-52-09 N long. 077-52-49 W; The town is named after the Canadian province.

•**ALEXANDRIA**, City; Pop. 111,183; Zip Code 22300; 6 mi. S of Washington D.C.; Lat. 38-47-05 N long. 077-00-51 W; The town is named after colonial settler John Alexander who came to the area in 1669. It is located on the western bank of the Potomac River.

Dictionary of Places

Although Captain John Smith ascended the Potomac to the falls in 1608, the west shore of the river was the last of Virginia's Tidewater fringe to be settled. In 1669 Governor Berkeley granted Robert Howsing 'six thousand acres of land situate . . . upon the freshes of Potomac River on the west side.' Captain John Alexander, who surveyed this tract, including the site of Alexandria, bought the Howsing grant the year following, and sporadic settlement began.

The section suffered in 1675 because of the Susquehannock War, when the Indians crossed the Potomac to attack new settlers. Colonel John Washington with a Virginia force joined Major John Truman's Maryland troops in a campaign against the Indians on Piscataway Creek (Maryland). During a truce, Maryland soldiers killed the Indian conferees. The Susquehannock, bent on revenge, advanced southward and aroused other Indians, thus bringing about conditions that led to Bacon's Rebellion. The century had ended before the Indians were driven out and permanent settlements established.

Plantations flourished after 1713, when Queen Anne's War ended and tobacco trade expanded. Indian trails then became 'rolling roads,' along which hogsheads of tobacco were drawn or 'rolled' by oxen or horses to public warehouses. The first warehouse in this vicinity was authorized in 1730 on the south side of Hunting Creek 'upon Broadwater's land.' The site was found unsuitable, and establishment of a warehouse 'upon Simon Pearson's land upon the upper side of Great Hunting Creek' was confirmed in 1732 by the general assembly. In 1740 a public ferry was established 'from Hunting Creek, warehouse, on land on Hugh West . . . to Frazier's point in Maryland,' and from 'the plantation of John Hareford in Doeg's Neck . . . to Prince George County in Maryland.' A tavern was erected here, on the main thoroughfare between New England and the South, and the community was called Belhaven. By 1742, when fees of tobacco inspectors were fixed, Hunting Creek Warehouse and that 'on the land of the Honourable Thomas Lee, Esquire, at the Falls of Patowmack,' were important shipping points.

In that year Fairfax County was cut from Prince William, and in 1748 the general assembly authorized the establishment of a town for Fairfax County 'at Hunting Creek warehouse,' to be named Alexandria for the family that had once owned the site. The following year the county surveyor, John West, Jr., assisted by young George Washington, laid off the town in streets and 84 half-acre lots. Among the purchasers were Lawrence Washington of Mount Vernon and his brother Augustine. Soon a busy port and an important stage stop, Alexandria grew quickly to commercial prominence. In 1752 it was made the county seat.

The export of wheat became in time even more important to Alexandria than that of tobacco. Grain growing increased as settlement pushed westward, making the colony self-sufficient in flour and meeting the demands of an expanding market in England and the West Indies. By 1776 caravans of 'flour waggons' were coming from as far as Winchester and returning laden with merchandise from England. In 1781 Alexandria was first on Virginia's flour inspection list.

Taverns such as the City Tavern, the Bunch of Grapes, and the Indian Queen opened for the accommodation of travelers and for the entertainment of the 'gentry'--Washingtons, Fairfaxes, Masons, and other plantation owners with fine mansions in or near town. Scottish merchant-shippers, like the partners Carlyle and Dalton, built handsome town houses, and George Washington had a house in town. Parties and balls were frequent, while the populace sought amusement in fairs, political rallies, and other gatherings held in Market Square. Washington, who raced his own horses, was a steward of the Alexandria Jockey Club.

Washington's first command-troops recruited in Alexandria-was drilled in Market Square before proceeding against the French in 1754. Alexandria was the mobilization point for Maryland troops and for one New York company in preparation for the second campaign in 1755. Here they joined Virginia troops and British regiments under the command of General Edward Braddock. Before starting, the general held a conference in Alexandria with the governors of four colonies. Washington set out as an aide to Braddock but assumed command after Braddock's death.

In July 1774 Washington presided in the courthouse here at a meeting to elect delegates to the first Virginia convention and to protest against the Boston Port Bill. 'If Boston is forced to submit, we will not,' the citizens declared. The Fairfax Resolves, drawn by George Mason, stated Virginia's position on taxation, Parliament, and the Crown, suggested a common platform, and affirmed that 'every little jarring interest and dispute which hath ever happened between these Colonies should be buried in eternal oblivion.

When the town was incorporated in 1779, Alexandria acquired a seal picturing 'a ship in full sail with a balance equally poised above the ship.' Some of the streets were paved by Hessian prisoners, labor procured through Dr. William Brown, one of the first surgeons general of the Revolutionary army and compiler during the war of the first American *Pharmacopoeia for the Use of Army Hospitals.* A lodge of Masons was organized in 1783. The next year a daily newspaper was established, now the oldest in America, and in 1785 an academy was founded in which Washington contributed annual gifts. He also endowed a short-lived charity school, the first free school in northern Virginia.

In that same year representatives from Virginia and Maryland met in Alexandria to discuss boundaries and commercial relations between the two states. This meeting, continued at Mount Vernon, led to the Annapolis Convention of 1786 and to the Constitutional Convention at Philadelphia in 1787.

Dictionary of Places

In 1789 Virginia gave Alexandria away. Along with a generous slice of Fairfax County, the city then became a part of the District of Columbia, laid out in 1791, and the stone marking the southern corner, still in place at Jones Point, was planted with a Masonic ceremony. The presiding official was Dr. Elisha Cullen Dick, who executed two oil paintings of Washington and was consulting physician during Washington's last illness.

Alexandria's exile had its highlights. The Bank of Alexandria, first in the present area of Virginia, was organized in 1792. Two years later the Library Company of Alexandria was founded; many sea captains subscribed, and carried its books on long voyages. A brick building (1767-73) had been erected to replace the wooden parish church, and the Presbyterian Meeting House, completed in 1790, was followed in 1795 by St. Mary's, the first permanent Roman Catholic church in Virginia. When the British sacked the city of Washington in 1814 and jeopardized Alexandria, town officials surrendered to the invaders, who burned a ship at anchor and loaded their vessels liberally with supplies. Alexandria's most serious fire occurred in 1824. An event of quite another sort took place in 1836: the tweaking of President Jackson's nose by Lieutenant Robert Randolph, U.S.N., aboard the steamboat *Sydney*. Randolph, whom Jackson had dismissed for defaulting with Government funds, was knocked down, then hustled ashore and placed under arrest; he was not punished for the assault.

In 1846 homesick Virginians asked Congress to give them back to the Old Dominion. Their petition was granted. In 1847 the general assembly created Alexandria County with Alexandria its seat. In 1898 Clarendon became the county seat, and in 1920 the name of the county was changed to Arlington.

But good fortune was mixed with alloy. The Baltimore & Ohio Railroad reached Winchester and the Cumberland coal fields, and in the 1840's it diverted trade to Baltimore. Though Alexandria achieved city status in 1852, it was soon outstripped by Baltimore and its new fleets of clipper ships.

The War between the States brought about another period of exile. After sending four companies, including a battalion of artillery, to Harpers Ferry in 1859 to suppress John Brown's raid, Alexandria at the beginning of the war was severed from the rest of Virginia. In April 1861, when Robert E. Lee assumed command of Virginia's armed forces, he was followed by many Alexandrians. The next month Federal troops took possession of the city. In August 1863, two months after West Virginia had been admitted to the Union, Governor Francis Pierpont proclaimed Alexandria capital of the 'reorganized government' of Virginia, and it remained so to the end of the war.

Safe behind Federal lines Alexandria escaped the havoc that obliterated evidences of the past in other Virginia cities.

Encyclopedia of Virginia

POINTS OF INTEREST:
- Ramsay House. 221 King St. at Fairfax Street.
- Lafayette House. 301 St. Asaph Street.
- Lee-Fendall House. 614 Oronoco Street. •Boyhood Home of Robert E. Lee. 607 Oronoco Street.
- Fort Ward Museum and Park. 4301 W. Braddock Road.
- The Athenaeum. 201 Prince Street.
- George Washington Masonic National Memorial. Shooter's Hill, West end of King Street.
- Torpedo Factory Arts Center. 105 N. Union Street.
- Pohick Bay Regional Park. 10651 Gunston Road, in Lorton.

HISTORICAL PLACES... (See Historical Places Section for details).
Carlyle House; Lyceum; Christ Church; Gadsby's Tavern Museum; Mount Vernon; Gunston Hall; Ppohick Church; Bank of Alexandria; Huntley

•**ALLEGHENY COUNTY,** W Virginia; 451 sq. mi.; Pop. 13,176; The county was named after Indian tribe Allegevi.

•**ALLEGHENY MOUNTAINS** This plateau segment of the Applachian Mountains stretches into Virginia as well as Pennsylvania and West Virginia. Overall the Alleghenies extend for more than 500 miles with an escarpment of over 4,800 feet. The average height is 3,000-4,500 feet.

•**ALTAVISTA,** Town; Campbell County; Pop. 3,686; Zip Code 24517; Elev. 596; 23 mi. S of Lynchurg; Lat. 37-06-59 N long. 079-17-28 W; The town is named for a farm owned by settler Henry Lane.

•**AMELIA COUNTY,** S central Virginia; 366 sq. mi.; Pop. 8,757; Named for second daughter of King George II.

•**AMHERST COUNTY,** W central Virginia; 467 sq. mi.; Pop. 28,578; Named for Jeffery Amherst (1717-1797) captain general and governor of Virginia (1759-68).

•**AMHERST,** Town; Amherst County Seat; Pop. 1,060; Zip Code 24521; 42 mi. SW of Charlottesville; Lat. 37-35-09 N long. 079-02-52 N; Established in 1761 and named in honor of French-Indian War commander, Lord Amherst.

•**APPALACHIA,** Town; Wise County; Pop. 1,994; Zip Code 24216; Elev. 1651; 40 mi. WNW of Bristol; Lat. 36-57-52 N long. 082-46-49 W; The town is named after the Appalachia Mountains.

•**APPOMATTOX COUNTY,** SE central Virginia; 343 sq. mi.; Pop. 12,298; Appomattox is an Algonquin Indian word meaning "a sinuous tidal estuary."

Dictionary of Places

•**APPOMATTOX RIVER** joins the James River 137 miles East of its origin in east Virginia. The name is derived from an Indian queen Apumetec according to records made in 1607.

•**APPOMATTOX**, Town; Appomattox County Seat; Pop. 1,707; Zip Code 24522; 18 mi. E of Lynchburg; Lat. 37-21-15 N long. 078-49-37 W; A famous Civil War historical site, the town's name derives from an early Indian tribe which lived in the area. Appomattox County was formed in 1845, but the courthouse was not erected here until 1892. A scattered community typical of Virginia county seats established late in the nineteenth century. Frame and brick dwellings circle a main street closely packed with nondescript store fronts. The town is the local tobacco market and ships lumber.

HISTORICAL PLACE... (See Historical Places Section for details).
Appomattox Court House National Historical Park

•**ARLINGTON COUNTY**, Suburb of Washington D.C.; 24 sq. mi.; Pop. 170,936; Named for old home of George Washington Parke Custus who named his estate to honor the earle of Arlington. Formerly Alexandria County, named changed to Arlington County in 1920.

•**ASHLAND**, Town; Hanover County; Pop. 5,864; Zip Code 23005; 16 mi. N of Richmond; Lat. 37-45-28 N long. 077-28-57 W; The town is named for the Kentucky home of statesman Henry Clay. In 1848, Edwin Robinson, president of the Richmond, Fredericksburg & Potomac Railroad, bought 155 acres of wilderness-'slashes'-and around a well of mineral water created a health resort, Slash Cottage. Richmond came to dance in the ballroom; trains waited to let hungry passengers dine here. Churches sprang up. By 1855 the village discarded its earlier name and adopted Ashland, the name of Henry Clay's estate in Kentucky. Selected as a mustering place for Confederate troops when the War between the States began, it was later occupied alternately by both Northern and Southern troops.

In Ashland lived the Sheltons, whose daughter, it is said, was the inspiration for Poe's *Lenore*. In 1866, the unsold part of land passed into the possession of the railroad company, which, to foster growth, induced the Methodist Church-by means of a land donation-to move Randolph-Macon College here. Randolph-Macon College was the first college founded in the United States by the Methodist Church.

POINTS OF INTEREST:
•Randolph-Macon College. 1 mile West of 1-95.
•Kings Dominion. 1 mile East on VA 54, then 7 miles North on 1-95 in Doswell.

Encyclopedia of Virginia

HISTORICAL PLACES... (See Historical Places Section for details).
Fork Church; Hickory Hill; Scotchtown (Patrick Henry House); Slash Church

•**AUGUSTA COUNTY**, W Virginia; 999 sq. mi.; Pop. 54,677; Named for Augusta (1719-1772) the princess of Saxe-Coburg-Gotha, daughter of King George II.

•**BALCONY FALLS** Is a series of rapids in the beautiful gap, four miles long, cut by the James through the Blue Ridge. Because the James and the Potomac are the only streams offering possibilities of water transportation between Chesapeake Bay the valleys beyond the range, plans were made for their utilization as early as 1772.

Although the first section of the James River Canal was opened in 1789, more than 50 years had passed and $8,000,000 had been spend before the canal was carried beyond Balcony Falls. However, sluice navigation was being used by 1816. Long narrow batteaux loaded with produce were guided through the tortuous channel by boatmen whose services drew high pay. The railroad through this pass was completed in 1881.

•**BATH**, County; W Virginia; 540 sq. mi.; Pop. 4,799; Descriptive name for warm sulphur springs.

•**BEDFORD COUNTY**, S central Virginia; 774 sq. mi.; Pop. 45,656;

•**BEDFORD**, City; Pop. 6,073; Zip Code 24523; 22 mi. WSW of Lynchburg; Lat. 37-20-20 N long. 079-31-15 W; Originally named Liberty, the name was changed in 1896 after the county name. Bedford, itself, comes from the fourth Duke of Bedford of England.

After Campbell County was taken from the large Bedford area in 1781, the county seat was moved from New London to a tract donated by William Downey and Joseph Fuqua. The new settlement was officially named Liberty, but local people called it Bedford Court House. In 1890 it was incorporated as Bedford City, shortened in 1912 to the present form. The Courthouse, a red brick building facing a small square, was constructed in 1930. The Confederate Monument, an attractive monolithic obelisk in the court square, is a pleasing departure from the conventional soldier statue. The large stone in the courthouse square was chipped from the block used in cutting the stone that caps the Washington Monument in the Nation's capital.

HISTORICAL PLACES... (See Historical Places Section for details).
Fancy Farm; Three Otters

Dictionary of Places

•BELLE HAVEN, Town; Accomack & Northampton Counties; Pop. 526; Zip Code 23306; Elev. 36; 53 mi. NNE of Norfolk; Lat. 37-31-53 N long. 075-52-04 W; A pioneer named Bell had a large oven in the area, so the place became Bell's Oven. In 1762 this was changed to Bell's Haven.

•BERRYVILLE, Town; Clarke County Seat; Pop. 3,097; Zip Code 22611; Elev. 575; 13 mi. E of Winchester; Lat. 39-09-04 N long. 077-59-08 W; In 1798 the town was laid out on land belonging to settler Benjamin Berry who divided the area into town lots. The general assembly named it Berryville in 1803. Between 1835 and 1860 the community prospered greatly. Several skirmishes took place near by in 1862-64, but no important engagement. Part of Lee's army camped here on the way to Gettysburg.

HISTORICAL PLACES... (See Historical Places Section for details).
Annefield; Fairfield; Long Branch

•BIG STONE GAP, Town; Wise County; Pop. 4,748; Zip Code 24219; 40 mi. WNW of Bristol; Lat. 36-56-09 N long. 082-46-35 W; Descriptively named for the gap in the mountains nearby through which the Powell River emerges. The settlement here, first called Three Forks, then Imboden, was chartered as Mineral City in 1888 and assumed its present name in 1890.

POINTS OF INTEREST:
•Southwest Virginia Museum Historical State Park. West 1st St. and Wood Avenue.
•Natural Tunnel State Park. 18 miles SE, off US 23.
•John Fox, Jr. House & Museum. 117 Shawnee Avenue.

HISTORICAL PLACES... (See Historical Places Section for details).
"June Tolliver" House; Fox, John Jr., House

•BLACKSBURG, Town; Montgomery County; Pop. 34,590; Zip Code 24060; Elev. 2080; 28 mi. W of Roanoke; Lat. 37-13-48 N long. 080-24-35 W; The town's name honors William Black who donated land for the town. Incorporated in 1798, the town is dominated by Virginia Polytechnic Institute. The college and town are on lands once owned by Colonel James Patton. Homesteads were surveyed and sold to a handful of pioneers who formed a settlement here-Draper's Meadows-in 1745. On Sunday July 8, 1755, a band of Shawnee, in an attempt to repossess their lands, swooped down on the whites, killed four, took six prisoners, and destroyed the homes. Colonel James Patton, visited here, cut down two Indians with his broadsword but was shot by another. William Ingles and John Draper escaped, but their wives and children were captured and taken to the Shawnee town on the Scioto River. After several months of captivity Mrs. Ingles, nee Dary Draper, escaped at Big Bone Lick (now in Kentucky). Armed with a tomahawk and accompanied by an old Dutch woman, she followed streams east, finally reaching the home of Adam Harmon just west of Draper's Meadow. Mrs. John Draper, adopted by the family of an Indian chief, remained in captivity until 1761, when she was ransomed.

POINTS OF INTEREST:
•Mountain Lake. 20 miles NW on US 460, VA 700.

HISTORICAL PLACE... (See Historical Places Section for details).
Smithfield Plantation

•**BLACKSTONE**, Town; Nottoway County; Pop. 3,497; Zip Code 23824; Elev. 427; 36 mi. WSW of Petersburg; Lat. 37-04-44 N long. 077-59-50 W; Incorporated in 1888 and named for the famous English jurist, Sir William Blackstone.

HISTORICAL PLACE... (See Historical Places Section for details).
Schwartz Tavern

•**BLAND COUNTY**, W central Virginia; 369 sq. mi.; Pop. 6,514; Named after Richard Bland (1745-75) Continental Congress (1774-75). Known as the "Virginian Antiquary."

•**BLOXOM**, Town; Accomack County; Pop. 357; Zip Code 23308; Lat. 37-49-50 N long. 075-37-14 W; The town is named for early postmaster, William Bloxom.

•**BLUE RIDGE MOUNTAINS** Although primarily stretching across southern Pennsylvania, North and South Carolina and Georgia the Blue Ridge also reaches into Virginia with the Shenandoah Valley as its western base. It reaches its highest point in Virginia, at its eastern front range, at Mt. Rogers, 5,720 feet.

•**BLUEFIELD**, Town; Tazewell County; Pop. 5,363; Zip Code 24605; Elev. 2389; 32 mi. WNW of Pulaski; Descriptively named for the blue-grass valley it lies in.

•**BOONES MILL**, Town; Franklin County; Pop. 239; Zip Code 24065; 12 mi. S of Roanoke; Lat. 37-07-00 N long. 079-57-08 W; Named in honor of Jacob Boone, cousin to Daniel Boone, who settled here in 1782 and built a mill. Because the Carolina Road was near by, a community soon grew around the mill. A house built in 1820 by John Boone, son of Jacob, stands on the mill site at the northern end of the hamlet.

•**BOTETOURT COUNTY**, W Virginia; 549 sq. mi.; Pop. 24,992; Named after Lord Botetourt who was Colonial governor of Virginia (1768-70).

Dictionary of Places

•**BOTTOM'S BRIDGE** Is at the crossing of Chickahominy River and the old road to Williamsburg. General Joseph E. Johnston, retreating before McClennan, halted here for five days before withdrawing to the vicinity of Richmond on May 17, 1862, McClellan occupied this position two days later.

•**BOWLING GREEN**, Town; Caroline County Seat; Pop. 727; Zip Code 22427; 35 mi. N of Richmond; Lat. 38-03-05 N long. 077-20-52 W; Major Thomas Hoomes received a land grant and settled in the area in 1670. The town is named for his family estate in England. In 1727 Essex, King William, and King and Queen Counties contributed territory that became Caroline County and by its name honored the wife of George II. In 1742 another section of King and Queen County was given to Caroline. The courthouse, at the first county seat, about two mils north of the present one, was not without regal air, for Charles Bridges, an English artist, was paid 1,600 pounds of tobacco in 1740 to decorate the facade with the king's arms. In the clerk's office at the old seat Edmund Pendleton served as apprentice and studied law. Later, Pendleton tutored in law two of his nephews who became men of note-John Penn (1741-88), who moved to North Carolina in 1774 and two years later was among the signers of the Declaration of Independence, and John Taylor.

The town grew up about a tavern at a junction of two roads on the Bowling Green estate of John Hoomes, who in 1794 donated four acres here for a new county seat and a building for a courthouse 'until one could be built of the same size and material as the former.' When, however, one Kenner petitioned for two additional acres for public use, Hoomes appealed to the general assembly, requesting that the seat of justice be re-established at its former site. Kenner's petition prevailed, more taverns were built, the clerk's office was moved here, and the present courthouse was erected.

In 1868, during Reconstruction, Alice Scott Chandler (1839-1904) founded The Home School, later renamed Bowling Green Female Seminary. In 1901 the school was removed to Buena Vista.

A bronze marker at the junction with County 626, within the town, commemorates the 'heroism' of Baptist ministers imprisoned in the jail at the old seat in 1771 for 'teaching and preaching the gospel without having episcopal ordination or a license from the General Court.' Brought to trial, the Reverend Bartholomew Chewning, James Goodrich, and Edward Herndon were remanded to gaol, there to remain till they gave 'security, each in the sum of twenty pounds for their good behaviour twelve months and a daye.' Similar charges were preferred against other ministers, and the same punishment was meted out. Patrick Henry, on one occasion, hurried from his home in Hanover County to the old courthouse to defend the ministers.

HISTORICAL PLACE... (See Historical Places Section for details).
Old Mansion

Encyclopedia of Virginia

•**BOYCE**, Town; Clarke County; Pop. 520; Zip Code 22620; 8 mi. SE of Winchester; Lat. 39-05-32 N long. 078-03-35 W; The town's name remembers U. L. Boyce who owned an estate nearby.

HISTORICAL PLACE... (See Historical Places Section for details).
Saratoga

•**BOYDTON**, Town; Mecklenburg County Seat; Pop. 453; Zip Code 239+; 35 mi. E of South Boston; Lat. 36-39-49 N long. 078-23- 29 W; The town was established in 1812 and named in honor of wealthy merchant and Judge, Alexander Boyd.

•**BOYKINS**, Town; Southampton County; Pop. 658; Zip Code 23827; 45 mi. SW of Suffolk; Lat. 36-35-07 N long. 077-11-47 W; Incorporated in 1884 and named for a local resident named Boykins.

•**BRANCHVILLE**, Town; Southampton County; Pop. 55; Zip Code 23828; Elev. 46; Lat. 36-34-31 N long. 077-14-57 W; The town is named after a family of early settlers.

•**BRIDGEWATER**, Town; Rockingham County; Pop. 3,918; Zip Code 22812; 7 mi. SW of Harrisonburg; Lat. 38-22-59 N long. 078- 58-34 W; Once the site of a ferry across the North River, ultimately a bridge was built and the town so named. Beginning as a port for flatboats, the community was first called Dinkletown for John and S.J. Dinkle, who has a carding machine, a sawmill, and a gristmill here in 1810.

•**BRISTOL**, City; Pop. 18,426; Zip Code 242+; SW Virginia on Tennesee-Virginia line; Lat. 36-36-25 N long. 082-10-57 W; Once called Goodson, the name was changed in 1890 to Bristol, after Bristol, England. Surveyed in 1749 by John Buchanan, the Sapling Grove tract, part of James Patton's 120,000-acre grant, became after the French and Indian War, the property of Colonel Evan Shelby and Isaac Baker, Sr. of Maryland. In 1771 they built their homes-Colonel Shelby on the present Tennessee section and Isaac Baker, Sr., on that which now lies in Virginia. When news was bruited about in 1850 that the State line would be the terminus of the Virginia and Tennessee Railroad, Colonel Samuel Goodson, who then owned the Baker area, envisioned the town of Goodsonville on his property, had it surveyed, and sold all the lots. When the railroad was completed in 1856, the flourishing town was incorporated as Goodson, a name that was changed to Bristol when it received a city charter in 1890.

The question of the long-disputed Virginia-North Carolina (and later Tennessee) boundary line-first run by Colonel William Byrd in 1728, continued in 1749 by Joshua Fry and Peter Jefferson, and momentarily settled by a compromise in 1803-flared up afresh in

Dictionary of Places

1897 and again in 1900 when commissioners were appointed to re-establish the boundary between White Top Mountain and Cumberland Gap. Because of this long dispute, finally settled in 1903 by the U.S. Supreme Court's decision sustaining the boundary established in 1803, the site has been under the jurisdiction of North Carolina (1779), the State of Franklin (1785-89), the Federal Government (1789) in the territory south of the Ohio River, Tennessee (1796), and Virginia.

POINTS OF INTEREST:
•Bristol Caverns. 5 miles SE on US 421, off 1-81.
•South Holston Dam and Lake. 8 miles SE on US 421.
•Steele Creek Park. 3 1/2 SW via Volunteer Pkwy and Broad Street.
•Rocky Mount Historic Shrine.

•BROADWAY, Town; Rockingham County; Pop. 1,209; Zip Code 22815; 13 mi. N of Harrisonburg; Lat. 38-36-50 N long. 078-47-41 W; A gathering place for rowdy types in the nineteenth century; townspeople warned they were on the "broadway to destruction," the name stuck on the town.

HISTORICAL PLACES... (See Historical Places Section for details).
Lincoln Homestead and Cemetery (Jacob Lincoln House); Tunker House (Yount-Zigler House)

•BRODNAX, Town; Brunswick & Mecklenburg Counties; Pop. 388; Zip Code 23920; Elev. 388; 54 mi. SW of Petersburg; Lat. 36-42-12 N long. 078- 01-55 W; Incorporated in 1915 and named for a prominent local family.

•BROOKNEAL, Town; Campbell County; Pop. 1,344; Zip Code 24528; Elev. 560; 30 mi. N of South Boston; Lat. 37-03-01 N long. 078-56-21 W; in rolling country near the confluence of the Falling and Staunton Rivers. This little settlement, named for the Brooke and Neal Families, is on land where was established a tobacco inspection depot about 1790. Soon, a ferry was bringing tobacco from plantations and a settlement had appeared that in 1802 was chartered as a town.

POINTS OF INTEREST:
•Patrick Henry Shrine (Red Hill). 3 miles East on VA 40, 2 miles South on VA 600 & 619.

•BRUINSWICK COUNTY, S Virginia; 579 sq. mi. Pop. 15,987;

•BUCHANAN COUNTY, W Virginia 508 sq. mi.; Pop. 31,333; Named after James Buchanan.

•BUCHANAN, Town; Botetourt County; Pop. 1,222; 25 mi. NE of Roanoke; The town is named in honor of the deputy surveyor of Augusta County, John Buchanan. To prevent the eastward trend of

French settlements, the Virginia government offered huge grants in this area on condition that homesteads be established. Colonel James Patton received a grant of 120,000 acres. His company-the Wood's River Land Company-and the Loyal Land Company, with Dr. Thomas Walker of Castle Hill as its agent, were the principal operators.

In 1811 this town was established and it eventually became the terminus of the James River and Kanawha Canal and of the Buchanan & Clifton Forge Railroad.

It is the birthplace of Mary Johnston, writer of historical novels. In this mountain village, Miss Johnston spent the first 15 years of her life, gaining from her father's large library the foundation for her literary career.

•BUCKINGHAM COUNTY, Central Virginia; 576 sq. mi.; Pop. 12,873; Named after the Duke of Buckingham.

•BUENA VISTA, Independent City; Pop. 6,406; Zip Code 24416; 25 mi. NW of Lynchburg; Lat. 37-44-04 N long. 079-21-12 W; A local iron furnace supplied cannonballs used in the Battle of Buena Vista in the Mexican-American War. The furnace was dubbed "Buena Vista" and the town's name followed.

Buena Vista was one of the boom towns brought forth by a promotion company in the last decades of the nineteenth century, when paper towns were being created throughout western Virginia. A report of 1889 reads, 'The landed estate of the Buena Vista Company has been made by the consolidation of the historic iron and agricultural lands of Sam'l F. Jordan, known as the Buena Vista property, the Green Forest farm and the Hart's Bottom farm; all together making about 13,000 acres . . . Most of the lands of Green Forest and Hart's Bottom, amounting to over 1,000 acres, have been laid off into streets and building lots.

HISTORICAL PLACES... (See Historical Places Section for details).

Southern Seminary; Main Building (Buena Vista Hotel)

•BURKEVILLE, Town; Nottoway County; Pop. 535; Zip Code 23922; Elev. 522; 45 mi. W of Petersburg; Lat. 37-11-19 N long. 078-12-05 W; The town's name remembers Colonel Samuel Burke (1794 -1880). As a railroad stop for the community near Burke's Tavern, the place was first called Burke's Junction. Tarleton's British dragoons came here pillaging in July 1781, and in June 1864 Union cavalry, in order to cut off Confederate supplies to Richmond and Petersburg, tore up railroad tracks in the vicinity. On April 3, 1865, Jefferson Davis and cabinet passed through as they fled from Richmond to Danville, and three days later Union troops, pursuing the retreating Confederates, camped here.

Dictionary of Places

•CAMPBELL COUNTY, Central Virginia; 530 sq. mi.; Pop. 47,572; The county was named after William Campbell (1745-1781) Capt. first reg.; Col. Ca., militia 1777-80; Brig. gen Va., militia 1780.

•CAPE CHARLES, Town; Northampton County; Pop. 1,398; Zip Code 23310; 33 mi. NNE of Norfolk; Lat. 37-16-18 N long. 076- 00-05 W; The town is named after the Cape. Cape Charles honored Charles, Duke of Yorke.

Although Cape Charles was reborn when the railroad arrived in 1884, it is a belated successor to the first two settlements on the Eastern Shore: Secretary's Plantation to the north and Dale's Gift to the south.

This area was occupied by Federal forces early in the Civil War as a precaution against use of the peninsula as an attacking base by the Confederacy. When the Federal troops landed here, the residents, thinking there was to be a battle, armed themselves with whatever odd weapons they could lay hands on, only to find that no fighting was contemplated. The false alarm has been called the Battle of Three Ponds.

Though General H.H. Lockwood, who commanded the Federal forces, established friendly relations with the people, most men of the Eastern Shore who enlisted chose the Confederate side.

•CAPE HENRY Forms with Cape Charles on the north, the entrance to the Chesapeake Bay. A Cluster of buildings is dominated by the towering Cape Henry Lighthouse, which was erected in 1879 and supplanted the Old Lighthouse, near by, built in 1791. Before there was any lighthouse, ships were guided by bonfires. A Granite Cross marks the spot where on April 26, 1607, the passengers of three storm-driven little ships--the *Sarah Constand,* the *Goodspeed,* and the *Discovery* came ashore. Here the adventurers opened the box that contained the sealed instructions of the London Company and here first encountered the Indians, who had not forgotten the vengeance of the Spanish after the killing of the Jesuits along the Potomac.

•CAPRON, Town; Southampton County; Pop. 144; Zip Code 23829; 38 mi. W of Suffolk; Lat. 36-42-39 N long. 077-12-00 W; Originally called Princeton, the name was later changed to Capron, who was a general passenger agent of the railroad.

HISTORICAL PLACE... (See Historical Places Section for details).
Belmont

•CARET Is near an early seat of the old Rappahannock County, which was cut from Lancaster County in 1656 and, extending westward indefinitely, had two seats, the one here for the 'South Side.' It ceased to exist in 1692. Here Thomas and Benjamin

Goodrich were ordered to appear in 1676 with halters around their necks to express penitence for participating in Bacon's Rebellion. The men, wearing strings around their necks, obeyed the order symbolically rather than literally.

•CAROLINE COUNTY, E central Virginia; 544 sq. mi.; Pop. 19,217; Named after Princess Wilhelmina Carolina of Anspach (1683-1737) Queen of England (1727-1737) and second wife of King George II.

•CARROLL COUNTY, SE Virginia; 496 sq. mi.; Pop. 26,564; Named after Charles Carroll.

•CEDAR BLUFF, Town; Tazewell County; Pop. 1,290; Zip Code 24609; 57 mi. NE of Bristol; Descriptively named for the cedar trees covering the bluff.

•CHANCELLORSVILLE Is a crossroads named for the Chancellor House, used by General Joseph Hooker as headquarters during the Battle of Chancellorsville. The structure, burned during the battle and restored in 1908, was later destroyed again.

The Battle of Chancellorsville was the last of a series of Federal failures in Virginia, after each of which Lincoln changed Union commanders. General Hooker, who had supplanted General Ambrose E. Burnside, was placed in command of 130,000 men north of the Rappahannock. General Robert E. Lee had 57,000 Confederates on the south bank. Beginning an offensive on April 29, 1863, Hooker sent his cavalry raiding toward Richmond and placed a corps near Fredericksburg. Then hurriedly moving the greater part of his army up the river, he crossed to the south side and intrenched here.

General Lee, opposed by two forces, either of which, with a common reserve, outnumbered his entire army, left a division at Fredericksburg and moved the remainder to oppose Hooker. Here he retained 14,000 men to oppose the Federal front and sent Jackson with the main body to attack Hooker from the west. On May 2, Jackson's corps struck the Union rear and drove the corps of General O. O. Howard in rout over the main body.

While riding across the front of his lines at dusk to reform his tired and scattered troops, Jackson was shot down by Confederate bullets. Eight days later he died.

At dawn the next morning General J. E. B. Stuart attacked from the west and Lee from the east. The Union Army, caught between these forces, fell back across the Rappahannock River. The Federals lost 17,000 men, and the Confederates about 13,000. The Union forces did not again cross the river until Gettysburg had been fought.

Dictionary of Places

•CHANTILLY Is a crossroads, sometimes called Ox Hill, which Stonewall Jackson reached on Sept. 1, 1862, in a movement to prevent the Federal troops under General Pope from retreating to Alexandria. During spirited action here General Philip Kearny was killed.

•CHARLES CITY COUNTY, SE Virginia; 184 sq. mi.; Pop. 6,282; Named after King Charles the First of England (1600-1649).

•CHARLOTTE COUNTY, S central Virginia; 468 sq. mi.; Pop. 11,688; The county was named after Charlotte Sophia (1774-1818), princess of Mecklenburg - Strelitz; married King George III of England.

•CHARLOTTE COURT HOUSE, Town; Charlotte County Seat; Pop. 531; Zip Code 23923; Elev. 596; 45 mi. SE of Lynchburg; Lat. 37-03-29 N long. 078-38-30 W; The town had a series of names, but was renamed in 1901 after the county. Charlotte was the wife of King George III.

•CHARLOTTESVILLE, Independent City; Pop. 40,341; Zip Code 229+; Elev. 594; 70 mi. WNW of Richmond; Lat. 38-02-12 N long. 078-29-06 W; Founded in 1762 and named for Princess Charlotte, wife of King George III.
It is situated among the foothills of the Blue Ridge Mountains near the Rivanna River and has been an important crossroads since late Colonial times.
In 1735, following the first patents for land hereabout in 1727, Abraham Lewis received 800 acres that embraced the present grounds of the university, and Nicholas Meriwether, 1,020 acres including land on which the eastern part of Charlottesville stands. Two years later William Taylor patented 1,200 acres between the Meriwether and Lewis grants, owned later by Richard Randolph. Meanwhile, Peter Jefferson acquired the estates of Shadwell and Monticello. Few patentees, however, settled upon their estates. Thomas Jefferson said that his father 'was the third or fourth settler, about the year 1737, on the part of the county in which I live.' In 1761 the county purchased a 1,000-acre tract from Richard Randolph, built a new courthouse, and laid out 50 acres in streets and lots adjacent to the courthouse square. In 1762, when it was 'represented' that 'a town for the reception of traders ... would be of great advantage to the inhabitants' of the county, the general assembly 'established a town,' which was named for Queen Charlotte, wife of George III. The county sold the town lots, and taverns and stores sprang up around the courthouse. Other acres of public grounds were sold as 'outlots,' for agricultural use by town residents. Until well into the nineteenth century the Rivanna River was Charlottesville's chief avenue for commercial traffic.

The tumult of war has never seriously disturbed Charlottesville, although the Revolution touched it immediately on two occasions. The establishment of 'The Barracks' near by the 'Convention Troops,' about 4,000 prisoners taken when Burgoyne surrendered at Saratoga in 1777, aroused no bitter feeling. These troops-English officers and soldiers and a large number of Hessian mercenaries-arrived in January 1779 and remained until October 1780, but many of the Germans escaped into the mountains, where their names survive among mountain folk today. Colonel Banastre Tarleton's raid in 1781 was a more serious business. Cornwallis hoped to capture the most important Revolutionary leaders and send them to England. Ex-governor Jefferson, Acting Governor Fleming, and members of the general assembly, warned in the nick of time by Jack Jouett, hastily fled to Staunton. Tarleton and his men destroyed military stores, clothing, and tobacco, raided the county courthouse, and destroyed all the public records, which dated from 1748.

In its youth Charlottesville and the county of which it was social and commercial center produced several men, besides Thomas Jefferson, whose lives contributed richly to the Nation. In order to be near Jefferson, James Monroe came to Charlottesville in 1789 and later moved to Ashlawn close by Monticello. James Madison was a frequent visitor here. Two men whose expeditions identify Charlottesville with the opening of the great West were George Rogers Clark, born at Buena Vista, town miles east, and Meriwether Lewis, born near Ivy, about seven miles west.

Though situated on one of the main east-west roads, Charlottesville remained a small social center until after the first quarter of the nineteenth century. Thomas Jefferson said in 1822: "In our village . . . there is a good degree of religion, with a small spice of fanaticism. We have four sects, but without either church or meeting house. The courthouse is the common temple, one Sunday in the month to each. Here Episcopalian and Presbyterian, Methodist and Baptist meet together, . . . listen with attention and devotion to each others preachers, and all mix in society in perfect harmony," Construction of the first church in the town was begun in 1824. When the university was opened a year later Charlottesville contained 'a courthouse, a half finished church, and three or four taverns, which constitute the whole of its public buildings,' and its inhabitants numbered about 600.

The Civil War only brushed Charlottesville. Most of the university buildings were turned into hospitals, and temporary structures were erected, in which university doctors looked after the wounded. During the last year of the war Union forces under Sheridan occupied the town, but did little damage.

After the Virginia Central Railroad, now the Chesapeake and Ohio, reached Charlottesville in 1848, putting an end to river traffic, industries were established on a modest scale. One of these, the

Dictionary of Places

Charlottesville Woolen Mills, reorganized in 1868, still survives. In 1851 Charlottesville was chartered as a town. In 1881 it was chartered as a city, its population then being 4,200.

POINTS OF INTEREST:
- Ash Lawn (1799). 4 1/4 miles SE on County 795.
- Historic Michie Tavern. 1 mile South on VA 20.
- Robert E. Lee Monument. Jefferson St. between 1st and 2nd Streets.
- Lewis and Clark Monument. Midway Park, Ridge and Main Streets.
- George Rogers Clark Memorial.

HISTORICAL PLACES... (See Historical Places Section for details).
Monticello; Albemarle County Court House; Castle Hill; Ash Lawn; Farmington; Oak Lawn; Rotunda, University of Virginia; University of Virginia Historic District

•**CHASE CITY**, Town; Mecklenburg County; Pop. 2,442; Zip Code 23924; Elev. 546; 28 mi. ENE of South Boston; Lat. 36-47-55 N long. 078-27-34 W; The town's name honors U. S. Supreme Court Justice Chase.

•**CHATHAM**, Town; Pittsylvania County Seat; Pop. 1,354; Zip Code 24531; 15 mi. N of Danville; Lat. 36-49-30 N long. 079-24-03 W; Chatham has been the county seat since 1777. When a permanent courthouse was to be built, a long dispute over where it should be rent the community. When in 1807 the legislature settled the matter, the town was designated Competition and so remained until 1874, when it was renamed in honor of William Pitt, Earl of Chatham, for whom the county had been named in 1767. Henry St. George Tucker, clerk of the House of Delegates, wrote on the blotter: "Immoral Pitt! How great thy fame, When Competition yields to Chatham's name!".

HISTORICAL PLACE... (See Historical Places Section for details).
Little Cherrystone

•**CHERITON**, Town; Northampton County; Pop. 515; Zip Code 23316; 34 mi. NNE of Norfolk; Lat. 37-17-18 N long. 075-58-13 W; Called at one time Cherry Stones, Dr. William Stockley shortened this to "Cheriton."

HISTORICAL PLACE... (See Historical Places Section for details).
Eyre Hall

•**CHESAPEAKE**, Independent City; Pop. 151,976; Zip Code 23320; SE Virginia just S of Norfolk; Lat. 36-41-47 N long. 076-03-25 W; An Indian word meaning "great salt water."

HISTORICAL PLACES... (See Historical Places Section for details).
Glebe Church (Bennett's Creek Church); Great Bridge Battle Site

Encyclopedia of Virginia

•**CHESTERFIELD COUNTY**, E central Virginia; 475 sq. mi.; Pop. 209,274; Named after Philip Dormer Stanhope, Earl of Chesterfield.

•**CHILHOWIE**, Town; Smyth County; Pop. 1,971; Zip Code 24319; Elev. 1950; 30 mi. NE of Bristol; Lat. 36-47-58 N long. 081-41-06 W; Settled in 1750 and named after an Indian phrase meaning "valley of many deer."

•**CHINCOTEAGUE**, Town; Accomack County; Pop. 3,572; Zip Code 233+; E Virginia on Chincoteague Island; Lat. 37-55-59 N long. 075- 22-20 W; The town takes its name from the Chinco- Teague Indians. The name means "beautiful land across the water."

POINTS OF INTEREST:
•Oyster Museum of Chincoteague. Beach Road.
•Chincoteague Miniature Pony Farm. 201 Maddox Blvd.

HISTORICAL PLACE... (See Historical Places Section for details).
Assateague Island/Lighthouse

•**CHRISTIANSBURG**, Town; Montgomery County Seat; Pop. 15,004; Zip Code 240+; 27 mi. WSW of Roanoke; Lat. 37-08-02 N long. 080-24-24 W; Founded in 1792 and later named in honor of colonial Indian fighter, William Christian.

•**CLAREMONT**, Town; Surry County; Pop. 358; Zip Code 23899; Elev. 112; 42 mi. SE of Richmond; Lat. 37-13-38 N long. 076-57-56 W; The town is named after "Claremont," a royal home in Surrey, England.

•**CLARKE COUNTY**, N Virginia; 174 sq. mi.; Pop. 12,101; Named for George Rogers Clarke.

•**CLARKSVILLE**, Town; Mecklenburg County; Pop. 1,243; Zip Code 23927; Elev. 91; 20 mi. SE of South Boston; Lat. 36-37-17 N long. 078-33-44 W; The town takes its name from an early property owner on the Roanoke River.

POINTS OF INTEREST:
•Occoneechee State Park. 1 1/2 miles East on US 58.

HISTORICAL PLACES... (See Historical Places Section for details).
Roanoke River Museum-Prestwould Foundation f1795); Prestwould

•**CLEVELAND**, Town; Russell County; Pop. 214; Zip Code 24225; Elev. 1534; 39 mi. N of Bristol; Lat. 36-56-36 N long. 082-09-13 W; Established in 1890 and named in honor of President Grover Cleveland.

Dictionary of Places

•CLIFTON, Town; Fairfax County; Pop. 176; Zip Code 22024; Lat. 38-46-58 N long. 077-23-09 W; The town is named after the Wyckliffe family of England, who were large property owners in colonial times.

•CLIFTON FORGE, City; Pop. 4,679; Zip Code 24422; 10 mi. E of Covington; Lat. 37-49-01 N long. 079-49-30 W; by the Jackson River. Incorporated in 1884 and named after James Clifton's iron furnace. In 1861 the Virginia Central Railroad, extending from the east through Charlottesville, Waynesboro, and Staunton, had reached the Jackson River at the edge of the present town, and a roadbed had been graded westward to connect it with the Ohio River. But the War between the States intervened and tracks were not laid westward until 1867. The James River and Kanawha Canal Company was authorized in 1876 to build the Buchanan and Clifton Forge Railway to connect the westernmost point of the canal with the railroad. Two years later the Richmond and Alleghany Company was authorized to build a road along the James from Richmond to Buchanan. Thus Clifton Forge became the division point of the large east-to-west system that resulted when the pioneer roads were combined under the Chesapeake and Ohio Railway Company.

POINTS OF INTEREST:
•Douthat State Park. 5 miles North on VA 629.
•Iron Gate Gorge. 2 miles South on US 220.
•Lucy Selina Furnace (1827). 12 miles East on US 60.

HISTORICAL PLACE... (See Historical Places Section for details).
Colonial National Historical Park

•CLINCH RIVER Located in southwest Virginia this river flows about 300 miles through the Great Appalachian Valley into Tennessee. According to Dr. Thomas Walker in 1750 it was named for a hunter of the same name.

•CLINTWOOD, Town; Dickenson County Seat; Pop. 1,542; Zip Code 24228; 77 mi. NW of Bristol; Lat. 37-08-59 N long. 082- 27-09 W; The town's name honors Senator Henry Clinton Wood.

•CLOVER, Town; Halifax County; Pop. 198; Zip Code 24534; Elev. 502; 14 mi. NE of South BostonLat. 36-50-09 N long. 078-44-07 W; The town is named for clover Creek. From this place, on the night of April 5, 1865, John S. Wise, 19-year-old son of the former governor, Henry A. Wise, secretly carried a telegram from President Davis, than at Danville, to General Lee, at Farmville. Leaving Farmville on April 7 with Lee's reply, young Wise recrossed the Federal lines and made his way back to Danville.

Encyclopedia of Virginia

•**COEBURN**, Town; Wise County; Pop. 2,165; Zip Code 24230; Elev. 1992; 50 mi. NW of Bristol; Lat. 36-59-38 N long. 082-28-03 W; Settled in the 1770's, and later renamed for chief railroad engineer, W. W. Coe and a judge named Burn. Coeburn is a railroad junction and mining center by the Guest River. The settlement, first called Guest's Station, was incorporated in 1894.

•**COLONIAL BEACH**, Town; Westmoreland County; Pop. 3,132; Zip Code 22443; 30 mi. E of Fredericksburg; Lat. 38-15-12 N long. 076-57-59 W; Called White Beach from colonial days, it was renamed by a developer in the 1880's to Colonial Beach. The town is a river resort. Many of the cottage owners work in Washington but spend summer vacations here and come down on election days to vote. Two of the cottages were built by Alexander Graham Bell, inventor of the telephone. In the Colonial Beach Hotel is incorporated a house once owned by 'Light Horse Harry' Lee. The little Tonic portico has echoed diminishing elegance during a century and a half, from powdered wigs and epaulettes, through crinoline to slacks and shorts, and from minuet and waltz to big apple and jitter-bug.

The Site of Monrovia is marked by a clump of locust trees. James Monroe, born here April 28, 1758, was the son of Spence Monroe and Elizabeth Jones Monroe and the great-grandson of Andrew Monroe, a Scot who came to Virginia in 1647. The following year Andrew returned to Scotland and fought in the Battle of Preston. Captured and banished, he came again to Virginia and in 1650 patented the first tract of the estate here.

•**COLONIAL HEIGHTS**, Independent City; Pop. 16,064; Zip Code 23834; 5 mi. SE of Petersburg; Lat. 37-00-03 N long. 076-40-07 W; Incorporated in 1926 and named for the general heritage of the area. The first building on this site was erected in 1770 by Thomas Shore, a shipping merchant. Luxuriously appointed with English furniture and numerous *objets d'art*, this earlier Violet Bank, named for the thousands of violets that grew under the oaks once shading the adjacent hill, was chosen by La Fayette as headquarters in 1781. The first mansion burned in 1810.

HISTORICAL PLACES... (See Historical Places Section for details).
Swift Creek Mill; Ellerslie

•**COLUMBIA**, Town; Fluvanna County; Pop. 58; Zip Code 23038; 43 mi. NW of Richmond; Lat. 37-45-10 N long. 078-09-33 W; at the confluence of the James and Rivanna Rivers. Settled in the 18th century and given the popular name for America in 1897. Rising on the site of Rassawek, capital of the Monacans, this was called Point of Fork until an act of the general assembly in 1788 directed that land here 'shall be alid off with convenient streets, and shall be established as a town by the name of Columbia.' Later the town became impor-

Dictionary of Places

tant as the meeting place of two canals. Produce from the north was floated down the Rivanna and its tributaries as early as 1756, for in that year the Reverend James Fontaine Maury of Albemarle wrote, 'Nothing is more common than to see two of these tottering vehicles **flatboats**, when lashed together side by side, carrying down our upland streams eight or nine heavy hogshead of tobacco.

In the latter part of the Revolution, Baron von Steuben, then in charge of Virginia militia, commanded a training post and supply depot here. When he thought that the forces of Simcoe and Tarleton were about to converge here, von Steuben moved the stores and most of his force across the Rivanna. On Simcoe's arrival her retreated, abandoning most of the supplies.

•**COURTLAND,** Town; Southampton County Seat; Pop. 819; Zip Code 23837; Elev. 32; 42 mi. SE of Petersburg; Lat. 36-42-58 N long. 077-03-45 W; Settled in 1750 and renamed Courtland in 1788.

•**COVINGTON,** City; Pop. 6,991; Zip Code 24426; 55 mi. NW of Roanoke; Lat. 37-46-56 N long. 079-59-22 W; Incorporated in 1833 and named for Prince Edward Covingtons.

POINTS OF INTEREST:
•Fort Young. Near exit 4 on I-64.
•Alleghany Central Scenic Railroad. 2 1/2 miles North on US 220 in Intervale.
•Moomaw Lake. 13 miles North via US 200, VA 687.

•**CRAIG COUNTY,** SE Virginia; 336 sq. mi.; Pop. 4,372; Named after Robert Craig (1792-1852) Virginia house of delegates 1817-18, 1825-29 and 1850-52.

•**CRAIGSVILLE,** Town; Augusta County; Pop. 812; Zip Code 24430; Elev. 23; 23 mi. SW of Staunton; Lat. 38-05-02 N long. 079-23-00 W; The town is named for an early settler.

•**CREWE,** Town; Nottoway County; Pop. 2,276; Zip Code 23930; 42 mi. W of Petersburg; Lat. 37-10-46 N long. 078-07-28 W; Founded in 1886 as a rail center, and named for the English railway town, Crewe.

•**CULPEPER COUNTY,** N Virginia; 389 sq. mi.; Pop. 27,791; Named for Lord Thomas Culpeper (1635-1689) second (Royal Province) governor of Virginia.

•**CULPEPER,** Town; Culpeper County Seat; Pop. 8,581; Zip Code 22701; Elev. 430; 42 mi. NE of Charlottesville; Lat. 38-28-24 N long. 077-59-39 W; The town is named for the county. Culpeper honors Lord Culpeper, Governor of Virginia 1680-83. A hill overlooking the western side of the town was the muster place in 1775 for the Culpeper Minute Men, volunteers from Culpeper, Orange, and Fau-

Encyclopedia of Virginia

quier Counties. With a coiled rattlesnake and the legends, 'Don't tread on me' and 'Liberty of Death' on their flag, fringed deerskin trousers and hunting shirts, bucktails flying from their hats and scalping knives and tomahawks at their belts, they had a warlike appearance as they marched to Williamsburg to answer Governor Patrick Henry's call for volunteers in 1777. John Marshall, statesman and Chief Justice of the U.S. Supreme Court, was a youthful lieutenant in the Fauquier company of his father, Captain Thomas Marshall.

Confederates camped not far away in the winter of 1862-63, and officers stayed at the old Virginia Hotel. That polished army boots bound for social events might escape the quagmire, a boardwalk was built across Main Street. Wounded from the battles of Cedar Mountain, from Kelly's Ford, and from Brandy Station were brought to churches, homes, and vacant buildings here. Later, Union officers made headquarters at the Virginia Hotel, and soldiers were billeted in public buildings; General Grant and his staff stayed at the hotel during April 1864.

POINTS OF INTEREST:
•Culpeper Cavalry Museum. 133 West Davis Street.

HISTORICAL PLACE... (See Historical Places Section for details).
Hill, A. P., Boyhood Home

•**CUMBERLAND COUNTY,** Central Virginia; 288 sq. mi.; Pop. 7,825; Named after the Duke of Cumberland.

•**DAMASCUS,** Town; Washington County; Pop. 918; Zip Code 24236; Elev. 1928; 32 mi. NE of Bristol; Lat. 36-38-29 N long. 081-46-50 W; The town is named after the ancient Syrian city.

•**DAN RIVER** From its origin in south Virginia it winds into North Carolina and back, then Northeast past South Boston and the Roanoke River-- a total of about 175 miles.

•**DANVILLE,** City; Pop. 53,056; Zip Code 245+; 3 mi. N of North Carolina border; Lat. 36-35-12 N long. 079-23-09 W; spread over hills that slope gradually toward a wide bend in the Dan River. Descriptively named for its location on river. Danville began as an inspection warehouse. In 1793, Piedmont planters, irked by the hardship of rolling hogsheads over red clay roads to Richmond or Petersburg for the required inspection, petitioned the legislature for inspection facilities at this central point by the river. The petition was granted and trustees were appointed to take over 25 acres of land, which were to be divided and sold in half-acre lots. Inspection began at once, but it was two years before the first tier of lots, hugging the old Salisbury road, now Main Street, was offered for sale.

Dictionary of Places

Early tobacco marketing was a haphazard business. Many inland growers sold their tobacco by the acre of barnful, letting the buyer worry about getting it out. First impetus to Danville's growth was improvement of river transportation, which began about 1820 when the Roanoke Navigation Company built a canal around the falls and opened the way for bateaux carrying tobacco to ships in Albemarle Sound. Real expansion began when the organized auction warehouse system was introduced in 1852-though the first was a small, poorly-lighted structure and a Black advertised the sales by blowing a horn along the streets.

Though Danville escaped material damage during the War between the States, its position at the junction with the railroad bringing food and military supplies to Richmond and the fighting zone from Atlanta and gulf ports made it a valuable base. Idle tobacco warehouses were turned into hospitals, and one became a prison for captured Yankees. For seven days-April 3-10, 1865-Danville was the capital of the fast dying Confederacy. When the Richmond-Petersburg area was evacuated, President Davis and his Cabinet came to Danville, and here the President called the last full cabinet meeting and issued his last official proclamation, going to a newspaper office to see it set up and printed. When news of Lee's surrender came on April 10, Davis set out immediately for Greensboro, N.C. The same day Governor William (Extra-Billy) Smith arrived on horseback from Richmond, having stopped first at Lynchburg. For five days thereafter the town was the seat of the State administration.

Danville's industrial era began in 1881 with the opening of a small yarn mill. The Riverside Mill, parent of the present Riverside and Dan River Cotton Mills, was organized in 1882 and by 1890 had taken over a small rival, Morotock Mills. With the harnessing of the Falls of the Dan to create cheap electric power, and the influx of cheap labor from farms and mountain settlements, the business has grown fairly steadily. In 1931, 4,000 textile workers struck, demanding union recognition in a wage dispute. The strike, which loomed large in National importance as an early attempt by organized labor to capture textile strongholds in the South, began in September with a huge parade led by blaring bands, mass meetings with National organizers exhorting the strikers, meetings of those with sympathy for the mill owners, and charges and counter-charges. By midwinter the strike had swindled to a bitter endurance test, with bread lines, soup kitchens, evictions from mill houses, and the guns of the National Guard policing the mill districts. The affair ended in early spring, neither side conceding defeat.

POINTS OF INTEREST:
- Tobacco auctions.
- National Tobacco-Textile Museum. 614 Lynn Street.
- "Last Capitol of the Confederacy" (Danville Museum of Fine Arts and History). 975 Main Street.

Encyclopedia of Virginia

HISTORICAL PLACES... (See Historical Places Section for details).
Danville Historic District; Danville Public Library

•**DAYTON,** Town; Rockingham County; Pop. 921; Zip Code 22821; 6 mi. SW of Harrisonburg; Lat. 38-24-51 N long. 078-56-33 W; Dayton may be named in honor of Jonathan Dayton, a ratifier of the Constitution.

HISTORICAL PLACES... (See Historical Places Section for details).
Fort Harrison

•**DENDRON,** Town; Surry County; Pop. 305; Zip Code 23839; 15 mi. SW of Williamsburg; Lat. 37-02-21 N long. 076-55-40 W; Founded in the 1880's and given a Greek name meaning tree, referring to the town's lumber industry.

•**DICKENSON COUNTY,** SE Virginia; 335 sq. mi.; Pop. 17,620; Named after William Dickenson.

•**DILLWYN,** Town; Buckingham County; Pop. 458; Zip Code 239+; 34 mi. S of Charlottesville; Lat. 37-28-09 N long. 078-33-52 W; Named for an early settler.

•**DRAKES BRANCH,** Town; Charlotte County; Pop. 565; Zip Code 23937; Elev. 383; 49 mi. SE of Lynchburg; Lat. 36-59-40 N long. 078-36-12 W; Named for the stream, Drakes Branch, that flows through town.

•**DUBLIN,** Town; Pulaski County; Pop. 2,012; Zip Code 24084; 7 mi. NE of Pulaski; Lat. 37-06-09 N long. 080-41-17 W; The first settler, Irishman William Christian, named the town for Dublin, Ireland.

•**DUFFIELD,** Town; Scott County; Pop. 54; Zip Code 24244; Elev. 1365; Lat. 36-43-11 N long. 082-47-37 W; The town is named for the Duff family who were early settlers.

•**DUMFRIES,** Town; Prince William County; Pop. 4,282; Zip Code 22026; 17 mi. SW of Alexandria; Lat. 38-35-47 N long. 077- 19-02 W; An early settler, John Graham, named the town for his home in Scotland. After the bars to Virginia profitable tobacco trade were lifted by the Navigation Law of 1707, Scottish merchants immediately concentrated their activities around Quantico Creek. As early as 1713 a 'factory' and an 'agent's house' had been built and by 1749 the town had been established. In 1759 Dumfries became the seat of Prince William County. Filled at the apogee of its commercial activity with 2,000 people concerned only with exporting tobacco, Dumfries reckoned without the vagaries of nature and more in-

Dictionary of Places

sidious mankind, Silt began to clog Quantico Creek and boats, in search of flour as well as tobacco, sailed by its entry to Alexandria's more approachable wharfs. Improvident Dumfries gradually forwent its tea drinking, balls, and drama, and dwindled to comparative nothingness.

HISTORICAL PLACE... (See Historical Places Section for details).
Old Hotel

•**DUNGANNON**, Town; Scott County; Pop. 250; Zip Code 24245; Elev. 1311; 46 mi. NW of Bristol; Lat. 36-49-52 N long. 082-28-07 W; Pioneer Captain Patrick Hagan named the town for his former home in Ireland.

•**DUNWIDDIE COUNTY**, SE Virginia; 507 sq. mi.; Pop. 20,960; Named after Robert Dunwiddie (1693-1770) Lt. governor of Virginia, (Royal Province) 1751-56 and 56-58.

•**EASTVILLE**, Town; Northampton County Seat; Pop. 185; Zip Code 23347; 39 mi. NNE of Norfolk; Lat. 37-21-09 N long. 075-56-17 W; Descriptively named for its relative location east of other nearby towns. When the county that formerly embraced all the Virginia Eastern Shore and was first call Accawmacke (Accomac) was divided, the new upper county assumed the old named, and the lower county retained the one adopted in 1643. Eastville became the county seat in 1680, succeeding Town's Field.

HISTORICAL PLACE... (See Historical Places Section for details).
Caserta; Pear Valley

•**EDINBURG**, Town; Shenandoah County; Pop. 860; Zip Code 22824; 34 mi. NE of Harrisonburg; Lat. 38-49-26 N long. 078-33-48 W; Incorporated in 1852 as Edinburg, even though it was described as a "Garden of Eden" and Edenburg suggested. Edinburg was founded on land owned by Philip Bishop. Captured by Indians, he had escaped and changed his name to Grandstaff. The town rose to prominence because of its rifle factory, which supplied many guns for the War of 1812.

For a month during 1862 the town was a basis of operations for General Turner Ashby, who involved the enemy in 28 skirmishes during that period. General Sheridan set the mills of the town on fire, but, persuaded by two young women that the people of the community depended on the mills for food, he had the flames extinguished.

•**ELKTON**, Town; Rockingham County; Pop. 1,935; Zip Code 22827; 17 mi. SE of Harrisonburg; Lat. 38-24-29 N long. 078-37-06 W; The town takes its name for Elk Run stream which flows through the town.

Encyclopedia of Virginia

•**EMPORIA**, Independent City; Pop. 5,306; Zip Code 23847; Elev. 119; 38 mi. S of Petersburg; Lat. 36-41-24 N long. 077-32-27 W; Settled as two villages, North Emporia and South Emporia, in the 1780's divided by the Meherrin River, the towns merged in 1887 and took the name Emporia. The name means "center of trade."

The town of Hicksford, or Hicksville, grew up near the site of a ford, named for Captain Robert Hix, an Indian trader who was captain of the garrison at Fort Christanna in 1717. He accompanied Governor Alexander Spotswood to Albany, N.Y. in 1722, to negotiate a treaty with the Five Nations, and in 1728 was a member of Colonel William Byrd's surveying expeditions.

On December 10, 1864, when Warren reached Belfield, he found Hampton protecting the railroad bridge from a well-fortified position. Repulsed, Warren returned to his lines at Petersburg. Hampton's cavalry remained here for a month while repairs were being made on the railroad.

HISTORICAL PLACE... (See Historical Places Section for details).
Klugel, H. T., Architectual Sheet Metal Work Building

•**ESSEX COUNTY**, E Virginia; 250 sq. mi.; Pop. 8,689; Named after Essex County, England.

•**EXMORE**, Town; Northampton County; Pop. 1,115; Zip Code 23350; Elev. 41; 54 mi. NNE of Norfolk; Lat. 37-26-56 N long. 075-54-56 W; So named because it was the tenth (x) railroad station to the south of Delaware.

•**FAIRFAX COUNTY**, NE Virginia; 416 sq. mi.; Pop. 818,584; Named after Lord Thomas Fairfax (1612-1671).

•**FAIRFAX**, Independent City; Pop. 19,622; Zip Code 22021; Elev. 447; 10 mi. NW of Alexandria; Lat. 38-53-44 N long. 077-25-59 W; The city is named for Lord Fairfax, one of the early great landowners.

POINTS OF INTEREST:
•Dulles International Airport. I-66 from Roosevelt Bridge.
•Bull Run Regional Park. From Beltway I-66 West, exit at Centreville, West on US 29, 211, 3 miles to park sign.

HISTORICAL PLACES... (See Historical Places Section for details).
George Mason University; Sully (1794); Earp's Ordinary (Ratcliff-Logan-Allison House); Fairfax County Courthouse

•**FALLS CHURCH**, Independent City; Pop. 9,578; Zip Code 22040; 10 mi. NW of Alexandria; Lat. 38-53-03 N long. 077-10-38 W; Descriptively named for the town's location on the falls of the Potomac and an Episcopal Church built in 1734. This Church, of Fairfax Parish,

Dictionary of Places

was erected in 1767-69 on the site of a structure built in 1734 by Colonel Richard Blackburn of Rippon Lodge, 'a builder of skill.' During the Revolution it was a military recruiting station. After the disestablishment of the Church of England, it was abandoned until 1830. During the Civil War it was used as a hospital and later a stable for cavalry horses.

HISTORICAL PLACES... (See Historical Places Section for details).
The Falls Church; Cherry Hill

•FARMVILLE, Town; Cumberland & Prince Edward Counties; Prince Edward County Seat; Pop. 6,046; Zip Code 23901; 45 mi. E of Lynchburg; Lat. 37-18-02 N, long. 078-23-29 W. The town is a distribution point for agricultural produce and so was named Farmville. On the afternoon of April 6, 1865, Lee's retreating army was attacked by Sheridan's cavalry and two crops of infantry at Sailor's Creek, 10 miles to the east. The Confederate rear was cut off, and 6,000 men and six generals were taken prisoners. The following morning the retreating army pushed westward.

POINTS OF INTEREST:
•Bear Creek Lake State Park. 20 miles NE on VA 45, then 4 1/2 on VA 622 West.

HISTORICAL PLACES... (See Historical Places Section for details).
Appomattox Court House National Historical Park
Sayler's Creek Battlefield Historical State Park

•FAUQUIER COUNTY, N Virginia; 660 sq. mi.; Pop. 48,741; Named for Francis Fauquier (170401768) Lt. governor of Virginia (1758-68).

•FINCASTLE, Town; Botetourt County Seat; Pop. 236; Zip Code 24090; 21 mi. NE of Roanoke; Lat. 37-30-00 N long. 079- 52-39 W; Named for Lord Fincastle. The town was founded in 1772 on land donated by Israel Christian for a county seat in 1770, one year after the original Botetourt County was formed and two years before much of its territory was separated to from Fincastle County.

In 1828 it was incorporated. Botetourt County was named for Norborne Berkeley, Baron de Botetourt, then governor of Virginia, when it was formed during the first of a series of divisions of Augusta County, necessitated by the rapid increase in the number of western Virginia settlements. Botetourt first covered an area now included in 19 Virginia counties, 32 West Virginia counties, and the state of Kentucky.

HISTORICAL PLACE... (See Historical Places Section for details).
Santillane

•FLOYD COUNTY, S Virginia; 383 sq. mi.; Pop. 12,0005; Named after John Floyd.

Encyclopedia of Virginia

•**FLOYD**, Town; Floyd County Seat; Pop. 396; Zip Code 24091; Elev. 2496; 35 mi. SW of Roanoke; Lat. 36-54-25 N long. 080-15-30 W; The town was named in honor of a prominent local citizen.

In Floyd was born Robley Dunglison Evans (1846-1912), commander of the *USS Iowa* at the Battle of Santiago Harbor, 1898, who after his appointment as rear admiral in 1901, commanded both the Asiatic (1902) and Atlantic Fleets (1905-08).

•**FLUVANNA COUNTY**, Central Virginia; 282 sq. mi.; Pop. 12,429; Named for Queen Anne of England (1665-1714).

•**FRANKLIN COUNTY**, S Virginia; 718 sq. mi.; Pop. 39,549; Named after Benjamin Franklin.

•**FRANKLIN**, City; Pop. 7,864; Zip Code 23851; 21 mi. W of Suffolk; Lat. 36-40-38 N long. 076-55-46 W; The city's name honors patriot Benjamin Franklin.

•**FREDERICK COUNTY**, N Virginia; Pop. 45,723; Named for Frederick Louis (1707-1751) Prince of Wales, eldest son of George II and Queen Caroline.

•**FREDERICKSBURG**, Independent City; Pop. 19,027; Zip Code 224+; 41 mi. SW of Alexandria; Lat. 38-22-39 N long. 077-27-23 W; Founded in 1727 and named in honor of Frederic, Prince of Wales.

It is located at the head of navigation on the Rappahannock River.

Fredericksburg's authenticated record begins in 1608 with a visit by Captain John Smith. In 1671 John Buckner, Robert Bryan, and Thomas Royston patented here a tract called later the Lease-land. In 1722 there was a public ferry across the river 'from Mrs. Fitzhugh's plantation . . . to the wharf on the leased land of Thomas Buckner and John Royston.' About 1723 William Levingston moved here and built 'a dwelling and kitchen.' In 1727 the general assembly directed that 50 acres of the Lease-land be laid out, and established a town for Spotsylvania County by the name of Fredericksburg-for Frederick, Prince of Wales and father of George III. Colonel William Byrd II, visiting the sparsely settled town five years later, was impressed by the stone prison, 'strong enough to hold Jack Shepherd,' and by the versatility of 'Mrs. Levistone,' who was a 'Doctress and Coffee Woman,' and qualify'd to exercise 2 other callings.' He noted that 'the Court-house and the Church are going to be built here, and then both Religion and Justice will help enlarge the Place.'

The town grew as a port. Ships lay 'close to the Wharf, within 30 yards of the Public Warehouses, which are built in the figure of a Cross.' Wagons jolted in from the countryside with wheat and tobacco for export. Rows of buildings, many brick, began to rise on Sophia and Caroline Streets, and mansions were built on the 'hill.' In 1734 a new ferry was authorized 'on Rappahannock river, from the warehouse landing, at the town of Fredericksburg 1765: "Back settlements send down to Fredericksburg great quantities of butter, cheese, flax, hemp, flower and some tobacco." Soon wheat and flour led the exports.

During the Revolution the town furnished leaders for the Continental Army and arms from its 'gunnery.' In an old order book, dated September 18, 1783, is an entry 'to Mary Driskell, a nurse in the Continental Hospital at Fredericksburg, from January 9, '79, to May '82, by which appears to be due the amount certified, 266:19.'

In 1781 Fredericksburg was incorporated as a town. After the Revolution it prospered steadily. In 1807, however, during the obsequies of William Stanard, an overturned candle started a fire that reduced half the town to ashes. But Fredericksburg recovered. As center for a large number of slaveholding landed proprietors, some of whom lived in town, it entered a period of luxury, when racecourses, wine cellars, and balls reached their apogee. Great canvas-covered wagons, some as high as 12 feet, lumbered in from 'up country' with loads of grain, tobacco, and other produce, drawn by four to eight horses with bells jangling on their collars. They returned laden with groceries, wines house furnishings, and other imported supplies. Two hundred of these huge conveyances were often in Fredericksburg at one time, 'bringing business for the many vessels, some of them large three-masted schooners, which came from all parts of the globe to anchor at the wharves.' In 1822 Fredericksburg was made a central point for the distribution of mail to five States, and the mails became so heavy that surveys were used instead of postriders. During this era of prosperity even funerals were occasions for entertaining, refreshments being served in dark wrappings and wine drunk from glasses festooned with long black ribbons. In 1840 there were 73 stores, 4 semiweekly newspapers, 3,974 inhabitants, and exports amounted to about $4,000,000 yearly.

Fredericksburg's distinguished men were not at all of the Revolutionary period. Matthew Fontaine Maury, the great marine cartographer, spent part of his life here. Another native was Maury's brother-in-law, William Lewis Herndon, who worked with him for a time at the National Observatory and, in 1851, was apparently the first to explore the Amazon to its headwaters.

The Civil War struck Fredericksburg down. Situated halfway between Washington and Richmond and on main roads and a rail route, it was a major objective of both armies. It changed hands seven times during the conflict and achieved, with its immediate neighborhood, the unhappy distinction of being one of the bloodiest battlegrounds of history.

In 1879 the general assembly created 'the city of Fredericksburg .. one body politic, in fact and in name.' By the

Encyclopedia of Virginia

beginning of the twentieth century the scars of battle and Reconstruction were fairly smoothed out, and since then improvements have changed a sleepy community into a modern little city. In 1912 Fredericksburg exchanged its councilmanic form of government for the city manager plan.

POINTS OF INTEREST:
- Rising Sun Tavern. 1306 Caroline Street.
- Presbyterian Church (1833).
- Masonic Cemetery. George and Charles Streets Street.
- Mary Washington House. 1200 Charles Street.
- St. James House. 1300 Charles Street.
- Confederate Cemetery. Washington Avenue between Amelia and William Streets.
- Old Stone Warehouse. 920 Sophia Street.

HISTORICAL PLACES... (See Historical Places Section for details).
St. George's Episcopal Church and Churchyard; Kenmore (1752); Belmont; Mary Washington College; Fredericksburg and Spotsylvania County Battlefields Memorial National Military Park; St. James Church; Fredericksburg Historic District; Monroe Law Office; Rising Sun Tavern; Fall Hill; Rapidan Dam Canal of the Rappahannock; Ferry Farm Site (George Washington's Boyhood Home Site); George Washington Birthplace National Monument

- **FRIES,** Town; Grayson County; Pop. 690; Zip Code 24330; Elev. 2180; 26 mi. SSW of Pulaski; Lat. 36-42-59 N long. 080-58-40 W; The town is named for a local resident.

- **FRONT ROYAL,** Town; Warren County Seat; Pop. 11,880; Zip Code 22630; Elev. 567; 20 mi. S of Winchester; Lat. 38-55-21 N long. 078-11-37 W; Front Royal was chartered in 1788, was at first a frontier village, called 'Hell Town,' on the packhorse road to the north. Two legends account for the name Front Royal. According to one, British officers during the Revolution, when drilling their men near a large oak tree, gave the command, 'Front the Royal Oak' and the sentence was shortened to 'Front Royal.' According to another story, the sentry's command 'Front' and the pass word 'Royal' were linked by common usage.

Front Royal was one of the bases from which the pretty Confederate spy Belle Boyd worked most effectively. In 1862 when a Federal regiment occupied Front Royal, she invited General Nathaniel P. Banks and his officers to a ball. While the weary officers slept after the festivities, according to the story, she made a daring horseback ride to give Jackson valuable information she had garnered. The next morning, May 23, 1862, the Confederates attacked the Union force here and captured 750 of the 1,000 men. In the afternoon General Jackson arrived.

Dictionary of Places

POINTS OF INTEREST:
•Skyline Caverns. 1 mile South on US 340.
•Thunderbird Museum and Archaeological Park. 7 miles South via US 340.
•Sky Meadows State Park. 20 miles East on US 66, 7 miles North on VA17.

•**GALAX**, City; Pop. 6,670; Zip Code 24333; Elev. 2382; 36 mi. N of Pulaski; Lat. 36-39-55 N long. 080-54-52 W; The town is named for the decorative mountain evergreen plant. Galax sits astride the Grayson-Carroll County line, sprang up in 1904, when a spur of Norfolk and Western Railway opened up the timber regions. For a year it was called Bonaparte.

POINTS OF INTEREST:
•Blue Ridge Parkway.

•**GATE CITY**, Town; Scott County Seat; Pop. 2,214; Zip Code 24251; Elev. 1304; 24 mi. W of Bristol; Lat. 36-37-43 N long. 082-34-06 W; Descriptively named for nearby Moccasin Gap, which was a gateway to western coal fields. An early tavern kept here by Elisha Faris was frequented by most travelers on the Boone trail. The Faris family was slain in 1791 by the notorious half-breed Benge, who led his red brothers in an attempt to drive out the intruding whites.

•**GILES COUNTY**, SE Virginia; 356 sq. mi.; Pop. 16,366; Named after Willian Branch Giles.

•**GLADE SPRING**, Town; Washington County; Pop. 1,435; Zip Code 24340; Elev. 2084; 30 mi. NE of Bristol; Lat. 36-47-51 N long. 081-46-03 W; The town is descriptively named for the spring found in a glade by the first settlers.

•**GLASGOW**, Town; Rockbridge County; Pop. 1,140; Zip Code 24555; 40 mi. NE of Roanoke; Lat. 37-37-51 N long. 079-26-52 W; The town was developed on the Glasgow homestead and so named. Established in 1890. General Fitzhugh Lee was president of the promotion company. Neither the large hotel nor the power plant, hopefully built, was ever operated, and industries failed to materialize.

In December 1742, Captain John McDowell and seven militiamen were killed near by in the first fight with the Indians in this vicinity. Captain McDowell had entertained the natives for a day on apparently friendly terms. But after the warriors left they hunted for a week or more along the South River and pillaged in the neighborhood. Captain McDowell raised a body of 34 men to expel the Indians from the area; in the fight that followed, there were casualties on both sides.

•GLEN LYN, Town; Giles County; Pop. 170; Zip Code 24093; Elev. 1537; 30 mi. NE of Blacksburg; Lat. 37-22-18 N long. 080-51-59 W; Settled in 1750 and named Montreal, the name was changed to Glen Lyn, or lovely glen, in 1883.

•GLOUCESTER COUNTY, SE Virginia; 225 sq. mi.; Pop. 30,131; Named after Henry, Duke of Glousester.

•GOOCHLAND COUNTY, Central Virginia; 289 sq. mi.; Pop. 14,163; Named after William Gooch (1681-1751) Lt col; governor of Virginia (Royal Province) Virginia col. governor 1727-1737 and 1737-40.

•GORDONSVILLE, Town; Orange County; Pop. 1,351; Zip Code 22942; Elev. 493; 25 mi. NE of Charlottesville; Lat. 078-11-21 W; Early settler Nathaniel Gorden purchased 1300 acres here in 1787. The town is named after him. The village had its first growth as the western terminus of the Louisa Railroad. In 1855 the Orange and Alexandria established its terminus here. To reach these, two toll roads were constructed in the 1850's across the Blue Bridge.

Interest in blooded horses began early here. Before the middle of the nineteenth century, local breeders set up a training stable under the care of an English trainer and dubbed it 'Horse College.' Here was kept Voltaire, a renowed sire.

HISTORICAL PLACES... (See Historical Places Section for details).
Boswell's Tavern; Hawkwood

•GOSHEN, Town; Rockbridge County; Pop. 366; Zip Code 24439; 30 mi. SW of Staunton; Lat. 37-59-28 N long. 079-29-55 W; The town's name is a biblical synonym of fruitfulness and fertility.

•GRAYSON COUNTY, SE Virginia; 451 sq. mi.; Pop. 16,278; Named after William Grayson.

•GREENE COUNTY, Central Virginia; 153 sq. mi.; Pop. 10,297; Named after Nathaniel Greene.

•GREENSVILLE COUNTY, S Virginia; 301 sq. mi.; Pop. 8,853; Named after Nanthanael Greene.

•GRETNA, Town; Pittsylvania County; Pop. 1,339; Zip Code 24557; Elev. 844; 34 mi. S of Lynchburg; Lat. 36-57-20 N long. 079-21-52 W; Called Franklin Junction until 1916 when the name was changed to Gretna.

HISTORICAL PLACES... (See Historical Places Section for details).
Yates Tavern

Dictionary of Places

•**GROTTOES**, Town; Augusta & Rockingham Counties; Pop. 1,455; Zip Code 24441; 16 mi. SE of Harrisonburg; Lat. 38-15-43 N long. 078-49-23 W; Descriptively named for the many grottoes, or limestone caverns in the nearby Shenandoah Mountains.

•**GRUNDY**, Town; Buchanan County Seat; Pop. 1,305; Zip Code 24614; Elev. 1050; 86 mi. N Bristol; Founded in the 1850's and named for a U. S. Senator from Texas in that era.

•**HALIFAX COUNTY**, S Virginia; 808 sq. mi.; Pop. 29,033; Named after George Montago Dunk, Earl of Halifax.

•**HALIFAX**, Town; Halifax County Seat; Pop. 688; Zip Code 24558; 6 mi. N of South Boston; Lat. 36-45-50 N long. 078-55-57 W; Founded in 1752 and named for George Dunk, Earl of Halifax. In 1890 new railroad facilities caused it to change its name from Banister to Houston for a railroad executive, who was to be asked to send factories into the town. Unfortunately, the committee sent to New York to acquaint the gentlemen with his new honor made the disastrous mistake of mispronouncing his name. Whereupon he denied his interest in the town and thereafter influenced no industries to come. In 1920 the little community went back to its historic designation as the county town of Halifax County.

•**HALLWOOD**, Town; Accomack County; Pop. 228; Zip Code 23359; Lat. 37-52-38 N long. 075-35-16 W; Although not incorporated until 1958 the town is named after an old colonial family, the Halls.

•**HAMILTON**, Town; Loudoun County; Pop. 700; Zip Code 22068; Elev. 275; Lat. 39-08-05 N long. 077-39-46 W; Established in 1829 and named after the town's first postmaster, Charles Hamilton.

HISTORICAL PLACE... (See Historical Places Section for details).
Clifton

•**HAMPTON**, Independent City; Pop. 133,793; Zip Code 236+; 7 mi. NE of Newport News; The city was founded in 1680 and named in honor of the Earl of Southampton.

Everywhere in Hampton are soldiers, enlisted men, and officers from the Coast Artillery post at Fort Monroe and from Langley Field. Crowds, far out of proportion to the size of the city, move in leisurely fashion, and army cars pass continually along Queen Street. From May through September holiday throngs go through Hampton to and from Buckroe Beach.

When in 1619 the colony was divided into four 'incorporations' with a proposed chief city for each division, a wide territory on both sides of the James was named Elizabeth City. When the 'incorporations' were divided into counties in 1634, the territory embracing Kecoughtan became Elizabeth City County. In 1620 the land between the creek and Chesapeake Bay was appropriated for public uses, and the portion on the bay called Buck Roe was assigned to the growing of grapes and mulberry trees.

Hampton's first businessman, William Claiborne, arrived in 1630 with authorization from the governor's council 'to make discoveries in the Chesapeake Bay and to trade with the Indians.' He established a profitable post on Kent Island, then thought to be a part of Virginia, and set up a storehouse and a trading base on his 150-acre grant at Kecoughtan. Here he lived during the tumultuous years after 1634 when Lord Baltimore's colonists, with a map that showed Kent Island within their domain, found him his underlings most mutinous subjects. When the system of inspecting and storing tobacco was inaugurated in 1633, one of the first seven warehouses was established at 'Southhampton river in Elizabeth City.' The town of Hampton was formally established and named in 1680.

The community knew too well the pirates that infested the Virginia coast in the late seventeenth century. Hampton citizens continually protested the drunkenness and inefficiency of Captain Aldred, who commanded the *Essex-Prize,* a pirate-chaser that always lay up for repairs when its services were needed. When the man-of-war *Shoreham* replaced the *Essex-Prize* in 1700, Peter Heyman, collector of customs for the James River, was among the Virginians killed in a ten-hour battle that resulted in defeat of the pirates. Governor Nicholson, who had risked his life aboard the *Shoreham* to watch the engagement, reported that 'Peter Heyman had behaved himself very well in the fight.' Heyman was appointed postmaster in 1692 for all the plantations in Virginia and Maryland, and endeavored to set up an efficient Colonial postal system. In 1718 Captain Henry Maynard, a citizen of Hampton, killed Edward Teach, alias Blackbeard, the most notorious of all the Colonial brigands of the sea, and helped bring piracy to an end.

More than 1,100 Acadians came to Hampton in 1755, and while their ships lay at anchor in Hampton Roads, Governor Dinwiddie and the council engaged in lengthy conferences and much letter writing. The poor exiles were greatly feared, for, said the governor, Virginia had been 'much harassed by that perfidious nation in our back country.' 'It was unkind of the Governor of Nova Scotia,' he continued, 'to send such a number of people here without the least previous notice.' Nevertheless, the Acadians were allowed to land and were cared for until the following spring when Virginia appropriated money for their deportation.

Dictionary of Places

Among the prominent citizens or natives of Hampton were George Wythe; James Barron, commodore of the American Navy during the Revolution; Commodore Samuel Barron, commander of a United States squadron in the Tripolitan War; another Commodore James Barron; and Commodore Lewis Warrington, commander of an American squadron during the War of 1812.

This seaport town also has a military history. Though the British several times skirted Hampton during the Revolution, and though Hampton furnished its share of soldiers, no fighting took place in the immediate vicinity. During the War of 1812, however, the British, exasperated by their failure to take Portsmouth, attacked Hampton in June 1813. Momentarily repulsed by Virginia militia under Major Stapleton Crutchfield, the British rallied and entered Hampton as the Virginians retreated westward. Hampton was incorporated as a town in 1849, though it was authorized by the 'Act of Cohabitation' in 1680. In August 1861 Hampton suffered its greatest loss when the town was burned by its own inhabitants to prevent occupation by the Federals; only five houses remained standing.

At the end of the war, ragged soldiers came home to rebuild the city. Hampton Institute became an important center of Black education. In 1882 a rail line was completed from Richmond to the mouth of the James. Another fire in 1884 wiped out 33 of the newly built residences and stores on Queen Street. Fishermen and oystermen began to bring in their wares for shipping; seafood plants were started on a small scale and flourished. The establishment of important industries in the Norfolk area helped to bring about Hampton's revival, and in 1908 it was chartered as a city.

POINTS OF INTEREST:
- Hampton Monument. 1/2 mile South, on grounds of the Veterans Admin., Medical Center between Hampton River and Mill Creek, off I-64 exits 4, 5.
- National Aeronautics and Space Administration Langley Research Center. 3 miles North on VA 134.
- Big Bethel Battlefield. Big Bethel Road.
- Aerospace Park. 413 W. Mercury Blvd., US 258.
- Syms-Eaton Museum. 418 West Mercury Blvd.
- Kecoughtan Indian Village. 418 West Mercury Blvd., 2 miles East on US 258 via I-64.
Avenue on Chesapeake Bay.
- Bluebird Gap Farm. 60 Pine Chapel Road.

HISTORICAL PLACES... (See Historical Places Section for details).
St. John's Church; Fort Monroe; Chesterville Plantation Site; Fort Wool; Hampton Institute; Herbert House; Old Point Comfort Lighthouse; St. John's Church

HAMPTON ROADS PORT, the channel through which the waters of the converging James, Nansemond, and Elizabeth Rivers flow into Chesapeake Bay.

From 1607, when Sir Christopher Newport brought his band of pioneers to effect the first permanent English settlement in America, throughout the Colonial period, Hampton Roads was a point of entry to the seat of government in Virginia. Ships bringing other settlers and supplies sailed through its broad waters into the James. Later it was the hunting place of pirates and hostile British ships, and, during the Civil War, the scene of important naval conflicts.

On June 22, 1807, occurred a naval engagement rising from the presence of four alleged British deserters on the American vessel, *Chesapeake*. The British frigate *Leopard* pursued the *Chesapeake* through the Capes, then fired a broadside into the American vessel, which surrendered without firing a shot. The *Chesapeake* was boarded and the deserters were taken. Commodore James Barron (1769-1821), commander of the *Chesapeake*, was afterwards court-martialed 'for neglecting in the probability of an engagement, to clear his ship for battle,' and deprived of rank and pay for five years. On his return to duty, he was refused an active command through the influence of Commodore Stephen Decatur, Jr. This resulted in a duel between Barron and Decatur in 1820, and Decatur was killed. Barron was later commandant of the Gosport Navy Yard in Portsmouth.

On the afternoon of March 8, 1862, occurred the battle that changed naval warfare. The *Virginia*, formerly the *Merrimac*, a wooden ship which had been sunk, raised by the Confederates, and converted into an ironclad, attacked the Federal fleet, which was armed with 204 guns and aided by land batteries. By six o'clock the *Virginia* had sunk the *Cumberland*, burned the *Congress*, driven the *Minnesota* ashore, and compelled the *St. Lawrence* and the *Roanoke* to seek shelter under the guns of Fort Monroe. On March 9 the *Virginia* encountered the *Monitor*, an ironclad more heavily armored and more efficient by reason of her light draught and revolving gun turret. For four hours the two ironclads battered each other, until at last a shell from the *Virginia* exploded on the eyeslit of the *Monitor's* pilot house, blinding her commander, Captain John L. Worden. 'Tactically,' said R.S. Henry in *The Story of the Confederacy*, 'it was a drawn fight, in its results a victory for the Monitor.'

•**HANOVER COUNTY**, E Virginia; 466 sq. mi.; Pop. 63,306; Named after the Duke of Hanover.

•**HARRISONBURG**, Independent City; Pop. 30,707; Zip Code 22801; Elev. 1352; 23 mi. NNE of Staunton; Lat. 38-26-46 N long. 078-52-15 W; Harrisonburg was founded by Thomas Harrison, who, with his wife

Dictionary of Places

Sarah, had settled about 1739 at this point where the Indian Road crossed the Spotswood Trail. In 1779 the couple conveyed land to the county for the erection of a courthouse, and the following year Harrison procured the passage of an act establishing the town. Popularly known in its infancy as Rocktown, the settlement grew rapidly, fostered by Harrison's sons Reuben and Robert, who supplied lands in 1797 for municipal expansion. In 1794 Bishop Asbury started a Methodist school here, in which not only were gaming and 'instruments of music' outlawed, but no scholar was 'permitted on any account whatever to wear Ruffles or powder his hair.'

At the turn of the century, hogs were excluded from the streets; in 1805 a new jail became part of the municipal equipment; in 1822 Lawrence Wartmen started the *Rockingham Register,* a vigorous weekly that lasted until 1912.

Charles Triplett O'Ferrall (1840-1905), a member of Congress (1882-93) and governor of Virginia (1894-98), was a citizen of Harrisonburg form 1869 to 1893.

POINTS OF INTEREST:
- Massanutten Caverns. 2 1/2 miles North on US 33 in Keezletown.
- Shenandoah Caverns. 24 miles North on US 11.
- Grand Caverns Regional Park. 12 miles South on I-81, then 6 miles East on VA 256 in Grottoes.
- Harrisonburg-Rockingham Historical Society. 301 South Main Street.
- James Madison University (1908). South Main Street.
- Miller Hall Planetarium and Sawhill Art Gallery.
- Menno Simons Historical Library.
- Natural Chimneys Regional Park. 15 miles SW off VA 42 in Mt. Solon.
- Shenandoah National Park. 24 miles East on US 33.
- George Washington National Forest. 10 miles West on US 33.

HISTORICAL PLACES... (See Historical Places Section for details).
Lincoln Homestead; Beery, John K., Farm; Baxter House; Harrison, Thomas, House; Morrison House

•**HAYMARKET,** Town; Prince William County; Pop. 483; Zip Code 22069; 30 mi. SW of Washington D.C.; Lat. 38-40-12 N long. 077-29-26 W; Pioneer William Skinner named the town for the famous race track in London. In the colonial days Haymarket was called Red House, for a tavern here. Federal troops burned all the buildings of the village except a church and two houses.

•**HAYSI,** Town; Dickenson County; Pop. 222; Zip Code 24256; Elev. 1266; 81 mi. N of Bristol; Lat. 37-12-21 N long. 082-17-40 W; General store merchants Charles Hay and Mr. Sypher had their last names combined for the town's name.

•**HENRICO COUNTY**, E Virginia; 241 sq. mi.; Pop. 217,881; Named after Henry Frederick, prince of Wales (1594-1612).

•**HENRY COUNTY**, S Virginia; 392 sq. mi.; Pop. 56,942; Named after Patrick Henry.

•**HERNDON**, Town; Fairfax County; Pop. 16,139; Zip Code 22070; 20 mi. NW of Washington D.C.; Lat. 38-57-56 N long. 077-21-37 W; The town's names commemorates Captain William Herndon who was lost at sea in 1857.

•**HIGHLAND COUNTY**, W Virginia; 416 sq. mi.; Pop. 2,635; Descriptively named.

•**HILLSBORO**, Town; Loudoun County; Pop. 72; 45 mi. NW of Washington D.C.; The town is descriptively named for its location on Short Hill Mountain.

•**HILLSVILLE**, Town; Carroll County Seat; Pop. 2,008; Zip Code 24343; Elev. 2557; 30 mi. SE of Wytheville; Lat. 36-45-40 N long. 080-44-03 W; the highway widens to become the main street, bordered by spic-and-span cottages with flowery front yards, general stores, the neon-signed drugstore, the new buff brick school, and the county courthouse. The town was named after the Hill family who were early Quaker settlers.

In the Carroll County Courthouse, a red brick building with white columned entrance, the mountain clan of Allen ran amok on March 12, 1912, during the trial of Floyd Allen, arraigned for freeing two youthful members of the clan who had been arrested for disturbing a church meeting. Trouble was expected when the mountaineers rode into town and the courtroom was crowded. After the jury's verdict of guilty and the refusal of a new trial, Judge Thorton L. Massie imposed a sentence of a year in jail. As the prisoners stood up and shouted, 'I ain't a-goin'! a volley blazed 'like the crackle of mountain laurel,' a witness said. The judge, the commonwealth attorney, the sheriff, the jury foreman, and a witness for the prosecution were killed, and the clerk of court was wounded. Then the Allens rode off into the hills. Subsequently caught, two were sentenced to death and four to prison. Of these, two were pardoned by Governor E. Lee Trinkle in 1924 and two by Governor Harry F. Byrd in 1926. In the mountains the shooting is remembered in the doleful ballad 'Claude Allen.'

Carroll County was cut from Grayson County in 1842 and named for Charles Carroll of Carrollton, who died in that year.

•**HONAKER**, Town; Russell County; Pop. 950; Zip Code 24260; Elev. 1860; 49 mi. NE of Bristol; Lat. 37-01-07 N long. 081-58-39 W; The town was named in honor of Squire Harve Honaker, a one-time postmaster.

Dictionary of Places

•**HOPEWELL,** Independent City; Pop. 23,101; Zip Code 23860; 10 mi. NE of Petersburg; Lat. 37-17-29 N long. 077-18-11 W; The city is named after the Quaker Hopewell meeting established in 1734. Hopewell owes its origin and its development to its position at the confluence of the two rivers, for ocean-going vessels can reach its harbor on the James and smaller vessels can run up the Appomattox to Petersburg.

City Point now a part of Hopewell, was planned in 1611 as the 'Chief City' of Bermuda Hundred, 'with a Pale cut over from River to River, about two miles long.' In 1619, when the four 'corporacouns' were formed, City Point was one of the hundreds in the Charles City Corporation. Its first designation, Bermuda City, was changed to Charles City, lengthened to Charles City Point, and later abbreviated to City Point. But on March 22, 1622 (N.S.), its population was almost entirely wiped out during the Indian attack and the city did not materialize for many years. However, the deep waters off shore served the cities of Petersburg and Richmond as a harbor and in both the Revolution and the War between the States it witnessed naval and military maneuvers.

Probably the most illustrious son of Hopewell, was John Randolph of Roanoke (1773-733), the site of whose birthplace, Cawsons, is within the limits of the new city. William Randolph of 'Turkey Island' was his great grandfather; John Randolph (1742-75), his father; and Frances, daughter of Theodoric Bland, Sr. (whose home Cawsons was) and sister of Theodoric Bland Jr. (1742-90), was his mother. Soon after his father's death, Mrs. Randolph married St. George Tucker, amiable and brilliant scholar of law, whose influence was of first importance in molding his stepson's mind. After attending private school and the College of William and Mary, Princeton, and Columbia intermittently, he studied law. In 1810 he moved permanently to Charlotte County.

POINTS OF INTEREST:
•Flowerdew Hundred. 10 miles SE on VA 10.
•City Point Unit. of Petersburg National Battlefield.

HISTORICAL PLACES... (See Historical Places Section for details).
Merchants Hope Church; Eppes Island; Shirley; Appomattox Manor; Weston Manor

•**HURT,** Town; Pittsylvania County; Pop. 1,294; Zip Code 24563; Elev. 736; 25 mi. N of Lynchburg; Lat. 37-05-50 N long. 079-18-09 W; The town's name honors John L. Hurt who helped develop the city.

•**INDEPENDENCE,** Town; Grayson County Seat; Pop. 988; Zip Code 24348; Elev. 2698; WSW of Galax; Lat. 36-37-15 N long. 081-09-06 W; high on the slopes of the Blue Ridge. In 1842 the county seat was moved here from Old Town, where it has been since Grayson County was created in 1792. Its name honored William Grayson, one of Virginia's first United States senators.

Encyclopedia of Virginia

•IRON GATE, Town; Allegheny County; Pop. 417; Zip Code 24448; 39 mi. N of Roanoke; Lat. 37-47-51 N long. 079-47-30 W; Named for the "Iron Gate" gap where the Jackson River cuts through the White Mountain.

•IRVINGTON, Town; Lancaster County; Pop. 496; Zip Code 22480; Elev. 1006; Lat. 37-39-48 N long. 076-25-08 W; The town was incorporated in 1891 and named for an early pioneer family, the Irvings. Irvington is by Carter's Creek, and noted for its seafood and fishing grounds. The winter occupation of those who live in the small frame houses, spread along the tree-lined streets in the newer section, is primarily oyster and herring packing. Plants here extract oil from menhaden and manufacture fertilizer from fish. But in summer the town becomes festive. Urban people open their cottages, motor launches arrive, and boats are made ready for fishing parties.

On Rappahannock Day, usually the Fourth of July, people from the entire Northern Neck come for the motorboat racing, athletic contests, and the crowning of 'Miss Rappahannock.'

POINTS OF INTEREST:
•Historic Christ Church (1732). 4 1/2 miles West, off VA 3.

•ISLE OF WIGHT COUNTY, SE Virginia; 321 sq. mi.; Pop. 25,053; Named after the Isle of Wight in England.

HISTORICAL PLACES... (See Historical Places Section for details).
Boykin's Tavern

•IVOR, Town; Southampton County; Pop. 324; Zip Code 23866; 30 mi. NW of Suffolk; Lat. 36-54-23 N long. 076-53-46 W; The town's name comes from a Walter Scott novel.

•JAMES CITY COUNTY, SE Virginia; 150 sq. mi.; Pop. 34,859; Named after James II (1633-1701) King of England, Scotland and Ireland 1685-88.

•JAMES RIVER The confluence of the Jackson and Cowpasture Rivers provide the source for the James flowing southeast past Buchanan then northeast across the Blue Ridge. It then generates the spectacular Balcony Falls and a series of Rapids and continues to Chesapeake Bay. Its name is derived from that of English King James I.

•JAMESTOWN ISLAND A flat, wooded oval nearly three miles long separated from the mainland by a marshy inlet, is the site of James Towne, where permanent settlement in British America began in 1607 and where in 1619 was set up the first representative Government in the New World. Besides the ruins of the church tower and graveyard, all that remains of the capital of the Virginia Colony from 1607 to 1699, are the foundations of several dwellings and of the third and fourth statehouses. Much of the western end of the island, on which the first buildings stood, where a neck of land joined the island to the mainland, had been washed away by tides before a sea wall was constructed in 1901. Scattered about in clumps are gnarled descendants of the mulberry trees planted by order of the assembly of 1621 to feed silkworms that would provide one of the colony's first industries.

Thirteen-year-old Pocahontas, daughter of the Indian leader, Powhatan, came often to the island to turn cartwheels about the stockade and to warn the English against attacks from her people, but particularly to see fascinating Captain Smith, whose life she had saved at Werowocomoco. Smith called her the only *Nonpariel'* of the country, but failed to realize the real love she bore him. Here in 1614, soon after she had been brought to Jamestown as a hostage, her first visit since Smith's departure in 1609, John Rolfe married her, not for any 'carnall affection; but for the good of this plantation, for the honour of our countrie...' When she met Smith again three years later in England, where she died, she was overcome with emotion-- lost on the unsentimental captain. Smith reported: 'After a modest salutation, without any word, she turned about, obscured her face, as not seeming well contented; and in that humour...we all left her two or three houres, repenting my selfe to have writ she could speake *English*. But not long after, she began to talke, and remembered mee well what courtesies shee had done...' They did tell us alwaies you were dead, and I knew no other till I came to Plimoth...because your Countriemen will lie much.'

It was to Jamestown that the 22 burgesses came in 1619 to sit in the first legislative body in America; that 20 blacks, forerunners of Virginia's future slaves, were brought and sold the same year; and that the first considerable number of Virginia 'maides' were consigned a year later. By 1623, a year after the first massacre, there were only 183 inhabitants and 22 dwellings in Jamestown itself, which had not extended beyond the four original acres.

In July 1781 Cornwallis, retreating with his British army before La Fayette, crossed the James here on his way to Portsmouth. In 1861 the Confederates built a Jamestown fort on the site of the first one; a year later the island was occupied by Union troops. It had become a briar-choked wilderness in 1893, when twenty-three and a half acres were acquired by the Assocation for the Preservation of Virginia Antiquities.

•**JARRATT**, Town; Greensville & Sussex Counties; Pop. 556; Zip Code 23867; 30 mi. S of Petersburg; Lat. 36-49-56 N long. 077-28-18 W; The Jarratt family settled in the county in 1652. The town was named in their honor.

Encyclopedia of Virginia

On May 8, 1864, the village was burned by General Kautz to delay Beauregard. On December 8, track was torn up here by a large Federal force operating under Warren on retreat from Belfield. Warren withdrew to his lines near Petersburg in time to avoid conflict with General A.P. Hill's 16,000 Confederates, concentrating here on the morning of December 11.

•JONESVILLE, Town; Lee County Seat; Pop. 927; Zip Code 24263; Elev. 1530; 45 mi. W of Bristol; Lat. 36-40-16 N long. 083-06-51 W; The town is named for pioneer Frederick Jones who donated the land for the townsite. In November 1781 Jonesville, a collection of log cabins, witnessed the arrival of a body of dissenters from upper Spotsylvania County on their way to Kentucky. These separate Baptists had long defied the Colonial law requiring that ministers be licensed. Led by the Reverend Lewis Craig, about 200 church members left Spotsylvania County with their children, slaves, and earthly possessions. Along the pioneer trail they were joined by other westbound pioneers anxious for company on the journey through the Indian country. By the time it left Jonesville the caravan of staid religious folk, shepherded by a dozen preachers who held daily prayer services, had been augmented by soldiers, adventurers, land grabbers, Indian traders, backwoodsmen, and homeseekers (600 in all) and was trailed by droves of domestic animals.

HISTORICAL PLACE... (See Historical Places Section for details).
Jonesville Methodist Campground

•KELLER, Town; Accomack County; Pop. 235; Zip Code 23401; Elev. 42; Lat. 37-14-06 N long. 075-55-52 W; The town's name honors the contractor who built the local railroad.

•KENBRIDGE, Town; Lunenburg County; Pop. 1,264; Zip Code 23944; 45 mi. SW of Petersburg; Lat. 36-57-38 N long. 078-07-29 W; The town was built on the Kennedy and Bridgeforth family farms. The town's name was coined from the two names.

•KEYSVILLE, Town; Charlotte County; Pop. 606; Zip Code 23947; Elev. 642; 38 mi. NE of South Boston; Lat. 37-02-20 N long. 078-28-54 W; The town was named after early settler and tavern owner, John Keys.
POINTS OF INTEREST:
•Goodwin Lake-Prince Edward State Park.

•KILMARNOCK, Town; Lancaster & Northumberland Counties; Pop. 1,109; Zip Code 22482; 45 mi. SE of Williamsburg; Lat. 37-42-40 N long. 076-23-18 W; Early settlers named the town for the city in Scotland.

HISTORICAL PLACES... (See Historical Places Section for details).
Christ Church

Dictionary of Places

•**KING AND QUEEN COUNTY**, E Virginia; 318 sq. mi.; Pop. 6,289; Named after King William of Orange (1650-1702) and Queen Mary II (1662-1694).

•**KING GEORGE COUNTY**, NE Virginia; 178 sq. mi.; Pop. 13,527; Named after King George I (1660-1727).

•**KING WILLIAM COUNTY**, E Virginia; 278 sq. mi. Pop. 10,913; The county was named after King William of Orange.

•**LA CROSSE**, Town; Mecklenburg County; Pop. 549; Zip Code 23950; Lat. 36-41-47 N long. 078-05-39 W; The town is named after the game of La Crosse.

•**LAKE DRUMMOND** Is in the heart of a swamp. William Drummond, the first governor of North Carolina, who was hanged in 1677 by Governor William Berkeley for his share in Bacon's Rebellion, discovered the lake while hunting. The growth of juniper, cypress, gum, maple, poplar, ash, and oak is dense and continuous along the ditch; the undergrowth is filled with flowering water plants. The lake, with an altitude of 22, is upon an elevation much like an inverted saucer. It is five miles long and is rimmed with stumps of giant trees.

•**LANCASTER COUNTY**, E Virginia; 142 sq. mi.; Pop. 10,896; Named after Lancaster, England.

•**LAWRENCEVILLE**, Town; Brunswick County Seat; Pop. 1,486; Zip Code 23868; 48 mi. SW of Petersburg; Lat. 36-45-33 N long. 077-50-55 W; Established in 1783 and named in honor of Captain James Lawrence.

   HISTORICAL PLACE...(See Historical Places Section for details).
   Bentfield (Melrose)

•**LEBANON**, Town; Russell County Seat; Pop. 3,386; Zip Code 24266; 40 mi. NNE of Bristol; Lat. 36-59-46 N long. 081- 58-32 W; Founded in 1819 and named after Biblical Lebanon for the many cedar trees in the area. The town grew up after the county seat was moved here from Dickensonville in 1816.

•**LEE COUNTY**, SW Virginia; 434 sq. mi.; Pop. 24,496; Named after Henry Lee (1756-1818) ninth governor of Virginia.

•**LEESBURG**, Town; Loudoun County Seat; Pop. 16,202; Zip Code 22075; Elev. 352; 38 mi. NW of Alexandria; Lat. 39-06-46 N long. 077-33-49 W; The first settlement here, log houses huddled at the intersection of the Carolina and Ridge Roads, was called Georgetown. But when 'proper streets' were laid off on lands of Captain Nicholas Minor near the new courthouse, the 1758 assembly ordered the town incorporated under the name of Leesburg, probably for Francis Lightfoot Lee and Philip Ludwell Lee, local landholders who were among the town's first trustees.

POINTS OF INTEREST:
- Loudoun Museum/Visitor Center. 16 West Loudoun Street.
- Oatlands (ca 1804). 6 miles South on US 15.
- American Work Horse Museum. 4 miles West of Leesburg via VA 7 on VA 662 in Paeonian Springs.
- Balls Bluff. North via US 15.
- Hill High Orchards. 15 miles West via VA 7.

HISTORICAL PLACES...(See Historical Places Section for details).
Waterford; Morven Park; Leesburg Historic District; Exeter; Oak Hill (James Monroe House)
Oatlands Historic District; Oatlands

•**LEXINGTON,** Independent City; Pop. 6,959; Zip Code 24450; Elev. 1084; Lat. 30 mi. NW of Lynchburg; 37-47-01 N long. 079-26-28 W; The town was named during the Revolutionary War in honor of the Battle of Lexington. A part of the Borden Grant, acquired in 1739 by Gilbert Campbell, who left his 'hoose and personality' to his son Isaac in 1750, this land became the town of Lexington in 1777. Wiped out by fire in 1796, it was rebuilt from the proceeds of a lottery.

Lexington's peaceful seclusion was distributed on June 10, 1864, by General David Hunter, who bombarded the town and later allowed his troops to burn many buildings.

POINTS OF INTEREST:
- George C. Marshall Research Library and Museum (1964). Faces parade ground of VMI.
- McCormick Farm and Workshop. 20 miles North on US 11.

HISTORICAL PLACES...(See Historical Places Section for details).
Stonewall Jackson House; Washington and Lee University; Lee Chapel, Washington and Lee University; Virginia Military Institute; Alexander-Withrow House; Barracks, Virginia Military Institute; Lexington Historic District

•**LOUDOUN COUNTY,** N Virginia; 517 sq. mi.; Pop. 86,129; Named after John Campbell, 4th earl of Loudoun.

•**LOUISA COUNTY,** Central Virginia; 514 sq. mi.; Pop. 20,325; Named after Queen Louisa of Denmark (1724-1751) youngest daughter of George II of England.

•**LOUISA,** Town; Louisa County Seat; Pop. 1,088; Zip Code 23093; Elev. 468; 29 mi. E of Charlottesville; Lat. 38-01-39 N long. 078-00-10 W; The town's beginning was in 1742 when it became the seat of Louisa County, taken from Hanover in 1742 and named for Queen Louisa of Denmark, daughter of George II of England.

Dictionary of Places

It was as a member from Louisa that the 29-year-old Patrick Henry in May 1765 began his fight for the common man when he spoke against the 'loan office,' an instrument intended to cloak certain questionable loans made from the public treasury by John Robinson, Speaker of the House and Treasurer of the Colony. Toward the end of this session when the House was in committee to consider the Greenville Stamp Act, Henry introduced his resolutions proposing 'That the General Assembly . . . have the only and sole exclusive right and power to lay taxes and impositions upon the inhabitants of this colony.' The startled members were brought to their feet when Henry cried, 'Caesar had his Brutus, Charles the First his Cromwell, and George the Third--' 'Treason, treason!' cried members of the assembly. Henry continued, ' . . . and George the Third may profit by example. If this be treason, make the most of it!'.

Though cautioned against sleeping at Louisa Courthouse-with 'the worst lodging . . . in all America'-the Marquis de Chastellux, when traveling in Virginia after the Revolution, had 'curiosity to judge of it by my own experience' and went in. 'This man, called Johnson, is become so monstrously fat, that he cannot move out of his armchair . . . A stool supported his enormous legs, in which were large fissures on each side, a prelude to what must soon happen to his belly . . .'

During the Revolution and again during the War between the States, Louisa lay in the path of hostile forces. Tarleton passed through in 1781; and on May 2, 1863, General George Stoneman's Union forces destroyed the railroad here. From the friendly side, however, came General Fitzhugh Lee, who camped near by on June 10, 1864, before the Battle of Trevilian.

•LOVETTSVILLE, Town; Loudoun County; Pop. 749; Zip Code 22080; 41 mi. NW of Washington D.C.; Lat. 39-16-24 N long. 077-38-22 W; The town was established in 1820 on David Lovett's land. It is named in his honor.

•LUNENBURG COUNTY, S central Virginia; 443 sq. mi.; Pop. 11,419; Named after the Duke of Brunswick-Lunenburg.

•LURAY, Town; Page County Seat; Pop. 4,587; Zip Code 22835; Elev. 789; 30 mi. NE of Harrisonburg; Lat. 38-40-02 N long. 078-27-25 W; Laid out in 1812 by William Staige Marye, son of Peter Marye, who built the first turnpike-a toll road-to cross the Blue Ridge from Culpeper into the Shenandoah Valley. The site of Luray was part of a tract that belonged to the family of William Mayre's wife. The town is named either for early Blacksmith Lewis Ray, or after Lorraine (Luray), France.

HISTORICAL PLACES...(See Historical Places Section for details).
Page County Courthouse; Aventine Hall

Encyclopedia of Virginia

•LYNCHBURG, Independent City; Pop. 66,049; Zip Code 24501; Elev. 818; 48 mi. ENE of Roanoke; Lat. 37-24-25 N long. 079-09-36 W; The town grew up around John Lynch's ferry which he built in 1756. The town is named after him.

Lynchburg is along the banks of the James River and extends into the foothills of the Blue Ridge on the northwest.

Seventeen-year-old John Lynch established a ferry here in 1757, supplanting a difficult ford, and dwellings were built on the navigable river near his ferry house. John Lynch was the son of Charles Lynch, an Irishman who served his indentureship in Louisa County, where in 1733 he married Sarah Clark, ardent Quakeress and daughter of his master. Somewhat later he patented land near the present Lynchburg and lived at a house named Chestnut Hill.

Tobacco was early the economic stimulus of this largely Quaker community. Before 1786, when the general assembly authorized a town on his land, John Lynch had built the first tobacco warehouse north of the river on the bluff above his ferry. Tobacco in hogsheads was 'rolled' in from the surrounding fields and let down by ropes from the warehouse to bateaux on the river below, and this point became a trade center for dark tobacco--a coarse-leaf variety used as chewing and pipe tobacco and for the making of cigars. The first warehouse on the south bank was built in 1791, and four more warehouses were added between 1800 and 1805. The village was incorporated as a town in the latter year.

Strict attention to quality at that time made the town the world center for dark leaf tobacco. Stemming was begun here in 1804 by Charles Johnson, and tobacco inspectorship was established in 1806. The partners Hare and Labby (L'Abbe) were the first to use licorice in the treatment of tobacco.

Before the days of canal and railroads, fleets of bateaux bore tobacco down to Richmond. Three husky slaves manned each bateaux. From planked gunwales the two strongest propelled it with long iron-shod poles, and the third used a large oar as rudder. They were furnished with 60 pounds of meat and two bushels of meal for the trip and helped themselves to potatoes, corn, and tobacco from the down cargoes and to salt, sugar, molasses, and whiskey from return cargoes. Poling demanded a high degree of strength, courage, and skill, and the Blacks took great pride in their job.

In 1829, when the population of the town was 4,630, a visitor recorded that 500 bateaux left the wharves of Lynchburg and described the place as a bustling business center with an incredible number of stores and 15 tobacco factories.

A curious figure of this period was Colonel Augustine Leftwich, born in Bedford, England, in 1794, who came here at 18 and made a fortune in tobacco. In summer he would stroll to his factory like an Indian nabob, dressed in spotless white linen with a slave behind him holding aloft a great green umbrella.

Dictionary of Places

The James River and Kanawha Canal reached Lynchburg from Richmond in 1840. In 1852, when the population was more than 8,000, Lynchburg received its city charter, and that year the first train steamed in. During the Civil War the city was an important Confederate supply base, with hospitals and an arsenal.

By 1870, when the community began to rise out of postwar depression, railroads were almost the exclusive carriers of industrial products. Former industries were continued; new ones were founded, including the manufacture of shoes, started in 1870. John W. Carroll the same year started the manufacture of 'Lone Jack' and 'Brown Dick,' widely known smoking and chewing tobaccos. A great gambler down on his luck, Carroll drew a 'lone jack,' which, with the three others he held, won a pot of more than $5,000 and the chance to recoup his fortunes. In 1882 James A. Bonsack revolutionized the tobacco industry by inventing a cigarette making machine. In 1886 more than 30,000,000 pounds of tobacco were marketed from Lynchburg. Soon thereafter other industries were established. At the close of the century the city had survived a depression that followed the boom and had increased its population to 19,700.

In 1883 Theodore Presser founded *The Etude*, a publication for music teachers and pianists; Randolph-Macon Woman's College was opened in 1893; the Art Club was organized in 1896 and revived in 1925; and the Civic Art League was established in 1932 by Bernard Gutmann; in 1912 Mrs. John H. Lewis organized the Equal Suffrage League; and the Little Theater came into being in 1920.

Lynchburg is the home of Carter Glass, United States senator, former Secretary of the Treasury, and author of the Federal Reserve Act.

POINTS OF INTEREST:
- Randolph-Macon Woman's College (1891). 2500 Rivermont Avenue.
- Quaker Meeting House. 5810 Fort Avenue.
- Anne Spencer House. 1313 Pierce Street.
- Blackwater Creek Natural Area. In the city.

HISTORICAL PLACES...(See Historical Places Section for details).

Point of Honor (1815); Hope Dawn; Poplar Forest; Academy of Music; Garland Hill Historic District; Lynchburg Courthouse; Western Hotel

•**LYNNHAVEN BAY** Is an arm of the Chesapeake. Captain John Smith called the inlet Morton's Bay, for Matthew Morton, who, with Captain Gabriel Archer, was wounded here by the Indians. The present name was given by Adam Thoroughgood for Lynn, England.

•**MCKENNEY**, Town; Dinwiddie County; Pop. 386; Zip Code 23872; Lat. 36-59-07 N long. 077-43-17 W; The town's name honors large area landowner William R. McKenney.

Encyclopedia of Virginia

•**MADISON COUNTY**, N Virginia; 327 sq. mi.; Pop. 11,949; Named after James Madison.

•**MADISON**, Town; Madison County Seat; Pop. 307; Zip Code 22719; Elev. 589; 27 mi. NE of Charlottesville; Lat. 38-31-45 N long. 078-15-38 W; Founded in 1801 and named in honor of James Madison. The community was established when a log courthouse was built here in 1793, the year in which William Wirt (1772-1834) began his practice of law here. He became attorney general under Monroe and John Quincy Adams and a prosecutor of Aaron Burr (1807). Wirt was the author of several books, of which *The Letters of the British Spy* (1803) is the best known.

HISTORICAL PLACES...(See Historical Places Section for details).
Madison County Courthouse; Hebron Lutheran Church

•**MANASSAS**, City; Pop. 27,957; Zip Code 22110; 25 mi. W of Alexandria; Lat. 38-46-37 N long. 077-27-54 W; Early settlers named the town for the Biblical Manasseh.

POINTS OF INTEREST:
•Prince William County Fair.

HISTORICAL PLACE...(See Historical Places Section for details).
Manassas National Battlefield Park

•**MANASSAS GAP** (950 alt.), the lowest pass in the Blue Ridge was early an important gateway through the range. John Lederer is believed to have used it in 1670. George Washington and John Wood surveyed it in 1761.

•**MANASSAS PARK**, City; ; Pop. 6,734; 24 mi. SW of Alexandira; A residential community of nearby Manassas, it is named after that city.

•**MARION**, Town; Smyth County Seat; Pop. 6,630; Zip Code 24354; Elev. 2178; 42 mi. ENE of Bristol; Lat. 36-50-26 N long. 081-31-03 W; Founded in 1831 and named for Revolutionary War hero, General Francis Marion or for the 'Swamp Fox' of South Carolina. Earlier this aggressive county mart had two newspapers, supposedly at political loggerheads but both edited by Robert Anderson, son of Sherwood Anderson.

POINTS OF INTEREST:
•Hungry Mother State Park. 3 miles North on VA 16.
•Mount Rogers National Recreation Area.

HISTORICAL PLACE...(See Historical Places Section for details).
Preston House (Herndon)

Dictionary of Places

•**MARTINSVILLE**, City; Pop. 16,162; Zip Code 241 ; 32 mi. W of Danville; Lat. 36-40-20 N long. 079-51-58 W; The city was founded in 1791 and named after General Joseph Martin, and its site was given by George Hairston, who reputedly bought his 30,000-acre tract in 1770 for 10 cents an acre. Martin was a robust figure in the history of the early frontier. He was born in Albemarle County in 1740, ran away to fight Indians at 17, became an Indian agent, land agent, and officer of militia, fighting Indians all up and down the frontier. In 1774 he came to Henry County, established himself at Belle Monte on Leatherwood Creek, for nine years sat for his district in the general assembly, and in 1793 was made a brigadier general of State militia. He was a brawny, picturesque man, more than six feet tall and the father of 18 children; wore buckled knee breeches and a great beard, braided and thrust inside his shirt.

POINTS OF INTEREST:
•Fairy Stone State Park. 21 miles NW via US 220/VA 57, VA 822.
•Blue Ridge Farm Museum. VA 40 in Ferrum.
•Stoneleigh (1929) Edgewood Drive.

HISTORICAL PLACE...(See Historical Places Section for details).
Martinsville Fish Dam

•**MATHEWS COUNTY**, E Virginia; 87 sq. mi.; Pop. 8,348; Named after Gen. Thomas Mathews.

•**MATTAPONI RIVER** Formed in east Virginia; Caroline county, this river flows about 120 miles southeast to form the York River. The name is derived from a Native American tribe recorded in 1608 as Mattapanient.

•**MECKLENBURG**, S Virginia; 665 sq. mi.; Pop. 29,241;

•**MELFA**, Town; Accomack County; Pop. 428; Zip Code 23410; Lat. 37-39-05 N long. 075-44-22 W; The town was named for an official of the Pennsylvania Railroad Company.

•**MIDDLESEX COUNTY**, E Virginia; 132 sq. mi.; Pop. 8,653; Named after Middlesex, England.

•**MIDDLEBURG**, Town; Loudoun County; Pop. 549; Zip Code 22117; Elev. 492; 33 mi. NW of Washington D.C.; Lat. 38-58-05 N long. 077-44-22 W; Once called Chinn, the name was later changed to reflect its "middle position" between Alexandria and Winchester. Once a night stop on the stagecoach between Alexandria and Winchester.

HISTORICAL PLACES...(See Historical Places Section for details).
Farmer's Delight; Welbourne

Encyclopedia of Virginia

•**MIDDLETOWN**, Town; Frederick County; Pop. 1,061; Zip Code 22645; 15 mi. S of Winchester; Lat. 39-01-38 N long. 078-16-39 W; Spread out on a low plateau and first known as Senseny Town, was chartered in 1796 by Dr. Peter Senseny. The name was later changed to Middletown for its location between Winchester and Woodstock. As early as 1776 this village was recognized as a clockmaking center, and its reputation increased as wooden-wheeled timepieces gave way to those with brass, which bowed in turn to elaborately patterned eight-day clocks. The same artisans fashioned watches and surveyors' implements. One of them, Jacob Danner, constructed compasses of such mathematical precision that their reputation endures today. Here in 1817 a threshing machine demonstrated its superiority over flail and threshing-floor.

POINTS OF INTEREST:

•Strasburg Museum. 5 miles SW on I-81 in Strasburg, on King Street.

HISTORICAL PLACES...(See Historical Places Section for details).

Belle Grove (1794); St. Thomas Chapel; Cedar Creek Battlefield; Fort Bowman

•**MINERAL**, Town; Louisa County; Pop. 471; Zip Code 23117; 36 mi. NW of Richmond; Lat. 38-00-37 N long. 077-54-02 W; Established around 1800 and descriptively named for the mineral deposits in the area. In 1848 Robert and Colonel James Hart, brothers, operated a furnace here that they called 'Rough and Ready' to honor Zachary Taylor. After the War between the States the demand for sulphur increased; and iron pyrites found near by, was mined and smelted for that product.

•**MONTEREY**, Town; Highland County Seat; Pop. 222; Zip Code 24465; Elev. 2881; 35 mi. NW of Staunton; Lat. 38-24-42 N long. 079-34-54 W; The name was changed to Monterey to honor President Zachary Taylor's victory during the Mexican-American War. As early as 1774 Samuel Black had a cabin here, in 1848 the site was still only a small clearing on the Staunton and Parkersburg Turnpike across the Allegheny Range.

The Highland County Courthouse was built in 1848. It was the first courthouse of Highland County, which was formed the year before from parts of Bath County and Pendleton County.

POINTS OF INTEREST:

•Maple Museum. South on US 220.

HISTORICAL PLACE...(See Historical Places Section for details).

Monterey Hotel

•**MONTGOMERY COUNTY**, S Virginia; 395 sq. mi.; Pop. 73,913; Named after Richard Montgomery.

Dictionary of Places

•**MONTPELIER** Nearby is the site of Cuckoo Tavern, from which Jack Jouette, the son of the proprietor, began his ride on the night of June 3, 1781, to warn Thomas Jefferson at Monticello and the Virginia assembly in Charlottesville of the approaching British dragoons under Colonel Tarleton. Jouette had learned of their mission while the British rested here. In gratitude for his warning, the assembly voted'. . .to present Captain John Jouette an elegant sword and a pair of pistols as a memorial of the high sense which the General Assembly entertains for his activity and enterprise. . .whereby the designs of the enemy were frustrated and many valuable stores preserved.'

Later, after Jouette moved to Kentucky, then a Virginia county, he served in the general assembly, where he sponsored a petition for the divorce of his brother-in-law, Lewis Robards, from Rachel Donelson who was later Mrs. Andrew Jackson.

•**MONTROSS,** Town; Westmoreland County Seat; Pop. 359; Zip Code 22520; Lat. 38-05-36 N long. 076- 49-38 W; The town was named for an early settler.

POINTS OF INTEREST:

•Stratford Hall Plantation (1725). 6 miles North on VA 3 to Lerty, then East on VA 214.
•Westmoreland State Park. 5 miles NW on VA 3, then North on VA 347.

HISTORICAL PLACE...(See Historical Places Section for details).
Chantilly

•**MOUNT CRAWFORD,** Town; Rockingham County; Pop. 228; Zip Code 22841; 7 mi. S of Harrisonburg; Lat. 38-21-17 N long. 078- 56-26 W; In 1835 *Martin's Gazetteer* credited the town with '25 dwelling houses, 1 house of public worship free for all denomination, 2 common schools, 2 taverns, and sundry stores and shops. The town is named after an early settler.

•**MOUNT JACKSON,** Town; Shenandoah County; Pop. 1,583; Zip Code 22842; 28 mi. N of Harrisonburg; Lat. 38-44-54 N long. 078- 38-39 W; The town's name honors President Andrew Jackson. Mount Jackson altered its homespun name of Mount Pleasant to honor the hero of New Orleans. Mount Jackson was for long the terminus of the valley division of the stage route and, until Reconstruction days, was the southern terminal of the valley's railroad.

•**MULBERRY ISLAND** Is a little peninsula where in June 1610 the starving colonists, who had abandoned Jamestown to return to England, stopped for the night. The following morning, when news came that Lord Delaware had arrived at Point Comfort with new colonists and supplies, all turned back.

•**NARROWS**, Town; Giles County; Pop. 2,082; Zip Code 24124; 22 mi. W of Blacksburg; Lat. 37-20-08 N long. 080-48-27 W; The New River cuts a deep gorge, or narrows, through the Alleghenies at this point. The town is named for this feature.

•**NASSAWADOX**, Town; Northampton County; Pop. 564; Zip Code 23413; Elev. 38; Lat. 37-28-35 N long. 075-53-23 W; Settled in 1656 and given an Indian name meaning "a stream between two streams." William Robinson, a Quaker who entered the colony about 1656 and was promptly arrested on the complaint of the Anglican churchmen, was eventually released and aided fellow-Quakers by pretending to help them leave the colony. Actually he landed the dissenters on Nassawadox Creek, where Levin Denwood provided them with a log-cabin meeting house.

•**NELSON**, Central Virginia; 468 sq. mi.; Pop. 12,778; named after Thomas Nelson.

•**NEW CASTLE**, Town; Craig County Seat; Pop. 152; Zip Code 24127; 55 mi. W of Lynchburg; Lat. 37-29-45 N long. 080-06-45 W; Founded as New Fincastle in 1756, but later changed as a result of confusion to New Castle.

HISTORICAL PLACE...(See Historical Places Section for details).

New Castle Historic District

•**NEW KENT COUNTY**, E Virginia; 212 sq. mi.; Pop. 10,445; Named after Kent, England.

•**NEW MARKET**, Town; Shenandoah County; Pop. 1,435; Zip Code 22844; 20 mi. N of Harrisonburg; Lat. 38-38-54 N long. 078- 40-20 W; Founded in 1784 and named for the famous racing town in England. In 1761 John Sevier, later governor of Tennessee, married and moved to this crossroads, where he established an inn and a store. In 1774 Sevier sold his land. In 1785 Peter Palsel laid off a town.

Lewis Summers wrote in 1808: 'Proceeded to New Market, a very handsome little town . . . The houses well built of brick, a good many stores & full of goods; containing 500 or 600 people.' In 1817 the New Market Academy was established, and in 1821, the Lutheran Seminary. Almost a century later, in 1908, another school joined these-the Shenandoah Valley Academy; a coeducational institution of the Seventh Day Adventists.

POINTS OF INTEREST:

•Shenandoah Caverns. 4 miles North, off I-81 exit 68.
•Shenandoah Vineyards. 20 miles North on I-81 in Edinburg.

HISTORICAL PLACES...(See Historical Places Section for details).

New Market Battlefield Park; New Market Historic District

Dictionary of Places

•NEW RIVER Flowing from North Carolina, where it is called South Fork, it enters southwest Virginia and continues through the Allegheny Mountains into West Virginia.

•NEWPORT NEWS, Independent City; Pop. 170,045; Zip Code 23600; 11 mi. NNW of Norfolk; Lat. 37-03-15 N long. 076-28-36 W; Founded in 1619 and named for Sir Christopher Newport and Sir William Newce, or gradually Newport News.
  The city is at the mouth of the James River and at the head of Hampton Roads.
  In 1607 the first English settlers entering the James River named the apex of the triangle Point Hope. In 1611 Robert Salford, with his wife and son, came to the creek now in the eastern part of the city. The name of the stream, Salford Creek, was changed through usage to Salter's. Other land within the limits of present Newport News was patented in 1621 by the Newce brothers, Thomas and Sir William, who came from Ireland. Sir William Newce had offered to transport 1,000 persons to Virginia, but brought 'only a few weak and unserviceable people, ragged and not above a fortnight's provisions, some bound for three years, and most upon wages.' For his failure William Capps impatiently dubbed him 'Sir William Naughtworth.' But there was some reason for Sir William's failure to bring the thousand persons-he died in 1621.
  Daniel Gookin, an Englishman who had moved to Port Newce in County Cork, Ireland, followed the Newces to this area, bringing with him 'fifty men of his owne, and thirty Passengers, exceedingly well furnished with all sort of Prouision.' It was he who probably named the community--some say for his home in Ireland; others, to honor Newce and Captain Christopher Newport; and still others, for the good news that Newport brought the starving colonists--the most likely origin since old inhabitants still call the city Newport's News. That the name was current in 1626 is attested by the minutes of the general court, which record a transfer to Daniel Gookin of land 'situate above Newport's News at a place called Marie's Mount.'
  Although tracing its ancestry to Kecoughtan and sharing in Colonial and American vicissitudes, Newport News was merely an area of farm lands and a fishing village until the coming of the railroad and the subsequent establishment of the great shipyard. In 1852, an act of the general assembly 'to legalize a wharf at Newport News,' gave the Warwick County Court 'the same powers in regard to said wharf as are possessed by the county court of James City in regard to the Grove Wharf on the lands of Thomas Wynne.' In 1873 Major Robert H. Temple surveyed a railway line from Richmond to the mouth of the James River. Seven years later Collis P. Huntington, the industrialist, found Major Temple's wooden markers intact and undertook to build the road along that route. The railroad was completed in 1882, and a town was plotted without formal

Encyclopedia of Virginia

authorization by the general assembly. Four years later the Chesapeake Dry Dock and Construction Company, now the Newport News Shipbuilding and Dry Dock Company, was begun and boom years followed. In 1900 the population was 19,635; and in 1920, 35,596.

POINTS OF INTEREST:
- The Mariners Museum. Jct. US 60 & Clyde Morris Blvd., 3 miles off I-64 exit 62A.
- War Memorial Museum of Virginia. 9285 Warwick Blvd. in Huntington Park, on US 60.
- Peninsula Nature and Science Center. 524 J. Clyde Morris Blvd., in Deer Park, 2 miles North.
- Fort Eustis. NW end of city on Mulberry Island.
- Peninsula Fine Arts Center. Museum Drive.

HISTORICAL PLACES...(See Historical Places Section for details).
Denbigh Plantation Site (Mathews Manor House); Fort Crafford; Hilton Village; Jones, Matthew, House; Lee Hall

•**NEWSOMS**, Town; Southampton County; Pop. 337; Zip Code 23874; Elev. 92; 26 mi. SW of Suffolk; Lat. 36-37-40 N long. 077-07-28 W; The town is named after pioneer merchant, Thomas Newsoms.

•**NICKELSVILLE**, Town; Scott County; Pop. 411; Zip Code 24271; 40 mi. NW of Bristol; The town is named for an early settler.

HISTORICAL PLACE...(See Historical Places Section for details).
Killgore Fort House

•**NORFOLK**, Independent City; Pop. 261,229; Zip Code 23500; just S of Hampton Roads; Lat. 36-40-40 N long. 075-48-43 W; Established in 1682 and named for county Norfolk in England.

The city stretches north from the eastern branch of the Elizabeth River to a curving sand beach on Chesapeake. Norfolk's site on the Elizabeth River embraces a grant made to Captain Thomas Willoughby in 1636. Development began here in 1680, when, in the 'Act of Cohabitation' providing for a town for each county, the general assembly directed that, 'in Lower Norfolk county . . . on the Easterne Branch on Elizabeth river at the entrance of the branch,' 50 acres be 'measured about, layd out and appointed for a towne.' Though Charles II in 1681 suspended the Act of 1680, 'the ffeoffees' proceeded with the purchase of the site, 'on Nicholas Wise his land,' effecting the transaction in 1682 for 'tenn thousand pounds of tobacco and caske.' When in 1691 the statute of 1680 was re-enacted to provide for 'ports of entry,' the town was described as 'the land appointed . . . and accordingly laid out and paid for and severall dwelling houses and ware houses already built.' In 1705 the house of burgesses named it Norfolk for Norfolk County, England.

Trade with the mother country and the West Indies made this the largest municipality in Colonial Virginia. The first wharves were built of pine logs fastened together by cross beams and extending from the shore to the channel. Here 'twenty brigs and smaller vessels rode constantly.' Norfolk ships carried tobacco, meat, flour, and lumber to the West Indies and returned with cargoes of sugar and molasses. Trade with the Carolinas, however, was hindered by pirates until Governor Alexander Spotswood took determined measures against the sea robbers (*see Hampton*).

In 1736 'the town of Norfolk' was 'erected into a borough, by the name of The borough of Norfolk . . . a body corporate, consisting of a major, recorder, eight aldermen, and sixteen common council men . . . with power to elect and send one burgess to sit in the house of burgesses.' Of 16 towns authorized in 1705 to acquire borough status-a unit politically separate from the county-Norfolk was the only one that became a borough.

Samuel Boush was the first mayor of Norfolk, and Sir John Randolph served as recorder. Male citizens took turns at patrolling the streets to restrain the exuberance of transient sailors. Early streets were improved and new ones were formed by filling in creek and marshes.

The town had to reclaim ground from tidal sloughs as the population grew. Church Street led across the neck of a peninsula to the mainland. Main (then Front) Street, bordering the waterfront, was crowded with warehouses, residences, shops, sailors' boarding houses, and ordinaries. Most of the early citizens quenched their thirsts at taverns, the only source of drinking water being a public spring near the corner of Main and Church Streets. Water for other uses came from the river and, in case of fire, was passed along from hand to hand by bucket brigades.

Norfolk by 1740 had a population of about 1,000 composed of English and Scottish residents and some Irish. The merchants were mainly anti-Jacobite Scots. Importing most of their luxuries from Great Britain and conducting a lucrative trade with the mother country, the well-to-do merchants leaned toward Tory conservatism. In recognition of their loyalty, Governor Robert Dinwiddie in 1753 presented the corporation with a mace.

Though Norfolk protested boldly against the Stamp Act and later contributed its share of minutemen, it became early in the Revolution a rallying point for Tories. Lord Dunmore, the royal governor, chose Norfolk and Portsmouth as bases for his ships. Landing at Norfolk, he dismantled the printing office of John Holt and seized two printers publishing revolutionary literature. He was finally forced to retire.

The Virginia regiments under Colonel William Woodford occupied Norfolk, and Dunmore attempted to drive them out by bombarding the borough, January 1, 1776. When firing ceased, the riflemen continued to plunder and burn buildings without the interference of officers. Finally Colonel Woodford forbade the burning of houses under severe penalty, but two-thirds of Norfolk was in ashes. In February the rest of the town was burned, by order of the

Colonial government, to rid it of Tories and to deprive Dunmore of shelter. Only the borough church (St. Paul's) was spared. After assisting 'poor people' in finding shelter elsewhere, troops abandoned the area.

After peace was signed in 1783, the Tories returned to Norfolk and began restoring the borough's former commercial prestige. In 1794 Norfolk was overrun with several thousand French refugees from the Black insurrection in Santo Domingo. It had then, said Moreau de St. Mery, a population of 3,000, a brick theater, a hospital, an academy, two gazettes, and a Catholic chapel where 'a zealous Irishman with a red face has come to preach to the wretched French refugees.' The women 'are pretty in Norfolk,' noted Moreau de St. Mery, 'but their complextion is sallow and . Norfolk soon became the port for water-borne trade from the inland country. The town suffered from a disastrous fire in 1799. During the Napoleonic wars Norfolk's commerce increased only to be lost to the French, Spanish, and British privateers. The anger of Norfolk shipowners reached a peak in 1807, when the *Chesapeake* was fired upon by the British frigate *Leopard.*

During the War of 1812 men of Norfolk, Portsmouth, and other towns, with a reinforcement of marines from the frigate *Constellation,* joined to form defenses. On June 22, 1813, Fort Norfolk and Fort Nelson repulsed a British attack on Portsmouth by land and afterwards, aided by batteries on Craney Island, routed an assault by barges.

Peace in 1815 promised to restore Norfolk's prosperity, though New York was a strong trade rival. In 1822 the first steam ferry made a trial trip between Norfolk and Portsmouth. In 1845 the general assembly made Norfolk a city. With a population of 14,000 in 1854, it began to regain some of its earlier prestige. In 1855, however, it met with a setback in an epidemic of yellow fever, which destroyed about a tenth of the population. The hero of the scourge was a Black gravedigger, who buried the dead until he, too, was struck down by the plague. He is remembered as 'Yellow Fever Jack,' and a monument in a cemetery here testifies to his faithfulness.

Margaret Douglas, a white woman from North Carolina, started Virginia's first Black free school in Norfolk in 1853. When the enrollment increased to 25 she was sentenced to 30 days in jail on the charge that several pupils were slaves.

Hardly had the city recovered from the epidemic when the Civil War brought on a new series of disasters. After the secession of Virginia, the Federal command evacuated and burned the navy yard in Portsmouth. But when Roanoke Island, south of Norfolk, was occupied in February 1862, the situation of Norfolk became precarious; and, though the *Virginia (Merrimac)* gained temporary victories in March, Norfolk fell to Union forces under General John Ellis Wool, May 10, 1862. The city was never again in Confederate hands.

Dictionary of Places

With the coming of peace, Norfolk had little trade and no apparent future, but a hope came to fulfillment through the development of railroads. The Norfolk and Petersburg Railroad, laid in 1858, was merged in 1870 with the Southside and the Virginia & Tennessee as the Atlantic, Mississippi and Ohio Railroad. This system, reorganized in 1881 as the Norfolk and Western Railroad Company, brought the first carload of coal into Norfolk in 1882 and began the traffic that made Norfolk a commanding coal port.

Meanwhile, the Norfolk and Southern (now Norfolk Southern) Railroad Company, chartered in 1875 as the Elizabeth City and Norfolk Railroad Company, laid tracks between Norfolk and Elizabeth City, North Carolina. When the road was extended to Albermarle Sound, Norfolk became a port through which fruit, vegetables, and other perishable products of South pass quickly to Northern markets. The Virginian Railway (organized as the Tidewater Railway in 1904), which brings coal from West Virginia, and the Belt Line, connecting all railroads with terminals at Norfolk and Portsmouth, are more recent developments in transportation.

Norfolk has extended its boundaries several times. In 1906 it annexed Berkley, a town on the east side of the river's southern branch.

POINTS OF INTEREST:
- Norfolk Botanical Gardens. 8 miles on Azalea Garden Road, adjacent to Norfolk Int'l Airport.
- Hermitage Foundation Museum. 7637 North Shore Road.
- St. Paul's Episcopal Church (1739). 201 St. Paul's Blvd., at City Hall Avenue.
- Norfolk Scope. Scope Plaza.
- Lafayette Zoological Park. 33rd and Granby Streets.
- Waterside. 333 Waterside Drive.
- Norfolk School of Boatbuilding. On the waterfront.

HISTORICAL PLACES...(See Historical Places Section for details).
Norfolk Naval Station and Norfolk Naval Air Station; Willoughby-Baylor House (1794); Cape Henry Memorial and Lighthouse; Allmand-Archer House; Boush-Tazewell House; Freemason Street Baptist Church; Myers, Moses, House; Norfolk Academy; Norfolk City Hall (Gen. Douglas Macarthur Memorial); St. Paul's Church; U.S. Customshouse; West Freemason Street Area Historic District; Whittle House (Taylor-Whittle House)

•**NORTH HAMPTON COUNTY,** E Virginia; 226 sq. mi. Pop. 13,061; Named after Northhampton, England.

•**NORTHUMBERLAND,** E Virginia; 454 sq. mi.; Pop. 10,524; Named after Northumberland County, England.

•**NORTON,** City; Pop. 4,247; Zip Code 24273; Elev. 2141; 35 mi. NW of Bristol; Lat. 36-59-19 N long. 082-37-31 W; First called Prince's

Flats for William Prince, who settled here in 1787, the town changed its name in the 1890's. The town is named in honor of Eckstein Norton, who was L & N Railroad president from 1886 -1891.

•**NOTTOWAY COUNTY,** S Virginia; 308 sq. mi.; Pop. 14,993; Nottoway was named after the Indian tribe.

•**OCCANEECHEE ISLAND** Was once a village of the peaceful and industrious Occaneechee, who traded with other Indians of a broad area. These Indians, having established a fur monopoly, saw the white man not as a new enemy but as a new customer. On the trail of the marauding Susquehannock, who had fled here, Nathaniel Bacon brought his militia to the island in 1676 and persuaded the Occaneechee to join in expelling the visitors. This accomplished, trouble flared up between the whites and their Indian allies, ending in a two-day battle in which Occaneechee village was destroyed.

•**OCCOQUAN,** Town; Fairfax & Prince William Counties; Pop. 361; Zip Code 22125; 10 mi. S of Alexandria; Lat. 38-40-56 N long. 077-15-39 W; The town's name is an Indian word meaning "at the river's end."

HISTORICAL PLACE...(See Historical Places Section for details).
Rockledge

•**ONANCOCK,** Town; Accomack County; Pop. 1,434; Zip Code 23417; 65 mi. NNE of Norfolk; Lat. 37-42-41 N long. 075-44-25 W; Founded in 1680 and eventually given an Indian name meaning "foggy place." Onancock was an Indian village when John Pory was a guest of Ekeeks, king of the Onancocks in 1621. At the feast the visitors were introduced to oysters and 'batata' or potatoes. After burning his mouth on hot potatoes, Master Pory said, 'I would not give a farthing for a shipload.' Onancock was established in 1680 as one of the 19 places designated by the general assembly in the Act of Cohabitation, to provide 'ports of entry.' Onancock became the county seat the year it was created, and so remained until 1786.

During the Revolution it was headquarters for the troops under General John Cropper. In these years the Eastern Shore suffered from frequent raids by British privateers. On November 30, 1782, occurred the Battle of the Barges, so called because of the crude craft used. Commodore Whaley of Maryland sallied forth with four barges to attack the marauders. He pursued the enemy vessels, caused them to strike their colors, but was killed when the powder on his barge exploded.

HISTORICAL PLACES...(See Historical Places Section for details).
Hopkins and Brother Stone; Kerr Place

Dictionary of Places

•ONLEY, Town; Accomack County; Pop. 532; Zip Code 23418; Lat. 37-41-33 N long. 075-42-57 W; The town was named for the estate of Virginia Governor Henry Wise. Onley is headquarters of the Eastern Shore Produce Exchange, a co-operative marketing agency, organized in 1899.

•ORANGE COUNTY, N central Virginia; 354 sq. mi.; Pop. 21,421; Named after Prince William of Orange.

•ORANGE, Town; Orange County Seat; Pop. 2,582; Zip Code 22960; Elev. 521; 27 mi. NE of Charlottesville; Lat. 38-13-19 N long. 078-06-17 W; The town is named for the county. Orange County, created in 1734, was named for the Prince of Orange, who became England's William III. As originally constituted, the county boundaries were loosely defined and court was held in various places until 1748, when Orange was divided to create Culpeper County, and the courthouse, then 'absurdly near the very edge of the county,' was ordered moved to a more central site.

Montpelier, once the home of James Madison, 'Father of the Constitution' and fourth President of the United States. From among ancient trees the long, two-story house faces a wide view of the Blue Ridge Mountains. The brick walls are stuccoed and the roof, built in several hipped sections, extends over a finely denticulated cornice. The four widely spaced Roman Doric columns of the great portico rise directly from the ground, quite independent of an iron-railed porch terrace. The exterior, with simple window frames, is ornamented only by well-proportioned fanlights in the pediments of the portico and front door. The numerous and very spacious reception rooms have simple white woodwork.

The central part of the house-two rooms on each side of the transverse hall on both floors-was built by Colonel James Madison, about 1760. His son and namesake added the portico in 1793 at the suggestion of other minor changes after plans drawn by William Thorton, amateur architect of the capitol in Washington. In 1907 new owners raised the wings to the level of the main part and extended the house toward the east, without destroying its fine proportions. The house was suited to the entertainment that President and Dolly Madison dispensed here, as in Washington, on a large and generous scale. On one occasion 90 persons were served dinner at Montpelier. Madison dealt graciously and successfully with a mother-in-law-in-the-house problem by giving his mother an apartment, with her own kitchen and servants. Behind the house is a natural amphitheater that has been made into a large formal garden on plans drawn by General La Fayette while visiting the Madisons in 1824. Until Madison's last years, the descending terraces, box-bordered paths, and geometrical flower beds were kept neatly groomed by a French gardener. The present owners have restored the garden. A charming little classical summer house, which concealed an icehouse and slave quarters, stands near by.

Encyclopedia of Virginia

Born at Port Conway, Virginia, James Madison was graduated from Princeton College in 1771 but remained for a year studying theology. As a member of the Virginia Constitutional Convention of 1776, he proposed unsuccessfully an article providing for religious freedom. In 1785, however, he pushed through the general assembly Jefferson's Statute of Religious Liberty. As a delegate in the Continental Congress in 1780 he drafted instructions to John Jay, then representing the United States in Spain, to insist on free navigation of the Mississippi River, but it was not until 1803, when he was Secretary of State under Jefferson, that he saw this objective attained through the purchase of the vast Louisiana Territory.

In 1781 he favored an amendment to the Articles of Confederation that would give the Congress power to enforce its requisitions. At the expiration of his term in 1783, he took up the study of law and in 1784 was elected to the Virginia general assembly, where he paved the way for the National Constitutional Convention. On his proposal the Virginia and Maryland commissioners met to discuss navigation and commerce. When the Alexandria and Mount Vernon conference led to the Annapolis Convention, Madison and Alexander Hamilton worked together on the proposal that all States be invited to send representatives to consider commercial questions, and the Constitutional Convention resulted. The Virginia Plan, which served as the basis of deliberation in Philadelphia, was Madison's handiwork. As delegate he took a leading part in the debates and convinced of the historical importance of the occasion, kept full and careful notes that are the chief source of information on what happened during the secret sessions.

Though the Constitution did not wholly satisfy him, he was able to swing the Virginia delegates for its adoption; later he worked for ratification by his State and wrote 20 of the 85 Federalist papers, which had circulated through the Union. After being elected to Congress in 1789, he fulfilled a promise made first to George Mason by introducing the first nine amendments, which, along with the tenth, became the Bill of Rights. He was an opponent of slavery and deplored the compromise that permitted the slave trade to continue until 1808 and failed to provide for ultimate emancipation. Pressure, especially from New England, forced him to abandon the policy of commercial sanctions against Great Britain and brought on the War of 1812, declared during his Presidency.

In 1789, in opposing the Alien and Sedition Laws, Madison wrote the Virginia Resolution, reiterating the limitations of Federal powers, which, together with Jefferson's Kentucky Resolutions, served as the foundation for Calhoun's nullification policy in 1832 and furnished the basic argument for the rights of secession in 1861.

When his term as President expired in 1817, he retired to Montpelier, where he died June 28, 1836. Here Dolley Payne Madison, the beautiful widow whom he had married in 1793, the

Dictionary of Places

year he began to make plans for a mansion that would be a fitting background for her social graces, won her laurels as America's most accomplished hostess.

POINTS OF INTEREST:

•Roaring Twenties Antique Car Museum. 3 miles North on US 15, then 15 miles NW on VA 230, in Hood.
•Courthouse (1858). Main Street.

HISTORICAL PLACES...(See Historical Places Section for details).

Montpelier (James Madison House); Mayhurst

•**PAGE COUNTY**, N Virginia; 316 sq. mi.; Pop. 21,690; Named after John Page (1743-1808) 13th governor of Virginia (Commonwealth).

•**PAINTER**, Town; Accomack County; Pop. 259; Zip Code 23420; Elev. 37; 55 mi. NNE of Norfolk; Lat. 37-35-19 N long. 075- 47-05 W; The town was named for an official of the Pennsylvania Railroad at the time the station was opened.

•**PARKSLEY**, Town; Accomack County; Pop. 779; Zip Code 23421; 72 mi. NNE of Norfolk; Lat. 37-47-12 N long. 075-39-07 W; Founded on land owned by Edmund Parkes in 1742. Originally called Matomkin, but later changed to Parksley.

•**PATRICK COUNTY**, S Virginia; 469 sq. mi.; Pop. 17,473; Named after Patrick Henry (1763-1799) govenor of Virginia 1774-76, 1776-69 and 1784-86.

•**PEARISBURG**, Town; Giles County; Pop. 2,064; Zip Code 24134; Elev. 1804; 15 mi. NW of Blacksburg; Lat. 37-19-47 N long. 080-43-44 W; The town is shadowed by a tall peak, Angel's Rest. In 1782, Captain George Pearis established a ferry here across New River. Later Captain Pearis provided land, together with timber and stone necessary to erect public buildings, as a seat for the court, and the town of Pearisburg was legally brought into existence. Pearisburg was founded in 1808 and named in Captain Pearis's honor.

POINTS OF INTEREST:

•White Rocks Recreation Area. 17 mile East via VA 613, 635, in Jefferson National Forest.

•**PEMBROKE**, Town; Giles County; Pop. 1,064; Zip Code 24136; 15 mi. NW of Blacksburg; Lat. 37-19-30 N long. 080-38-08 W; The town was named after Pembroke in Wales.

•**PENNINGTON GAP**, Town; Lee County; Pop. 1,922; Zip Code 24277; Elev. 1377; Lat. 36-45-35 N long. 083-01-55 W; An early family named Pennington settled near the mountain gap, and gave the town their name.

•PETERSBURG, City; Pop. 38,386; Zip Code 23801; 23 mi. S of Richmond; Lat. 37-14-40 N long. 077-20-02 W; Founded in 1646 and later named for trader Peter Jones.

The beginning of Petersburg dates from 1645, when the general assembly directed that Fort Henry be built at the falls of the Appomattox River. The next year the assembly provided that the fort be given to Abraham Wood for three years, on condition that he keep ten men there for its protection. He established a trading post and cultivated friendly relations with Indians, who furnished guides and hunters. Thus reinforced, between 1650 and 1671 Wood undertook two journeys of exploration westward.

Peter Jones, who married Wood's daughter, succeeded his father-in-law as manager and proprietor of the trading post, which became known as Peter's Point. The settlement figured prominently in Bacon's Rebellion (1676), when unfriendly Indians were driven from the village.

William Byrd II in 1733 envisaged two cities, 'one . . . to be called Richmond, and the other at the Point of the Appamattuck River, to be nam'd Petersburgh.' The strategic position at the head of navigation indicated to him the future growth of Petersburg. As it is today, the city represents the amalgamation of Petersburg, laid out in 1748; Blandford, established the same year; Pocahontas, constituted a town in 1752; and Ravenscroft, a settlement that meanwhile had grown up on a triangle enclosed today by Halifax, Sycamore, and Shore Streets. These four were united and incorporated in 1784, and 'stiled the town of Petersburg.'

During the Revolutionary War the city was too important to be overlooked by the adversary. In 1781 General Benedict Arnold and General William Phillips, commanding 2,500 British troops, destroyed stores in Petersburg and pillaged the community despite the valiant efforts of General von Steuben and General Muhlenburg. British forces, augmented on May 20, 1781, by the army of Cornwallis, started from Petersburg four days later on the journey that ended at Yorktown.

For years before the Revolution and until the Civil War, a race track, a theater, many comfortable and merry taverns, and hospitable homes made Petersburg a popular stopping-place for travelers and a jolly center for long visits. When George Washington paused here on his southern tour (1791), he found, according to his diary, that Petersburg, containing 'near 3,000 souls,' received 'at the Inspections nearly a third of the Tobacco exported from the whole State besides a considerable quantity of wheat and flour.' He wrote also of telling a lie: 'Having suffered very much by the dust yesterday, and finding that parties of Horse, and a number of other Gentlemen were intending to attend me part of the way to day, I caused their enquiries respecting the time of my setting out, to be answered that, I should endeavor to do it before eight o'clock; but did it a little after five.' The mayor of Petersburg is said to have bestowed upon Washington during his visit the title 'father of this country.'

Dictionary of Places

Across from the town of Petersburg, according to Thomas Anburey's *Travels in the Interior Parts of America* (1776-81), was 'a kind of suburb, independent of Petersburg, called Pocahunta . . . the principal trade of Petersburg arises from the exporting of tobacco, deposited in warehouses and magazines . . . up to which sloops, schooners, and small vessels continually sail.'

During the War of 1812 the territory furnished a company under Richard McRae, which distinguished itself at Fort Meigs. These soldiers, jauntily wearing cockades, gave President Madison occasion to call Petersburg the 'Cockade City,' a name that has held through the years. In Petersburg, John Daly Burk, Irish refugee, began his history of Virginia; Aaron Burr and his daughter, Theodosia, lived here in 1805; Winfield Scott started his brief law career; and the returning La Fayette was lavishly entertained here. Joseph Jenkins Roberts (1809-76), who migrated to Liberia in 1829, was born in Petersburg. The American Colonization Society appointed him in 1842 the first Black governor of Liberia; when the country was proclaimed a republic in 1847, Roberts was elected the first president.

After 1812 Petersburg overshadowed Richmond in many respects. Theatrical companies, booked for Petersburg, went to Richmond incidentally. Disastrous fires occurred in 1815 and 1826. The first general conference of the Methodist Episcopal Church, South, meeting in Petersburg in 1846, made history through the organization of Southern Methodism. Four years later Petersburg achieved the status of city. The *Southern Star,* the first steamboat to reach Petersburg, was appropriately welcomed in 1858.

The Civil War ravaged the little city on the Appomattox. Though at first no battles were fought near by, Petersburg sent 17 companies to the front. In 1864 the city became the 'last ditch of the Confederacy.' Railroad lines through Petersburg constituted an artery of supply for Richmond and made the city a Federal objective. The long and terrible siege of Petersburg marked the downfall of the Confederacy. Here the South made its last stand against superior Federal forces. The fall of Petersburg led directly to the surrender at Appomattox.

The city made a new start after 1865. By 1880 there were 70 more industries than existed here 20 years earlier. Census tabulations of ensuing years showed steady gains.

POINTS OF INTEREST:
- Poplar Grove (Petersburg) National Cemetery. South off I-85.
- Old Blandford Church (1735) and Cemetery (1702). 321 South Crater Road.
- Trapezium House (1817). Market & Banks Streets.
- Lee Memorial Park. South part of town, off Johnson Road.
- Fort Lee. 3 miles NE on VA 36.

Encyclopedia of Virginia

HISTORICAL PLACES...(See Historical Places Section for details).
Petersburg National Battlefield; Siege Museum; Courthouse (1839); Centre Hill Mansion (ca 1823); Five Forks Battlefield; Mayfield Cottage; Wales; Battersea; Blandford Church; Exchange Building; Farmers Bank; Petersburg Courthouse; Strawberry Hill

•**PHENIX**, Town; Charlotte County; Pop. 260; Zip Code 23959; Elev. 462; 38 mi. SE of Lynchburg; Lat. 37-05-03 N long. 078-44-48 W; The town was named after the "phenix" legend, where it arose from its own ashes.

•**PITTSYLVANIA COUNTY**, S Virginia; 1,022 sq. mi.; Pop. 55,655; Named after William Pitt.

•**POCAHONTAS**, Town; Tazewell County; Pop. 513; Zip Code 24635; 52 mi. W of Blacksburg; Named for the famous Indian princess, the name means "stream between two hills." With nondescript frame houses beside huge black shafts, is the focal point of the great Pocahontas semi-bituminous coal fields. The town sprang into existence around the first mine in the field, with the coming of the Norfolk & Western Railroad in 1882. A blacksmith discovered this field, used the coal for his forge, and allowed neighbors to dig enough for their homes. His frugal wife, fearing the supply would be exhausted, advised against such wanton generosity.

HISTORICAL PLACE...(See Historical Places Section for details).
Pocahontas Historic District

•**PORT ROYAL**, Town; Caroline County; Pop. 204; Zip Code 22535; 23 mi. SE of Fredericksburg; Lat. 38-10-09 N long. 077-11-32 W; Named by Thomas Roy and called Port Roy for its shipping activity. The name evolved to Port Royal.

HISTORICAL PLACES...(See Historical Places Section for details).
Camden; Gay Mont; Hazelwood

•**PORTSMOUTH**, Independent City; Pop. 103,907; Zip Code 23700; SE Virginia, opposite Norfolk; Lat. 36-49-34 N long. 076-20-33 W; Established in 1752 and named for the city in England.

The palisaded village of the Chesapeake Indians had long disappeared when Captain William Carver, mariner, acquired a plantation in 1664 along the brackish southern banks of the Elizabeth River. Later, despite the high offices he held, Captain Carver, 'deciding to risk his old bones against the Indian rogues,' participated in Bacon's Rebellion (1676), even attempting to capture Governor Berkeley. For this treasonable escapade, he was afterwards hanged. His confiscated land was granted in 1716 to Colonel William Crawford, who in 1750 'laid out a parcel of land... into one hundred and twenty-two lots, commodious streets, places for a

Dictionary of Places

court house, market, and public landings for a town . . . and made sale . . . to divers persons . place Portsmouth, he presented it to Norfolk County. In 1752 the general assembly 'enacted . . . that the said . . . parcel of land be . . . established a town . . . and retain the name of Portsmouth.'

Among the traders, merchants, and shipbuilders, chiefly Scots, who flocked to the new town, was Andrew Sprowle. Acquiring land immediately to the south, he started the village of Gosport-named after the town opposite Portsmouth, England-by building a marine yard and tenements for workers. The British Government, recognizing the value of this enterprise, soon took over the yard as a repair station and appointed Andrew Sprowle navy agent.

When royal government ended in Virginia in 1775, Governor Dunmore fled to Sprowle's home in Gosport, where he lived 'riotously upon his friend.' For several months, he rallied Tories and Negroes about him and plundered the countryside, until his defeat at Great Bridge. Immediately afterwards he joined the British fleet, accompanied by Sprowle.

Following the burning of Norfolk in 1776, Dunmore and his Tories took possession of Portsmouth and remained until the eccentric General Charles Lee arrived with his forces, and Dunmore sailed away with his whole following. Finding the town a hotbed of Tories, General Lee, 'to quell this Toryism,' had the houses 'of the most notorious Traitors' demolished. Sprowles's property and the abandoned marine yard were seized. Later, Fort Nelson, named for General Thomas Nelson, was erected on Windmill Point.

One May morning of 1779, a great gray British fleet, carrying 2,000 men and commanded by Sir George Collier, anchored in Elizabeth River. General Edward Mathew of the fleet burned Fort Nelson and the marine yard, and the British departed. Portsmouth was the landing place and base for three other invading British expeditions under Leslie, Arnold, and Phillips.

The Revolution had repercussions in Portsmouth. Filled with refugees from burned Norfolk, the town, tolerant at first, soon flamed with indignation. About 1784 'those execrable miscreants called Tories' were told 'to leave this town immediately' or 'measures' would be taken. Thus banished, the 'Tories' went back to ruined Norfolk.

In 1784 Andrew Sprowle's confiscated property, Gosport, was divided into lots and made a part of Portsmouth. A decade later, the navy yard, which the State had retained, was lent to the Federal Government, Captain Richard Dale was placed in command, and the keel of a frigate was laid. The *Chesapeake*, the first ship built by the Federal Government, was completed in 1799. In 1801 the Government purchased the Gosport Navy Yard (now Norfolk Navy Yard) for $12,000. In 1798 a visitor marked that 'one might walk from Portsmouth to Norfolk on the decks of vessels at anchor.'

In an attempt to take Portsmouth and the navy yard during the War of 1812, the British landed 2,600 men at Port Norfolk (now a part of Portsmouth), but the guns of Fort Nelson and Fort Norfolk stopped the invasion. A fresh onslaught was made on sandy Craney Island, lined with redoubts. Approaching in barges, the British were met with a bombardment that sank several vessels and caused an immediate retreat.

After extending its town limits in 1811, a 'boat containing 10,000 shingles' being the first to pass over the mingled waters of Chesapeake Bay and Albemarle Sound. In 1821, when the first horseboat ferry was built, the town was swept by a fire of incendiary origin, but it was soon rebuilt. The land on which Fort Nelson lay was augmented by a 61-acre tract in 1826, the old fort was demolished, and on its site a naval hospital was begun. The town's first railroad was chartered in 1834, and public schools were established in 1846.

During this period Portsmouth attended its jockey, cricket, and quoit clubs; frequented racecourses; watched the launching of the *Lady of the Lake* (1830), which 'moved by its own steam'; and welcomed such visitors as Andrew Jackson (1833) and Henry Clay (1844).

Yellow fever, brought by a ship just returned from the tropics, decimated the inhabitants of Portsmouth in 1855. Of the 4,000 people who remained in the town during the epidemic, 1,089 died. In 1858 Portsmouth was chartered as a city.

When Virginia seceded from the Union, the Gosport Navy Yard was evacuated and burned, after which Virginia troops occupied the area. In May 1862 the Confederates burned the navy yard and evacuated the area. Then Federal forces moved in, established martial law in Portsmouth, and again took possession of the navy yard.

Another phase of Portsmouth's commercial era began in 1837 with the completion of the Portsmouth and Roanoke Railroad, which in 1900 became the Seaboard Air Line Railway, with its coastal terminus at Portsmouth. Branches of two other railroads, the Atlantic Coast Line and the Southern, bring inland produce to the city. Since taking over the lines of the Atlantic and Danville Railway in 1894, the Southern gas built an elaborate system of freight piers on the Western Branch.

At the beginning of the twentieth century, Portsmouth started extending its wharves along the water front, and, as necessity demanded, demolished its old houses to make way for modern business establishments.

POINTS OF INTEREST:

•Portsmouth Naval Shipyard Museum. 2 High Street on Elizabeth River.

•Portsmouth Lightship Museum. London Slip and Water Street.

Dictionary of Places

HISTORICAL PLACES...(See Historical Places Section for details).
US Naval Hospital; Trinity Episcopal Church; Monumental United Church; Cradock Historic District; Drydock No. 1; Portsmouth Courthouse (Norfolk County Courthouse); Portsmouth Historictal District; Portsmouth Naval Hospital; Quarters A, B, and C, Norfolk Naval Shipyard

•**POTOMAC RIVER** About 290 miles in length the Potomac rises near the Appalachian plateau. Its north branch comes near the headquarters of the Ohio River. It is joined by the Shenandoah on the south bank.

Washington, D.C. is on the left bank of the river. The outlet is is into Chesapeake Bay. The name was first recorded in 1608 by John Smith as Patawomeck. Its derivation is unknown but probably has an association with the Native American Algonquin nation.

•**POUND,** Town; Wise County; Pop. 995; Zip Code 24279; 70 mi. NW of Bristol; Lat. 37-08-02 N long. 082-36-13 W; Site of an early pioneer mill built here in 1815 by James Mullins. Settlers brought grain to be milled or "pounded," and gave the town its name. Here in 1935 Edith Maxwell, a young school teacher, was charged with killing her father when she struck him as her sought to punish her for staying out late at night. The code of the hills, as interpreted in the newsrooms, furnished a basis for many sensational stories. Edith Maxwell was convicted, retired, and sentenced to serve 20 years.

•**POWHATAN COUNTY,** Central Virginia; 268 sq. mi.; Pop. 15,328; Named after Indain chief Powhatan of the Powhatan Indian tribe. Father of Indian maiden Pocahontas.

•**PRINCE EDWARD,** S central Virginia; 357 sq. mi.; Pop. 17,320; Named after Prince Edward (1733-1761) second Prince of Wales.

•**PRINCE GEORGE COUNTY,** SE Virginia; 286 sq. mi.; Pop. 27,394; Named after Prince George (1653-1708) prince of Denmark.

•**PRINCE WILLIAM COUNTY,** N Virginia; 347 sq. mi.; Pop. 215,686; Named after Prince William (1721-1765); third son of George II and Queen Caroline.

•**PULASKI COUNTY,** SW Virginia; 333 sq. mi.; Pop. 34,496; Named after Casimir Pulaski.

•**PULASKI,** Town; Pulaski County Seat; Pop. 9,985; Zip Code 24301; 52 mi. WSW of Roanoke; Lat. 37-03-38 N long. 080-46-34 W; The town was founded in 1839 and named in honor of Polish-American Revolutionary War hero Count Casimir Pulaski.

Coal discovered to the northwest in 1877 suddenly rocketed this railroad flag stop, Martin's Tank, into industrial importance and a more dignified name, Martin's Station. Cheap fuel soon lured zinc and iron furnaces, nuclei for the town's subsequent growth.

•**PUNGOTEAGUE** Seat of Accomac from 1662 to 1677. Court was held at the tavern of John Cole, who vainly attempted to keep the court day trade by offering to furnish bricks and woodwork for a courthouse. On August 27, 1665, the first theatrical performance in Virginia was given in this town. For presenting *Ye Bare and Ye Cubb,* Cornelius Wilkinson, Phillip Howard, and William Derby were ordered to appear before the court (on the complaint of a busybody named Edward Martin) 'in those habilmets that they then acted in, and give a draught of such verses, or other speeches and passages which were then acted by them.' After presenting their wares, the men were acquitted of the charge of immorality; the complainant was fined.

On May 30, 1814, the British admiral, Sir George Cockburn, landed on Pungoteague Creek with 500 marines and fought the Eastern Shore militia. Fearing capture, he retired to Tangier Island.

•**PURCELLVILLE,** Town; Loudoun County; Pop. 1,744; Zip Code 22078; Elev. 576; 32 mi. NW of Washington D.C.; Lat. 39-06-54 N long. 077-41-42 W; The Purcell family opened the first store and post office in 1832. The town is named after them.

•**QUANTICO,** Town; Prince William County; Pop. 670; Zip Code 22134; 18 mi. NNE of Fredericksburg; Lat. 38-31-15 N long. 077-17-43 W; An Indian word meaning "place of dancing." Quantico was a 'naval base,' established to serve the vessels of the 'Potomac Navy' during the Revolution. When the United States entered World War I in 1917, Quantico was selected as a training camp and maneuver field for the Marine Corps, and in 1918 became a permanent post.

•**RADFORD,** City; Pop. 15,940; Zip Code 24141; Elev. 1023; 14 mi. ENE of Pulaski; Lat. 37-08-04 N long. 080-34-18 W; The city takes its name from the original landowner, Dr. John Bane Radford. On the New River's deep gorge, hides behind its corporate mask two separate units, Radford and East Radford, each with its own business center.

Successor to the village of Lovely Mount, Central Depot, equidistant from Lynchburg and Bristol, grew up after the Virginia & Tennessee Railroad established machine shops here in 1856. In the wake of the New Division of the Norfolk & Western Railway, opened in 1881, came a stove foundry, brick kilns, and iron furnace. Four years later the little town was incorporated and named for the man who had formerly owned the property, Dr. John Bane Radford.

Dictionary of Places

POINTS OF INTEREST:
•Radford University (1910). On US 11, I-81 exit 35.
•Claytor Lake State Park. On VA 660, 6 miles SW, just South of I-81 exit 33.

HISTORICAL PLACE...(See Historical Places Section for details).
Ingles Ferry

•**RAPPAHANNOCK COUNTY,** N Virginia; 267 sq. mi.; Pop. 6,622; Named after the Indian tribe.

•**RAPPAHANNOCK RIVER** The source of the river is the Manassas Gap in the Blue Ridge Mountains. Its name is from the Algonquin Indian meaning "back and forth stream." It was the early location of the Powhatan Indian Confederacy.

Its main tributary, the Rapidan, joins about twenty miles north of Fredericksburg. At its southeastern extremity it widens into a 50-mile-long estuary.

Ridge Mountains •**REMINGTON,** Town; Fauquier County; Pop. 460; Zip Code 22734; 25 mi. S of Manassas; Lat. 38-32-09 N long. 077-48-32 W; Originally called Millview, the name was changed in 1890 to Remington. It was known during the War between the States as Rappahannock Station.

•**RICH CREEK,** Town; Giles County; Pop. 670; Zip Code 24147; Lat. 37-23-09 N long. 080-49-15 W; A large, cool set of creeks run through the town. Water is bottled from one stream because of its medicinal effects. This business named the town.

•**RICHLANDS,** Town; Tazewell County; Pop. 4,456; Zip Code 24641; Elev. 1967; the high-quality pastures in the area gave the town its name.

•**RICHMOND COUNTY,** E Virginia; 192 sq. mi.; Pop. 7,273; Named after Richmond, Surry County, England.

•**RICHMOND,** Independent City; Pop. 203,056; Zip Code 230+; Central Virginia; Lat. 37-17-55 N long. 076-50-26 W; Founded in 1742 and named for Richmond on Thames in England.

It is the capital of Virginia, and is at the head of navigation on the James River.

A week after the English landed at Jamestown in 1607, Captain Christopher, Newport set out to explore the James River. On the '27th daye of May,' coming upon some falls, the party set up a cross on a small island near the foot of the present 9th Street. Two years later, sent by John Smith, Captain Francis West purchased a site at the falls from the Indians and erected a fort that he called Fort

West. After trouble with the Indians the settlement was abandoned. In 1610 Lord Delaware led an expedition to the falls, vainly sought minerals, and returned to Jamestown. In 1637 Thomas Stegg established a trading post at the head of navigation on the James and was later granted lands about the falls, His son, Thomas Stegg II, who had acquired property on both sides of the river, in 1670 left his holding to William Byrd I, a nephew, then only 18.

After the massacre of 1644 the settlers established Fort Charles at the head of navigation and offered freedom from taxation to anyone who would establish a home near by. Young Nathaniel Bacon had taken up land near the falls. In this neighborhood the Susquehannock incited other Indians to the depredations that precipitated Bacon's Rebellion in 1676. The settlement at Fort Charles, encouraged by 'certain privileges' granted William Byrd I for inducing able-bodied men to live there as a defense against Indians, became a trading post for furs, tobacco, and other commodities and was known as Byrd's Warehouse of Shocco.

In 1733 William Byrd II 'laid the foundation of two Citys': Petersburg and Richmond. Colonel Byrd combined truth with prophecy when he wrote: '. . . these two places being the uppermost Landing of James and Appamattux Rivers, are naturally intended for Marts, where the Traffick of the Outer Inhabitants must Center.' Four years later Major William Mayo plotted on what is now Church Hill 32 squares for Richmond 'with Streets 65 feet wide,' and named the place after Richmond on the Thames. In 1742, when the population was 250, the general assembly enacted that 'piece or parcel of land . . . at the falls of the James River...constituted...a town.' In 1769 William Byrd III 'laid out another parcel of his lands, on the north side of the James river later called Manchester was established at Rocky Ridge on the south side of the river.

During the next two decades Richmond grew slowly, with vicissitudes that included the destructive 'great freshet' of 1771. The First Virginia Convention, held in Williamsburg in August 1774, had elected delegates to the First Continental Congress and adopted a system of nonintercourse with Great Britain. The Second Convention opened on March 20, 1775, at St. John's Church in Richmond. Patrick Henry made his impassioned plea for liberty or death and put through his resolution for 'embodying, arming, and disciplining' the militia. The Third Convention, meeting in Richmond in July, appointed the Committee of Safety, proposed the enlisting of recruits, and inaugurated a plan for financing the war; and the Fourth Convention was organized in Richmond but adjourned to Williamsburg.

In 1779 Richmond was made the capital of Virginia. The following year, when Governor Jefferson moved into a rented house and the assembly convened in temporary quarters, there were but 684 people living in Richmond. The town played an important part in

Dictionary of Places

the last days of the Revolution, suffered pillaging by Benedict Arnold in January 1781, was rescued from the British under Arnold and Phillips the following April by the arrival of La Fayette, and in June was on Cornwallis's line of march eastward.

With peace came a new era of growth. The *Virginia Gazette* was moved from Williamsburg to Richmond, and three other newspapers were established in the new capital. In 1782 Richmond was incorporated as a town, though it was called a city in deference to its status as capital. William Foushee was elected mayor. The general assembly held sessions that led to a convention of other states for the framing of a Federal Constitution, which-amid verbal fireworks-Virginia ratified in 1788. Thomas Jefferson's beautiful building went up on Capitol Square. By 1790 the population had increased to 3,761, and by 1800 had reached 5,730.

In 1802 Benjamin Henfry, a Scotsman, demonstrated lighting by gas before citizens in Haymarket Garden, present terminus of the Atlantic Coast Line Railway, and heard his 'tea kettle apparatus' ridiculed; Richmond missed the opportunity of being the first American city to install street lighting. In 1803 came Tome Moore, Irish poet, 'whose songs were sung to every guitar and harpsichord in Richmond.' In 1807 Aaron Burr was tried for high treason behind the portico of the Jeffersonian capitol. In 1811 a theater fire took the lives of 73 people. That year the Allans of Richmond adopted Edgar Allan Poe, an orphaned baby. His youth here and his later connection with the *Southern Literary Messenger* are justification for Poe's declaring, 'I am a Virginian. At least, I call myself one.'

Like most cities Richmond grew with the development of transportation. Though its was not until 1840 that freight was shipped by canal between Richmond and Lynchburg, a canal was proposed by the Reverend Robert Rose in 1750. The general assembly passed an act in 1764 'for extending navigation of the James River from Westham (seven miles) downward through the Falls.' In 1784 the James River Navigation Company was chartered, and the following year George Washington was elected its president. In 1790 the canal was opened from Richmond to Westham, and in 1836 the Richmond, Fredericksburg and Potomac Railroad carried its first passengers out of Richmond, at the terrifying speed of 10 miles per hour. When the James River and Kanawha Canal was completed in 1840, Richmond was linked with the Piedmont country.

The city became as joyful and fashionable as Williamsburg had been in its heyday. Hostesses vied with each other in elaborate entertaining. In 1842, the year that Richmond became a city in reality as well as in name, Charles Dickens at a dinner given in the Exchange Hotel was toasted as 'the artful dodger' because he had 'dodged Philadelphia and Baltimore,' but not Richmond. Theaters presented stars of the European and American stage-the Booths, Joe Jefferson, Jenny Lind.

But the 'Fiery Epoch' had begun. Sectional misunderstanding had thwarted a movement within the State for the emancipation of slaves. The capital city was caught up in the excitement of war. On the night of April 19, 1861, Richmond blazed with fireworks and 'ten thousand hurrahing men and boys carried torches' to celebrate Virginia's secession. On May 29, the Confederate capital was moved to Montgomery, Alabama, to Richmond.

For a time the city was headily gay. Officers, resplendent in new uniforms, strolled beside hoop-skirted beauties, whose very curls danced with patriotism. Sewing circles culminated in 'danceable teas,' and pretty heads were forever planning balls, parties, and theatricals. But there was bickering, too. Richmond ladies were critical of wives of new officialdom. 'The Cabinet of ours,' wrote Mary Boykin Chestnut on July 27, 'are in such bitter quarrels among themselves-everybody abusing everybody.'

As the war years deepened Richmond was the center of political wrangling and the objective of an invading army. Privation stifled gaiety and feuds. Wounded soldiers were brought to hurriedly equipped hospitals. In May 1862, McClellan came within sight of Richmond. Defeated in Seven Days' Campaign, he changed his base from the York to the James, where he remained until recalled in midsummer.

Foremost among the war heroines was Sally Tompkins, who as head of a hospital was commissioned captain in the Confederate army. Elizabeth Van Lew heroically toiled for the Union and emancipation, sending daily communications to Federal officers and helping blue-clad soldiers to escape from crowded Libby Prison, a ship chandlery and tobacco warehouse built by William Libby in 1845 at Twentieth and Cary Streets. On February 9, 1864, she aided Colonel Thomas E. Rose and 108 Federals in a daring break from the prison. On April 3, 1865, Richmond was evacuated and burned by its own people.

After the war Richmond began the slow task of rebuilding. Elizabeth Van Lew became postmaster-the only woman ever to hold so important a government post in the city; the canal was reopened; railroads were repaired; a system of public education was established; and the emancipated slave began to find his place in the economic scheme. In 1887 horsedrawn streetcars, which had been running since 1861, were supplanted by electric cars.

A romantic literature, characterized by nostalgia for bygone days, gave place in time to the writing of history and realism. Mary Johnston became America's foremost historical novelist; Ellen Glasgow held the mirror before the people she knew-too close for their happiness; and James Branch Cabell created a medieval realm in which he ridiculed the Philistia about him. Edward V. Valentine, Sir Moses Ezekiel, Dugald Stewart Walker, and others achieved National recognition in the world of art. John Powell took front rank among musicians. Schools and colleges increased in

Dictionary of Places

number and size and strengthened their curricula. Richmond became a hospital center for Virginia and other Southern States. In 1910 Manchester across the river was annexed as a unit of greater Richmond. Women, under such leaders as Lila Meade Valentine and Mary Cooke Branch Mumford, began to participate in public affairs. Blacks set out to learn the use of new tools that freedom and education had given them. Commerce and the arts built a new Richmond, which while celebrating its bicentennial in 1937, refreshed its memory by means of historical pageant.

POINTS OF INTEREST:
- Virginia State Library. 12th and Broad Streets.
- Virginia Museum of Fine Arts.
- Battle Abbey, Virginia Historical Society. 428 North Blvd.
- Edgar Allan Poe Museum. 1914 East Main Street.
- Museum of the Confederacy. 1201 East Clay Street.
- Richmond Children's Museum. 740 North 6th Street.
- Science Museum of Virginia. 2500 West Broad Street.
- Virginia House. 4301 Sulgrave Road, 1/4 mile off VA 147 (Cary Street) in Windsor Farms.
- Pocahontas State Park. SW on US 360, then SE on VA 655.

HISTORICAL PLACES...(See Historical Places Section for details).
State Capitol (1785-1788); Governor's Mansion (1813); Monument Avenue; St. Paul's Church; St. John's Episcopal Church (1741); Monumental Church; Valentine Museum; James River and Kanawha Canal Locks; Richmond National Battlefield Park; Tree Hill; Bell Tower; Barret House; Beers, William, House; Branch Building; Broad Street Station; Cabell, Henry Coalter, House; City Hall; Confederate Memorial Chapel; Crozet House (Curtis Carter House; Donnan-Asher Iron-Front Building; Egyptian Building; First African Baptist Church; First Baptist Church; Glasgow, Ellen, House; Hancock-Wirt-Caskie House; Haxall, Bolling House; Hollywood Cemetery; Kent-Valentine House; Leigh-Benjamin Watkins, House; Leigh Street Baptist Church; Linden Row; Main Street Station; Marshall, John, House; Maupin-Maury House; Maymont; Mayo Memorial Church House; Monroe, James, Tomb; Monument Avenue Historic District; Monumental Church; Morson's Row; Old Stone House; Putney Houses; Scott-Clarke House; Second Presbyterian Church; Sheltering Arms Hospital (William H. Grant House); Shockoe Slip Historic District; St. John's Church Historic District; St. Peter's Church; Stearns Iron-Front Building; Stewart-Lee House; Tredegar Ironworks; U.S. Post Office and Customhouse; West Franklin Street Historic District; White House of the Confederacy (Brockenbrough Mansion); William J. Clark Library and Barco-Stevens Hall, Virginia Union University (Belgian Building); Woodward House; Ruffin, Edmund, Plantation (Marlbourne); Flood Marker of 1771; Malvern Hill

- **RIDGEWAY**, Town; Henry County; Pop. 752; Zip Code 24148; Elev. 638; 37 mi. W of Danville; Lat. 36-32-55 N long. 079-51-27 W; Early settler Samuel Sheffield descriptively named the town. The Virginia Commission, to establish the Virginia-North Carolina line, camped on its banks in 1728. William Byrd II, who headed the party of Virginians, wrote that the creek was 'called so by an unfortunate marry'd man because it was exceedingly noisy and impetuous. However, tho the stream was clamorous, like those women who make themselves plainest heard, it was perfectly clear and unsully'd.'

•ROANOKE COUNTY, SW Virginia; 292 sq. mi.; Pop. 79,332; Indian word for a shell used for money.

•ROANOKE, Independent City; Pop. 96,397; Zip Code 24001; 148 mi. W of Richmond; Lat. 37-16-36 N long. 079-57-23 W; The city's name is from an Indian word meaning "swell money".

When Augusta County was formed in 1738, the valley of the Roanoke lay within its boundaries. Settlements were made here as early as 1740. In 1749 Dr. Thomas Walker of Albermarle organized the Loyal Land Company and on a trip to explore the country found squatters in the valley. At the 'Great Lick they bought corn for their horses from Michael Campbell' and farther on 'lodged at James Robinson's.'

The French and Indian War almost wrecked these frontier settlements, yet a few stalwart people continued to hold their homes, and others came to set up homesteads. About the turn of the century Old Lick, already a stage on the Great Road down the valley, became an important crossroads when it was reached by the turnpike running west from Lynchburg.

In 1834 the community made its first effort to become a town. Streets were laid out and lots were sold, but only the little town of Gainsborough materialized. Salem, and not Big Lick, was made the seat of Roanoke County when it was created in 1838.

In 1852 the Virginia and Tennessee Railroad built a depot at Big Lick and a few shops and stores followed immediately. In 1858 Isham M. Ferguson established a tobacco factory in the village, and 10 years later a canning factory was put in operation. Big Lick was chartered as a town in 1874; John Trout was elected mayor; the council met regularly in Rorer's Hall; and the town even erected a calaboose 12 feet square. Four years later *The Big Lick News* printed its first edition.

In 1881 its was announced abroad that two railroads, the Shenandoah Valley and the Norfolk and Western, were seeking a junction point. John C. Moomaw suggested that the council offer inducements that would bring the terminal to Big Lick and started on a 50-mile ride to Lexington, where he was to confer the next day with railroad officials. He had arranged that a messenger convey to him at Buchanan, in the morning, details of the town's offer. The council promised a terminal and $10,000. Charles W. Thomas rode to Buchanan and delivered the papers to Mr. Moomaw, who hurried on the Lexington. The junction was awarded to Big Lick.

Dictionary of Places

In 1882 the town changed its name to Roanoke (Ind., shell money) and extended its limits. In 1881 there had been less than 700 inhabitants; in 1883 there were 5,000, and Roanoke received its city charter the next year. In 1906 the Virginian Railway came, bringing its shops and its great coal traffic. Mark Twain was a passenger on the first Virginian coach that entered the city.

POINTS OF INTEREST:
- Mill Mountain Zoo. Off US 220/I-581 and Blue Ridge Pkwy.
- Roanoke Transportation Museum. 802 Wiley Drive in Wasena Park.
- Blue Ridge Pkwy. 6 miles East on US 460 or 3 miles South on US 220.
- Showplace at the Barn. 6071 Airport Road.

HISTORICAL PLACES...(See Historical Places Section for details).
Hollins College; Buena Vista; Fire Station No. 1; St. Andrew's Roman Catholic Church; Deyerle, Benjamin, Place; Monterey

- **ROANOKE RIVER** Cutting through the Blue Ridge Mountains by the town of Roanoke this river rises to a height of about 1,000 feet. It is joined from the south by the Dam above Clarksville. Below Clarksville is the J. H. Kerr Dam power project and drainage basin. Flowing southeastward it crosses into North Carolina. Its name probably derives from the Native American Algonquin but its meaning is indefinite.

- **ROCKBRIDGE COUNTY,** W Virginia; 604 sq. mi.; Pop. 18,350; Descriptive name for a natural bridge over Cedar Creek.

- **ROCKINGHAM COUNTY,** N Virginia; 869 sq. mi.; Pop. 57,482; Named after the Marquis of Rockingham.

- **ROCKY MOUNT,** Town; Franklin County Seat; Pop. 4,098; Zip Code 24151; 22 mi. S of Roanoke; Lat. 36-59-58 N long. 079- 53-23 W; Settled in 1760 and descriptively named for an abrupt precipice in the area. For nearly 100 years the community was two rival villages, Rocky Mount and Mount Pleasant. Though in 1873 Rocky Mount swallowed its smaller rival, the town buildings of the two villages still glare at each other across a narrow street.

HISTORICAL PLACES...(See Historical Places Section for details).
Washington Iron Furrnace; Booker T. Washington National Monument

- **ROUND HILL,** Town; Loudoun County; Pop. 514; Zip Code 22141; Elev. 97; 45 mi. NW of Washington D.C.; Lat. 39-08-03 N long. 077-46-09 W; The town was settled in 1735 and named for a prominent "round hill" landmark nearby.

- **RURAL RETREAT,** Town; Wythe County; Pop. 972; Zip Code 24368; Elev. 2510; 55 mi. NE of Bristol; Lat. 36-53-43 N long. 081-16-27 W; Named after an early inn on the stage route which was a "retreat" for weary travelers.

Encyclopedia of Virginia

•**RUSSELL COUNTY**, SW Virginia; 483 sq. mi.; Pop. 28,667; Named after William Russell.

•**ST. CHARLES**, Town; Lee County; Pop. 206; Zip Code 24282; 57 mi. NW of Bristol; Lat. 36-49-01 N long. 083-03-28 W; The town was named in honor of early coal developer Charles Bondurant.

•**ST. PAUL**, Town; Russell & Wise Counties; Pop. 1,007; Zip Code 24283; Elev. 1492; 41 mi. NW of Bristol; Lat. 36-58-04 N long. 082-18-28 W; St. Paul is a railroad junction and a lively shopping center that grew up near the old Wheeler's Ford on the Clinch River. Here, in the 1770s, was Moore's Fort. In the 1890s a promotion company, anticipating the construction a railroad, acquired land on both sides of the river and proposed to establish twin cities, to be named St. Paul and Minneapolis. Originally Estonoa, the name was changed when the company paid $100 to the postmaster of another St. Paul, in Carroll County, for the exclusive use of the name, and laid out streets; but the project was abandoned when the financing of the railroad failed. It was not until the Carolina, Clinchfield & Ohio Railway was built in 1904 that St. Paul began to grow.

In 1790, Baron Francois Pierre de Tubeuf, a French political exile, traded houses in London to one Richard Smith for 55,000 acres of land in this neighborhood. The next year Tubeuf arrived with his wife, a son, and servants, and among other supplies, a pair of specially made boots designed as a protection against snakes. In 1794 two visitors killed Tubeuf, his wife, and all the servants except one maid, who escaped but was drowned during her flight. Alexandre de Tubeuf, the son, was left for dead but recovered. The house was stripped of its valuables and burned by the brigands. Later the men were captured and placed in the Abingdon jail, from which they freed themselves.

•**SALEM**, Independent City; Pop. 23,756; Zip Code 24153; Elev. 1060; 8 mi. W of Roanoke; Lat. 37-16-49 N long. 080-03-01 W; Named for Salem, New Jersey. After purchasing 31 acres of the 625-acre grant made to Andrew Lewis in 1768, James Simpson laid out Salem on 16 acres in 1802. On the main line of travel down the Valley, Salem became a stopping-place with numerous inns: The Old Time Tavern, The Bull's Eye, The Indian Queen, the Globe, and the Mermaid Tavern-the last a 'tippling place' run by James Simpson's son-in-law, Griffin Lumpkin, whose interests ran to profitable horse-races and cock-fights.

POINTS OF INTEREST:
•Lakeside Park. 1526 East Main Street.
•Dixie Caverns. 5 miles West off I-81 exit 39.
•Roanoke College (1842). College Avenue, off I-81.

HISTORICAL PLACES...(See Historical Places Section for details).

Evans House; Main Campus Complex, Roanoke College; Salem Presbyterian Church; Williams-Brown House and Store

Dictionary of Places

•**SALTVILLE**, Town; Smyth & Washington Counties; Pop. 2,300; Zip Code 24370; Elev. 1718; 32 mi. NE of Bristol; Lat. 36-52-41 N long. 081- 46-10 W; Incorporated in 1896 and named for its two century old salt production industry.

•**SAVAGE STATION** Was formerly a railroad stop that gave its name to the third battle in the Seven Days' Campaign. Following the Battle of Gaines' Mill, both armies spent June 28 seeking new positions. On this day McClellan abandoned his supply base at White House Landing and began his retreat toward Harrison's Landing on the James. One the morning of June 29 half of McClellan's army was beyond White Oak Swamp, several miles south, and the remainder grouped around this station, awaited withdrawal. Lee's scattered army moved rapidly to intercept McClellan. In mid-morning, General John B. Magruder's division encountered General E. V. Sumner's Federal corps about a mile to the southwest. Sumner easily repulsed Magruder, then withdrew to this place. In the afternoon Sumner repelled a second attack by Magruder and withdrew southward during the night.

•**SAXIS**, Town; Accomack County; Pop. 367; Zip Code 23427; Lat. 37-55-35 N long. 075-43-12 W; The name is a corruption of seventeenth century settler Robert Sike's name.

•**SCOTT COUNTY**, SW Virginia; 539 sq. mi.; Pop. 23,204; Named after Winfield Scott.

•**SCOTTSBURG**, Town; Halifax County; Pop. 152; Zip Code 24589; Elev. 380; 8 mi. NE of South Boston; Lat. 36-45-28 N long. 078-47-28 W; The town's name honors John Scott, a Revolutionary War soldier and officer.

•**SCOTTSVILLE**, Town; Albemarle & Fluvana Counties; Pop. 239; Zip Code 24562; 19 mi. S of Charlottesville; Lat. 37-43-53 N long. 078-39-32 W; The town is named after the Scott family, who were prominent early settlers. It was the seat of Albemarle County until Charlottesville was established in 1762. Later it became the terminal of the James River-Staunton Turnpike.

•**SEVEN PINES** Was a field of action in indecisive fighting on May 31 and June 1, 1862, when McClellan's army, quiescent on the Chickahominy, was attacked by the Confederate Army under Johnston. General Johnston, wounded at Fair Oaks one mile north, was succeeded by General G. W. Smith. During the afternoon of June 1, General Robert E. Lee was assigned to command the Confederate Army in Virginia.

•**SHENANDOAH COUNTY**, N Virginia; 507 sq. mi.; Pop. 31,636; Indian word for "sprucy stream."

Encyclopedia of Virginia

•SHENANDOAH, Town; Page County; Pop. 2,213; Zip Code 22849; 15 mi. E of Harrisonburg; Lat. 38-29-14 N long. 078-37-19 W; Incorporated in 1884 and given an Indian name meaning "beautiful daughter of the stars."

•SHENANDOAH RIVER With its source in Augusta County, Virginia the Shenandoah flows between the Blue Ridge Mountains and the Appalachians. It has two paralled forks separated by the Massanutten Mountains. It rises to about 1,500 feet to less than 500 feet when it outlets into the Potomac River. It is about 200 miles in length. The name is probably derived from the Native American Algonquin making reference to the abundance of spruce trees.

When Governor Spotswood's party camped by this river, they named it Euphrates. According to the diary of one of the members of the party, 'The Governor buried a bottle with a paper inclosed, on which he writ that he took possession of this place in the name and for King George the First of England...and we drank the king's health in champagne and fired a volley, the Princess's health in Burgundy, and fired a volley, and all the rest of the Royal Family in Claret, and fired a volley. We had several sorts of liquors, viz: Virginia red wine, Irish usquebaugh, brandy shrub, two sorts of rum, champagne, canary, cherry punch, water cider, etc.

•SKINQUARTER Was so named, according to the story, because Indians gathered at spring close by after hunts to skin and quarter their game.

Nearby, in July 1781, General 'Mad Anthony' Wayne's Continentals took position to halt British troops, moving southward. On April 3, 1865, Hill's Longstreet's and Gordon's Corps of Lee's army crossed here in retreat from Petersburg.

•SMITHFIELD, Town; Isle of Wight County; Pop. 4,686; Zip Code 23430; Elev. 45; 13 mi. W of Newport News; Lat. 36-59-20 N long. 076-37-49 W; Founded in 1662 on land owned by settler Arthur Smith, and so named. A tobacco warehouse was here in 1633 and in the eighteenth century the place was the seat of Isle of Wight County. From the Indians here, the first settlers learned the process of curing the meat of razorback hogs. In the eighteenth century Mallory Todd perfected the primitive technique. According to an invoice, Mallory Todd, founder of E. M. Todd & Co., was shipping hams to the West Indies in 1779. The best hams come from the hog that is allowed to roam through the woods and fields in the spring and summer and thus grow strong and lean. In the fall he is turned into fields from which the major part of the peanut crop has been taken but where enough has been left to fatten him. After killing, hams are packed with salt, then subjected to a slow smoking above smoldering hickory fires. Afterward they are stored for at least a year, though the thicker the mold the more the connoisseur is pleased. In and

Dictionary of Places

around Smithfield real 'Virginia hams' are procurable. Local cooks advise that hams be boiled 20 minutes to the pound, allowed to cool, be skinned, baked, and, for serving, sliced to paper thinness. The experts disdain coatings of brown sugar, cloves, and dressings of wine. Well-cured and cooked, Smithfield ham is deep red, with the fat translucent amber. In Smithfield are preserved orders from Windsor Castle for hams that were sent to Queen Victoria.

HISTORICAL PLACES...(See Historical Places Section for details).

Old Isle of Wight Courthouse; Smithfield Historic District; St. Luke's Church; Wolftrap Farm

•**SMYTH COUNTY**, SW Virginia; 435 sq. mi.; Pop. 32,370; Named after Alexander Smyth (1765-1830) Virginia House of Delegates 1792, 1796, 1801, 1802, 1804-08. Representative from Virginia 1817-25 and 1827-30.

•**SOUTH BOSTON**, City; Pop. 6,997; Zip Code 24592; 28 mi. ENE of Danville; Lat. 36-42-30 N long. 078-54-17 W; on the Dan River in Halifax County in one of the country's leading tobacco markets. The town was chartered in 1796, nearly a century before it was incorporated in 1884. The settlement was made on land bought from George Carrington for $2,000 and disposed of in half-acre plots by lottery. Buyers were given five years to build dwellings with brick or stone chimneys. Originally slated to be called Boston, post office objections forced a name change to South Boston.

POINTS OF INTEREST:

•Staunton River State Park. 8 miles NE on VA 304, then 11 miles SE on VA 344.

HISTORICAL PLACE...(See Historical Places Section for details).

Berry Hill

•**SOUTHAMPTON COUNTY**, SE Virginia; 607 sq. mi.; Pop. 17,550; Named after Henry Wriothesley, second earl of Southampton (1573-1624).

•**SOUTH HILL**, Town; Mecklenburg County; Pop. 4,217; Zip Code 23970; Elev. 440; 45 mi. E of South Boston; Lat. 36-43-45 N long. 078-07-25 W; The town is south of a large hill, and was so descriptively named. South Hill is one of the leading cotton markets in Virginia. On the Roanoke River, one of the first waterways used for transportation to the western part of the State, a well-organized fleet of flatboats operated as early as 1825.

Returning from a trip to 'settle the bound' between Virginia and North Carolina, William Byrd II and the other Virginia commissioners crossed here in November 1728.

•**SPOTSYLVANIA COUNTY**, NE Virginia; 413 sq. mi.; Pop. 57,403; Named after Alexander Spotswood (1676-1640) Lt. governor of Virginia 1710-22.

Encyclopedia of Virginia

•**STAFFORD**, NE Virginia; 271 sq. mi.; Pop. 61,236; Named after the county Stafford in England.

•**STANARDSVILLE**, Town; Greene County Seat; Pop. 257; Zip Code 22973; 22 mi. N of Charlottesville; Lat. 38-17-53 N long. 078-26-17 W; The name honors Robert Standards who donated the land for the courthouse.

HISTORICAL PLACES...(See Historical Places Section for details).
Greene County Courthouse; Octonia Stone

•**STAUNTON**, Independent City; Augusta County Seat; Pop. 24,461; Zip Code 24401; 110 miles NW of Richmond. Founded in 1736 on land granted to William Beverly by King George II and named for Rebecca Staunton wife of Sir William Gooch, a colonial governor.

In 1736 Beverly was granted a large tract of land embracing the present city of Staunton, 'in consideration for inducing a large number of settlers to the community.' In 1738, when Augusta County was formed, extending from the Blue Ridge Mountains to the Mississippi River and south from the Great Lakes to North Carolina, no provision was made for a county seat. Beverly gave a small stone building, Mill Place, the earliest name of the settlement, for use as the county courthouse. In 1761 the general assembly authorized the town of Staunton. Some say the name honored Lady Gooch, wife of Governor William Gooch and a member of the Staunton family, others that the town was named for Staunton, England.

The town was advantageously situated at the crossing of the Valley Pike and the Midland Trail. Travelers westward bound and those journeying southward or northward stopped in Staunton. Here they refreshed themselves at taverns, rested their horses, and replenished their supplies. Through Staunton were shipped luxuries that East sent West, and along the streets of the frontier city great droves of hogs passed on their way to eastern markets. In 1796 Isaac Weld, and Irish traveler, wrote, 'As I passed along the road in the great valley and the village called Staunton, I met with great numbers of people from Kentucky and the new state of Tennessee, going towards Philadelphia and Baltimore and with many others going in a contrary direction, "to explore," as they call it, that is to search for lands conveniently situated for new settlements in the western country. This town called Staunton carries on a considerable trade with the back country and contains nearly two hundred dwellings, mostly built of stone, together with a church. Nowhere, I believe, is there such a superfluity of . . . military personages as in the town of Staunton,' In 1797 the Duc de la Rochefoucauld-Liancourt, a French philosopher, visited Staunton on his way to Monticello, and commented in his diary upon the town: 'There are eight Inns, fifteen to eighteen stores and about 800 inhabitants fond of gambling and betting.'

Dictionary of Places

Throughout vast Augusta County Indians gave no end of trouble, for they resented the white men's theft of their land. Among the Indian fighters was 'Mad Ann' Bailey, intermittently a resident of Staunton. She came to America from England as an indentured servant, married Richard Trotter, and brought forth a son. After her husband was killed by the Indians, Ann set out to avenge his death. She 'halways carried a hax and a hauger and could chop as well as hany man.' Dressed in men's clothes, equipped with rifle, tomahawk, and knife, she became a spy, messenger, and scout, killed more than one person's share of Indians, saved stockades, and lived to the creditable age of 83.

Staunton was once the capital of Virginia, though the distinction was unpremeditated and short-lived. In 1781, when the British Colonel Tarleton approached Charlottesville, the general assembly fled to Staunton and continued its sessions in Old Trinity Church.

After the Revolution, Dr. Alexander Humphreys, a pioneer surgeon and teacher of medical science, who died in 1802, lived in Staunton. Ephraim McDowell, pioneer in the science of ovariotomy, William Wardlaw, Samuel Brown, and other distinguished physicians were pupils of Dr. Humphreys. In 1788, after the disappearance of a visiting Englishman, Dr. Humphreys was suspected of murder when a bag that bore his name and contained the bones of a man was found in a cave. He sued his accuser and received a verdict of 'slander.' Later Dr. McDowell positively identified the hair as that of a Black man whose corpse Dr. Humphreys probably had used for dissection.

The town was chartered in 1801. The Central Railroad completed its tracks as far west as Staunton in 1854. During the Civil War no battles were fought in the immediate vicinity of Staunton, but both armies used the city as a base for supplies. Staunton became a city in 1871.

POINTS OF INTEREST:
- Woodrow Wilson Birthplace. 24 North Coalter Street, off US 11.
- Gypsy Hill Park. Off Churchville and Thornrose Avenues.

HISTORICAL PLACES...(See Historical Places Section for details).
Mary Baldwin College; Trinity Episcopal Church; Augusta Stone Church; Folly; Sears House; Stuart Hall (Main Building); Stuart House); Virginia School For The Deaf and Blind; Western State Hospital Complex; Wharf Area Historic District; Wilson, Woodrow, Birthplace

- **STUART**, Town; Patrick County Seat; Pop. 965; Zip Code 24171; 55 mi. W of Danville; Lat. 36-38-16 N long. 080-16-00 W; Founded in the 1700's. First called Taylorsville, the town in 1884 changed its name to honor Confederate general, J. E. B. Stuart, born in the county February 6, 1833.

Encyclopedia of Virginia

HISTORICAL PLACE...(See Historical Places Section for details).
Patrick County Courthouse

•**STUART'S DRAFT** Spreads over rolling lands to the northwest of acres that Colonel James Patton, monarch of Southwest Virginia, bought from William Beverley in 1736 and 1740. Patton's house, Spring Hill, stood about two miles from the hamlet. Patton, a sea captain, transported colonists to Virginia and carried products from the New World to England. His sister Elizabeth, with her husband, John Preston, and several children, settled near Stuart's Draft in 1740.

•**SUFFOLK**, Independent City; Pop. 52,141; Zip Code 234+; 18 mi. WSW of Portsmouth; The city was named for Sulfolk County in England. Suffolk is the peanut capital of the world and the birthplace of 'Mr. Peanut.' The city was at the head of the Nansemond River in 1608, and Edward Waters settled here in 1868. The first group of Puritans to reach Virginia settled in this section but were driven out of the colony by orthodox Governor Berkeley just as the Puritan revolt triumphed in England; the 300 of them who migrated from Nansemond to tolerant Maryland and established Providence on the Severn River took their turn at carrying on religious persecution in that State.

Suffolk itself did not come into being until 1742 when the general assembly established a town at Constance's Warehouse, to care for the then dominant tobacco business. It was not until 1808 that the town was incorporated. The town early began to look out for its poor. It took seriously a law passed in 1755 by the general assembly that every person receiving aid must wear a badge with the name of his parish, under penalty of loss of allowance or lashers not to exceed five. A vestry book of this period reveals that 500 pounds of tobacco were paid to a doctor for 'salevating Mary Brinkley and keeping her salevated.'

The little town suffered during the Revolution and the War between the States. On May 13, 1779, General Matthews burned it, and on May 12, 1862, Federal troops took possession.

•**SURRY COUNTY**, SE Virginia; 280 sq. mi.; Pop. 6,145; Named after Surry County, England.

•**SURRY**, Town; Surry County Seat; Pop. 192; Zip Code 23883; 33 mi. NW of Newport News; Lat. 37-08-10 N long. 076-49-56 W; Founded in the later 1700's and first called the Cross Roads, McIntosh's

Cross Roads, Scuffletown, and Smithville before it settled down to its courthouse town designation. It was named after an area in England.

Herein the early days stagecoaches changed horses and travelers stopped for the night. In 1782 Robert McIntosh, tavern keeper, was hauled to court for failing to keep his liquor prices posted. Revolutionary officers and soldiers slept beneath this roof, and officers in the War of 1812 stopped here on their way to Norfolk.

HISTORICAL PLACES...(See Historical Places Section for details).
Chippokes Plantation State Park; Four-Mile Tree; Smith's Fort; Warren House

•SUSSEX COUNTY, SE Virginia; 496 sq. mi.; Pop. 10,248;

•TANGIER, Town; Accomack County; Pop. 659; Zip Code 23440; Lower Chesapeake Bary; Lat. 37-49-29 N long. 075-59-34 W; Settled in 1680 and named for small clay bowls, or tanga, which reminded the colonists of similar products of North Africa.

•TANGIER ISLAND In Chesapeake Bay about 12 miles from the mainland. When Captain John Smith explored the bay in 1608, he found Tangier inhabited by the Pocomokes. On his map of 1612 Tangier and Watt Islands bear the name 'Russels Isles,' honoring Dr. Walter Russell, the physician who accompanied Smith. In 1670 Tangier was granted to Ambrose White; and in 1686 John Crockett and his eight sons settled here. About a third of the present inhabitants bear the name of Crockett.

The hero of the island is the early minister, Joshua Thomas, whose prayers were those of a righteous man. As a fisher lad, he prayed for large catches and was heard. He prayed that the girl he loved would marry him; and then, praying for a home, he was led to Tangier. That was not so long after America became a republic. Then came the War of 1812, when the British used the island as a base for their operations in the Bay. Brother Joshua, sorely distressed, invited the enemy to come to his temple in the grove. There he prayed that their efforts would meet failure and, in a stirring sermon, declared their cause to be unrighteous and prophesied their defeat.

•TAPPAHANNOCK, Town; Essex County Seat; Pop. 1,550; Zip Code 22560; Elev. 22; 46 mi. NE of Richmond; Lat. 37-55-27 N long. 076-51-39 W; on the Rappahannock River. An Indian name meaning "on the running water."

Encyclopedia of Virginia

Tappahannock was constituted a town in 1680 when the general assembly, considering 'the greate necessity, usefullnesse, and advantage of cohabitation,' directed that 19 towns be established, one for each county. Everything went well until Charles II in 1681 vetoed the act 'for cohabitation and. . . trade and manufacture,' because planters objected violently to the provision that they should ship their tobacco only from the towns and only during stipulated periods. But in 1691, after William and Mary had ascended the throne, the towns were again made ports on entry-one 'for Rappahannock County at Hobs his hole warehouses are already built.' But in 1693 the general assembly, grown bolder, itself suspended the ports act. In 1705, after Anne had become Queen, ports were again constituted , this time only 16 but among them Hobbs' Hole, then renamed Tappahannock.

Tappahannock prospered. When created in 1680, it had been made the seat of Rappahannock County, and in 1692 after the old county was divided to from Essex and Richmond Counties it became the seat of Essex. Though the town was formally named, Washington, stopping here in 1752, referred to it as 'Hobs Hole'. A century and a half ago ships went hence to the remotest parts of the world and the town was something of a social center. But its importance declined after the construction of railroads. It was shelled in December 1814 by the British navy, under orders of Admiral Cockburn.

HISTORICAL PLACE...(See Historical Places Section for details).
Tappahannock Historic District

•**TAZEWELL COUNTY,** SW Virginia; 522 sq. mi.; Pop. 45,960; Named after Henry Tazewell (1753-1799) senator 1794-99.

•**TAZEWELL,** Town; Tazewell County Seat; Pop. 4,176; Zip Code ; Elev. 2519; 77 mi. NE of Bristol; The town is named for Henry Tazewell, a U. S. Senator from 1794-1799. After the formation of Tazewell County in 1799, two communities had champions in the contest for the seat of government. Those favoring Tazewell argued that here were the prime essentials of a frontier town-a grist mill and a blacksmith shop. A skull and fist fight settled the controversy. First called Tazewell Courthouse, then Jeffersonville, the town of Tazewell was incorporated in 1866.

•**THE PLAINS,** Town; Fauquier County; Pop. 219; Zip Code 22171; 40 mi. W of Washington D.C.; Lat. 38-51-52 N long. 077-46-22 W; Formerly White Plains, the name was shortened to avoid confusion with a similarly named city in New York.

•**TIMBERVILLE,** Town; Rockingham County; Pop. 1,596; Zip Code 22853; 47 mi. N of Staunton; Lat. 38-38-09 N long. 078- 46-24 W; Established in the late 1700's and named for the abundant timber nearby.

Dictionary of Places

•**TOMS BROOK,** Town; Shenandoah County; Pop. 227; Zip Code 22660; Lat. 38-56-50 N long. 078-26-28 W; An early settler's cabin named a local stream "Tom's Creek"; this was later changed to Tom's Brook and given to the town.

•**TROUTDALE,** Town; Grayson County; Pop. 196; Zip Code 24378; 58 mi. NE of Bristol; Lat. 36-42-05 N long. 081-26-23 W; Excellent trout fishing in nearby Fox Creek gave the town its name.

HISTORICAL PLACE...(See Historical Places Section for details).
Ripshin

•**TROUTVILLE,** Town; Botetourt County; Pop. 455; Zip Code 24175; Lat. 37-24-54 N long. 079-52-46 W; The town was named in honor of the Trout family.

•**URBANNA,** Town; Middlesex County; Pop. 529; Zip Code 23175; Lat. 37-38-28 N long. 076-34-22 W; Founded in 1705 and named in honor of Queen Anne, or Urb-Anna.

HISTORICAL PLACE...(See Historical Places Section for details).
Mills, James, Storehouse (Old Tobacco Warehouse)
Rosegill

•**VICTORIA,** Town; Lunenburg County; Pop. 1,830; Zip Code 23974; 51 mi. WSW of Petersburg; Lat. 36-59-28 N long. 078-13-34 W; The town's name honors Great Britain's Queen Victoria.

•**VIENNA,** Town; Fairfax County; Pop. 14,852; Zip Code 22027; 10 mi. NW of Alexandria; Lat. 38-53-26 N long. 077-13-39 W; The town was named after Vienna, New York.

•**VINTON,** Town; Roanoke County; Pop. 7,665; Zip Code 24179; 4 mi. NE of Roanoke; Lat. 37-22-35 N long. 079-48-36 W; Founded in 1794 as Gish's Mill, but later given a coined name combining pioneer names Vineyard and Preston, or Vinton.

•**VIRGILINA,** Town; Halifax County; Pop. 161; Zip Code 24598; Elev. 534; The town is situated on the Virginia-North Carolina boundary. The name is derived from a combination of the two state names.

•**VIRGINIA BEACH,** Independent City; Pop. 393,069; Zip Code 234+; SE Virginia on Atlantic Ocean; 18 mi. E of Norfolk; Lat. 36-50-51 N long. 076-05-52 W; Descriptively named for the state and its ocean location. Virginia Beach is a seaside playground where from May to October holiday throngs line the six miles of white beach and jostle each other on the concrete walk above it in front of cottages, hotels, and amusement halls.

Encyclopedia of Virginia

POINTS OF INTEREST:
- Maritime Historical Museum. 24th Street and Oceanfront.
- Princess Anne Court House (1824) 9 miles SW via VA 615, 149 in Princess Anne.
- Seashore State Park. 5 miles North on US 60 near Cape Henry.

HISTORICAL PLACES...(See Historical Places Section for details).

Cape Henry Memorial; Keeling House; Old Donation Church; Pembroke Manor; Pleasant Hall; Thoroughgood House; Weblin House; Wishart-Boush House

- **WACHAPREAGUE,** Town; Accomack County; Pop. 291; Zip Code 23480; 65 mi. NNE of Norfolk; Lat. 37-36-29 N long. 075-41-18 W; Incorporated in 1902 and given an Indian name meaning "little city by the sea."

- **WAKEFIELD,** Town; Sussex County; Pop. 1,070; Zip Code 23888; 27 mi. SE of Petersburg; Lat. 36-58-12 N long. 076-58-44 W; Incorporated in 1902 and given the name of a place in a Walter Scott novel.

- **WARREN COUNTY,** N Virginia; 219 sq. mi.; Pop. 26,142; Named after Joseph Warren.

- **WARRENTON,** Town; Fauquier County Seat; Pop. 4,830; Zip Code 22186; 35 mi. NNW of Fredericksburg; Lat. 38-44-02 N long. 077-44-18 W; The town was named in honor of Revolutionary War Bunker Hill hero, Dr. Joseph Warren. The town was incorporated in 1810. But Fauquier Courthouse already had a history coupled with that of the county. As early as 1712 there were settlers in this vicinity and Thomas Lee received a large grant of land here in 1718. By direction of his son, Richard Henry Lee, a survey was made in 1790 and 12 half-acre lots were staked.

HISTORICAL PLACE...(See Historical Places Section for details).

Little Fork Church

- **WARSAW,** Town; Richmond County Seat; Pop. 961; Zip Code 22572; 61 mi. NE of Richmond; Lat. 37-57-33 N long. 076-45-30 W; Originally Richmond Courthouse, renamed in 1845 because of its local sympathy for the Poles, who were fighting for independence.

HISTORICAL PLACES...(See Historical Places Section for details).

Richmond County Courthouse; Mount Airy

- **WASHINGTON COUNTY,** SW Virginia; 581 sq. mi.; Pop. 45,887; Named after George Washington.

Dictionary of Places

•**WASHINGTON**, Town; Rappahannock County Seat; Pop. 198; Zip Code 22747; 54 mi. SE of Washington D.C.; Lat. 38-42-47 N long. 078-09-35 W; Established by George Washington in 1749, and named for him by Lord Fairfax. A stone monument, setting forth the town's principal claim to fame, recites: 'The First Washington of All, surveyed and platted by George Washington, with the assistance of John Lonem and Edward Corder as chairman, August 4, 1749 . . . Town organized Dec. 14, 1796-Incorporated Feb. 12, 1894.'

•**WAVERLY**, Town; Sussex County; Pop. 2,223; Zip Code 23890; 27 mi. SE of Petersburg; Lat. 37-02-06 N long. 077-06-54 W; Incorporated in 1879 and given the name from a Walter Scott novel.

•**WAYNESBORO**, City; Pop. 18,549; Zip Code 22980; 12 mi. ESE of Staunton; Lat. 38-04-27 N long. 078-53-34 W; The city was named to honor the Great Revolutionary War General, Anthony Wayne.

On March 2, 1865, General Philip H. Sheridan, with a force of Union cavalry, drove General Jubal A. Early and 1,000 Confederates from their strategic position near by. Early's force was captured almost to a man, but the general and his staff escaped to the woods. This was one of the last contests of the war in western Virginia.

About 1895, citizens of Waynesboro were victims of an oil hoax. A group proclaiming it had found oil in the vicinity began to sell stock and made a show of drilling. As the work progressed with no signs of oil, the sale of stock began to lag. One night several barrels of oil were poured into the drilled hole. The next day this hopeful evidence stimulated sales, and several business men retired to enjoy their oil royalties. The only product of the well was good drinking water.

POINTS OF INTEREST:
•Sherando Lake Recreation Area. 16 miles SW on Blue Ridge Pkwy, in George Washington National Forest.
•Wintergreen Ski Resort. 34 miles East via US 250, 6 S, 151, 664.

HISTORICAL PLACE...(See Historical Places Section for details).
Swannanoa

•**WEBER CITY**, Town; Scott County; Pop. 1,377; 26 mi. W of Bristol; The town's name is copied from radio era show "Amos and Andy" who lived in mythical "Weber City."

•**WESTMORELAND COUNTY**, NE Virginia; 236 sq. mi.; Pop. 15,480; Named after the county in England.

•**WEST POINT**, Town; King William County; Pop. 2,938; Zip Code 230+; 38 mi. E of Richmond; Lat. 37-31-48 N long. 076-41-19 W; On the peninsula made where the Mattaponi and the Pamunkey unite to form the York, developed after the completion of the railroad between West Point and Richmond in 1861. Called "The Point" in the 18th century and later given the additional name west for the West brothers, Thomas, Francis, Nathaniel, and John-three of them governor of Virginia-but especially for John, who patented the land embracing the town's site. In 1607 West Point was called Pamunkee or Pamunkey and was the chief village of the Pamunkey of the Powhatan Confederacy. From Pamunkey, Powhatan's brother and successor, Opechancanough carried out the massacres of 1622 and 1644. In 1646 Governor Berkeley led a company of soldiers against the chief, captured him, and bore him wounded on a stretcher to Jamestown, where he was shot by a sentry appointed to guard him. Opechancanough was succeeded by Necotowance, son of Powhatan's eldest sister, then by the Queen of Pamunkey, who was reigning in 1676. In that year, she went to Jamestown to confer with the governor and council. The chairman asked her how many men she could furnish the colony in the war that seemed impending. At first she declined to speak, but finally uttered vehement reproaches against the English for their injustice and ingratitude. Her husband, Totopotomoi, had been slain with many of his men while assisting the settlers against the Ricahecreans, and she had never had 'any compensation for her loss.' After further parley, she 'abruptly quitted the room.'

In 1691, the general assembly directed that West Point be created a port of entry and in 1705 the burgesses authorized the town to qualify as a 'free borough' and named it Delaware, for Governor Thomas West, third Lord Delaware. The old name resumed when the railroad was constructed.

HISTORICAL PLACE...(See Historical Places Section for details).
Chelsea

•WHITE STONE, Lancaster County; Pop. 372; Zip Code 22578; Elev. 51; 68 mi. NE of Richmond; Lat. 37-38-42 N long. 076- 23-20 W; The town is descriptively named for White Stone Beach.

•WILLIAMSBURG, Independent City; Pop. 11,530; Zip Code 23081; Elev. 86; 27 mi. NNW of Newport News; Lat. 37-12-28 N long. 076-46-29 W; Settled in 1632 and named in honor of William III of England.

This city which was the capital of Virginia from 1699 to 1780, is spread upon a ridge in the peninsula between the James and York Rivers. Queen's Creek and College Creek (called in early days Archer's Hope) partly encircle the city.

The 'Act for the Seatinge of the Middle Plantation,' passed in 1633, and encouraged settlement in the area where Dr. John Pott was living. Middle Plantation stood just within the six-mile palisade built across the peninsula to protect settlers from a repetition of the Massacre of 1622. The 'pallisades . . . bounded in by two large

Dictionary of Places

Creekes' gave 'all the lower part of Virginia . . . a range for their cattle, near fortie miles in length and in most places twelve miles broade.' Middle Plantation suffered in the Massacre of 1644, and two years later a new palisade was ordered to replace the neglected original. On August 3, 1676, at the house of Otho Thorpe occurred the taking of the 'Oath of Middle Plantation,' an important event in Bacon's Rebellion. Here William Drummond and other principals in that abortive assertion of independence were hanged by Governor Berkeley. Jamestown having been destroyed by Bacon, Middle Plantation became for a short time the seat of restored royal Government. Though citizens of York signed a petition urging the temporary capital as most fit to become permanent, Jamestown was rebuilt.

The choice of Middle Plantation by the assembly in 1693 as the site of 'a free school and college to be known as William and Mary' and the burning of the State House in Jamestown caused Middle Plantation, still only a loose concentration of plantation dwellings, to be designated in 1699 as the new capital, renamed Williamsburg in honor of William III. Immediate provision was made for construction of a capitol and for platting the new city according to the survey of Theodoric Bland.

The new capital rapidly attained the size and appearance it presents today. Alexander Spotswood, who arrived in Virginia as lieutenant governor in 1710, had several ravines filled and the streets leveled, and assisted in erecting college buildings, a church, and a magazine for the storage of arms. He was patron of one of the earliest theaters in America, built in 1716 by William Levingston, who brought musicians and actors from England to perform 'comedies, drolls, and other kinds of stage plays.' The theater was conducted by Charles Stagg and his wife Mary, America's first 'leading lady.' The first successful printing press in Virginia was set up at Williamsburg in 1728 by William Parks, who founded the colony's first newspaper eight years later and Virginia's first paper mill in 1744.

Incorporated in 1722, Williamsburg became the political and educational center of Virginia and the scene of the most 'fashionable' social life in Colonial America. During legislative sessions substantial planters emerged from rural isolation to occupy 'town houses,' comfortable rooms at inns or taverns or to lodge with friends. Sycophants and adventurers swelled the throng. English visitors testified that balls, races, fairs, and other entertainment composed a 'season' not greatly inferior to London's in amusement and elegance.

The tranquillity of this scene was broken in 1765 when Patrick Henry, undeterred by cries of 'Treason!' incited the burgesses to pass resolutions against the Stamp Act. Here in 1773 were developed the intercolonial activities of a committee of correspondence that grew out of the standing committee originated in

1759 to communicate with the colony's London agents. The House of Burgesses, meeting in Williamsburg in 1774, called the First Continental Congress. The First Virginia Convention, indirectly resulting from closure of the port of Boston, met at Williamsburg in the summer of 1774 to elect delegates to a general Colonial congress. Fear of Lord Dunmore and of a British man-of-war nearby in the York River caused the next three conventions to meet in Richmond. The fifth and most noted Virginia Convention met in Williamsburg on May 6, 1776, and began the open move toward American freedom by declaring Virginia an independent commonwealth and by instructing the Virginia delegates to the Second Continental Congress to propose American independence.

Williamsburg began to decline when the capital was moved to Richmond in 1780 to escape the invading British. In 1781, before and during the Siege of Yorktown, Williamsburg was headquarters first of the British and then of the Continental and French forces. From the capitulation of Cornwallis in October until the following summer, the French army was quartered near by. Though these closing events of the war temporarily animated Williamsburg, the population dwindled from more than 2,000 in 1779 to about 1,200 in 1795, and in 1804 the former capital was described as very 'decayed'. Between 1770 and 1790 the Reverend Mr. Moses, who seems to have been the first black preacher in Virginia, had organized the Williamsburg Baptist Church, undaunted by opposition that was at times physical.

Except for brief revivals brought about by two wars, Williamsburg dozed for a century and a half as shopping center for the surrounding country. Many residents owned small farms near by and managed to live with a minimum of enterprise. The Battle of Williamsburg took place on May 5, 1862, when a Union corps engaged Confederates retreating from Yorktown toward Richmond. The city suffered at the hands of the Union troops, and reached the nadir of its fortunes when the College of William and Mary was closed in 1881. After 1889, when the college reopened, a slow recovery began and continued until the little community was aroused suddenly in 1917 by the location on its outskirts of a munitions factory with nearly 15,000 workers. Hastily constructed cheap building disfigured the Colonial city.

In its newborn ugliness Williamsburg dozed again. In 1926 John D. Rockefeller, Jr., came to Williamsburg at the invitation of Dr. W.A.R. Goodwin, who had been responsible for the restoration of Bruton Paris Church, of which he was rector, and of the Wythe House. Mr. Rockefeller was enthusiastic over Dr. Goodwin's plan for restoring the city to its eighteenth-century appearance. On Mr. Rockefeller's authorization most of the property in the Colonial area was acquired by Colonial Williamsburg, Inc., and within a decade most of the research and restoration was completed. Research covered Colonial documents and records in libraries, museums, and family archives in America, England, and France.

Dictionary of Places

Buildings totaling 459 were torn down, 91 of the Colonial period rebuilt, 67 restored, and a new shopping center in Colonial style was provided.

POINTS OF INTEREST:
- Abby Aldrich Rockefeller Folk Art Center. 307 South England Street, 1 block South of Francis Street.
- Craft House.
- Busch Gardens "The Old Country." 3 miles East on US 60.
- York River State Park. 8 miles NW via I-64, Croaker exit, then 1 mile North on VA 607 to VA 606E.

HISTORICAL PLACES...(See Historical Places Section for details).
Wren Building, College of William and Mary; Carter's Grove Plantation; Williamsburg Historic District; Governor's Land Archeological District; Kingsmill Plantation; Porto Bello; Bruton Parish Church; Randolph, Peyton, House; Semple, James, House; Wythe House

- **WINCHESTER**, Independent City; Pop. 21,947; Zip Code 22601; Elev. 720; 70 mi. WNW of Alexandria; Lat. 39-11-02 N long. 078-09-32 W; The city which was settled in 1738 and named for Winchester, England is the seat of Frederick County and the oldest Virginia city west of the Blue Ridge.

In 1732 Joist Hite crossed the Potomac at Pack Horse Ford, near present Shepherdstown, West Virginia, bringing 16 families from Pennsylvania to settle at Opequon, five miles south of Winchester. From Isaac and John Van Meter, Hite purchased lands that were a part of the Northern Neck proprietary of Thomas, Lord Fairfax.

Though Frederick County was sliced in 1738 from Orange County, the story of Winchester, first Fredericktown, did not begin until 1744, when James Wood laid out a courthouse square and 26 lots. Frederick County held its first court in a log house Wood built at the present Glen Burnie. If Lord Fairfax had his way, Stephens City would have been made the county seat. James Wood, however, outwitted him by serving one of the justices enough toddy, and the deciding vote was cast for Frederick. In 1752 the town was laid out and named for Winchester, England.

Already settlers knew the lad, George Washington, who had been surveying Lord Fairfax's vast holdings since 1748. Washington was 16 years old-redheaded, freckle-faced, and very eager-when he set out in March 1748 for Winchester and his first job, and his eyes were busy as he 'went through most beautiful groves of Sugar Trees and spent ye best part of ye Day in admiring ye Trees and richness of ye Land.'

After General Braddock's defeat in 1755, Lieutenant Colonel Washington, placed in command of frontier forces, 'rid post to this place . . . and found everything in the greatest hurry and Confusion, by the back Inhabitants flocking in, and those of the town removing out... No Orders are obey'd, but what a Party of Soldiers, or my own drawn Sword, Enforces.' He set about to quiet a frightened people and to build Fort Loundoun for their protection.

Men of Winchester played a conspicuous part in the Revolutionary War. Their leader was Daniel Morgan, who moved there from New Jersey in 1753. After the Battle of Bunker Hill he organized a company of northern Virginia riflemen. Commissioned captain of militia under General Benedict Arnold, he pressed with his company into Canada, was held prisoner in Quebec, fought in both battles of Saratoga, and as hero of the Battle of Cowpens is given credit for the defeat of General Tarleton. Morgan spent the last ten years of his life in Winchester.

Between the Revolution and the 1860's Winchester grew and prospered. In 1779 the general assembly authorized its incorporation as a town. Early in the nineteenth century stage lines operated between Winchester and Harpers Ferry, continuing even after the Winchester and Potomac Railroad was completed in 1836.

From the beginning till the end of the Civil War Winchester was a center of military activities. Crops and cattle, mills and factories made the valley an important requisitioning area for the Confederacy, and Winchester was a vantage point coveted by both armies. When General Thomas J. Jackson was given command of the Department of the Shenandoah in October 1861, he cleared Winchester of invading Federal troops; in March 1862 Union forces under General Banks forced him to evacuate the town; but on May 25 he moved again. Until the summer of 1864 Winchester changed hands many times, and more than 100 military engagements took place in the surrounding area.

Fighting at an end, Frederick County looked again to fields and orchards, and its principal town to marketing. Winchester was chartered as a city in 1874 and adopted the city manager form of government in 1918.

POINTS OF INTEREST:
- Washington's Office-Museum. Corner Cork and Braddock Streets.
- Stonewall Jackson's Headquarters. 415 North Braddock Street.
- Lloyd Logan Home. Braddock and Piccadilly Streets.
- Old Stone Presbyterian Church (1788). 306 Piccadilly Street.
- Abram's Delight and Log Cabin (1754). 1340 South Pleasant Valley Road.
- Old Frederick County Courthouse. Loudoun Street Mall.
- Springdale. 5 miles South on US 11.

HISTORICAL PLACES...(See Historical Places Section for details).
Abram's Delight; Handley Library; Jackson, Thomas J., Headquarters

•**WINDSOR,** Town; Isle of Wight County; Pop. 1,025; Zip Code 23487; 20 mi. NW of Suffolk; Lat. 36-48-37 N long. 076-44-46 W; The town is named after the location in one of Walter Scott's novels.

Dictionary of Places

•**WISE COUNTY**, SW Virginia; 414 sq. mi.; Pop. 39,573; Named after Henry Alexander Wise.

•**WISE**, Town; Wise County Seat; Pop. 3,193; Zip Code 24923; Elev. 2,454; 58 mi. NW of Bristol; Lat. 37-01-14 N, long. 082-34-42 W. The town was named for former governor of Virginia, Henry A. Wise.

•**WOODSTOCK**, Town; Shenandoah County Seat; Pop. 3,182; Zip Code 22664; 30 mi. SW of Winchester; Lat. 38-52-49 N, long. 078-30-39 W. Named by founder Jacob Miller in 1761. First called Mullerstadt for Jacob Miller, it was legally established in 1761. Miller, with his wife and six children, came from Pennsylvania in 1752. In 1761 he set aside 1,200 of his acres for a town. In 1766 John Peter Gabriel Muhlenburg (1746-1807), a Lutheran minister, arrived to take charge of the church here. Son of the Reverend Henry Melchior Muhlenburg, organizer of the first Lutheran synod in America, John Muhlenburg was educated at the universities of Pennsylvania and Halle. Muhlenburg went to London in 1772, and was ordained a priest in the Established Church, but he and his parishioners met June 16,1774, and drafted a resolution declaring they would 'pay due submission to such acts of government as His Majesty has a right to exercise over his subjects and to such only.' The smoldering rebellion reached its climax on a Sunday in January 1776. Muhlenburg mounted the pulpit of the log church and announced as his text Eccl. 3.1-8: 'There is a time to every purpose . . . a time to war, and a time to peace.' The sermon rose to a dramatic finale: 'The time to fight has come!' he cried and, flinging aside the black folds of his cassock, he stood forth in the blue and buff of a Continental colonel and began to enroll his parishioners in the Eighth Virginia Regiment.

A weekly newspaper, the *Shenandoah Herald,* established in 1817 by Major Benjamin Hogan, a cousin of Washington's, was published here.

In 1859 the artist Benjamin West Clinedinst was born in Woodstock. Educated at the Virginia Military Institute and the Ecole des Beaux-Arts, this *genre* painter is best known in Virginia for his panorama of the Battle of New Market.

POINT OF INTEREST:
•Shenandoah Vineyards. South via US 11, right on VA 605 to first left onto VA 686 near Edinburg.

HISTORICAL PLACE...(See Historical Places Section for details).
Shenandoah County Court House (1792)

•**WYTHE COUNTY**, SW Virginia; 460 sq. mi.; Pop. 25,466; Named after George Wythe (1726-1806) Virginia house of burgesses 1758-68; professor of law of William and Mary College 1779-91.

•**WYTHEVILLE,** Town; Wythe County Seat; Pop. 8,038; Zip Code 24382; Elev. 2,284; 19 mi. WSW of Pulaski; Lat. 36-56-47 N, long. 081-05-04 W. Named for George Wythe, the first professor of law in America, teacher of Thomas Jefferson, John Marshall and James Monroe; and first Virginia signer of Declaration of Independence.

First called Abbeville, honoring the South Carolina birthplace of Jesse Evans, the settlement was legally established in 1792 as Evansham, a name that clung until its incorporation in 1839.

Being near the lead mines and the only salt works in the South, Wytheville was in a constant state of turmoil as the contending forces intermittently poured through. In July 1863 a Union cavalry detachment descended on the town intending to tear up the railroad, but was routed by the home guards forewarned by Mary Tynes.

Two Virginia governors were born here: Henry Carter Stuart (1855-1933), governor from 1914 to 1918, and Elbert Lee Trinkle (1876-1939), governor from 1922 to 1926. Henry Carter Stuart's administration was characterized by efforts to promote agriculture and to raise the living standards in rural Virginia. Deeply interested in education and social problems, E. Lee Trinkle emphasized human welfare and did much to eradicate for a time sectionalism in Virginia.

POINTS OF INTEREST:
•Big Walker Lookout. 12 miles North on US 52.
•Rock House Museum. Monroe and Tazewell Streets.

HISTORICAL PLACE...(See Historical Places Section for details).
Shot Tower Historical Park

•**YORK COUNTY,** SE Virginia; 123 sq. mi.; Pop. 42,422; Named after the Duke of York.

PICTORIAL SCENES IN VIRGINIA

Colonnade on the front campus of Washington & Lee University, Lexington.

Pictorial Scenes

Stature of Stonewall Jackson on the VMI post, Lexington.

Lee's office as he left it at Washington & Lee University.

Little Sorrel, Stonewall Jackson's war horse in the VMI Museum.

Pictorial Scenes

Red Hill, Patrick Henry's last home and burial place.

Virginia Military Institute cadets on parade.

Mount Vernon, the beautiful plantation of George and Martha Washington.

Pictorial Scenes

"The Old Country" in Busch Gardens is a marvelously re-created Europe of yesterday.

Goshen pass, one of Rockbride County's most scenic attractions.

Pictorial Scenes

Modern-day couples still marry in famous old Bruton Parish Church, Williamsburg.

Robotic Triceratops at the Virginia Museum of Natural History.

Pictorial Scenes

Monticello, home of Thomas Jefferson is a architectural masterpiece.

Encyclopedia of Virginia

With the exuberance of today and the grace of yesterday, Richmond is an exiting study in contrasts.

Virginia Beach is famous for marvelous surf and warm summers.

Pictorial Scenes

Clifton Forge from Cemetery Hill.

International Street, a glittering plaza of inviting shops, European restaurants and dancing fountains.

Crabbing and fishing are popular family pastimes.

Pictorial Scenes

Natural Bridge, a towering limestone structure, carved over eons by tiny Cedar Creek.

Virginia's eastern shore.

Pictorial Scenes

Martinsville Speeday annually attracts some 150,000 people to the Martinsville-Henry County area.

Encyclopedia of Virginia

Humpback Bridge; Virginia's oldest standing covered bridge.

Pittsyvania County

Pictorial Scenes

Yorktown Victory Monument.

World Famous Coloniel Williamsburg

GUIDE TO HISTORICAL PLACES IN VIRGINIA

Designations of Historical Places

Frequently the designations NHL, HABS, HAER, and/or G follow the ownership and accessibility. These are explained as follows:

NHL — A National Historic Landmark is a building, structure, site, district, or object declared eligible for recognition as a property of national significance by the Secretary of the Interior under the provisions of the Historic Sites Act of 1935. These properties are not administered by the National Park Service.

HABS — A Historic American Buildings Survey designation indicates that documentation by photographs, measured drawings, and/or data sheets has been made as evidence of a building's architectural or historical significance. The Historic American Buildings Survey is conducted by the National Park Service in cooperation with the American Institute of Architects and the Library of Congress where the records are deposited. A HABS designation is included in the description of historic districts when at least one property has been documented by the Historic American Buildings Survey.

HAER — A Historic American Engineering Record designation means that the property has been recognized and recorded as an important example of American engineering. The Historic American Engineering Record is conducted by the National Park Service in cooperation with the American Society of Civil Engineers. Records are kept at the Library of Congress.

G — A grant designation means that the property has received a National Park Service grant-in-aid under the National Historic Preservation Act of 1966.

HISTORICAL PLACES

ACCOMACK COUNTY

Accomac. **BANK BUILDING,** No. 1 Court House Ave., c. 1820. Brick, 2 stories, rectangular, gabled roof with fanlight in front gable, rear interior end chimney, denticulated cornice, 1st- and 2nd-story center entrances; modern alterations include remodeling of the 1st-story entrance and the interior and the removal of the cat's head and hoist above the 2nd-story window. Federal style commercial structure. Built by Michael Higgins and Alexander McCollum, 2 local businessmen. *Public.*

Accomac. **ST. JAMES CHURCH,** Daugherty Rd. between Back St. and Ocean Hwy., 1838. Brick, stuccoed front facade; 1 story, rectangular, gabled roof, full-width tetrastyle Doric entrance portico with 2 doors, square Gothic Revival bell tower, rubbed-brick jack arched windows, interior contains finely executed illusionistic apsidal painting and original box pews. Greek Revival. *Private:* G.

Chincoteague vicinity. **ASSATEAGUE LIGHTHOUSE,** S of Chincoteague at S end of Assateague Island, 1867. 129'-high circular tower of brick, with painted red and white bands, metal and glass cupola, and projecting gabled brick entrance building; interior cast iron circular staircase; adjacent oil house. Ironwork imported from Paris firm of Barbier and Fenestre. State's sole surviving lighthouse of period; on site of first light, 1832. *Federal/USCG; not accessible to the public.*

Guilford vicinity. **MASON HOUSE,** N of Guilford off VA 658, 18th C.. Brick (English and Flemish bonds), 1 1/2 stories, rectangular, slightly bell-cast gabled roof, interior end chimneys, front gabled dormers; center entrance, windows, and corners marked by raised brickwork; area between raised sections features brickwork set in a diaper pattern with glazed headers forming a double lozenge design, unique in VA. Excellent example of dwelling featuring early building techniques and early Georgian elements. *Private; not accessible to the public:* HABS.

Hallwood vicinity. **WESSELLS ROOT CELLAR,** NE of jct. of Rtes. 701 and 692, 18th C.. Brick, 1 story, rectangular, steeply gabled roof, central chimney, gable end entrance partially below ground level, wooden batten door with large iron hinges may be original, interesting glazed header pattern in front gable. Unusual because most root cellars were contained in foundations of other buildings. *Private; not accessible to the public.*

Horntown vicinity. **CORBIN HALL,** E of Horntown on VA 679, c. 1787. Brick (Flemish bond), 2 1/2 stories, rectangular, gabled roof, interior end chimneys, modillion cornice, rubbed brick belt course, center door, gauged brick arches above center Palladian windows on front and rear facades; notable original interior paneling and woodwork; gabled entrance porch, early-20th C.; 1-story frame service wing, rebuilt 1951. Fine example of Georgian house with superb interior work. *Private; not accessible to the public:* HABS.

Mappsville vicinity. **WHARTON PLACE,** 0.7 mi. NE of jct. of VA 762 and 679, c. 1800. Brick (Flemish bond), 2 stories, rectangular, hipped roof with deck, 2 interior chimneys, bracketed cornice, center entrance with fanlight and open pediment, splayed marble lintels, wooden panels between 1st and 2nd floors, 1-story side wing; fine interiors with composition ornamentation by Robert Wellford of Philadelphia; frame outbuildings; restored. Federal. Among best-preserved houses of type in state; built for prosperous merchant, John Wharton. *Private; not accessible to the public:* HABS.

Metomkin Island vicinity. **BOWMAN'S FOLLY,** SE of jct. of Rtes. 652 and 13, c. 1815. Frame, clapboarding, brick (Flemish bond in gable ends); 2 1/2 stories, L-shaped, gabled roof, dormers with fanlights in pediments, 1 1/2-story E wing, interior end chimneys, center pedimented entrance portico with Palladian window above, central hall plan, several outbuildings. Georgian Colonial. Built by John Cropper, Jr., member of the VA senate and House of Delegates. *Private; not accessible to the public.*

Onancock. **HOPKINS AND BROTHER STORE,** Market St., 19th C.. Frame, clapboarding; 2 1/2 stories, L-shaped, gabled roof, interior chimney, bracketed cornice with gable end returns, pointed arched window in pediment above entrance, corner pilasters, 2-story ell and lean-to section. Moved from original site. Founded as Eastern Shore commercial and maritime trading center, 1842, by Capt. Stephen Hopkins. *Private.*

Onancock. **KERR PLACE,** NE corner of Crockett Ave. and Market St., 18th–19th C.. Brick (Flemish bond), 2 stories, Greek cross shape, gabled roof with intersecting gable, interior and interior end chimneys, center projecting front and rear section with roundels in pediments, 2-story side wing, fine Adamesque mantels and woodwork. One of the most elaborate Federal mansions on state's Eastern Shore. *Private·* HABS; G.

Pungoteague. **ST. GEORGE'S CHURCH**, VA 178, NE of jct. with VA 180, c. 1738. Brick (Flemish bond in contrasting blue and red stretchers and headers), square front belfry, central entrance in gable end with diamond-shaped window above. Georgian. Built early-18th C., ruinous after Civil War; rebuilt without transepts, 1885. One of only 2 colonial churches on state's Eastern Shore. *Private:* HABS.

ALBEMARLE COUNTY

Charlottesville vicinity. **ASH LAWN**, SE of Charlottesville off VA 53, 1799. Frame, clapboarding; 1 story, L-shaped, gabled roof, central and interior end chimneys, 1-bay entrance porch, large addition (c. 1860), 3 outbuildings. Early colonial elements. Home of President James Monroe until 1830. *Private:* HABS.

Charlottesville vicinity. **FARMINGTON**, W of jct. of U.S. 250 and U.S. 29/250 bypass, 18th-19th C.. Brick, 2 stories, rectangular, gabled roof, 2 interior end chimneys; octagonal front section with large tetrastyle pedimented Tuscan portico with fanlight in the pediment, center doorway flanked by triple-hung windows on either side with roundels above. Jeffersonian Classicism. Octagonal addition designed by Thomas Jefferson. *Private:* HABS.

Charlottesville vicinity. **MONTICELLO**, 2 mi. S of Charlottesville on VA 53, 1770-1789, Thomas Jefferson, architect. Brick (Flemish bond), 2 stories, modified rectangle, balustraded hipped roof with central balustraded deck, slightly projecting E and W Tuscan porticos with a fanlight in each pediment, front section partially supporting octagonal dome with roundels and fanlights. Interior contains many of Jefferson's ingenious devices and some

Historical Places

original furnishings. Numerous outbuildings including earliest completed guest cottage (1769–1770). Structural renovations. Jeffersonian Classicism. Home of Thomas Jefferson, 3rd U.S. President, author of Declaration so Independence, and founder and architect of the University of Virginia (see also University of Virginia Historic District, VA). *Private:* NHL; HABS.

Cismont vicinity. **CASTLE HILL,** NE of Cismont near jct. of VA 231 and 640, 1764, 1825. Two connected houses: 1764 frame 1 1/2-story rectangular Georgian dwelling with steeply gabled roof, interior and interior end chimneys, gabled dormers, center entrance porch with slender Doric columns, and fine interior woodwork; and 1825 2-story rectangular Jeffersonian Classical dwelling with low gabled roof, interior end chimneys, center entrance with fanlight and side lights, tetrastyle Tuscan portico with Chinese Chippendale railing, elliptical interior stair, c. 1845 wings with Tuscan colonnades, numerous outbuildings, and finely landscaped grounds. Early dwelling built for Dr. Thomas Walker, prominent physician, politician, and pioneer; site where Walker detained British troops under Tarletan long enough for Jefferson and VA legislators to flee Charlottesville, 1781; 19th C. house built for William Cabel Rives, lawyer and politician. *Private; not accessible to the public:* HABS.

Cobham vicinity. **COBHAM PARK,** S of VA 22, c. 1856. Brick, 2 1/2 stories, rectangular, hipped roof, dormers, large paneled interior chimneys, modillion cornice, front and rear verandas with Doric columns, Chinese lattice railing, cornices over 1st-floor windows. Unusual mid-19th C. example of Georgian Revival. Grounds treated as landscaped park in 18th C. English manner with vistas, sloping lawns and planting. *Private; not accessible to the public.*

Covesville vicinity. **REDLANDS**, Jct. of Rtes. 708 and 627, 1798–1808. Brick (Flemish bond), 2 1/2 stories, rectangular, hipped roof with gabled dormer additions, 2 interior chimneys, modillion cornice, 3-bay entrance portico with flat roof and balustrade, shuttered windows, rear center 2-story bow projection, notable Adamesque woodwork. One of Piedmont area's notable Federal mansions. Built by John Carter and remains in the same family. *Private.*

Keene vicinity. **CHRIST CHURCH GLENDOWER**, On VA 713, 0.4 mi. SW of jct. with VA 712, 1831–1832. Brick (Flemish bond), 1 story, rectangular, gabled roof, interior chimney, full Doric entablature around building; temple-form front contains 2 double-door entrances with louvered fans, lunettes above and in pediment; windows and doors set in recessed panels; small frame rear vestry added later; interior altered, 1958. Jeffersonian Classicism. Nice little church probably built by William Phillips, brickmason who had worked for Thomas Jefferson at the University of Virginia. Illustrates the dissemination of the style into the surrounding area. *Private.*

Simeon vicinity. **MORVEN**, W of Simeon off VA 20, 1821, Martin Thacker, builder. Brick, 2 1/2 stories, rectangular, gabled roof sections, paired interior end chimneys, hipped dormers, modillion cornice, center entrance with fanlight and pedimented Tuscan tetrastyle portico, center entrance on wing with distyle pedimented porch, brick flat arches over 1st-story front windows; Carrara marble fireplaces; outbuildings include late-18th C. frame office, brick kitchen, frame smokehouse and cottages. Excellent example of Jeffersonian Classical country house and farm complex. *Private; not accessible to the public.*

Historical Places

Yancey Mills vicinity. **MILLER SCHOOL OF ALBEMARLE,** SE of Yancey Mills off VA 635, 1874–1882, Albert M. Lybrock and D. Wiley Anderson, architects. Complex of 3 brick buildings each with a mansard roof, pointed arched entrances and windows, towers and turrets, decorative belt courses, and extensive use of brick and stone trim. Excellent example of High Victorian Gothic. Established as charitable school from bequest of Samuel Miller, philanthropist; pioneer in industrial education under direction of first school superintendent, C. E. Vawter. *Private.*

ALEXANDRIA (independent city)

ALEXANDRIA HISTORIC DISTRICT, 18th–19th C.. Probably the state's largest concentration of late-18th and early-19th C. urban architecture; mostly brick or frame buildings in the Federal style, with some Colonial and Victorian period structures. Formally authorized as a town in 1748; George Washington was one of the original surveyors. Served as principal upstate seaport and commercial center until the Civil War. Retains picturesque quality. *Multiple public/private:* NHL; HABS.

BANK OF ALEXANDRIA, 133 N. Fairfax St., 1807. Brick, painted and stuccoed; 3 1/2 stories, L-shaped, center entrance with fanlight and engaged columns, stone lintels with raised keystones over 1st-story front windows, side entrance; altered mid-19th C. with stucco, large side addition, balcony, and probably attic. Federal elements. Built to serve state's first chartered bank. *Municipal:* HABS.

CARLYLE HOUSE, 123 N. Fairfax St., 1752. Brick, stuccoed; 2 1/2 stories, rectangular, hipped roof, gabled dormers, 2 interior chimneys, stone quoins, original front stone cornice, dated keystone above entrance, arcaded ground-floor facade with balustrade above, some original interior trim. Georgian. Built for John Carlyle, an original incorporator of Alexandria. *Public:* HABS.

CHRIST CHURCH, SE corner of Cameron and Columbus Sts., 1767-1773, James Wren, architect. Brick (Flemish bond), 2 stories, rectangular, hipped roof, modillion cornice, stone quoins and keystones painted white, E Palladian window. Exterior is original and unaltered except for the square brick front tower with octagonal belfry and cupola which is an 1818 addition. Georgian. *Private:* NHL; HABS.

GADSBY'S TAVERN, 128 N. Royal St., 18th C.. Combines 2 buildings: 1752 Coffee House, brick, 2 stories, rectangular, gabled roof with 3 pedimented dormers, interior end chimneys, front center recessed entrance with fanlight framed by pediment and pilasters; 1792 City Hotel, brick, 3 1/2 stories, rectangular, gabled roof with 3 pedimented dormers, interior end chimneys; restored. Georgian. Original 2-story tavern enlarged by John Wise in 1792; named Gadsby's Tavern when John Gadsby leased both buildings and established a single management in 1794. Meetingplace for patriot groups during colonial and early national periods; headquarters for George Washington during French and Indian War; meetingplace of 1785 conference which resulted in Virginia's invitation to the colonies to attend a commercial convention in Annapolis in 1786 (see also Maryland Statehouse, MD). *Private:* NHL.

LYCEUM, THE, 201 S. Washingon St., c. 1837. Brick, stuccoed; 2 1/2 stories, rectangular, gabled roof, 4 interior chimneys, center entrance bay articulated by pilasters; full-height, pedimented, tetrastyle Doric entrance portico with fluted columns; late-19th C. rear addition;

restored. Greek Revival. Built to provide meeting space for the Lyceum, a society for scholarly activities, founded by Benjamin Hallowell. *Municipal; not accessible to the public:* HABS; G.

ALLEGHANY COUNTY

Covington vicinity. **HUMPBACK BRIDGE,** Over Dunlop Creek, SW of jct. of U.S. 60 and CR 651, 1835. Oak timber construction with locust joining pins, stone foundations with no center support; center 8' higher than the ends, producing low arch shape. State's oldest covered bridge and the only one of its type in the country. *State.*

Earlhurst vicinity. **SWEET CHALYBEATE SPRINGS,** S of Earlhurst on VA 311, 1850's. Hotel complex: frame main building with weatherboarding, 2 1/2 stories, rectangular, gabled roof, 2-story balustraded gallery with Doric columns. Other buildings include frame guest ranges, 2 stories with Doric galleries; 2 1-story frame cottages with hipped roofs and galleries; servants' quarters; original bandstand; and foundations of original bathhouses. Commercialized by Philip Rogers and other members of Red Spring Co. Typical of fashionable resorts developed during 2nd-half of 19th C. Closed, 1918. *Private.*

AMELIA COUNTY

Amelia vicinity. **HAW BRANCH,** N of Amelia off VA 667, Late-18th C.. Frame, clapboarding; 2 1/2-story main block with 1-story symmetrical wings over full basement, modified rectangle, hipped roof sections, exterior end chimneys, gabled dormers, modillion cornice; center entrance with fanlight, side lights, and 1-

story hipped porch with balustrade and Chinese Chippendale railing surrounding roof; finely detailed interior woodwork c. 1815; outbuildings include schoolhouse, kitchen, and smokehouse. Excellent area example of Federal dwelling. *Private.*

Chula vicinity. **WIGWAM,** 8 mi. NW of Chula, 18th–19th C.. Frame, clapboarding; 1 1/2 stories, L-shaped, gabled roof, dormers, 2 interior end chimneys, center double-door entrance with side lights and transom, simple gabled porch; rear 18th C. ell altered; 19th C. front block retains much original woodwork. Home of William Branch Giles, U.S. congressman, senator, and VA governor. *Private; not accessible to the public.*

AMHERST COUNTY

Clifford. **WINTON,** W of VA 151, Early-1770's. Frame, clapboarding; 2 stories, rectangular, hipped roof; 2-story entrance portico, entrance features and rear wings added later. Smokehouse and family burial plot. Georgian elements. Built by Col. Joseph Cabell, prominent colonial and state official. Home of Col. Samuel Meredith, Jr., VA militiaman, politician, and Patrick Henry's brother-in-law. *County.*

Sweet Briar. **SWEET BRIAR HOUSE,** SW of jct. of U.S. 29 and VA 624, Early-19th C.. Brick, 2-story central block with 3-story end pavilions, modified H shape, low hipped roof, 2-story projecting arcaded center portico opening onto 1st- and 2nd-story verandas, round and flat arched windows, ornamental iron balconies, much original interior trim in older center section; tower, wings, and arcaded portico added c. 1851. Federal and Italian Villa elements. Owned by newspaper publisher,

Historical Places

Elijah Fletcher in mid-19th C.; now serves as president's house of Sweet Briar College (est. 1901). *Private.*

APPOMATTOX COUNTY

Appomattox vicinity. **APPOMATTOX COURT HOUSE NATIONAL HISTORICAL PARK,** 3 mi. NE of Appomattox on VA 24, 19th C.. Park includes the courthouse, houses, tavern, jail, and store; frame and brick construction, 1-3 stories. Robert E. Lee surrendered Confederate troops to Union commander Ulysses S. Grant in the McLean House, Apr. 9, 1865. *Private/federal/NPS:* HABS.

ARLINGTON COUNTY

Arlington. **ARLINGTON HOUSE, THE ROBERT E. LEE MEMORIAL,** Arlington National Cemetery, 1802-1817, George Hadfield, architect. Brick, stuccoed; 2 stories, rectangular, gabled roof, 4 interior end chimneys, Doric entrance portico, 1-story hipped flanking wings; restored. Greek Revival. Built by George Washington Parke Custis; home of Robert E. Lee from 1831 until 1861. *Federal/NPS:* HABS.

Arlington. **FORT MYER HISTORIC DISTRICT,** Arlington Blvd. (U.S. 50), 1863-20th C.. Military post including numerous brick and frame structures; features the 6-building post headquarters, stables, Post Exchange, and General's Row, a series of large officers' residences. Constructed as Fort Whipple, defensive fortification of Washington, D.C.; name changed in honor of Brig. Gen. Albert J. Myer, commanding officer of Signal School of Instruction located here, 1872; site of aviation experiments by Orville Wright, 1809; home of the Air Force Chiefs of Staff and the Chairmen of the Joint Chiefs of Staff. *Federal/USA:* NHL.

Arlington. **GLEBE, THE,** 4527 N. 17th St., 19th C.. Brick, 1 1/2 stories, modified rectangle, gabled roof, 2 interior end chimneys, gabled dormers; 2-story octagonal block topped by octagonal cupola with scalloped eaves added, 1850's; 1-story veranda with sawn-work brackets surrounding building; remodeled, early-20th C. Octagonal Mode. Site of Fairfax Parish glebe house; present house used as studio by American sculptor Clark Mills. *Private; not accessible to the public.*

AUGUSTA COUNTY

Fishersville vicinity. **TINKLING SPRING PRESBYTERIAN CHURCH,** VA 608, 1 mi. S of jct. with VA 636 and VA 631, c. 1850, Robert Lewis Dabney, architect. Brick, 1 story, modified rectangle, hipped roof; projecting pedimented distyle in antis Doric portico, center entrance topped by pediment, recessed vertical panels in flanking facade bays, pilasters between stained glass windows on sides; rear and side additions. Greek Revival. Area's 2nd oldest Presbyterian church, built for congregation formed in 1830's. *Private.*

Fort Defiance. **AUGUSTA STONE CHURCH,** U.S. 11, 1749. Stone, 1 1/2 stories, cross-shaped, jerkinhead roof, round arched stone entrance porch with similar roof, round arched center door, large transom over side entrance; porch, transepts, rear wing, and crossing spire added, 20th C. State's oldest Presbyterian church in continuous use. *Private:* HABS.

Jolivue vicinity. **VALLEY RAILROAD STONE BRIDGE,** S of Jolivue off VA 654, 1874 (?). Stone, quadruple arch totaling 130', 15' wide, slightly projecting imposts set on splayed piers, keystones. Built for Valley Railroad, later part of Baltimore & Ohio RR.; branch discontinued, ties and rails removed, 1942. *State:* HAER.

Historical Places

Spottswood vicinity. **OLD PROVIDENCE STONE CHURCH,** Jct. of VA 613 and VA 620, 1793. Fieldstone, 1 story, rectangular, gabled roof, center doors in gable ends and sides; only walls remained following 1959 fire. Among oldest Presbyterian meetinghouses in area. *Private.*

Staunton vicinity. **FOLLY,** S of Staunton on U.S. 11, 1818. Brick (Flemish bond), 1 story, rectangular, hipped roof with deck and simple wooden balustrade. E entrance portico with lunette in pediment, similar portico on N; W portico replaced by wing (1856); 1 1/2-story S wing. Several outbuildings. Modified serpentine wall. Federal. Built for Joseph Smith, VA legislator; continuous family ownership. *Private; not accessible to the public:* HABS.

Waynesboro vicinity. **MT. TORRY FURNACE,** SW of Waynesboro on VA 664 in the George Washington National Forest, 1804. Stone laid without mortar, pyramidal, 4 sides. Originally 35' above the firebox, 8' interior diameter. Typical of 19th C. furnaces. Following repair of Civil War damage, furnace operated until 1892. *Federal/USFS.*

Waynesboro vicinity. **SWANNANOA,** S of jct. of VA 610 and U.S. 250 (also in Nelson County), 1913, Baskerville and Noland, architects. Marble, 3-story block with 2 slightly projecting 4-story front towers and 2-story end pavilions, modified rectangle, tile hipped roof, interior chimneys, bracketed cornice, 1-story vaulted front center arcade with balustraded balcony connects with open corner galleries, classical details, rustication, large Tiffany stained glass window on staircase landing. Second Renaissance Revival. Summer home of railroad magnate James Dooley. *Private.*

BATH COUNTY

Bacova vicinity. **HIDDEN VALLEY (WARWICKTON),** N of Bacova near jct. of Rtes. 621 and 39 in George Washington National Forest, c. 1858. Brick (Flemish bond), 2 stories, rectangular, hipped roof, 4 interior end chimneys, full-height pedimented tetrastyle entrance portico with fluted Ionic columns. Greek Revival. Built by Judge James Woods Warwick, VA legislator and county judge. *Federal/USFS; not accessible to the public.*

Warm Springs vicinity. **WARM SPRINGS BATHHOUSES,** NE of Warm Springs off Rt. 220, 1761 (men's bathhouse), 1836 (women's bathhouse). Men's bathhouse: frame, clapboarding; 1 story, octagonal, steeply pitched pyramidal roof with deck, gabled and shed wings with dressing rooms added later. Women's bathhouse: frame, vertical siding; 1 story, 20 sides, low pitched polygonal roof with shed roof over enclosed gallery. Traditional starting point for annual tour of springs in VA by Southern aristocrats; bathhouses in use. *Private.*

BEDFORD COUNTY

Bedford vicinity. **FANCY FARM,** On VA 43, N of jct. with VA 682, 1780's. Brick (Flemish bond), 2 1/2 stories, rectangular, gabled roof, interior end chimneys, modillion cornice; center door with fanlight, Ionic pilasters, and pediment; notable interior woodwork; outbuildings; restored, 1969–1971. Fine Late Georgian house with noteworthy drawing room. *Private; not accessible to the public.*

Bedford vicinity. **THREE OTTERS,** W of jct. of Rte. 838 and VA 43, c. 1830. Brick (Flemish bond), 2 stories, L-shaped, low hipped roof, interior end chimneys, full Doric entablature in which nearly all metopes are single pane windows; 1-story, front and rear Doric entrance porticos with balustraded decks; several brick outbuildings. Greek Revival with details based on Asher Benjamin's handbook, *The Practical House Carpenter* (1830). Built by merchant Abel Beach Nichols. *Private; not accessible to the public.*

Forest vicinity. **ELK HILL,** NW of Forest on VA 663, c. 1797. Brick (Flemish bond), 2-story center block with 1 1/2-story wings, modified rectangle, 2 exterior end chimneys on S wall of main block, modillion cornice, center door with transom and side lights, porch with projecting pedimented center section; interior paneling and trim; one wing and porch added, 20th C.; outbuildings including small brick office. Federal. *Private.*

Forest vicinity. **NEW LONDON ACADEMY,** 0.1 mi. E of jct. of VA 297 and VA 211, c. 1837–1839. Brick, 2 stories, rectangular, low hipped roof, interior end chimneys, center entrance with transom; altered; adjacent 1-story frame kitchen building, serving as museum. Academy inc. 1795 as classical school for boys; affiliated, late-19th C., with public school system. *Private.*

Forest vicinity. **WOODBOURNE,** NE of Forest off VA 609, 18th–19th C.. Frame, stuccoed brick; 2 stories, rectangular, gabled roof, 2 interior chimneys, denticulated main pediment and broken pediment over door. Finely carved mantel and woodwork in center section. Original center block (1810) added onto W (1780's) and E (1820) sides. Once owned by Thomas Jefferson; purchased c. 1808 by William Radford, great grandfather of present owner. *Private.*

Lynchburg vicinity. **HOPE DAWN,** NW of Lynchburg off VA 761, 19th C.. Brick (Flemish bond), 1 1/2 stories, rectangular, gabled roof, interior end chimneys, dormers, corbeled cornice, pedimented entrance porch, center door with fanlight, side wing with porch recessed under roof; interior contains finely carved mantels; restored, 1960's; outbuildings. Federal. Originally the country home of Dr. Howell Davies, noted Lynchburg druggist. *Private.*

Lynchburg vicinity. **POPLAR FOREST,** S of jct. of Rtes. 661 and 460, Early-19th C., Thomas Jefferson, gentleman architect. Brick (Flemish bond), 1 1/2 stories on high basement, octagonal, hipped roof with gabled dormers, 4 interior chimneys, 2 Tuscan porticos supported by brick arcades, hipped section, several brick dependencies. Rebuilt according to original plan after fire c. 1840. Jeffersonian Classicism. Designed and built by Jefferson as his summer retreat. *Private:* HABS.

Perrowville vicinity. **OLD RECTORY,** S of Perrowville on VA 663, c. 1787. Frame, beaded siding; 2 1/2 stories, T-shaped, gabled roof, exterior end chimneys; 2-story pedimented center entrance portico with fanlight and fluted columns, 2 windows flanking either side. Interior woodwork almost completely intact. Georgian with Greek Revival detailing. Served as rectory of St. Stephen's Episcopal Church from 1828 to 1904. *Private.*

BOTETOURT COUNTY

Fincastle. **FINCASTLE HISTORIC DISTRICT,** 18th–19th C.. Contains numerous buildings, unified by scale and use of local materials; wide variety of styles including Greek and Gothic Revival, and the Victorian styles. Small agricultural courthouse community. *Multiple public/private:* HABS.

Historical Places

Fincastle vicinity. **SANTILLANE,** W of U.S. 220, 1830's. Brick (Flemish bond), 2 stories, modified rectangle, low hipped roof, 4 interior end chimneys; center entrance with side lights, transom, and a wide, full-height balustraded tetrastyle porch with a Chinese Chippendale rail at roof; side gabled kitchen wing, central hall plan; several brick outbuildings. Federal and Greek Revival elements. *Private; not accessible to the public.*

Glen Wilton vicinity. **CALLIE FURNACE,** 1.5 mi. N of Glen Wilton in the George Washington National Forest, 1873, D. S. Cook, builder. Cut stone set without mortar, pyramidal, 4 sides, interior diameter of 8', 33' above firebox, 1 iron stack 6' high, enlarged, 1880. Typical of furnaces constructed during 19th C. industrial expansion. *Federal/USFS.*

BRUNSWICK COUNTY

Lawrenceville. **BRUNSWICK COUNTY COURTHOUSE SQUARE,** U.S. 58, 19th C.. Complex of brick county government buildings including the Greek Revival courthouse with 2-story tetrastyle pedimented portico (1854), clerk's office (1893), county jail and library; Confederate war monument nearby. Area example of 19th C. courthouse square. *County.*

Lawrenceville vicinity. **BENTFIELD (MELROSE),** SW of Lawrenceville off U.S. 58 and VA 656, 1810. Brick (Flemish bond), 2 1/2 stories, rectangular, gabled roof, 2 exterior end chimneys, 7 bays wide, center N and S entrances, central hall plan; frame kitchen wing added, mid-19th C; Adamesque interior detailing; damaged by fire, 1974; 3 wooden outbuildings. Federal. Built on Melrose plantation for John Jones, Revolutionary War colonel and state senator; later purchased and renamed Bentfield by Thomas Flournoy who helped establish Union Presbyterian Church. Flournoy family retained ownership for 114 years. *Private.*

BUCKINGHAM COUNTY

Buckingham. **BUCKINGHAM COURTHOUSE HISTORIC DISTRICT,** Both sides of U.S. 60, 19th C.. Complex of court buildings including 2-story Greek Revival courthouse with tetrastyle portico, several taverns, and number of brick and frame 19th C. dwellings in Federal, Greek Revival, and Italian Villa styles. Typical 19th C. village which developed around courthouse establishment. *Multiple public/private.*

Dillwyn vicinity. **FRANCISCO, PETER, HOUSE (LOCUST GROVE)** , SE of Dillwyn, 0.9 mi. S of SR 626, 18th C.. Frame, clapboarding; 1 1/2 stories, rectangular, gabled roof, shed dormers, exterior end chimneys; in semiruinous condition. Home of Revolutionary War hero Peter Francisco from 1794 to mid-1820's. *Private; not accessible to the public.*

BUENA VISTA (independent city)

SOUTHERN SEMINARY MAIN BUILDING (BUENA VISTA HOTEL) , Jct. of Ivy and Park Aves., 1890's, S. W. Foulks, architect. Brick, frame with clapboarding and shingling; 3 1/2 stories with high basement, irregular shape, gabled roof with cross gables, interior chimneys, dormers, center gable flanked by circular brick towers; frame galleries on 3 levels flanking entrance, joined at 3rd story by pedimented arch with latticework spandrels, round arched entrances, gabled bays with Palladian windows,

Historical Places

round end towers; interior woodwork. Queen Anne. Erected as hotel for land development company during land boom of eastern Shenandoah Valley; converted, 1901, to join Southern Seminary System of Schools by Dr. Edgar H. Rowe. *Private.*

CAMPBELL COUNTY

Long Island vicinity. **GREEN HILL,** SW of Long Island near jct. of Rtes. 633 and 728, c. 1800. Brick (Flemish bond), 2 1/2 stories, L-shaped, gabled roof, 2 interior end chimneys, small center gabled entrance porch with 2 windows on either side, open side shed, original section is rear ell. Federal elements. Independent kitchen with stone chimney the width of the gable end. Built by Samuel Pannill, a member of the Virginia General Assembly and a navigation company president. *Private; not accessible to the public:* HABS.

CAROLINE COUNTY

Bowling Green. **CAROLINE COUNTY COURTHOUSE,** Main St. and Court House Lane, 1830. Brick (Flemish bond), 2 1/2 stories, rectangular, gabled roof, pedimented front gable, 1st-floor arcaded loggia, lunette in tympanum, full entablature; renovated and rear wing added, 1970. Jeffersonian Classical. *County:* HABS.

Bowling Green vicinity. **OLD MANSION,** S of jct. of U.S. 301 and VA 207, c. 1670. Brick (Flemish bond), 1 1/2 stories, L-shaped, gabled roof with jerkinheads with hipped dormers, gambrel roof on rear ell, interior end chimneys; full-width front porch and ell are later additions; most original interior features remain. Colonial elements. Built by Maj. John Hoomes; important social center, noted for its stables. *Private; not accessible to the public:* HABS.

Port Royal. **PORT ROYAL HISTORIC DISTRICT,** 18th–19th C.. Predominantly residential community with notable 18th and early-19th C. architecture and few modern intrusions. Founded in 1744, quickly developed into major shipping port for tobacco; commercial importance lessened with advent of railroad. *Multiple public/private:* HABS.

Port Royal vicinity. **CAMDEN,** N of jct. of Rte. 686 and U.S. 17, 1857–1859, Norris G. Starkwether, architect. Frame, horizontal flush siding; 2 1/2 stories, T-shaped, hipped roof with intersecting gables, projecting eaves, interior and interior end chimneys, paired and single segmental arched windows, triple arched windows, projecting pedimented front pavilion, 1-story front and rear porch, 2-story side wing. Well-preserved Italian Villa country house. *Private; not accessible to the public:* HABS.

Port Royal vicinity. **GAY MONT,** Off U.S. 17 near jct. with U.S. 301, Late-18th–early-19th C.. Brick, stuccoed; 2-story central block with flanking 1-story wings, modified rectangle, gabled and low hipped roof sections, exterior end chimneys, interior chimneys in wings, box cornice, center entrance behind colonnade of cylindrical columns, circular windows in gable ends; wings and colonnade added, 1819; polygonal wing extension, 1834; center block reconstructed and wings restored following 1959 fire; brick outbuilding; landscaped gardens. Neo-Classical elements. Original building expanded by later owner John Hipkins Bernard, who had been impressed with French landscaping and architecture while traveling in France. *Private:* HABS.

Port Royal vicinity. **HAZELWOOD,** NW of Port Royal off U.S. 17, Mid-18th C.. Site of 18th C. plantation containing brick fragments, domestic artifacts, and brick walls of outbuildings. Originally a prosperous complex including main house, slave quarters, and outbuildings. Home of John Taylor, prominent lawyer, writer, and delegate to Virginia General Assembly and U.S. Senate. *Private; not accessible to the public.*

CARROLL COUNTY

Fancy Gap vicinity. **ALLEN, SIDNA, HOUSE,** N of Fancy Gap on U.S. 52, 1911, Preston Dickens, builder. Frame, clapboarding; 1 1/2 stories, modified L shape, gabled roof; dormers, gables, tower, and conical roofed porch section; several porches, decorative woodwork and shingling, iron cresting, chimneys with corbeled caps. Elaborate Queen Anne house. Built for Sidna Allen, member of "Allen Clan" involved in local 1912 courtroom shootout; sentenced to life imprisonment a year after completion of house. *Private; not accessible to the public.*

CHARLES CITY COUNTY

Charles City. **CHARLES CITY COUNTY COURTHOUSE,** VA 5, 18th C.. Brick (Flemish bond), 1 story, T-shaped, hipped roof, 2 interior chimneys, modillion cornice, segmental arched windows, 1-story front porch added later, extensive alterations. Sophisticated example of colonial courthouse in an isolated setting much as it was in 18th C. *County:* HABS.

Charles City vicinity. **BELLE AIR,** N of VA 5, c. 1700. Frame, clapboarding; 1 1/2 stories, rectangular, gabled roof, interior end and central chimneys, dormers, 2 transomed front entrances; 3-bay extension and elaboration, c. 1800; later rear ell, exposed framing inside old section. Federal elements. Oldest house on old Williamsburg-to-Richmond road. *Private.*

Charles City vicinity. **BERKELEY (BENJAMIN HARRISON V BIRTHPLACE)**, 8 mi. W of Charles City, 1726. Brick (Flemish bond), 2 1/2 stories, rectangular, gabled roof with end pediments defined by lower pent, interior chimneys, gabled dormers, modillion cornice, center entrance with 4-light transom and pediment supported by pilasters, projecting string course above 1st story, gabled side basement entrance, flat arched windows; 2 flanking brick dependencies; interior altered and remodeled in Adamesque style, c. 1790–1800; restored, 1937–1938. Georgian with early appearing end pediments. Birthplace and home of Benjamin Harrison V, a signer of the Declaration of Independence, planter, politician, and VA governor; birthplace of William Henry Harrison, 9th U.S. President. Museum. *Private:* NHL; HABS.

Charles City vicinity. **GREENWAY**, On VA 5, Late-18th C.. Frame, clapboarding; 1 1/2 stories, T-shaped, gabled roof with dormers, 2 exterior end chimneys, much original woodwork and hardware, early-19th C. rear ell. Colonial elements. Birthplace of John Tyler, state governor and 10th U.S. President. *Private; not accessible to the public:* HABS.

Charles City vicinity. **TYLER, JOHN, HOUSE (SHERWOOD FOREST)**, 4 mi. E of Charles City on VA 5, 1780. Frame, clapboarding; 2 1/2 stories, modified H shape, gabled roof, exterior end chimneys, dormers, balustraded front entrance porch, flanking 1 1/2-story gabled wings, connecting 1-story hyphens and dependencies. Last home of John Tyler, 10th U.S. President. *Private;* NHL; HABS.

Charles City vicinity. **WESTOVER CHURCH**, 5 mi. W of Charles City off VA 5, 1731. Brick (Flemish bond with glazed headers), 1 1/2 stories, rectangular, jerkinhead roof, modillion

Historical Places

cornice, round arched windows, center arched entrance under segmental pediment framed by pilasters; gallery added, 1867; renovated and restored, 1956 and 1970. Georgian. Second church to serve the Westover Parish, one of the oldest parishes in the country. *Private.*

Charles City vicinity. **WESTOVER,** 7 mi. W of Charles City on VA 5, 1730–1734. Brick (Flemish bond), 2 1/2 stories, rectangular, steeply pitched hipped roof, 4 tall interior end chimneys, hipped dormers; exceptional center entrance with broken pediment above the S entrance and arched pediment above the N; flanking 1 1/2-story wings connected by hyphens. Georgian. Constructed for William Byrd II, founder of Richmond. *Private:* NHL; HABS.

Hopewell vicinity. **EPPES ISLAND,** At confluence of the James and Appomattox rivers, 17th–20th C.. Island containing sites of Shirley Hundred, a 17th C. village; 18th C. houses, slave quarter ruins, Woodland and Archaic sites, and boundary ditches reflecting some of the oldest property lines in U.S.; some excavations. Occupied since 1624 by members of the Eppes family; considered the oldest family farm in state still held by descendants of original owners. *Private; not accessible to the public.*

Hopewell vicinity. **SHIRLEY,** 5 mi. N of Hopewell off VA 608, 1770. Brick (Flemish bond), 2 1/2 stories, nearly square, double hipped roof surmounted by large ornament in pineapple motif, dormers, 2 tall interior chimneys, modillion cornice, 2-story tetrastyle pedimented N and S porticos (early-19th C.), molded brick water table and string course; interior suspended stair with scrolled soffit; 2 brick L-shaped dependencies (c. 1740) form outer forecourt, several brick outbuildings.

Georgian. Homestead of distinguished Carter Family and birthplace of Robert E. Lee's mother, Ann Hill Carter. *Private:* HABS.

Tettington vicinity. **MARGOTS,** NE of Tettington off VA 621, c. 1700. Brick with glazed headers on main facades, 2 stories (frame 2nd-story 19th C. addition), rectangular, gabled roof, interior end chimney and unusual exterior end chimney with splay around 3 sides. *State; not accessible to the public.*

CHARLOTTE COUNTY

Brookneal vicinity. **STAUNTON HILL,** SW of jct. of Rtes. 619 and 693, 1848, John E. Johnson, designer. Brick, stuccoed; 2 stories with 3-story central pavilion, modified square, flat roof, crenelated parapet, octagonal crenelated towers at pavilion corners, full-width 1-story Tudor veranda. Excellent Gothic Revival structure. Built for Charles Bruce, son of merchandising magnate. *Private; not accessible to the public.*

Charlotte Court House vicinity. **GREENFIELD,** E of Charlotte Court House on VA 656, 1771. Frame, clapboarding; 2 stories, rectangular, gabled roof, 2 interior end chimneys, modillion cornice, 1 1/2-story side wings, center door, gabled porch, rear shed gallery; good interior woodwork; renovated, kitchen wing added. Georgian elements. Built for Isaac Read, prominent planter; remains in family. *Private; not accessible to the public.*

Randolph vicinity. **MULBERRY HILL,** N of Randolph on VA 641, 18th C.. Frame, clapboarding; 2 1/2 stories, T-shaped, cross-gable roof, interior and exterior end chimneys, center entrance with transom and side lights, Doric portico with roof railing; paneled wainscoting and fine stair; 2-story rear and side wings and entrance porch, mid-19th C.; unusually complete complex of outbuildings. Greek Revival elements. Home plantation of VA jurist and politician, Paul Carrington. *Private; not accessible to the public:* HABS.

Saxe vicinity. **ROANOKE PLANTATION,** W of Saxe off VA 746, Early-19th C.. Frame, clapboarding; 1 1/2 stories, rectangular, steeply gabled roof incorporating shed porch, exterior end chimneys, center entrance, exterior stair to attic; outbuildings include smokehouse and frame cottage possibly of later date. Remaining cottage from Roanoke Plantation, home of John Randolph, politician and delegate to the Virginia Constitutional Convention, 1829-1830. *Private:* HABS.

CHARLOTTESVILLE (independent city)

ALBEMARLE COUNTY COURTHOUSE HISTORIC DISTRICT, Courthouse Sq. and surrounding properties, Early–mid-19th C.. Small court square district including Federal and Greek Revival public buildings and town houses lining 2 sides of a rectangular green; Albemarle County Courthouse with pedimented tetrastyle Ionic portico on the green and Levy Opera House included. Original heart of town; retains 19th C. character. *Multiple public/private.*

OAK LAWN, Cherry Ave. and 9th St., 1822. Brick (Flemish bond), 2-story central block with flanking 1-story wings, rectangular, gabled roof, interior end and 2 exterior chimneys, center entrance, 1-story Tuscan portico with cast iron balustraded deck on pedimented main block, lunette in tympanum; 1-story rear additions; brick outbuilding. Jeffersonian Classical.

Probably constructed by builders working on the University of Virginia nearby (see also University of Virginia Historic District, VA). *Private; not accessible to the public.*

ROTUNDA, UNIVERSITY OF VIRGINIA, University of Virginia campus, 1819, Thomas Jefferson, gentleman architect. Brick, 2 stories, modified circle, domed roof, front flat section with Corinthian entrance portico, center entrance, rotunda space. Designed after the ancient Roman Pantheon; rebuilt and altered by Stanford White; being restored to a Jeffersonian Classical appearance. Built by Jefferson as the library and educational and architectural focal point of his "academical village." (See also University of Virginia Historic District, VA.) *State:* NHL; HABS.

UNIVERSITY OF VIRGINIA HISTORIC DISTRICT, Bounded by University and Jefferson Park Aves., and Hospital and McCormick Rds., 19th–20th C., Thomas Jefferson, planner and architect. University complex including red brick classroom and dormitory buildings flanking a series of grassy terraces, the domed Rotunda (see also Rotunda, University of Virginia, VA) at the N end and Stanford White's Cabell Hall (1952) at the S end. Later additions by Stanford White and J. R. Thomas. Predominately Jeffersonian Classicism. Realization of Jefferson's ambition to form an academic village, or a community of scholars living and studying in an architecturally unified complex. Chartered 1819. *State:* NHL; HABS.

CHESAPEAKE (independent city)

GREAT BRIDGE BATTLE SITE, Both sides of the Albemarle and Chesapeake Canal between Oak Grove and Great Bridge, 1775. Site of colonial bridge and causeway over marsh and water, fortified by British as vital link in land route to Norfolk. Location of first armed conflict between British soldiers and state's patriot forces, Dec. 1775, in which British were driven from area; fortified later during Revolution by Queen's Rangers, Loyalist unit under command of John Simcoe. *Private.*

CHESTERFIELD COUNTY

Colonial Heights vicinity. **SWIFT CREEK MILL,** N of Colonial Heights on U.S. 1, Late-17th C.; 19th C.. Brick, rubble stone foundation; 2 stories, gabled roof, stepped parapeted ends, interior end chimneys. Restored. Replacement of mill wheel with modern turbine machinery (mid-19th C.). Brick and stone wing added, 1965. Built for Henry Randolph adjacent to his plantation, Bloomesburg. Scene of Civil War action at Swift Creek during Gen. Butler's Drewry's Bluff Campaign, May 1864; except for brief period as distillery, served continuously as gristmill until 1950's. *Private.*

Midlothian vicinity. **BELLONA ARSENAL,** Off VA 673, NW of jct. with Rte. 147, Early-19th C.. Powder magazine and 3 2-story, brick workshops with hipped roofs, remains of original 8-building arsenal enclosed by stone walls. Arsenal stored cannon and arms from nearby Bellona Foundry, a major supplier of government ordnance through the antebellum period, 1817-1837. *Private:* HABS.

Winterpock vicinity. **EPPINGTON,** S of jct. of VA 621 and 602, Late-1760's. Frame, clapboarding; 2 1/2-story central block with symmetrical 1-story wings, rectangular, steeply hipped roof with gabled dormers, 2 exterior end chimneys, modillion cornice, later 3-bay entrance portico and rear ell, central hall plan.

Home of John Wayles Eppes, U.S. congressman and senator and son-in-law of Thomas Jefferson. *Private; not accessible to the public.*

CLARKE COUNTY

Berryville vicinity. **ANNEFIELD,** E of jct. of Rtes. 633 and 652, c. 1790. Stone, 2 stories, rectangular, hipped roof with balustraded deck, 4 tall interior end chimneys, denticulated cornice, center entrance with 2-story Ionic portico with Chinese Chippendale balustrade at 2nd level and fanlight in pediment, later stuccoed rear ell, several outbuildings. Georgian with Palladian elements. Built by Mathew Page. *Private; not accessible to the public:* HABS.

Berryville vicinity. **FAIRFIELD,** E of jct. of Rtes. 340 and 610, c. 1770. Limestone, 2 1/2 stories, central block with symmetrical T-shaped wings, hipped roof with round arched dormer additions, interior and exterior end stone chimneys, pedimented entrance porch (19th C.), flanking 1-story dependencies and rear ells (20th C.), several outbuildings. Five-part Georgian country house. Built by Warner Washington, a first cousin of George Washington. *Private; not accessible to the public.*

Berryville vicinity. **LONG BRANCH,** W of jct. of CR 626 and 624, 19th C., Benjamin H. Latrobe, architect. Brick, 2 stories, rectangular, hipped roof with balustraded deck, central rectangular cupola, 4 interior chimneys, 2-story front and rear pedimented tetrastyle entrance porticos, 1-story service wing with castelated roof. Georgian with Greek Revival elements. One of 4 extant houses in U.S. known to have been designed by Latrobe; built for Robert Carter Burwell. *Private; not accessible to the public.*

Historical Places

Boyce vicinity. **SARATOGA,** SE of jct. of Rtes. 723 and 617, Late-18th C.. Limestone, 2 1/2 stories, modified L shape, gabled roof with dormers, 2 interior end chimneys, 1-story tetrastyle pedimented center entrance porch with round arched window above, later additions, several original stone outbuildings. Georgian. One of the Shenandoah Valley's largest and best preserved Revolutionary period mansions; built by Revolutionary War general Daniel Morgan. *Private; not accessible to the public:* HABS.

Millwood. **MILLWOOD MILL (BURWELL-MORGAN MILL),** At jct. of Rtes. 723 and 255, c. 1785. Frame, clapboarding, stone; 2 1/2 stories, rectangular, gabled roof. Building, water wheel, and machinery restored. Built by prominent businessman, Col. Nathaniel Burwell and Revolutionary War general, Daniel Morgan; operative until 1943. *Private:* HABS.

Millwood vicinity. **CARTER HALL,** NE of Millwood off VA 255, 1792–1800. Limestone, 2-story central block with low hipped roof, 2- and 1-story gabled symmetrical wings, interior end chimneys at end of each of the 5 sections, 2-story Ionic portico across main block. Outbuilding. Extensively remodeled, 1930. Georgian with Greek Revival elements. Built for Nathaniel Burwell, wealthy planter and Lt. Col. of the James City Militia. Temporary headquarters for Gen. "Stonewall" Jackson, 1862. *Private; not accessible to the public:* HABS.

Millwood vicinity. **OLD CHAPEL,** 3 mi. N of Millwood off U.S. 340, 1793. Stone (rubble), 1 story, rectangular, gabled roof, interior chimney, center door with transom, paneled window shutters with iron strap hinges; interior contains high pulpit with plain sounding board, gallery. Oldest Episcopal church W of the Blue Ridge Mountains. *Private:* HABS.

White Post vicinity. **GREENWAY COURT,** 1 mi. S of White Post on VA 277, c. 1762. Limestone, 1 story, rectangular, gabled roof, thick wall construction, narrow windows. Served as land office for the vast Northern Neck proprietary of Lord Thomas Fairfax. Site of Fairfax's home from 1751 until his death in 1781, is marked by paving stones and has been replaced by 1828 farmhouse. *Private; not accessible to the public:* NHL; HABS.

White Post vicinity. **TULEYRIES, THE,** 1.5 mi. E of White Post off VA 628, c. 1833. Brick, painted white; 2 stories, modified rectangle, low hipped roof, interior chimneys; central octagonal cupola with round arched windows, octagonal dome, and apex orb; double-door center entrance with fanlight and side lights, 2nd-story window with similar elements; 2-story pedimented Corinthian entrance portico; entrance hall with low rotunda and coffered vault, basement kitchen; numerous outbuildings include garden house with large elaborate cupola, and brick barn and stable buildings, each with stepped gabled roof. Federal and Greek Revival elements. Well-preserved example of antebellum VA estate. *Private; not accessible to the public:* HABS.

COLONIAL HEIGHTS (independent city)

ELLERSLIE, Ellerslie Rd., c. 1857, Robert Young, architect. Stucco, 2 1/2 stories, modified rectangle, hipped roof sections, hipped N tower section, gables, end 3-story bays interrupt roof line, full-width veranda with porte-cochere at center bay, narrow belt course separating 1st and 2nd stories, rear service wing; extensive alterations include replacement of flat roof and addition of dormers. Italian Villa. Built for David Dunlap, wealthy tobacco merchant; headquarters for Gen. Pierre G. T. de Beauregard during Civil War; Confederate rest camp, 1864. *Private; not accessible to the public.*

OAK HILL, 151 Carroll Ave., c. 1825. Frame, clapboarding; 1 story, modified H shape, hipped roof, polygonal ends on main wing with triple-hung sash, porch with 4 square columns, semielliptical fan over center door, side gallery on middle section; later additions. Federal and Greek Revival elements. *Private; not accessible to the public:* HABS.

VIOLET BANK, Royal Oak Ave., 1815. Frame, clapboarding; 1 story, rectangular with octagonal end bays, modified hipped roof, exterior end chimneys; front recessed entrance bay with center double doors with fanlight and side lights, flanking full-height windows on each side, and a tetrastyle porch; original N 2-story wing removed. Excellent interior Adamesque detailing. Federal. Served as Lee's headquarters from June 8, 1864, to Nov. 1, 1864. *Municipal:* HABS.

CRAIG COUNTY

New Castle. **NEW CASTLE HISTORIC DISTRICT,** Main and Court Sts., 19th C.. Five county and commercial buildings, including an impressive Greek Revival courthouse, the sherriff's house, a hotel, and 2 late-19th C. commercial structures which attracted enterprise and became nucleus of county's commercial center. Most complete antebellum county seat complex in area. Became county seat in 1851; still the major commercial center of an essentially rural county. *Multiple public/private:* HABS.

CULPEPER COUNTY

Culpeper. **HILL, A. P., BOYHOOD HOME,** 102 N. Main St., 1820. Brick (Flemish bond), painted; 3 stories, rectangular, low hipped roof, central cupola with bracketed hipped roof; interior chimneys along S, W, and N; original 2nd-story entrances no longer used, ground-floor entrances. Italian Villa elements added, 1860's. Federal. Boyhood home of Confederate general Ambrose Powell Hill. *Multiple private.*

Stevensburg vicinity. **SALUBRIA,** E of jct. of Rtes. 3 and 663, 18th C.. Brick (Flemish bond), 2 stories, rectangular, hipped roof, denticulated cornice, 2 tall corbel-capped interior end chimneys, segmental arched openings, fine interior trim. Georgian. Built by John Thompson, Anglican minister. *Private; not accessible to the public.*

Warrenton vicinity. **LITTLE FORK CHURCH,** Jct. of Rtes. 624 and 726, 1774–1776. Brick (Flemish bond), 1 story, rectangular, steeply hipped roof with denticulated cornice, round arched center door and flanking windows; original reredos and some interior trim. One of state's finer and better preserved colonial churches. *Private;* HABS.

CUMBERLAND COUNTY

Cartersville vicinity. **AMPTHILL,** W side of VA 602, 3 mi. N of jct. with VA 45, c. 1835. Brick, 1 story, modified T shape, hipped roof sections, interior chimneys, slightly off-center front entrance with pedimented tetrastyle Doric portico, marble lintels; 1-story frame passage connects to 2-story 18th C. frame dwelling; extensively altered, mid-19th C.; brick outbuildings. Jeffersonian Classicism. Built for Randolph Harrison, great-grandson of Robert "King" Carter, possibly after sketch prepared by Thomas Jefferson. *Private; not accessible to the public.*

Historical Places

Cartersville vicinity. **CARTERSVILLE BRIDGE,** VA 45 over James River (also in Goochland County), 1884. Two end spans and piers remaining from timber and cast iron bridge; modified Pratt truss of 6 spans with original total length of 843', 25' above James River; stone piers and abutments survive from 1822 bridge. Rare example of composite construction; seriously damaged by flood in June 1972. *Private:* HAER.

Cartersville vicinity. **MUDDY CREEK MILL,** S of Cartersville off VA 684, 1785. Complex containing mill, miller's house, farmhouse, post office, and related outbuildings; of primary importance is 2 1/2-story gabled mill of brick over stone basement with clapboard gable ends and double tier of dormers. Large mill reflects evolution of gristmilling techniques; operated until 1950's. *Private; not accessible to the public.*

Hamilton vicinity. **CLIFTON,** N of Hamilton off VA 690, 18th C.. Frame, clapboarding; 2 stories, rectangular, hipped roof, 2 interior chimneys, modillion cornice, center door, 3-bay gabled entrance porch with slender columns and Chinese Chippendale lattice balustrade, 1-story side wing shed porch; read shed additions; numerous outbuildings. Georgian. Built for Carter Henry Harrison, author of the Instructions for Independence presented to the Virginia Convention of May 1776. *Private; not accessible to the public.*

DANVILLE (independent city)

·**DANVILLE HISTORIC DISTRICT,** 19th C.. Residential district containing 2–2 1/2-story brick, frame and stucco dwellings; includes fine examples of buildings with elements of various Victorian styles. Area supported by tobacco, textile, and other industries developed mid–late-19th C.; maintains turn-of-the-century character. *Multiple public/private.*

Encyclopedia of Virginia

DANVILLE PUBLIC LIBRARY, 975 Main St., 1857–1858. Stuccoed, 2 stories, modified L shape, shallow hipped roof with large square cupola, bracketed cornice, segmental arched windows with simple hood molds, 2 1-story wings. Italian Villa. Confederate President Jefferson Davis signed his last official proclamation here on Apr. 4, 1865. *Municipal.*

DINWIDDIE COUNTY

Dinwiddie. **DINWIDDIE COUNTY COURTHOUSE,** Jct. of U.S. 1 and VA 619, 1851. Brick, painted; 2 stories, modified T shape with main rectangular temple-form block, gabled roof sections, full entablature, 1933 full-height pedimented Doric portico with lunette in tympanum, altered center entrance beneath balcony, 2-story brick pilasters between bays; remodeled 1858; 19th and 20th C. rear and side wings. Greek Revival. Scene of Gen. Philip Sheridan's decisive Union victory over Gen. George Pickett at Five Forks during last phase of the Civil War. *County.*

Dinwiddie vicinity. **BURNT QUARTER,** SW of jct. of Rtes. 627, 613, and 645, Late-18th C.. Frame, clapboarding; 2 stories, central block with symmetrical wings, hipped roof, exterior end chimneys, off-center entrance porch, 1 1/2-story gabled wings with dormers, rear ell, early-19th C. additions. Federal with Greek Revival details. Battle of Five Forks fought nearby on Apr. 1, 1865; house served as hospital and headquarters for Union general Wesley Merritt. *Private; not accessible to the public:* HABS.

Petersburg vicinity. **FIVE FORKS BATTLEFIELD,** 12 mi. W of Petersburg on CR 627 at Church Rd., 1865. Site of decisive battle assuring success of Gen. Ulysses S. Grant's 11 month Appomattox Campaign to drive Confederates from Petersburg and Richmond

370

Historical Places

defenses. Gen. Philip H. Sheridan successfully cut Gen. Robert E. Lee's last supply line, forcing withdrawal of Confederate forces. Small portion of Confederate breastworks remains. *Private:* NHL.

Petersburg vicinity. **MAYFIELD COTTAGE,** Central State Hospital Grounds, Mid-18th C.. Brick (Flemish bond), 1 1/2 stories, rectangular, gabled roof with jerkinheads, gabled dormers, 2 interior end chimneys, center door with later porch, beveled water table and gauged flat arches, fine interior paneling. Georgian. Scene of fierce fighting during the siege of Petersburg in 1865. *Private; not accessible to the public:* G.

Petersburg vicinity. **PETERSBURG NATIONAL BATTLEFIELD,** SE, S, and SW of Petersburg (also in Prince George County), 1864–1865. Site of portion of 10-month struggle of Union army under command of Gen. Ulysses S. Grant to capture Petersburg and cut Gen. Robert E. Lee's railroad supplies from the South, June 1864–Apr. 1865. After unsuccessfully attempting direct assaults, Grant began seige; Lee evacuated city on Apr. 2, 1865, one week before his surrender at Appomattox Courthouse (see also Appomattox Court House National Historical Park, VA). *Federal/NPS/non-federal.*

Petersburg vicinity. **WALES,** W of Petersburg off VA 632, 1730. Frame, clapboarding; 1 1/2-story main block connected to flanking 1-story symmetrical wings by 1-story hyphens, rectangular, gabled roof sections, exterior end chimneys, hipped dormers, modillion cornice, center and hyphen entrances; contains much original interior paneling and hardware; original center section enlarged by construction of wings, c. 1752; outbuildings. Georgian plantation. Home of prominent area Briggs family. *Private; not accessible to the public:* HABS.

371

Encyclopedia of Virginia

Rowanta vicinity. **WILLIAMSON SITE,** NE of jct. of Rtes. 693 and 703, Paleo-Indian (c. 9000 B.C.). Assorted debris and tool assemblage recovered in excavations indicate site was quarry workshop; one of 4 such workshops in eastern U.S. Investigated. *Private.*

EMPORIA (independent city)

KLUGEL, H. T., ARCHITECTURAL SHEET METAL WORK BUILDING, 135 Atlantic St., 1914. Brick, sheet metal trim; 2 stories, rectangular, flat roof, side stepped parapets, front balustraded parapet with raised center pediment with side volutes, 5-bay facade with large round arched openings, 2 front entrances; worked sheet metal ornament on front facade, painted silver and black; concrete block rear section added. Eclectic. Excellent example of sheet metal decorated facade; serves as advertisement for Klugel firm. *Private.*

ESSEX COUNTY

Caret vicinity. **BLANDFIELD,** E of jct. of Rtes. 624 and U.S. 17, c. 1850. Brick (Flemish bond), 2-story central block with flanking 2-story wings and 1-story hyphens, U-shaped, hipped and double-hipped roof, interior chimneys, modillion cornice, center 1-story porch across projecting pedimented entrance pavilion. Georgian. One of the state's largest colonial plantation mansions; built for William Beverly, member of prominent VA family. *Private; not accessible to the public.*

Loretto vicinity. **BROOKE'S BANK,** 1 mi. E of Loretto, 1.4 mi. N of VA 17, 1751. Brick, 2-story main block with 1-story wings, hipped roof, tall interior end chimneys with unusual glazed brick lozenge decoration, denticulated

Historical Places

cornice, molded belt course, flat arches over windows; fine interior woodwork and staircase; additions include late-18th C. and mid-20th C. 1-story wings, 1-story entrance porch; smokehouse and rebuilt dependencies. Fine example of a Tidewater Virginia Georgian plantation. *Private; not accessible to the public:* HABS.

Loretto vicinity. **ELMWOOD,** SW of jct. of Rtes. 640 and U.S. 17, c. 1774. Brick (Flemish bond), 2 1/2 stories, rectangular, hipped roof, 2 interior chimneys, center projecting entrance pavilion with open tympanum above 2nd-story Palladian window, molded brick water table and brick string course, some original woodwork. Georgian. Built for landowner Muscoe Garnett, member of prominent county family. *Private; not accessible to the public:* HABS.

Loretto vicinity. **VAUTER'S CHURCH,** 1 mi. NW of Loretto on U.S. 17, 1719. Brick (Flemish bond with glazed headers), 1 1/2 stories, T-shaped, steeply gabled roof, modillion cornice, center entrance with small pediment, flanking small segmental arched gallery windows, round arched windows; believed to have been built in 2 stages with wing added, 1831; interior remodeled, 1827; renovated, 1970. Georgian. *Private:* HABS.

Tappahannock. **TAPPAHANNOCK HISTORIC DISTRICT,** 18th–20th C.. District associated with town's maritime and political history; contains commercial, residential, government, and religious structures in a wide variety of 18th and 19th C. styles; notable are Anderson House (c. 1750) and Scot's Arms Tavern (early-19th C.). Town chartered in 1682, developed into prominent port facility; politically active as center of strong protest against the Stamp Act 10 years before the Revolution. *Multiple public/private:* HABS.

Encyclopedia of Virginia

FAIRFAX (independent city)

EARP'S ORDINARY (RATCLIFF-LOGAN-ALLISON HOUSE), 200 E. Main St., c. 1805-1813. Brick, 2 stories, L-shaped, gabled roof, interior chimneys, corbeled brick cornice, 2 front entrances, flat arches over windows; built in 2 sections; 2-story porch over W section added late-19th C.; 2-story frame rear wing added 20th C. Federal elements. Early-19th C. postal station and stagecoach stop. *Private; not accessible to the public.*

FAIRFAX COUNTY COURTHOUSE, 4000 Chain Bridge Rd., 1799-1800, James Wren, builder-architect. Brick, 2 stories, rectangular, gabled roof, 1-story arcade beneath 2nd story on front gabled wall, stone imposts and keystones, 3 interior chimneys, octagonal cupola. Interior destroyed during Civil War, restored. Federal. 20th C. wings added. Invaded, 1863, by Gen. John S. Mosby, leader of the Partisan Rangers, a Confederate group specializing in guerilla warfare. *County.*

FAIRFAX COUNTY

Accotink vicinity. **POPE-LEIGHEY HOUSE**, E of Accotink off U.S. 1, 1940-1941. Frank Lloyd Wright, architect. Wood (broad horizontal cypress sheathing), brick, and glass; 1 story, modified L shape, flat roof with broad overhang, emphasis on the horizontal, interior divided into overlapping spaces with much built-in furniture. Moved and reconstructed on present site, 1965. Typical of Wright's practical, economical, and well designed "Usonian" house for contemporary Americans. *Private:* HABS.

Accotink vicinity. **WOODLAWN PLANTATION,** W of jct. of U.S. 1 and Rte. 235, 1800-1805, William Thornton, architect. Brick (Flemish bond), 2 1/2 stories, central block with 1 1/2-story end pavilions and hyphens, gabled roof with jerkinhead ends, 2 pairs of interior end chimneys, modillion cornice; center round arched entrance with oval window in pediment above. Georgian. Located on land given by George Washington to his ward, Eleanor Parke Custis, as a wedding gift. *Private:* HABS.

Alexandria vicinity. **GUNSTON HALL,** 15 mi. S of Alexandria on VA 242, 1755–1758, William Buckland, architect. Brick (Flemish bond), 1 1/2 stories, rectangular, gabled roof with splayed eaves, pedimented dormers, 2 pairs of interior end chimneys, modillion cornice, stone quoins, pedimented hexastyle entrance porch on NW, polygonal entrance porch on SE, central hall plan, notable interior trim. Georgian. Built for George Mason, author of the Virginia Declaration of Rights. *State:* NHL; HABS.

Alexandria vicinity. **HUNTLEY,** 6918 Harrison Lane, c. 1820. Brick, 1 1/2 stories, modified U shape, gabled roof sections, elongated rectangular interior chimneys, center entrance with fanlight and side lights; 3-bay porch flanked by projecting wings, each with front windows set in recessed rectangular panel; original truncated gabled roof raised; frame addition; numerous outbuildings including tenant house, root cellar, and icehouse. Federal elements. Built for Thomson Francis Mason, grandson of George Mason IV. *Private.*

Alexandria vicinity. **MOUNT VERNON,** 7 mi. S of Alexandria on George Washington Memorial Pkwy., 1743, Augustine Washington, builder. Frame, 2 1/2 stories, U-shaped, hipped roof, pedimented dormers, central cupola with finial and weathervane, 2 interior chimneys, full-width 2-story portico on river facade, 3 entrances, gabled dependencies connected to main house by curved open arcades. Georgian. Home of George Washington. *Private:* NHL; HABS.

Chantilly vicinity. **SULLY,** N of jct. of Rtes. 28 and U.S. 50, 1794. Frame, clapboarding; 2 1/2 stories, rectangular, gabled roof, pair of exterior end chimneys, 1-story porch with scrollwork and square fluted piers; later 1 1/2-story E wing and 1-story W wing; side hall plan, most original interior woodwork; several outbuildings. Colonial elements. Built by Richard Bland Lee, state legislator and member of first U.S. Congress, 1789. *County:* HABS.

Dranesville vicinity. **DRANESVILLE TAVERN,** 11919 Leesburg Pike, 1830's. Log construction, 2 stories, rectangular, gabled roof, central and exterior end stone chimneys; original dogtrot dwelling joined to 1-story log kitchen; 2nd story added to kitchen, rear porch enclosed, clapboarded, 1850; moved, 1968. Served travelers on the heavily used pike; catered largely to teamsters. *County.*

Fort Belvoir. **BELVOIR MANSION RUINS AND FAIRFAX GRAVE SITE,** SE of jct. of 23rd St. and Belvoir Rd., 18th C.. Brick foundations and drains of mansion house built, c. 1740, for Col. William Fairfax; early home of prominent VA family. Gravesite with wrought iron fence surrounding obelisk marks graves of Col. Fairfax and wife. *Federal/USA COE; not accessible to the public.*

Lorton. **POHICK CHURCH,** 9201 Richmond Hwy., 1772, attributed to James Wren, architect. Brick (Flemish bond), 2 stories, rectangular, hipped roof, modillion cornice, round arched 2nd-floor windows, 2 pedimented entrances, stone quoins, restored. Georgian elements. George Washington served on building committee. *Private:* HABS.

Historical Places

McLean. **SALONA,** 1214 Buchanan St., c. 1812. Brick (Flemish bond), 2 stories, rectangular, gabled roof with brackets, 2 interior end chimneys, center entrance, regular fenestration. Late-19th C. 2-story N wing addition with shallow hipped roof, 2 interior chimneys, 1-bay entrance porch and cornice with Eastlake modillions and brackets. Unusual floor plan with T-shaped hall. Federal with Eastlake details. Temporary headquarters for Gen. George B. McClellan, commanding officer of the Army of the Potomac, during Civil War. *Private; not accessible to the public.*

FALLS CHURCH (independent city)

CHERRY HILL, 312 Park Ave., c. 1840. Frame, clapboarding; 2 1/2 stories, rectangular, gabled roof, 2 interior end chimneys, center hall plan, later additions include full-width porch with box cornice and small brackets (c. 1870) and kitchen wing (c. 1900). Barn and shed appear to be largely original. Home of Judge Joseph Riley, alderman, founder of movement for a town public school, and instrumental in incorporating Falls Church; and of his son, J. Harvey Riley, ornithologist. *Municipal:* HABS.

FALLS CHURCH, 115 E. Fairfax St., 1767–1769, James Wren, architect. Brick (Flemish bond), 2 stories, rectangular, hipped roof, modillion cornice, round arched 2nd-story windows and rectilinar lower windows with rubbed brick arches, center pedimented doorway with flanking pilasters. Extensive alterations (1959) included a new gallery and enlarged chancel. Georgian. Replaced first church building in Falls Church. *Private:* HABS.

Encyclopedia of Virginia

FAUQUIER COUNTY

Delaplane vicinity. **ASHLEIGH,** S of Delaplane, off U.S. 17, 1840. Stone, stuccoed and painted; 1 story, central block with symmetrical wings, gabled roof, 2 interior end chimneys, 1-bay Doric tetrastyle portico with cast iron balustrade, 1 outbuilding. Greek Revival. Built for and designed by Margaret Marshall, granddaughter of Chief Justice John Marshall. *Private; not accessible to the public.*

Delaplane vicinity. **OAK HILL,** 2.2 mi. S of Delaplane, 18th–19th C.. Frame, clapboarding, stuccoed brick; 1 1/2–2 1/2 stories, L-shaped, gabled roof sections, exterior end and interior chimneys, front pediment with denticulated modillion cornice and fanlight, center entrance with fluted fan and side lights; finely detailed interior woodwork; original 1773 frame structure enlarged, 1819, by Greek Revival addition with 1-story frame connection; 1-story Doric portico removed; numerous outbuildings. Home of Chief Justice John Marshall and his sons. *Private; not accessible to the public.*

Upperville. **UPPERVILLE HISTORIC DISTRICT,** On VA 50, 18th–20th C.. Mile-long linear village along VA 50; contains primarily residential and religious structures and some commercial buildings at one end; features 2-story brick, frame, and stone rectangular dwellings, 3–5 bays wide with end chimneys, gabled roofs, and Federal elements. Retains rural qualities; associations with equine sports. *Multiple public/private:* HABS.

FLUVANNA COUNTY

Bremo Bluff vicinity. **BREMO,** N of the jct. of Rtes. 15 and 656, Early-19th C.. Brick (Flemish bond), 1 story with high basement,

Historical Places

modified L shape; low hipped roof with balustraded deck over main section, gabled roof over rear section; interior chimneys, pedimented Tuscan porticos, loggia and side porches. Jeffersonian Classicism. Stone and brick outbuildings include brick Jacobethan style houses with curvilinear end gables and diagonally set chimney stacks. Built by Gen. John Hartwell Cocke, noted planter, social reformer, and a leader of the American Colonization Society. *Private; not accessible to the public:* HABS.

Columbia. **POINT OF FORK ARSENAL**, SE of jct. of Rtes. 624 and 656, 18th C.. Two visible ruins, probably the 1788 stone magazine and one of the "long-house" arsenals. Arsenal raided and burned during the American Revolution. Later rebuilt, it was used for manufacture and repair of arms and equipment and as stockpile of weapons for frontier fighting; state arsenal from 1783 until 1801 when abandoned for more favorable site. *Private.*

Columbia vicinity. **POINT OF FORK PLANTATION**, W of Columbia off VA 624, 1820's. Brick, 2 stories over high basement, rectangular, hipped roof, 4 interior end chimneys, 2-story tetrastyle Doric portico; entrance flanked by pilasters, side lights, and transom; marble sills, lintels and water table; interior alterations. Outbuildings include interesting temple-form office building with 2 Doric columns in antis. Greek Revival. Plantation on confluence of James and Rivanna rivers; headquarters for invading general Philip Sheridan, Mar. 1865. Home of James Galt, state representative, 1865–1867. *Private; not accessible to the public.*

Palmyra. **FLUVANNA COUNTY COURTHOUSE HISTORIC DISTRICT**, Roughly bounded by VA 601, VA 15, and the Rivanna River, Mid-19th C.. County seat complex; contains 1829 stone jail built by John G. Hughes, 1831 Greek Revival temple-form courthouse locally attributed to Gen. John Hartwell Cocke, and contemporary lawyer's office. Maintains original appearance in undeveloped setting. *County:* G.

FRANKLIN COUNTY

Rocky Mount. **WASHINGTON IRON FURNACE,** 108 Old Furnace Rd., c. 1770. Rock-faced granite furnace set against hillside; pyramid set on square base with hearth and bellows openings at base. Important industry for small town, employing 10 in 1773 and 100 in 1836. *Private.*

Rocky Mount vicinity. **BOOKER T. WASHINGTON NATIONAL MONUMENT,** 16 mi. E of Rocky Mount on VA 122, Mid-19th C.. Farm includes reconstruction of slave cabin. Birthplace of of Booker T. Washington (1856), nationally prominent black leader who founded founded Tuskegee Institute (see also Tuskegee Institute, AL) and wrote famous autobiography *Up From Slavery. Federal/NPS.*

FREDERICK COUNTY

Middletown. **ST. THOMAS CHAPEL,** Jct. of SR 1102 and 1105, 1837. Brick, stuccoed; 1 story, modified rectangle, gabled roof with stepped ends and rising pilasters articulating end bays, small square frame belfry, center W entrance recessed under pointed arch, pointed arched entry with double doors surmounted by tripartite tracery window and doors set in reveals, side pointed arched tracery windows; S side shed addition; restoration in process, will raise belfry to original height. Gothic Revival. *Private.*

Historical Places

Middletown vicinity. **CEDAR CREEK BAT-TLEFIELD AND BELLE GROVE,** On I 81 between Middletown and Strasburg (also in Warren County), c. 1790. Stone, 1 1/2 stories, rectangular, hipped roof, 4 tall stone interior chimneys, quoins, windows with splayed lintels and keystones, later wings and front and rear pedimented entrance porticos. Georgian. Served as headquarters for Maj. Gen. Philip H. Sheridan during Battle of Cedar Creek, which gave the Union final control over the Shenandoah Valley. Battlefield contains trenches and earthworks. *County/private:* NHL; HABS.

FREDERICKSBURG (independent city)

FREDERICKSBURG HISTORIC DISTRICT, 18th–20th C.. Original downtown area containing commercial, government, transit, religious, and residential structures; features 1–2 1/2-story brick and frame 18th and 19th C. dwellings and the Fredericksburg Courthouse, by architect James Renwick. Chartered 1727; developed into important trading center, 1748, with establishment of ferry across Rappahannock River. *Multiple public/private:* HABS; G.

KENMORE, 1201 Washington Ave., Mid-18th C.. Brick (Flemish bond), 2 stories, rectangular, gabled roof with jerkinhead ends, 4 interior end chimneys, modillion cornice, center 1-story pedimented Doric entrance portico, magnificent plasterwork, retains mostly original paneling and woodwork. Restored. Georgian. Revolutionary patriot Fielding Lewis built Kenmore for his bride, Betty Washington, sister of George Washington. *Private:* NHL; HABS.

MONROE LAW OFFICE, 908 Charles St., 1758. Brick, 1 1/2 stories, rectangular, gabled roof and dormers, interior end chimneys, 2 front entrances, some original furnishings, 1961 rear library ell. James Monroe's Law office (1786–1789) between his service in the Congress of the Confederation and his return to public life as a U.S. senator and later 5th U.S. President. *State:* NHL.

RISING SUN TAVERN, 1306 Caroline St., 1760, Charles Washington, builder. Frame, clapboarding, horizontal flush boarding; 1 1/2 stories, rectangular, gabled roof, pedimented dormers, 2 interior end chimneys, pedimented center entrance, later rear addition, restored 1956. Colonial elements. Important political and social meetingplace; bill which later became Thomas Jefferson's Statute of Virginia for Religious Liberty outlined here; site of the 1781 Peace Ball, celebrating the victory at Yorktown. *Private:* NHL; HABS.

GLOUCESTER COUNTY

Gloucester. **GLOUCESTER COUNTY COURTHOUSE SQUARE HISTORIC DISTRICT,** 18th–20th C.. Contains numerous civic, commercial, and private buildings on and bordering square. Wide variety of mid-18th C.–mid-20th C. styles represented. Notable are the brick Greek Revival and the 2-story Botetourt Hotel with slate-shingled gabled roof, restored for office use (1968). Typical of early VA county seat complexes. *Multiple public/private:* HABS.

Gloucester. **GLOUCESTER WOMEN'S CLUB (LONG BRIDGE ORDINARY),** On U.S. 17, Mid-18th C.. Frame, clapboarding; 1 1/2 stories, rectangular, gabled roof with dormers, exterior end chimney, 1st-story SE gallery with wooden railing supported on basement piers. High masonry basement on W, extensive later

Historical Places

additions and alterations, 19th C. lean-to additions. Much original paneling, roof framing, and batten doors. Colonial elements. 18th and 19th C. commercial building; purchased by Gloucester Woman's Club, 1919. *Private:* HABS.

Gloucester vicinity. **ABINGDON GLEBE HOUSE,** S of jct. of U.S. 17 and VA 615, Early-18th C.. Brick, painted; 1 1/2 stories, T-shaped, high-pitched gabled roof with dormers, 1 interior and 2 exterior end chimneys, flanking 1-story hipped pavilion on each end; rear ell added soon after construction. One of the few early glebe houses remaining in VA. *Private; not accessible to the public:* HABS.

Gloucester vicinity. **LITTLE ENGLAND,** E of Gloucester on VA 672, 18th C., attributed to John Ariss, architect. Brick, 2 1/2 stories, modified L shape, gabled roof, interior end chimneys, gabled dormers, modillion cornice, center front entrance with transom, raised entrance platform with railing, belt course, flat arches over windows; elaborate interior paneling; restored; center 1-story frame wing moved N, 1939; 1 1/2-story S frame wing added, 1954; formal gardens. Well-preserved example of Georgian plantation house. *Private:* HABS.

Gloucester vicinity. **REED, WALTER, BIRTHPLACE,** SW of Gloucester at jct. of VA 614 and 616, 19th C.. Frame, weatherboarding; 1 1/2 stories, rectangular with rear shed addition, steeply gabled roof, 2 exterior chimneys, center entrance with window on either side, 1-room main interior section, attic, shed room; restored. Birthplace of Walter Reed who discovered the cause of yellow fever in 1851. *Private:* HABS.

Gloucester vicinity. **ROARING SPRING,** 0.3 mi. E of VA 616, 18th C.. Frame, clapboarding; 1 1/2 stories, rectangular; gambrel roof, partially shingled; interior end chimneys, gabled dormers, slightly off-center front entrance with hipped porch on paneled posts; handsome paneled interior end wall with fireplace on 1st floor, elaborate stairway; built in 2 sections; 19th C. renovations, front doorway and porch addition; smokehouse. *Private; not accessible to the public.*

Gloucester vicinity. **ROSEWELL,** W of Carter Creek, SE of VA 644, c. 1725-1744. Remains of wall sections of early 3-story brick dwelling, one of the state's largest and finest colonial mansions; burned, 1916. Home of John Page, U.S. congressman (1789-1797) and VA governor (1802-1805). *Private; not accessible to the public:* HABS.

Gloucester vicinity. **TODDSBURY,** E of jct. of Rtes. 662 and 14, 17th-18th C.. Brick, stuccoed; 2 stories, cross shaped, gambrel roof with gabled dormers, gabled roof section, interior end chimneys, porch; later additions include gabled kitchen and hyphen. Colonial elements. Home of Thomas Todd, Gloucester justice of the peace. *Private; not accessible to the public:* HABS.

Gloucester vicinity. **WARE PARISH CHURCH,** NE of Gloucester on VA 14, 1715. Brick (Flemish bond with glazed headers), 1 story, rectangular, steeply gabled roof, modillion cornice; center entrance in gable end with pilasters and molded brick archivolt, oculus above; pedimented side entrances, large round arched windows, molded brick water table; remodeled 1854. Georgian. Among earliest churches in the state, with original entrances unaltered. *Private:* HABS.

Naxera vicinity. **LANDS END,** SE of Naxera on VA 614, 1796-1800. Brick (Flemish bond), 2 stories over high basement, L-shaped, gambrel

Historical Places

roof, interior end chimneys, gabled dormers, center basement and 1st-story entrance, small gabled entrance porch supported by brick screened-in block; 1840's 1-story frame section incorporated in rear 2 1/2-story brick veneer addition, 1927. Colonial elements. Home of Revolutionary War sea captain, John Sinclair. *Private; not accessible to the public.*

Ware Neck vicinity. **LOWLAND COTTAGE,** SW of Ware Neck, 0.5 mi. S of VA 623, 17th C.. Frame, clapboarding; 1 1/2 stories, modified rectangle, gambrel roof, gabled dormers, 2 exterior end and interior chimneys, center entrance with 3-light transom, side gabled wing with shed porch; rear and side wing added, c. 1800; remodeled, 1854; restored, 1935. Colonial elements. Built by Robert Bristow, prosperous merchant and planter; one of few frame 17th C. structures remaining in VA. *Private.*

White Marsh vicinity. **ABINGDON CHURCH,** U.S. 17, S of jct. with VA 614, c. 1755. Brick (Flemish bond), 1 story, Latin cross shape, gabled roof, modillion cornice and eaves, 3 original doorways framed by rubbed and molded brick designs; round arched windows, original wooden reredos and transept galleries; altered, mid-19th C. Georgian. *Private:* HABS.

White Marsh vicinity. **FAIRFIELD SITE,** W of White Marsh near jct. of VA 633 and 614, 1692. Site of plantation reputedly built by Lewis Burwell, member of governor's council. Inherited by grandson Lewis, president of the council and acting VA governor. aboveground remains. *Private; not accessible to the public.*

GOOCHLAND COUNTY

CARTERSVILLE BRIDGE, *Reference—see Cumberland County*

385

Cedar Point. **LOCK-KEEPER'S HOUSE,** Off VA 6 at James River, c. 1836. Frame, clapboarding; 2 stories built into hillside on full stone basement, rectangular, gabled roof, central chimney, main entrance on basement level, 2nd-story full-width shed porch above front basement section. Last remaining lock-keeper's house of the James River and Kanawaha Canal system; ceased operation after acquisition by the railroad. *Private; not accessible to the public.*

Goochland. **GOOCHLAND COUNTY COURT SQUARE,** On VA 6, 19th C.. Complex arranged around brick, 2-story, gabled roof courthouse (1826) with full-height pedimented tetrastyle Tuscan portico. Jeffersonian Classicism. Enclosed by original brick wall, the square includes a 2-story, hipped stone jail (1848); a 1-story brick clerk's office; and a Confederate monument. *County:* HABS.

Goochland vicinity. **BOLLING HALL,** W of Goochland off VA 600, 18th C.. Frame, clapboarding; 1–2 stories, modified rectangle, gabled roof sections, interior chimneys, box cornice, front center entrance with transom and 1-story classical portico, small off-center front entrance with portico; interior Georgian paneling; many 19th C. additions and alterations; 1947 renovation. Home of William Bolling, who donated property for school for the education of the deaf. *Private.*

Manakin vicinity. **POWELL'S TAVERN,** On VA 650, 18th–19th C.. Two connected structures—frame, clapboarding, brick; 2–2 1/2 stories, H-shaped, gabled roof sections with shed wings, exterior and interior end chimneys, center front entrance with Tuscan portico, center rear and side entrances with gabled porches on posts; late-18th C. frame structure; c. 1815 shed wings; frame structure connected

Historical Places

to 1820 brick structure by 2-story frame hyphen, 1958. Federal elements. Operated as tavern from 1808 on road between Richmond and Charlottesville. *Private; not accessible to the public:* HABS.

Manakin vicinity. **TUCKAHOE,** SE of Manakin near jct. of Rtes. 650 and 647, Early-18th C.. Frame, clapboarding, brick on S wing end; 2 stories, H-shaped, gabled roof, exterior and interior end chimneys, prominent modillion cornice, center pedimented entrance porch, much original interior woodwork. Several outbuildings. Georgian and Federal elements. Built by Thomas Randolph; early home of Thomas Jefferson. *Private; not accessible to the public.*

Oilville vicinity. **WOODLAWN,** SE of Oilville at jct. of VA 250 and VA 612, Late-18th C.. Brick, 2 stories, modified rectangle, gabled roof, paired exterior end chimneys with 2-story pent connection between, denticulated cornice and bargeboards, front center entrance with transom and hipped porch with Ionic columns and Chippendale railing, stuccoed lintels over front and rear windows; interior paneling; front entrance porch added, 1810; 1-story frame side kitchen and rear porch added during 1937 restoration. Federal elements. Associated with prominent local families. *Private; not accessible to the public.*

Pemberton vicinity. **HOWARD'S NECK PLANTATION,** 1 mi. NW of Pemberton, c. 1825. Brick, 2 stories, rectangular, hipped roof with deck, interior end chimneys, mutule cornice, center entrance with transom, small pedimented Tuscan portico; interior spiral staircase and marble mantels. Unusually complete set of outbuildings include 1-story frame house, possibly 18th C.; early-19th C. brick kitchen, log slave quarters, and carriage houses. Jeffersonian Classicism. Well-preserved VA plantation; locally attributed to Robert Mills. *Private; not accessible to the public.*

Rock Castle vicinity. **ROCK CASTLE,** Rte. 600, c. 1732. Frame, clapboarding; 1 1/2 stories, rectangular, gabled roof with jerkinhead ends, pedimented dormers, 2 interior end chimneys, prominent modillion cornice, center entrance with 8-panel door flanked by similar panels, exquisitely paneled interior. Moved to nearby site in 1935. Colonial elements. Purchased, 1843, by John Rutherfoord, state governor, 1841–1842. *Private; not accessible to the public.*

GRAYSON COUNTY

Trout Dale vicinity. **RIPSHIN,** 0.1 mi. NE of jct. of VA 603 and 732, 1927, William Spratling, architect. Random fieldstone, log construction; 1 1/2 stories, U-shaped, gabled roof sections, interior chimneys, front center entrance, glassed rear porch between log wings; irregular fenestration; 2 guest cottages, log cabin for writing. Home of noted American author Sherwood Anderson. *Private; not accessible to the public:* NHL.

GREENE COUNTY

Stanardsville. **GREENE COUNTY COURTHOUSE,** S of jct. of U.S. 33 and VA 649, 1839. Brick (Flemish bond), 2 stories, rectangular, gabled roof, central cupola, pilasters, dividing front bays. Full-height tetrastyle Tuscan portico, added 1928. Greek Revival elements. Flanked by county jail and clerk's office. *County.*

Stanardsville vicinity. **OCTONIA STONE,** N of Stanardsville, off VA 637, c. 1721. Granite-

Historical Places

type rock, part of natural outcropping with engraving of a figure 8 with a cross touching the top. Unusual early use of inscribed stone to mark the terminus of the W boundary of the 1722 Octonia Grant made by Lt. Gov. Alexander Spotswood to 8 prominent Virginians. *Private; not accessible to the public.*

HALIFAX COUNTY

Ingram vicinity. **CARTER'S TAVERN,** SE of Ingram, c. 1773. Frame, clapboarding; 2 1/2 stories, rectangular, gabled roof, paired exterior end chimneys, off-center door with transom, earlier 1 1/2-story side wing with full-width shed porch; much original interior woodwork; restored, 1972. Federal. Built by Joseph Dodson; enlarged c. 1807 by Samuel Carter; important stage stop on main road from New York to New Orleans. *Private; not accessible to the public.*

South Boston vicinity. **BERRY HILL,** S of jct. of Rtes. 659 and 682, c. 1839. Brick, stuccoed; 2 stories, rectangular, gabled roof, 4 interior side chimneys, full-width Doric pedimented portico with 8 fluted columns. Identical flanking 1-story outbuildings with tetrastyle Doric pedimented porticos. Greek Revival. *Private; not accessible to the public:* HABS.

HAMPTON (independent city)

CHESTERVILLE PLANTATION SITE, On Langley NASA Research Center, 17th–18th C.. Site of 2-story mansion includes brick ruins, a ballast stone and brick kiln foundation, and a cemetery. Purchased, 1692, by Thomas Wythe. Reputedly the birthplace of George Wythe, signer of the Declaration of Independence, and prominent legal educator. Destroyed by fire, 1911. *Federal/NASA*

Encyclopedia of Virginia

FORT MONROE, Old Point Comfort, 1819–1834, General Simon Bernard, designer. Brick fort of 40 acres within modern army fort; 3 casemates restored as museum exhibitions; anchoring place of the U.S. fleet. One of the few Union forts in the South not captured by the Confederates; strategically important because of proximity to C.S.A. capital. Overlooks site of nearby battle between the U.S.S. *Monitor* and the C.S.S. *Virginia* (*Merrimack*), the first confrontation of ironclad ships. Confederate President Jefferson Davis was imprisoned here after the Civil War. *Federal/USA:* NHL.

FORT WOOL, Island between Willoughby Spit and Old Point Comfort, 19th C.. Fort remains including granite walls, original ramparts, and batteries dating from the Civil War and WWI and WWII towers. Most of the original wall passages, powder and storage rooms, guncrew shelters, and lower tier gun positions remain. Built as Fort Calhoun as part of coastal fortification plan; renamed during Civil War. *State; not accessible to the public.*

HAMPTON INSTITUTE, NW of jct. of U.S. 60 and the Hampton Roads Bridge Tunnel, 19th C.. Academic institution on 200 acres, contains over 100 structures including Richard Morris Hunt's Virginia Hall and Academic Hall, and J. C. Cady's Memorial Church. As a post-Civil War gathering place for freed slaves under the protection of the Union Army, Hampton became the location of a school for teaching and training freedmen. Opened in 1868 under guidance of Samuel Chapman Armstrong, chief of the local Freedmen's Bureau; chartered as a normal and industrial institute, 1870; received college accreditation, 1932–1933. Famous alumni includes Booker T. Washington. *Private:* NHL.

Historical Places

HERBERT HOUSE, E end of Marina Rd. on Hampton Creek, 1753. Brick (Flemish bond), 2 stories, U-shaped, gabled roof sections, interior end chimneys, center entrance, later 2-story portico with upper level enclosed, flat arched windows, belt course; 19th C. frame wing added to rear ell. Georgian elements. Oldest house in Hampton; here the empaled head of Blackbeard was posted as a warning to other pirates. *Private; not accessible to the public.*

OLD POINT COMFORT LIGHTHOUSE, Fenwick Rd., SW of E gate of Fort Monroe, 1802. Ashlar, 47'-high tapered tower, octagonal, glass and metal cupola, 4 windows; interior stone spiral stair; c. 1900 2-story frame lightkeeper's house nearby. Guides ships entering Hampton Roads; still in use. *Federal/USCG; not accessible to the public.*

ST. JOHN'S CHURCH, NW corner of W. Queen and Court Sts., c. 1728. Brick (Flemish bond), 1 story, Latin cross shape, gabled roof, rubbed brick around windows and at corners, round arched windows, entrances covered by modern vestibules, 1901 tower. Cemetery. Burned during the Civil War, only the walls are original. Serves the oldest active parish of the Anglican Church in America. *Private;* G.

HANOVER COUNTY

Ashland vicinity. **FORK CHURCH,** At jct. of Rtes. 738 and 685, c. 1736–1740. Brick (Flemish bond), 1 story, rectangular, gabled roof, modillion cornice; rubbed brick at jambs, window arches, and corners; segmental arched windows. Small pedimented entrance porches added later. Original gallery largely intact. Typical VA colonial church. Services attended by notables such as Patrick Henry, Dolley Madison, and novelist Thomas Nelson Page. *Private;* HABS.

Ashland vicinity. **HICKORY HILL,** E of Ashland off VA 646, 19th C.. Plantation complex containing large brick dwelling (1875) with a 2-story front center pedimented portico with paneled piers, matching 1-story frame kitchen and office buildings (1820's), smokehouse, greenhouse, Gothic Revival cottage, frame dovecote, and extensive woods and formal gardens and lawns. Original frame plantation house (1820) and gardens planned by William and Anne Butler Carter Wickham, later home of prominent VA military leader, statesman, and businessman, Gen. Williams Carter Wickham; remains in Wickham family. *Private; not accessible to the public.*

Ashland vicinity. **SCOTCHTOWN (PATRICK HENRY HOUSE),** 10 mi. NW of Ashland on VA 685, c. 1719. Frame, clapboarding; 1 1/2 stories, rectangular, gabled roof with jerkinhead ends, large interior chimneys, denticulated cornice, small center entrance porch with fanlight in the pediment; restored, 1953. Outbuildings. Federal. Home of Revolutionary War leader and state's first governor, Patrick Henry, from 1771 to 1777. *Private:* NHL; HABS.

Ashland vicinity. **SLASH CHURCH,** VA 656, N of jct. with VA 657, 1729, Thomas Pinchbeck and Edward Chambers, builders. Frame, clapboarding; 1 1/2 stories, rectangular, steeply gabled roof, modillion cornice, double-door entrance in gable end and sides; recent 2-story side block connected by gallery; restored, 1970's. Colonial elements. One of small number of frame colonial churches in state; served as hospital during Civil War. *Private.*

Hanover. **HANOVER COUNTY COURTHOUSE HISTORIC DISTRICT,** 18th–20th C.. Historic core of village; contains c. 1735 Hanover County Courthouse (see also Hanover County Courthouse, VA), c. 1835 jail (renovated 1916), c. 1835 clerk's office, and 18th C. Hanover Tavern, a frame 2-story building with exterior and interior end chimneys, full-width front shed porch, and 2-story wing. Courthouse community in little altered surroundings. Patrick Henry first distinguished himself as an orator here, pleading the Parson's Cause, 1763. *Multiple public/private:* HABS.

Hanover Court House. **HANOVER COUNTY COURTHOUSE,** Jct. of Rte. 1006 and U.S. 301, c. 1735. Brick (Flemish bond), 1 story, T-shaped, steeply hipped roof, 3 interior end chimneys, modillion cornice; front arcade with 5 openings, each with rubbed brick trim; front center double-door entrance with transom. Well-preserved example of Georgian courthouse. Scene of Patrick Henry's first well-known case, the Parson's Cause. *County:* NHL; HABS.

Mechanicsville vicinity. **HANOVER TOWN,** NE of Mechanicsville off VA 605, 18th C.. Site of 18th C. port village; contains remains beneath unexcavated plow zone, including domestic and commercial structures situated alongside 2 earlier tobacco warehouses. Village's early demise enhances potential for archeological study. Map drawn by French cartographer during encampment of Rochambeau's troops (1782) survives as only early picture of village. *Multiple private.*

Montpelier. **SYCAMORE TAVERN,** W of U.S. 33, Late-18th C.. Frame, clapboarding; 1 1/2 stories, rectangular, gabled roof with shed extensions, exterior end chimneys, full-width balustraded front porch under roof extension supported by square wooden posts. Colonial elements. Built as a tavern and stagecoach stop. Donated as county library by VA author Thomas Nelson Page, early-20th C. *County.*

Montpelier vicinity. **OAKLAND,** N of Montpelier, c. 1898. Frame, clapboarding; 1 1/2- and 2 1/2-story sections, modified L shape, gabled roof sections, dormers, porches. Rebuilt on lines of original 1812 house following fire in 1898. Federal elements. Home of Thomas Nelson Page, popular VA author of late-19th and early-20th C., and later ambassador to Italy. *Private; not accessible to the public:* HABS.

Richmond vicinity. **RICHMOND NATIONAL BATTLEFIELD PARK,** E of Richmond (also in Henrico County and Richmond), 1862–1865. Portions of several battlefields and other sites associated with Union attempt to capture Confederate capital, including Seven Days Battles sites (June 25–July 1, 1862), and Cold Harbor (May 31–June 12, 1864) in which Grant's assault was repulsed with heavy losses. Richmond fell, Apr. 3, 1865, after evacuation of Petersburg (see also Petersburg National Battlefield, VA), and shortly before Confederate surrender at Appomattox (see also Appomattox Court House National Historical Park, VA). *Federal/NPS:* HABS.

Richmond vicinity. **RUFFIN, EDMUND, PLANTATION (MARLBOURNE),** 11 mi. NE of Richmond on U.S. 360, 1843. Frame, clapboarding; 2 1/2 stories, irregular shape, gabled roof sections, exterior end chimneys, modillion cornice, 2-tier entrance porch, later additions, numerous outbuildings. Greek Revival elements. Home of Edmund Ruffin, southern agricultural reformist and secessionist who established this plantation for farming experimentation. *Private; not accessible to the public:* NHL.

Historical Places

HARRISONBURG (independent city)

HARRISON, THOMAS, HOUSE, 30 W. Bruce St., c. 1750. Limestone, 1 1/2 stories, rectangular, gabled roof with dormers, interior end chimney, flat arched windows, molded box cornice with short returns. Oldest house in Harrisonburg; built by Thomas Harrison, major landowner and city founder. Scene of first courts after town became county seat. *Private.*

MORRISON HOUSE, W. Market and N. Liberty Sts., c. 1820–1824. Brick (Flemish bond), 2 1/2 stories, L-shaped, gabled roof, interior end chimneys, center entrance with transom, flat arched windows; interior open string stair to attic level; 1845 rear wing. Federal. Fine example of Shenandoah Valley town house of period; ell served as post office, later as tavern. *Private; not accessible to the public.*

HENRICO COUNTY

RICHMOND NATIONAL BATTLEFIELD PARK, *Reference—see Hanover County*

Dutch Gap vicinity. **HENRICO,** Farrar Island, 1611–1624. Site of the town of Henrico constructed in 1611 by the Virginia Company as part of a plan by Thomas Dale to relocate the Virginia colony from Jamestown to a more defensible and healthy location further up the James River. Revocation of the Virginia Company's charter in 1624 resulted in loss of support for the settlement which was subsequently abandoned. Unexcavated. *Multiple private.*

Glen Allen. **RANDOLPH, VIRGINIA E., COTTAGE,** 2200 Mountain Rd., 1937. Brick, 1 1/2 stories, rectangular, gabled roof, interior chimney, gabled dormers, front center entrance. Built as home economics building of the Virginia Randolph Training School; named for the black teacher who, as the first Jeanes teacher, worked to upgrade vocational training for blacks. Museum. *County:* NHL.

Glen Allen vicinity. **MEADOW FARM,** Mountain and Courtney Rds., Late-18th C.. Frame, clapboarding; 1 1/2 stories, modified L shape, gabled roof, exterior end chimneys, gabled dormers, small hipped center entrance portico, E shed wing, rear wing with 2-story E addition. Home of Mosby Sheppard, first planter to learn of the plot to capture Richmond, instigated by the slave Gabriel in 1800. Sheppard's report to Gov. James Monroe prevented the insurrection, resulted in the execution of many slaves, and increased the atmosphere of fear and distrust among slaveholders throughout the South. *Private; not accessible to the public.*

Richmond vicinity. **FLOOD MARKER OF 1771,** 0.8 mi. SE of jct. of VA 5 and VA 156, 1771–1772. 18'-high stone obelisk set on 6'-sq. base, 20th C. restoration; inscriptions include one to memorialize Richard and Jane Randolph, prominent area residents. Traditionally thought to designate high-water mark of May 1771 flood, state's worst natural disaster until that time. *Private; not accessible to the public.*

Richmond vicinity. **JAMES RIVER AND KANAWHA CANAL HISTORIC DISTRICT,** Extends from Ship Locks to Bosher's Dam (also in Richmond city), 1840. Richmond vicinity section of canal containing earthen excavations, stone locks, bridges, culverts, basins, and towpaths. Canal completed 1840 by James River and Kanawha Co. from Richmond to Lynchburg, later extended to Buchanan; included Tidewater Connection of 5 stone locks, now partially destroyed, to connect Piedmont and Tidewater Virginia. Mid-19th C. commercial importance of canal waned with growth of railroads and with Civil War destruction. *Multiple public/private:* HAER.

Richmond vicinity. **MALVERN HILL,** SE of jct. of Rtes. 5 and 156, 17th C.. Destroyed by fire (c. 1905), only end wall and chimney survive, contains excellent example of 17th C. diaper brickwork. Original 1 1/2-story, gabled structure in cruciform plan. Built by Thomas Cocke, high sheriff of Henrico and member of the House of Burgesses. Property involved in at least 3 Civil War occasions, the last being the battle between Gens. Lee and McClellan, July 1, 1862, which temporarily removed Union threat to Confederate capital of Richmond. *Private:* HABS.

Richmond vicinity. **TREE HILL,** VA 5, Late-18th C.. Frame, clapboarding; 2 stories, rectangular, gabled roof, 4 semiexterior end chimneys, 2-story screened tetrastyle portico, lunette in pediment, flanking 1-story wings, rear shed porch; separate kitchen. Greek Revival. Home of U.S. congressman and senator, William Roane. *Private; not accessible to the public.*

Tuckahoe vicinity. **WOODSIDE,** SW of Tuckahoe off VA 157, 1858. Brick, stuccoed; 2 1/2 stories, rectangular, gabled roof, 4 interior chimneys, full-width entrance porch with flanking floor-length windows, rear 1 1/2-story addition, central hall plan, original black marble mantel in NE room. Several outbuildings. Built for Littleton Waller Tazewall Wickham, son of John Wickham, a defender of Aaron Burr in his treason case. *Private; not accessible to the public.*

Encyclopedia of Virginia

HENRY COUNTY

Martinsville vicinity. **MARTINSVILLE FISH DAM**, Off U.S. 220, S of Martinsville in Smith River, Prehistoric (c. 1300). Stone pile wall with V-shaped layout, original opening now filled with stones. Fish trap probably associated with nearby prehistoric Indian village. *Private*.

Ridgway vicinity. **BELLEVIEW**, S of VA 641, 1783. Frame, clapboarding; 2 stories, U-shaped, gabled roof, exterior end chimneys, pedimented and balustraded 2-story center entrance portico with Ionic columns, fanlighted entrances, later rear additions; renovated, 1950's; fine interior detail. Notable example of late-18th C. plantation architecture with classical detail. Built for early settler Maj. John Redd; home of state Supreme Court Justice Kennon C. Whittle. *Private; not accessible to the public.*

HIGHLAND COUNTY

Monterey. **MONTEREY HOTEL**, Main St. (U.S. 250), 1904. Frame, clapboarding; 3 1/2 stories, L-shaped, hipped roof with 1/2-story gabled dormers, 2 interior chimneys, full-width 2-story porch with turned posts and elaborately carved frieze and balustrade, off-center main entrance with transom. Eastlake elements. Built for S. W. Crummett of Staunton. Prominent hotel during period of fashionable mountain resorts, instrumental in economic growth of area; guests included Harvey Firestone and Henry Ford. *Private.*

HOPEWELL (independent city)

APPOMATTOX MANOR, Cedar Lane, at confluence of James and Appomattox rivers, 18th C.. Frame, clapboarding; 1 1/2 stories, modified rectangle, gabled roof with pedi-

Historical Places

mented dormers, exterior end and interior chimneys, center entrance with pedimented overhang above and flat roofed porch, 1-story latticework side porch, central hall plan. Several outbuildings. Colonial elements. Property owned by the Eppes family since 1635; house served as headquarters for Gen. Ulysses S. Grant from June 1864 to Apr. 1865. *Private; not accessible to the public:* HABS.

WESTON MANOR, Off VA 10 on S bank of Appomattox River, c. 1780's. Frame, clapboarding; 2 stories, rectangular, hipped roof, paired interior end chimneys with corbeled caps, modillion cornice, center front entrance with transom and gabled porch with posts; original interior mantels and detailing; riverfront porch altered; under restoration. Example of late Georgian frame plantation house. *Private; not accessible to the public:* G.

ISLE OF WIGHT COUNTY

Isle of Wight. **BOYKIN'S TAVERN,** W of U.S. 258, 1780. Frame, clapboarding, end walls of lower floor brick; 2 1/2 stories, gabled and gambrel roofed sections, 4 exterior end chimneys on main block, projecting pedimented 2-story front porch with slender columns, rear gambrel roof ell and upper story of main block from 19th C. Altered and remodeled, early-20th C. Federal elements. *County.*

Smithfield. **OLD ISLE OF WIGHT COURTHOUSE,** NE corner of Main and Mason Sts., Mid-18th C.. Brick (Flemish bond), 1 story, modified T shape, hipped roof, 2 interior end chimneys, modillion cornice, rear center circular apse, full-width front arcaded porch. Federal doorway dating from 1812 alteration. Detached brick jail and clerk's office. Colonial elements. *Private:* HABS.

Smithfield. **SMITHFIELD HISTORIC DISTRICT,** 18th–20th C.. One of the best preserved and most picturesque of prosperous colonial seaport towns in VA. Contains balance of architectural styles from 1750 to the present; predominantly 19th C. residential district with some modern structures interspersed within small commercial district. World famous for production of ham; one packing house in business since c. 1779. *Multiple public/private:* HABS.

Smithfield vicinity. **ST. LUKE'S CHURCH,** 4 mi. S of Smithfield on VA 10, 1632. Brick (Flemish bond), 1 story, rectangular, gabled roof with gabled step ends, buttresses, 3-story tower with pyramidal roof, some original molded brick mullions, paired lancet windows in round arched openings, gable end large tracery window, detached pediment above main entrance. Restored. Medieval colonial elements. *Private:* NHL; HABS.

Smithfield vicinity. **WOLFTRAP FARM,** NW of Smithfield off VA 627, 1920's. Frame, clapboarding; 2 1/2 stories, L-shaped, steeply gabled roof, 4 exterior end chimneys, 2 rows of symmetrically-placed dormers; full-width front shed porch and rear porch later additions. Only known example of early VA farmhouse with double tier of dormer windows. *Private; not accessible to the public.*

JAMES CITY COUNTY

Five Forks vicinity. **POWHATAN,** N of jct. of Rtes. 615 and 5, 18th C., Attributed to Richard Taliaferro, builder-architect. Brick (Flemish bond), 2 1/2 stories, rectangular, steeply hipped roof, 2 tall interior end chimneys. Gutted by fire during the Civil War, only the

Historical Places

masonry portions are original. Restored. Georgian. Home of Richard Taliaferro, prominent area builder-architect. *Private; not accessible to the public:* HABS.

Jamestown. **JAMESTOWN NATIONAL HISTORIC SITE,** Jamestown Island, 1607. Portion of site of the oldest permanent English settlement in America contains the church tower, the settlement's only 17th C. structure still standing; a 1907 memorial church built on the site of an earlier church; foundations of a church, dwellings, and 2 statehouses; and 18th and 19th C. structures including a plantation house and remains of a Confederate fort. Principal VA town and colonial capital until 1700; among those associated with early history are Capt. John Smith, John Rolfe and his wife Pocahontas, and Lord De La Warr. Museum. *Private:* HABS.

Jamestown and vicinity. **COLONIAL NATIONAL HISTORICAL PARK,** VA 359 (also in York County), 17th–18th C.. Includes site and ruins of Jamestown, first permanent English settlement in New World, and Yorktown and Yorktown Battlefield, where Americans aided by French under Rochambeau, Lafayette, and Adm. de Grasse fought the last important conflict of the War for Independence, forcing Cornwallis' surrender to Gen. Washington, Aug. 30–Oct. 19, 1781. *Federal/NPS/nonfederal.*

Lightfoot vicinity. **PINEWOODS (WARBURTON HOUSE)**, 1.4 mi. SW of jct. of VA 613 and 614, Late-17th C.. Brick, 1 1/2 stories, L-shaped, gabled roof; T-shaped interior end chimneys with corbeled caps, set into jerkinhead roof ends; gabled dormers, front center entrance with full-width screened porch, rear porch; rebuilt after fire destroyed all but brick portions. Georgian elements. Example of 17th C. planter's house. *Private:* HABS.

Toano vicinity. **HICKORY NECK CHURCH**, N of Toano on U.S. 60, 18th C.. Brick, 1 story, rectangular, gabled roof, interior end chimney, later brick entrance porch and vestry. Present structure is fragment of original colonial church—N part is 1773-1774 extension, S bay is c. 1825 alteration. *Private:* HABS.

Toano vicinity. **STONE HOUSE SITE,** NE of Toano, off VA 600, 17th C.. Foundation remains indicate rectangular structure of solid stone construction, unusual for area; form and location indicate use as defensive outpost. Unexcavated. *Private; not accessible to the public.*

Williamsburg vicinity. **CARTER'S GROVE,** SE of jct. of Rte. 667 and U.S. 60, Mid-18th C.. Brick (Flemish bond), 2 1/2-story main block with 1 1/2-story symmetrical wings, hipped roof and dormers, interior and interior end chimneys, modillion cornice. Gabled wings connected by smaller hyphens. Magnificent interior woodwork. Altered, 1927-1928. Excellent 5-part Georgian country house. *Private:* HABS.

Williamsburg vicinity. **GOVERNOR'S LAND ARCHEOLOGICAL DISTRICT,** W of Williamsburg, 17th-18th C.. Area contains a concentration of 18 known structure sites dating from the 17th and 18th C. and the 17th C. road connecting Green Spring with Jamestown. Green Spring excavated by National Park Service (1954-1955). *Multiple public/private; not accessible to the public.*

Williamsburg vicinity. **KINGSMILL PLANTATION,** 5 mi. S of Williamsburg, c. 1736. Remains of early brick plantation complex; includes mansion foundations and cellar and brick 1 1/2-story rectangular office and kitchen, each with gabled roof, flat arched windows, and interior end chimneys. Dependencies originally placed in front of main building at right angles form U-shaped complex with formal forecourt. 1782 map locates outbuildings to reveal nearby landing site important in 18th C. local economy. Excellent example of early colonial plantation complex. *Private:* HABS.

KING AND QUEEN COUNTY

Aylett vicinity. **HOLLY HILL,** NE of Aylett off U.S. 360, Early-19th C.. Brick (Flemish bond), 2 stories, L-shaped, hipped roof; 3 interior end chimneys, modillion cornice, simple 1-bay gabled entrance porch with iron balustrade. Exceptional interior woodwork. Georgian. *Private; not accessible to the public.*

Cumnor vicinity. **MATTAPONI CHURCH,** 0.5 mi. S of Cumnor off VA 14, 1730–1734, c. 1755. Brick, 1 1/2 stories, Latin cross shape, cross-gable roof, N transept end chimneys, box cornice, rubbed brick at corners and surrounding round arched windows, nave with double-door entrance and fanlight set under segmental brick arch; transept entrances, each with brick pediments; interior galleries in nave and transept ends; interior renovation 1922, chimneys added. Excellent example of Georgian ecclesiastical architecture. *Private.*

Shanghai vicinity. **UPPER CHURCH, STRATTON MAJOR PARISH,** SE of Shanghai on VA 14, 1724–1729. Brick, 1 story, modified rectangle, gabled roof sections, interior chimneys, box cornice, off-center side S entrance with brick pediment, original W entrance set under segmental arch now obscured by brick structure and forms interior doorway to gabled addition; round arched side windows and circular gable windows, both with colored glass; gauged brick window and door trim, rubbed brick at corners. Example of Georgian ecclesiastical structure. *Private.*

Walkerton vicinity. **HILLSBOROUGH,** 2 mi. SE of Walkerton off SR 633, Mid-18th C.. Frame, clapboarding, brick end walls; 2 stories, modified rectangle, hipped roof, paired tapered interior end chimneys, modillion cornice, center entrance with small pedimented porch; fine interior staircase; entrance porch, 2-story side frame wing, entrance porch, and rear screened porch added; outbuildings include frame smokehouse and 1 1/2-story brick storehouse. Georgian elements. *Private; not accessible to the public:* HABS.

KING GEORGE COUNTY

Comorn vicinity. **MARMION,** NE of jct. of Rtes. 649 and 609, 18th C.. Frame, clapboarding; 2 stories, rectangular, gabled roof with jerkinhead ends, 2 interior end chimneys with exposed shafts, modillion cornice, fine interior trim. Full-width 1-story front shed porch and N wing are later additions. House sits in balanced quadrangle formed by the smokehouse, dairy, kitchen, and office. *Private; not accessible to the public:* HABS.

King George Court House vicinity. **NANZATICO,** S of jct. of Rtes. 650 and 625, c. 1770. Frame, clapboarding; 2 stories, rectangular, hipped roof, 2 interior end chimneys, dentil cornice, 3 center bays supporting gabled pediment are articulated by Ionic pilasters, center entrance; frame outbuildings. Excellent wooden interpretation of common brick style. *Private; not accessible to the public:* HABS.

Owens vicinity. **ST. PAUL'S CHURCH,** W of Owens off VA 206, 1766. Brick, 2 stories, Greek cross shape, hipped roof sections, interior chimney, modillion cornice, E and S entrances, segmental arched 1st-story windows, round arched 2nd-story windows, rubbed brick at corners and window jambs; E, S, and W interior galleries; restored and altered, 1813. One of few remaining Georgian churches with Greek cross format. *Private:* HABS.

Port Conway. **BELLE GROVE,** On U.S. 301, 1790–1796. Frame, clapboarding; 2-story hipped main block with 1-story pedimented wings connected by hyphens, some gabled roof sections, interior and interior end chimneys, modillion cornice; landfront center entrance with transom and side lights, full-width 2-story Doric portico, and convex corner entrances at wings, each with transom and side corbeled scrolls; riverfront center entrance with fanlight and side lights, 2-story center portico with Doric order below and Ionic order above with denticulated cornice; altered and enlarged after 1839; frame kitchen, brick smokehouse. Georgian and Greek Revival elements. Excellent example of local plantation house. *Private; not accessible to the public:* HABS.

Sealston vicinity. **LAMB'S CREEK CHURCH,** On VA 607, 1769–1770, attributed to John Ariss, builder-architect. Brick, 1 story, rectangular, hipped roof, modillion cornice; entrances at W end and S side, each with pediment; round arched windows with gauged brick trim, rubbed brick at corners; interior altered; repairs in 1908, 1939, and 1954. Fine example of Georgian ecclesiastical structure. *Private:* HABS.

KING WILLIAM COUNTY

King William. **KING WILLIAM COUNTY COURTHOUSE,** Rte. 619, off VA 30, c. 1725. Brick (Flemish bond), 1 story, T-shaped, steeply hipped roof, interior end chimneys, modillion cornice, open arcade extends across front. Colonial elements. Considered oldest courthouse still in use in U.S. *County:* HABS.

Mangohick. **MANGOHICK CHURCH,** VA 638, S of VA 30, c. 1730. Brick (Flemish bond), 1 1/2 stories, modified rectangle, gabled roof sections, interior chimney, modillion cornice; double-door entrances on end and side walls, each with transom; rubbed brick at corners and around openings, flat arches over side windows, segmental arches over end windows; interior gallery; recent rear addition with separate entrance. Colonial elements, influenced by late medieval European styles. *Private:* HABS.

Sweet Hall vicinity. **ST. JOHN'S CHURCH,** N of Sweet Hall on VA 30, 1734. Brick, 1 1/2 stories, T-shaped, intersecting gabled roof, W round arched entrance with segmental arched pediment, N entrance with triangular pediment, rubbed brick at corners and around openings, round arched 1st-floor windows, segmental and flat arched gable windows; interior galleries; wing added, 1755–1765. Fine example of T-shaped Georgian church. *Private:* HABS.

Tunstall vicinity. **ELSING GREEN,** SW of jct. of Rtes. 632 and 623, 18th–19th C.. Brick (Flemish bond), 2 stories, U-shaped, hipped roof, interior end chimneys, modillion cornice, belt course gauged brickwork. 1 1/2-story E dependency (c. 1690) was probably earlier than main house. Several outbuildings. Built by Carter Braxton, a signer of the Declaration of Independence. *Private; not accessible to the public:* HABS.

West Point vicinity. **CHELSEA,** N of jct. of Chelsea Rd. and Rte. 30, c. 1709. Brick (Flemish bond), 2 stories, T-shaped, hipped and gambrel roof sections, interior end chimneys, modillion cornice, 2-story pedimented front center portico, 1 1/2-story rear gambrel ell with pedimented dormers. Fine interior paneling. Georgian. Built by Augustine Moore, a prominent local planter. *Private; not accessible to the public:* HABS.

Historical Places

LANCASTER COUNTY

Kilmarnock vicinity. **CHRIST CHURCH**, 3 mi. S of Kilmarnock on VA 3, 1732. Brick (Flemish bond), 1 story, Greek cross shape, cross-hipped roof with splayed eaves, denticulated cornice, tall round arched windows, entrance set in pilastered frame with segmental arched pediment with oval window above. Exceptionally fine interior woodwork. Colonial elements. Built by Robert Carter who is buried here. *Private:* NHL; HABS.

Lancaster vicinity. **BELLE ISLE**, SW side of W end of VA 683, Mid-18th C.. Brick, 2-story rectangular hipped main block with 1-story gabled wings, interior end chimneys, modillion cornice, front center entrance with transom and 1-story pedimented Tuscan portico with railing, side wing entrance with transom, segmental arches over windows and side door, flat belt course; c. 1790 wings, 19th C. portico, 1940 restoration by Thomas T. Waterman included new 1st-floor woodwork; original woodwork installed in Winterthur Museum, Wilmington, DE (see also Winterthur Museum and Gardens, DE); 2 1-story brick outbuildings set perpendicular to house facade to form forecourt; handsome gardens. Georgian elements. Well-preserved example of Tidewater Virginia plantation complex. *Private; not accessible to the public:* HABS.

Lively vicinity. **ST. MARY'S WHITECHAPEL**, NW of jct. of Rtes. 354 and 201, 1740–1741.. Brick (Flemish bond), 1 story, rectangular, hipped roof, modillion cornice, round arched windows. Originally formed the transepts of a 1669 cruciform church; nave and chancel removed, 1832; only original interior trim is the S gallery. Colonial elements. *Private:* HABS.

Weems vicinity. **COROTOMAN,** Jct. of Rtes. 222 and 631, Early-18th C.. Site of dwelling of Robert "King" Carter, wealthy VA colonist. Destroyed by fire, 1729; ruins remain. Investigated by James Wharton (1930's) and later by Ivor Noel Hume. *Private; not accessible to the public.*

LEE COUNTY

CUMBERLAND GAP NATIONAL HISTORICAL PARK, *Reference—see Bell County, KY*

Jonesville vicinity. **JONESVILLE METHODIST CAMPGROUND,** W of Jonesville at jct. of VA 652 and U.S. 58, 1810. Includes rectangular, 1-story frame auditorium with gabled roof and open N end below gable; 8 panels that can be raised for ventilation hinged together to form side walls; and broad lawn area. Established as meeting ground for revival services; in continuous use since completion. *Private.*

LEXINGTON (independent city)

ALEXANDER-WITHROW HOUSE, Main and Washington Sts., c. 1790. Brick, limestone 1st story; 3 stories, modified rectangle, low hipped roof, corner chimneys, prominent cornice brackets, front center 1st-story entrance surmounted by 2nd-story entrance and iron balustraded balcony, side entrance, flat arched 2nd- and 3rd-story openings; glazed headers form diaper-patterned brickwork; original interior woodwork, fine stairway; level of adjacent streets lowered 10' in 1850's necessitating limestone 1st story; mid-19th C. roof alteration; 2nd-story rear porch added. Italianate elements added. Built in center of town for prominent merchant William Alexander. *Private; not accessible to the public.*

Historical Places

BARRACKS, VIRGINIA MILITARY INSTITUTE, N edge of Lexington on U.S. 11, Mid-19th C.. Military educational complex containing 2 connecting quadrangles along the parade ground with barracks as the focal point. Founded in 1839 on the state arsenal site, patterned after West Point. Noted for graduating outstanding military leaders including Thomas "Stonewall" Jackson and George C. Marshall. Burned in 1864, it now contains 40 major buildings. *State:* NHL.

JACKSON, STONEWALL, HOUSE, 8 E. Washington St., c. 1801. Brick, 2 stories with high basement, L-shaped, cross-gable roof with off-center front pediment with oculi in tympanum, interior end chimneys, modillion cornice, full-height pilasters on facade, front center ground-floor entrance with wide interior stair to 1st floor, stone lintels over all front openings; rear random stone ell probably predates main block, 20th C. front facade renovations. Neo-Classical Revival elements. Owned and occupied by Thomas J. "Stonewall" Jackson, 1858–1861. *Private.*

LEE CHAPEL, WASHINGTON AND LEE UNIVERSITY, Washington and Lee University campus, c. 1866. Brick, 1 story above raised basement, modified rectangle, gabled roof, projecting entrance tower with pyramidal roof. High Victorian Gothic. Houses Lee's burial vault and the office he used while president of the college. *Private:* NHL; HABS.

LEXINGTON HISTORIC DISTRICT, 18th–20th C.. Sections of town containing campuses of Washington and Lee University (see also Washington and Lee University Historic District, VA) and Virginia Military Institute (see also Virginia Military Institute, VA) and commercial, residential, and religious structures. Variety of 19th C. styles featured; notable are the Jeffersonian Classical Washington Hall by John Jordan, 1823; and Gothic Revival examples such as Virginia Military Institute's buildings by A. J. Davis and small brick and frame cottages. Pleasing setting for education-oriented community retaining late-19th C. character. *Multiple public/private:* HABS; G.

LOUDOUN COUNTY

Aldie. **ALDIE HISTORIC DISTRICT,** Both sides of U.S. 50 from E of Rte. 612 to W of Rte. 732, Early-19th C.. Contains early-19th C. mill complex including a mill, miller's house, and manor house. Still in operation, the 3-part brick mill with twin overshot wheels is one of the best outfitted and preserved mills in the state. Built by Charles Fenton Mercer, Revolutionary War general and U.S. congressman. *Multiple private.*

Atoka vicinity. **GOOSE CREEK STONE BRIDGE,** NW of Atoka off U.S. 50, c. 1820. Fieldstone, 4 spans totaling about 200'; demiconical stone buttresses extending entire height of bridge and separating the segmental arched spans, low walls with concrete slab cap framing roadway. Part of Ashby's Gap Turnpike which extended from the Little River Turnpike to the Shenandoah River; no longer in use. *State.*

Leesburg. **LEESBURG HISTORIC DISTRICT,** Area of the original town centered at jct. of U.S. 15 and VA 9, 18th–19th C.. Residential community containing large number of late-18th and early-19th C. houses and commercial and public buildings. Notable is the Greek Revival courthouse and the county office building (c. 1844). Est. 1758, designated county seat. Growth slowed after Civil War. *Multiple public/private:* HABS.

Historical Places

Leesburg vicinity. **EXETER,** E of Leesburg on Edwards Ferry Rd., 1790. Frame, brick rear walls; 2 stories, central block with symmetrical wings, gabled and gambrel roofs, 2-tier Doric portico with lattice railing (1830's), 2-story brick rear wing (1850's), 1-story passages connect house to hipped dependencies. Numerous outbuildings. Colonial building with later Greek Revival and Victorian additions. *Private.*

Leesburg vicinity. **OAK HILL (JAMES MONROE HOUSE),** 8 mi. S of Leesburg on U.S. 15, 1820–1823, James Hoban, architect. Brick, 2 1/2-story main block with 1 1/2-story symmetrical wings, gabled roof, interior and exterior end chimneys, full-height pedimented Tuscan portico set on arcaded foundation, numerous outbuildings including law office. Jeffersonian Classicism. Built for President James Monroe; outline of Monroe Doctrine written here. *Private; not accessible to the public:* NHL.

Leesburg vicinity. **OATLANDS HISTORIC DISTRICT,** S of Leesburg off U.S. 15, 19th C.. Plantation acreage containing the elegant mansion of George Carter (see also Oatlands, VA); Mountain Gap School (c. 1827), the county's last operating 1-room school; the Church of Our Savior (c. 1875); and the ruins of a mill complex. *Private:* HABS.

Leesburg vicinity. **OATLANDS,** S of jct. of Rtes. 15 and 651, c. 1800. Brick, stuccoed; 2 1/2–3 1/2 stories, central block superimposed on larger block with symmetrical 2-story wings ending in octagonal sections, hipped roof with parapet, 2-story tetrastyle Corinthian entrance portico added, 1826. Numerous outbuildings. Federal with Adamesque detailing. Designed and built by George Carter. *Private.*

Lincoln. **GOOSE CREEK MEETINGHOUSE COMPLEX,** S of VA 7, 18th–early-19th C.. Complex containing 1765 stone meetinghouse, 1817 brick meetinghouse still in use, 1815 schoolhouse now used as a Sunday school, and a Quaker cemetery. Symbolizes continuity of Quaker tradition in northern VA; complex contains state's 2nd oldest Friends meetinghouse and county's oldest public school. *Private.*

Middleburg vicinity. **FARMER'S DELIGHT,** About 3 mi. N of Middleburg off Rte. 745, 19th C.. Brick (Flemish bond), 2 1/2-story central block with 2-story symmetrical wings, gabled roof with pedimented dormers, 2 interior end chimneys, gauged brick flat arches over door and windows, cornice with scroll modillions and dentils. Federal. Built by Col. Joseph Lane, member of Virginia General Assembly and the army during Whiskey Rebellion of 1793. *Private; not accessible to the public.*

Middleburg vicinity. **WELBOURNE,** NW of jct. of VA 743 and 6111, c. 1770. Stone and brick, stuccoed; 2 1/2-story main block with flanking 1-story polygonal ended wings, each with Chippendale balustrade; T-shaped, gabled roof sections, front center entrance with fanlight and side lights; front full-width 2-story shed porch, similar rear porch; 2-story rear wing with bay window; main portion of rear wing, c. 1770; main block, c. 1820; side wings with Greek Revival entrances, 1830's; porticos, 1850's; rear wing addition, 1870's; numerous outbuildings include a schoolhouse, springhouse, and tenant house. Federal, Greek Revival, and Italianate elements. Evolution of stone farmhouse into mansion through 5 generations of one family; mid-18th C. owned by Richard Henry Dulany, founder of the Upperville Colt and Horse Show, 1853, oldest horse show in U.S. *Private.*

Historical Places

Sterling vicinity. **BROAD RUN BRIDGE AND TOLLHOUSE,** Jct. of Rtes. 7 and 28 with Broad Run, c. 1820. Tollhouse: stone, 1 story, modified rectangle, gabled roof, interior end chimneys, enlarged by 3 wings; connected by low parapet walls to stone bridge of double-arched span supported by central pier and massive abutments; damaged by flood, 1972. Built by Leesburg Turnpike Co. as part of 1809 road project from Leesburg to Alexandria's Little River Turnpike. *Public (bridge)/private (tollhouse); not accessible to the public.*

Waterford. **WATERFORD HISTORIC DISTRICT,** NW of Leesburg on Rte. 665, 18th–19th C.. Predominately residential, this is a good example of a little altered 18th–19th C. mill town. Contains about 90 stone, brick, wood, and log historic structures; 25 date from the 18th C., 40 from the period 1801 to 1835, 15 from 1836 to 1853, and 10 from 1854 to 1882. First settled, 1733, by Quakers from PA; maintains country character. *Multiple public/private:* NHL; HABS.

Waterford vicinity. **CATOCTIN CREEK BRIDGE,** Rte. 673, N of Waterford, c. 1900. Iron Pratt truss of 150' single span, 14' wide; dismantled and moved to present location, 1932. Manufactured by Variety Iron Works of Cleveland, OH. One of a diminishing number of iron bridges once common in area. *State.*

LOUISA COUNTY

Gordonsville vicinity. **BOSWELL'S TAVERN,** Jct. of VA 22 and U.S. 15, Mid-18th C.. Frame, clapboarding; 2 1/2 stories, rectangular, gabled roof, 2 exterior end chimneys, 2-story E wing contained innkeeper's quarters; pedimented entrance porch, 1-story rear and side ell, later additions. Retains original stairway, wainscoting, and hat pegs. Colonial elements. *Private:* HABS.

Gordonsville vicinity. **HAWKWOOD,** S of Gordonsville off U.S. 15, 1854–1855, Alexander Jackson Davis, architect. Brick, stuccoed; 2-story central block with flanking 1-story hipped wings, 1 surrounded by open arcade; gabled roof, tower, bracketed cornice, front Palladian window at 2nd level; 2-story rear wing added, 1969; outbuildings. Picturesque Italian Villa. Built for Richard O. Morris, VA planter. *Private; not accessible to the public:* HABS.

Gum Spring vicinity. **PROVIDENCE PRESBYTERIAN CHURCH,** NW of Gum Spring off U.S. 250, 1747. Frame, clapboarding; 1 1/2 stories, rectangular, gabled roof, central chimney, entrances on front (off-center) and side, single wooden shutter on 1st-story front windows; interior galleries, some original woodwork. One of few remaining frame churches from colonial period. *Private.*

Trevelians vicinity. **IONIA (CLOVER PLAINS)** 0.1 mi. E of VA 640 and 0.8 mi. N of jct. with VA 613, c. 1775. Frame, clapboarding; 1 1/2 stories, L-shaped, gabled roof sections, exterior end chimneys, gabled dormers, front center twin entrances with shed porch; oak-grained pine interior woodwork; additions include side wings, 2 porches (now partially enclosed), and kitchen wing. Home of locally prominent Watson family. *Private; not accessible to the public.*

Trevilians vicinity. **GRASSDALE,** W of Trevilians off U.S. 15, 1861. Brick, 2 stories, T-shaped, low hipped roof with overhanging bracketed eaves, 3 interior chimneys, projecting center entrance bay, full-width front and partial side porch with bracketing. Outbuildings include frame smokehouse and 2-story, board-and-batten kitchen. Rare rural example of Italian Villa. Built by James Maury Morris, Jr., member of prominent local family. *Private; not accessible to the public.*

Historical Places

Trevilians vicinity. **GREEN SPRINGS,** 0.2 mi. S of VA 617 and 1.5 mi. SW of jct. with VA 640, 18th C.. Frame, clapboarding; 2 stories, modified rectangle, gabled roof sections, exterior end chimneys, front center twin entrances with gabled balustraded porch; excellent interior woodwork; contemporary 1-story rear shed addition with porch extension, later 2-story side addition; 3 renovated frame outbuildings. 18th C. farm dwelling in tranquil setting; home of locally prominent Morris family. *Private.*

Trevilians vicinity. **WESTEND,** S of jct. of Rtes. 22 and 638, 1849. Brick, painted; 2-story central block with flanking 1-story dependencies, one still an orangery; full-height pedimented tetrastyle Tuscan portico. Outbuildings. Greek Revival. *Private:* HABS.

Zion Crossroads vicinity. **GREEN SPRINGS HISTORIC DISTRICT,** NE of Zion Crossroads on U.S. 15, 18th–20th C.. Agricultural district of broad fields and some forested areas featuring fine examples of a variety of 19th C. buildings and styles; included are Italian Villa style Hawkwood (1854–1855) by Alexander Jackson Davis, Greek Revival style Westend (1849), and Gothic Revival style St. John's Chapel (1888) (see also Hawkwood and Westend, VA). Prosperous farm area first settled c. 1720 with nationally important wheat crop in mid-19th C. *Private:* NHL.

LUNENBURG COUNTY

Lunenburg and vicinity. **LUNENBURG COURTHOUSE HISTORIC DISTRICT,** Town of Lunenburg and environs on VA 40/49, 19th C.. Small village containing 19th C. buildings and outbuildings; features courthouse square dominated by Jeffersonian Classical courthouse (1827), and a notable frame house, later altered and used as a tavern, and frame Hotel Gary, both early-19th C. Picturesque courthouse community. *Multiple public/private.*

LYNCHBURG (independent city)

ACADEMY OF MUSIC, 522-526 Main St., 1905, E. G. Frye and Aubrey Chesterman, architects. Brick (stuccoed front facade), 3 stories, rectangular, rusticated ground floor, center entrance with marquee, facade bays articulated by pilasters supporting entablature and parapet with modillions, center 3 bays with windows surmounted by semielliptical panels and flanking 2nd-story pedimented windows, interior contains full range of classical plaster decoration. Beaux-Arts Classicism. One of state's few turn-of-the-century theaters. *Private; not accessible to the public:* G.

GARLAND HILL HISTORIC DISTRICT, Bounded roughly by 5th St., Federal Ave., and Norfolk Western Ry. tracks, 19th-20th C.. Small residential district containing 2-3-story dwellings; features early-19th C. 2-story brick and frame houses with low hipped roofs and Greek Revival elements, and numerous late-19th-early-20th C. brick, frame, and stone houses in Queen Anne and eclectic Victorian styles. Notable are the Watkins House at 400 Madison St. (1898) by Edward Frye and the Burroughs House at 220 Madison St. (1899) by J.M.B. Lewis. Prosperous late-Victorian neighborhood developed by industrialists of local tobacco and shoe industries. *Multiple public/private.*

LYNCHBURG COURTHOUSE, 9th St., between Court and Church Sts., 1855, Andrew Ellison, Jr., architect. Brick, stuccoed; 2 stories, rectangular, cross-gable roof, interior end chimneys, central dome with cupola; full-width

Historical Places

tetrastyle Doric portico with triglyph frieze and mutule cornice, and early-19th C. clock in tympanum; full-width tetrastyle Doric portico with front center double-door entrance; side and rear projecting sections each with pilasters and pediment ending in projecting boars' heads, and double flight of stairs leading to center entrance; interior altered; pentagonal rear addition. Excellent example of Greek Revival-courthouse. *Municipal.*

OLD CITY CEMETERY, 4th, Monroe, 1st Sts. and Southern RR. tracks, 19th C.. Cemetery in open park-like setting in developed center city; variety of markers in marble, granite, soapstone, slate, and local greenstone exemplify 19th C. funerary art. Served, 1806–1965, as burial place for all social and economic classes including over 2,000 Confederate dead. *Municipal.*

POINT OF HONOR, 112 Cabell St., 1806. Brick, stuccoed; 2 stories, 3-bay center section with flanking octagonal projections, hipped roof, 3 exterior end chimneys, bracketed cornice, center entrance, later additions include the 1-story Italianate porch and rear sections, exceptional interior woodwork. Federal. Built by Dr. George Cabell, prominent Lynchburg physician. *Municipal; not accessible to the public:* HABS; G.

WESTERN HOTEL, 5th and Madison Sts., Pre-1815. Brick, 2 stories, L-shaped, hipped roof, early main block with simple cornice, interior front chimneys, round arched center door; later ell with 3-part door behind Doric porch. Federal elements. Sole remaining antebellum tavern in town; in use as early as 1815. *Private; not accessible to the public:* HABS.

417

MADISON COUNTY

Madison. **MADISON COUNTY COURTHOUSE,** U.S. 29, 1828, Malcolm F. Crawford, builder. Brick (Flemish bond), 2 stories, rectangular, gabled roof, front octagonal cupola with dome, 4-bay open ground-floor arcade, pediment contains large fanlight, slightly altered; some original furnishings. Jeffersonian Classicism. *County:* HABS.

Madison vicinity. **HEBRON LUTHERAN CHURCH,** 1 mi. NE of Madison off U.S. 29, 1740. Frame, clapboarding; 1 1/2 stories, T-shaped, intersecting gabled roof, with slight end kicks, box cornice with end returns, S center front entrance through gabled narthex, E entrance; interior galleries; S wing added and Tannenburg pipe organ installed, 1800; remodeled, 1850; 1961 renovations including narthex addition and rebuilt vestry. Colonial elements, based on late medieval European styles. One of few remaining colonial frame churches. *Private:* HABS.

MATHEWS COUNTY

Cobbs Creek vicinity. **HESSE,** E of Cobbs Creek off VA 631, Early-18th C.. Brick, 2 1/2 stories, rectangular, gabled roof, 2 interior end chimneys, denticulated cornice, original E porch replaced by 3-bay center porch with hipped roof (c. 1900), S wing and breezeway added. Federal. Plantation home of the Armisteads, prominent colonial VA family. *Private; not accessible to the public.*

Hudgins vicinity. **CRICKET HILL (FORT CRICKET HILL),** NE of Hudgins, E of jct. of Rtes. 669 and 223, 1776. Earthworks 2' above grade and 150 yards long. Hastily constructed by VA forces under Gen. Andrew Lewis who forced the last royal governor to sail for England, ending the last vestiges of British rule in state. *Private; not accessible to the public.*

Historical Places

New Point vicinity. **NEW POINT COMFORT LIGHTHOUSE,** Jct. of Chesapeake Bay and Mobjack Bay, 1805. Tapered octagonal ashlar sandstone tower with glass and metal cupola, 3 windows, interior stone spiral stair. Guided ships entering Mobjack Bay; discontinued 1963. *Federal/GSA; not accessible to the public.*

Williams vicinity. **POPLAR GROVE MILL AND HOUSE,** SW of jct. of Rtes. 14 and 613, Early-18th–19th C.. House: frame, clapboarding; 2 1/2 stories, L-shaped, gabled and gambrel roof sections, 2-story front pedimented portico, 5-part construction incorporating original 1 1/2-story gambrel roof cottage. Mill: frame, weatherboarding; 2 1/2 stories, rectangular, gabled roof; tide-operated large wooden mill wheel, some original mechanisms. Site of mill from colonial times; present mill in operation from Civil War to 1912. *Private; not accessible to the public.*

MECKLENBURG COUNTY

Clarksville vicinity. **PRESTWOULD,** N of Clarksville, c. 1795. Coursed stone, 2 stories, rectangular, hipped roof, 2 interior stone chimneys, modillion cornice, 1-story pedimented entrance portico added later, much original interior trim and furnishings. Several outbuildings. Georgian. Built by Sir Peyton Skipwith. *Private:* HABS; G.

MIDDLESEX COUNTY

Hartfield vicinity. **LOWER CHURCH,** W of Hartfield on VA 33, 1717. Brick, 1 1/2 stories, modified rectangle, jerkinhead roof with slight end kicks, W center entrance with gabled porch on brick piers and oculi above, off-center S entrance, E chancel recess, round arched windows; interior gallery; brick S addition with passageway to main building. Example of Georgian church. *Private*.

Saluda vicinity. **CHRIST CHURCH,** Off VA 638, N of jct. with VA 33, 1712-1714. Brick, 1 1/2 stories, modified rectangle, gabled roof, box cornice; W center double-door entrance through gabled vestibule with brick pediment and blind oculus in tympanum, bisected fanlight forms part of entrance door; rubbed brick at corners and as trim for openings; interior low box pews; vestibule added in 1843 restoration; N side sacristy added in 1931 renovation. Early Georgian church. *Private:* HABS.

Saluda vicinity. **DEER CHASE,** SE of Saluda off VA 629, Mid-18th C.. Brick, 1 1/2 stories, rectangular, gabled roof with jerkinheads, dormers, 2 interior end chimneys, substantially unaltered. Only remaining outbuilding is 3-bay frame schoolhouse. Typical colonial dwelling. *Private; not accessible to the public.*

Urbanna. **LANSDOWNE,** Virginia St. at Upton Lane, 1740-1750. Brick (Flemish bond), 2 1/2 stories, T-shaped, gabled roof sections, interior end chimneys, 2-story center entrance portico with lunette in pediment and balustraded 2nd story, 1st- and 2nd-story window entrances, beveled water table, 3-course rubbed brick belt course; rear brick wings added later, 1880 rear frame wing; interior and exterior alterations; rear graveyard. Georgian. Home of Arthur Lee, major 18th C. American diplomat. *Private; not accessible to the public.*

Urbanna. **MILLS, JAMES, STOREHOUSE (OLD TOBACCO WAREHOUSE)**, S side of Rte. T-1002, 1763-1767. Brick, 1 1/2 stories on high basement, rectangular, interior end chimney, twin frame stairs leading to full-width shed porch with railing on raised brick founda-

Historical Places

tion, 2 front entrances, hoist and loft door on end wall, cellar doors on each end wall; interior restored and adapted for use as town library, 1964. Built for Scottish merchants as tobacco storehouse; important in pre-Revolutionary tobacco trade. *Private:* HABS.

Urbanna vicinity. **ROSEGILL**, E of Urbanna off VA 227, Mid-17th C.. Brick, stuccoed 1st story and clapboarded 2nd story, rectangular, gabled roof, 2 interior end chimneys, center entrance with 3-bay porch with balustraded flat roof below diamond-shaped window. Numerous alterations include addition of story and bays and removal of gambrel roof and N wings. Extensive remodeling, c. 1850 and early-1940's. Outbuildings include brick washhouse, kitchen and storage house, and 19th C. bake oven and frame smokehouse. Colonial elements. Built for Ralph Wormeley, early settler and member of Governor's Council; inherited by Ralph Wormeley II, burgess president of Governor's Council, VA secretary of state. *Private; not accessible to the public.*

MONTGOMERY COUNTY

Blacksburg vicinity. **SMITHFIELD**, W of Blacksburg, 1773–1774. Frame, clapboarding; 1 1/2 stories, L-shaped, gabled roof with dormers, interior and interior end chimneys, center entrance with bracketed hood, interior features unusual Chinese trellis balustrade on main staircase. Renovated. Rare example of Tidewater-type house in western VA. Built by William Preston, soldier and member of Virginia House of Burgesses. *Private.*

Elliston vicinity. **FOTHERINGAY**, S of jct. of Rtes. 11 and 631, c. 1796. Brick (Flemish bond), 2 stories, L-shaped, gabled roof, end chimneys, modillion cornice, splayed lintels with keystones, 2-level pedimented entrance portico, excellent interior woodwork. S facade extended, 1950's. Georgian elements. Built by Col. George Hancock, Revolutionary War soldier and U.S. congressman. *Private; not accessible to the public:* HABS.

NELSON COUNTY

SWANNANOA, *Reference—see Augusta County*

Lovingston. **NELSON COUNTY COURTHOUSE,** Off U.S. 29, 1809, Shelton Crostwait, designer. Brick, stuccoed; 2 stories, T-shaped, low pitched gabled roof, hexagonal cupola on rectangular base, side modillion cornice, blind lunette in front gable, recessed front 5-bay arcaded entrance porch with center entrance; 2 rear wings added 1940; remodeled 1968; outbuildings include 2 1-story brick structures. Jeffersonian Classical elements. Example of arcaded-front VA courthouse; designed by Justice Shelton Crostwait. *Multiple public/private:* HABS.

Midway Mills. **MIDWAY MILL,** On the James River at end of VA 743, 1787. Uncoursed ashlar, 3 1/2 stories, rectangular, gabled roof, 2 front entrances, granite lintels and sills on all openings; intact inoperable mill machinery; nearby late-19th C. frame miller's dwelling. Master Italian shipwrights thought responsible for highly skilled craftsmanship; built for William H. Cabell, VA governor, 1805–1808; part of mid-19th C. settlement promoted due to adjacent James River and Kanawha Canal (see also James River and Kanawha Canal Historic District, VA). *Private.*

Historical Places

NEW KENT COUNTY

New Kent. **ST. PETER'S CHURCH,** CR 642, Early-18th C.. Brick (English and Flemish bond), 1 story, rectangular, gabled roof, curvilinear Jacobethan gable ends, segmental arched windows, projecting square 2-story entrance tower with pyramidal roof (mid-18th C.) and open 1st-floor arches. Colonial elements. One of the state's oldest remaining churches. *Private:* HABS.

New Kent vicinity. **CRISS CROSS,** SW of New Kent off VA 608, c. 1690. Brick, clapboarded gables; 1 1/2–2 stories, T-shaped, gabled roof sections, exterior end chimneys, front center entrance in projecting wing, flat belt course on wing; interior woodwork from various periods; 19th C. alterations; 1953 restoration. Georgian with unusual porch projection (see also Bacon's Castle, VA). *Private; not accessible to the public:* HABS.

Tunstall vicinity. **FOSTER'S CASTLE,** NE of Tunstall off VA 608, 1685–1690. Brick, 2 stories, T-shaped, gabled roof sections, interior end chimney, front center entrance with hipped porch on projecting front gable section, string courses on side facades; interior woodwork from various periods; raised 1/2 story, 1873; windows altered; 20th C. rear section and porch added. Georgian with unusual front projection (see also Bacon's Castle, VA). *Private; not accessible to the public:* HABS.

Tunstall vicinity. **HAMPSTEAD,** 1 mi. NW of jct. of Rtes. 606 and 607, c. 1825. Brick (Flemish bond), 2 stories, rectangular, hipped roof with deck and balustrade, 4 interior end chimneys, elaborate entablature, identical N and S facades with full-height tetrastyle pedimented entrance porticos, central hall with freestanding spiral stair. Several outbuildings. Federal. Plantation house with Greek Revival elements. *Private.*

NEWPORT NEWS (independent city)

DENBIGH PLANTATION SITE (MATHEWS MANOR HOUSE), SW of the southern end of Lukas Creek Rd., Mid-17th C.. Remains of the 2nd Mathews Manor House, including exposed foundations, evidence of early blacksmithing and other industrial activities, and artifacts including earliest known porcelain discovered in VA. Archeological investigations have provided information about plantation life between 1620 and 1670. *Private.*

FORT CRAFFORD, Fort Eustis Military Reservation on Mulberry Island Point, 1861–1862. Well-preserved fort built on orders of Gen. Robert E. Lee; served to control advance of Union shipping; significant in delaying Union approach to Richmond during Apr.–May 1862 Peninsular Campaign; abandoned May 3, 1862, when Confederate forces withdrew to Williamsburg. *Federal/USA.*

HILTON VILLAGE, Bounded by the James River, Post St., Chesapeake and Ohio RR. tracks, and Hopkins St., 20th C., Francis Y. Joannes, architect. Contains groups of frame houses with stucco or clapboard exteriors and steeply pitched slate roofs. Includes play areas, 1- and 2-family dwellings, and row houses, stores, schools, parks, churches, and a city square. One of the first planned communities financed with federal funds; built to alleviate WWI housing shortage. *Multiple private.*

JONES, MATTHEW, HOUSE, MacAuliffe Ave. and James River Rd., c. 1727. Brick (Flemish bond), 2 stories, T-shaped, gabled roof, large exterior end chimneys, round arched

Historical Places

front door. Original 1-story structure enlarged by addition of 2-story enclosed porch and 1-story rear lean-to; 2nd story added, late-19th C. Colonial elements. *Federal/USA:* HABS.

LEE HALL, Near jct. of U.S. 60 and VA 238, 1848–1859. Brick, 2 stories over high basement, rectangular, low hipped roof, paired interior end chimneys, ornate bracketed cornice, front center entrance with transom; 1-story hipped entrance porch with denticulated cornice, square posts, and balustrade; restored 1964–1965; 2-story brick guesthouse. Greek Revival and Italianate elements. Used as headquarters by Confederate general J. B. Magruder, 1862. *Private.*

NORFOLK (independent city)

ALLMAND-ARCHER HOUSE, 327 Duke St., 1790's. Brick, stuccoed; 2 1/2 stories, square, gabled roof, 1 pair interior end chimneys, denticulated cornice, front off-center recessed entrance with pediment above and flanking columns, stone lintels above front windows, stucco quoins; 19th C. remodeling with Greek Revival elements; rear frame addition. Federal and Greek Revival. *Private.*

BOUSH-TAZEWELL HOUSE, 6225 Powhaten Ave., 1783–1784. Frame, clapboarding; 2 stories, main block with flanking recessed 2-story wings, hipped roof with deck, 2 pairs of interior end chimneys, small front tetrastyle entrance portico, 2-story rear pedimented portico and 1-story wing porches, modillion cornice and pediments, central hall plan; dismantled and rebuilt, c. 1902. Late Georgian town mansion. Home of Littleton Waller Tazewell, prominent VA political leader who served as U.S. senator and state governor. *Private; not accessible to the public.*

425

FREEMASON STREET BAPTIST CHURCH, NE corner of Freemason and Bank Sts., 1850, Thomas U. Walter, architect. Brick, stuccoed; 1 1/2 stories, rectangular, gabled roof with crenelated end parapets; projecting front center tower with crockets, finials and pointed arched double-door entrance; side buttresses with crockets and finials, pointed arched openings; interior gallery; steeple replaced after 1879, renovated 1941 and 1970; education wing added, 1958. Excellent example of Gothic Revival church. *Private.*

MYERS, MOSES, HOUSE, SW corner of E. Freemason and N. Bank Sts., c. 1792. Brick (Flemish bond), 2 1/2 stories, rectangular, gabled roof with fanlight in pediment, interior chimneys, denticulated cornice, broken pedimented entrance vestibules; stone belt course, lintels, and keystones; octagonal ended wing, service wing, and kitchen added later. Unusually rich interior, some original furnishings. Federal style. *Municipal.*

NORFOLK ACADEMY, 420 Bank St., 1840, Thomas U. Walter, architect. Brick, stuccoed; 2 stories, rectangular, gabled roof, front and rear hexastyle pedimented Doric porticos; restored. Greek Revival. Est. 1728, the school occupied the building until 1915. *Private.*

NORFOLK CITY HALL (GEN. DOUGLAS MACARTHUR MEMORIAL), 421 E. City Hall Ave., 1847–1850, William R. Singleton, architect. Stone, stuccoed, granite-faced front facade; 2 stories, rectangular, gabled roof, central dome on colonnaded base, front Tuscan pedimented portico; double-door front and side entrances, front bays articulated by pilasters; interior gutted 1961, and converted to museum and tomb for Gen. Douglas MacArthur featuring rotunda with Italian marble walls and floor and murals by Alton S. Tobey. Greek Revival

Historical Places

elements. Served as courthouse and city hall until 1918 and as courthouse until 1961. *Municipal.*

ST. PAUL'S CHURCH, 201 St. Paul's Blvd., 1739. Brick, 1 1/2 stories, modified Latin cross shape, gabled roof sections, central cupola, 3-story brick bell tower connected to W end by a flat roof brick vestibule, double-door entrance with fanlight set in W vestibule, transept frame vestibules, rubbed brick at corners and around round arched openings; 1776 fire destroyed all except walls; additions include brick bell tower (1901), vestibules, and vestry, and 1913 interior restoration; parish house. Georgian elements. City's oldest building. *Private.*

U.S. CUSTOMSHOUSE, 101 E. Main St., 1852–1859, Ammi B. Young, architect. Granite, 3 stories on high rusticated basement, rectangular, hexastyle pedimented Corinthian entrance portico, center entrance flanked by projecting bays, cast iron columns and capitals on pilasters articulating each bay. Interior features double staircase with openwork cast iron. Greek Revival. *Federal/USCS.*

WEST FREEMASON STREET AREA HISTORIC DISTRICT, Both sides of Bute and Freemason Sts. between Elizabeth River, and York and Duke Sts., 18th–20th C.. Predominantly residential district at edge of center city; contains 2–3-story detached or semidetached brick dwellings set close to the street on deep narrow lots; variety of 19th and early-20th C. styles; notable are the 1791 Federal Whittle House (see also Whittle House, VA), the Italianate dwelling at 419 Duke St. (mid-19th C.), the Second Empire John Cary Weston House (1890's), and the Georgian Revival Roper House (1893). Excellent illustration of city's architectural development. *Multiple public/private:* HABS.

Encyclopedia of Virginia

WHITTLE HOUSE (TAYLOR-WHITTLE HOUSE), 225 W. Freemason St., c. 1791. Brick, 2 1/2 stories, modified rectangle, gabled roof with pedimented ends, interior chimneys, denticulated modillion cornice, fanlight in end tympanums, off-center front entrance with fanlight and small pedimented portico, stone Welsh arches over front windows and belt course; original interior woodwork; 2-story Italianate side porch and brick and frame rear wing added; under restoration. Well-preserved Federal house. Home of C.S.A. general Richard Lucian Page. *Private; not accessible to the public:* HABS; G.

WILLOUGHBY-BAYLOR HOUSE, 601 Freemason St., 1790's. Brick, 2 1/2 stories, modified rectangle, gabled roof, 1 pair of interior end chimneys, modillion cornice, off-center front entrance with transom and 1-story Doric portico, flat arched front windows, flattened arches over 1st-story side windows, 1-story rear wing; entrance portico remodeled early-19th C.; brick caretaker's cottage on grounds. Georgian and Greek Revival elements. Well-preserved medium-sized town house. Museum. *Municipal.*

NORTHAMPTON COUNTY

Bridgetown. **HUNGARS CHURCH,** E of jct. of Rtes. 619 and 622, 1842–1751. Brick (Flemish bond), 1 story, rectangular, gabled roof, 2 entrance doors, round arched door and window openings with gauged rubbed brick and fluted brick tiles. Extensively altered, 1851, 1892, 1922, 1950, and 1955. Colonial elements. Built as the 3rd parish church of Nuswattocks (laters Hungars) Parish. *Private.*

Historical Places

Bridgetown vicinity. **VAUCLUSE,** S of jct. of Rtes. 619 and 657, 18th–19th C.. Frame, clapboarding, brick ends; 2 1/2 stories, L-shaped, gabled roof, interior and interior end chimneys, modillion cornice, 2 small pedimented entrance porches, shed section on ell end. Home of Abel Parker Upshur, Secretary of the Navy (1841–1842) and Secretary of State (1843–1844). *Private; not accessible to the public:* HABS.

Bridgetown vicinity. **WESTERHOUSE HOUSE,** W of Bridgetown off VA 619, c. 1700. Brick (Flemish bond), 1-story, rectangular, gabled roof; exterior end chimneys, one with pyramidal base and freestanding stack; W wall and chimney replaced, mid-19th C. Apparently influenced by English cottage styles. Title to land secured, 1661, by William Westerhouse, house believed to have been built by him or descendants around 1700. *Private.*

Bridgetown vicinity. **WINONA,** NE of jct. of Rtes. 619 and 622, 17th C.. Frame, clapboarding, shingling, brick (Flemish bond); 1 1/2 stories, rectangular, gabled roof with gabled dormers, original brick structure expanded later on E and W. Renovated. Colonial elements. One of 2 known 17th C. VA houses to have diagonally placed triple chimney stacks (see Bacon's Castle, VA). *Private; not accessible to the public:* HABS.

Cheapside vicinity. **CUSTIS TOMBS,** NW of jct. of Rtes. 644 and 645, 17th–18th C.. Contains 2 tombs enclosed by high iron fence; marble tomb with pyramidal top decorated with sculpture, including drapery carvings, family crest, and a human skull motif within a shield—rare funerary sculpture for VA. These are the graves of Maj. Gen. John Custis, progenitor of the Custis family, and of John Custis IV, his grandson. *Private:* G.

Cheriton vicinity. **EYRE HALL,** N of jct. of Rte. 680 and U.S. 13, 18th C.. Frame, clapboarding; 2 1/2 stories, L-shaped, gambrel and gabled roof sections, 3 interior end chimneys, hipped dormers, 1-story entrance porch, side hall plan; original gabled 2 1/2-story dwelling expanded, c. 1796. Much original woodwork and furnishings; hall features entrance and stair hall space. Outbuildings and cemetery. Colonial elements. *Private; not accessible to the public:* HABS.

Eastville. **NORTHAMPTON COUNTY COURTHOUSE HISTORIC DISTRICT,** 18th–19th C.. Courthouse district around court square; features government and some commercial structures. Notable are 1731 brick courthouse, much altered; mid-18th C. brick clerk's office; 1899 Georgian Revival brick courthouse; and late-18th C. frame Eastville Inn, altered. One of the state's most complete courthouse complexes. *County/private:* HABS.

Eastville vicinity. **CASERTA,** NW of jct. of Rtes. 630 and US 13, 18th–19th C.. Frame, clapboarding, brick gable end; 1 1/2–2 1/2 stories, modified L shape, gabled roof sections, exterior and interior end chimney, 1 1/2-story side wing with hyphen; roof over main side hall raised to accommodate extension of hall beyond rear wall, forming rear ell; 3-story interior stairwell. *Private; not accessible to the public:* HABS.

Eastville vicinity. **PEAR VALLEY,** S of jct. of Rtes. 689 and 628, 17th C.. Frame, clapboarding, brick gable ends; 1 1/2 stories, rectangular, gabled roof, exterior pyramidal end chimney. Colonial elements. Rare example of small yeoman cottage with some original interior trim. *Private; not accessible to the public.*

Historical Places

Franktown vicinity. **GLEBE OF HUNGAR'S PARISH,** NW of jct. of Rtes. 622 and 619, 17th–18th C.. Brick (Flemish bond), 1 1/2 stories, rectangular, gabled roof with dormers, 2 interior end chimneys, some original interior paneling. Colonial elements. *Private; not accessible to the public.*

Jamesville vicinity. **SOMERS HOUSE,** SE of jct. of Rtes. 183 and 691, Mid-18th C.. Brick (Flemish bond), 1 1/2 stories, rectangular, gabled roof with dormers, pair of interior end chimneys, modillion cornice, side hall plan; entrances altered, very little original interior. Colonial elements. *Private; not accessible to the public:* HABS.

Nassawadox vicinity. **BROWNSVILLE,** SW of jct. of Rtes. 608 and 600, 1806. Brick (Flemish bond), 2 1/2 stories, rectangular, gabled roof, interior end chimney, white marble lintels, small screened pedimented entrance Doric vestibule, 1 1/2-story side wing connects house with frame kitchen, side hall plan, excellent interior trim. Several outbuildings. Federal style. *Private; not accessible to the public:* HABS.

NOTTOWAY COUNTY

Blackstone. **SCHWARTZ TAVERN,** 111 Tavern St., 1798. Frame, 1 1/2 stories, rectangular, gabled roof sections; 4-part length with oldest block dating from late-18th C. and others over course of 19th C.; 3 interior chimneys, hyphen with projecting polygonal bay, interior trim intact. Federal elements. Built as one of 2 taverns at crossroads. *Private.*

Nottoway. **NOTTOWAY COUNTY COURTHOUSE,** Off U.S. 460 on VA 625, 1843, Branch H. Ellington, builder-architect. Brick (Flemish bond), wood, stucco; 1 story, central block with symmetrical wings, gabled roof, pedimented tetrastyle portico with stuccoed columns, wings with pedimented gable ends, central double-door entrance set in paneled jamb with transom and windows with triple-hung sashes on either side, white marble sills and lintels. Jeffersonian Classicism. *County;* HABS.

ORANGE COUNTY

Barboursville vicinity. **BARBOURSVILLE,** S of jct. of Rtes. 777 and 678, c. 1822, Thomas Jefferson, gentleman architect. Fire in 1884 destroyed all but exterior brick walls, interior masonry partitions, and portico columns of mansion which closely resembled Jefferson's Monticello (see also Monticello, VA). Two service buildings (c. 1790) remain. Jeffersonian Classicism. Built for James Barbour, state governor, U.S. senator, and Secretary of War. *Private; not accessible to the public.*

Gordonsville. **EXCHANGE HOTEL,** S. Main St., 1860, attributed to Benjamin F. Faulconer, builder. Frame, brick; 3 stories, rectangular, low hipped roof, 2 interior chimneys, full-width 2-tier front and rear portico, 2-story brick dependency. Greek Revival elements. Used as hospital during Civil War; believed to be quarters of Dr. Brewerton Monroe Lebby, surgeon-in-charge. *Private.*

Orange vicinity. **MAYHURST,** SW of jct. of Rte. 647 and U.S. 15, 1860. Frame, horizontal flush boarding scored to resemble stone; 2 1/2 stories, modified square, hipped roof with center cross-gable sections, central belvedere with similar cross gables and elaborate brackets and finials, roundel, 2 large ornamented interior chimneys, paired and single round arched windows, 2 front Palladian windows, wide eaves

Historical Places

with elaborate paired brackets and pendants. Front center entrance porch, rear and side additions. Italian Villa. Headquarters for Confederate general A. P. Hill during the winter of 1863–1864. *Private; not accessible to the public:* HABS.

Orange vicinity. **MONTPELIER (JAMES MADISON HOUSE),** 4 mi. W of Orange on VA 20, c. 1760. Brick, stuccoed; 2 1/2 stories, modified rectangle, hipped roof, interior end chimneys, denticulated cornice, full-height pedimented center Doric portico, wings added later. Georgian with classical detailing. Home of President James Madison for 76 years; burial site of both James and Dolley Madison. *Private; not accessible to the public:* NHL.

PAGE COUNTY

Luray. **AVENTINE HALL,** 143 S. Court St., 1852. Frame, clapboarding, horizontal flush siding; 2 stories, square, low hipped roof with central columned and shuttered cupola, 2 pairs of interior end chimneys, 2-story Corinthian tetrastyle entrance portico, corner pilasters, Doric frieze and cornice, center entrance with side lights and transom framed by columns, ornate interior trim. Moved to present site, 1937. Greek Revival with minimal Italian Villa elements. Built by Peter Bock Borst, the Commonwealth's attorney in 1868, 1870. *Private; not accessible to the public.*

Luray. **PAGE COUNTY COURTHOUSE,** 116 S. Court St., 1833, Malcolm Crawford, William B. Philips, builders. Brick 2 1/2-story main block with 1-story side wings, modified rectangle, gabled roof sections, interior end chimneys; central cupola with louvered openings and cross-gable roof, pedimented main block with fanlight in tympanum, full-width ground-floor front arcade, front center entrance; cupola added. Jeffersonian Classical. Built by Malcolm Crawford and William B. Philips, masons for Thomas Jefferson at the University of Virginia (see also Rotunda, University of Virginia). *County:* G.

Newport vicinity. **CATHERINE FURNACE,** 2 mi. W of Newport in George Washington National Forest, 1836. Hand-laid stone without mortar, pyramidal; interior originally 8' in diameter and 32' high above firebox, enlarged during Civil War. Produced high quality pig iron used in Mexican War and by the Confederacy during Civil War; abandoned, 1885. *Federal/USFS.*

Stanley vicinity. **FORT PHILIP LONG,** Off VA 616 on Shenandoah River, 18th–19th C.. Remains of building complex consisting of an underground fort, now partially exposed, connected by a tunnel to a 1 1/2-story stone gabled house; a later (1856) 2-story brick dwelling featuring living room walls painted to resemble paneling with molding; and rear stone slave quarters. Built by descendant of German immigrant who settled here during German migration into area in late 1720's and early 1730's. Example of fortifications constructed by area families during and after the French and Indian War. *Private.*

PATRICK COUNTY

Critz vicinity. **REYNOLDS HOMESTEAD,** VA 798 off VA 626, 1843. Brick, 2 stories, rectangular, hipped roof; 1st- and 2nd-story center entrances, each with a transom and side lights; small 1-story shed entrance porch with Doric and Ionic columns; original 1843 structure enlarged by 1855; restored 1970; outbuildings. Greek Revival elements. Birthplace of Richard

Historical Places

Joshua Reynolds, founder of the R. J. Reynolds Tobacco Co., which played a leading role in the development of the Nation's tobacco industry. Museum. *Private.*

Stuart. **PATRICK COUNTY COURTHOUSE,** SE corner of Main and Blue Ridge Sts., 1821-1822, Abram Staples, builder. Brick, 2 stories, T-shaped, gabled roof sections, front center projecting pedimented 3-bay section with center pedimented entrance (1928) and full-width Tuscan portico set on piers, center staircase; jail added, 1928; remodeled, 1928, 1936, and 1971. Jeffersonian Classicism. *County.*

Woolwine vicinity. **BOB WHITE COVERED BRIDGE,** About 2.5 mi. S of Woolwine off VA 618, over Smith River, 1920-1921, Walter Weaver, builder. Frame with vertical siding, Burr arch truss of 80' double span, 11' wide, interior diagonal sheathing, concrete abutments and pier; reinforced 1972. Built as part of state highway system; still in use. *State.*

Woolwine vicinity. **JACK'S CREEK COVERED BRIDGE,** About 2 mi. S of Woolwine off VA 8, over Jack's Creek, 1914, Walter Weaver, designer. Frame with vertical siding, Burr arch truss of 48' single span, 9' wide, interior diagonal sheathing, concrete abutments; reinforced and restored 1969. One of 11 covered bridges remaining in VA. *County:* G.

PETERSBURG (independent city)

BATTERSEA, 793 Appomattox St., c. 1765-1770. Brick, stuccoed; 2 stories, modified U shape, hipped and gabled roof sections, center 1-story entrance portico, central block connected by hyphens to flanking 1-story pedimented wings. Retains much original interior woodwork and Chinese trellis stair. Extensive early-19th C. alterations. Georgian. Built for Col. John Banister, colonial legislator and congressman, and first mayor of Petersburg. *Private; not accessible to the public:* HABS.

BLANDFORD CHURCH, 319 S. Crater Rd., c. 1736. Brick (Flemish bond with glazed headers), 1 1/2 stories, L-shaped, gabled roof with splayed eaves, modillion cornice, center entrance, water table, round arched windows with rubbed brick voussoirs; vaulted interior with gallery; 18th C. brick wall with molded cap; restored 1901. Georgian. Fine example of 18th C. Anglican church architecture, with excellent brickwork. Museum. *Municipal.*

CENTRE HILL, N of Franklin St. at end of Centre Hill Lane, c. 1820. Brick (Flemish bond), 2 stories, rectangular, low hipped roof, paired interior end chimneys, central cupola, denticulated cornice, front center entrance with fanlight and side lights; full-width 1-story hexastyle Ionic entrance portico; full-height 1st-story front windows; 1850 S side wing. Federal and Greek Revival. Headquarters of Union general G. L. Hartsuff after siege of Petersburg, June 1864–Apr. 1865 (see also Petersburg National Battlefield, VA). Museum. *Private:* HABS.

CITY MARKET, Rock and W. Old Sts., 1878–1879, B. J. Black, architect. Brick, 1 story, octagonal, hipped roof with octagonal louvered cupola, 2 interior end chimneys at alternating corners, 3 round arched bays on each side, projecting shed roof with ornamental cast iron brackets around entire building over exterior market space; altered, 1952. Market site since 1787. *Municipal:* HABS.

Historical Places

EXCHANGE BUILDING, 15-19 W. Bank St., 1841. Brick, stuccoed; 2 stories on raised basement, rectangular, low hipped roof and dome with 10-sided lantern, interior end chimney, roundels in frieze, 5-bay front facade articulated by pilasters, center pedimented tetrastyle Doric portico, central rotunda with surrounding balcony. Greek Revival. Built by members of the Petersburg Exchange to house tobacco and cotton displays, auctions, and sales. Museum. *Municipal:* NHL; HABS.

FARMERS' BANK, NW corner of Bollingbrook St. and Cockade Alley, 1817. Brick, 3 stories, rectangular, pyramidal roof behind parapet, 4 interior end chimneys, molded brick cornice, belt courses between floors, lintels with keystones over windows, 2 pedimented entrances with fanlights; reconstructed brick smokehouse and guardhouse at rear; restored 1970's. Federal. Served bank established in Richmond with branches in several cities; remained in operation until 1866 when all state banks had to be liquidated. Museum. *Private.*

MCILWAINE HOUSE, Market Square at corner of Pellam and Cockade alleys, 1815. Frame, beaded weatherboarding; 2-story central block with 1 1/2-story wing, gabled roof, 2 exterior chimneys, off-center entrance with side lights and transom, pedimented open entrance porch, 2 rear additions. Adamesque interior. Built by George H. Jones, mayor of Petersburg, 1815-1816; home of Archibald Graham McIlwaine, industrialist and financier. *Private.*

PETERSBURG COURTHOUSE, Court House Sq., 1838-1840, Calvin Pollard, architect. Brick, stuccoed; 2 stories, rectangular temple-form, gabled roof; center double-door entrance, small iron balustraded balcony above; hexastyle pedimented portico; 3-stage bell and clock tower; interior altered 1877; extension added 1965. Fine Greek Revival courthouse by New York architect Calvin Pollard. *Municipal.*

STRAWBERRY HILL, 231-235-237 Hinton St., Early-19th C.. Frame, clapboarding; 2 stories, U-shaped, hipped roof sections, interior and interior end chimneys, small cupola, projecting front center 3-bay entrance section with off-center pedimented entrance, W polygonal wing with porch; excellent interior designs; original cross-shaped house enlarged, 1816 and 1900; entrance moved from center bay when house divided into 3 dwellings, 1884. Federal. *Private; not accessible to the public.*

PITTSYLVANIA COUNTY

Chatham vicinity. **LITTLE CHERRYSTONE,** N of jct. of Rtes. 703 and 832, 18th–19th C.. Frame, clapboarding, brick; 1 1/2–2 1/2 stories, L-shaped, gabled roof sections, exterior end chimneys. Original 1 1/2-story wooden structure enlarged c. 1800 by a 2 1/2-story brick structure connected by wooden hyphen. Federal wing has off-center round arched entrance and plaster flat arches with keystones at each window. Fine interior woodwork. *Private; not accessible to the public.*

Gretna vicinity. **YATES TAVERN,** S of Gretna on U.S. 29, 18th C.. Frame, weatherboarding; 2 stories on raised stone basement, rectangular, large exterior end chimney with freestanding stack, 2nd story extends over 1st-story side walls by 8", front and rear entrances; Tidewater hall-and-parlor plan. *Private; not accessible to the public:* HABS.

Historical Places

PORTSMOUTH (independent city)

CRADOCK HISTORIC DISTRICT, Bounded by Paradise Creek, Victory Blvd., and George Washington Hwy., 1918, George B. Post and Sons, planners and architects. Residential neighborhood with small commercial center and town square, laid out with streets forming anchor shape. Contains approximately 760 predominantly frame dwellings representing a range of eclectic architectural styles including modified English cottage, Bungaloid, and Colonial Revival. One of Nation's first planned 20th C. communities built according to 1918 Act of Congress by federal government to accommodate influx of workers at Norfolk Navel Station; designed in-conjunction with the U.S. Housing Corp. facilities planned to be within walking distance of one another, connected by streetcar line to city; early effort made to conceal utility lines. Government sponsorship of the development ended after the Armistice. *Multiple public/private.*

DRYDOCK NO. 1, Norfolk Naval Shipyard, 1827–1834. Granite, 319.5' long, series of stepped tiers, 2 flights of stairs at land end. Unaltered except replacement of original caisson. During the Civil War the Confederates reconstructed the captured Union steamer *Merrimack* into an ironclad renamed the *Virginia* (see also U.S.S. *Merrimack*, VA). *Federal/USN.*

PORTSMOUTH COURTHOUSE (NORFOLK COUNTY COURTHOUSE), NE corner of Court and High Sts., 1846, William B. Singleton, architect. Brick, painted; 1 story over high basement, rectangular, center tetrastyle Doric entrance portico set on an arcade and surmounted by a paneled parapet. Greek Revival. City's oldest public building. *Municipal.*

Encyclopedia of Virginia

PORTSMOUTH HISTORIC DISTRICT, Bounded by Crawford Pkwy., London St., the Elizabeth River, and extending 0.1 mi. W of Washington St., 18th–20th C.. District encompasses the entire area of Olde Towne; contains primarily brick and wood 2- and 3-story Federal and Greek Revival town houses and some post-Civil War and early-20th C. structures. The high English basement, a characteristic feature of Portsmouth architecture, gives the district a distinctive quality. *Multiple public/private.*

PORTSMOUTH NAVAL HOSPITAL, On Hospital Point at Washington and Crawford Sts., 1827–1832, John Haviland, architect. Ashlar granite and freestone, 3 stories over high basement, modified U shape, gabled and hipped roof sections behind parapet, full-height pedimented decastyle Doric portico; remodeled with shallow central dome and wings added, interior altered, and verandas removed, 1907; additions, 1909, 1942. Greek Revival. Established following 1798 Congressional act creating the Marine Hospital Service; architecturally an example of developing hospital design in first half 19th C., by noted architect John Haviland. *Federal/USN.*

QUARTERS A, B, AND C, NORFOLK NAVAL SHIPYARD, 1837–1842. Group of 3 Greek Revival brick dwellings; notable are the rear 2-story frame sun porch on Quarters A and the decorative details, probably derived from Asher Benjamin's building books, applied to all 3 structures. Built as the Commandant's House, Master Commandant's House, and the Surgeon's House on the expanded Gosport Navy Yard, later the Norfolk Naval Shipyard. *Federal/USN.*

Historical Places

TRINITY EPISCOPAL CHURCH, High and Court Sts., 1828–1830. Brick, stuccoed; 1 1/2 stories, modified rectangle, gabled roof sections, modillion cornice, triglyph frieze, center door in projecting pedimented entrance pavilion; round arched windows and doors; side annex and square 4-stage bell tower added 1893; remodeled 1961. Greek Revival elements. Built on site of original 1762 church; used as hospital during Civil War; churchyard contains many old tombstones, the oldest dating from 1763. *Private.*

POWHATAN COUNTY

Powhatan. **POWHATAN COURTHOUSE HISTORIC DISTRICT,** Jct. of Rtes. 13 and 300, 19th C.. Local government building complex containing relatively unaltered group of 19th C. structures, including 1-story Greek Revival courthouse (1848–1849), 18th C. clerk's office, a 1-story Italianate frame office building, and the early-19th C. former jail. Several frame and brick structures adjacent to the green. *Multiple public/private.*

Powhatan vicinity. **BELMEAD,** NW of jct. of Rtes. 663 and 600, c. 1845, Alexander Jackson Davis, architect. Brick, stuccoed; 2 stories, modified rectangle, gabled roof with cross gable, circular and polygonal chimney stacks, stepped gable ends; central 3-story square tower with corner piers, crenelations, ground-level Tudor-arched openings, diamond-pane casement windows on upper levels, bay windows. Gothic Revival. *Private.*

Powhatan vicinity. **KESWICK,** NE of Powhatan off VA 711, Early-19th C.. Frame, clapboarding; 2 stories, H-shaped, gabled roof sections, stepped exterior end chimneys, front center entrance with small gabled porch, rear ell entrance with gabled hood; excellent interior woodwork; outbuildings include wellhouse, circular structure, 2-story brick house, and laundry. Federal. Example of early-19th C. area plantation. *Private; not accessible to the public:* HABS.

PRINCE EDWARD COUNTY

Briery vicinity. **BRIERY CHURCH,** N of jct. of Rtes. 747 and 671, c. 1855; Robert Lewis Dabney, architect. Frame, board and batten; 1 story, T-shaped, steeply gabled roof with wide overhanging eaves, 3 cross gables, simple finials on gable ends, pointed arched lancet windows, pointed arched entrance with gabled hoods. The pulpit has lancet arched recessed panel with a row of pendants hung from the top; ceiling gives the appearance of vaulting. Gothic Revival. *Private.*

Hampden-Sydney. **HAMPDEN-SYDNEY COLLEGE HISTORIC DISTRICT,** Bounded approximately by the Hampden-Sydney College campus, 19th C.. Contains mostly 19th C. buildings in original settings combined with 20th C. Georgian Revival structures. Two of the earliest buildings are the Alamo (1817) and Cushing Hall (1822). One of state's oldest educational institutions; opened in 1776. *Private.*

Worsham. **DEBTOR'S PRISON,** On U.S. 15, 1787. Log construction, 1 story, rectangular, steeply gabled roof, interior end chimney; center door, small flanking windows; finely fitted square logs form ceiling and floor; converted into residence, c. 1820; restored 1951. Colonial elements. Oldest public building in the county. Museum. *Private.*

Historical Places

PRINCE GEORGE COUNTY

PETERSBURG NATIONAL BATTLEFIELD, *Reference—see Dinwiddie County*

Brandon vicinity. **BRANDON,** W bank of the James River at the end of Rte. 611, 17th–18th C.. Brick (Flemish bond), 2-story central block with symmetrical 2- and 1-story wings, U-shaped, hipped roof, 1-story balustraded center entrance portico. Handsome interior paneling. Georgian. *Private:* HABS.

Hopewell vicinity. **MERCHANT'S HOPE CHURCH,** W of jct. of Rte. 641 and VA 10, 17th C.. Brick (Flemish bond), 1 1/2 stories, rectangular, gabled roof with splayed eaves, modillion cornice, rubbed brick arched entrances and windows, original Portland stone flooring tiles, most of the interior dates from 1870. Restored, 1957. Reputedly the state's oldest church, the date 1657 appears on a roof timber. Colonial elements. *Private:* HABS; G.

PRINCE WILLIAM COUNTY

Dumfries. **OLD HOTEL,** U.S. 1, 18th C.. Brick (all header bond front facade), 2 stories, rectangular, hipped roof, denticulated cornice, 2 pairs of interior end chimneys; center doorway with pedimented stone quoins, door frames, and lintels with keystones; side porch. Georgian. *Private; not accessible to the public:* HABS.

Manassas vicinity. **MANASSAS NATIONAL BATTLEFIELD PARK,** NW of Manassas off VA 215, 1861, 1862. Site of 2 important Confederate victories: July 21, 1861, and Aug. 28–30, 1862. In the first encounter, the opening battle of the Civil War, Gen. McDowell's unseasoned troops fled from Gen. Beauregard's equally inexperienced Confederates; first indication of strength of resistance South could demonstrate against Union; battle in which Gen. Thomas Jackson earned nickname "Stonewall." Lee's victory over Gen. Pope in 2nd battle permitted Confederate penetration into Northern territory (see also Antietam National Battlefield Park, MD). *Federal/NPS/nonfederal:* HABS.

Minnieville vicinity. **BEL AIR,** W of Rte. 640, Mid-18th C.. Brick, 1 1/2 stories over high stone basement, rectangular, steeply gabled roof with small pedimented dormers, interior and exterior end chimneys, center doorway. Extensive alterations. Federal. Home of Mason Locke Weems (1759–1825), first biographer of George Washington. *Private; not accessible to the public:* HABS.

Occoquan. **ROCKLEDGE,** Telegraph Rd., c. 1760, attributed to William Buckland, architect. Random stone, 2 1/2 stories, modified rectangle, gabled roof sections, interior and interior end chimneys, gabled dormers, modillion cornice, off-center entrance with transom; 1 1/2-story side wing connects brick kitchen wing; under restoration. Georgian. Built for John Ballendine, wealthy industrialist. *Private; not accessible to the public:* HABS.

Plains vicinity. **BEVERLEY MILL (CHAPMAN MILL)** , Jct. of VA 600 and 55, Mid-18th C.. Random stone, 4 1/2 stories over basement on sloping site, rectangular, gabled roof, interior end chimney, large hood on brackets shelters center entrance; 2 upper stories added, 1850's; 29' metal waterwheel installed 1900; remodeled 1940's; sluice gate and stone mill race remain. Built for Jonathan Chapman; designed for corn milling, later expanded to grind limestone and flour; in operation through WWII. *Private; not accessible to the public.*

Historical Places

Woodbridge vicinity. **RIPPON LODGE,** 0.8 mi. N of jct. of U.S. 1 and VA 642, Mid-18th C.. Frame, clapboarding; 1 1/2-story main block with 1-story side wings, modified rectangle, jerkinhead roof, interior and interior end chimneys, gabled dormers; front facade recessed behind 1-story porch with balustraded deck extending between side wings, center entrance with fanlight; fine interior paneling; late-18th C. side addition; restored, flanking side wings and porch added 1924. Georgian elements. Built for Richard Blackburn, wealthy planter and builder. *Private; not accessible to the public:* HABS.

PULASKI COUNTY

Radford vicinity. **INGLES FERRY,** N of jct. of Rtes. 611 and 624, 18th C.. Ferry site including 1-story log section (1772) and early-19th C. 2-story frame wing of tavern, and the chimneys of the ferry house which burned in 1967. Across the river is Ingleside, a 2-story frame house (1790) built by William Ingles, ferry owner. Ferry operations began, 1762, and continued intermittently until 1948; used by settlers moving W to KY and TN. Tavern was a local social center. *Multiple private; not accessible to the public.*

RAPPAHANNOCK COUNTY

Sperryville vicinity. **MONTPELIER,** S of Sperryville on VA 231, 18th C.. Brick, stuccoed; 2 1/2 stories, rectangular, gabled roof, interior end chimneys, bracketed cornice, center entrance with transom, center cross gable with paired round arched windows; full-width 2-story veranda with 8 Tuscan columns; expanded and veranda added, 19th C.; ornate interior; outbuildings. Greek Revival and Italianate elements. Landmark in region, built for Francis Thornton, wealthy landowner. *Private; not accessible to the public.*

RICHMOND (independent city)

BARRET HOUSE, 15 S. 5th St., 1844, Anderson Barret, builder. Brick, stuccoed; 2 stories over high basement, rectangular, low hipped roof, paired interior end chimneys, front entrance with transom with 1-story Ionic distyle portico; front 1st-story tripartite windows, each with raked lintel; rear full-height frame porch; original woodwork and fireplaces; restored 1937; 2-story brick outbuilding. Greek Revival. Built for William Barret, the original manufacturer of Lucky Strike chewing tobacco, and son of John Barret, city's mayor for 3 terms in 1790's; construction supervised by owner's cousin, AndersonBarret. *Private:* HABS.

BEERS, WILLIAM, HOUSE, 1228 E. Broad St., 1839. Brick, 3 stories, rectangular, low hipped roof, bracketed cornice, entrance porch with paired Greek Doric columns, side hall plan; 3rd story added, 1860; most of interior intact. Federal with Greek Revival elements. *Private; not accessible to the public.*

BELL TOWER, Capitol Sq., 1824. Brick, 3 stories, square, flat roof with balustraded deck, central open octagonal bell cupola, wide recessed arched panels on 2nd and 3rd story of each facade containing rectangular window with roundel above. Federal. Erected by Levi Swain as a guardhouse and signal tower. *State:* HABS.

BRANCH BUILDING, 1015 E. Main St., c. 1866. Brick, cast iron facade; 4 stories, rectangular, low shed roof, ornate cornice, recessed

Historical Places

Corinthian entrance porch with 1-bay-wide stair up to entrance landing and 3-bay stair down to basement entrance, upper floors separated by engaged balustrades, Corinthian pilasters articulate round arched window frames. Fine example of post-Civil War iron-front commercial building. High Victorian Italianate. *Private:* HABS.

BROAD STREET STATION, Broad and Robinson Sts., 1919, John Russell Pope, architect. Masonry, 3 stories, cruciform shape, flat roof with large central dome on cross-shaped base with large lunettes on each side, entablature with denticulated cornice; parapet with raised front section, front hexastyle-in-antis Tuscan portico with barrel-vaulted coffered ceiling, cast iron and glass canopies with ornamental brackets wrap around side wings at 1st-floor level, rear concourse; central 1-story octagonal rotunda with Ionic columns and pilasters. Neo-Classical Revival. Designed to handle city's increased railroad activity in early-20th C. *Private.*

CABELL, HENRY COALTER, HOUSE, 116 S. 3rd St., 1847. Brick, painted; 2-story main block with smaller 2-story wings, modified L shape, low pitched roof sections, denticulated cornice, main-block tetrastyle portico with entablature and fluted columns with lotus flower capitals, front off-center entrance, main-block 2nd-story balcony with wrought iron railing with anthemion ornament; wings with front bay windows, 2nd-story paired round arched windows with molded architrave; railing added c. 1880; bay windows added; interior remodeled, rear 2-story wing added 1947–1948. Eclectic with Greek Revival and Egytian Revival elements. Home for 3 decades ofHenry C. Cabell, lawyer and son of Gov. William H. Cabell. *Private.*

Encyclopedia of Virginia

CITY HALL, Bounded by 10th, Broad, 11th, and Capitol Sts., 1887–1894, Elijah E. Myers, architect. Granite, 4 stories, rectangular, mansard roof with gabled and pyramidal roof sections, projecting gabled entrance pavilions with recessed or pointed arched entrances, ornamental gables, dormers, crockets, and chimneys; 7-story NW corner clock tower balanced by a 4-story NE tower. Interior features 4-story skylit well surrounded by cloistered tiers. High Victorian Gothic. *Municipal.*

CONFEDERATE MEMORIAL CHAPEL, 2900 Grove Ave., 1887, Marion J. Dimmock, Sr., architect. Frame, clapboarding and shingling; 1 story, cross-shaped, gabled roof sections, belfry, 2 front entrances with shingled hipped porch with posts and pierced braces joining to form lancet arches, half-lancet window in gable, side lancet windows with 19th C. stained glass; restored 1960–1961. Picturesque eclectic. Interdenominational chapel constructed with contributions from veterans; in use as Confederate Soldiers Home until 1941. *State.*

CROZET HOUSE (CURTIS CARTER HOUSE), 100 E. Main St., 1814. Brick, 2 stories over high basement, U-shaped, gabled roof, interior end chimneys; double stairway ascends to front center entrance with brick segmental pediment and flanking pilasters, basement entrance below; stuccoed Welsh arches over front windows, stuccoed belt course; 19th C. interior woodwork; rear porch partially enclosed with clapboarding, 2nd-story oriel added; restored 1940, porch and entrance added, modeled after 18th C. prototypes. Well-preserved example of house with Federal elements. *Private:* HABS.

DONNAN-ASHER IRON-FRONT BUILDING, 1207–1211 E. Main St., c. 1866. Brick, cast iron facade; 4 stories, rectangular, low shed

Historical Places

roof, bracketed cornice, ground-floor storefronts, floors separated by engaged balustrades, double round arched windows set in round arched frames articulated by Corinthian pilasters. Interior extensively altered. Italian Renaissance Revival. One of city's finest and most ornate iron-front rows. *Private:* HABS.

EGYPTIAN BUILDING, SW corner of E. Marshall and College Sts., 1845, Thomas Stewart, architect. Brick, stuccoed; 3 stories, rectangular, low hipped roof, torus cornice, recessed portico containing 2 acanthus capital columns with flanking elongated pylons, pylon motif repeated as pylon side window enframements. Excellent example of Egyptian Revival. South's oldest medical college building. *State.*

FIRST AFRICAN BAPTIST CHURCH, NE corner of College and E. Broad Sts., 1876. Brick, 2 stories, rectangular, gabled roof, recessed Doric entrance portico, Roman Corinthian entablature with modillions and dentils. Greek Revival elements. Originally housed one of the earliest black congregations in VA. *State.*

FIRST BAPTIST CHURCH, NW corner of 12th and E. Broad Sts., 1839–1841, Thomas U. Walter, architect. Brick, stuccoed; 2 stories, T-shaped, gabled roof, recessed front entrance portico with 2 fluted Doric columns, Doric entablature, bays articulated by pilasters. Greek Revival. Used as hospital during Civil War. *State.*

GLASGOW, ELLEN, HOUSE, 1 W. Main St., 1841. Brick, stuccoed front facade; 2 stories over high basement, L-shaped, hipped roof, 4 interior chimneys, denticulated cornice; center entrance with transom, side lights, and a small Doric portico; rear veranda; rear ell added, c. 1900; interior altered for office use, bedroom and study remain intact; carriage house. Federal and Greek Revival elements. Home (1877–1945) of Ellen Glasgow, significant 20th C. novelist noted for her realistic presentations of VA social history from the 1850's into the 20th C. *Private:* NHL; HABS.

HANCOCK-WIRT-CASKIE HOUSE, 2 N. 5th St., 1808–1809. Brick (Flemish bond), 2 stories, modified H shape, hipped roof with wide eaves supported by long narrow brackets, 2 interior chimneys, 2-story wooden arcaded entrance porch between 3-part bow projections, frame and brick rear additions. Much original interior trim. Federal. Home of William Wirt, U.S. and VA attorney general, from 1816 to 1818, during which time he completed his biography, the *Life of Patrick Henry. Private:* HABS.

HAXALL, BOLLING, HOUSE, 211 E. Franklin St., 1858. Brick, scored stucco imitating ashlar; 2 1/2 stories over high basement, modified rectangle, low pitched roof, paired interior end paneled chimneys, central square cupola with paired round arched windows, modillion cornice with paired brackets and paneled frieze; projecting front center pavilion with semicircular pediment raised above cornice, entrance with side lights, 1-story entrance porch with fluted columns, and round arched front windows, each with cast-iron hood molds; recessed side wing with front entrance; rear 2nd-story porch; interior double-spiral walnut staircase with stained glass skylight above, 1st-story cove molding, original pink marble fireplaces; interior renovated, 1880's; auditorium added, 1916 and enlarged, 1924; portions of rear full-height porch removed. Italian Villa elements. Built for prominent businessman, Bolling W. Haxall. *Private.*

Historical Places

HOLLYWOOD CEMETERY, 412 S. Cherry St., Mid-19th C., John Notman, architect. Contains classic funerary sculpture and famous Richmond ironwork, including the impressive Gothic iron "cage" surrounding the James Monroe tomb. Laid out to follow the contours of the land. Became most fashionable cemetery in Richmond by 1860; well-known persons buried here include Presidents James Monroe and John Tyler, Jefferson Davis, and J.E.B. Stuart. Stone pyramid at N end of grounds marks burial place of 18,000 Confederates. *Private:* HABS.

JAMES RIVER AND KANAWHA CANAL HISTORIC DISTRICT, *Reference—see Henrico County*

JEFFERSON HOTEL, 104 W. Main St., 1895, Carrere and Hastings, architects. Brick, terra cotta and stone trim; 4-story center block with loggia flanked by 2 6-story towers and 3-story wings, gabled and hipped balustraded roof sections, bracketed eaves, varied window forms, rich architectural ornaments, rear 8-story wings. Interior contains 2-story lobby with double tier of columns supporting the mezzanine and cove ceiling. Beaux-Arts Classical elements. *Private:* HABS.

KENT-VALENTINE HOUSE, 12 E. Franklin St., 1845, Isaiah Rogers, architect. Brick, stuccoed; 3 stories, L-shaped, low hipped roof, 2 pairs of interior end chimneys, bracketed cornice; 2-story tetrastyle Ionic portico with balustraded roof added later; original ground floor and center balcony lattice ironwork. Extensively altered, 1904. Rear outbuilding. Greek Revival. *Private; not accessible to the public:* HABS.

LEIGH, BENJAMIN WATKINS, HOUSE, 1000 E. Clay St., 1812–1816. Brick, stuccoed; 3 stories, rectangular, low hipped roof, interior chimney center entrance. Later additions include 3-story side wing, bracketed cornice, and entrance porch. Little original woodwork remains. Federal with Italian Villa detailing. Home of Benjamin Leigh, noted jurist, lawyer, and U.S. senator. *State; not accessible to the public.*

LEIGH STREET BAPTIST CHURCH, 517 N. 25th St., 1854-1857, Samuel Sloan, architect. Brick, stuccoed; 1-2 stories over high basement, irregular shape, gabled and flat roof sections, interior end chimneys, full entablature, front hexastyle Doric pedimented portico; 2 entrances, each with transom and crosseted raked architrave; pilasters articulate bays; interior gallery; 1-story side wing added 1870's; granite stairs and porch with cast iron railing added 1880's; rear wing added 1911; 3-bay-wide Sunday school wing (1917) extends across front facade; annex added 1930; interior altered. Greek Revival. Designed by Philadelphia architect, Samuel Sloan; city's oldest white Baptist Church to continuously occupy the same building. *Private:* HABS.

LINDEN ROW, 100-114 E. Franklin St., 1847, 1853. Row of 8 town houses, each brick, 3 stories over high basement, rectangular, with low pitched roof, interior chimney, front side entrance with small 1-story Doric portico with mutules and triglyph frieze, windows with stone lintels and sills, and rear full-width 3-story porch; each house 3 bays wide, except for one wider house with late-19th C. rear addition; outbuildings removed except for 2 houses, one with separate brick dependency, and one with attached brick building. Greek Revival. 19th C. home of city's prominent citizens; converted 20th C. to apartment and commercial use. *Private:* HABS.

Historical Places

MAIN STREET STATION, 1520 E. Main St., 1900–1901, Wilson, Harris, and Richards, architects. Brick with stone and terra cotta trim, 3 stories with 2 half-stories under hipped roof, rectangular, interior end chimneys, 2 rows of hipped and ornately gabled dormers, 6-story front corner clock tower surmounted by dome, ground-floor segmental arches, round arched windows at 2nd level, rear iron train shed. Chateauesque. *Private.*

MARSHALL, JOHN, HOUSE, 9th and Marshall Sts., 1790. Brick, 2 1/2 stories, modified square, gabled roof, 2 interior chimneys, roundel in front pediment, modillion cornice and pediment, pedimented entrance porch with 2 windows flanking either side, excellent Adamesque woodwork, rear wing added 1810. Federal. Home of John Marshall, Chief Justice of the Supreme Court from 1801 to 1835. *Municipal:* NHL; HABS.

MASON'S HALL, 1807 E. Franklin St., 1785–1786. Frame, clapboarding; 2 stories, square, low hipped roof, central octagonal cupola, 2 interior chimneys, center pedimented section with 2nd-story 3-part window and 1st-story pedimented entrance portico. Extensive remodeling, mid-19th C. Federal with Greek Revival detailing. First building erected for Masonic purposes and continuously used as such; members included John Marshall and Edmund Randolph. *Private; not accessible to the public:* HABS.

MAUPIN-MAURY HOUSE, 1105 E. Clay St., 1846. Brick, 3 stories over high basement, rectangular, gabled roof, interior end chimneys, decorative open entrance vestibule supported by Ionic columns, side hall plan, some original trim. Federal and Revival elements. Built for Dr. Socrates Maupin, a founder of the medical department of Hampden-Sydney College; later occupied by Matthew F. Maury, famous oceanographer. *Private; not accessible to the public.*

MAYMONT, Hampton St. (Spottswood Rd.), 1890, Edgerton S. Rogers, architect. Rock-faced sandstone, 2 1/2 stories over high basement, irregular shape; hipped, gabled, conical, and polygonal roof sections; interior chimney, hipped dormer, front slightly off-center entrance with transom, front 1-story wrap-around porch with denticulated cornice and small columns, front corner 2-story turret, front 3-story polygonal tower at opposite corner, transoms with stained glass above most windows, side porte-cochere with massive round arches; restored; outbuildings include stone stable with central cobblestone courtyard, brick and stone carriage house, and manager's house of brick and frame with shingling and with octagonal tower at one side; extensive gardens. Queen Anne and Richardsonian Romanesque elements. Built for Maj. James H. Dooley, wealthy industrialist and member of Virginia House of Delegates. Museum. *Municipal.*

MAYO MEMORIAL CHURCH HOUSE, 110 W. Franklin St., 1845. Brick, stuccoed; 2 stories over high basement, L-shaped, low pitched roof sections, paneled chimneys, denticulated cornice, front double-door entrance with pediment and pilasters; center 2-story Ionic pedimented portico, 1st-story windows with pediments, 2nd-story windows with cornices on consoles; other windows with label molds, rear enclosed porches; interior paneled stair hall with carved oak staircase; 1-story side wings raised to 2 stories during 1880's renovation; rear addition; woodwork replaced with many exotic woods. Greek Revival. Purchased in 1883 by Peter H. Mayo, wealthy tobacco man. *Private:* HABS.

Historical Places

MONROE, JAMES, TOMB, Hollywood Cemetery, 412 S. Cherry St., 1858-1859, Albert Lybrock, architect. Cast-iron "cage" containing granite sarcophagus; features delicate tracery onion dome surmounted by finial, decorative openwork parapet, board-and-batten motif above pointed arched tracery openings on each side, corner columns surmounted by engaged pinnacles, decorative ironwork at base; surrounded by 2'-high stone wall. Gothic Revival. Built after reinterment of James Monroe, 5th U.S. President. *State:* NHL; HABS.

MONUMENT AVENUE HISTORIC DISTRICT, Bounded by Grace and Birch Sts., Park Ave., and Roseneath Rd., 19th-20th C.. Predominantly residential section along an unusually wide avenue, virtually unaltered, containing Georgian Revival and Second Renaissance Revival town houses and terrace rows, several Greek Revival churches, and monuments honoring Confederate heroes. *Multiple public/private:* G.

MONUMENTAL CHURCH, 1224 E. Broad St., 1812-1814, Robert Mills, architect. Stone, partially stuccoed; 2 stories, octagonal, low domed roof with circular lantern; entrance portico, surmounted by triangular parapet on a wide entablature supported by corner piers and freestanding Doric columns; later 2-story wing (1840). Greek Revival. Built on the site of the American French Academy as a monument to 72 victims of the Academy's 1811 fire. *Private.*

MORSON'S ROW, 219-223 Governor St., 1853. Three brick, stuccoed attached town houses; each 3 stories with flat roof, bracketed denticulated cornice, bracketed hood over doors with fanlights, drip molding over windows, bow fronts, retain most of original interiors. Italian Renaissance Revival. Built as rental properties. *Multiple public/private; not accessible to the public:* HABS; G.

OLD STONE HOUSE, 1914 E. Main St., Mid-18th C.. Stone, 1 1/2 stories, rectangular, gabled roof with dormers, 2 interior end chimneys, 3-bay facade, cut stone lintel with keystone over front door. Richmond's only surviving colonial dwelling, rare regional example of colonial stone construction. *Private:* HABS.

PUTNEY HOUSES, 1010–1012 E. Marshall St., 1859. Two brick town houses, each stuccoed with 3 stories and classical detailing. More elaborate than the Stephen Putney House is the Samuel Putney House with its round arched windows, decorative cornice, and ornamental front entrance porch and side 2-story iron veranda. Italian Renaissance Revival. *Municipal.*

RICHMOND NATIONAL BATTLEFIELD PARK, *Reference—see Hanover County*

SCOTT-CLARKE HOUSE, 9 S. 5th St., 1841. Brick, 2 stories over high basement, rectangular, flat roof, interior end chimneys, front center entrance with transom and side lights, small 1-story distyle Doric portico; rear 2-story frame porch with Doric columns, 2nd story partially enclosed; interior altered; brick and stone outbuilding. Greek Revival. Built for James Scott, tobacco merchant. *Private:* HABS.

SECOND PRESBYTERIAN CHURCH, 9 N. 5th St., 1848. Brick, 1 story, T-shaped, gabled roof sections, crenelated parapet, front center pointed arched double-door entrance in base of square tower with corner pinnacles, front facade with similar corner pinnacles, lancet-shaped openings with label molds, side buttresses, brownstone trim; interior galleries;

Historical Places

transept added 1873, galleries extended; several renovations. Gothic Revival. Design was probably taken from Minard Lafever's *Young Builder's General Instructor* of 1829. *Private:* HABS.

SHELTERING ARMS HOSPITAL (WILLIAM H. GRANT HOUSE), 1008 E. Clay St., 1857. Brick, 3 stories, almost square, low hipped roof, center entrance with richly ornamented 1fstory open vestibule, single and double round arched windows with hood moldings, rear additions and 3-story side wing added later. Italian Villa. *State; not accessible to the public.*

SHOCKOE SLIP HISTORIC DISTRICT, Roughly along E. Carey St. between S. 14th and S. 12th Sts., 18th–19th C.. Commercial district consists of 5-block area centered around triangular-shaped plaza with fountain; features 2–4-story brick buildings, some stuccoed, many with Italianate elements, constructed primarily late-19th C.; many buildings with storefronts incorporating iron columns and pilasters. District named for narrow passage along 13th St. to nearby Shockoe Canal; provides area of human scale adjacent to center city and to nearby high rise development. *Multiple public/private:* HABS.

ST. JOHN'S CHURCH HISTORIC DISTRICT, Bounded roughly by 22nd, Marshall, 32nd, Main, and Franklin Sts. and Williamsburg Ave., 18th–19th C.. Predominantly residential area with architectural styles ranging from Federal and Greek Revival to the Victorian styles. Majority are brick and frame side hall plan town houses. The city's oldest row houses compose the Federal stuccoed brick Carrington Row (1818). Focal point of the district is the frame 1-story St. John's Church, the site of the Virginia Convention of 1775. *Multiple public/private:* HABS.

ST. JOHN'S EPISCOPAL CHURCH, E. Broad St. between 24th and 25th Sts., 1740–1741. Frame, clapboarding; 1 story, rectangular, gabled roof, entrance tower with louvered belfry and cupola added later. Georgian elements. Grounds contain oldest public cemetery in Richmond; scene of Patrick Henry's "Liberty or Death" speech. *Municipal/private:* NHL; HABS.

ST. PAUL'S CHURCH, 815 E. Grace St., 1845, Thomas B. Stewart, architect. Brick, stuccoed; 2 stories, rectangular, gabled roof with octagonal cupola on square base, Roman temple-form with Greek Revival detailing, Corinthian entrance portico, bays articulated by pilasters; interior gallery, original pews, and baptismal font by Alexander Galt. *Private.*

ST. PETER'S CHURCH, 800 E. Grace St., 1834. Brick, stuccoed; 1 story, Latin cross shape, gabled roof with stepped parapet, front octagonal cupola, Doric entablature, pedimented front entrance portico with Doric columns. Greek Revival. Oldest Roman Catholic church in Richmond. *Private.*

STEARNS IRON-FRONT BUILDING, 1007–1013 E. Main St., c. 1865–1869. Brick with cast iron front, 4 stories, rectangular, low shed roof, bracketed ornate cornice, round arched windows with keystones are separated by engaged Corinthian columns. Interior divided into 4 commercial units. Italian Renaissance Revival. *Private:* HABS.

STEWART-LEE HOUSE, 707 E. Franklin St., 1844. Brick, 3 stories over high basement, L-shaped, low hipped roof, paired interior end chimneys; front side entrance with transom and side lights, small distyle Doric portico; front basement entrance, stone lintels over front and

Historical Places

side windows, side 2-story wing, rear 3-story full-width porch; balustraded parapet removed; rear wing taken down and reconstructed c. 1913; annex attached to side wing 1933. Fine example of Greek Revival town houses popular in Richmond during mid-1840's; built for tobacco merchant Norman Stewart; residence of Robert E. Lee's family, 1864–1865, and his place of retirement for period after Appomattox. Museum. *Private:* HABS.

TREDEGAR IRONWORKS, Roughly bounded by the James River, Kanawha Canal, and VA 1/U.S. 301, 19th–20th C.. Remains of extensive ironworks including some ruins and the restored (mid-1970's) brick gabled gun foundry with corbeling and adjacent chimney stack; chartered 1837, and successfully developed by Joseph Reid Anderson, who purchased the company, 1843; became the J. R. Anderson Co.—one of America's largest and best equipped ironworks; produced at 1/3 full capacity during Civil War's drain on skilled manpower and materials; redeveloped after the Civil War but again decreased production with the panic of 1873, when rail customers went bankrupt and with the development of steel production, an operation to which the ironworks could not adapt; in operation until 1952 when gutted by fire. *Private:* HAER.

U.S. POST OFFICE AND CUSTOMHOUSE, 1000 E. Main St., 1858, Ammi B. Young, architect. Granite, 3 stories, modified rectangle, hipped roof, center 1-story triple-arched porch, original round arched windows with keystones, quoins, bracketed cornice; wings added in 1889, 1910, 1930. Renaissance Revival. Site of Jefferson Davis' trial for treason, 1867. *Federal/USPS.*

VALENTINE MUSEUM (WICKHAM-VALENTINE MUSEUM), 1005–1015 E. Clay

St., 1812, attributed to Robert Mills, architect. Brick, stuccoed; 2 stores over high basement, rectangular, hipped roof, 2 interior chimneys; front center entrance with semielliptical fanlight and side lights, 1-story portico with mutule cornice and paired columns; front facade with tripartite windows, those on 1st story set within shallow round arched recesses; rear 1-story veranda with bowed center; attached are 3 Italianate town houses (c. 1870) and the Greek Revival Bransford-Cecil House (1840) moved to this site in 1954. Federal. Built for John Wickham, distinguished lawyer who served as defense counsel at the trial of Aaron Burr; purchased in 1882 by Mann Valentine II, who left the house to the city as a museum for his collection of historic artifacts. Museum. *Private:* NHL; HABS.

VIRGINIA GOVERNOR'S MANSION, Capitol Sq., 1810-1813, Alexander Parris, architect. Brick, painted; 2 stories, rectangular, low hipped roof with balustraded deck, 4 interior chimneys, projecting center entrance bay with 1-story portico supported by 2 pairs of Corinthian columns and a triple 2nd-level window, semioctagonal ended rear wing added 1906. Little original interior remains. Federal. Home of VA governors since 1813. *State.*

VIRGINIA STATE CAPITOL (CONFEDERATE CAPITOL), Capitol Sq., 1785-1792, Thomas Jefferson and Louis Clerisseau, architects. Brick, stuccoed; 2 stories, rectangular, gabled roof, full-width pedimented hexastyle Roman Ionic portico, denticulated modillion cornice and pediment, bays articulated by Ionic pilasters; flanking wings added, 1904-1906; altered. Jeffersonian Classicism. Design based on a Roman temple, La Maison Carree. State capitol of VA and capitol of the Confederacy during the Civil War. *State:* NHL.

Historical Places

WEST FRANKLIN STREET HISTORIC DISTRICT, W. Franklin St. between Laurel and Ryland Sts., 19th–20th C.. Urban residential district containing attached and detached town houses, apartment buildings, and religious structures; features primarily 2 1/2–3-story residences of brick and stone in a variety of late-19th–early-20th C. styles; notable is the Second Renaissance Revival residence at 810 W. Franklin St. (c. 1900), and the Millhiser House with Jacobethan Revival elements (late-19th C.). Fashionable residential area after the Civil War; parts of district now incorporated successfully into the Virginia Commonwealth University and the Richmond Professional Institute. *Multiple public/private.*

WHITE HOUSE OF THE CONFEDERACY (BROCKENBROUGH MANSION), Clay and 12th Sts., 1818, attributed to Robert Mills, architect. Brick, stuccoed; 3 stories, rectangular, low hipped roof with cupola, modillion cornice, center Ionic entrance porch, 2-story Doric portico on garden facade, modified central hall plan. Federal. Served as the executive mansion of the Confederacy during the Civil War. *Private:* NHL; HABS.

WILLIAM J. CLARK LIBRARY AND BARCO-STEVENS HALL, VIRGINIA UNION UNIVERSITY (BELGIAN BUILDING) , Lombardy St. and Brook Rd., 1939, Victor Bourgeois, Leo Stijnen, and Henri Van de Velde, architects. Red tile, 1 story, modified U shape, flat roof, slate-faced water table and companile-like tower with glass corner and louvered lantern. International Style. Built as the Belgian Pavilion for New York World's Fair. *Private.*

WOODWARD HOUSE, 3017 Williamsburg Ave., 18th C.. Frame, clapboarding; 2 1/2 stories, rectangular, gabled roof, dormers, 3 exterior chimneys on 1 side; enlarged from small 1-story structure, 1828-1829; shed rear wing, 20th C. front porch. One of city's oldest structures; last significant structure representing active 18th C. maritime district of old Richmond. Owned by sea captain John Woodward *Municipal; not accessible to the public.*

2900 BLOCK GROVE AVENUE HISTORIC DISTRICT , 2901, 2905, 2911, and 2915 Grove Ave., 19th-20th C.. Residential district consists of 4 stone and brick 2 1/2-story dwellings, 3 constructed in late-1890's, each with irregular shape with turrets and porches in Queen Anne style, and one square dwelling constructed in 1912; behind houses are frame carriage houses with cupolas and scrollwork. Block developed after 1886 sale to West End Land Improvement Co.; retains quiet residential atmosphere. *Private; not accessible to the public.*

RICHMOND COUNTY

Ethel vicinity. **MENOKIN,** NW of jct. of Rtes. 690 and 621, c. 1769. Stone, stuccoed; 2 stories, rectangular, hipped roof with deck, 2 interior chimneys, double belt course, quoins, round arched center doorway, molded window architrave with rusticated blocks; ruinous. Georgian. Home of Francis Lightfoot Lee, signer of the Declaration of Independence. *Private; not accessible to the public:* HABS.

Farnham. **FARNHAM CHURCH,** VA 3, 1737. Brick (Flemish bond), glazed above water table; 1 story, Latin cross shape, intersecting gabled roofs, semicircular arched and circular windows. 1921 restoration. Early colonial structure with imported Gothic elements. *Private:* HABS.

462

Historical Places

Tappahannock vicinity. **SABINE HALL,** S of jct. of Rtes. 624 and 360, c. 1730. Brick (Flemish bond); 2 stories, rectangular, hipped roof, 4 interior end chimneys, flanking 1 1/2-story gabled wings, full-height rusticated center bay, stone window lintels with raised keystones, 2-story pedimented tetrastyle entrance portico. Much fine original woodwork. Georgian. Built by Landon Carter, colonial burgess and political writer. House remains in family. *Private; not accessible to the public:* NHL; HABS.

Warsaw. **RICHMOND COUNTY COURTHOUSE,** Jct. of U.S. 360 with VA 3, 1748–1750. Brick, 1 story, rectangular, hipped roof, interior end chimneys, modified bracketed cornice, segmental arched double-door entrance through vestibule; each side with 6-bay arcade, some bays bricked in, some with windows; remodeled 1877; cornice raised; chimneys possibly added late-19th C.; fenestration altered; rear shed addition; passage added to clerk's office. Georgian elements. Colonial courthouse with unusual side arcade. *County:* HABS.

Warsaw vicinity. **MOUNT AIRY,** W of Warsaw on U.S. 360, 1758–1762, John Ariss, architect. Stone, 2 stories, rectangular, hipped roof, 2 pairs of interior chimneys, quoins, pedimented 3-bay projecting entrance pavilion flanked by 2 windows on either side, rectangular 2-story dependencies with hipped roof and central chimney are connected to the house by quadrant passages. Interior rebuilt after fire in 1844. Georgian. Rare 18th C. stone house built by Col. John Tayloe, remains in family. *Private; not accessible to the public:* NHL; HABS.

ROANOKE (independent city)

BUENA VISTA, Penmar Ave. and 9th St., c. 1840. Brick, 2 stories, modified L shape, hipped roof sections, paired interior end chimneys, center entrance with side lights and 6-light transom surmounted by a window with side lights, full-height distyle Doric entrance porch, bays articulated by pilaasters, side wing; altered, c. 1889. Greek Revival. Built for prominent VA resident George P. Tayloe, son of the Tayloes of Mount Airy (see also Mount Airy, VA). *Municipal.*

FIRE STATION NO. 1, 13 E. Church Ave., 1907–1908, - Huggins and Bates, architects. Rock-faced limestone foundation, brick, rusticated at 1st-story level; 2 1/2 stories, rectangular, low pitched roof, denticulated modillion cornice; parapet, square base above with belfry with pediments and bell-cast dome; 2 large segmental arched entrances with pedestrian entrance between with tall round arched transom, 2nd-story paired windows set in round arched panels with flanking pilasters; interior with 1st-story stamped metal ceiling, 2nd story with 2 hay lofts, hoists and runners to lift hay. Renaissance Revival elements. Well-preserved exampleof early fire station. *Municipal.*

ST. ANDREW'S ROMAN CATHOLIC CHURCH, 631 N. Jefferson St., 1900–1902, William P. Ginther, architect. Brick, 1 story, Latin cross shape, gabled roof sections, roof cresting, fleche at crossing, gabled vents, brick corbeling below cornice; stone steps lead to 3 front entrances, each under compound pointed arch; rose window above within pointed arched frame; flanking tall towers, each with spire and corner pinnacles; beveled stone water table and belt courses, side buttresses, pointed arched openings, stained glass; interior decorated with polychrome paint, 1940's. Late Gothic Revival. Catholic congregation establishedhere by Father John W. Lynch in 1882; church is a city landmark. *Private.*

ROANOKE COUNTY

Hollins. **HOLLINS COLLEGE QUADRANGLE,** Hollins College campus, 19th–20th C.. Campus architectural focal point; contains 6 brick structures grouped around quadrangular green. Includes the first structure built especially for the school, East Building (1856–1858), Main Building (1861), Bradley Chapel (1883), the octagonal Botetourt Building (1890), West Building (1890), and the Charles Cocke Memorial Library (1900), all displaying classically derived elements. Part of educational facility which began as popular resort and developed from a female seminary (1839) into an excellent women's college (1911). *Private.*

Roanoke vicinity. **DEYERLE, BENJAMIN, PLACE,** 3402 Grandin Road Extension SW., c. 1852, Benjamin Deyerle, builder. Brick, 2 stories over high basement, L-shaped, low hipped roof, interior end chimneys, cornice with wide frieze, double curving staircase leads to front center entrance with transom and side lights, 1-story tetrastyle Doric pedimented portico, basement entrance below; wooden lintels, corner pilasters, rear facade and ell with screened porch; some original interior woodwork; stairs added 20th C.; brick outbuildings. Greek Revival. Home of Benjamin Deyerle, important area contractor, also a farmer and local entrepreneur. *Private:* HABS.

Roanoke vicinity. **MONTEREY,** Tinker Creek Lane, NE, 1840's. Brick; 1-story front, 2-story rear; L-shaped, hipped roof, interior end chimneys, center entrance with transom and side lights, full-width front veranda, 2-story rear L-shaped porch; ell and rear porches added after 1871. Greek Revival with some details copied from Asher Benjamin's *The Practical House Carpenter* (1830). *Private; not accessible to the public.*

ROCKBRIDGE COUNTY

Brownsburg. **BROWNSBURG HISTORIC DISTRICT,** On VA 252, 19th–20th C.. Contains residential and commercial structures in styles popular during early-19th C. and between 1870 and 1910. Prominent is a local interpretation of the Federal style in simple brick and frame 2-story structures with gabled roofs and molded brick cornices. Typical early valley village; once a commercial center. Maintains 19th C. character. *Multiple public/private.*

Lexington vicinity. **TIMBER RIDGE PRESBYTERIAN CHURCH,** SW of jct. of Rtes. 11 and 716, 1755–1756. Stone, 1 story, T-shaped, gabled roof; numerous alterations include enlarged round arched windows and transepts (1900). Only 3 of the stone walls and several roof timbers remain of original church. Second oldest Presbyterian meetinghouse in the Valley of Virginia. *Private.*

Staunton vicinity. **MCCORMICK, CYRUS, FARM AND WORKSHOP,** S of Staunton on U.S. 11 and CR 606 at Walnut Grove, Early-1800's. Log construction, 1-story on high foundation, gabled roof. Workshop of Cyrus McCormick, inventor of the mechanical reaper, foremost among the inventions that revolutionized agriculture. Also includes the 2-story brick farmhouse. *State:* NHL.

Historical Places

ROCKINGHAM COUNTY

Broadway vicinity. **LINCOLN HOMESTEAD AND CEMETERY (JACOB LINCOLN HOUSE)**, S of jct. of VA 684 and 42, Early–mid-19th C.. Brick, 2 1/2 stories, L-shaped, gabled roof, interior end chimneys, denticulated cornice with fretted molding, front center entrance with fanlight set partially within pediment supported by fluted pilasters, 1-story balustraded front porch, Welsh arches over some windows, belt course between stories; rear ell constructed 1849, joined to main house early-20th C. Federal. Home of Jacob Lincoln, great-uncle of President Abraham Lincoln; nearby is family cemetery in which are buried 5 generations of the family, including the President's great-grandfather. *Private:* HABS.

Broadway vicinity. **TUNKER HOUSE (YOUNT-ZIGLER HOUSE)**, S of Broadway at jct. of VA 786 and 42, c. 1798. Brick, frame; 1–2 1/2 stories, modified L shape, gabled and flat roof sections, exterior end chimneys, front center entrance with 1-story shed porch; large pine partitions separating 2 front rooms can be raised; original 1 1/2-story dwelling incorporated into rear wing; front 2 1/2-story block added, 1802–1806; rear 1- and 2-story additions. Main room of house used for religious services until 1830 by the German Baptists (or Tunker Brethren). *Private; not accessible to the public.*

Dayton vicinity. **FORT HARRISON**, NE of Dayton on VA 42, c. 1749. Limestone, stuccoed; 2 1/2 stories, T-shaped, gabled roof, interior end chimneys, front entrance porch, rear N wing built early-1800's. Built by Daniel Harrison and used during French and Indian War. *Private; not accessible to the public.*

Harrisonburg vicinity. **BAXTER HOUSE,** N of Harrisonburg on VA 42, Late-18th C.. Timber construction, 2 stories, rectangular, gabled roof, 1 exterior end chimney, 3-bay center front porch; sections with 1/2-dovetail notching and rock-and-daub chinking, and those with full dovetail notching; N frame board-and-batten shed addition. Typical of colonial log construction. Reputedly built by George Baxter, Scottish immigrant whose family gained local prominence. *Private.*

Harrisonburg vicinity. **BEERY, JOHN K., FARM,** N of Harrisonburg off VA 42, 1838-1839. Farm complex containing numerous buildings such as barn, loom house, and springhouse arranged around limestone farmhouse. 2-story, L-shaped dwelling has gabled roof, 3 interior end chimneys; 1-story, late-19th C. bracketed porch with simple sawn balustrade; central hall plan. Scotch-Irish and German construction techniques. Following tradition, one wing served as meeting room for large congregation of Mennonites. *Private.*

RUSSELL COUNTY

Dickersonville vicinity. **OLD RUSSELL COUNTY COURTHOUSE (DICKENSON-FUGATE HOUSE)**, W of Dickersonville on U.S. 58A, 18th-19th C.. Stone courthouse: 2 stories, rectangular, gabled roof, interior end chimney; attached to a brick, 2-story, mid-19th C. farmhouse. Outbuildings include a 19th C. smokehouse. Built in 1799 to replace the first courthouse which burned, used until 1818 when the county seat was moved. Russell County originally included the greater part of southwestern VA. *Private; not accessible to the public.*

Historical Places

SALEM (independent city)

EVANS HOUSE, 312 Broad St., 1882. Brick, 1 1/2 stories, L-shaped; mansard roof with side section exposing brick wall, framed by outline of convex mansard roof; decorative bracketed cornice with wide frieze; ornate gabled dormers, each with round arched window; slightly projecting front center 2 1/2-story tower with double-door entrance with segmental arched transom; paired 2nd-story round arched windows with decorative moldings, and convex mansard roof with oculi dormers; small 1-story entrance porch with carved supports, side bay window, segmental and round arched windows, rear ell; elaborately decorated interior; patterned brass hardware. Excellent area exampleof Second Empire dwelling. Reflects area's new prosperity brought by activities made possible by the connection of the Norfolk and Western and Shenandoah Valley railroads. *Private; not accessible to the public:* HABS.

MAIN CAMPUS COMPLEX, ROANOKE COLLEGE, Roanoke College, 19th–20th C.. Campus complex includes 4 adjacent buildings; features 1–3-story brick structures with Greek Revival and High Victorian Gothic elements; notable are the 3-story Administration Building constructed 1847 and substantially altered with Georgian Revival elements 1903; and Bittle Hall constructed 1876–1879 as a library and altered 1894 for use as a chapel with a library annex. College founded 1842 at Mount Tabor as Virginia Collegiate Institute, moved to Salem 1847, and rechartered as a college 1853; these buildings form the focal point of the college and the town. *Private:* HABS.

SALEM PRESBYTERIAN CHURCH, E. Main and Market Sts., 1851–1852. Brick, 1 story, modified rectangle, gabled roof, front square belfry with louvered openings and octagonal domed lantern over Ionic entrance portico, front pediment, bays articulated by paneled pilasters, wide Ionic entablature, large rectangular windows with wide lintels with Greek fret motifs; later side and rear additions. Federal and Greek Revival elements. Built primarily by slave labor; slave gallery torn down after Civil War; architectural details influenced by popular contemporary builders' handbooks. *Private:* HABS.

WILLIAMS-BROWN HOUSE AND STORE, 523 E. Main St., c. 1837. Brick, frame; 2 1/2 stories, modified L shape, gabled and shed roof sections, interior end chimneys; front 2-story porch, each level with balustrade, round arched openings at either side; front center entrance, 2nd-story entrance above with transom, side lights, and crosseted architrave; 5 rear frame additions; 1st-floor openings altered. Federal and Greek Revival elements. Main St. storehouse became solely a dwelling when adjacent store was constructed, 1876; prominent local landmark. *Private:* HABS.

SCOTT COUNTY

Nickelsville vicinity. **KILLGORE FORT HOUSE,** SW of Nickelsville off VA 71, Late-18th C.. Log construction, 2 stories, rectangular, gabled roof, stone exterior end chimney, front center entrance, timbers V-notched at corners. Colonial elements. The last in a chain of frontier forts extending from Castlewood to Cumberland Gap; an example of the fortified housetype that succeeded earlier stockaded forts; built for Robert Killgore, a farmer and prominent Baptist minister. *Private.*

Historical Places

SHENANDOAH COUNTY

Middletown vicinity. **FORT BOWMAN,** NE of jct. of Rtes. 660 and U.S. 11, c. 1753. Stone, 2 1/2 stories, rectangular, gabled roof, 2 interior end chimneys, segmental flat stone lintels, later kitchen wing and 1-story columned entrance porch, original interior woodwork, fortified basement room demolished. Outbuildings. Reflects German construction common in PA. *Private; not accessible to the public:* HABS.

New Market. **NEW MARKET HISTORIC DISTRICT,** Jct. of U.S. 11 and 211, 18th–19th C.. Linear town along old Valley Pike; contains primarily 2-story frame and brick gabled residential, commercial, and religious structures, most constructed early–mid-19th C.; notable are the limestone Henkel family house (c. 1800) with Federal elements, and the Emmanuel Lutheran Church with Romanesque Revival elements. Town laid out in 1785, became an active mercantile center in early-19th C.; prominent among many German inhabitants was Ambrose Henkel, founder of the Henkel Press, the oldest Lutheran Press in America (1806); growth ceased in late-19th C. *Multiple public/private:* HABS.

New Market vicinity. **NEW MARKET BATTLEFIELD PARK,** N of jct. of U.S. 11 and U.S. 211, 1864. 160-acre park containing the Bushong House, used as a hospital during the Civil War, and full-scale models of field pieces. Here Union troops, commanded by Maj. Gen. Franz Sigel, were successfully repulsed by Maj. Gen. John C. Breckinridge. The delay in the Union advance enabled crops to be harvested and the railroads to continue operation. *Private.*

Encyclopedia of Virginia

Woodstock. **SHENANDOAH COUNTY COURTHOUSE,** W. Court and S. Main Sts., c. 1790. Rock-faced limestone, coursed front facade; 2 stories, modified T shape, gabled roof sections, interior end chimneys, central hexagonal cupola with pyramidal roof with ball finial set on ogee dome, front center entrance with pediment on pilasters; 3-bay-wide Tuscan tetrastyle portico with pediment, oculus in tympanum; front side entrance with transom; rear 1-story courtroom wing added, 1840; 1-story clerk's office added to rear wing, 1880; molding added to each gable end to imitate pediment; center entrance surround added. Eclectic. One of the oldest courthouses still in use W of Blue Ridge Mountains in town settled 1761 by German immigrants. *County.*

SMYTH COUNTY

Marion vicinity. **PRESTON HOUSE (HERNDON),** S of jct. of Rtes. 645 and U.S. 11, 1842. Brick, 2 1/2 stories, rectangular, gabled roof, 2 pairs of end chimneys, Doric entablature; center entrance porch with balustraded roof, similar doors on each level; 2-story brick rear ell. Greek Revival elements. Built as an inn by John Montgomery Preston. *Private; not accessible to the public.*

SOUTHAMPTON COUNTY

Capron vicinity. **BELMONT,** NE of Capron off VA 652, Late-18th C.. Frame, clapboarding; 1 1/2 stories, L-shaped, gabled roof with dormers, 3-bay front, rear shed porch (later addition). Several 19th C. outbuildings. Site of the unsuccessful Nat Turner slave revolt and the capture of many of his followers, Aug. 13, 1831. *Private; not accessible to the public.*

Historical Places

SPOTSYLVANIA COUNTY

Fredericksburg vicinity. **FALL HILL,** NW of Fredericksburg off VA 639, 18th C.. Brick (Flemish bond), 2 stories, rectangular, hipped roof, 2 interior chimneys, center entrance with transom, small hipped Doric porch; frame service wing; outbuildings; remodeled 1830. Georgian and Greek Revival elements. Home of distinguished Colonial family; thought to be part of the original grant patented by Francis Thornton I in 1720; situated in battle area during Fredericksburg campaign (1862). *Private; not accessible to the public.*

Fredericksburg vicinity. **FREDERICKSBURG AND SPOTSYLVANIA COUNTY BATTLEFIELDS MEMORIAL NATIONAL MILITARY PARK,** Fredericksburg and W and SW areas in Spotsylvania County, 1862–1864. Area encompassing 4 major Civil War battlefields; Fredericksburg, Chancellorsville, the Wilderness, and Spotsylvania Courthouse, and Jackson Shrine. At Fredericksburg, midway between Washington, D.C., and Richmond, VA, Gen. Robert E. Lee defeated Union General A. E. Burnside (May 11–13, 1862). In the battle of Chancellorsville, Lee defeated Burnside's replacement, Gen. Joseph Hooker, but lost Stonewall Jackson who was accidentally shot by his own men, May 1863. From Chancellorsville, Lee conducted an unsuccessful invasion into PA (see also Gettysburg National Military Park, PA). The battles of the Wilderness (May 5–7, 1864) and Spotsylvania Courthouse (May 9–19, 1864) were bloody but inconclusive, and Grant advanced toward Richmond (see also Petersburg National Battlefield and Richmond National Battlefield Park, VA). *Federal/NPS/non-federal.*

Fredericksburg vicinity. **RAPIDAN DAM CANAL OF THE RAPPAHANNOCK**

NAVIGATION, NW of Fredericksburg, 1829–1849, John Couty, engineer (rebuilding). Dry canal bed with stone walls and locks. Minimum damage. Complete rebuilding in 1847–1849. Batteau and lock dam navigation parallels Rappahannock River, provided economic outlet to area farmers and focused trade on Fredericksburg. *Municipal.*

STAFFORD COUNTY

Brooke vicinity. **POTOMAC CREEK SITE,** 1.8 mi. SE of jct. of Rt. 621 and Rt. 608, Powhatan (early-17th C.). Site of the Indian village of Patawomeke, described by Capt. John Smith in 1608, and repeatedly visited by traders until 1630. Abandoned in 1635 when the site was patented by Giles Brent. Excavations begun 1935 by Judge William H. Graham and continued, 1938–1940, by Dr. T. Dale Stewart of the U.S. National Museum. *Multiple private.*

Falmouth. **BELMONT (GARI MELCHERS HOUSE),** Off U.S. 1, Early-1900's. Frame, clapboarding; 2 1/2 stories, modified rectangle, gabled roof, 2 pairs of exterior end chimneys, tetrastyle Ionic entrance porch with 2 flanking windows on either side, polygonal side wing. Outbuildings include 1-story fieldstone studio built by Gari Melchers, landscape and portrait artist who painted *The Arts of War* and *The Arts of Peace* in the Library of Congress. *Public:* NHL.

Falmouth. **CARLTON,** 501 Melchers Dr., Late-18th C.. Frame, clapboarding; 2 stories, rectangular, hipped roof, 2 interior end chimneys, E and W entrances with shutters and 8-light transoms, porch and pedimented frontispiece with fluted pilasters added to W entrance, narrow side addition with shed roof, central hall plan. Outbuildings include frame kitchen and dairy and brick meat house; family cemetery. Georgian. Built for John Short, prosperous Falmouth merchant and landowner. *Private; not accessible to the public.*

Falmouth. **FALMOUTH HISTORIC DISTRICT,** Jct. of U.S. 1 and U.S. 17, 18th–19th C.. Residential area of predominantly frame, brick, and stone dwellings with few sophisticated decorative features; brick commercial structures. Architecture varies from low riverside rows of houses to the larger houses overlooking the town. Mostly Federal in style. Laid out in 1727, the port was a leading VA mercantile centers until early-19th C. *Multiple public/private:* HABS.

Falmouth vicinity. **HUNTER'S IRONWORKS,** W of Falmouth off U.S. 17, Mid-18th C.. Contains stone foundations of more than 20 buildings, stone rubble in creek indicating dam, and brick remains of one building. Uninvestigated. Founded by James Hunter, leading Falmouth merchant; supplied equipment for American forces during Revolutionary War. *Private; not accessible to the public.*

Fredericksburg vicinity. **FERRY FARM SITE (GEORGE WASHINGTON'S BOYHOOD HOME SITE)**, E of Fredericksburg at 712 Kings Hwy., 18th C.. Farm site includes late-19th C. farmhouse, smokehouse, and barns; a surveying office that reputedly dates from colonial times; and a road that led to the ferry in colonial days. Site of George Washington's boyhood home; he owned this land from his father's death in 1743 until its sale in the 1770's; main house destroyed in late-18th C. fire. *Private:* HABS.

Garrisonville vicinity. **AQUIA CHURCH,** N of jct. of U.S. 1 and Va. 610, 1751. Brick (Flemish bond), 2 stories, Greek cross shape, hipped roof with tower and cupola, modillion cornice; stone keystones, quoins, and pedimented and rusticated doorways; retains interior original triple-tier pulpit, reredos, sounding board, and box pews. Damaged by fire, 1754; rebuilt, 1757; some 20th C. restoration. One of the best preserved VA colonial churches. *Private:* HABS.

STAUNTON (independent city)

MARY BALDWIN COLLEGE, MAIN BUILDING, Mary Baldwin College campus, 1844. Brick, painted; 2 stories, central block with symmetrical wings, gabled roof, 2 interior end chimneys; full-height, tetrastyle, pedimented portico with cast iron balcony above the center entrance. Greek Revival. Founded as Augusta Female Seminary, 1842; name changed, 1895, in honor of Mary Julia Baldwin, first principal of the seminary. *Private.*

SEARS HOUSE, Sears Hill Rd. in Woodrow Wilson City Park, 1866. Frame, board-and-batten siding; 1 1/2 stories, modified U shape, gabled roof with cross gable, interior chimney, bracketed cornice, off-center front entrance with transom and side lights, 3-bay arcaded porch with slender paired posts; rectangular and round arched openings, 3-story octagonal tower with polygonal roof at rear corner, rear 1-story service wing with porch. Picturesque cottage style. Home of prominent educator Dr. Barnas Sears, president of Brown University and administrator of the Peabody fund which helped establish free schooling in the postwar South. *Municipal; not accessible to the public.*

STUART HALL (MAIN BUILDING), 235 W. Frederick St., 1846, Edwin Taylor, architect. Brick, painted; 2 stories, rectangular, hipped roof with central belvedere, 4 interior chimneys, 2-story Doric entrance portico with full entablature, projecting side entrance bays framed by pilasters, side porch. Greek Revival. State's oldest preparatory school for girls, est. 1843 as Virginia Female Institute; Board of Visitors headed by Robert E. Lee after Civil War; renamed Stuart Hall (1907) in honor of Flora Stuart, widow of J.E.B. Stuart and headmistress, 1880–1898. *Private.*

STUART HOUSE, 120 Church St., 1791. Brick; 2-story main block with 2 1/2-story wing, over high basement; L-shaped, gabled roof sections, interior end chimneys, gabled dormers, main-block denticulated cornice, front center entrance with transom and swan's neck pediment; full-width balustraded 2-story portico with pediment, 2 windows and painted oculus in tympanum; side wing with 1-story porch on brick piers with latticework balustrade and supports; original interior woodwork including swan's neck pediments used over some doorways and mantelpieces; wing added 1844; outbuildings include smokehouse and 2-story frame residence and law office erected after 1783. Early example of building with elements of Jeffersonian Classicism. Home of Archibald Stuart, lawyer and judge; inherited by his son, Alexander H. H. Stuart, lawyer, state and Federal legislator, and Secretary of the Interior under Millard Fillmore. *Private; not accessible to the public:* HABS.

TRINITY EPISCOPAL CHURCH, Beverley and Lewis Sts., 1855. Brick, 1 1/2 stories, modified rectangle, gabled roof; front projecting 3-stage tower with crenelated parapet, double-door entrance with rose window above, 3rd stage with tall louvered openings; lancet openings, diagonal corner buttresses, side buttresses; choir loft; stained glass windows, including 7 Tiffany windows; rear additions,

1870; chancel enlarged, 1888; brick rectory (1872) and parish house (1872–1873, enlarged 1924). Excellent example of Early Gothic Revival style; 3rd church constructed for this parish, founded in 1746. *Private.*

VIRGINIA SCHOOL FOR THE DEAF AND BLIND, E. Beverly St. and Pleasant Ter., 1846, Robert Cary Long, Jr., architect. Brick (Flemish bond), 3 stories, center block with symmetrical wings, gabled roof, full-height hexastyle Greek Doric pedimented portico, frieze contains 3rd-floor windows, piazzas front flanking wings; 2 asymmetrical rear wings, one connecting to later (1885) chapel. Greek Revival. One of the country's oldest schools for the deaf and blind. *State.*

WESTERN STATE HOSPITAL COMPLEX, Jct. of U.S. 11 and U.S. 250, 1830's–1840's, William Small and Thomas Blackburn, architects. Administration building: brick (Flemish bond), 3-story center block with flanking 2-story wings and end pavilions with Ionic porticos, hipped and gabled sections, central cupola, front Greek Ionic portico. Complex also contains 4 buildings for patient accommodations and the chapel. Greek Revival. Founded in 1825, one of the best of its type in the country. *State.*

WHARF AREA HISTORIC DISTRICT, Middlebrook Ave. between S. New and S. Lewis Sts., including S. Augusta St. to Johnson St., 19th–20th C.. Warehouse and commercial district that includes elongated plaza; features primarily 2–3-story brick buildings with Italianate elements, constructed late-19th–early-20th C.; notable are the eclectic Chesapeake and Ohio RR. passenger station, the building at 119–123 S. Augusta St. with cast iron facade elements, and the building at 120–124 S. Augusta St. with frame front carved to imitate masonry and metallic forms. Exemplified town's growth and prosperity in late-19th C. due to railroad; active during Civil Warera when town served as military post, supply depot, and training and hospital center. *Multiple public/private.*

WILSON, WOODROW, BIRTHPLACE, N. Coalter St. between Beverly and Frederick Sts., 1846. Brick, 2 stories, rectangular, hipped roof, 4 interior end chimneys, Doric entrance porch with a flanking window on either side; restored, c. 1941. Greek Revival elements. Birthplace of Woodrow Wilson, 28th President of the U.S. *Private:* NHL; HABS.

SUFFOLK (independent city)

RIDDICK HOUSE, 510 Main St., 1837. Brick, 2 1/2 stories, rectangular, gabled roof, parapeted end chimneys; small, pedimented distyle Doric entrance portico with coffered ceiling on W front, full-width 20th C. porch on S side. Federal and Greek Revival elements. Home of prominent local Riddick family. *County.*

Chesapeake City vicinity. **GLEBE CHURCH (BENNETT'S CREEK CHURCH)**, W of Chesapeake City on VA. 337, 1737-1738. Brick, 1 1/2 stories, modified rectangle, gabled roof with frame pediment; front center entrance with transom, marble lintel, and plaque; segmental arched openings, 19th C. colored glass windows; interior gallery; vestry added in 1856 renovation; recent 1-story brick addition. One of 2 colonial churches remaining in county. *Private.*

Chuckatuck vicinity. **ST. JOHN'S CHURCH (CHUCKATUCK CHURCH)**, E of Chuckatuck on VA 125, 1755. Brick, 1 1/2 stories, rectangular, gabled roof, exterior side chimney, box cornice, front center entrance, rubbed brick at corners and around openings, round arched windows; interior gallery; original jerkinhead roof altered; late-19th C. interior paneling added. Georgian elements. *Private.*

SURRY COUNTY

Bacon's Castle. **BACON'S CASTLE,** Off VA 10, c. 1655. Brick, 2 1/2 stories, modified rectangle, gabled roof with curvilinear Flemish gable ends, 2 exterior diagonally set triple chimneys, E mid-19th C. addition. Cruciform plan Jacobethan colonial structure. Seized and fortified by followers of Nathaniel Bacon during Bacon's Rebellion of 1676. *Private; not accessible to the public:* NHL; HABS.

Jamestown vicinity. **CHIPPOKES PLANTATION,** S bank of the James River opposite Jamestown Island, 17th–19th C.. Plantation consisting of a working farm with 1 1/2-story frame house (c. 1810), the present main 2-story brick Greek Revival dwelling (c. 1850), and numerous outbuildings and farm dependencies. One of the earliest plantations, named for Indian chief from whose domain the land derived; first English owner was William Powell, a shareholder in the Virginia Co. of 1609. *State.*

Surry vicinity. **FOUR-MILE TREE,** NE of the jct. of VA 618 and VA 610, 18th–19th C.. Brick, stuccoed; 1 1/2 stories, rectangular, hipped-on-gambrel roof, pedimented dormers, 2 pairs of interior end chimneys, denticulated cornice, Ionic center entrance porch, 19th C. alterations, outbuildings. One of county's more prosperous early plantations; home of the Brownes, a leading Surry family. Grounds contain oldest legible tombstone in VA (1650). *Private:* HABS.

Historical Places

Surry vicinity. **SMITH'S FORT,** NE of jct. of Rts. 31 and 620, Early-17th C.. Fort mound, 2' high, intersecting a penisula and enclosing a triangle 200' on a side; originally twice as high and surmounted by palisades; constructed by Capt. John Smith during the first two years of the Jamestown colony. *Private; not accessible to the public.*

Surry vicinity. **WARREN HOUSE,** NE of Surry off VA 31, Mid-17th C.. Brick (Flemish bond), 1 1/2 stories, rectangular, gabled roof with 3 front gabled dormers, 2 interior end chimneys with molded brick caps, stepped entrance landing with wooden railing, segmental arch of rubbed and gauged brick. Restored after 1933. Colonial elements. Unusually sophisticated for period. Built by Thomas Warren who purchased land from Thomas Rolfe, son of John Rolfe and Pocahontas to whom land descended from Indian King Powhatan. *Private;* HABS.

SUSSEX COUNTY

Grizzard vicinity. **FORTSVILLE,** SE of the jct. of Rtes. 612 and 611, 19th C.. Frame, clapboarding; 2-story pedimented center block with symmetrical 1-story wings, modified T shape, gabled roof, 2 prominent exterior chimneys, pedimented 1-story entrance porch, denticulated cornice. Greek Revival. Home of John Y. Mason (1799–1859), U.S. congressman, Secretary of the Navy, U.S. Attorney General, and minister to France. *Private; not accessible to the public.*

Homeville vicinity. **CHESTER,** N of jct. of Rtes. 625 and 35, 1773. Frame, clapboarding; 2 1/2 stories, rectangular, pitched gabled roof, 2 exterior chimneys connected at 1st and 2nd floors forming brick pent closets, off-center entrance; later 2-story, early-19th C. S wing. Little altered; nearly all interior woodwork remains. Colonial elements. *Private; not accessible to the public:* HABS.

Sussex. **SUSSEX COUNTY COURTHOUSE HISTORIC DISTRICT,** 19th–20th C.. Consists largely of buildings essential to county government including the clerk's office, county office building, jail, and treasurer's office. Focal point is the courthouse, designed under the influence of Jefferson's structures. Despite a few modern structures, the town, with its brick Greek Revival county buildings and white frame residences, retains its 19th C. character. *Multiple public/private.*

TAZEWELL COUNTY

Maiden Spring vicinity. **INDIAN PAINTINGS,** 2.7 mi. S of jct. of Rts. 610 and 19 (460), Prehistoric. Site consists of pictographs of birds, animals, women, and warriors halfway up Paint Lick Mountain. Executed in locally available ochre by either Shawnees or Cherokees. *Public.*

Pocahontas and vicinity. **POCAHONTAS HISTORIC DISTRICT,** Corporate boundaries of Pocahontas including N cemetery, Late 19th–20th C.. Mining town contains residential and commercial areas including religious and government structures; features primarily 2-story duplex frame dwellings with weatherboarding or board-and-batten siding and front 1-story shed porches, and 2-story brick commercial buildings, many with Italianate elements and a few with pressed metal facades; of interest is the Italianate city hall (1895) and nearby brick bank building with Richardsonian Romanesque elements. Town est. c. 1881 by Southwest Virginia Improvement Co. which

Historical Places

acquired 31,000 acres of land and began mining operations; the company constructed housing and support facilities; mining continued until 1955. *Multiple public/private.*

VIRGINIA BEACH (independent city)

CAPE HENRY LIGHTHOUSE, Atlantic Ave. at U.S. 60, 1792, John McComb, Jr., architect. Stone, 90' high, octagonal, glass-enclosed light. Third oldest lighthouse in U.S.; first one authorized and constructed by the federal government. *Private:* NHL.

KEELING HOUSE, 3157 Adam Keeling Rd., 1695–1715. Brick (Flemish bond with glazed headers), chevron pattern in gables; 1 1/2 stories, rectangular, gabled roof, interior end chimneys, modillion cornice, gabled dormers, front entrance; belt courses, flat arches over windows; main-level room with paneled end wall, closed-string stair with pulvinated frieze; side wing added. Colonial elements. Well-preserved late-18th–early-19th C. manor house. *Private; not accessible to the public:* HABS.

OLD DONATION CHURCH, 4449 N. Witch Duck Rd., 1736. Brick (Flemish bond with glazed headers and Queen closers), 1 story, L-shaped, gabled roof sections, interior chimney, front gabled vestibule with double-door entrance with fanlight, beveled water table, round arched windows, rear side addition; restored 1916. Georgian elements. Third church erected in Lynnhaven Parish. *Private.*

PEMBROKE MANOR, E of jct. of Rtes. 627, 647, and U.S. 58, Mid-18th C.. Brick (Flemish bond), 2 stories, rectangular, low hipped roof, modillion cornice, 2 interior chimneys, center entrance with segmental wooden pediment, regular fenestration, unmolded belt course; altered. Georgian. Probably built by Jonathan Saunders. *Private; not accessible to the public.*

PLEASANT HALL, 5184 Princess Anne Rd., 1779. Brick, 2 1/2 stories, rectangular, gabled roof, interior end chimneys, modillion cornice; front center entrance with transom, 1-story gabled porch with paired columns; belt course, brick flat arches over front windows, side 1-story porch with balustraded deck; original interior woodwork; rear shed structure; front porch added; rear addition 1890's; side porch added early-20th C. Georgian elements. Erected for wealthy landowner Peter Singleton, who donated the plot behind the house for the Princess Anne County Courthouse, now demolished. *Private; not accessible to the public:* HABS.

THOROUGHGOOD HOUSE, E of Norfolk on Lynnhaven River, c. 1636–1640. Brick (Flemish and English bonds), 1 1/2 stories, rectangular, gabled roof, a massive exterior end chimney and an interior end chimney, center entrance with flanking windows. Restored. One of the oldest houses in the English-speaking colonies. Built by Adam Thoroughgood, who came to VA in 1621 as an indentured Servant became a prominent citizen, burgess, and landowner. *Private:* NHL; HABS.

WEBLIN HOUSE, 5588 Moore's Pond Rd., c. 1700. Brick, 1 1/2 stories, rectangular, gambrel and gabled roof sections, large exterior end chimneys, front entrances, irregular fenestration with gauged brick flat arches, 1-story S addition; gambrel roof added, early-19th C. Contains excellent area colonial dwelling elements. *Private; not accessible to the public.*

Historical Places

WISHART-BOUSH HOUSE, E of jct. of VA 649 and Absalom Rd., 17th C.. Brick, 1 1/2 stories, rectangular, steeply gabled roof, connected shed dormers, 2 large T-shaped exterior end chimneys, rear ell added later, much original interior woodwork. One of the oldest brick dwellings in the U.S., extraordinary intact example of 17th C. medieval design. *Private; not accessible to the public:* HABS; G.

WARREN COUNTY

CEDAR CREEK BATTLEFIELD AND BELLE GROVE, *Reference—see Frederick County*

Milldale. **MOUNT ZION,** NE of jct. of Rtes. 624 and 639, 1771–1772. Fieldstone, 2 stories, rectangular, hipped roof, modillion cornice, 2 pairs of stone interior end chimneys, center entrance, round arched center window at 2nd level, 2-story frame addition, central hall plan. Georgian. Built for Rev. Charles Mynn Thruston, prominent member of the VA legislature. *Private; not accessible to the public:* HABS.

WASHINGTON COUNTY

Abingdon. **ABINGDON BANK,** 225 E. Main St., c. 1845. Brick, 3 stories, rectangular, flat roof, elaborate wide cornice, corbeled belt course between 1st and 2nd floor; off-center and center door, the latter with transom and side lights; center triple windows at 2nd and 3rd levels, retains bank entrance flanked by full-size windows. Later rear additions. Federal elements. Built by Robert Preston, first resident cashier, as combination bank and residence. *Private; not accessible to the public.*

Abingdon. **ABINGDON HISTORIC DISTRICT,** Both sides of Main St., 18th–19th C.. Predominantly residential area with brick, frame, and stuccoed structures, some with stepped gables; many fine Federal and other 19th C. revival designs. Est. 1778; typical 19th C. rural VA town. Multiple public/private.

Abingdon. **MONT CALM,** W of VA 75, c. 1827. Brick, 2 stories, L-shaped, gabled roof, interior end chimneys, 20th C. porch and side extension, full entablature, fanlighted central entrance; altered and expanded. Federal. Owned by line of important local citizens. *Private; not accessible to the public:* HABS.

Abingdon vicinity. **WHITE'S MILL,** NW of Abingdon on White Mill Rd., Mid-19th C.. Frame, weatherboarding, board-and-batten siding; 2 1/2 stories, L-shaped, gabled roof, front gabled entrance section; main gears and area for waterpowered sawmill on basement level, grinding apparatus on 1st floor, bolting and sifting equipment on 2nd, and grain elevator mechanism in attic; run by waterpowered overshot wheel; 19th C. alterations. Built along ideas outlined in 1795 edition of *The Young Millwright and Miller's Guide* by Oliver Evans. Rare working example showing various stages of gristmill design. *Private.*

WESTMORELAND COUNTY

Fredericksburg vicinity. **GEORGE WASHINGTON BIRTHPLACE NATIONAL MONUMENT,** E of Fredericksburg off U.S. 301 and VA 3, 1732. Site of George Washington's birthplace; symbolized by a memorial house built in 1932 to represent a typical 18th C. VA plantation house; also includes a commemorative granite shaft, a colonial period frame kitchen, other farm buildings, exhibits, and the family burial plot. *Federal/NPS.*

Historical Places

Hague vicinity. **JONES, MORGAN, 1677 POTTERY KILN**, NW of Hague, 1677. Remains of earthenware pottery kiln and associated waster concentration, and artifacts. Established by Morgan Jones for making and selling earthenware, probably used only a short time; not completely excavated. *Private; not accessible to the public.*

Lerty vicinity. **STRATFORD HALL,** N of Lerty on VA 214, 1725-1730. Brick (Flemish bond), 1 story on full raised basement, H-shaped, hipped roof with twin sets of 4 chimneys joined by arches and balustrade, central hall plan, outbuildings, formal gardens. Noted example of Georgian architecture. Home of historic Lee family; birthplace of Robert E. Lee and 2 signers of the Declaration of Independence, Richard Henry Lee and Francis Lightfoot Lee. *Private:* NHL; HABS.

Montross vicinity. **CHANTILLY,** NE of jct. of VA 609 and 622, 18th C.. Site of plantation and dwelling owned by Richard Henry Lee, signer of the Declaration of Independence and member of the Continental Congress, the Virginia House of Burgesses, and the U.S. Senate. Dwelling probably burned during War of 1812. *Private.*

Tucker Hill vicinity. **YEOCOMICO CHURCH,** SW of Tucker Hill on Rte. 606, Early-18th C.. Brick, 1 story, modified rectangle, steeply gabled roof with flared eaves and modillion cornice, round window in E gable, entrance vestibule with flared eaves and fine diaper pattern above triple arched head over doorway; massive battened door with smaller wicket door set within. Medieval colonial elements. Only surviving colonial church in county. *Private:* NHL; HABS.

Westmoreland. **SPENCE'S POINT (JOHN R. DOS PASSOS FARM)**, On Sandy Point Neck, on VA 749, 1806. Brick, 2 stories, rectangular, gabled roof sections, interior end chimneys, off-center entrance, flat arched openings, rear enclosed porch; original 1806 structure remodeled and enlarged by a 2-story side section, 1940's. Federal. Home of John Dos Passos, influential modern American writer of the 1920's and 1930's, noted for such works as the *U.S.A.* trilogy. *Private; not accessible to the public:* NHL.

WILLIAMSBURG (independent city)

BRUTON PARISH CHURCH, Duke of Gloucester St., 1712–1715, Alexander Spotswood, builder-architect Alexander Spotswood, builder-architect. Brick, 1 story, modified Latin cross shape, gabled roof, round arched windows, modillion cornice, roundels in chancel and transept and walls; square 3-story tower with spire added, 1769; altered; restored, 1905 and 1939. Georgian. Designed by Royal Governor Alexander Spotswood; for many years the court church of VA. *Private:* NHL; HABS.

COLONIAL NATIONAL HISTORICAL PARK, *Reference—see James City County*

RANDOLPH, PEYTON, HOUSE, Corner of Nicholson and N. England Sts., c. 1715. Frame, clapboarding; 2 stories (1 1/2-story E section), modified rectangle, hipped and gabled roof sections, 3 interior chimneys, modillion cornice, center entrance, regular fenestration. Erected in 3 stages, the E section was connected to the older house by Sir John Randolph, c. 1724. Notable paneling, most of which is original, in main rooms; restored. Georgian. *Private:* NHL; HABS.

SEMPLE, JAMES, HOUSE, S side of Frances St. between Blair and Walker Sts., c. 1770. Frame, clapboarding; 2 1/2-story main block, flanking 1-story wings; rectangular, gabled roof sections, interior end chimneys, circular window in pediment, denticulated modillion cornice, center Doric entrance porch; restored, 1932. Federal. Design derived from plate of Robert Morris' *Select Architecture* (London, 1757). *Private; not accessible to the public:* NHL; HABS.

WILLIAMSBURG HISTORIC DISTRICT, Bounded by Francis, Waller, Nicholson, N. England, Lafayette, and Nassau Sts., 17th–18th C.. 130-acre district containing more than 490 1–2 1/2-story brick and frame structures, reconstructed or restored to 18th C. appearance. First settled in 1633; center of leadership and influence throughout period preceding Revolution; VA capital, 1699–1779. Location of College of William and Mary (est. 1693), one of the oldest in the U.S. *Multiple public/private:* NHL; HABS.

WREN BUILDING, COLLEGE OF WILLIAM AND MARY, College of William and Mary campus, 1702, attributed to Sir Christopher Wren, architect. Brick, 2 1/2 stories, rectangular, hipped roof, dormers, center pedimented pavilion, central cupola, rear ells added later. Burned and rebuilt several times; restored, 1927. Oldest academic building in the U.S. *State:* NHL; HABS.

WYTHE HOUSE, W side of the Palace Green, c. 1755, Richard Taliaferro, architect. Brick (Flemish bond), 2 stories, rectangular, hipped roof, 2 interior chimneys, modillion cornice, regular fenestration, center entrance with 2 flanking windows on either side. Georgian. Home of George Wythe, a signer of the Declaration of Independence. *Private:* NHL.

WINCHESTER (independent city)

ABRAM'S DELIGHT, Parkview St. and Rouss Spring Rd., 1754. Rock-faced random limestone, 2 1/2 stories, modified rectangle, gabled roof sections, interior end chimneys, main block with slightly off-center front entrance with transom; wing with front and rear entrances, each with transom; doors and windows with molded trim with corner blocks with rosettes; wing added before 1801, brick addition removed; fenestration altered. Colonial elements. Town's oldest house; former home of the Hollingsworth family. Museum. *Municipal:* HABS.

HANDLEY LIBRARY, NW corner of Braddock and Piccadilly Sts., 1908–1913, J. Stewart Barney and Henry Otis Chapman, architects. Stone, 2 stories, L-shaped, gabled sections, oval dormer lights, central dome with circular windows over octagonal base, arched entrance portico with Corinthian columns, flanking 2 1/2-story wings with colonnaded porches topped by balustrade. One of state's outstanding examples of Beaux-Arts Classicism. *Municipal.*

JACKSON, THOMAS J., HEADQUARTERS, 415 N. Braddock St., 1854. Brick, 1 1/2 stories, rectangular, gabled roof, 2 interior chimneys, center entrance section with pointed arched entranceway and window on either side, decorative bargeboards. Gothic Revival elements. Headquarters of "Stonewall" Jackson prior to his famous Shenandoah Valley campaign of 1862. *Private:* NHL.

WISE COUNTY

Big Stone Gap. **FOX, JOHN JR., HOUSE,** 117 Shawnee Ave., 1890. Frame, shingling; 2 stories, irregular shape, gabled and shed roof sections, interior and exterior chimneys, many additions enlarging 4-room cottage into 22-room house. Home of novelist John Fox, Jr., whose best known works include *The Little Shepherd of Kingdom Come* and *The Trail of the Lonesome Pipe*. Museum. *Private.*

Big Stone Gap. **"JUNE TOLLIVER" HOUSE,** On VA 613, 19th C.. Brick, 2 1/2 stories, rectangular, intersecting gabled and flat roof sections, projecting wooden end bays. Queen Anne elements. June Morris, prototype of June Tolliver, heroine of *The Trail of the Lonesome Pine* by John Fox, Jr., boarded here. One of the first best sellers of the century, the story describes the boom which followed the discovery of coal in the mountains. *Private.*

WYTHE COUNTY

Fosters Falls vicinity. **MARTIN SITE,** Late Archaic–Woodland (2000 B.C.–1300 A.D.). Woodland village site with an earlier Archaic component. Unexcavated. *Private.*

Max Meadows vicinity. **FORT CHISWELL MANSION,** I 81 near jct. of U.S. 52 and VA 121, 1839–1840. Brick, 2 1/2 stories, L-shaped, gabled roof with stepped gable ends, slightly projecting end chimneys, center 2-story distyle pedimented entrance portico, 2-story front Italianate porches with balustrades, 1-story E kitchen wing and 2-story rear ell. Greek Revival. Built by Stephen and Joseph McGavock, prominent planters. *Private; not accessible to the public.*

Max Meadows vicinity. **SHOT TOWER,** W of jct. of Rte. 608 and U.S. 52, c. 1807. Limestone, 75' high, square, pyramidal roof, 1 interior chimney, simple wooden balcony on one side at top. Room at top, reached by winding wooden staircase, contains a fireplace and shaft through which molten metal was poured through a sieve into a kettle of water below to form shot. One of 3 shot towers remaining in U.S. Built by Thomas Jackson to manufacture shot for frontiersmen and settlers. *State.*

Wytheville. **HALLER-GIBBONEY ROCK HOUSE,** Monroe and Tazewell Sts., 1822–1823. Random limestone, 2 stories, L-shaped, gabled roof sections, interior end chimneys, front center slightly recessed entrance with transom, side bay window; rear 2-story ell with polygonal end, 1-story porch, and shed wing; fenestration altered slightly, ell added c. 1900. Greek Revival elements. One of several remaining stone houses built late-18th–early-19th C. in area which was then a frontier. *Municipal:* HABS.

YORK COUNTY

COLONIAL NATIONAL HISTORICAL PARK, *Reference—see James City County*

Lackay vicinity. **LEE HOUSE (KISKIACK),** NE of jct. of VA 238 and 168, 17th C.. Brick (Flemish bond), 1 1/2 stories, rectangular, gabled roof with pedimented dormers, 2 T-shaped interior end chimneys with molded caps; projecting enclosed center entrance vestibule added, 1937. Colonial elements. Typical early VA country house. Tract patented in 1641 and remained in Lee family until 1918. *Federal/USN; not accessible to the public:* HABS.

Williamsburg vicinity. **PORTO BELLO,** On Queens Creek, in Camp Peary Military Reservation, c. 1800. Brick, 1 1/2 stories, rectangular, mansard roof, dormers, front entrance with hipped porch; alterations after 1915 fire damage included rebuilding interior and

Historical Places

replacement of modified gambrel roof. Built on property of Porto Bello plantation; country home possibly occupied by Lord Dunmore, colonial governor of VA, in late-18th C. *Federal/USA; not accessible to the public.*

Yorktown. **GRACE CHURCH,** Rte. 1003 and Main St., 1848. Marl, stuccoed; 1 story, rectangular, gabled roof, decorative center entrance; 1926 additions include the octagonal belfry, W door, and roundel in pediment. Greek Revival. May be the only extant early marl structure. Replaced original York-Hampton Parish Church which burned in 1814. Prominent parishioners included Thomas Nelson, signer of the Declaration of Independence. *Private.*

Yorktown vicinity. **GOOCH, WILLIAM, TOMB AND YORK VILLAGE ARCHEOLOGICAL SITE,** E of Yorktown on U. S. Coast Guard Reserve Training Center, 17th C.. Site of colonial settlement containing brick foundations of York Church surrounding limestone slab tomb (1655) of Maj. William Gooch, VA burgess; below ground village remains; and Confederate earthworks constructed by Confederate Gen. John B. Magruder in defense of Richmond, 1862. *Federal/USCG.*

Yorktown vicinity. **YORKTOWN WRECKS,** 4 mi. of York River between Gloucester and York County shores at Yorktown, 1781. Underwater site containing remains of British war fleet sunk in seige of Yorktown 1781; undetermined number of ships. Partially investigated by National Park Service and Mariner's Museum 1934–1935; and by Fort Eustis, 1954. *State/federal/USA; not accessible to the public.*

THE CONSTITUTION OF VIRGINIA

ARTICLE I

Bill of Rights

A DECLARATION OF RIGHTS made by the good people of Virginia in the exercise of their sovereign powers, which rights do pertain to them and their posterity, as the basis and foundation of government.

Section 1. Equality and rights of men.

That all men are by nature equally free and independent and have certain inherent rights, of which, when they enter into a state of society, they cannot, by any compact, deprive or divest their posterity; namely, the enjoyment of life and liberty, with the means of acquiring and possessing property, and pursuing and obtaining happiness and safety.

Section 2. People the source of power.

That all power is vested in, and consequently derived from, the people, that magistrates are their trustees and servants, and at all times amenable to them.

Section 3. Government instituted for common benefit.

That government is, or ought to be, instituted for the common benefit, protection, and security of the people, nation, or community; of all the various modes and forms of government, that is best which is capable of producing the greatest degree of happiness and safety, and is most effectually secured against the danger of maladministration; and, whenever any government shall be found inadequate or contrary to these purposes, a majority of the community hath an indubitable, inalienable, and indefeasible right to reform, alter, or abolish it, in such manner as shall be judged most conducive to the public weal.

Section 4. No exclusive emoluments or privileges; offices not to be hereditary.

That no man, or set of men, is entitled to exclusive or separate emoluments or privileges from the community, but in consideration of public services; which not being descendible, neither ought the offices of magistrate, legislator, or judge to be hereditary.

Section 5. Separation of legislative, executive, and Judicial departments; periodical elections,

That the legislative, executive and judicial departments of the Commonwealth should be separate and distinct; and that the members thereof may be restrained from oppression, by feeling and participating the burthens of the people, they should, at fixed periods, be reduced to a private station, return into that body from which they were originally taken, and the vacancies be supplied by regular elections, in which all or any part of the former members shall be again eligible, or ineligible, as the laws may direct.

Section 6. Free elections; consent of governed.

That all elections ought to be free; and that all men, having sufficient evidence of permanent common interest with, and attachment to, the community, have the right of suffrage, and cannot be taxed, or deprived of, or damaged in, their property for public uses, without their own consent, or that of their representatives duly elected, or bound by any law to which they have not, in like manner, assented for the public good.

Section 7. Laws should not be suspended.

That all power of suspending laws, or the execution of laws, by any authority, without consent of the representatives of the people, is injurious to their rights, and ought not to be exercised.

Section 8. Criminal prosecutions.

That in criminal prosecutions a man hath a right to demand the cause and nature of his accusation, to be confronted with the accusers and witnesses, and to call for evidence in his favor, and he shall enjoy the right to a speedy and public trial, by an impartial jury of his vicinage, without whose unanimous consent he cannot be found guilty. He shall not be deprived of life or liberty, except by the law of the land or the judgment of his peers, nor be compelled in any criminal proceeding to give evidence against himself, nor be put twice in jeopardy for the same offense.

Laws may be enacted providing for the trial of offenses not felonious by a court not of record without a jury, preserving the right of the accused to an appeal to and a trial by jury in some court of record having original criminal jurisdiction. Laws may also provide for juries consisting of less than twelve, but not less than five, for the trial of offenses not felonious, and may classify such cases, and prescribe the number of jurors for each class.

In criminal cases, the accused may plead guilty. If the accused plead not guilty, he may, with his consent and the concurrence of the Commonwealth's Attorney and of the court entered of record, be tried by a smaller number of jurors, or waive a jury. In case of such waiver or plea of guilty, the court shall try the case.

State Constitution

The provisions of this section shall be self-executing.

Section 9. Prohibition of excessive bail and fines, cruel and unusual punishment, suspension of habeas corpus, bills of attainder, and ex post facto laws.

That excessive bail ought not to be required, nor excessive fines imposed, nor cruel and unusual punishments inflicted; that the privilege of the writ of habeas corpus shall not be suspended unless when, in cases of invasion or rebellion, the public safety may require; and that the General Assembly shall not pass any bill of attainder, or any ex post facto law.

Section 10. General warrants of search or seizure prohibited.

That general warrants, whereby an officer or messenger may be commanded to search suspected places without evidence of a fact committed, or to seize any person or persons not named, or whose offense is not particularly described and supported by evidence, are grievous and oppressive, and ought not to be granted.

Section 11. Due process of law; obligation of contracts; taking of private property; prohibited discrimination; jury trial in civil cases.

That no person shall be deprived of his life, liberty, or property without due process of law; that the General Assembly shall not pass any law impairing the obligation of contracts, nor any law whereby private property shall be taken or damaged for public uses, without just compensation, the term "public uses" to be defined by the General Assembly; and that the right to be free from any governmental discrimination upon the basis of religious conviction, race, color, sex, or national origin shall not be abridged, except that the mere separation of the sexes shall not be considered discrimination.

That in controversies respecting property, and in suits between man and man, trial by jury is preferable to any other, and ought to be held sacred. The General Assembly may limit the number of jurors for civil cases in courts of record to not less than five.

Section 12. Freedom of speech and of the press; right peaceably to assemble, and to petition.

That the freedoms of speech and of the press are among the great bulwarks of liberty, and can never be restrained except by despotic governments; that any citizen may freely speak, write, and publish his sentiments on all subjects, being responsible for the abuse of that right; that the General Assembly shall not pass any law abridging the freedom of speech or of the press, nor the right of the people peaceably to assemble, and to petition the government for the redress of grievances.

Section 13. Militia; standing armies; military subordinate to civil power.

That a well regulated militia, composed of the body of the people, trained to arms, is the proper, natural, and safe defense of a free state, therefore, the right of the people to keep and bear arms shall not be infringed; that standing armies, in time of peace, should be avoided as dangerous to liberty; and that in all cases the military should be under strict subordination to, and governed by, the civil power.

Section 14. Government should be uniform.

That the people have a right to uniform government; and, therefore, that no government separate from, or independent of, the government of Virginia, ought to be erected or established within the limits thereof.

Section 15. Qualities necessary to preservation of free government.

That no free government, nor the blessings of liberty, can be preserved to any people, but by a firm adherence to justice, moderation, temperance, frugality, and virtue; by frequent recurrence to fundamental principles; and by the recognition by all citizens that they have duties as well as rights, and that such rights cannot be enjoyed save in a society where law is respected and due process is observed.

That free government rests, as does all progress, upon the broadest possible diffusion of knowledge, and that the Commonwealth should avail Itself of those talents which nature has sown so liberally among its people by assuring the opportunity for their fullest development by an effective system of education throughout the Commonwealth.

Section 16. Free exercise of religion; no establishment of religion.

That religion or the duty which we owe to our Creator, and the manner of discharging it, can be directed only by reason and conviction, not by force or violence; and, therefore, all men are equally entitled to the free exercise of religion, according to the dictates of conscience; and that it is the mutual duty of all to practice Christian forbearance, love, and charity towards each other. No man shall be compelled to frequent or support any religious worship, place, or ministry whatsoever, nor shall be enforced, restrained, molested, or burthened in his body or goods, nor shall otherwise suffer on account of his religious opinions or belief; but all men shall be free to profess and by argument to maintain their opinions in matters of religion, and the same shall in nowise diminish, enlarge, or affect their civil capacities. And the General Assembly shall not prescribe any religious test

State Constitution

whatever, or confer any peculiar privileges or advantages on any sect or denomination, or pass any law requiring or authorizing any religious society, or the people of any district within this Commonwealth, to levy on themselves or others, any tax for the erection or repair of any house of public worship, or for the support of any church or ministry; but it shall be left free to every person to select his religious instructor, and to make for his support such private contract as he shall please.

Section 17. Construction of the Bill of Rights.

The rights enumerated in this Bill of Rights shall not be construed to limit other rights of the people not therein expressed.

ARTICLE II

Franchise and Officers

Section 1. Qualifications of voters.

In elections by the people, the qualifications of voters shall be as follows: Each voter shall be a citizen of the United States, shall be eighteen years of age, shall fulfill the residence requirements set forth in this section, and shall be registered to vote pursuant to this article. No person who has been convicted of a felony shall be qualified to vote unless his civil rights have been restored by the Governor or other appropriate authority. As prescribed by law, no person adjudicated to be mentally incompetent shall be qualified to vote until his competency has been reestablished.

The residence requirements shall be that each voter shall be a resident of the Commonwealth and of the precinct where he votes. A person who is qualified to vote except for having moved his residence from one precinct to another may in the following November general election and in any intervening election vote in the precinct from which he has moved.

Residence, for all purposes of qualification to vote, requires both domicile and a place of abode. The General Assembly may provide, in elections for President and Vice-President of the United States, alternatives to registration for new residents of the Commonwealth.

Any person who will be qualified with respect to age to vote at the next general election shall be permitted to register in advance and also to vote in any intervening primary or special election.

The amendment ratified November 7, 1872 and effective January 1, 1872- In paragraph one, the voting age, formerly "twenty©e", was reduced to "eighteen".

Encyclopedia of Virginia

The amendment ratified November 2, 1876 and effective January 1, 1877- In paragraph two, substituted "be" for "have been" and removed the durational residency requirement of "six months" in the Commonwealth and "thirty days" in the precinct in the first sentence. The second sentence removed the language "fewer than thirty days prior to an election" and after the word "may" added the language "in the following November general election and (in any) intervening". In the last sentence of the paragraph the less than six months residency requirement for presidential elections was removed to conform with the first sentence.

Section 2. Registration of voters.

The General Assembly shall provide by law for the registration of all persons otherwise qualified to vote who have met the residence requirements contained in this article, and shall ensure that the opportunity to register is made available. Registrations accomplished prior to the effective date of this section shall be effective hereunder. The registration records shall not be closed to new or transferred registrations more than thirty days before the election in which they are to be used.

Applications to register shall require the applicant to provide under oath the following information on a standard form: full name, including the maiden and any other prior legal name; age; date and place of birth; social security number, if any; whether the applicant is presently a United States citizen; address and place of abode and date of residence in the precinct; place of any previous registrations to vote; and whether the applicant has ever been adjudicated to be mentally incompetent or convicted of a felony, and if so, under what circumstances the applicant's right to vote has been restored. Except as otherwise provided in this Constitution, all applications to register shall be completed in person before the registrar and by or at the direction of the applicant and signed by the applicant, unless physically disabled. No fee shall be charged to the applicant incident to an application to register.

Nothing in this article shall preclude the General Assembly from requiring as a prerequisite to registration to vote the ability of the applicant to read and complete in his own handwriting the application to register.

The amendment ratified November 2, 1876 and effective January 1, 1877- In paragraph two, substituted "date of residence in the precinct" for "length of residence in the Commonwealth and In the precinct" and removed "time" of any previous registrations to vote.

The amendment ratified November 2, 1882 and effective January 1, 1882- In paragraph two, after "maiden" added "and any other prior legal" and deleted "of a woman, if married" and after "birth;" deleted "marital status; occupation;".

State Constitution

Section 3. Method of voting.

In elections by the people, the following safeguards shall be maintained: Voting shall be by ballot or by machines for receiving, recording, and counting votes cast. No ballot or list of candidates upon any voting machine shall bear any distinguishing mark or symbol, other than words identifying political party affiliation; and their form, including the offices to be filled and the listing of candidates or nominees, shall be as uniform as is practicable throughout the Commonwealth or smaller governmental unit in which the election is held.

In elections other than primary elections, provision shall be made whereby votes may be cast for persons other than the listed candidates or nominees. Secrecy in casting votes shall be maintained, except as provision may be made for assistance to handicapped voters, but the ballot box or voting machine shall be kept in public view and shall not be opened, nor the ballots canvassed nor the votes counted, in secret. Votes may be cast only in person, except as otherwise provided in this article.

Section 4. Powers and duties of General Assembly.

The General Assembly shall establish a uniform system for permanent registration of voters pursuant to this Constitution, including provisions for appeal by any person denied registration, correction of illegal or fraudulent registrations, proper transfer of all registered voters, and cancellation of registrations in other jurisdictions of persons who apply to register to vote in the Commonwealth. The General Assembly shall provide for maintenance of accurate and current registration records and shall provide for cancellation of the registration of any voter who has not voted at least once during four consecutive calendar years and who fails to return a written response indicating a desire to remain registered at the residence address currently on record in response to a notice of pending cancellation.

The General Assembly may provide for registration and voting by absentee application and ballot for members of the Armed Forces of the United States in active service, persons residing temporarily outside of the United States by virtue of their employment, and their spouses and dependents residing with such persons, who are otherwise qualified to vote, and may provide for voting by absentee ballot for other qualified voters.

The General Assembly shall provide for the nomination of candidates, shall regulate the time, place, manner, conduct, and administration of primary, general, and special elections, and shall have power to make any other law regulating elections not inconsistent with this Constitution.

Encyclopedia of Virginia

The amendment ratified November 2, 1876 and effective January 1, 1977- In paragraph two, added "persons residing temporarily outside of the United States by virtue of their employment," and "and dependents residing with such persons".

The amendment ratified November 4' 1886 and effective July 1, 1887- In paragraph one, after "consecutive calendar years" added "and who fails to return a written response"

Section 5. Qualifications to hold elective office.

The only qualification to hold any office of the Commonwealth or of its governmental units, elective by the people, shall be that a person must have been a resident of the Commonwealth for one year next preceding his election and be qualified to vote for that office, except as otherwise provided in this Constitution, and except that:

(a) the General Assembly may impose more restrictive geographical residence requirements for election of its members, and may permit other governing bodies in the Commonwealth to impose more restrictive geographical residence requirements for election to such governing bodies, but no such requirements shall impair equal representation of the persons entitled to vote;

(b) the General Assembly may provide that residence in a local governmental unit is not required for election to designated elective offices in local governments, other than membership in the local governing body; and

(c) nothing in this Constitution shall limit the power of the General Assembly to prevent conflict of interests, dual officeholding, or other incompatible activities by elective or appointive officials of the Commonwealth or of any political subdivision.

The amendment ratified November * 1876 and effective January 1, 1877- In paragraph one, after "one year" added the language "next preceding his election".

Section 6. Apportionment.

Members of the House of Representatives of the United States and members of the Senate and of the House of Delegates of the General Assembly shall be elected from electoral districts established by the General Assembly. Every electoral district shall be composed of contiguous and compact territory and shall be so constituted as to give, as nearly as is practicable, representation in proportion to the population of the district. The General Assembly shall reapportion the Commonwealth into electoral districts in accordance with this section in the year 1971 and every ten years thereafter.

State Constitution

Any such reapportionment law shall take effect Immediately and not be subject to the limitations contained in Article IV, Section 13, of this Constitution.

Section 7. Oath or affirmation.

All officers elected or appointed under or pursuant to this Constitution shall, before they enter on the performance of their public duties, severally take and subscribe the following oath or affirmation:

"I do solemnly swear (or affirm) that I will support the Constitution of the United States, and the Constitution of the Commonwealth of Virginia, and that I will faithfully and Impartially discharge all the duties incumbent upon me as............, according to the best of my ability (so help me God)."

Section 8. Electoral boards; registrars and officers of election.

There shall be in each county and city an electoral board composed of three members, selected as provided by law. In the appointment of the electoral boards, representation, as far as practicable, shall be given to each of the two political parties which, at the general election next preceding their appointment, cast the highest and the next highest number of votes. The present members of such boards shall continue in office until the expiration of their respective terms; thereafter their successors shall be appointed for the term of three years. Any vacancy occurring in any board shall be filled by the same authority for the unexpired term.

Each electoral board shall appoint the officers of election and general registrar for Its county or city. In appointing such officers of election, representation, as far as practicable, shall be given to each of the two political parties which, at the general election next preceding their appointment, cast the highest and next highest number of votes.

No person, nor the deputy of any person, who is employed by or holds any office or post of profit or emolument, or who holds any elective office of profit or trust, under the governments of the United States, the Commonwealth, or any county, city, or town, shall be appointed a member of the electoral board or general registrar. No person, nor the deputy or the employee of any person, who holds any elective office of profit or trust under the government of the United States, the Commonwealth, or any county, city, or town of the Commonwealth shall be appointed an assistant registrar or officer of election.

The amendmeat ratified November 4, 1986 and effective January 1, 1987- In paragraph two, after "officers" deleted the words "and registrars" id added "and general registrar" after "of election". In paragraph three, after "the electoral board or" added the word "general" before "rear" and deleted a reference to officer of election, ad added the last sentence: "No person, nor the deputy or the employee of any person .

Section 9. Privileges of voters during election.

No voter, during the time of holding any election at which he is entitled to vote, shall be compelled to perform military service, except in time of war or public danger, nor to attend any court as suitor, juror, or witness; nor shall any such voter be subject to arrest under any civil process during his attendance at election or in going to or returning therefrom.

ARTICLE III

Division of Powers

Section 1. Departments to be distinct.

The legislative, executive, and judicial departments shall be separate and distinct, so that none exercise the powers properly belonging to the others, nor any person exercise the power of more than one of them at the same time; provided, however, administrative agencies may be created by the General Assembly with such authority and duties as the General Assembly may prescribe. Provisions may be made for judicial review of any finding, order, or judgnient of such administrative agencies.

ARTICLE IV

Legislature

Section 1. Legislative power.

The legislative power of the Commonwealth shall be vested in a General Assembly, which shall consist of a Senate and House of Delegates.

Section 2. Senate.

The Senate shall consist of not more than forty and not less than thirty-three members, who shall be elected quadrennially by the voters of the several senatorial districts on the Tuesday succeeding the first Monday in November.

Section 3. House of Delegated

The House of Delegates shall consist of not more than one hundred and not less than ninety members, who shall be elected biennially by the voters of the several house districts on the Tuesday succeeding the first Monday in November.

Section 4. Qualifications of senators and delegates.

Any person may be elected to the Senate who, at the time of the election, is twenty-one years of age, is a resident of the senatorial district which he is seeking to represent, and is qualified to vote for members of the General Assembly. Any person may be elected to the House of Delegates who, at the time of the election, is twenty©e years of age, is a resident of the house district which he is seeking to represent, and is qualified to vote for members of the General Assembly. A senator or delegate who moves his residence from the district for which he is elected shall thereby vacate his office.

No person holding a salaried office under the government of the Commonwealth, and no judge of any court, attorney for the Commonwealth, sheriff, treasurer, assessor of taxes, commissioner of the revenue, collector of taxes, or clerk of any court shall be a member of either house of the General Assembly during his continuance in office; and his qualification as a member shall vacate any such office held by him. No person holding any office or post of profit or emolument under the United States government, or who is in the employment of such government, shall be eligible to either house.

Section 5. Compensation; election to civil office of profit.

The members of the General Assembly shall receive such salary and allowances as may be prescribed by law, but no increase in salary shall take effect for a given member until after the end of the term for which he was elected. No member during the term for which he shall have been elected shall be elected by the General Assembly to any civil office of profit in the Commonwealth.

Section 6. Legislative sessions.

The General Assembly shall meet once each year on the second Wednesday in January. Except as herein provided for reconvened sessions, no regular session of the General Assembly convened in an even-numbered year shall continue longer than sixty days; no regular session of the General Assembly convened in an odd-numbered year shall continue longer than thirty days; but with the concurrence of two-thirds of the members elected to each house, any regular session may be extended for a period not exceeding thirty days. Neither house shall, without the consent of the other, adjourn to another place, nor for more than three days.

The Governor may convene a special session of the General Assembly when, in his opinion, the interest of the Commonwealth may require and shall convene a special session upon the application of two-thirds of the members elected to each house.

The General Assembly shall reconvene on the sixth Wednesday after adjournment of each regular or special session for the purpose of considering bills which may have been returned by the Governor with recommendations for their amendment and bills and items of appropriation bills which may have been returned by the Governor with his objections. No other business shall be considered at a reconvened session. Such reconvened session shall not continue longer than three days unless the session be extended, for a period not exceeding seven additional days, upon the vote of the majority of the members elected to each house.

The amendment ratified November 4, 1880 and effective January 1, 1881- Alter the first sentence In the first paragraph added "Except as herein provided for reconvened sessions,". Added a third paragraph "The General Assembly shall reconvene on the sixth Wednesday .

Section 7. Organization of General Assembly.

The House of Delegates shall choose its own Speaker; and, in the absence of the Lieutenant Governor, or when he shall exercise the office of Governor, the Senate shall choose from its own body a president pro tempore. Each house shall select its officers and settle its rules of procedure. The houses may jointly provide for legislative continuity between sessions occurring during the term for which members of the House of Delegates are elected. Each house may direct writs of election for supplying vacancies which may occur during a session of the General Assembly. If vacancies exist while the General Assembly is not in session, such writs may be issued by the Governor under such regulations as may be prescribed by law. Each house shall judge of the election, qualification, and returns of its members, may punish them for disorderly behavior, and, with the concurrence of two-thirds of its elected membership, may expel a member.

Section 8. Quorum.

A majority of the members elected to each house shall constitute a quorum to do business, but a smaller number may adjourn from day to day and shall have power to compel the attendance of members in such manner and under such penalty as each house may prescribe. A smaller number, not less than two-fifths of the elected membership of each house, may meet and may, notwithstanding any other provision of this Constitution, enact legislation if the Governor by proclamation declares that a quorum of the General Assembly cannot be convened because of enemy attack upon the soil of Virginia. Such legislation shall remain effective only until thirty days after a quorum of the General Assembly can be convened.

Section 9. Immunity of legislators.

Members of the General Assembly shall, in all cases except treason, felony, or breach of the peace, be privileged from arrest during the sessions of their respective houses; and for any speech or debate in either house shall not be questioned in any other place. They shall not be subject to arrest under any civil process during the sessions of the General Assembly, or during the fifteen days before the beginning or after the ending of any session.

State Constitution

Section 10. Journal of proceedings.

Each house shall keep a journal of its proceedings, which shall be published from time to time. The vote of each member voting in each house on any question shall, at the desire of one-fifth of those present, be recorded in the journal. On the final vote on any bill, and on the vote in any election or impeachment conducted in the General Assembly or on the expulsion of a member, the name of each member voting in each house and how he voted shall be recorded in the journal.

Section 11. Enactment of laws.

No law shall be enacted except by bill. A bill may originate in either house, may be approved or rejected by the other, or may be amended by either, with the concurrence of the other.

No bill shall become a law unless, prior to its passage:

(a) it has been referred to a committee of each house, considered by such committee in session, and reported;

(b) it has been printed by the house in which it originated prior to its passage therein;

(c) it has been read by its title, or its title has been printed in a daily calendar, on three different calendar days in each house; and

(d) upon its final passage a vote has been taken thereon in each house, the name of each member voting for and against recorded in the journal, and a majority of those voting in each house, which majority shall Include at least two-fifths of the members elected to that house, recorded in the affirmative.

Only in the manner required in subparagraph (d) of this section shall an amendment to a bill by one house be concurred in by the other, or a conference report be adopted by either house, or either house discharge a committee from the consideration of a bill and consider the same as if reported. The printing and reading, or either, required In subparagraphs (b) and (c) of this section, may be dispensed with in a bill to codify the laws of the Commonwealth, and in the case of an emergency by a vote of four-fifths of the members voting in each house, the name of each member voting and how he voted to be recorded in the journal.

No bill which creates or establishes a new office, or which creates, continues, or revives a debt or charge, or which makes, continues, or revives any appropriation of public or trust money or property, or which releases, discharges, or commutes any claim or demand of the Commonwealth, or which imposes, continues, or revives a tax, shall be passed except by the affirmative vote of a majority of all the members elected to each house, the name of each member voting and how he voted to be recorded in the journal.

Every law imposing, continuing, or reviving a tax shall specifically state such tax. However, any law by which taxes are imposed may define or specify the subject and provisions of such tax by reference to any provision of the laws of the United States as those laws may be or become effective at any time or from time to time, and may prescribe exceptions or modifications to any such provision.

The presiding officer of each house or upon his inability or failure to act a person designated by a majority of the members elected to each house shall, not later than three days after each bill is enrolled, sign each bill that has been passed by both houses and duly enrolled. The fact of signing shall be recorded in the journal.

The amendment ratified November 4, 1989 and effective January 1, 1981- In the last paragraph substituted "or upon his inability or failure to act a person designated by a majority of the members elected to each house shall, not later than three days after each bill is enrolled, sip each" for "shall, not later than twenty days after adjouramenL sign every".

Section 12. Form of laws.

No law shall embrace more than one object, which shall be expressed in its title. Nor shall any law be revived or amended with reference to its title, but the act revived or the section amended shall be reenacted and published at length.

Section 13. Effective date of laws.

All laws enacted at a regular session, including laws which are enacted by reason of actions taken during the reconvened session following a regular session, but excluding a general appropriation law, shall take effect on the first day of July following the adjournment of the session of the General Assembly at which it has been enacted; and all laws enacted at a special session, including laws which are enacted by reason of actions taken during the reconvened session following a special session but excluding a general appropriation law, shall take effect on the first day of the fourth month following the month of adjournment of the special session; unless in the case of an emergency (which emergency shall be expressed in the body of the bill) the General Assembly shall specify an earlier date by a vote of four-fifths of the members voting in each house, the name of each member voting and how he voted to be recorded in the journal, or unless a subsequent date is specified in the body of the bill or by general law.

The amendment ratified November 4, 1989 and effective January 1, 1981- Rewrote the section so that all laws enacted at regular sessions and reconvened sessions which follow will take effect on July 1 rather than on the first day of the fourth month following the month of adjournment, and all laws enacted at special sessions and reconvened sessions which follow will take effect on tne fourth month following the month of adjournment, excluding the general appropriation laws.

State Constitution

Section 14. Powers of General Assembly; limitations

The authority of the General Assembly shall extend to all subjects of legislation not herein forbidden or restricted; and a specific grant of authority in this Constitution upon a subject shall not work a restriction of its authority upon the same or any other subject. The omission In this Constitution of specific grants of authority heretofore conferred shall not be construed to deprive the General Assembly of such authority, or to Indicate a change of policy In reference thereto, unless such purpose plainly appear.

The General Assembly shall confer on the courts power to grant divorces, change the names of persons, and direct the sales of estates belonging to infants and other persons under legal disabilities, and shall not, by special legislation, grant relief in these or other cases of which the courts or other tribunals may have jurisdiction.

The General Assembly may regulate the exercise by courts of the right to punish for contempt.

The General Assembly shall not enact any local, special, or private law In the following cases:

(1) For the punishment of crime.

(2) Providing a change of venue in civil or criminal cases.

(3) Regulating the practice in, or the jurisdiction of, or changing the rules of evidence In any judicial proceedings or inquiry before the courts or other tribunals, or providing or changing the methods of collecting debts or enforcing judgfnents or prescribing the effect of judicial sales of real estate.

(4) Changing or locating county seats.

(5) For the assessment and collection of taxes, except as to anamals which the General Assembly may deem dangerous to the farming interests.

(6) Extending the time for the assessment or collection of taxes.

(7) Exempting property from taxation.

(8) Remitting, releasing, postponing, or diminishing any obligation or liability of any person, corporation, or association to the Commonwealth or to any political subdivision thereof.

(9) Refunding money lawfully paid into the treasury of the Commonwealth or the treasury of any political subdivision thereof.

(10) Granting from the treasury of the Commonwealth, or granting or authorizing to be granted from the treasury of any political subdivision thereof, any extra compensation to any public officer, servant, agent, or contractor.

(11) For registering voters, conducting elections, or designating the places of voting.

(12) Regulating labor, trade, mining, or manufacturing, or the rate of Interest on money.

(13) Granting any pension.

(14) Creating, increasing, or decreasing, or authorizing to be created, Increased, or decreased, the salaries, fees, percentages, or allowances of public officers during the term for which they are elected or appointed.

(15) Declaring streams navigable, or authorizing the construction of booms or dams therein, or the removal of obstructions therefrom.

(16) Affecting or regulating fencing or the boundaries of land, or the running at large of stock.

(17) Creating private corporations, or amending, renewing, or extending the charters thereof.

(18) Granting to any private corporation, association, or individual any special or exclusive right, privilege, or immunity.

(19) Naming or changing the name of any private corporation or association.

(20) Remitting the forfeiture of the charter of any private corporation, except upon the condition that such corporation shall thereafter hold its charter subject to the provisions of this Constitution and the laws passed in pursuance thereof.

The General Assembly shall not grant a charter of incorporation to any church or religious denomination, but may secure the title to church property to an extent to be limited by law.

Section 15. General laws.

In all cases enumerated in the preceding section, and in every other case which, in its judgment, may be provided for by general laws, the General Assembly shall enact general laws. Any general law shall be subject to amendment or repeal, but the amendment or partial repeal thereof shall not operate directly or indirectly to enact, and shall not have the effect of enactment of, a special, private, or local law.

State Constitution

No general or special law shall surrender or suspend the right and power of the Commonwealth, or any political subdivision thereof, to tax corporations and corporate property, except as authorized by Article X. No private corporation, association, or individual shall be specially exempted from the operation of any general law, nor shall a general law's operation be suspended for the benefit of any private corporation, association, or individual.

Section 16. Appropriations to religious or charitable bodies.

The General Assembly shall not make any appropriation of public funds, personal property, or real estate to any church or sectarian society, or any association or institution of any kind whatever which is entirely or partly, directly or indirectly, controlled by any church or sectarian society. Nor shall the General Assembly make any like appropriation to any charitable institution which is not owned or controlled by the Commonwealth; the General Assembly may, however, make appropriations to nonsectarian institutions for the reform of youthful criminals and may also authorize counties, cities, or towns to make such appropriations to any charitable institution or association.

Section 17. Impeachment.

The Governor, Lieutenant Governor, Attorney General, judges, members of the State Corporation Commission, and all officers appointed by the Governor or elected by the General Assembly, offending against the Commonwealth by malfeasance in office, corruption, neglect of duty, or other high crime or misdemeanor may be impeached by the House of Delegates and prosecuted before the Senate, which shall have the sole power to try impeachments. When sitting for that purpose, the senators shall be on oath or affirmation, and no person shall be convicted without the concurrence of two-thirds of the senators present. Judgment in case of impeachment shall not extend further than removal from office and disqualification to hold and enjoy any office of honor, trust, or profit under the Commonwealth; but the person convicted shall nevertheless be subject to indictment, trial, judgment, and punishment according to law. The Senate may sit during the recess of the General Assembly for the trial of impeachments.

Section 18. Auditor of Public Accounts.

An Auditor of Public Accounts shall be elected by the joint vote of the two houses of the General Assembly for the term of four years. His powers and duties shall be prescribed by law.

Encyclopedia of Virginia

ARTICLE V

Executive

Section 1. Executive power; Governor's term of office.

The chief executive power of the Commonwealth shall be vested in a Governor. He shall hold office for a term commencing upon his inauguration on the Saturday after the second Wednesday in January, next succeeding his election, and ending in the fourth year thereafter immediately upon the inauguration of his successor. He shall be ineligible to the same office for the term next succeeding that for which he was elected, and to any other office during his term of service.

Section 2. Election of Governor.

The Governor shall be elected by the qualified voters of the Commonwealth at the time and place of choosing members of the General Assembly. Returns of the election shall be transmitted, under seal, by the proper officers, to the State Board of Elections, or such other officer or agency as may be designated by law, which shall cause the returns to be opened and the votes to be counted in the manner prescribed by law. The person having the highest number of votes shall be declared elected; but if two or more shall have the highest and an equal number of votes, one of them shall be chosen Governor by a majority of the total membership of the General Assembly. Contested elections for Governor shall be decided by a like vote. The mode of proceeding in such cases shall be prescribed by law.

Section 3. Qualifications of Governor.

No person except a citizen of the United States shall be eligible to the office of Governor; nor shall any person be eligible to that office unless he shall have attained the age of thirty years and have been a resident of the Commonwealth and a registered voter in the Commonwealth for five years next preceding his election.

Section 4. Place of residence and compensation of Governor.

The Governor shall reside at the seat of government. He shall receive for his services a compensation to be prescribed by law, which shall neither be increased nor diminished during the period for which he shall have been elected. While in office he shall receive no other emolument from this or any other government.

Section 5. Legislative responsibilities of Governor.

The Governor shall communicate to the General Assembly, at every regular session, the condition of the Commonwealth,

State Constitution

recommend to its consideration such measures as he may deem expedient, and convene the General Assembly on application of two-thirds of the members elected to each house thereof, or when, in his opinion, the interest of the Commonwealth may require.

Section 6. Presentation of bills; veto powers of Governor.

Every bill which shall have passed the Senate and House of Delegates shall, before It becomes a law, be presented to the Governor. If he approve, he shall sign it; but, If not, he may return it with his objections to the house in which it originated, which shall enter the objections at large on its journal and proceed to reconsider the same. If, after such consideration, two-thirds of the members present, which two-thirds shall include a majority of the members elected to that house, shall agree to pass the bill, it shall be sent, together with the objections, to the other house, by which it shall likewise be reconsidered, and If approved by two-thirds of all the members present, which two-thirds shall include a majority of the members elected to that house, it shall become a law, notwithstanding the objections; provided, however, if the General Assembly has adjourned from a regular or special session pending a reconvened session, and the Governor has objections to any bill presented to him or has refused to sign such bill from such session, he shall return such bill to the clerk of the house from which the bill originated pending the reconvened session, as provided by Article IV, Section 6, and such bill shall be considered by such reconvened session.

The Governor shall have the power to veto any particular item or items of an appropriation bill, but the veto shall not affect the item or items to which he does not object. The Item or items objected to shall not take effect except in the manner heretofore provided In this section as to bills returned to the General Assembly without his approval.

If the Governor approve the general purpose of any bill but disapprove any part or parts thereof, he may return it, with recommendations for its amendment, to the house in which It originated, whereupon the same proceedings shall be had in both houses upon the bill and his recommendations in relation to its amendment as is above provided in relation to a bill which he shall have returned without his approval, and with his objections thereto; provided that, if after such reconsideration both houses, by a vote of a majority of the members present in each, shall agree to amend the bill in accordance with his recommendation in relation thereto, or either house by such vote shall fail or refuse to so amend It, then and in either case the bill shall be again sent to him, and he may act upon it as if it were then before him for the first time; provided further, that if the Governor so return any bill to a reconvened session and (i) a majority of the members present in each house shall agree to amend the bill in accordance with his recommendation, the bill as amended shall become law or (ii) two-thirds of all the members present in each house, which

Encyclopedia of Virginia

tw hirds shall include a majority of the members elected to that house, shall agree to the bill in the form originally sent to the Governor, the bill shall become law.

In all cases above set forth, the names of the members voting for and against the bill or item or items of an appropriation bill, shall be entered on the journal of each house.

If any bill shall not be returned by the Governor within seven days after it shall have been presented to him, the same shall be a law in like manner as if he had signed it, unless the General Assembly shall, by adjournment from a regular or special session, pending a reconvened session, prevent such return; In which case it shall be a law if approved by the Governor, in the manner and to the extent above provided, within thirty days after such adjournment. If the General Assembly in a reconvened session shall have been unable (i) by a majority of the members present in each house to agree to amend a bill returned by the Governor in accordance with his recommendation and (ii) by two-thirds of all the members present in each house, which two-thirds shall include a majority of the members elected to that house, to agree to the bill in the form originally sent to the Governor, it shall be returned to the Governor and shall become a law only if approved by the Governor, in the manner and to the extent above provided, within thirty days after adjournment of the reconvened session, but not otherwise.

The amendment ratified November 4, 1980 and effective January 1, 1981- At the end of paragraph one, after "notwitnstandlng the objections" added "; provided, however, if the General Assembly has adjourned . . .". In paragraph three, after "for the first time" added "; provided further, that if the Governor so return any bill to a reconvened session and . . . the bill shall become law". Made the previous second sentence of paragraph three a separate paragraph. In the last paragraph, substituted "adjournment from a regular or special session, pending a reconvened session" for "final adjournment", substituted "such adjournment" for "adjournment, but not otherwise", and added the last sentence of the paragraph.

Section 7. Executive and administrative powers.

The Governor shall take care that the laws be faithfully executed.

The Governor shall be commander-in-chief of the armed forces of the Commonwealth and shall have power to embody such forces to repel invasion, suppress insurrection, and enforce the execution of the laws.

The Governor shall conduct, either in person or in such manner as shall be prescribed by law, all intercourse with other and foreign states.

The Governor shall have power to fill vacancies in all offices of the Commonwealth for the filling of which the Constitution and laws make no other provision. If such office be one filled by the election of the people, the appointee shall hold office until the next general election, and thereafter until his successor qualifies, according to law. The General Assembly shall, if it is in session, fill vacancies in all offices which are filled by election by that body.

Gubernatorial appointments to fill vacancies in offices which are filled by election by the General Assembly or by appointment by the Governor which is subject to confirmation by the Senate or the General Assembly, made during the recess of the General Assembly, shall expire at the end of thirty days after the commencement of the next session of the General Assembly.

Section 8. Information from administrative officers.

The Governor may require information in writing, under oath, from any officer of any executive or administrative department, office, or agency, or any public institution upon any subject relating to their respective departments, offices, agencies, or public institutions; and he may inspect at any time their official books, accounts, and vouchers, and ascertain the conditions of the public funds in their charge, and in that connection may employ accountants.
He may require the opinion in writing of the Attorney General upon any question of law affecting the official duties of the Governor.

Section 0. Administrative organization.

The functions, powers, and duties of the administrative departments and divisions and of the agencies of the Commonwealth within the legislative and executive branches may be prescribed by law.

Section 10. Appointment and removal of administrative officers.

Except as may be otherwise provided in this Constitution, the Governor shall appoint each officer serving as the head of an administrative department or division of the executive branch of the government, subject to such confirmation by the General Assembly may prescribe. Each officer appointed by the Governor pursuant to this section shall have such professional qualifications as may be prescribed by law and shall serve at the pleasure of the Governor.

Section 11. Effect of refusal of General Assembly to confirm an appointment by the Governor.

No person appointed to any office by the Governor, whose appointment is subject to confirmation by the General Assembly, under the provisions of this Constitution or any statute, shall enter upon, or continue in, office after the General Assembly shall have refused to confirm his appointment, nor shall such person be eligible for reappointment during the recess of the General Assembly to fill the vacancy caused by such refusal to confirm.

Section 12. Executive clemency.

The Governor shall have power to remit fines and penalties under such rules and regulations as may be prescribed by law; to grant reprieves and pardons after conviction except when the prosecution has been carried on by the House of Delegates; to remove political disabilities consequent upon conviction for offenses committed prior or subsequent to the adoption of this Constitution; and to commute capital punishment.

He shall communicate to the General Assembly, at each regular session, particulars of every case of fine or penalty remitted, of reprieve or pardon granted, and of punishment commuted, with his reasons for remitting, granting, or commuting the same.

Section 13. Lieutenant Governor; election and qualifications.

A Lieutenant Governor shall be elected at the same time and for the same term as the Governor, and his qualifications and the manner and ascertainment of his election, in all respects, shall be the same, except that there shall be no limit on the terms of the Lieutenant Governor.

Section 14. Duties and compensation of Lieutenant Governor.

The Lieutenant Governor shall be President of the Senate but shall have no vote except in case of an equal division. He shall receive for his services a compensation to be prescribed by law, which shall not be increased nor diminished during the period for which he shall have been elected.

Section 15. Attorney General.

An Attorney General shall be elected by the qualified voters of the Commonwealth at the same time and for the same term as the Governor; and the fact of his election shall be ascertained in the same manner. No person shall be eligible for election or appointment to the office of Attorney General unless he is a citizen of the United States, has attained the age of thirty years, and has the qualifications required for a judge of a court of record. He shall perform such duties and receive such compensation as may be prescribed by law, which compensation shall neither be increased nor diminished during the period for which he shall have been elected. There shall be no limit on the terms of the Attorney General.

State Constitution

Section 16. Succession to the office of Governor.

When the Governor-elect is disqualified, resigns, or dies following his election but prior to taking office, the Lieutenant Governor-elect shall succeed to the office of Governor for the full term. When the Governor-elect falls to assume office for any other reason, the Lieutenant Governor-elect shall serve as Acting Governor.

Whenever the Governor transmits to the President pro tempore of the Senate and the Speaker of the House of Delegates his written declaration that he is unable to discharge the powers and duties of his office and until he transmits to them a written declaration to the contrary, such powers and duties shall be discharged by the Lieutenant Governor as Acting Governor.

Whenever the Attorney General, the President pro tempore of the Senate, and the Speaker of the House of Delegates, or a majority of the total membership of the General Assembly, transmit to the Clerk of the Senate and the Clerk of the House of Delegates their written declaration that the Governor is unable to discharge the powers and duties of his office, the Lieutenant Governor shall Immediately assume the powers and duties of the office as Acting Governor.

Thereafter, when the Governor transmits to the Clerk of the Senate and the Clerk of the House of Delegates his written declaration that no inability exists, he shall resume the powers and duties of his office unless the Attorney General, the President pro tempore of the Senate, and the Speaker of the House of Delegates, or a majority of the total membership of the General Assembly, transmit within four days to the Clerk of the Senate and the Clerk of the House of Delegates their written declaration that the Governor is unable to discharge the powers and duties of his office. Thereupon the General Assembly shall decide the issue, convening within forty-eight hours for that purpose if not already in session. If within twenty-one days after receipt of the latter declaration or, if the General Assembly is not in session, within twenty-one days after the General Assembly is required to convene, the General Assembly determines by three-fourths vote of the elected membership of each house of the General Assembly that the Governor is unable to discharge the powers and duties of his office, the Lieutenant Governor shall become Governor; otherwise, the Governor shall resume the powers and duties of his office.

In the case of the removal of the Governor from office or in the case of his disqualification, death, or resignation, the Lieutenant Governor shall become Governor.

If a vacancy exists in the office of Lieutenant Governor when the Lieutenant Governor is to succeed to the office of Governor or to serve as Acting Governor, the Attorney General, if he is eligible to serve as Governor, shall succeed to the office of Governor for the unexpired term or serve as Acting Governor. If the Attorney General is ineligible to serve as Governor, the Speaker of the House of Delegates, if he is eligible to serve as Governor, shall succeed to the office of Governor for the unexpired term or serve as Acting Governor. If a vacancy exists in the office of the Speaker of the House of Delegates or if the Speaker of the House of Delegates is ineligible to serve as Governor, the House of Delegates shall convene and fill the vacancy.

Section 17. Commissions and grants.

Commissions and grants shall run in the name of the Commonwealth of Virginia, and be attested by the Governor, with the seal of the Commonwealth annexed.

ARTICLE VI

Judiciary

Section 1. Judicial power; jurisdiction.

The judicial power of the Commonwealth shall be vested in a Supreme Court and in such other courts of original or appellate jurisdiction subordinate to the Supreme Court as the General Assembly may from time to time establish. Trial courts of general jurisdiction, appellate courts, and such other courts as shall be so designated by the General Assembly shall be known as courts of record.

The Supreme Court shall, by virtue of this Constitution, have original jurisdiction in cases of habeas corpus, mandamus, and prohibition, in matters of judicial censure, retirement, and removal under Section 10 of this article, and to answer questions of state law certified by a court of the United States or the hest appellate court of any other state. All other jurisdiction of the Supreme Court shall be appellate. Subject to such reasonable rules as may be prescribed as to the course of appeals and other procedural matters, the Supreme Court shall, by virtue of this Constitution, have appellate jurisdiction in cases Involving the constitutionality of a law under this Constitution or the Constitution of the United States and in cases involving the life or liberty of any person.

No appeal shall be allowed to the Commonwealth in a case Involving the life or liberty of a person, except that an appeal by the Commonwealth may be allowed In any case involving the violation of a law relating to the State revenue. The General Assembly may also allow the Commonwealth a right of appeal In felony cases, before a jury is impaneled and sworn if tried by jury or, in cases tried without a jury, before the court begins to hear or receive evidence or the first witness is sworn, whichever occurs first, from (1) an order of a circuit court dismissing a warrant, information or indictment or any count or charge thereof on the grounds that a statute upon which it was based is unconstitutional and (2) an order of a circuit court proscriblng the use of certain evidence at trial on the grounds such evidence was obtained In violation of the provisions of the Fourth, Fifth or Sixth Amendments to the Constitution of the United States or Article 1, Sections 8, 10 or 11 of this Constitution proscribing illegal searches and seizures and protecting rights against self-incrimination, provided the Commonwealth certifies the evidence is essential to the prosecution.

Subject to the foregoing limitations, the General Assembly shall have the power to determine the original and appellate jurisdiction of the courts of the Commonwealth.

The amendment ratified November 4' 1886 and effective December 1, 1886- In parngraph two, after "mandamus, and prohibition" deleted "and" and added to the sentence ", and to answer questions of state law certified by a court of the United States...".

The amendment ratified November 4' 1886 and effective December 1, 1888- In paragraph three, after "relating to the State revenue." added the last sentence "The 0eneral Assembly may also allow the commonwealth..

Section 2. Supreme Court.

The Supreme Court shall consist of seven justices. The General Assembly may, If three-fifths of the elected membership of each house so vote at two successive regular sessions, Increase or decrease the number of justices of the Court, provided that the Court shall consist of no fewer than seven and no more than eleven justices. The Court may sit and render final judgment en banc or in divisions as may be prescribed by law. No decision shall become the judgment of the Court, however, except on the concurrence of at least three justices, and no law shall be declared unconstitutional under either this Constitution or the Constitution of the United States except on the concurrence of at least a majority of all justices of the Supreme Court.

Section 3. Selection of Chief Justice.

The Chief Justice shall be selected from among the justices In a manner provided by law. Section 4. Administration of the judicial system.

The Chief Justice of the Supreme Court shall be the administrative head of the judicial system. He may temporarily assign any judge of a court of record to any other court of record except the Supreme Court and may assign a retired judge of a court of record, with his consent, to any court of record except the Supreme Court. The General Assembly may adopt such additional measures as it deems desirable for the Improvement of the administration of justice by the courts and for the expedition of judicial business.

Section 5. Rules of practice and procedure.

The Supreme Court shall have the authority to make rules governing the course of appeals and the practice and procedures to be used in the courts of the Commonwealth, but such rules shall not be in conflict with the general law as the same shall, from time to time, be established by the General Assembly.

Section 6. Opinions and judgments of the Supreme Court

When a judgment or decree is reversed, modified, or affirmed by the Supreme Court, or when original cases are resolved on their merits, the reasons for the Court's action shall be stated in writing and preserved with the record of the case. The Court may, but need not, remand a case for a new trial. In any civil case, it may enter final judgment, except that the award in a suit or action for unliquidated damages shall not be increased or diminished.

Section 7. Selection and qualification of judges.

The justices of the Supreme Court shall be chosen by the vote of a majority of the members elected to each house of the General Assembly for terms of twelve years. The judges of all other courts of record shall be chosen by the vote of a majority of the members elected to each house of the General Assembly for terms of eight years. During any vacancy which may exist while the General Assembly is not in session, the Governor may appoint a successor to serve until thirty days after the commencement of the next session of the General Assembly. Upon election by the General Assembly, a new justice or judge shall begin service of a full term.

All justices of the Supreme Court and all judges of other courts of record shall be residents of the Commonwealth and shall, at least five years prior to their appointment or election, have been admitted to the bar of the Commonwealth. Each judge of a trial court of record shall during his term of office reside within the jurisdiction of one of the courts to which he was appointed or elected; provided, however, that where the boundary of such jurisdiction is changed by annexation or otherwise, no judge thereof shall thereby become disqualified from office or ineligible for reelection if, except for such annexation or change, he would otherwise be qualified.

Section 8. Additional judicial personnel.

The General Assembly may provide for additional judicial personnel, such as judges of courts not of record and magistrates or justices of the peace, and may prescribe their jurisdiction and provide the manner in which they shall be selected and the terms for which they shall serve.

The General Assembly may confer upon the clerks of the several courts having probate jurisdiction, jurisdiction 'of the probate of wills and of the appointment and qualification of guardians, personal representatives, curators, appraisers, and committees of persons adjudged insane or convicted of felony, and in the matter of the substitution of trustees.

Section 9. Commission; compensation; retirement.

All justices of the Supreme Court and all judges of other courts of record shall be commissioned by the Governor. They shall receive such salaries and allowances as shall be prescribed by the General Assembly, which shall be apportioned between the Commonwealth and its cities and counties in the manner provided by law. Unless expressly prohibited or limited by the General Assembly, cities and counties shall be permitted to supplement from local funds the salaries of any judges serving within their geographical boundaries. The salary of any justice or judge shall not be diminished during his term of office.

The General Assembly may enact such laws as it deems necessary for the retirement of justices and judges, with such conditions, compensation, and duties as it may prescribe. The General Assembly may also provide for the mandatory retirement of justices and judges after they reach a prescribed age, beyond which they shall not serve, regardless of the term to which elected or appointed.

Section 10. Disabled and unfit judged

The General Assembly shall create a Judicial Inquiry and Review Commission consisting of members of the judiciary, the bar, and the public and vested with the power to investigate charges which would be the basis for retirement, censure, or removal of a judge. The Commission shall be authorized to conduct hearings and to subpoena witnesses and documents. Proceedings before the Commission shall be confidential.

If the Commission finds the charges to be well-founded, it may file a formal complaint before the Supreme Court.

Upon the filing of a complaint, the Supreme Court shall conduct a hearing in open court and, upon a finding of disability which is or is likely to be permanent and which seriously interferes with the performance by the judge of his duties, shall retire the judge from office. A judge retired under this authority shall be considered for the purpose of retirement benefits to have retired voluntarily.

If the Supreme Court after the hearing on the complaint finds that the judge has engaged in misconduct while in office, or that he has persistently failed to perform the duties of his office, or that he has engaged In conduct prejudicial to the proper administration of justice, it shall censure him or shall remove him from office. A judge removed under this authority shall not be entitled to retirement benefits, but only to the return of contributions made by him, together with any Income accrued thereon.

This section shall apply to justices of the Supreme Court, to judges of other courts of record, and to members of the State Corporation Commission. The General Assembly also may provide by general law for the retirement, censure, or removal of judges of any court not of record, or other personnel exercising judicial functions.

Section 11. Incompatible activities

No justice or judge of a court of record shall, during his continuance In office, engage In the practice of law within or without the Commonwealth, or seek or accept any nonjudicial elective office, or hold any other office of public trllst, or engage In any other Incompatible activity.

Section 12. Limitation; judicial appointment

No judge shall be granted the power to make any appointment of any local governmental official elected by the voters except to fill a vacancy In office pending the next ensuing general election or, if the vacancy occurs within one hundred twenty days prior to such election, pending the second ensuing general election, unless such election falls within sixty days of the end of the term of the office to be filled.

The amendment ratified November 2, 1870 and effeetive January 1, 1877- At the end of the section, after the word "election" added the langnage ", ualess such election faiis within sixty days of the end of the term of the office to be filled".

ARTICLE VII

Local Government

Section 1. Definitions.

As used in this article (1) "county" means any existing county or any such unit hereafter created, (2) "city" means an independent Incorporated community which became a city as provided by law before noon on the first day of July, nineteen hundred seventy-one, or which has within defined boundaries a population of 5,000 or more and which has become a city as provided by law, (3) "town" means any existing town or an incorporated community within one or more counties which became a town before noon, July one, nineteen hundred seventy-one, as provided by law or which has within defined boundaries a population of 1,000 or more and which has become a town as provided by law, (4) "regional government" means a unit of general government organized as provided by law within defined boundaries, as determined by the General Assembly, (5) "general law" means a law which on its effective date applies alike to all counties, cities, towns, or regional governments or to a reasonable classification thereof, and (6) "special act" means a law applicable to a county, city, town, or regional government and for enactment shall require an affirmative vote of two-thirds of the members elected to each house of the General Assembly.

The General Assembly may increase by general law the population minima provided in this article for cities and towns. Any county which on the effective date of this Constitution had adopted an optional form of government pursuant to a valid statute that does not meet the general law requirements of this article may continue its form of government without regard to such general law requirements until it adopts a form of government provided in conformity with this article. In this article, whenever the General Assembly is authorized or required to act by general law, no special act for that purpose shall be valid unless this article so provides.

he amendment ratified November 7, 197* Added language to the definition of city in (2) to include those communities which became cities before July 1, 1971. Added language to the definition of town in (3) to include those communities which became towns before July 1, 1971.

Section 2. Organization and government.

The General Assembly shall provide by general law for the organization, government, powers, change of boundaries, consolidation, and dissolution of counties, cities, towns, and regional governments. The General Assembly may also provide by general law optional plans of government for counties, cities, or towns to be effective if approved by a majority vote of the qualified voters voting on any such plan in any such county, city, or town.

The General Assembly may also provide by special act for the organization, government, and powers of any county, city, town, or regional government, including such powers of legislation, taxation, and assessment as the General Assembly may determine, but no such special act shall be adopted which provides for the extension or contraction of boundaries of any county, city, or town.

Every law providing for the organization of a regional government shall, in addition to any other requirements imposed by the General Assembly, require the approval of the organization of the regional government by a majority vote of the qualified voters voting thereon in each county and city which is to participate in the regional government and of the voters voting thereon in a part of a county or city where only the part is to participate.

Section 3. Powers.

The General Assembly may provide by general law or special act that any county, city, town, or other unit of government may exercise any of its powers or perform any of its functions and may participate in the financing thereof jointly or in cooperation with the Commonwealth or any other unit of government within or without the Commonwealth. The General Assembly may provide by general law or special act for transfer to or sharing with a regional government of any services, functions, and related facilities of any county, city, town, or other unit of government within the boundaries of such regional government.

Section 4. County and city officers.

There shall be elected by the qualified voters of each county and city a treasurer, a sheriff, an attorney for the Commonwealth, a clerk, who shall be clerk of the court in the office of which deeds are recorded, and a commissioner of revenue. The duties and compensation of such officers shall be prescribed by general law or special act.

Regular elections for such officers shall be held on Tuesday after the first Monday in November. Such officers shall take office on the first day of the following January unless otherwise provided by law and shall hold their respective offices for the term of four years, except that the clerk shall hold office for eight years.

The General Assembly may provide for county or city officers or methods of their selection, including permission for two or more units of government to share the officers required by this section, without regard to the provisions of this section, either (1) by general law to become effective in any county or city when submitted to the qualified voters thereof in an election held for such purpose and approved by a majority of those voting thereon in each such county or city, or (2) by special act upon the request, made after such an election, of each county or city affected. No such law shall reduce the term of any person holding an office at the time the election is held. A county or city not required to have or to elect such officers prior to the effective date of this Constitution shall not be so required by this section.

The General Assembly may provide by general law or special act for additional officers and for the terms of their office.

Section 5. County, city, and town governing bodies.

The governing body of each county, city, or town shall be elected by the qualified voters of such county, city, or town in the manner provided by law.

State Constitution

If the members are elected by district, the district shall be composed of contiguous and compact territory and shall be so constituted as to give, as nearly as is practicable, representation in proportion to the population of the district. When members are so elected by district, the governing body of any county, city, or town may, In a manner provided by law, increase or diminish the number, and change the boundaries, of districts, and shall in 1971 and every ten years thereafter, and also whenever the boundaries of such districts are changed, reapportion the representation in the governing body among the districts in a manner provided by law. Whenever the governing body of any such unit shall fall to perform the duties so prescribed in the manner herein directed, a suit shall lie on behalf of any citizen thereof to compel performance by the governing body.

Unless otherwise provided by law, the governing body of each city or town shall be elected on the second Tuesday in June and take office on the first day of the following September. Unless otherwise provided by law, the governing body of each county shall be elected on the Tuesday after the first Monday in November and take office on the first day of the following January.

Section 6. Multiple offices

Unless two or more units exercise functions jointly as authorized in Sections 3 and 4, no person shall at the same time hold more than one office mentioned In this article. No member of a governing body shall be eligible, during the term of office for which he was elected or appointed, to hold any office filled by the governing body by election or appointment, except that a member of a governing body may be named a member of such other boards, commissions, and bodies as may be permitted by general law and except that a member of a governing body may be elected or appointed to fill a vacancy In the office of mayor or board chairman if permitted by general law or special act.

The amendment ratified November 0, 1080 and effeetive January 1, 1081- After "as may he permitted by general law" added "and except that a member of a governing body may be elected or appointed to fill a vacancy in the office of mayor or board chairman If permitted by general law or special act".

Section 7. Procedures.

No ordinance or resolution appropriating money exceeding the sum of five hundred dollars, imposing taxes, or authorizing the borrowing of money shall be passed except by a recorded affirmative vote of a majority of all members elected to the governing body. In case of the veto of such an ordinance or resolution, where the power of veto exists, it shall require for passage thereafter a recorded affirmative vote of two-thirds of all members elected to the governing body.

On final vote on any ordinance or resolution, the name of each member voting and how he voted shall be recorded.

Section 8. Consent to use public property.

No street railway, gas, water, steam or electric heating, electric light or power, cold storage, compressed air, viaduct, conduit, telephone, or bridge company, nor any corporation, association, person, or partnership engaged In these or like enterprises shall be permitted to use the streets, alleys, or public grounds of a city or town without the previous consent of the corporate authorities of such city or town.

Section 9. Sale of property and granting of franchises by cities and towns.

No rights of a city or town in and to its waterfront, wharf property, public landings, wharves, docks, streets, avenues, parks, bridges, or other public p@ces, or its gas, water, or electric works shall be sold except by an ordinance or resolution passed by a recorded affirmative vote of three-fourths of all members elected to the governing body.

No franchise, lease, or right of any kind to use any such public property or any other public property or easement of any description in a manner not permitted to the general public shall be granted for a longer period than forty years, except for air rights together with easements for columns of support, which may be granted for a period not exceeding sixty years. Before granting any such franchise or privilege for a term in excess of five years, except for a trunk railway, the city or town shall, after due advertisement, publicly receive bids therefor. Such grant, and any contract in pursuance thereof, may provide that upon the termination of the grant, the plant as well as the property, if any, of the grantee In the streets, avenues, and other public places shall thereupon, without compensation to the grantee, or upon the payment of a fair valuation therefor, become the property of the said city or town; but the grantee shall be entitled to no payment by reason of the value of the franchise. Any such plant or property acquired by a city or town may be sold or leased or, unless prohibited by general law, maintained, controlled, and operated by such city or town. Every such grant shall specify the mode of determining any valuation therein provided for and shall make adequate provisions by way of forfeiture of the grant, or otherwise, to secure efficiency of public service at reasonable rates and the maintenance of the property in good order throughout the term of the grant.

Section 10. Debt.

(a) No city or town shall issue any bonds or other Interest-bearing obligations which, including existing indebtedness, shall at any time exceed ten per centum of the assessed valuation of the real estate in the city or town subject to taxation, as shown by the last preceding assessment for taxes. In determining the limitation for a city or town there shall not be included the following classes of indebtedness:

(1) Certificates of indebtedness, revenue bonds, or other obligations issued in anticipation of the collection of the revenues of such city or town for the then current year; provided that such certificates, bonds, or other obligations mature within one year from the date of their issue, be not past due, and do not exceed the revenue for such year.

(2) Bonds pledging the full faith and credit of such city or town authorized by an ordinance enacted in accordance with Section 7, and approved by the affirmative vote of the qualified voters of the city or town voting upon the question of their uance, for a supply of water or other specific undertaking from which the city or town may derive a revenue; but from and after a period to be determined by the governing body not exceeding five years from the date of such election, whenever and for so long as such undertaking fails to produce sufficient revenue to pay for cost of operation and administration (including interest on bonds issued therefor), the cost of insurance against loss by injury to persons or property, and an annual amount to be placed into a sinking fund sufficient to pay the bonds at or before maturity, all outstanding bonds issued on account of such undertaking shall be included in determining such limitation.

(3) Bonds of a city or town the principal and interest on which are payable exclusively from the revenues and receipts of a water system or other specific undertaking or undertakings from which the city or town may derive a revenue or secured, solely or together with such revenues, by contributions of other units of government.

(4) Contract obligations of a city or town to provide payments over a period of more than one year to any publicly owned or controlled regional project, If the project has been authorized by an interstate compact or if the General Assembly by general law or special act has authorized an exclusion for such project purposes.

(b) No debt shall be contracted by or on behalf of any county or district thereof or by or on behalf of any regional government or district thereof except by authority conferred by the General Assembly by general law. The General Assembly shall not authorize any such debt, except the classes described in paragraphs (1) and (3) of subsection (a), refunding bonds, and bonds Issued, with the consent of the school board and the governing body of the county, by or on behalf of a county or district thereof for capital projects for school purposes and sold to the Literary Fund, the Virginia Supplemental Retirement System, or other State agency prescribed by law, unless in the general law authorizing the same, provision be made for submission to the qualified voters of the county or district thereof or the region or district thereof, as the case may be, for approval or rejection by a majority vote of the qualified voters voting in an election on the question of contracting such debt. Such approval shall be a prerequisite to contracting such debt.

Any county may, upon approval by the affirmative vote of the qualified voters of the county voting in an election on the question, elect to be treated as a city for the purposes of issuing its bonds under this section. If a county so elects, it shall thereafter be subject to all of the benefits and limitations of this section applicable to cities, but in determining the limitation for a county there shall be included, unless otherwise excluded under this section, indebtedness of any town or district in that county empowered to levy taxes on real estate.

Tne amendment ratified November 4, 1888 and effective January 1, 1881- In subsection (a) substituted "ten per centum" for "eighteen per centum".

ARTICLE VIII

Education

Section 1. Public schools of high quality to be maintained.

The General Assembly shall provide for a system of free public elementary and secondary schools for all children of school age throughout the Commonwealth, and shall seek to ensure that an educational program of high quality is established and ly maintained.

Section 2. Standards of quality; State and local support of public schools.

Standards of quality for the several school divisions shall be determined and prescribed from time to time by the Board of Education, subject to revision only by the General Assembly.

The General A:,:,£mbly shall determine the manner in which funds are to be provided for the cost of maintaining an educational program meeting the prescribed standards of quality, and shall provide for the apportionment of the cost of such program between the Commonwealth and the local units of government comprising such school divisions. Each unit of local government shall provide its portion of such cost by local taxes or from other available funds.

Section 3. Compulsory education; free textbooks.

The General Assembly shall provide for the compulsory elementary and secondary education of every eligible child of appropriate age, such eligibility and age to be determined by law. It shall ensure that textbooks are provided at no cost to each child attending public school whose parent or guardian is financially unable to furnish them.

Section 4. Board of Education.

The general supervision of the public school system shall be vested in a Board of Education of nine members, to be appointed by the Governor, subject to confirmation by the General Assembly. Each appointment shall be for four years, except that those to fill vacancies shall be for the unexpired terms. Terms shall be staggered, so that no more than three regular appointments shall be made in the same year.

Section 5. Powers and duties of the Board of Education.

The powers and duties of the Board of Education shall be as follows:

(a) Subject to such criteria and conditions as the General Assembly may prescribe, the Board shall divide the Commonwealth into school divisions of such geographical area and school-age population as will promote the realization of the prescribed standards of quality, and shall periodically review the adequacy of existing school divisions for this purpose.

(b) It shall make annual reports to the Governor and the General Assembly concerning the condition and needs of public education in the Commonwealth, and shall in such report identify any school divisions which have failed to establish and maintain schools meeting the prescribed standards of quality.

(c) It shall certify to the school board of each division a list of qualified persons for the office of division superintendent of schools, one of whom shall be selected to fill the post by the division school board. In the event a division school board fails to select a division superintendent within the time prescribed by law, the Board of Education shall appoint him.

(d) It shall have authority to approve textbooks and instructional aids and materials for use in courses in the public schools of the Commonwealth.

(e) Subject to the ultimate authority of the General Assembly, the Board shall have primary responsibility and authority for effectuating the educational policy set forth in this article, and it shall have such other powers and duties as may be prescribed by law.

Section 6. Superintendent of Public Instruction.

A Superintendent of Public Instruction, who shall be an experienced educator, shall be appointed by the Governor, subject to confirmation by the General Assembly, for a term coincident with that of the Governor making the appointment, but the General Assembly may alter by statute this method of selection and term of office. The powers and duties of the Superintendent shall be prescribed by law.

Section 7. School boards.

The supervision of schools in each school division shall be vested in a school board, to be composed of members selected in the manner, for the term, possessing the qualifications, and to the number provided by law.

Section 8. The Literary Fund.

The General Assembly shall set apart as a permanent and perpetual school fund the present Literary Fund; the proceeds of all public lands donated by Congress for free public school purposes, of all escheated property, of all waste and unappropriated lands, of all property accruing to the Commonwealth by forfeiture, of all fines collected for offenses committed against the Commonwealth, and of the annual interest on the Literary Fund; and such other sums as the General Assembly may appropriate. But so long as the principal of the Fund totals as much as eighty million dollars, the General Assembly may set aside all or any part of additional moneys received into its principal for public school purposes, including the teachers retirement fund.

The Literary Fund shall be held and administered by the Board of Education in such manner as may be provided by law. The General Assembly may authorize the Board to borrow other funds against assets of the Literary Fund as collateral, such borrowing not to involve the full faith and credit of the Commonwealth.

The principal of the Fund shall include assets of the Fund in other funds or authorities which are repayable to the Fund.

Section 0. Other educational institutions

The General Assembly may provide for the establishment, maintenance, and operation of any educational institutions which are desirable for the intellectual, cultural, and occupational development of the people of this Commonwealth. The governance of such institutions, and the status and powers of their boards of visitors or other governing bodies, shall be as provided by law.

Section 10. State appropriations prohibited to schools or institutions
learning not owned or exclusively controlled by the State or some subdivision thereof; exceptions to rule.

No appropriation of public funds shall be made to any school or institution of learning not owned or exclusively controlled by the State or some political subdivision thereof; provided, first, that the

General Assembly may, and the governing bodies of the several counties, cities and towns may, subject to such limitations as may be imposed by the General Assembly, appropriate funds for educational purposes which may be expended in furtherance of elementary, secondary, collegiate or graduate education of Virginia students in public and nonsectarian private schools and institutions of learning, in addition to those owned or exclusively controlled by the State or any such county, city or town; second, that the General Assembly may appropriate funds to an agency, or to a school or institution of learning owned or controlled by an agency, created and established by two or more States under a joint agreement to which this State is a party for the purpose of providing educational facilities for the citizens of the several States joining in such agreement; third, that counties, cities, towns, and districts may make appropriations to nonsectarian schools of manual, Industrial, or technical training, and also to any school or institution of learning owned or exclusively controlled by such county, city, town, or school district.

Section 11. Aid to nonpublic higher education.

The General Assembly may provide for loans to, and grants to or on behalf of, students attending nonprofit institutions of higher education In the Commonwealth whose primary purpose Is to provide collegiate or graduate education and not to provide religious training or theological education. The General Assembly may also provide for a State agency or authority to assist in borrowing money for construction of educational facilities at such Institutions, provided that the Commonwealth shall not be liable for any debt created by such borrowing. The General Assembly may also provide for the Commonwealth or any political subdivision thereof to contract with such institutions for the provision of educational or other related services.

The amendment ratified November $, 1874 and effeetive January 1, 18711- Provided for "grants to or on behalf or' in addition to loans to students, in the first sentence. Added the last sentence to permit "the commonwealth or any political subdivision thereof to contract with" nonprofit institutions of higher education.

ARTICLE IX

Corporations

Section 1. State Corporation Commission.

There shall be a permanent commission which shall be known as the State Corporation Commission and which shall consist of three members. The General Assembly may, by majority vote of the members elected to each house, Increase the size of the Commission to no more chan five members. Members of the Commission shall be elected by the General Assembly and shall serve for regular terms of six years. At least one member of the Commission shall have the qualifications prescribed for judges of courts of record, and any Commissioner may be impeached or removed in the manner provided for the Impeachment or removal of judges of courts of record. The General Assembly may enact such laws as it deems necessary for the retirement of the Commissioners, with such conditions, compensation, and duties as it may prescribe. The General Assembly may also provide for the mandatory retirement of Commissioners after they reach a prescribed age, beyond which they shall not serve, regardless of the term to which elected or appointed. Whenever a vacancy in the Commission shall occur or exist when the General Assembly is in session, the General Assembly shall elect a successor for such unexpired term. If the General Assembly Is not In session, the Governor shall forthwith appoint pro tempore a qualified person to fill the vacancy for a term ending thirty days after the commencement of the next regular session of the General Assembly and the General Assembly shall elect a successor for such unexpired term.

The Commission shall annually elect one of Its members chairman. Its subordinates and employees, and the manner of their appointment and removal, shall be as provided by law, except that its heads of divisions and assistant heads of divisions shall be appointed and subject to removal by the Commission.

Section 2. Powers and duties of the Commission.

Subject to the provisions of this Constitution and to such requirements as may be prescribed by law, the Commission shall be the department of government through which shall be issued all charters, and amendments or extensions thereof, of domestic corporations and all licenses of foreign corporations to do business in this Commonwealth.

Except as may be otherwise prescribed by this Constitution or by law, the Commission shall be charged with the duty of administering the laws made in pursuance of this Constitution for the regulation and control of corporations doing business in this Commonwealth. Subject to such criteria and other requirements as may be prescribed by law, the Commission shall have the power and be charged with the duty of regulating the rates, charges, and services and, except as may be otherwise authorized by this Constitution or by general law, the facilities of railroad, telephone, gas, and electric companies.

The Commission shall in proceedings before it ensure that the interests of the consumers of the Commonwealth are represented, unless the General Assembly otherwise provides for representation of such interests.

The Commission shall have such other powers and duties not inconsistent with this Constitution as may be prescribed by law.

State Constitution

Section 3. Procedures of the Commission.

Before promulgating any general order, rule, or regulation, the Commission shall give reasonable notice of its contents.

In all matters within the jurisdiction of the Commission, it shall have the powers of a court of record to administer oaths, to compel the attendance of witnesses and the production of documents, to punish for contempt, and to enforce compliance with its lawful orders or requirements by adjudging and enforcing by its own appropriate process such fines or other penalties as may be prescribed or authorized by law. Before the Commission shall enter any finding, order, or judgment against a party it shall afford such party reasonable notice of the time and place at which he shall be afforded an opportunity to introduce evidence and be heard.

The Commission may prescribe its own rules of practice and procedure not inconsistent with those made by the General Assembly. The General Assembly shall have the power to adopt such rules, to amend, modify, or set aside the Commission's rules, or to substitute rules of its own.

Section 4. Appeals from actions of the Commission.

The Commonwealth, any party in interest, or any party aggrieved by any final finding, order, or judgment of the Commission shall have, of right, an appeal to the Supreme Court. The method of taking and prosecuting an appeal from any action of the Commission shall be prescribed by law or by the rules of the Supreme Court. All appeals from the Commission shall be to the Supreme Court only.

No other court of the Commonwealth shall have jurisdiction to review, reverse, correct, or annul any action of the Commission or to enjoin or restrain it in the performance of its official duties, provided, however, that the writs of mandamus and prohibition 'hall lie from the Supreme Court to the Commission.

Section 5. Foreign corporations.

No foreign corporation shall be authorized to carry on in this Commonwealth the business of, or to exercise any of the powers or functions of, a public service enterprise, or be permitted to do anything which domestic corporations are prohibited from doing, or be relieved from compliance with any of the requirements made of similar domestic corporations by the Constitution and laws of this Commonwealth. However, nothing in this section shall restrict the power of the General Assembly to enact such laws specially applying to foreign corporations as the General Assembly may deem appropriate.

Section 6. Corporations subject to general laws.

The creation of corporations, and the extension and amendment of charters whether heretofore or hereafter granted, shall be provided for by general law, and no charter shall be granted, amended, or extended by special act, nor shall authority in such matters be conferred upon any tribunal or officer, except to ascertain whether the applicants have, by complying with the requirements of the law, entitled themselves to the charter, amendment, or extension applied for and to issue or refuse the same accordingly. Such general laws may be amended, repealed, or modified by the General Assembly. Every corporation chartered in this Commonwealth shall be deemed to hold its charter and all amendments thereof under the provisions of, and subject to all the requirements, terms, and conditions of, this Constitution and any laws passed in pursuance thereof. The police power of the Commonwealth to regulate the affairs of corporations, the same as individuals, shall never be abridged.

Section 7. Exclusions from term "corporation" or "company."

The term "corporation" or "company" as used In this article shall exclude all municipal corporations, other political subdivisions, and public institutions owned or controlled by the Commonwealth.

ARTICLE X

Taxation and Finance

Section 1. Taxable property; uniformity; classification and segregation.

All property, except as hereinafter provided, shall be taxed. All taxes shall be levied and collected under general laws and shall be uniform upon the same class of subjects within the territorial limits of the authority levying the tax, except that the General Assembly may provide for differences in the rate of taxation to be imposed upon real estate by a city or town within all or parts of areas added to its territorial limits, or by a new unit of general government, within its area, created by or encompassing two or more, or parts of two or more, existing units of general government. Such differences in the rate of taxation shall bear a reasonable relationship to differences between nonrevenue-producing governmental services giving land urban character which are furnished in one or several areas in contrast to the services furnished in other areas of such unit of government.

The General Assembly may define and classify taxable subjects. Except as to classes of property herein expressly segregated for either State or local taxation, the General Assembly may segregate the several classes of property so as to specify and determine upon what subjects State taxes, and upon what subjects local taxes, may be levied.

State Constitution

Section 2. Assessments.

All assessments of real estate and tangible personal property shall be at their fair market value, to be ascertained as prescribed by law. The General Assembly may define and classify real estate devoted to agricultural, horticultural, forest, or open space uses, and may by general law authorize any county, city, town, or regional government to allow deferral of, or relief from, portions of taxes otherwise payable on such real estate if it were not so classified, provided the General Assembly shall first determine that classification of such real estate for such purpose is in the public interest for the preservation or conservation of real estate for such uses. In the event the General Assembly defines and classifies real estate for such purposes, it shall prescribe the limits, conditions, and extent of such deferral or relief. No such deferral or relief shall be granted within the territorial limits of any county, city, town, or regional government except by ordinance adopted by the governing body thereof.

So long as the Commonwealth shall levy upon any public service corporation a State franchise, license, or other similar tax based upon or measured by its gross receipts or gross earnings, or any part thereof, its real estate and tangible personal property shall be assessed by a central State agency, as prescribed by law.

Section 3. Taxes or assessments upon abutting property owners.

The General Assembly by general law may authorize any county, city, town, or regional government to impose taxes or assessments upon abutting property owners for such local public improvements as may be designated by the General Assembly; however, such taxes or assessments shall not be in excess of the peculiar benefits resulting from the improvements to such abutting property owners.

Section 4. Property segregated for local taxation; exceptions.

Real estate, coal and other mineral lands, and tangible personal property, except the rolling stock of public service corporations, are hereby segregated for, and made subject to, local taxation only, and shall be assessed for local taxation in such manner and at such times as the General Assembly may prescribe by general law.

Section 5. Franchise taxes; taxation of corporate stock.

The General Assembly, in imposing a franchise tax upon corporations, may in its discretion make the same in lieu of taxes upon other property, in whole or in part, of such corporations. Whenever a franchise tax shall be imposed upon a corporation doing business in this Commonwealth, or whenever all the capital, however invested, of a corporation chartered under the laws of this Commonwealth shall be taxed, the shares of stock issued by any such corporation shall not be further taxed.

Section 6. Exempt property.

(a) Except as otherwise provided in this Constitution, the following property and no other shall be exempt from taxation, State and local, including inheritance taxes:

(1) Property owned directly or indirectly by the Commonwealth or any political subdivision thereof, and obligations of the Commonwealth or any political subdivision thereof exempt by law.

(2) Real estate and personal property owned and exclusively occupied or used by churches or religious bodies for religious worship or for the residences of their ministers.

(3) Private or public burying grounds or cemeteries, provided the same are not operated for profit.

(4) Property owned by public libraries or by institutions of learning not conducted for profit, so long as such property is primarily used for literary, scientific, or educational purposes or purposes incidental thereto. This provision may also apply to leasehold Interests in such property as may be provided by general law.

(5) Intangible personal property, or any class or classes thereof, as may be exempted in whole or in part by general law.

(6) Property used by its owner for religious, charitable, patriotic, historical, benevolent, cultural, or public park and playground purposes, as may be provided by classification or designation by a three-fourths vote of the members elected to each house of the General Assembly and subject to such restrictions and conditions as may be prescribed.

(7) Land subject to a perpetual easement permitting inundation by water as may be exempted in whole or in part by general law.

(b) The General Assembly may by general law authorize the governing body of any county, city, town, or regional government to provide for the exemption from local property taxation, or a portion thereof, within such restrictions and upon such conditions as may be prescribed, of real estate and personal property designed for continuous habitation owned by, and occupied as the sole dwelling of, persons not less than sixty-five years of age or persons permanentiy and totally disabled as established by general law who are deemed by the General Assembly to be bearing an extraordinary tax burden on said property in relation to their income and financial worth.

(c) Except as to property of the Commonwealth, the General Assembly by general law may restrict or condition, in whole or in part, but not extend, any or all of the above exemptions.

State Constitution

(d) The General Assembly may define as a separate subject of taxation any property, including real or personal property, equipment, facilities, or devices, used primarily for the purpose of abating or preventing pollution of the atmosphere or waters of the Commonwealth or for the purpose of transferring or storing solar energy, and by general law may allow the governing body of any county, city, town, or regional government to exempt or partially exempt such property from taxation, or by general law may directly exempt or partially exempt such property from taxation.

(e) The General Assembly may define as a separate subject of taxation household goods, personal effects and tangible farm property and products, and by general law may allow the governing body of any county, city, town, or regional government to exempt or partially exempt such property from taxation, or by general law may directly exempt or partially exempt such property from taxation.

(f) Exemptions of property from taxation as established or authorized hereby shall be strictiy construed; provided, however, that all property exempt from taxation on the effective date of this section shall continue to be exempt until otherwise provided by the General Assembly as herein set forth.

(g) The General Assembly may by general law authorize any county, city, town, or regional-government to Impose a service charge upon the owners of a class or classes of exempt property for services provided by such governments.

(h) The General Assembly may by general law authorize the governing body of any county, city, town, or regional government to provide for a partial exemption from local real property taxation, within such restrictions and upon such conditions as may be prescribed, of real estate whose improvements, by virtue of age and use, have undergone substantial renovation, rehabilitation or replacement.

(l) The General Assembly may by general law allow the governing body of any county, city, or town to exempt or partially exempt from taxation any generating equipment Installed after December 'thirty-one, nineteen hundred seventy-four, for the purpose of converting from oil or natural gas to coal or to wood, wood bark, wood residue, or to any other alternate energy source for manufacturing, and any co-generation equipment Installed since such date for use in manufacturing.

The amendment ratified November 5 1870 and effeetive January 1, 1877- After (a) (6) added subdivision (7) "land subject to a perpetual easement . . .". In subsection (b) after "sixty-five years of age" added the language "or persons permanentiy and totally disabled as established by general law". In subsection (d) after "—monweaith" added the language "or for the purpose of transferring or storing solar energy". In subsection (e) after "personal effects" added the language "and tangible farm property and products".

The amendment ratified November 7, 1878 and effeeflve January 1, 1878- Added a new subsection (h).

The amendment ratified November 4, 1880 ad effective January 1, 1881- In subsection (b) substituted "exemption from local property taxation" for "exemption from local real property taxation". After "of real estate" added "and personal property designed for continuous habitation". Substituted "property" for "real estate" near the end of subsection (b).

The amendment ratified November 4, 1880 and effective January 1, 1881- Added a new subsection (l).

Section 7. Collection and disposition of State revenues.

All taxes, licenses, and other revenues of the Commonwealth shall be collected by its proper officers and paid into the State treasury. No money shall be paid out of the State treasury except in pursuance of appropriations made by law; and no such appropriation shall be made which is payable more than two years and six months after the end of the session of the General Assembly at which the law is enacted authorizing the same.

Other than as may be provided for in the debt provisions of this Constitution, the Governor, subject to such criteria as may be established by the General Assembly, shall ensure that no expenses of the Commonwealth be incurred which exceed total revenues on hand and anticipated during a period not to exceed the two years and six months period established by this section of the Constitution.

The amendment ratified November 0, 1884 and effective July 1, 1888- Added the second paragraph.

Section 8. Limit of tax or revenue.

No other or greater amount of tax or revenues shall, at any time, be levied than may be required for the necessary expenses of the government, or to pay the indebtedness of the Commonwealth.

Section 9. State debt.

No debt shall be contracted by or in behalf of the Commonwealth except as provided herein.

(a) Debts to meet emergencies and redeem previous debt obligations.

State Constitution

The General Assembly may (1) contract debts to suppress insurrection, repel invasion, or defend the Commonwealth in time of war; (2) contract debts, or may authorize the Governor to contract debts, to meet casual deficits in the revenue or in anticipation of the collection of revenues of the Commonwealth for the then current fiscal year within the amount of authorized appropriations, provided that the total of such indebtedness shall not exceed thirty per centum of an amount equal to 1.15 times the average annual tax revenues of the Commonwealth derived from taxes on income and retail sales, as certified by the Auditor of Public Accounts, for the preceding fiscal year and that each such debt shall mature within twelve months from the date such debt is incurred; and (3) contract debts to redeem a previous debt obligation of the Commonwealth.

The full faith and credit of the Commonwealth shall be pledged to any debt created under this subsection. The amount of such debt shall not be included in the limitations on debt hereinafter established, except that the amount of debt incurred pursuant to clause (3) above shall be included in determining the limitation on the aggregate amount of general obligation debt for capital projects permitted elsewhere in this article unless the debt so incurred pursuant to clause (3) above is secured by a pledge of net revenues from capital projects of institutions or agencies administered solely by the executive department of the Commonwealth or of institutions of higher learning of the Commonwealth, which net revenues the Governor shall certify are anticipated to be sufficient to pay the principal of and interest on such debt and to provide such reserves as the law authorizing the same may require, in which event the amount thereof shall be included in determining the limitation on the aggregate amount of debt contained in the provision of this article which authorizes general obligation debt for certain revenue-producing capital projects.

(b) General obligation debt for capital projects and sinking fund.

The General Assembly may, upon the affirmative vote of a majority of the members elected to each house, authorize the creation of debt to which the full faith and credit of the Commonwealth is pledged, for capital projects to be distinctly specified in the law authorizing the same; provided that any such law shall specify capital projects constituting a single purpose and shall not take effect until it shall have been submitted to the people at an election and a majority of those voting on the question shall have approved such debt. No such debt shall be authorized by the General Assembly if the amount thereof when added to amounts approved by the people or authorized by the General Assembly and not yet submitted to the people for approval, under this subsection during the three fiscal years immediately preceding the authorization by the General Assembly of such debt and the fiscal year in which such debt is authorized shall exceed twenty-five per centum of an amount equal to 1.15 times the average annual tax revenues of the Commonwealth derived from taxes on income and retail sales, as certified by the Auditor of Public Accounts, for the three fiscal years immediately preceding the authorization of such debt by the General Assembly.

No debt shall be incurred under this subsection if the amount thereof when added to the aggregate amount of all outstanding debt to which the full faith and credit of the Commonwealth is pledged other than that excluded from this limitation by the provisions of this article authorizing the contracting of debts to redeem a previous debt obligation of the Commonwealth and for certain revenue-producing capital projects, less any amounts set aside in sinking funds for the repayment of such outstanding debt, shall exceed an amount equal to 1.15 times the average annual tax revenues of the Commonwealth derived from taxes on income and retail sales, as certified by the Auditor of Public Accounts, for the three fiscal years immediately preceding the incurring of such debt.

All debt incurred under this subsection shall mature within a period not to exceed the estimated useful life of the projects as stated in the authorizing law, which statement shall be conclusive, or a period of thirty years, whichever is shorter; and all debt incurred to redeem a previous debt obligation of the Commonwealth, except that which is secured by net revenues anticipated to be sufficient to pay the same and provide reserves therefor, shall mature within a period not to exceed thirty years. Such debt shall be amortized, by payment into a sinking fund or otherwise, in annual installments of principal to begin not later than one-tenth of the term of the bonds, and any such sinking fund shall not be appropriated for any other purpose; if such debt be for public road purposes, such payment shall be first made from revenues segregated by law for the construction and maintenance of State highways. No such installment shall exceed the smallest previous installment by more than one hundred per centum. If sufficient funds are not appropriated in the budget for any fiscal year for the timely payment of the interest upon and installments of principal of such debt, there shall be set apart by direction of the Governor, from the first general fund revenues received during such fiscal year and thereafter, a sum sufficient to pay such interest and installments of principal.

(c) Debt for certain revenue-producing capital projects.

The General Assembly may authorize the creation of debt secured by a pledge of net revenues derived from rates, fees, or other charges and the full faith and credit of the Commonwealth, and such debt shall not be included in determining the limitation on general obligation debt for capital projects as permitted elsewhere in this article, provided that

(1) the creation of such debt Is authorized by the affirmative vote of two-thirds of the members elected to each house of the General Assembly; and

State Constitution

(2) such debt is created for specific revenue-producing capital projects (Including the enlargement or improvement thereof), which shall be distinctly specified In the law authorizing the same, of institutions and agencies administered solely by the executive department of the Commonwealth or of Institutions of higher learning of the Commonwealth.

Before any such debt shall be authorized by the General Assembly, and again before it shall be incurred, the Governor shall certify in writing, filed with the Auditor of Public Accounts, his opinion, based upon responsible engineering and economic estimates, that the anticipated net revenues to be pledged to the payment of principal of and interest on such debt will be sufficient to meet such payments as the same become due and to provide such reserves as the law authorizing such debt may require, and that the projects otherwise comply with the requirements of this subsection, which certifications shall be conclusive.

No debt shall be incurred under this subsection if the amount thereof when added to the aggregate amount of all outstanding debt authorized by this subsection and the amount of all outstanding debt incurred to redeem a previous debt obligation of the Commonwealth which is to be included in the limitation of this subsection by virtue of the provisions of this article authorizing the contracting of debts to redeem a previous debt obligation of the Commonwealth, less any amounts set aside in sinking funds for the payment of such debt, shall exceed an amount equal to 1.15 times the average annual tax revenues of the Commonwealth derived from taxes on income and retail sales, as certified by the Auditor of Public Accounts, for the three fiscal years immediately preceding the incurring of such debt.

This subsection shall not be construed to pledge the full faith and credit of the Commonwealth to the payment of any obligation of the Commonwealth, or any institution, agency, or authority thereof, or to any refinancing or reissuance of such obligation which was incurred prior to the effective date of this subsection.

(d) Obligations to which section not applicable.

The restrictions of this section shall not apply to any obligation incurred by the Commonwealth or any institution, agency, or authority thereof if the full faith and credit of the Commonwealth is not pledged or committed to the payment of such obligation.

Section 10. Lending of credit, stock subscriptions, and works of internal improvement

Neither the credit of the Commonwealth nor of any county, city, town, or regional government shall be directly or indirectly, under any device or pretense whatsoever, granted to or in aid of any person, association, or corporation; nor shall the Commonwealth or any such unit of government subscribe to or become interested in the stock or obligations of any company, association, or corporation for the purpose of aiding in the construction or maintenance of its work; nor shall the Commonwealth become a party to or become interested in any work of internal improvement, except public roads and public parks, or engage in carrying on any such work; nor shall the Commonwealth assume any indebtedness of any county, city, town, or regional government, nor lend its credit to the same. This section shall not be construed to prohibit the General Assembly from establishing an authority with power to insure and guarantee loans to finance industrial development and industrial expansion and from making appropriations to such authority.

Section 11. Governmental employee retirement system fund.

The General Assembly shall maintain a state employees retirement system to be administered in the best interest of the beneficiaries thereof and subject to such restrictions or conditions as may be prescribed by the General Assembly.

ARTICLE XI

Conservation

Section 1. Natural resources and historical sites of the Commonwealth.

To the end that the people have clean air, pure water, and the use and enjoyment for recreation of adequate public lands, waters, and other natural resources, it shall be the policy of the Commonwealth to conserve, develop, and utilize its natural resources, its public lands, and its historical sites and buildings. Further, it shall be the Commonwealth's policy to protect its atmosphere, lands, and waters from pollution, impairment, or destruction, for the benefit, enjoyment, and general welfare of the people of the Commonwealth.

Section 2. Conservation and development of natural resources and historical sites.

In the furtherance of such policy, the General Assembly may undertake the conservation, development, or utilization of lands or natural resources of the Commonwealth, the acquisition and protection of historical sites and buildings, and the protection of its atmosphere, lands, and waters from pollution, impairment, or destruction, by agencies of the Commonwealth or by the creation of public authorities, or by leases or other contracts with agencies of the United States, with other states, with units of government in the Commonwealth, or with private persons or corporations. Notwithstanding the time limitations of the provisions of Article X, Section 7, of this Constitution, the Commonwealth may participate for any period of years in the cost projects which shall be the subject of a joint undertaking between the Commonwealth and any agency of the United States or of other states.

Section 3. Natural oyster beds.

The natural oyster beds, rocks, and shoals in the waters of the Commonwealth shall not be leased, rented, or sold but shall be held in trust for the benefit of the people of the Commonwealth, subject to such regulations and restriction as the General Assembly may prescribe, but the General Assembly may, from time to time, define and determine such natural beds, rocks, or shoals by surveys or otherwise.

ARTICLE XII

Future Changes

Section 1. Amendments.

Any amendment or amendments to this Constitution may be proposed in the Senate or House of Delegates, and if the same shall be agreed to by a majority of the members elected to each of the two houses, such proposed amendment or amendments shall be entered on their journals, the name of each member and how he voted to be recorded, and referred to the General Assembly at its first regular session held after the next general election of members of the House of Delegates. If at such regular session or any subsequent special session of that General Assembly the proposed amendment or amendments shall be agreed to by a majority of all the members elected to each house, then it shall be the duty of the General Assembly to submit such proposed amendment or amendments to the voters qualified to vote in elections by the people, in such manner as it shall prescribe and not sooner than ninety days after final passage by the General Assembly. If a majority of those voting vote in favor of any amendment, it shall become part of the Constitution on the date prescribed by the General Assembly in submitting the amendment to the voters.

Section 2. Constitutional convention.

The General Assembly may, by a vote of two-thirds of the members elected to each house, call a convention to propose a general revision of, or specific amendments to, this Constitution, as the General Assembly in its call may stipulate.

The General Assembly shall provide by law for the election of delegates to such a convention, and shall also provide for the submission, in such manner as it shall prescribe and not sooner than ninety days after final adjournment of the convention, of the proposals of the convention to the voters qualified to vote in elections by the people. If a majority of those voting vote in favor of any proposal, it shall become effective on the date prescribed by the General Assembly in providing for the submission of the convention proposals to the voters.

SCHEDULE

Section 1. Effective date of revised Constitution.

This revised Constitution shall, except as is otherwise provided herein, go into effect at noon on the first day of July, nineteen hundred and seventy-one.

Section 2. Officers and elections

Unless otherwise provided herein or by law, nothing in this revised Constitution shall affect the oath, tenure, term, status, or compensation of any person holding any public office, position, or employment in the Commonwealth, nor affect the date of filling any State or local office, elective or appointive, which shall be filled on the date on which it would otherwise have been filled.

Section 3. Laws, proceedings, and obligations unaffected.

The common and statute law in force at the time this revised Constitution goes into effect, so far as not in conflict therewith, shall remain in force until they expire by their own limitation or are altered or repealed by the General Assembly. Unless otherwise provided herein or by law, the adoption of this revised Constitution shall have no effect on pending judicial proceedings or judgments, on any obligations owing to or by the Commonwealth or any of its officers, agencies, or political subdivisions, or on any private obligations or rights.

Section 4. Quaiifications of judges.

The requirement of Article VI, Section 7, that justices of the Supreme Court and judges of courts of record shall, at least five years prior to their election or appointment, have been members of the bar of the Commonwealth, shall not preclude justices or judges who were elected or appointed prior to the effective date of this revised Constitution, and who are otherwise qualified, from completing the term for which they were elected or appointed and from being reelected for one additional term.

Section 5. First session of General Assembly following adoption of revised Constitution.

The General Assembly shall convene at the Capitol at noon on the first Wednesday in January, nineteen hundred and seventy©e. It shall enact such laws as may be deemed proper, including those necessary to implement this revised Constitution. The General Assembly shall reapportion the Commonwealth into

State Constitution

electoral districts in accordance with Article II, Section 6, of this Constitution. The General Assembly shall be vested with all the powers, charged with all the duties, and subject to all the limitations prescribed by this Constitution except that this session shall continue as long as may be necessary; that the salary and allowances of members shall not be limited by Section 46 of the Constitution of 1902 as amended and that effective date limitation of Section 53 of the Constitution of 1902 as amended shall not be operative.

BOOKS ABOUT VIRGINIA

Abernethy, Thomas Perkins. *The South in the New Nation, 1789-1819.* Baton Rouge, LA: LA State University Printing, 1957.
-----*Three Virginia Frontiers.* 1940.
Adams, James Truslow. *The Living Jefferson.* New York, NY and London: Charles Scribner's Sons, 1936.
-----*America's Tragedy.* New York, NY: Charles Scribner's Sons, 1934.
Alden, John Richard. *The South in the Revolution, 1763-1789.* Baton Rouge, LA: LA State University, 1957.
Allan, William. *History of the Campaigns of Gen. T. J. (Stonewall.) Jackson in the Shenandoah Valley of Virginia from November 4, 1861, to June 17, 1862.* Philadelphia, PA: J. B. Lippincott Co. 1880.
Alvord, Clarence Walworth, and Lee Bidgood. *Travels in Virginia.* Cleveland, OH: Arthur H. Clark Co., 1912.
American Anthropologist. *Aboriginal Shell-Heaps of the Middle Atlantic Tidewater Region.* Washington, DC: 1907.
Andrews, Charles M. *The Colonial Period of American History.* New Haven, CT and London: Yale Univ. Press, Oxford Univ. Press, 1934.
Andrews, Matthew Page. *Virginia: The Old Dominion.* Garden City, NY: Doubleday, Doran and Company, Inc., 1937.
-----*Women of the South in War Times.* Baltimore, MD: The Norman Remington Co., 1927.
Arnold, Benjamin William. *History of the Tobacco Industry in Virginia from 1860 to 1894.* Baltimore, MD: John Hopkins Press, 1897.
Ashe, Dora J. *An Anthology.* Lanham, MD: Univ., Press of America, 1985.
-----*Four Hundred Years of Virginia, 1584-2984.* Lanham, MD: University Press of America, 1985.
Baily, Harold H. *The Birds of Virginia.* Lynchburg, VA: J. P. Bell Co., 1913.

Ballagh, James Curtis. *A History of Slavery in Virginia.* Baltimore, MD: John Hopkins Press, 1902.

Bayne, Howard R. *A Rebellion in the Colony of Virginia.* New York, NY: Society of Colonial Wars in the State of New York, 1904.

Billings, Warren M. *The Old Dominion in the Seventeenth Century: A Documentary History of Virginia, 1606-1689.* Chapel Hill, NC: University of North Carolina Press, 1975.

Boyd, Julian P. *The Papers of Thomas Jefferson.* Princeton University Printing, 1950.

Brown, Alexander. *The First Republic in America.* Boston, MA, and New York, NY: Houghton Mifflin Co., 1898.

Bruce, Philip Alexander. *Economic History of Virginia in the Seventeeth Century.* New York, NY and London: The Macmillan Co., 1896.

-----*History of the University of Virginia, 1819-1919.* New York, NY: The Macmillan Co., 1920-22.

-----*History of Virginia.* Chicago, IL and New York, NY: American Historical Society, 1924.

-----*Institutional History of Virginia in the Seventeenth Century.* New York, NY and London: G. P. Putnam's Sons, 1910.

-----*Social Life of Virginia in the Seventeeth Century.* Lynchburg, VA: J. P. Bell, Inc., 1927.

Brydon, George M. *Virginia's Mother Church.* Richmond, VA: Virginia Historical Society, 1875 reprinted 1947, 1952.

Buni, Andrew. *The Negro in Virginia Politics, 1902-1965.* Charlottesville: University Press of Virginia, 1967.

Bushnell, David I. Jr., *The Five Manocan Towns in Virginia, 1607.* Washington, DC: Government Printing Office, 1930.

-----*Native Villages and Village sites East of the Mississippi.* Washington, DC: Government Printing Office, 1919.

Butler, Stuart Lee. *Virginia Soldiers in the United States Army, 1800-1815.* Athens, GA: Iberian Publishing Co., 1986.

Campbell, Charles. *History of the Colony and Ancient Dominion of Virginia.* Philadelphia, PA: J. B. Lippincott and Company, 1860.

Caperton, Helena Lefroy. *Legends of Virginia.* Richmond, VA: Garrett and Massie, 1931.

Cappon, Lester J. and Stella F. Duff. *Bibliography of Virginia History Since 1865.* University of Virginia, 1930.

-----*Virginia Gazette Index, 1736-1780.* 1950.

Bibliography

Chesson, Michael. *Richmond After the War, 1865-1890.* Richmond, VA: Virginia State Library, 1981.

Cooke, John Esten. *Virginia: A History of the People.* New York, NY: Houghton, Mifflin and Co., 1891.

Craven, Avery O. *The Growth of Southern Nationalism, 1848-1861.* Baton Rouge, LA: LA State University Printing, 1953.

Craven, Wesley Frank. *The Colonies in Transition, 1660-1713.* 1968.

-----*The Southern Colonies in the Seventeenth Century, 1607-1689.* Baton Rouge, LA: 1949.

Cunningham, Noble E. Jr. *The Jeffersonian Republicans: The Formation of Party Organization, 1789-1801.* Chapel Hill, NC: University of North Carolina Press, 1957.

-----*The Jeffersonian Republicans in Power, 1801-1809.* Chapel Hill, NC: University of North Carolina Press, 1963.

Dabney, Virginius. *Richmond: The Story of a City.* Garden City, NY: Doubleday, 1976.

-----*Virginia: The New Dominion.* Charlottesville, VA: University Press of Virginia, 1983.

Davis, Arthur Kyle. *Traditional Ballad of Virginia.* Cambridge: Harvard Univ. Press, 1929.

-----*Virginians of Distinguished Service of the World War.* Richmond, VA: Published by Order of the Executive Committee, 1923.

Davis, Jefferson. *The Rise and Fall of the Confederate Government.* New York, NY: Appleton & Co., 1881.

Davis, Richard Beale. *Intellectual Life in Jefferson's Virginia, 1790-1830.* Knoxville, TN: University of Tennessee Press, 1972.

Degler, Carl N. *The Other South: Southern Dissenters in the Nineteenth Century.* New York, NY: Harper and Row, 1974.

Department of Agriculture of Virginia. *Virginia.* Richmond, VA: Edited by Charlotte Allen under direction of George W. Koiner, Commissioner, 1937.

Dodd, William E. *Jefferson Davis* Philadelphia, PA: George W. Jacobs, 1907.

Dowdey, Clifford. *The Virginia Dynasties.* Boston, MA: Little, Brown, 1969.

Eaton, Clement. *The Mind of the Old South.* Baton Rouge, LA: Louisiana State University Press, 1967.

Eckenrode, Hamilton James. *Political History of Virginia during the Reconstruction.* Baltimore, MD: John Hopkins Press, 1904.

-----*The Revolution in Virginia.* Boston, MA and New York, NY: Houghton Mifflin Co., 1916.

-----*Separation of Church and State in Virginia.* Richmond, VA: D. Bottom, Supt. Public Printing, 1910.

Edelhart, Mike. *The Virginians.* Garden City, NY: Doubleday, 1982.

Eubank, H. Radland. *Historic Northern Neck of Virginia.* Richmond, VA: Northern Neck Association, 1934.

Ezekiel, Herbert T. and Lichtenstein, Gaston. *History of the Jews of Richmond, 1769-1917.* Richmond, VA: H. T. Ezekiel, 1917.

Farrax, Emmie Ferguson. *Old Virginia Houses: The Mobjack Bay Country and Along the James.* New York, NY: American Legacy Press, 1981.

Federal Writers' Project. *Virginia: A Guide to the Old Dominion.* New York, NY: Somerset, 1980. (orig. 1940)

Fishe, John. *Old Virginia and Her Neighbours.* Bost, MA, and New York, NY: Houghton, Mifflin and Co., 1900.

Fitzgerald, Ruth Coder. *A Different Story: Black History of Fredericksburg, Stafford, and Spotsylvania, Virginia.* Greensboro, NC: Unicorn, 1979.

Foote, Rev. William Henry. *Sketches of Virginia-Historical and Biographical.* Philadelphia, PA: J. B. Lippincott Co., 1850-1856.

Fowke, Gerard. *Archeologic Investigations in James and Potomac Valleys.* Washington, DC: Government Printing Office, 1894.

Freehling, Alison Goodyear. *Drift Toward Dissolution: The Virginia Slavery Debate of 1831-1832.* LA State University Printing, 1982.

Freeman, Douglas Southall. *George Washington.*, 1948-54. (Note: 7/8 vols. - biographies of Virginians) Kelley Press, 1951 reprinted 1975.

Friddell, Guy. *What Is It About Virginia?* Richmond, VA: Dietz, 1983 (orig. 1966.)

Gordon, Armistead C. *In the Picturesque Shenandoah Valley.* Richmond, VA: Garrett and Massie, Inc., 1930.

Gottmann, Jean. *Virginia at Mid-Century.* New York, NY: Henry Holt, 1955.

-----*Virginia in Our Century.* Charlottesville, VA: University Press of Virginia, 1969.

Bibliography

Government Printing Office. *Aboriginal Pottery of the Eastern United States.* (In the Twentieth Annual Report of the Bureau of American Ethnology...1898-99.) Washington DC, 1903.
-----*The Manahoac Tribes in Virginia, 1608.* Washington DC, 1935.
-----*Tribal Migrations East of the Mississippi.* Washington DC, 1934.
Hall, Wilmer L. *A Bibliography of Virginia, part IV & V.* Richmond, VA: D. Bottom, 1916 reprinted 1932, 1955.
Harvard William C. *The Changing Politics of the South.* Baton Rouge, LA: Louisiana State University Press, 1972.
Hatch, Charles E. *Colonial Yorktown's Main Street and Military Entrenchments.* New York, NY: Eastern Acorn Press, 1980.
Hawkins, Van. *Jamestown, Williamsburg, Yorktown: a pictorial history of America's historic triangle.* Virginia Beach, VA: Donning Co., 1980.
Henderson, Col. G.F.R. *Stonewall Jackson and the American Civil War.* New York, NY and London: Longmans, Green & Co., 1927.
Henderson, William D. *Gilded Age City: Policics, Life and Labor in Petersburg, Virginia, 1874-1889.* Washington DC: University Press of America, 1980.
Hoffer, F. B. *Bibliography of Virginia Geology and Mineral Resources, 1941-1949.* 1968.
Holmes, William Henry. *Stone Implements of the Potomac-Chesapeake Tidewater Province.* Washington, DC: Government Printing Office, 1897.
Howison, Robert Reed. *A History of Virginia, from Its Discovery and Settlement by Europeans to 1848.* Philadelphia, PA: Carey and Hart, 1845.
Jack, George S. *History of Roanoke County.* Roanoke, VA: Roanoke, Stone, 1912.
Jacob, Diane B. and Judith Moreland Arnold. *A Virginia Military Album, 1839-1910.* Charlottesville, VA: University Press of Virginia, 1982.
Jefferson, Thomas. *Notes on the State of Virginia.* Richmond, VA: Prof. Schele de vere, 1853.
Jennings, John M. and James A. Servies. *Selected Bibliography of Virginia, 1607-1699.* 1957.
-----*Virginia Historical Index.* 1934, 1936.
Jensen, Merrill. *the New Nation: A History of the United states During the Confederation, 1781-1789.* New York, NY: Vintage Boos, 1950.

Johnson, F. Roy. *The Nat Turner Slave Insurrection.* 1966.
Kercheval, Samuel. *History of the Valley of Virginia.* 1925.
Kern, M. Ethel Kelley. *The Trail of the Three Notched Road.* Richmond, VA: The William Byrd Press, Inc., 1929.
Kilpatrick, James Jackson. *The Sovereign States: Notes of a Citizen of Virginia.* Chicago, IL: Henry Regnery, 1957.
Kirby, Jack T. *Westmoreland Davis...1859-1942.* 1968.
Kukla, Jon. *Speakers and Clerks of the Virginia House of Burgess, 1643-1776.* Richmond, VA: Virginia State Library, 1981.
Lancaster, Robert A., Jr. *Historic Virginia Homes and Churches.* Philadelphia, PA: and London, J. B. Lippincott Co., 1915.
Lingley, Charles R. *The Transition in Virginia from Colony to Commonwealth.* AMS Printing. 1910.
Maddox, Jack P. Jr. *The Virginia Conservatives, 1867-1879.* Chapel Hill, NC: University of North Carolina Press, 1970.
Malone, Dumas. *The Age of Jefferson.* 1948.
-----*Jefferson and His Time.* Boston, MA: Little, Brown, 1948.
Mapp, Alf J., Jr. *Frock Coats and Epaulets: Confederate Political and Military Leaders.* New York, NY: A. S. Barnes, 1963.
-----*The Virginia Experiment: The Old Dominion's Role in the Making of America, 1607-1781.* La Salle, IL: Open Court, 1975.
Mayer, Henry. *A Son of Thunder: Patrick Henry and the American Republic.* New York, NY: 1986.
Mays, David John. *Edmund Pendleton 1721-1802: A Biography.* Cambridge, MA: Harvard University Press, 1952.
McBain, Howard L. *Government and Politics in Virginia.* Richmond, VA: The Bell Book and Stationery Co., 1922.
McGregor, James C. *Disruption of Virginia.* 1922.
Moger, Allen W. *Virginia: Bourbonism to Byrd, 1870-1925.* Charlottesville, VA: University Press of Virginia, 1968.
Mooney, James. *The Siouan Tribes of the East.* Washington, DC: Government Printing Office, 1894.
Morgan, Edmund S. *American Slavery, American Freedom: The Ordeal of Colonial Virginia.* New York, NY: Norton, 1975.
Morgan, George. *The Life of James Monroe.* Boston, MA: Small, Maynard and Company, 1921.
Morris, Shirley. *The Pelican Guide to Virginia.* Gretna, LA: Pelican Publication Co., 1981.

Bibliography

Morrison, A. J. *The Beginnings of Public Education in Virginia, 1776-1860.* Richmond, VA: D. Bottom, Supt. of Public Printing. 1917.

Morton, Frederic. *The Story of Winchester in Virginia, the oldest town in the Shenandoah Valley.* Strasburg, VA: Publishing House, 1925.

Morton, Richard L. *Colonial Virginia.* Chapel Hill, NC: University of North Carolina Press, 1960.

----- *The Negro in Virginia Politics, 1865-1902.* Charlottesville, VA: Univ. Press. 1919.

----- *Virginia Since 1861.* 1924.

Muse, Benjamin. *Virginia's Massive Resistance.* Bloomington, IN: Indiana University Press, 1961.

Noel Hume, Ivor. *Martin's Hundred.* New York, NY: Knopf, 1982.

Nordstrom, Julie V. *The Eastern Shore of Virginia in Days Past.* Exmore, VA: J. Nordstrom, 1981.

Page Mary Mann. *The Story of Virginia's First Century.* Philadelphia, PA: J. B. Lippincott Co., 1928.

Pierce, Neal R. *The Border South States: People, Politics and Power in the Five Border South States.* New York, NY: W. W. Norton, 1975.

Pollard, Jno. *Virginia Born Presidents.* New York, NY and Boston, MA: American Book Company, 1932.

Pomfret, John E. and F. M. Shummway. *Founding the American Colonies, 1583-1660.* 1970.

Pulley, Raymond H. *Old Virginia Restored: An Interpretation of the Progressive Impulse, 1870-1930.* Charlottesville, VA: University Press of Virginia, 1968.

Roberts, Joseph K. *Annotated Geological Bibliography of Virginia.* 1942.

----- *The Road from Monticello...the Slavery Debate of 1832.* , 1941.

Rouse, Parke Jr. *James Blair of Virginia.* Chapel Hill, NC: University of North Carolina Press, 1971.

Rubin, Louis D., Jr. *Virginia: A Bicentennial History.* New York, NY: Norton, 1977.

Russell, John H. *The Free Negro in Virginia, 1619-1865.* Baltimore, MD: Johns Hopkins Press, 1913.

Sams, Conway Whittle. *The Conquest of Virginia: the Forest Primeval.* New York, NY: J. P. Putnam's Sons, 1916.

Semple, Robert B. *History of the Rise and Progress of the Baptists in Virginia.* Church History, 1811, reprinted 1894, 1976.

Shanks, Henry T. *The Secession Movement in Virginia,* 1847-1861.
Sheldon, William D. *Populism in the Old Dominion: Virginia Farm Politics, 1885-1900.* VA: 1935.
Speck, Frank G. *Chapters on the Ethnology of the Powhatan tribes of Virginia.* New York, NY: Museum of the American Indian, Heye Foundation, 1928.
Standard, Mary Newton. *The Story of Virginia's First Century.* Philadelphia, PA: Lippincott, 1938.
Summers, Lewis Preston. *History of Southwest Virginia, 1746-1786, Washington County, 1777-1870.* Richmond, VA: J. L. Hill Printing Co., 1903.
Surface, G. T. *Physiography of Virginia.* in American Geographical Society Bulletin, vol. xxxviii, 1906.
Swem, Earl G. *The Brothers and the Spade.* VA: Historical Index, 1934, Peter Smith, 1949.
-----*The Jamestown 350th Anniversary Historical Booklets. Vol. 23.* 1957.
Syndor, Charles S. *The Development of Southern Sectionalism, 1819-1848.* Baton Rouge, LA: 1948.
-----*Gentleman Freeholders: Political Practices in Washington's Virginia.* Chapel Hill, NC: University of North Carolina Press, 1952.
Thwaites, Reuben Gold. *Original Journals of the Lewis and Clark Expedition, 1804-1806.* New York, NY Dodd, Mead & Co., 1904-05.
Tindall, George Brown. *The Emergence of the New South, 1913-1945.* Baton Rouge, LA: LA State University Printing, 1969.
Tooker, William Wallace. *The Algonquian Names of the Siouan tribes of Virginia.* New York, NY: F. P. Harper, 1901. (Repr. from *American Anthropologist.*
Tyler, Lyon Gardiner. *Narratives of Early Virginia.* New York, NY: Charles Scribner's Sons, 1907.
-----*Williamsburg, the Old Colonial Capitol.* Richmond, VA: Whittet and Shepperson, 1907.
Virginia, Commonwealth Of. *Virginia Facts and Figures 1984.* Richmond, VA: Division of Industrial Development, 1984.
Virginia Conservation Commission. *Common Forest Trees of Virginia.* Charlottesville, VA: Virginia Forest Service Publication No. 26, 1936.

Bibliography

Virginia Council. *Legislative Journals of the Council of Colonial Virginia.* Richmond, VA: Virginia State Library, (Reprint of the 1918-1919 published by the Colonial Press, Richmond) 1979.
-----*Minutes of the Council and General Court of Colonial Virginia.* Richmond, VA: Virginia State Library, 1979.
Virginia Historical Society. *Portraits in the Collection of the Virginia Historical Society.* Charlottesville, VA: University Press of Virginia, 1980.
Washington, Booker T. *My Larger Education.* 1911.
-----*Story of My Life and Work.* Negro University Printing, Greenwood, 1900.
Waterman, Thomas Tileston, and Barrows, John A. *Domestic Colonial Architecture of Tidewater Virginia.* New York, NY and London: Charles Scribner's Sons, 1932.
Watson, Thomas Leonard. *Mineral Resources of Virginia.* Lynchburg, VA: J. P. Bell Co., 1907.
Wayland, John W. *Historic Homes of Northern Virginia and the Eastern Panhandle of West Virginia.* Staunton, VA: McClure Co., Inc., 1937.
Wertenbaker, Thomas J. *Bacon's Rebellion, 1676.* University Printing of Virginia, 1957.
-----*The Planters of Colonial Virginia.* Princeton, NJ: Princeton University Press, 1918.
Wilkinson, J. Harvie III. *Harry Byrd and the Changing Face of Virginia Politics, 1945-1966.* Charlottesville, VA: University Press of Virginia, 1968.
Williams, Lloyd Haynes. *Pirates of Colonial Virginia.* Richmond, VA: The Dietz Press, 1937.
Wilstach, Paul. *Mount Vernon, Washington's Home and the Nation's Shrine.* Indianapolis, IN: The Bobbs-Merrill Co., 1930.
-----*Potomac Landings.* Indianapolis, IN: The Bobbs-Merrill Co., 1932.
Wood, Amos D. *Floyd County: A History of its People and Places.* Radford, VA: Commonwealth Press, 1981.
Woodberry, George E. *Edgar Allan Poe.* Boston, MA: and New York, NY: Houghton Mifflin Co., 1892.
Woodward, C. Vann. *Origins of the New South, 1877-1913.* Baton Rouge, LA, 1877-1913.
Wright, Louis B. *The First Gentlemen of Virginia.* Charlottesville, VA: University Press of Virginia, 1940.
Younger, Edward. *The Governors of Virginia, 1860-1978.* Charlottesville, VA: University Press of Virginia, 1982.

INDEX

Abingdon, 221
Abingdon Bank, 485
Abingdon Church, 385
Abingdon Glebe House, 383
Abingdon Historic District, 486
Abolitionists, 79
Abram's Delight, 490
Academy of Music, 416
Accomac, 222,247
Accomack County, 222
Act of Cohabitation, 257,276,280
Adams, H. R., 85
Adams, John Quincy, 60,152,153,157, 161,167,168,201,270
Adams, John, 57,135,137,140
Adkins, Mrs. I. W., 86
African Company, 122
Agriculture and Immigration, 69
Agriculture, 104,234
AIDS, 89
Air Force Chiefs of Staff, 347
Albany Conference, 28
Albemarle and Chesapeake Canal, 362
Albemarle County Courthouse Historic District, 361
Albemarle County, 222
Alberta, 222
Aldie Historic District, 410
Aldred, Captain, 256
Alexander, Captain John, 222,223
Alexander, William, 408
Alexander-Withrow House, 408
Alexandria, 64,89,125,222
Alexandria Constitution, 64
Alexandria Historic District, 343
Alien and Sedition Laws, 55,56,77
Allegheny County, 226
Allegheny Mountains, 1,25 46-47,75,226
Allen, Claude, 260
Allen, Floyd, 260
Allen, Sidna, House, 357
Allmand-Archer House, 425
Almond, Governor J. L., 84

Almond, James Lindsay, 194-195
Altavista, 226
Ambrose Powell Hill, 368
Amelia County, 226
American (Know-Nothing) Party, 176
American Antiquarian Society, 97
American Colonization Society, 60, 285,379
American French Academy, fire, 455
American System, 58-59
Amherst County, 226
Amherst, 226
Amherst, Jeffery, 226
Amherst, Lord, 226
Amoroleck, 26
Ampthill, 368
An Enquiry into the Rights of the *British Colonies*, 48
Anderson House, 373
Anderson, Henry, 188
Anderson, J. R., Co., 459
Anderson, Joseph Reid, 459
Anderson, Robert, 270
Anderson, Sherwood, 270,388
Andros, Governor, 119
Andros, Sir Edmund, 117-119
Angel's Rest, 283
Annapolis, 125
Annapolis Convention of 1786, 224
Annapolis Convention, 53,77,156
Annefield, 364
Ante-bellum debt, 64,66,82,86
Anti-war protests, 86
Appalachia, 226
Appalachian Mountains, 11,14-15,121,
Appalachian Plateau, 11,13
Appalachian Valley, 12,17
Appomattox, 63,81,176,227,394,459
Appomattox Campaign, 370
Appomattox County, 226
Appomattox Court House National Historical Park, 347
Appomattox Courthouse, 371

557

Encyclopedia of Virginia

Appomattox Manor, 398
Appomattox River, 227
Apumetec, 227
Aquia Church, 475
Archeozoic era, 14
Archer, Captain Gabriel, 269
Archer, William Segar, 201
Argall, Captain Samuel, 105
Argall, Samuel, 106-107
Argall, Sir Samuel, 35
Ariss, John, 383,405,463
Arlington County, 227
Arlington House/Robert E. Lee
   Memorial, 347
Arlington, Lord, 73
Arms of Virginia, 2
Armstrong, Samuel Chapman, 390
Army of Northern Virginia, 62
Army of the Potomac, 377
Arnold, Benedict, 52,76,138,284,293
Art Club, 269
Articles of Confederation, 53,76,145
Ash Lawn, 340
Ashburton, Lord, 164
Ashby, General Turner, 247
Ashland, 227
Ashleigh, 378
Assateague Lighthouse, 337
Association for the Preservation
   of Virginia Antiquities, 263
Assumption Bill, 55
Assumption Bill, 77
Atherton Gag, 60
Atlantic Coast Line, 288
Atlantic and Danville Railway, 288
Atlantic Coast Line Railway, 293
Atlantic Fleet, 81
Atlantic Ocean, 1,11
Augusta County, 228
Augusta Female Seminary, 476
Augusta Stone Church, 348
Austin, Stephen F., 78
Aventine Hall, 433
Bacon's Castle, 423,480
Bacon's Rebellion, 40-42,73,111,
   114-115,223,236,265,284,286,292,
   480
Bacon, Nathaniel, 40,41,69,111,
   116-117,280,292,311,480
Bacon, Nathaniel, Jr., 28,116
Bakker, Jim, 89
Balcony Falls, 228
Baldwin, Mary Julia, 476
Baliles, Gerald L., 198
Ballendine, John, 444

Baltimore & Ohio Railroad, 225
Baltimore, Lord, 38,72,108,109,111-
   113,256
Banister, Col. John, 436
Bank Building, 337
Bank of Alexandria, 343
Bank of the United States, 55,166,
   168,171
Banks, General Nathaniel P., 252
Banks, Lynn, 173
Barbour, Governor, 169
Barbour, James, 59,157-158,201-202,
   213,432
Barbour, John Strode, Jr., 202
Barboursville, 432
Barco-Stevens Hall, 461
Barnard, Henry, 61
Barney, J. Stewart, 490
Barracks, Virginia Military
   Institute, 409
Barret House, 446
Barret, Anderson, 446
Barret, John, 446
Barret, William, 446
Barron, Commodore James, 257,258
Barron, Commodore Samuel, 257
Barron, James, 257
Bath, 228
Battersea, 435
Battle of Bunker Hill, 137,314
Battle of Cedar Creek, 381
Battle of Chancellorsville, 80,236
Battle of Cowpens, 314
Battle of Five Forks, 370
Battle of Fredericksburg, 80
Battle of Gettysburg, 207
Battle of Greenspring, 53
Battle of Harlem Heights, 211
Battle of Kernstown, 80
Battle of New Market, 315
Battle of Petersburg, 80
Battle of Point Pleasant, 47
Battle of Santiago Harbor, 250
Battle of Scary Creek, 176
Battle of Spotsylvania Courthouse, 80
Battle of the Barges, 280
Battle of the Wilderness, 204
Battle of Three Ponds, 235
Battle of Trevilian, 267
Battle of Wilderness, 80
Battle of Williamsburg, 312
Battle, Governor J. S., 84
Battle, John Stewart, 193
Batts, Thomas, 27
Baxter House, 468

Index

Baxter, George, 468
Beauregard, General, 443
Bedford, 228
Bedford County, 228
Beers, William, House, 446
Beery, John K., Farm, 468
Bel Air, 444
Belgian Building, 461
Bell Tower, 446
Bell's Oven, 229
Bell, Alexander Graham, 242
Belle Air, 357
Belle Grove, 405
Belle Haven, 229
Belle Isle, 407
Belleview, 398
Bellona Arsenal, 363
Bellona Foundry, 363
Belmead, 441
Belmont, 472,474
Belvoir Mansion Ruins and Fairfax Grave Site, 376
Benedict, Arnold, 314
Benge, 253
Benjamin, Asher, 440,466
Bennett's Creek Church, 479
Bennett, Captain Richard, 38
Bennett, Governor, 112
Bennett, Richard, 111-112
Bentfield, 353
Berkeley, 358
Berkeley, Governor, 73,114,116,223 265,286,304,310,311,
Berkeley, Norborne, 127-128,249
Berkeley, Sir William, 38-41,110-111 113-114,116
Berkeley, William, 110-111
Bernard, General Simon, 390
Bernard, John Hipkins, 356
Berry Hill, 389
Berry, Benjamin, 229
Berry, Sir John, 114
Berryville, 229
Beverley Mill, 444
Beverley, Robert, 28,42
Beverley, William, 304
Beverly, William, 302,372
Big Stone Gap, 229
Bill of Rights, 43,51,54,77
Black population, 64
Black voter registration, increase of, 84
Black, B. J., 436
Black, Samuel, 272
Black, William, 229
Blackbeard, 1,44,256,391

Blackburn, Colonel Richard, 249
Blackburn, Richard, 445
Blackburn, Thomas, 478
Blacksburg, 83,229
Blackstone, 230
Blackstone, Sir William, 230
Blair, James, 119,123
Blair, John, 54,126
Bland County, 230
Bland, Edmund, 73
Bland, Edward, 44
Bland, James, 8
Bland, Richard, 48,127,230
Bland, Theodoric, 311
Bland, Theodoric, Jr., 261
Bland, Theodoric, Sr., 261
Bland, Theodorick, 205
Blandfield, 372
Blandford Church, 436
Bloxom, 230
Bloxom, William, 230
Blue Bridge, 254
Blue Ridge Mountains, 1,186,230,237, 291,300,472
Blue Ridge Plateau, 12
Blue Ridge Province, 11,12,14,16,17
Bluefield, 230
Board of Charities and Corrections, 68
Board of Trade and Plantations, 47
Board of War, 145
Bob White Covered Bridge, 435
Bolling Hall, 61,386
Bolling, William, 386
Bondurant, Charles, 298
Bonsack, James A., 269
Books About Virgina, 547-555
Boone trail, 253
Boone, Daniel, 230
Boone, Jacob, 230
Boone, John, 230
Boones Mill, 230
Borst, Peter Bock, 433
Boston Port Bill, 75
Boswell's Tavern, 413
Botetourt County, 230
Botetourt, Governor, Botetourt, Lord, 126-128
Bottom's Bridge, 231
Bourgeois, Victor, 461
Boush, Samuel, 277
Boush-Tazewell House, 425
Bowden, Lemuel Jackson, 202
Bowen, Henry, 207
Bowling Green Female Seminary, 231
Bowling Green, 231

559

Bowman's Folly, 339
Boyce, 232
Boyce, U. L., 232
Boyd, Belle, 252
Boyd, Judge Alexander, 232
Boydton, 232
Boykins, 232
Boykin's Tavern, 399
Bradby, J. N., 86
Bradby, Sheriff, J. N., death of, 86
Braddock, General Edward, 46,74
Braddock, General, 313
Branch Building, 446
Branchville, 232
Brandon, 443
Braxton, Carter, 406
Brazil, 176
Breckinridge, Maj. Gen. John C., 471
Breeder of slaves, 60
Bremo, 378
Brent, Giles, 474
Brent, Richard, 201-202
Bridgewater, 232
Briery Church, 442
Bristol, 232
Bristow, Robert, 385
Britain, 106
British, 74
British Army, 46-47
British colonization, 33
British Debts, 135
British encroachment, 126
British fleet, 78,138,144
British government, 122,155,287,
British guardship, 41
British House of Commons, 166
British officers, 252
British policy, 48
British rule, 26,75,418
British ships, *Chesapeake*, 56
British ships, *Diamond*, 98
British ships, *Discovery*, 33,98,235
British ships, *Falcon*, 98
British ships, *Fowly*, 129
British ships, *God-Speed*, 98
British ships, *Goodspeed*, 33,235
British ships, *Leopard*, 56,78,154, 258,278,
British ships, *Sarah Constand*, 33, 235
British ships, *Sarah Constant*, 33
British ships, *Sea Adventure*, 98
British ships, *Sea Venture*, 104
British ships, *St. Domingo*, 57
British ships, *Susan Constant*, 98
British soldiers, 363

British subjects, 36,156
British territory, 125
British trade, 155
British troops, 51-53,79,78,151,257
273,284,288,300,312,341
Broad Run Bridge and Tollhouse, 413
Broad Street Station, 447
Broadway, 233
Brockenbrough Mansion, 461
Brodnax, 233
Brooke's Bank, 372
Brooke, Robert, 149
Brookneal, 233
Brown University, 476
Brown, Dr. William, 224
Brown, John, 60,80,176,222,225
Brown, Samuel, 303
Brownsburg Historic District, 466
Brownsville, 431
Bruce, Charles, 360
Bruinswick County, 233
Brunswick County Courthouse Square, 353
Bruton Parish Church, 488
Bryan, Robert, 250
Buchanan & Clifton Forge Railroad, 234
Buchanan and Clifton Forge Railway, 241
Buchanan County, 233
Buchanan, 233
Buchanan, James, 233
Buchanan, John, 233
Buckingham County, 234
Buckingham Courthouse Historic District, 354
Buckland, William, 444
Buckner, John, 250
Buena Vista, 234,464
Buffon, 139
Bull, John, 138
Burch, Thomas Granville, 202-203
Bureau of Refugees, Freedmen, and Abandoned Lands, 64
Burk, John Daly, 285
Burke, Colonel Samuel, 234
Burke, Edmund, 48
Burkeville, 234
Burnside, Gen. A. E., 473
Burnside, General Ambrose E., 236
Burnt Quarter, 370
Burr, Aaron, 78,140,141,154,168,270
285,293,397,460
Burwell Morgan Mill, 365
Burwell, Col. Nathaniel, 365
Burwell, Lewis, 124-125,385
Burwell, Robert Carter, 364
Bush, President George, 89

Index

Bushong House, 471
Butler, Gen., Drewry's Bluff Campaign, 363
Byrd, Colonel William Byrd, II, 250
Byrd, Colonel William, 232,248
Byrd, Governor Harry F., 82,189,203, 260
Byrd, Governor Harry Flood, 68,82, 189,203-204
Byrd, Harry Flood, Jr., 203-204
Byrd, William I, 42,292
Byrd, William II, 45,284,292,296,301
Byrd, William, 30,31
Byrd, William, III, 44,292,359
C.S.S Virginia, 390
Cabell, Colonel George C., 183
Cabell, Colonel Joseph, 346
Cabell, Dr. George, 417
Cabell, Gov. William H., 447
Cabell, Henry Coalter House, 447
Cabell, James Branch, 294
Cabell, William H., 154,422
Cady, J. C., 390
Calhoun, John C., 152
California, 164,172
Callie Furnace, 353
Camden, 356
Cameron, Simon, 174
Cameron, William Evelyn, 181-182
Camp Humphreys, 68
Camp Lee, 68
Camp Peary Military Reservation, 492
Camp Stuart, 68
Campbell County, 235
Campbell, David, 169-170,222
Campbell, John, 221
Canada, 57,121
Canning, 296
Cape Charles, 33,235
Cape Cod, 106
Cape Hatteras, 62
Cape Henry Lighthouse, 235,483
Cape Henry, 33,81,100,235
Capital of Virginia, 292
Capital, 43
Capitol Building, 9
Capitol of the colony, 74
Capps, William, 275
Capron, 235
Caret, 235
Carleill, Captain Christopher, 103
Carlton, 474
Carlyle House, 343
Carlyle, John, 344
Carolina, Clinchfield & Ohio Railway, 298

Caroline County Courthouse, 355
Caroline County, 236
Carrington Row, 457
Carrington, George, 301
Carrington, Paul, 361
Carroll County, 236
Carter Family, 360
Carter Hall, 365
Carter's Grove, 402
Carter's Tavern, 389
Carter, George, 411
Carter, John, 342
Carter, Landon, 463
Carter, Robert, 122-123,407
Carter, Samuel, 389
Cartersville Bridge, 369,385
Carver, Captain William, 286
Cary, Archibald, 127
Caserta, 430
Castle Hill, 341
Catoctin Creek Bridge, 413
Cavaliers, 42
Cedar Bluff, 236
Cedar Creek Battlefield and Belle Grove, 381,485
Cenozoic era, 15
Central Hospital, 182
Central-Southside, 1
Centre Hill, 436
Chambers, Edward, 392
Chancellor House, 236
Chancellorsville, 236
Chanco, 36
Chantilly, 237,487
Chapman Mill, 444
Chapman, Henry Otis, 490
Chapman, Jonathan, 444
Charles City County Courthouse, 357
Charles City County, 237
Charles City Point, 35
Charles I, 38,106,108-110,124
Charles II, 39,41,73,115,276,306
Charleston, 62
Charlotte County, 237
Charlotte Courthouse, 237
Charlottesville, 237,387
Charlottesville Woolen Mills, 239
Charlottesville *Daily Progress*, 199
Chase City, 239
Chase, Samuel, 213
Chase, U.S. Supreme Court Justice, 239
Chatham, 239
Chelsea, 406
Cheriton, 239
Cherry Hill, 377

561

Encyclopedia of Virginia

Chesapeake and Ohio Railway Company, 238,241,478
Chesapeake Bay, 1,11,12,25,28,32,39, 41,47,99,106,129,,198,235,239,258, 262,289,305
Chesapeake, 154,258,278,287
Chester, 481
Chesterfield County, 240
Chesterman, Aubrey, 416
Chesterville Plantation Site, 389
Chestnut, Mary Boykin, 294
Chewning, Reverend Bartholomew, 231
Chicheley, Henry, 114-115
Chicheley, Sir Henry, 40,115
Chickahominy River, 26,99
Chickohocki River, 102
Children's Home Society of Southwestern Virginia, 189
Chilhowie, 240
Chincoteague, 240
Chippokes Plantation, 480
Christ Church Glendower, 342
Christ Church, 344,407,420
Christanna Indians, 28
Christian, Israel, 249
Christian, William, 240,246
Christiansburg, 240
Chronology of Virginia, 71-89
Chuckatuck Church, 479
Church of England, 118,249
Churches, 46
CIA, 87,88
City Hall, 448
City Market, 436
City of Henricus, 35
Civic Art League, 269
Civil War, 4,61-64,176,177,179,180, 181,183-186,204,207,209,214,219, 225,227,235,238,241,245,249,251, 258,261,267,269,272,278,284,285, 291,304,314,340,343,349,363,366, 370,377,390-392,397,400,410,419, 419,432,434,439,440,441,443,447, 449,459,460,461,470,471,473,477, 479
Civil War, battlefields, 1
Civil War, end of, 63-64
Civil War, Reconstruction Act, 65,81
Civil War, Reconstruction, 64
Civil War, surrender of Lee, 63
Claiborne, Captain William, 111
Claiborne, William, 38,107,256
Claremont, 240
Clark, George Rogers, 52,76
Clark, William J., Library, 461
Clark, William, 56
Clarke County, 240
Clarke, George Rogers, 240
Clarksville, 240
Clay's Compromise of 1850 60
Clay, Henry, 58,153,161-164,166,171 227,288
Clerisseau, Louis, 460
Cleveland, 240
Cleveland, Grover, 183,219,240
Clifton Forge, 241
Clifton, 241,369
Clifton, James, 241
Climate, 13-14
Clinch River, 241
Clinedinst, Benjamin West, 315
Clintwood, 241
Clockmaking, 272
Clopton, John, 160,217
Clover, 241
Coal, 253
Coastal Plain, 11,12
Cobham Park, 341
Cockade City, 285
Cockburn, Admiral George, 57
Cockburn, Sir George, 290
Cocke, Charles, Memorial Library, 465
Cocke, Gen. John Hartwell, 379,380
Cocke, Thomas, 397
Code of Virginia, 4-7
Coe, W. W., 242
Coeburn, 242
Coke, Richard, 175
Cold Harbor, 394
Coleman, J. Marshall, 198
College of William and Mary, 43,74, 76,117,489
College of William and Mary, admission of women, 82
College of William and Mary, closing of, 312
College of William and Mary, fire, 121
Colleges, 66
Collier, Sir George, 52
Colonial Beach, 242
Colonial Congress, 133
Colonial Council, 154
Colonial Governors, 97-129
Colonial Heights, 242
Colonial law, 264
Colonial legislature, 126
Colonial National Historical Park, 401,488,492

Index

Colonial Virginia, 45,73
Colonies, founding of, 102
Colonists, 26,33-36,38,39,72,97,98, 102,106,109,110-112,116,118-119, 127-129,256,273,275
Colonists, of Plymouth Company, 71
Colonization of Virginia, 71,103
Colony of Virginia, 3
Colony, desolate condition, 104
Columbia, 242
Commission on State and Local Revenues and Expenditures, 194
Commission to Revise the Constitution of Virginia, 195
Committee of Safety, 51
Committee of Ways and Means, 177
Commonwealth, 39,73,111
Commonwealth of Virginia, 5,7
Compromise Tariff of 1833, 161,162
Compulsory Education Act, 188
Confederacy, 63,80,173,181,183,222 235,245,285,314
Confederate Army, 173,174,184,207, 209,214,219,366,394,439
Confederate Capitol, 460
Confederate cavalry, 184
Confederate Congress, 173,217
Confederate fort, 401
Confederate government, 177
Confederate heroes, 455
Confederate House of Representatives, 165
Confederate Memorial Chapel, 448
Confederate Monument, 228
Confederate Provincial Congress, 207
Confederate Provisional Congress, 217
Confederate Soldiers Home, 448
Confederate States, 60,80
Confederate storehouses, 221
Confederate supplies, 234
Confederate supply base, 269
Confederate surrender, 394
Confederate troops, 227,244,263,264 ,278,309,312,347,370,371,390,424
Congress, 65,78,79,207,225
Congressional Cemetery, 202
Congressional declaration of war on England, 78
Congress, 258
Connecticut, 118
Conservation and Development, 69
Constellation, 278
Constitution, 246
Constitution, adoption of, 53
Constitution, ratification by Virginia, 54
Constitution of 1868, 66

Constitution of Virginia, 495-545
Constitutional Convention of 1787, 224
Constitutional Convention of Virginia, 175
Constitutional Convention, 77
Continental Army, 52-53,75,211,251,
Continental Congress, 75,79,134,137, 143,157,206,208,211,218,230,487
Cook, D. S., 353
Corbin Hall, 338
Cornwallis, 238,263,284,293,312
Cornwallis, General, 53,76,401
Cornwallis, Lord, 138
Corotoman, 408
Corporal's Guard, 175
Corporations, 69
Cortez, 99
Cotton, 58,59,119
Cotton industry, 301
Count of Gondomar, 37
Courtland, 243
Couty, John, 474
Covington, 243
Cradock Historic District, 439
Craig County, 243
Craig, Reverend Lewis, 264
Craig, Robert, 243
Craigsville, 243
Crawford, Colonel William, 286
Crawford, Malcolm F., 418,433
Crawford, William H., 152,160,161
Crewe, 243
Cricket Hill, 418
Criss Cross, 423
Cromwell, Oliver, 110,111
Cropper, General John, 280
Cropper, John, Jr., 339
Crostwait, Justice Shelton, 422
Crowninshield, Benjamin W., 152
Crozet House, 448
Crummett, S. W., 398
Crutchfield, Major Stapleton, 257
Culpeper, 243
Culpeper County, 243
Culpeper Minute Men, 243
Culpeper, Lord, 42,55,73,114-116,243
Cumberland County, 244
Cumberland Gap, 1,11
Cumberland Gap National Historical Park, 408
Cumberland Mountains, 1,13
Cumberland, 258
Curtis Carter House, 448
Cushing, Caleb, 165

Custis Tombs, 429
Custis, Eleanor Parke, 375
Custis, George Washington Parke, 347
Custis, John, IV, 429
Custis, Maj. Gen. John, 429
Custis, Major John, 175
Custus, George Washington Parke, 227
Dabney, Robert Lewis, 348,442
Dale, Sir Thomas, 34,101,103,104,105
Dale, Thomas, 104-105,395
Dalton, John Nicholas, 197
Dalton, Ted, 194
Damascus, 244
Dan River, 244
Daniel, John Warwick, 204,216
Daniel, Senator, 183
Danner, Jacob, 272
Danville, 244
Danville Historic District, 369
Danville Public Library, 370
Darden, C. W., Jr., 83
Darden, Colgate Whitehead, 192
Davies, Dr. Howell, 352
Davis, A. J., 410
Davis, Alexander Jackson, 414,415,441
Davis, Captain John, 169
Davis, Governor Westmoreland, 68,82
Davis, Jefferson, 65,81,174,234,241, 245,370,451,459
Davis, President Jefferson, 390
Davis, Westmoreland, 187-188
Daylight savings time bill, 195
Dayton, 246
Dayton, Jonathan, 246
de Beauregard, Gen. Pierre G. T., 366
de Botetourt, Baron, 249
de Grasse, Admiral, 53, 401
De la Warr, Lord, 101,104,106,401
De la Warre, Lord, 34,36
de Tubeuf, Baron Francois Pierre, 298
Deane, Silas, 138
Death penalty restored, 87
Death with dignity bill, 196
Debtor's Prison, 442
Decatur, Commodore Stephen, Jr., 258
Declaration of Independence, 37,41, 48,51,75,76,128,136,137,142-145, 208,231,341,358,389,406,462,487, 489,493
Declaration of Independence, signing of, 138
Declaration of war against Germany, 82
Declaratory Act, 145
Deer Chase, 420

Delaware, 119
Delaware, Lord, 71,100,273,292
Democratic Leadership Council, 198
Democratic National Convention, 191
Democratic Party, 66,161,162,166, 170,173,175,180
Democratic State Convention, 191
Democratic-Republicans, 152
Denbigh Plantation Site, 424
Dendron, 246
Denwood, Levin, 274
Department of Conservation and Economic Development, 195
Derby, William, 290
Deyerle, Benjamin, Place, 465
Dick, Dr. Elisha Cullen, 225
Dickens, Charles, 293
Dickens, Preston, 357
Dickenson County, 246
Dickenson, William, 246
Dickenson-Fugate House, 468
Dictionary of Places, 221-317
Digges, Gove . .or Edward, 112,113
Dillwyn, 246
Dimmock, Marion J., Sr., 448
Dinwiddie County Courthouse, 370
Dinwiddie, Governor Robert, 46,125, 126,256,277
Directory of State Services, 91-96
Discourse of Virginia, A, 97
District of Columbia, 225
Doddridge, Philip, 175
Dodson, Joseph, 389
Donnan-Asher Iron-Front Building, 448
Donne, John, 42
Dooley, James, 349
Dooley, Maj. James H., 454
Dos Passos, John R., 487-488
Douglas, Margaret, 278
Douglass, Frederick, 179,198
Downey, William, 228
Drake-Sidney voyage, 103
Drakes Branch, 246
Dranesville Tavern, 376
Draper's Meadows, 229
Draper, John, 229
Dred Scott Decision, 60
Drewry's Bluff, 62
Drummond, Governor William, 265,311
Drummond, Richard, 222
Drydock No. 1, 439
Drysdale, Hugh, 122
Dublin, 246
Duffield, 246

Index

Dulany, Richard Henry, 412
Dulles International Airport, 1
Dumfries, 246
Dunbar, Paul Lawrence, 198
Dungannon, 247
Dunk, George Montago, 255
Dunlap, David, 366
Dunmore, Governor, 47,128,287
Dunmore, Lord, 51,134,143,155,277, 312,493
Dunwiddie County, 247
Durand, M., 42
Dutch, 39
Dutch Gap Canal, 63
Dutch vessels, 73
Earl of Southampton, 37
Earl of Warwick, 107
Earliest books, 42
Early, General Jubal A., 309
Early, General, 63
Earp's Ordinary, 374
East India Company, 50
East India School, 35,36
Eastern Shore, 1
Eastville, 247
Education, 46,69
Effingham, Lord, 117
Eggleston, Joseph, 201
Egyptian Building, 449
Ekeeks, 280
Elk Hill, 351
Elkton, 247
Ellerslie, 366
Ellington, Branch H., 431
Ellison, Andrew, Jr., 416
Elmwood, 373
Elsing Green, 406
Emancipation, 60,62
Embargo Act of 1807, 56
Emigrants, 108,165
Emporia, 248
England, 147
Eppes family, 359
Eppes Island, 359
Eppes, John Wayles, 205,213,364
Eppington, 363
Equal Rights Amendment, 196,197
Equal Suffrage League, 269
Essex County, 248
Essex-Prize, 256
Establishment of towns in each county, 73-74
Etude, The, 269 Evans House, 468
Evans, Oliver, 486
Evans, Rear Admiral Robley D., 81

Evans, Robley Dunglison, 250
Ewing, Thomas, 163
Exchange Building, 437
Exchange Hotel, 432
Exchange National Bank, 179
Exchequer Bill, 164
Exeter, 411
Exmore, 248
Expansion, 43
Eyre Hall, 430
Ezekiel, Sir Moses, 294
F-15 fighter planes, 89
Factories, 46,66
Fairfax, 248
Fairfax County, 58,248
Fairfax County Courthouse, 374
Fairfax Resolves, 224
Fairfax, Col. William, 376
Fairfax, Lord Thomas, 122,248, 309,313,366
Fiarfield, 364
Fairfield Site, 385
Fall Hill, 473
Falling Creek, 72
Falls Church, 248,377
Falmouth Historic District, 475
Famine, 97
Fancy Farm, 350
Faris, Elisha, 253
Farmer's Bank, 437
Farmer's Delight, 412
Farmington, 340
Farms, 46,61
Farmville, 249
Farnham Church, 462
Fast Day, 75
Faulconer, Benjamin F., 432
Fauquier County, 249
Fauquier, Francis, writings, 127
Fauquier, Governor Francis, 29,48, 126,127
Federal Act, 77
Federal banks, 58
Federal Bureau of Investigation, 195
Federal Constitution, 146,206,208, 211,212,293
Federal Party, 141,161,166,179
Federal Reserve Act, 269
Federal Reserve Bank Act, 82
Federal Social Security Act, 83
Federal Whittle House, 427
Ferguson, Isham M., 296
Ferry Farm Site, 475
Fiery Epoch, 294
Fifteenth Amendment, 65

565

Fifth Virginia Convention, 51,75
Fillmore, Millard, 477
Finance, 69
Fincastle Historic District, 352
Fincastle, 249
Fire Station No. 1, 464
Fire, American French Academy, 455
Fire, College of William and Mary, 121
Fire, Fredericksburg, 251
Fire, Gosport Navy Yard, 288
Fire, Haymarket, 259
Fire, Lexington, 266
Fire, Norfolk, 129,278,287
Fire, Petersburg, 285
Fire, Portsmouth, 288
Fire, Suffolk, 304
Firestone, Harvey, 398
First African Baptist Church, 449
First Baptist Church, 449
First Battle of Manassas, 80
First Congress, 211
First Continental Congress, 50,75,145 ,292,312
First Supply, 34,71
First Virginia Convention, 75,143,292 312
First, Bank of Alexandria, 225
First, biographer of George Washington, 444
First, Black admitted to University of Virginia, Martinsville, 85
First, Black Clerk of Charles City County, 86
First, Black county supervisor, 69
First, Black elected to the County Supervisors Board, 83
First, black free school, 278
First, black Lieutenant Governor of Virginia, 198
First, Black Mayor, 69,87
First, Black member of the State Legislature since 1891, 86
First, black preacher in Virginia, 312
First, Black Sheriff of Charles City County, 86
First, Black to be elected to General Assembly since 1891, 86
First, Black to hold a statewide post since the reconstruction, 88
First, Black to serve in a Virginia Governor's office, 86
First, Blacks arrive in Jamestown, 72
First, blacks brought to Virginia, 35

First, college founded in U.S. by the Methodist Church, 227
First, college, 117
First, colonial Governor of Virginia, 97
First, colonists, 101
First, constitution of a free and independent state, 76
First, customhouse in the colonies, 128
First, democratically-elected legislative body, 35
First, educational institution endowed, 72
First, eight counties formed, 72
First, elected Black Governor in America, 89
First, elected Governor in America, 69
First, English colony, 33
First, formal invasion of Virginia, 76
First, foundry in America, 72
First, Governor of colony, 34,71
First, governor of the Commonwealth, 76
First, group of Puritans to reach Virginia, 304
First, incorporated municipality, 74
First, Indian massacre of colonists, 72
First, integration order for Charlottesville public schools, 85
First, intercollegiate fraternity in, America, 76
First, Jewish settlements in Virginia, 61
First, law school in America, 76
First, legislative body in America, 263
First, legislature in America, 106
First, massacre of colonists by Indians 107
First, mayor of Norfolk, 277
First, National Thanksgiving Day proclamation, 208
First, navigation act passed by Parliament, 73
First, newspaper in colony, 311
First, newspaper, 74
First, organized resistance to British authority, 41
First, paper mill, 311
First, permanent English settlement in America, 69,258
First, permanent English settlement in the New World, 71,401

Index

First, planters of the colony, 97
First, Portsmouth railroad, 288
First, postwar railroad magnate, 66
First, president of initial council of first colony in America, 97
First, President of the United States, 77
First, professor of law in America, 316
First, representative legislature in America, 72
First, settlers of Virginia at Roanoke Island, 71
First, ship built by the Federal Government, 287
First, ship constructed by the Federal Government, 77
First, shipload of women to arrive, 72
First, slaves brought into the English colonies, 106
First, stockade, at Jamestown, 25
First, successful printing press in Virginia, 311
First, successful smelting furnace, 44
First, theater in America, 74
First, theatrical performance in Virginia, 290
First, tobacco crop, 35
First, treaty with China, 165
First, turnpike built, 267
First, U.S. Congress (1789), 376
First, Virginia signer of Declaration of Independence, 316
First, windmill in America, 35
First, woman Attorney General of Virginia, 88
First, woman attorney general, 198
Fitzhugh, William, 42
Five Forks Battlefield, 370
Five Nations, 248
Fleming, Governor, 238
Fletcher, Elijah, 347
Flood Marker of 1771, 396
Floods, 84
Flora and Fauna, 20-23
Florida, 37,57,99,168
Flour, 223,247,251,277,284
Flournoy, Thomas, 354
Floyd, 250
Floyd County, 249
Floyd, John Buchanan, 173-174,222
Floyd, John, 166-167,170,249
Fluvanna County Courthouse Historic District, 379

Fluvanna County, 250
Folly, 349
Ford, Henry, 398
Fork Church, 391
Formation of new government, 51-55
Fort Bowman, 471
Fort Calhoun, 390
Fort Charles, 292
Fort Chiswell Mansion, 491
Fort Christanna, 28,121,248
Fort Crafford, 424
Fort Cricket Hill, 418
Fort Donelson, 62,174
Fort Duquesne, 46,74,75,126
Fort Eustis Military Reservation, 424
Fort Eustis, 493
Fort Harrison, 467
Fort Henry, 61-63,81,255,258, 284,390,391
Fort Myer Historic District, 347
Fort Necessity, 46
Fort Nelson, 278,287,288
Fort Norfolk, 278,288
Fort Philip Long, 434
Fort Sumter, 60
Fort Trent, 125
Fort West, 291
Fort Whipple, 347
Fort Wool, 390
Fortress Monroe, 179
Fortsville, 481
Foster's Castle, 423
Fotheringay, 421
Four-Mile Tree, 480
Fourteenth Amendment, 65
Fourth Congressional District, 66
Fourth Virginia Convention, 51
Foushee, William, 293
Fox, Charles James, 166
Fox, John Jr., House, 490
France, 98,147,166,168,176
Francisco, Peter, 354
Francisco, Peter, House, 354
Franklin, 250 Franklin County, 250
Franklin, Benjamin, 122,137,138,139, 142,250
Frederick County, 250
Frederick, Henry, 260
Fredericksburg and Spotsylvania Cty. Nat'l. Military Park, 473
Fredericksburg Historic District, 381
Fredericksburg, 250,473,474
Freedmen's Bureau, 65,390
Freemason Street Baptist Church, 426
French and Indian War, 29,46,74,75, 226,232,296,344,434,467

French, 121,151,401
French Huguenots, 74
French settlements, 234
French troops, 53
French, encroachment of, 125
French, settlements, 106
Fries, 252
Frobisher, 99
Front Royal, 252
Fry, Colonel Joshua, 46
Fry, Joshua, 232
Frye, E. G., 416
Fuqua, Joseph, 228
Fur trade, 44
Furnace, Catherine, 434
Furs, 292
Gadsby's Tavern, 344
Gadsby, John, 344
Galax, 253
Galloway, Joseph, 133
Galt, Alexander, 458
Galt, James, 379
Garfield, James, 178
Garland Hill Historic District, 416
Garnett, Muscoe, 373
Gate City, 253
Gates, Sir Thomas, 34,71,100-102 106
Gay Mont, 356
General Congress, 127
Geographical configuraton, 11-23
Geology, 14-17
George II, 250,266,289
George III, 47,250
George Washington Birthplace National Monument, 486
Georgian Revival Roper House, 427
Gettysburg, 63,229
Gilbert, Sir Humphrey, 33
Giles County, 253
Giles, William Branch, 165-167,205, 210,253,346
Giles, William Branch, writings, 166
Gilmer, B. T., 8
Gilmer, Francis W., 170
Gilmer, Pendey R., 170
Gilmer, Thomas Walker, 79,170-171
Ginther, William P., 464
Glade Spring, 253
Glasgow, 253
Glasgow, Ellen, 294,450
Glasgow, Ellen, House, 449
Glass works, 107
Glass, Carter, 82,203,205-206,215,269
Glebe Church, 479

Glebe of Hungar's Parish, 431
Glebe, The, 348
Glen Lyn, 254
Gloucester County Courthouse Square Historic District, 382
Gloucester County, 41,254
Gloucester Women's Club, 382
Godwin, Mills Edwin, 85,86,195-196
Goggin, W. L., 171
Gooch, Sir William, 122-124,254,302
Gooch, William, Tomb and York Village Archeological Site, 493
Goochland County Court Square, 386
Goochland County, 254
Goodrich, James, 231
Goodwin, Governor Mills E., 69
Goodwin, W. A. R., Dr., 312
Gookin, Daniel, 275
Goose Creek Meetinghouse Complex, 412
Goose Creek Stone Bridge, 410
Gorden, Nathaniel, 254
Gordon, Colonel James, 45
Gordonsville, 254
Goshen, 254
Gosnold, Bartholomew, 33
Gosnold, Captain, 98
Gosport Navy Yard, 258,287,288,440
Governor's Commission on Reorganization of the State Government, 203
Governor's Council, 421
Governor's Land Archeological District, 402
Governors of Virginia, 131-199
Governors, Colonial, 97-129
Grace Church, 493
Graham, John, 246
Graham, Judge William H., 474
Grant, Ulysses S., 63,65,174,209,347, 370,371,394,399
Grant, William H., House, 457
Grassdale, 414
Grayson County, 254,206,211,218,254 261
Great Appalachian Valley, 241
Great Bridge Battle Site, 362-363
Great Britain, 62,124,133,157,158, 164,166,168
Great Britain, general boycott of, 50
Great Depression, 190
Great Kanawha River, 47
Great Lakes, 54
Great Seal, 5
Green Hill, 355
Green Spring, 39,41,402
Green Springs Historic District, 415

Index

Green Springs, 415
Greene County 254
Greene County Courthouse, 388
Greene, General Nathanael, 52
Greene, Nathanael, 149,254
Greenfield, 360
Greensville County, 254
Greenville Stamp Act, 267
Greenway, 358
Greenway Court, 366
Gregory, John Munford, 171-172
Gretna, 254
Gristmill, 232
Grottoes, 255
Grundy, 255
Guest's Station, 242
Gulf of Mexico, 121
Gunston Hall, 375
Gwynn's Island, 129
Hagan, Captain Patrick, 247
Hairston, George, 271
Halifax, 255
Halifax County, 255
Haller-Gibboney Rock House, 492
Hallowell, Benjamin, 345
Hallwood, 255
Hamilton, 255
Hamilton, Alexander, 53,55,56,166
Hamilton, Charles, 255
Hamilton, George, 120
Hampden-Sydney College, 453
Hampden-Sydney College Historic District, 442
Hampstead, 423
Hampton Institute, 257,390
Hampton Roads, 80,82,391
Hampton Roads Port, 258
Hampton, 30,57,75,129,255
Hancock, Col. George, 422
Hancock, John, 138,145
Hancock-Wirt-Caskie House, 450
Handley Library, 490
Hanover County Courthouse Historic District, 392
Hanover County Courthouse, 393
Hanover County, 47
Hanover Town, 393
Harpers Ferry, 80
Harrison, Albertis Sydney, 195
Harrison, Benjamin, 145-146,156
Harrison, Benjamin, V, birthplace of, 358
Harrison, Carter Henry, 369
Harrison, Daniel, 467
Harrison, Governor Albertis, 196

Harrison, Governor, 85
Harrison, Nicholas, 134
Harrison, Randolph, 368
Harrison, Thomas, 258
Harrison, Thomas House, 395
Harrison, William Henry, 59,79,146, 162,164,170,217,358
Harrisonburg Daily News-Record, 189
Hart, Colonel James, 272
Hart, Robert, 272
Hartsuff, G. L., 436
Harvard University, 119
Harvey, John, 38,72,108-110
Haviland, 440
Haw Branch, 345
Hawkwood, 414
Haxall, Bolling, House, 450
Hay, Robert, 5
Hayes, Rutherford, 209
Haymarket, 259
Haysi, 259
Hazelwood, 356
Health, Public Welfare, Law, and Workmen's Compensation, 69
Heath, Sir Robert, 38,72
Hebron Lutheran Church, 418
Hell Town, 252
Henfry, Benjamin, 293
Henkel Press, 471
Henkel, Ambrose, 471
Henrico County, 260
Henrico, 104,105,395
Henry County, 260
Henry, Patrick, 40,48,50,69,76,126, 127,129,131-135,137,143,155,174, 214,231,244,260,267,391-3
Henry, Prince, 104
Henry, R. S., 258
Henry, William Wirt, 135
Herbert House, 391
Herndon, 260
Herndon, Captain William, 260
Herndon, Edward, 231
Herndon, William Lewis, 251
Hesse, 418
Heyman, Peter, 256
Hickory Hill, 392
Hickory Neck Church, 402
Hidden Valley, 350
Highest mountains, 12
Highland County, 260
Highlands, 1
Highways, 69
Hill, A. P., Boyhood Home, 368

Encyclopedia of Virginia

Hill, General A. P., 264,433
Hillsboro, 260
Hillsborough, 404
Hillsville, 260
Hilton Village, 424
Hinckley, John W., Jr., 87
Historical Places, 337-493
Historie of Virginia, 42
History of the World's Columbian
    Exposition, 182
History, 33-69
Hite, Joist, 313
Hix, Captain Robert, 248
Hoban, James, 411
Hogan, Major Benjamin, 315
Hoge, S. Harris, 189
Holliday, Frederick William Mackey, 180-181
Hollins College Quadrangle, 465
Holly Hill, 403
Hollywood Cemetery, 451
Holt, John, 277
Holton, Abner Linwood, 196-197
Holton, Governor Linwood, 86
Holton, L., 86
Holton, Linwood, 195
Holy Alliance, The, 58
Home School, 231
Honaker, 260
Hooker, Gen. Joseph, 473
Hoomes, John, 231
Hoomes, Maj. John, 355
Hoomes, Major Thomas, 231
Hope Dawn, 352
Hopewell, 261
Hopkins and Brother Store, 339
Hopkins, Capt. Stephen, 339
Hopkins, George W., 222
Horse College, 254
House of Burgesses, 35-40,72,73,110, ,113,116,122,124,127,132,133,136, ,143,144,145,147,148,150,154,157, 397
Housing, 45,46
Houston, Sam, 79
Howard's Neck Plantation, 387
Howard, Francis Lord Effingham, 116
Howard, General O. O., 236
Howard, Phillip, 290
Howard, Sir Charles, 116
Howe, General, 51
Howell, H. E., 86
Howell, Henry, 196,197
Howsing, Robert, 223
Hubard, Mathew, 42
Hudson Bay Fur Co., 165

Hudson River, 36
Hudson, Henry, 102
Huggins and Bates, 464
Hughes, John G., 380
Huguenot colony, 26
Hume, Ivor Noel, 408
Humpback Bridge, 345
Hungars Church, 428
Hunt, Richard Morris, 390
Hunter's Ironworks, 475
Hunter, General David, 266
Hunter, James, 475
Hunter, Robert Mercer, 206-207
Huntington, Collis P., 275
Huntley, 375
Hunton, Eppa, 207
Hurricane Agnes, 86
Hurricane Charley, 88
Hurricane David, 87
Hurricane Hugo, 88
Hurt, 261
Hurt, John L., 261
Illness, 97
Immigrants, 106,107
Immigrants, Dutch settlement, 106
Immigrants, Dutch, 44
Immigrants, English Quakers, 45
Immigrants, French Huguenot, 45
Immigrants, French, 44,46,52
Immigrants, German, 44-46,121,434,472
Immigrants, Irish, 44
Immigrants, Jewish, 44,61
Immigrants, Polish, 44,308
Immigrants, Scotch-Irish, 45-46
Immigrants, Scottish, 44,45,468
Immigrants, Swedish, 44
Immigrants, Welsh, 45
Incorporators of the new colony, 103
Indentured servants, 35,41,42
Independence, 261
Indian depredations, 148
Indian outbreak, 128
Indian Paintings, 482
Indian tribes, 102,118,119,121,122, 218,247,253,269,271,284,303
Indian tribes, Accomac, 222
Indian tribes, Akenatzy, 27
Indian tribes, Algonquian 25,31,32, 226,289,297,300
Indian tribes, Allegevi, 226
Indian tribes, Appamatuck, 25,227
Indian tribes, Arrowhatock, 25
Indian tribes, Catawba, 29
Indian tribes, Cherokee chiefs, 125
Indian tribes, Cherokee, 25,29,31, 221,482

Index

Indian tribes, Chesapeake, 286
Indian tribes, Chichominys, 28
Indian tribes, Chickahominy, 29
Indian tribes, Chiefs of the Five
  Nations, 116
Indian tribes, children, 121
Indian tribes, Chinco-Teague, 240
Indian tribes, Conestoga, 25
Indian tribes, Creek, 152
Indian tribes, Delaware, 29
Indian tribes, depredation of the
  colonists, 110
Indian tribes, encroachment of, 114
Indian tribes, Five Nations of the
  Iroquois, 28
Indian tribes, Florida, 164
Indian tribes, Hanohaskie, 27
Indian tribes, Iroquoian, 25,27-29,
124 Indian tribes, kind treatment of, 99
Indian tribes, Manahoac, 25-27
Indian tribes, massacre of March of
  1621, 110
Indian tribes, Mattapament, 25
Indian tribes, Mattapanient, 271
Indian tribes, Mattaponi, 28,29
Indian tribes, Monacan, 25-27
Indian tribes, Nansemond, 28,29
Indian tribes, Nottoway, 25,28,29,
  125,280
Indian tribes, Nuntaneuck, 27
Indian tribes, Occaneechee, 280
Indian tribes, Occaneechi, 28
Indian tribes, outbreak of fighting
  against colonists, 110
Indian tribes, Pamunkee, 25
Indian tribes, Pamunkey, 26-29
Indian tribes, peace conference, 114
Indian tribes, peace with, 105
Indian tribes, Pomeioc, 29
Indian tribes, Powhatan, 25,27-29,
  113,289
Indian tribes, Rappahannock, 291
Indian tribes, Rechahecrian, 25
Indian tribes, religion, 105
Indian tribes, Rickohockan, 25
Indian tribes, Saponeys, 29
Indian tribes, Saponi, 27,28
Indian tribes, Secotan, 29
Indian tribes, Seminoles, 57,152
Indian tribes, Shawanese, 150
Indian tribes, Shawnee, 329
Indian tribes, Shawnee, 28,29,75,
  229,482
Indian tribes, signing of a peace
  treaty, 116

Indian tribes, Siouan, 25-32
Indian tribes, Susquehanna, 28
Indian tribes, Susquehannock, 40,
  280,292
Indian tribes, Tuncaroras, 29
Indian tribes, Tuscarora, 28
Indian tribes, Tutelo, 27,28
Indian tribes, Youghtanund, 25
Indian tribes, Yuchi, 25
Indian village, prehistoric, 398
Indian-Catholic massacre, 43
Indians, Appomattox, 105
Indians, attacks on settlers, 36
Indians, burial customs, 31
Indians, Christianity, 36
Indians, costumes, 31
Indians, customs, 31
Indians, displacement, 25
Indians, encroachment by French, 46
Indians, religion, 31
Indians, remnants of their
  civilization, 32
Indians, second Indian massacre
  of colonists, 73
Indians, subservience to British
  rule, 26
Indians, warfare, 47
Indians, western tribes, 125
Industrial economy, 66
Infanta, 37
Ingles Ferry, 445
Ingles, William, 229,445
Instructions for Independence, 369
Introduction to Virginia, 1-9
Ionia (Clover Plains), 414
Iron foundry, 35
Iron Gate, 262
Iron, 59,107,121,234,241,380,434
Irvington, 262
Isle of Kent, 38
Isle of Wight County, 262
Ivor, 262
Jack's Creek Covered Bridge, 435
Jackson, Andrew, 57,59,160,161,167,
  168,170,172,175,181,213,225,252,
  273,288
Jackson, Gen. Thomas Stonewall, 152,
Jackson, Stonewall, House, 409
Jackson, Thomas J., Headquarters, 490
Jacksonian Party, 214
James City County, 262
James I, 71,103-105
James II, 41,43,118,119,262
James River and Kanawah Canal
  Company, 241

571

Encyclopedia of Virginia

James River and Kanawha Canal Historic District, 396,451
James River and Kanawha Canal, 234, 293
James River Canal, 63
James River, 25-27,32,35,36,62,97, 99,102,111,115,120,128,262,386, 395,396,422,424,443,459,480
Jamestown Exposition, 81
Jamestown Island, 262,480
Jamestown National Historic Site, 401
Jamestown, 26,33,36,39,40,41,43,53, 69,71,72,83,97-100,102,104-109, 114,117,395,401,402
Jarratt, 263
Jay, John, 54,55,151,166
Jefferson Hotel, 451
Jefferson Literary Society, 180
Jefferson's Embargo Act, 78
Jefferson's Ten Rules, 142
Jefferson, Martha, 159
Jefferson, Peter, 232,237
Jefferson, Thomas, 9,51,52, 55-58,65,69,76,77,125,127,135-142,151, 153-156,158-161,167,168,211,237,238 273,292,316,342,351,364,382,387,434
Jefferson, Thomas, as architect, 293,340,341,352,362,368,432,460
Jeffersonian Classical Washington Hall, 410
Jeffreys, Herbert, 114
Jenings, Edmund, 120
Jim Crow law, 81
Joannes, Francis Y., 424
Johnson, Charles, 268
Johnson, John E., 360
Johnson, Joseph, 174-175
Johnson, Lynda Bird, 198
Johnson, President Andrew, 64
Johnson, President Lyndon B., 87,198
Johnson, Walter, 193
Johnston, Charles Clement, 207
Johnston, General Albert Sidney, 62
Johnston, General Joseph E., 62,231, 299
Johnston, John Warfield, 207-208
Johnston, Joseph Eggleston, 207,221
Johnston, Mary, 234,294
Joint Chiefs of Staff, 347
Jones, Frederick, 264
Jones, George H., 437
Jones, John, 353
Jones, Joseph, 211
Jones, Matthew, House, 424
Jones, Morgan, 1677 Pottery Kiln, 487

Jones, Peter, 284
Jonesville Methodist Campground, 408
Jonesville, 264
Jordan, John, 410
Jouette, Jack, 76,238,273
Judicial Inquiry and Review Commission, 196
Judiciary system of Virginia, 154
Juvenile and Domestic Relations Court, 82
Kanawaha Canal, 386
Kanawha Canal, 422,459
Kanawha Co., 396
Kansas-Nebraska Bill, 60
Kearny, General Philip, 237
Kecoughtan, 29
Keeling House, 483
Keller, 264
Kemp, Richard, 110
Kemper, James Lawson, 180
Kenbridge, 264
Kendall, George, 33
Kenmore, 381
Kent-Valentine House, 451
Kentucky, 11,62,76
Kerr Place, 339
Keswick, 441
Keys, John, 264
Keysville, 264
Killgore Fort House, 470
Killgore, Robert, 470
Kilmarnock, 264
King and Queen County, 265
King Charles I, 237
King Cotton, 59
King George County, 265
King George I, 265
King George II, 226,228,231,236,302
King George III, 237
King James, 33,97,262
King James, death, 108
King Philip's War, 118
King William County Courthouse, 405
King William County, 265
King's Bench, 37,72
King, Dr. Martin, Jr., 199
Kings Dominion, 1
Kingsmill Plantation, 402
Klugel, H. T., Architectural Sheet Metal Work Building, 372
Knollys, Ann, 108
Korean War, 193,199
La Crosse, 265
La Fayette, 285,293
La Fayette, General, 52,53,76,401
Labor and Industry, 69

Index

Lady of the Lake, 288
Lafever, Minard, 457
Lake Drummond, 265
Lamb's Creek Church, 405
Lancaster County, 265
Landreth, S. Lloyd, 192
Lands End, 384
Lane, Col. Joseph, 412
Lane, Henry, 226
Langley Air Force Base, 89
Langley Field, 68
Langley NASA Research Center, 389
Lansdowne, 420
LaRouche, Lyndon H., 88
Latrobe, Benjamin H., 364
Laurnence, W., 69
Lawrence, Captain James, 265
Lawrenceville, 265
Lead mines, 316
Leaseland, 250
Lebanon, 265
Lebby, Dr. Brewerton Monroe, 432
Lederer, John, 26,27,31,270
Lee Chapel, Washington and Lee University, 409
Lee County, 265
Lee Hall, 425
Lee House (Kiskiack), 492
Lee's Legion, 148
Lee, Arthur, 420
Lee, Fitzhugh, 183
Lee, Francis Lightfoot, 266,462,487
Lee, General Charles, 287
Lee, General Fitzhugh, 267,353
Lee, General Henry, 135
Lee, General Robert E., 236,299
Lee, Henry, 148-149,265
Lee, Light Horse Harry, 148,242
Lee, Philip Ludwell, 266
Lee, Richard Bland, 376
Lee, Richard Henry, ,1,3-5,48,51,54, 76,77,127,134,137,155,208,308,487
Lee, Richard, 124
Lee, Robert E., 1,60,62,63,69,80,81, 149,181,225,229,241,347,360,367,371 ,397,424,459,473,477,487
Lee, Robert E., home of, 347
Lee, Robert E., surrender, 184,245
Lee, Thomas, 124,308
Leedstown Resolutions, 75
Leedstown, 48
Leesburg Historic District, 410
Leesburg Turnpike Co., 413
Leesburg, 265
Leftwich, Colonel Augustine, 268
Leigh Street Baptist Church, 452

Leigh, Benjamin Watkins, 173,212,208,452
Leigh, Benjamin Watkins, House, 451
Length of Virginia, 11
Lenore, 227
Leslie, General Alexander, 52
Letcher, Governor John, 60,177
Letters of the British Spy, 270
Levingston, William, 311
Levy, Com. Uriah P., 142
Levy, Jefferson M. 142
Lewis and Clark, 78
Lewis, Abraham, 237
Lewis, Andrew, 298
Lewis, Fielding, 381
Lewis, General Andrew, 75,418
Lewis, John Francis, 208-209
Lewis, Major Andrew, 47
Lewis, Meriwether, 56
Lewis, Thomas, 212
Lexington Historic District, 409
Lexington, 266
Libby Prison, 294
Libby, William, 294
Liberal Charter of 1612, 36
Libraries, 45
Library Company of Alexandria, 225
Library of Congress, 474
Life and Character of Robert E. Lee, 182
Life of Patrick Henry, 134,450
Lincoln Homestead and Cemetery, 467
Lincoln, Abraham, 5,62,63,164,165,207 236,467
Lincoln, Jacob, House, 467
Lind, Jenny, 293
Linden Row, 452
Liquor, 122
Little Cherrystone, 438
Little England, 383
Little Fork Church, 368
Little River Turnpike, 410,413
Livingston, R. R., 137
Livingston, Robert R., 56
Lock-Keeper's House, 386
Lockwood, General H. H., 235
Lodge, The, 201
London Company, 25,33-37,71,72,106, 235
Long Branch, 364
Long Bridge Ordinary, 382
Long, Robert Cary, Jr., 478
Lords of Trade and Plantation, 29
Loudoun County, 266
Louis, Frederick, 250
Louisa County, 266
Louisa Railroad, 254
Louisa, 266

Encyclopedia of Virginia

Louisiana Purchase, 151
Louisiana Territory, 56,57,141
Lovett, David, 267
Lovettsville, 267
Lower Church, 419
Lowland Cottage, 385
Loyal Company, 44,74
Lumber, 227,277
Lunenburg County, 267
Lunenburg Courthouse Historic District, 415
Luray, 267
Lutheran Press, oldest in America, 471
Lybrock, Albert, 455
Lyceum, The, 344
Lynch, Father John W., 465
Lynch, John, 268
Lynchburg Courthouse, 416
Lynchburg News, 219
Lynchburg, 268,417
Lynching, 189
Lynnhaven Bay, 57,269
MacArthur, Gen. Douglas, Memorial, 426
Mad Ann Bailey, 303
Madison, 270
Madison County, 270
Madison County Courthouse, 418
Madison's Virginia Plan, 77
Madison, Dolley, 57,78,391,433
Madison, James, 53,54,57,58,77,78, 152,155,157,159,160,166,168,171, 211,238,270,285,433
Madison, James, House, 433
Magruder, Gen. John B., 299,425,493
Mahock, 26
Mahone, General William 66
Mahone, William, 183, 209
Main Campus Complex, Roanoke College 469
Main Street Station, 453
Maine, 118,119
Malvern Hill, 397
Manassas, 61,62,270 Manassas Gap, 270
Manassas National Battlefield Park, 443
Manassas Park, 270
Mangohick Church, 406
Maningkinton, 26
Mann Act, 185,187
Mann, William Hodges, 186-187
Manual of Parliamentary Practice, 140
Margots, 360
Marine Hospital Service, 440
Marion, 270
Marion, General Francis, 270

Marlbourne, 394
Marmion, 404
Marsh, Henry L., 3rd, 87
Marshall, Captain Thomas, 244
Marshall, Chief Justice John, 78, 244,378,453
Marshall, George C., 409
Marshall, John, 157,167,244,316,453
Marshall, John, House, 453
Marshall, Margaret, 378
Marshall-Whyte School of Law, 216
Martin Site, 491
Martin's Gazetteer, 273
Martin, Captain, 98
Martin, Edward, 290
Martin, General Joseph, 271
Martin, John, 33
Martin, Thomas, 30
Martin, Thomas Staples, 206,209
Martinsville Fish Dam, 398
Martinsville, 271
Mary Baldwin College, 476
Marye, Peter, 267
Marye, William Staige, 267
Maryland, 11,39,44,53,62,88,109-112, 119,256
Maryland territory, 38
Mason House, 338
Mason, Armistead Thomson, 209-210
Mason, George, 51,54,224
Mason, George, IV, 375
Mason, James M., 219
Mason, James Murray, 210
Mason, John Y., 481
Mason, Stevens, Thomson, 210-211
Mason, Thomson Francis, 375
Mason's Hall, 453
Massachusetts, 48,118,119,126,151, 163
Massachusetts Bay colony, 38
Massacre of 1622, 310
Massacre of 1644, 311
Massanutten Mountain, 13,300
Massie, Judge Thorton L., 260
Massinacack, 26
Massive resistance, 85
Mathews County, 271
Mathews Manor House, 424
Mathews, General Thomas, 271
Mathews, Governor, 39
Mattaponi Church, 403
Mattaponi River, 271
Mattapony River, 115
Matthews, Samuel, 111-113
Maupin, Dr. Socrates, 453
Maupin-Maury House, 453

Index

Maury, Matthew Fontaine, 251,454
Maury, Rev. James Fontaine, 243
Maxwell, Edith, 289
May Campaign of 1905, 68
May, 1771 Flood, 396
Mayfield Cottage, 371
Mayhurst, 432
Maymont, 454
Maynard, Captain Henry, 256
Mayo Memorial Church House, 454
Mayo, Major William, 292
Mayo, Peter H., 454
McCarty, John Mason, 210
McClellan, Gen. George B., 62,377,397
McClurg, James, 54
McComb, John, Jr., 483
McCormick, Cyrus, Farm and Workshop, 466
McDowell, Captain John, 253
McDowell, Ephraim, 303
McDowell, General, 443
McDowell, James, 172,173
McGavock, Joseph, 491
McGavock, Stephen, 491
McIlwaine House, 437
McIlwaine, Archibald Graham, 437
McKenney, William R., 269
McKinney, Philip Watkins, 182
McLean House, 347
Meadow Farm, 396
Mecklenburg, 271
Melchers, Gari, 474
Melfa, 271
Mennonites, 468
Menokin, 462
Mercer, Charles Fenton, 410
Merchant's Hope Church, 443
Meredith, Colonel Samuel, 346
Merrimac, 62,80
Merrimack, 390,258,278,439
Merritt, Wesley, 370
Mesozoic era, 15
Metal, 107
Methodist Episcopal Church, South, 79
Mexican War, 59,434
Mexican-American War, 234,272
Mexico, 60,99,164
Michel, Francis Louis, 26
Michigan, 11
Middle Plantation, 40,74,114,117,120
Middleburg, 271
Middlesex County, 271
Middletown, 272
Midway Mill, 422
Military District No. 1, 65
Miller Manual Labor School, 209
Miller School of Albemarle, 343

Miller, Jacob, 315
Miller, Samuel, 343
Millhiser House, 461
Mills, 46
Mills, Clark, 348
Mills, James, Storehouse, 420
Mills, Robert, 388,455,460,461
Millwood Mill, 365
Mineral, 272
Mining, 242
Minnesota, 258
Minor, Captain Nicholas, 266
Mississippi River, 11,99
Missouri Compromise, 58,59
Mobjack Bay, 419
Moccasin Gap, 253
Monacan Town, 26
Monitor, 62,80,258,390
Monroe Doctrine, 58,78,153,411
Monroe Law Office, 381
Monroe, James, 56-58,78,79,150-154, 157,166,168,211,238,242,316,340, 382,396,451
Monroe, James, House, 411
Monroe, James, Tomb, 455
Mont Calm, 486
Montague, Andrew Jackson, 185-186
Monterey, 272,465
Monterey Hotel, 398
Montgomery County, 272
Montgomery, Richard, 272
Monticello, 140,141,159,238,273,340, 432
Montpelier, 273,433,445
Montross, 273
Monument Avenue Historic District, 455
Monumental Church, 157,455
Moore, Andrew, 211-212
Moore, Augustine, 406
Morgan, Daniel, 51,52,314,365
Morris, James Maury, Jr., 414
Morris, June, 491
Morris, Richard O., 414
Morris, Robert, 489
Morrison House, 395
Morson's Row, 455
Morton, Matthew, 269
Morven, 342
Moryson, Col. Francis, 111,113-114
Mosby, Gen. John S., 374
Mosco, 26
Moses, Reverend, 312
Mount Airy, 463
Mount Crawford, 273
Mount Desert, 106

Encyclopedia of Virginia

Mount Jackson, 273
Mount Rogers, 12
Mount Vernon, 1,53,375
Mount Zion, 485
Mountain Gap School, 411
Mowhemenchouch, 26
Mt. Torry Furnace, 349
Mt. Vernon Conference, 77
Muddy Creek Mill, 369
Muhlenburg, John Peter Gabriel, 315
Muhlenburg, Reverend Henry Melchior, 315
Mulberry Hill, 360
Mulberry Island Point, 424
Mulberry Island, 34,273
Mullins, James, 289
Mumford, Mary Cooke Branch, 295
Murray, John, 128-129
Myer, Brig. Gen. Albert J., 347
Myers, Elijah E., 448
Myers, Moses, House, 426
Nanzatico, 404
Napoleon, 141
Narrows, 274
Nassawadox Creek, 274
Nassawadox, 274
Nat'l Conference of Lieut. Governors' Drug Interdiction Task Force, 199
National Democratic Convention, 183
National Democratic Lieutenant Governors' Association, 199
National Guard, 245
National House of Representatives, 66
National Republican Party, 161, 162
Natural Resources, 18-20
Navigation Act of 1660, 39
Navigation Act, 39,111
Navigation Law of 1707, 246
Necotowance, 310
Nelson County Courthouse, 422
Nelson House, 128
Nelson, 274
Nelson, General Thomas, 287
Nelson, Thomas, 128,274,
Nelson, Thomas, Jr., 143-144
Nelson, William, 128,143
New Castle Historic District, 367
New Castle, 274
New England Co., 108
New England, 106,118,119
New England, cod fisheries, 100
New Hampshire, 118
New Kent County, 274
New London Academy, 351
New Market, 274 New Market Battlefield Park, 471

New Point Comfort Lighthouse, 419
New River, 275
New York World's Fair, 461
New York, 117,118,151
Newce, Sir William, 275
Newce, Thomas, 275
Newport News, 275
Newport News Shipbuilding and Dry Dock Company, 276
Newport, Captain Christopher, 26,33, 34,291
Newport, Captain, 98,100
Newport, Sir Christopher, 258,275
Newsoms, 276
Newsoms, Thomas, 276
Newspaper founded, 76
Nicholas, Robert Carter, 127
Nicholas, Wilson Cary, 158,205,212,
Nichols, Abel Beach, 351
Nicholson, Governor, 256
Nicholson, Sir Francis, 117,120
Nickelsville, 276
Nicknames, 2-4
Nineteenth Amendment, 82
Nixon, Richard, 196
No-fault divorce, 198
Non-Importation Agreement, 49
Non-Intercourse Act, 56
Norfolk, 12,51,57,58,62,276
Norfolk, burning of, 129
Norfolk & Petersburg Railroad, 209
Norfolk & Western Railroad, 209,286, 296,469
Norfolk & Western Railway, 253,290
Norfolk Academy, 426
Norfolk and Western Railroad Company, 279
Norfolk City Hall, 426
Norfolk County Courthouse, 439
Norfolk Naval Shipyard, 439,440
Norfolk Navy Yard, 209,287
Norfolk *Virginian*, 181
Norfolk *Virginian-Pilot*, 199
Norfolk-Virginian, 182
Normal and Collegiate Institute for Negroes, 182
North, Lord 50,129
North Carolina, 11,12,19,54,63,88, 89,123
North Hampton County, 39,279
Northampton County Courthouse Historic District, 430
Northampton County, 48
Northern Neck, 39,42,55,73,122
Northumberland, 279

576

Index

Northwest Territory, 54
Norton, 279
Norton, Captain William, 107
Norton, Eckstein, 280
Notes on Virginia, 139,140
Notman, John, 451
Nott, Edward, 120
Nottoway, 30
Nottoway County, 280
Nottoway County Courthouse, 431
Nuclear power plants, 87
O'Ferrall, Charles Triplett, 184,259
Oak Hill, 367,378,411
Oak Lawn, 361
Oakland, 394
Oatlands, 411
Oatlands Historic District, 411
Occaneechee Island, 280
Occoquan, 280
Octonia Stone, 388
Ohio Company, 44,74
Ohio River, 47,124,125
Ohio Valley, 74
Old Chapel, 365
Old City Cemetery, 417
Old Dominion, 2,3,11,54,65,170,225
Old Donation Church, 483
Old Hotel, 443
Old Isle of Wight Courthouse, 399
Old Lick, 296
Old Lighthouse, 235
Old Mansion, 355
Old Point Comfort Lighthouse, 391
Old Providence Stone Church, 349
Old Rectory, 352
Old Russell County Courthouse, 468
Old Stone House, 456
Old Tobacco Warehouse, 420
Oldest daily newspaper in America, 224
Onancock, 280
Onancocks, 280
Onley, 281
Opechancanough, 26,36,38,310
Operation Desert Shield, 89
Oppecancanough, 110
Orange & Alexandria Railroad Co., 202
Orange and Alexandria Railroad, 254
Orange, 281
Orange County, 281
Oregon, 167
Origin of name, 2,99
Original patent of Virginia, 97
Otey, Peter J., 206
Otho Thorpe, 311

Pace, Richard, 36
Page County, 283
Page County Courthouse, 433
Page, John, 153-154,283,384
Page, Mathew, 364
Page, Richard Lucian, 428
Page, Thomas Nelson, 2,393,394
Paine, Tom, 140
Paint Lick Mountain, 482
Painter, 283
Paleozoic era, 14,15
Palsel, Peter, 274
Pamunkey River, 26
Panama, 168
Pannill, Samuel, 355
Parker, Richard E., 215,212
Parkes, Edmund, 283
Parks, William, 311
Parksley, 283
Parris, Alexander, 460
Parson's Cause, 75,132,393
Partisan Rangers, 374
Patawomeke, 474
Patrick County, 283
Patrick County Courthouse, 435
Patrick Henry House, 392
Patton, Colonel James, 229,234,304
Peace Conference, 80
Pear Valley, 430
Pearis, Captain George, 283
Pearisburg, 283
Pearson, H. Clyde, 195
Peery, George Campbell, 190-191
Pembroke, 283
Pembroke Manor, 483
Penn, John, 231
Pennington Gap, 283
Pennsylvania Railroad Company, 271
Pennsylvania Railroad, 283
Pennsylvania, 11,37,43,54,63,119,122
Pennybacker, Isaac S., 210
Percy, Captain George, 34,100-102,104 108
Percy, George, writings, 101
Peru, 99
Petersburg, 52,76,79,81,284,436
Petersburg Courthouse, 437
Petersburg Exchange, 437
Petersburg National Battlefield, 371,436,443
Petersburg *Index*, 181
Peyton, Bailie, 175
Phenix, 286
Phi Beta Kappa Society, 76
Philanthropic Society, 183

Encyclopedia of Virginia

Philips, William B., 433
Phillips, General William, 52,284
Phillips, William, 342
Pickering, John, 213
Pickett, General George, 370
Piedmont Province, 11,12
Piedmont, 13,14,16,17,19,26,27,31,41 44,45,49,54,58-61,293,396
Pierce, William, 113
Pierpont, Francis H., 177-178
Pierpont, Governor Francis. H., 64, 177,178,225
Pilgrims, 72
Pilgrim Fathers, 36
Pinchbeck, Thomas, 392
Pinewoods, 401
Pitt, William, 286
Pittsylvania County, 286
Pizarro, 99
Plains, The 306
Plantations, 44,61
Pleasant Hall, 484
Pleasants, James, 201,212-213
Pleasants, James, Jr., 159
Pleasants, John Hampden, 159,167
Plymouth, 72,103
Plymouth Company, 33,35
Pocahontas, 26,34-36,71,100,102,106, 263,284,286,289,401,481
Pocahontas Historic District, 482
Pocahontas, marriage to John Rolfe, 105
Poe, Edgar Allan, 79,227,293
Pohick Church, 376
Point Comfort, 35,71,102,113,273
Point of Fork, 242
Point of Fork Arsenal, 379
Point of Fork Plantation, 379
Point of Honor, 417
Point Pleasant, 75,128
Political Saviour of Virginia, 179
Polk, James, 180
Pollard, Calvin, 437,438
Pollard, John Garland, 189-190
Pollard, John Garland, writings, 190
Pope Paul VI, 87
Pope, General, 444
Pope, John Russell, 447
Pope-Leighey House, 374
Poplar Forest, 352
Poplar Grove Mill and House, 419
Population, 72-74,76-78,80-87,89
Populations, 79
Port Royal, 286
Port Royal Historic District, 356
Porto Bello, 492

Portsmouth, 52,53,57,286
Portsmouth and Roanoke Railroad, 288
Portsmouth Courthouse, 439
Portsmouth Historic District, 440
Portsmouth Naval Hospital, 440
Pory, John, 280
Post, George B., and Sons, 439
Potomac Creek Site, 474
Potomac Navy, 290
Potomac River, 11,18,25,31,39,106, 115,289
Pott, Dr. John, 38,310
Pott, John, 107-109
Pound, 289
Powell's Tavern, 386
Powell, John, 294
Powell, William, 480
Powhatan, 25,26,30,35,36,98,99,106 108,263,289,400,481
Powhatan Confederacy, 310
Powhatan County, 289
Powhatan Courthouse Historic District, 441
Powhatan Indian Confederacy, 291
Practical House Carpenter, 466
Pre-History and Archeology, 25-32
Presser, Theodore, 269
Preston House (Herndon), 472
Preston, James, P., 158
Preston, John Montgomery, 472
Preston, Robert, 485
Preston, William, 421
Prestwould, 419
Price, James Hubert, 191
Prince Edward, 289
Prince Edward Action Group, 85
Prince George County, 289
Prince, William, 280
Prince William County, 289
Princess Anne County Courthouse, 484
Printing press, 42
Proclamation by the Governor, 7
Prohibition, 187
Providence Presbyterian Church, 414
Province of Carolina, 72
Province of Maryland, 72
Provisional Congress of the Confederacy, 210
Public Assistance Act, 83
Public records, destruction of, 238
Pulaski, 289
Pulaski County, 289
Pulaski, Count Casimir, 289
Pungoteague, 290
Purcellville, 290
Purchase of Louisiana Territory, 78

Index

Puritans, 38,110
Putney Houses, 456
Putney, Samuel, House, 456
Putney, Stephen, House, 456
Quaker community, 268
Quaker settlers, 260
Quantico, 290
Quarters A, B, and C, Norfolk Naval Shipyard, 440
Queen Anne, 250
Queen Anne's War, 223
Queen Caroline, 250
Queen Louisa of Denmark, 266
Queen of Pamunkey, 310
Queen's Rangers, 363
Quincy, John, 79
Racial integration, 85,194
Radford, 290
Radford, Dr. John Bane, 290
Radford, William, 351
Railroads, 66,269,275,279,285,306, 310,397,471
Rainfall, 14
Raleigh, Sir Walter, 2,33,71,99
Randolph, Beverley, 147-148
Randolph, Edmund, 54,137,146,147,155 453
Randolph, Governor Edmund, 53,77
Randolph, Henry, 363
Randolph, Jane, 396
Randolph, John, 137,159,161,166,213, ,261,361
Randolph, Lieutenant Robert, 225
Randolph, Peyton, 75,127,145,146
Randolph, Peyton, House, 488
Randolph, Richard, 237,396
Randolph, Sir John, 44,488
Randolph, Thomas, 387
Randolph, Thomas Mann, 158-159
Randolph, Virginia E., Cottage, 395
Randolph, William, 261
Randolph-Macon College, 216,227
Randolph-Macon Woman's College, 269
Rapidan Dam Canal of the Rappahannock, 473
Rapidan-Rappahannock, 26
Rappahannock, 62
Rappahannock County, 291
Rappahannock Day, 262
Rappahannock Military Academy, 209
Rappahannock River, 18-19,25,39,57, 115,121,123,250,291,474
Rappahannock-Rapidan, 32
Ratcliff-Logan-Allison House, 374
Ratcliffe, John, 33-34,97-98

Ratification of Federal Constitution, 77
Ratification of State constitution, 81
Read, Isaac, 360
Readjuster Party, 66,181,209,214
Reagan, President Ronald. 87
Reconstruction, 231,252,273
Redd, Maj. John, 398
Redlands, 342
Reed, Walter, birthplace, 383
Reid, Dr. William Ferguson, 86
Religious freedom, 45
Remedial reading program for Black children, 85
Remington, 291
Renwick, James, 381
Republican Party, 66,69,140,141,149 154,160,180
Restoration, 39
Revenue Act, 49
Revolution, 39,46,47,49,51-53,127, 363,373,379
Revolutionary Army, 210,212
Revolutionary troops, 305
Revolutionary War, 144,146,148,149, 152,154,174,206,211,216,218,238, 243,249,251,252,257,261,266,267, 270,277,280,284,287,289,290,293, 299,303,304,308,309,314,353,354, 365,385,392,410,422,475,489
Reynolds Homestead, 434
Reynolds, R J., Tobacco Co., 435
Reynolds, Richard Joshua, 434-435
Rhode Island, 118,156,164
Rich Creek, 291
Rich, Sir Robert, 36
Richlands, 291
Richmond, 1,9,12,52,61-65,69,76,78, 80,81,83,84,86,291,387,394,451,456 458,459,473,493
Richmond County, 291
Richmond County Courthouse, 463
Richmond Enquirer, 181
Richmond Fayette Artillery, 171
Richmond Inquirer, 166
Richmond National Battlefield Park, 394,395,456
Richmond Professional Institute, 461
Richmond Theatre, 157
Richmond, founder of, 359
Richmond, Fredericksburg & Potomac Railroad Company, 191,227
Richmond, plot to capture, 396
Riddick House, 479

579

Riddleberger, Harrison Holt, 214
Ridge Province, 11
Ridgeway, 295
Rifle factory, 247
Rights of Man, 140
Riley, J. Harvey, 377
Riley, Judge Joseph, 377
Rippon Lodge, 445
Ripshin, 388
Rising Sun Tavern, 382
Rivanna River, 27
Riverside and Dan River Cotton Mills, 245
Rives, William C., 162,171,214,314
Roane, William Henry, 214-215
Roane, William, 397
Roanoke, 296
Roanoke, 258
Roanoke Colony, 34
Roanoke County, 296
Roanoke Island, 62
Roanoke Navigation Company, 245
Roanoke Plantation, 361
Roanoke River, 27,28,297
Roaring Spring, 383
Robb, Charles Spittal, 87,197-198
Roberts, Joseph Jenkins, 285
Robertson, Absalom Willis, 215,216
Robertson, William B., 86
Robertson, Wyndham, 168-169,222
Robertson, Wyndham, writings, 169
Robinson, Edwin, 227
Robinson, John, 123-124,267
Robinson, William, 274
Rochambeau, General, 53, 401
Rock Castle, 388
Rockbridge County, 297
Rockefeller, John D., Jr., 312
Rockingham County, 297
Rockingham Register, 259
Rockledge, 444
Rocky Mount, 297
Rocky Mountains, 167
Rogers, Edgerton S., 454
Rogers, Isaiah, 451
Rogers, Philip, 345
Rolfe, John, 26,34,36,72,100,263, 401,481
Rolfe, John, marriage to Pocahontas, 105
Rolfe, Thomas, 481
Roosevelt, Franklin D., 186,206,216
Rose, Colonel Thomas E., 294
Rosegill, 421
Rosewell, 384
Rotunda, University of Virginia, 362

Round Hill, 297
Rowe, Dr. Edgar H., 355
Roy Clark Day, 87
Royal colony, 72
Royal grant, 72
Royston, Thomas, 250
Ruebush, Will H., 8
Ruffin, Edmund, 60
Ruffin, Edmund, Plantation, 394
Ruffner, Dr. William H., 65
Rural Retreat, 297
Russell, Dr. Walter, 305
Russell, William, 298
Rutherfoord, John, 388,171
Sabine Hall, 463
Sadat, Anwar, 87
Salem Presbyterian Church, 469
Salem, 298
Salona, 377
Salt industry, 299
Salt works, 316
Saltville, 299
Salubria, 368
Sandys, George, 107
Sandys, Sir Edwin, 36,37,104
Santillane, 353
Saratoga battle, 52
Saratoga, 365
Saunders, Jonathan, 484
Savage Station, 299
Sawmill, 232
Saxis, 299
Schofield, General John M., 65,178
School for the deaf, 386
Schwartz Tavern, 431
Scot's Arms Tavern, 373
Scotchtown, 392
Scott County, 299
Scott, General Winfield, 79
Scott, James, 456
Scott, John, 299
Scott, Walter, 308,309,314
Scott, William, 219
Scott, Winfield, 59,299
Scott-Clarke House, 456
Scottsburg, 299
Scottsville, 299
Seaboard Air Line Railway, 288
Sears House, 476
Sears, Dr. Barnas, 476
Secession approval by Convention, 80
Secession Convention, 80,176,180,
Secession, 59,165,169,174,177,183, 208,278,288,294
Second Battle of Cold Harbor, 80
Second Battle of Manassas, 80,181

Index

Second Company of Virginia, 101
Second Confederate Congress, 214
Second Empire John Cary Weston House, 427
Second institution of higher learning in America, 74
Second Presbyterian Church, 456
Second Revolutionary Convention of Virginia, 133
Second Virginia Convention, 50,75
Select Architecture, 489
Semple, James, House, 488
settlement of North America, 99
Seven Days' Battles, 80,294
Seven Days' Campaign 294,299
Seven Decades of the Union, 176
Seven Pines, 62,299
Sevier, John, 274
Seward, William, 63
Sheep, 59
Sheffield, Samuel, 295
Sheltering Arms Hospital, 457
Shenandoah, 300
Shenandoah County, 299
Shenandoah County Courthouse, 472
Shenandoah Herald, 315
Shenandoah Mountains, 255
Shenandoah River, 300,410
Shenandoah Valley Academy, 189
Shenandoah Valley Railroad, 296,469
Shenandoah Valley, 1,13,18,29,230,365 381,395,490
Sheppard, Mosby, 396
Sheridan, Gen. Philip H., 63,247,309, 370,371,379,381
Sherman, Roger, 137
Sherman, William, 63
Shirley, 359
Shockoe Canal, 457
Shockoe Slip Historic District, 457
Shore, Thomas, 242
Shoreham, 256
Short, John, 475
Shot Tower, 491
Sickle cell anemia, 199
Siege of Yorktown, 312
Sigel, Maj. Gen. Franz, 471
Signal School of Instruction, 347
Sike, Robert, 299
Simcoe, Colonel John G., 52
Simcoe, John, 363
Simpson, James, 298
Sinclair, John, 385
Singleton, Peter, 484
Singleton, William B., 439

Singleton, William R., 426
Six Nations, 29,121
Skinner, William, 259
Skinquarter, 300
Skipwith, Sir Peyton, 419
Skyline Drive, 1
Slash Church, 392
Slash Cottage, 227
Slave insurrection, 79
Slave, Gabriel, 396
Slavery, 35,41-43,45,50-52,54,58,59, 60,61,79,105,115,122,127,139,146, 150,152,156,162,167,170,172,177, 251,263,264,264,268,278,294,396
Slavery, promise of freedom, 129
Sloan, Samuel, 452
Small, William, 478
Smith's Fort, 481
Smith's Rude Answer, 34
Smith, Arthur, 300
Smith, Capt. John, 25-27,33,34,42, 71,98-101,108,223,250,263,269, 289,291,305,401,474,481
Smith, General G. W., 299
Smith, General W. F. (Baldy), 176
Smith, George William, 157
Smith, Gov. William (Extra-Billy), 245
Smith, Governor William, 59
Smith, John, writings, 100
Smith, Joseph, 349
Smith, Lillian, 8
Smith, Sir Thomas, 105
Smith, William, 172-173
Smithfield Historic District, 400
Smithfield, 300,421
Smyth County, 301
Smyth, Alexander, 301
Smyth, Sir Thomas, 36
Snowfall, 14
Snyder, Carlile John, 204
Social Security Act, 191
Somers House, 431
Somers, Sir George, 100,102,106
South America, 152
South Boston, 301
South Carolina, 11,62,165,167,168, 170,172
South Carolina's Nullification Act 59
South Hill, 301
Southampton County, 301
Southern Literary Messenger, 79,293
Southern Planter, 188
Southern Seminary Main Building, 354
Southern Seminary System of Schools, 355

Encyclopedia of Virginia

Southern Star, 285
Southwest Virginia Improvement Co., 482
Southwest Virginia Livestock Association, 185
Spain, 37,78,101,151,152,168
Spaniards, 97
Spanish ambassador, 37
Spelman, Henry, 31
Spence's Point, 487
Spencer, Nicholas, 116
Spong, William Belser, Jr., 215-216
Spotswood, Alexander, 28,44,45,120-122,134,180,248,277,300,301,311,389,488
Spotsylvania County, 301
Spratling, William, 388
Sprowle, Andrew, 287
St. Andrew's Roman Catholic Church, 464
St. Charles, 298
St. George, 121
St. George's Church, 340
St. James Church, 337
St. John's Church, 391,406,479
St. John's Church Historic District, 457
St. John's Episcopal Church, 458
St. Lawrence, 258
St. Luke's Church, 400
St. Mary's Whitechapel, 407
St. Paul, 298
St. Paul's Church, 404,427,458
St. Peter's Church, 423,458
St. Pierre, 125
St. Thomas Chapel, 380
Stafford, 302
Stagg, Charles, 311
Stagg, Mary, 311
Stamp Act, 48,49,75,132,133,135,145,155,277,311,373
Stamp Tax, 48
Stanard, William, 251
Stanardsville, 302
Standards, Robert, 302
Stanley, Governor T. B., 84
Stanley, Thomas Bahnson, 193-194
Starving Time, 71
State Alcoholic Beverage Control Board, 191
State Bird, 9
State Board of Agriculture, 203
State Board of Charities and Corrections, 82
State Board of Education, 203
State Board of Public Welfare, 68,82

State Constitution, 51
State Constitution, revised, 197
State Convention of Virginia, 176
State Corporation Commission, 187
State Flag, 4
State Flower, 8
State Government departments, 69
State Health Department, 199
State Highway Commission, 82
State Industrial Commission, 188
State Labor Bureau, 185
State Milk Commission, 191
State Motto, 5
State Services Directory, 91-96
State Song, 8
State symbols, 2-9
State Teachers College, 8
State Transportation and Public Utility Advisory Commission, 203
State Tree, 9
State university, 68
States'-rights, 160-162,164,169-171
Statute for Religious Liberty, 77
Statute of Virginia for Religious Liberty, 382
Statutes of Virginia for Religious Freedom, 142
Staunton, 81,302
Staunton Hill, 360
Staunton, Rebecca, 302
Steamships, 66
Stearns Iron-Front Building, 458
Stegg, Thomas, 292
Stewart, Dr. T. Dale, 474
Stewart, Norman, 459
Stewart, Thomas B., 449,458
Stewart-Lee House, 458
Stijnen, Leo, 461
Stone House Site, 402
Stone, Governor, 111,112
Stoneman, General George, 221,267
Stonewall Brigade, 181
Story, William J., Jr., 195
Story of the Confederacy, 258
Stratford Hall, 487
Strawberry Hill, 438
Stuart, 303
Stuart Hall, 476
Stuart House, 477
Stuart's Draft, 304
Stuart, Alexander. H. H., 477
Stuart, Archibald, 477
Stuart, Flora, 477
Stuart, General J. E. B., 236
Stuart, Henry Carter, 187,316
Stuart, J. E. B., 303,451,477

582

Index

Stuart, King Charles, 2,3
Suffolk, 304
Suffolk, peanut capital 304
Sugar Bill, 48
Sully, 376
Sulphur, 272
Summers, Judge George W., 175
Summers, Lewis, 274
Sumner, General E. V., 299
Supreme Court, 66,163
Surrender at Appomattox, 285
Surry, 305
Surry County, 305
Susquehanna River, 100
Susquehannock Indian War, 73
Susquehannock War, 223
Sussex County Courthouse Historic District, 482
Sussex County, 305
Swain, Levi, 446
Swannanoa, 349,422
Swanson, Claude Augustus, 186,189, 203,216
Swanton, John Reed, 25
Sweet Briar House, 346-347
Sweet Chalybeate Springs, 345
Swift Creek, 363
Swift Creek Mill, 363
Sycamore Tavern, 393
Sydney, 225
Syms Free School, 72
Taliaferro, Richard, 400,489
Tangier, 305
Tangier Island, 305
Tappahannock, 305
Tappahannock Historic District, 373
Tariff of Abominations, 59,79
Tarleton, Colonel Banastre, 52,76, 238,273,303
Taxation, 37,41,43,48,69,72,83,126, 127,155,182,224,292
Tayloe, Col. John, 463
Tayloe, George P., 464
Tayloes of Mount Airy, 464
Taylor, Edwin, 476
Taylor, Elizabeth, 87
Taylor, John, 160,216,231,357
Taylor, William, 172,237
Taylor, Zachary, 59,79,272
Taylor-Whittle House, 428
Tazewell, 306
Tazewell County, 306
Tazewell, Henry, 158,216,306
Tazewell, Littleton W., 160,167-169, 214,425

Teach, Edward, 121,256
Temple, Major Robert H., 275
Tennessee, 11,12,62
Tenth Legion Banner, 214
Territory of Virginia, 115
Terry, General Alfred H. 64
Terry, Sue, 88
Texas, 59,78,79,255
Texas, acquisition of, 164
Texas, annexation of, 165,170,171
Texas, Republic of, 170
Textile, 245,369
Textile mills, 190
Theodore Roosevelt Island, 210
Third Virginia Convention, 50
Thomas, J. R., 362
Thomas, Joshua, 305
Thompson, John, 368
Thornton, Francis I, 446,473
Thornton, William, 374
Thoroughgood House, 484
Three Otters, 350
Thruston, Rev. Charles Mynn, 485
Tidewater, 1,12,13,18,19,41,44-46, 54,58-61,223,396,407,421,438
Tidewater Connection, 396
Tidewater Railway, 279
Timber, 253,306
Timber Ridge Presbyterian Church, 466
Timberville, 306
Tinkling Spring Presbyterian Church, 348
Tippecanoe and Tyler too, 162
Tobacco Rebellion, 115
Tobacco Riots, 42
Tobacco, 18,37,38,39,42-45,47,58,59, 74,106,112,115,121,202,223,227, 231,233,238,243,245,246,250,251, 256,268,269,277,284,285,292,294, ,296,300,301,304,306,366,369,416, 421,435,437,446,454,456,459
Tobacco, introduction of, 72
Tobey, Alton S., 426
Todd, E. M., & Co., 300
Todd, Mallory, 300
Todd, Thomas, 384
Toddsbury, 384
Toleration Act, 45
Tolliver, June, House, 491
Tompkins, Sally, 294
Toms Brook, 307
Tories, 155,277,278,287
Total area of Virginia, 1,11
Totopotomoi, 27,310

Encyclopedia of Virginia

Trail of the Lonesome Pine, 491
Tramontaine Order, 121
Travels in the Interior Parts of America, 285
Treaty of Annexation, 165
Treaty of Ghent, 57
Treaty of Paris, 46,47
Treaty of Utrecht, 43
Treaty of Washington, 59
Treaty with Russia, 58,79
Tredegar Ironworks, 459
Tree Hill, 397
Trent Affair, 62
Triassic period, 15
Trible, Paul Seward, Jr., 217
Trinity Episcopal Church, 441,477
Trinkle, Elbert Lee, 68,188-189,260, 316
Trout, John, 296
Troutdale, 307
Troutville, 307
True Travels, Adventures, and Observations of Cpt. John Smith, 100
Tuck, Governor, 84
Tuck, William Munford, 192-193
Tuckahoe, 387
Tucker, St. George, 261
Tuleyries, The, 366
Tunker House, 467
Turner, Gabriel, 167
Turner, Nat, 60,79,472
Turner, Nat, insurrection, 167,172
Tuscarora War, 28
Tuscaroras, 121
Tuskegee Institute, 380
Twain, Mark, 297
Two Penny Act, 47
Tyler, James Hoge, 184-185
Tyler, John, 59,79,154-157,159-165, 170,172,175,214,217,358,451
Tyler, John, House, 358
Tyler, President, 171
Tynes, Mary, 316
U.S. Arsenal, 80
U.S. Customshouse, 427
U.S. Housing Corp., 439
U.S. National Museum, 474
U.S. Post Office and Customhouse, 459
U.S. Supreme Court, 78,82,84,86,244
U.S.S. Dolphin, 57
Uncle Tom's Cabin, 60
Underwood, Judge John C., 65
Unemployment Compensation Comm., 83, 191

Union Army, 236,371,390,394
Union commanders, 236
Union forts, 390
Union Presbyterian Church, 354
Union Theological Seminary, 185
Union troops, 234,252,263,267,278, 309,312,316,471
Unionist Party, 204,219
United State Senators from Virginia, 201-219
United States Bank, 161
United States Centennial Exposition, 181
University of Virginia Historic District, 362
University of Virginia, 59,78,83,141, 158,341,342,362,434
University of Virginia, admission of women, 82
University of Virginia, student protest, 86
Up From, 380
Upper Church, Stratton Major Parish, 403
Upperville Colt and Horse Show, 412
Upperville Historic District, 378
Upshur, Abel Parker, 429
Urbanna, 307
USS Iowa, 250
Valentine Museum, 459
Valentine, Edward V., 294
Valentine, Lila Meade, 295
Valentine, Mann, II, 460
Valley Field, 19
Valley of Virginia, 16,19,44-46,61,63
Valley Province, 11
Valley Railroad Stone Bridge, 348
Valley Star, 177
Van Buren, Martin, 162,164
Van de Velde, Henri, 461
Van Lew, Elizabeth, 294
Van Meter, Isaac, 313
Van Meter, John, 313
Vaucluse, 429
Vauter's Church, 373
Vawter, C. E., 343
Venable, Abraham B., 205,212 218
Vermont, 145
Victoria, 307
Vienna, 307
Vietnam War, 198
Vinton, 307
Violet Bank, 242 367
Virgilina, 307
Virgin Queen Elizabeth, 33
Virginia & Tennessee Railroad, 290

Index

Virginia Advocate, The, 170
Virginia Agricultural and Mechanical College, 182,186
Virginia and Tennessee Railroad, 232,296
Virginia Assembly, 128
Virginia Beach, 307
Virginia Central Railroad, 63,238, 241
Virginia Co. of 1609, 480
Virginia Collegiate Institute, 469
Virginia Colonization Society, 162
Virginia Commission on Uniform State Laws, 190
Virginia Commonwealth University, 461
Virginia Company of London, 33,37, 102
Virginia Company, 104,107,108,395
Virginia Constitution of 1621, 37
Virginia Constitutional Convention, 182,190
Virginia Convention of 1775 457
Virginia Convention of 1776, 5
Virginia Convention of May 1776, 369
Virginia Dynasty, 79
Virginia Electric and Power Company, 87,88,193
Virginia Female Institute, 477
Virginia Gazette, 293
Virginia General Assembly, 412
Virginia House of Burgesses, 421,487
Virginia House of Delegates, 454
Virginia Iron, Coal & Coke Company, 190
Virginia Legislature, 76,77
Virginia Military Institute, 187, 203,209
Virginia Military Institution, 180
Virginia Militia, 209-211
Virginia Mutual Assurance Society, 171
Virginia National Guard, 191
Virginia Pay-As-You-Go Association, 187
Virginia Pay-As-You-Go Association, 190
Virginia Plan 53
Virginia Polytechnic Institute, 83, 188,216,229
Virginia Provinces, 11
Virginia Randolph Training School, 395-396
Virginia readmitted to Union, 81
Virginia Republican Committee, 197
Virginia Resolutions, 77,154

Virginia Resolves, 48
Virginia School for the Deaf and Blind, 478
Virginia State Bar, 199
Virginia State Board of Education, 189
Virginia State Capitol, 460
Virginia State Corporation Commission, 191
Virginia State Fair Association, 188
Virginia State Farmers' Institute, 185,188
Virginia State Treasury, 197
Virginia Union University, 86,199,461
Virginia Volunteers, 209
Virginia's cession of land to the U.S. for seat of government, 77
Virginia's cession of Northwest Territory to U.S. 76
Virginia's Education Governor, 195
Virginia's first rebellion, 40
Virginia, oldest colony, 117
Virginia, original territory, 3
Virginia, Senators, 201-219
Virginian Antiquary, 230
Virginian Railway, 279,297
Virginian-Pilot, 182
Virginia, 258,278,439
von Steuben, General, 52,53,243
Wachapreague, 308
Wakefield, 308
Wales, 371
Walker, Dr. Thomas, 221,241,296,341
Walker, Dugald Stewart, 294
Walker, Gilbert Carlton, 178-179
Walker, John, 218
Walpole Company, 47
Walter, Thomas U., 426,449
War for Independence, 401
War Industries Board, 187
War memorial dedicated, 84
War of 1812, 157,159,160,172,175,208, 209,212,247,257,278,285,288,305, 487
War of the Spanish Succession, 43
Warburton House, 401
Wardlaw, William, 303
Ware Parish Church, 384
Warehouse of Shocco, 292
Warm Springs Bathhouses, 350
Warner, John W., 87
Warner, John Williams, 218-219
Warren County, 308
Warren House, 481
Warren, Admiral Borlasse, 57

Warren, Dr. Joseph, 308
Warren, Thomas, 481
Warrenton, 308
Warrington, Commodore Lewis, 257
Warsaw, 308
Warsh, Henry L., III, 69
Wartmen, Lawrence, 259
Warwick, Judge James Woods, 350
Washington and Lee Law School, 212, 217,218
Washington County, 308
Washington Iron Furnace, 380
Washington Monument, 228
Washington *Post*, 199
Washington, 309
Washington, Augustine, 223,375
Washington, Betty, 381
Washington, Booker T., 390
Washington, Booker T., National Monument, 380
Washington, Charles, 382
Washington, Colonel John, 223
Washington, D.C., 11,227,289
Washington, George 1,46,50,51,53-56, 74,75,77,125,127,134,135,137,140, 145-147,149,152,206,210-212,218, 223-225,270,284,293,308,309,313, 315,343,344,364,375,376,381,401,
Washington, George, boyhood home site, 475
Washington, George, National Forest, 349,350
Washington, George, National Forest, 353,434
Washington, Lawrence, 223
Washington, Warner, 364
Waterford Historic District, 413
Waterman, Thomas T., 407
Waverly, 309
Wayland, Dr. John W., 8
Wayne, General Anthony, 52,309
Waynesboro, 309
Weaver, Walter, 435
Weber City, 309
Weblin House, 484
Webster, Daniel, 162,164
Weems, Mason Locke, 444
Welbourne, 412
Weld, Isaac, 302
Well, Henry Horatio, 178
Wells, General H. H., 179
Wells, H. H., Jr., 178
Werowocomoco, 25,29,263
Wessells Root Cellar, 338
West Franklin Street Historic District, 461
West Freemason Street Area Historic District, 427
West Point, 309
West Virginia, 11,12,66,75,80
West, Captain Francis, 108,291
West, Francis, 37,38,108,310,
West, John Jr., 223
West, John, 38,110,113,310
West, Nathaniel, 310
West, Thomas, 71,108,110,310
West, Thomas, (Lord De la Warr), 101-103
Westend, 415
Westerhouse House, 429
Westerhouse, William, 429
Western Hotel, 417
Western State Hospital Complex, 478
Westmoreland County, 309
Westmoreland Militia, 208
Weston Manor, 399
Westover Church, 358
Westover, 359
Wharf Area Historic District, 478
Wharton Place, 338
Wharton, James, 408
Wheat, 59,61,223,250,251,284
Whig Convention of 1839, 59
Whig Convention, 158
Whig National Convention, 202
Whig Party, 162,163,164,170,170,171, 172,173,201,206,208,214,217
Whiskey Rebellion of 1793 412
Whitaker, Jabez, 107
White Beach, 242
White House of the Confederacy, 461
White Stone, 310
White's Mill, 486
White, Ambrose, 305
White, Hugh, 162
White, Stanford, 362
Whitetop Mountain, 12
Whittle House, 428
Whittle, Kennon, C., 398
Wickham, Anne Butler Carter, 392
Wickham, Gen. Williams Carter, 392
Wickham, John, 397,460
Wickham, Littleton Waller Tazewall, 397
Wickham, William, 392
Wickham-Valentine Museum, 459
Wigwam, 346
Wilder, L. Douglas, 69,88
Wilder, L. Douglas, elected as Governor, 89
Wilder, Lawrence Douglas, 198-199
Wilkinson, Cornelius, 290
Willey, Waitman Thomas, 219

Index

William and Mary, 43
William and Mary College, 119,120, 122,126,160,201,208-210,210,211
William C. Rives, 208
William III, 281,310,311
Williams-Brown House and Store, 470
Williamsburg, 40,43,49,52,53,74,75, 76,87,114,117,120,121,122,125, 128,201,202,310,424 Williamsburg Convention of 1774, 137
Williamsburg Historic District, 489
Williamson Site, 372
Willoughby, Captain Thomas, 276
Willoughby-Baylor House, 428
Wilmot Proviso, 60
Wilson, Edwin P., 87
Wilson, Harris, and Richards, 453
Wilson, President Woodrow, 82,187, 206
Wilson, Woodrow, birthplace, 479
Winchester Star, 189
Winchester, 61
Windsor, 314
Wingfield, E. M., 98
Wingfield, Edward Maria, 33-34,97
Winona, 429
Winton, 346
Wirt, William, 135,152,156,161,270, 450
Wise, 315
Wise County, 315
Wise, Captain O. Jennings, 176
Wise, Governor Henry, 241,281
Wise, Henry Alexander, 175-176,222, 315
Wise, John S., 241,344
Wishart-Boush House, 485
Withers, Robert Enoch, 219
Wolftrap Farm, 400
Wood, Abraham, 44,73
Wood, James, 150,313
Wood, John, 270
Wood, Senator Henry Clinton, 241
Woodbourne, 351
Woodford, Colonel William, 277
Woodlawn, 387
Woodlawn Plantation, 374
Woodside, 397
Woodstock, 315

Woodward House, 461
Woodward, John, 462
Wool, General John Ellis, 278
Worden, Captain John L., 258
World War I, 187,190-194,,215,290, 390,424
World War II, 195,196,390
Wormeley, Colonel Ralph, 42,421
Wormeley, Ralph, II, 421
Wren Building, College of William and Mary, 489
Wren, James, 374,376,377
Wren, Sir Christopher, 120,489
Wright, Frank Lloyd, 374
Wright, Orville, 347
Wyatt, Francis, 37,107-108
Wyatt, Hawte, 107
Wyatt, Sir Francis, 38,106,108,110
Wythe County, 315
Wythe House, 489
Wythe, George, 54,165,257,315,316, 389,489
Wythe, Marshall, School of Government and Citizenship, 190
Wythe, Thomas, 389
Wytheville Military Academy, 188
Wytheville, 316
Yates Tavern, 438
Ye Bare and Ye Cubb, 290
Yeardley, George, 35,37,105-108,109
Yellow fever epidemic, 278
Yellow Fever Jack, 278
Yellow fever, 288
Yeocomico Church, 487
York County, 316
York River, 25
Yorktown Battlefield, 401
Yorktown Wrecks, 493
Yorktown, 53,76,128,129,210
Young Builder's General Instructor of 1829, 457
Young Republican Federation of Virginia, 197
Young Millwright and Miller's Guide, 486
Young, Ammi B., 427,459
Young, Robert, 366
Yount-Zigler House, 467

587

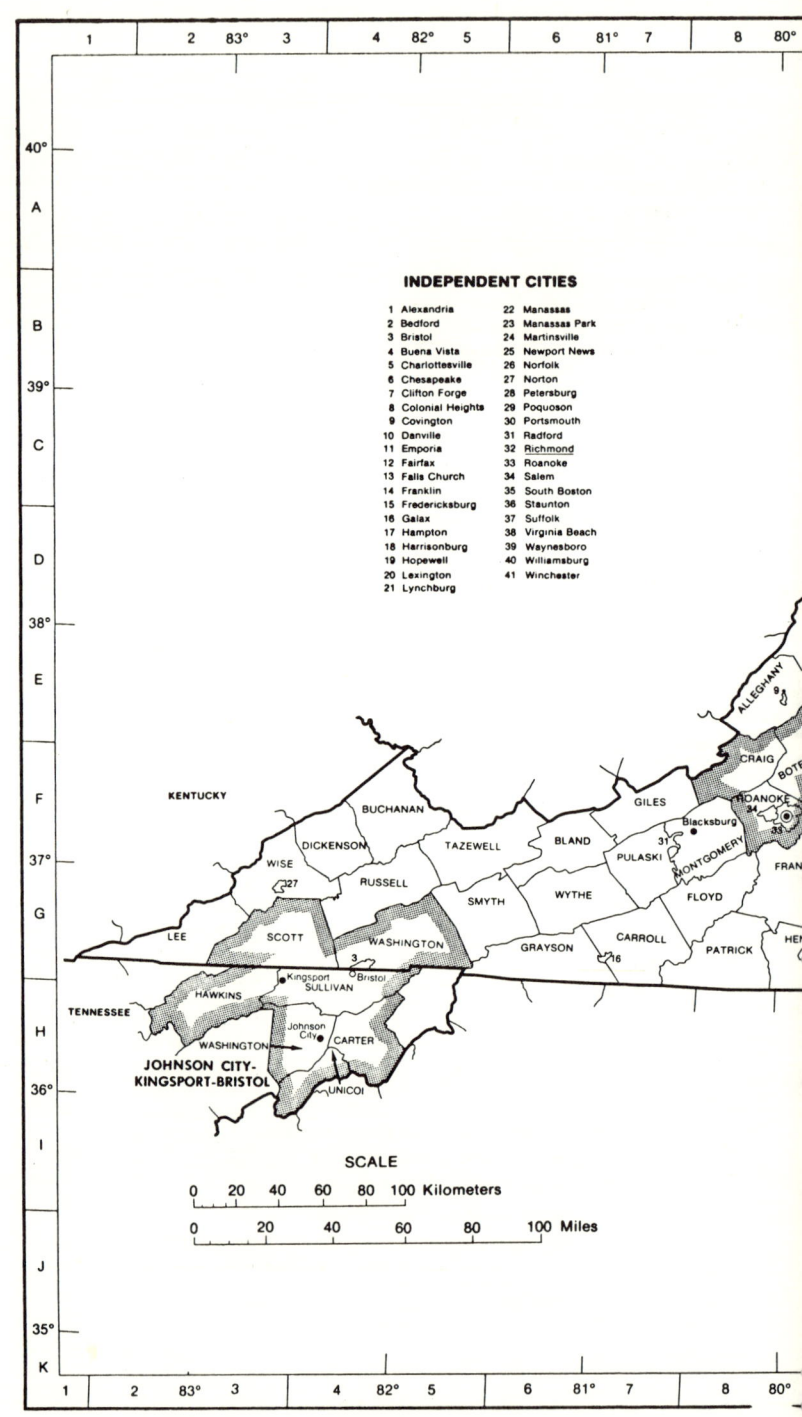

INDEPENDENT CITIES

1	Alexandria	22	Manassas
2	Bedford	23	Manassas Park
3	Bristol	24	Martinsville
4	Buena Vista	25	Newport News
5	Charlottesville	26	Norfolk
6	Chesapeake	27	Norton
7	Clifton Forge	28	Petersburg
8	Colonial Heights	29	Poquoson
9	Covington	30	Portsmouth
10	Danville	31	Radford
11	Emporia	32	Richmond
12	Fairfax	33	Roanoke
13	Falls Church	34	Salem
14	Franklin	35	South Boston
15	Fredericksburg	36	Staunton
16	Galax	37	Suffolk
17	Hampton	38	Virginia Beach
18	Harrisonburg	39	Waynesboro
19	Hopewell	40	Williamsburg
20	Lexington	41	Winchester
21	Lynchburg		

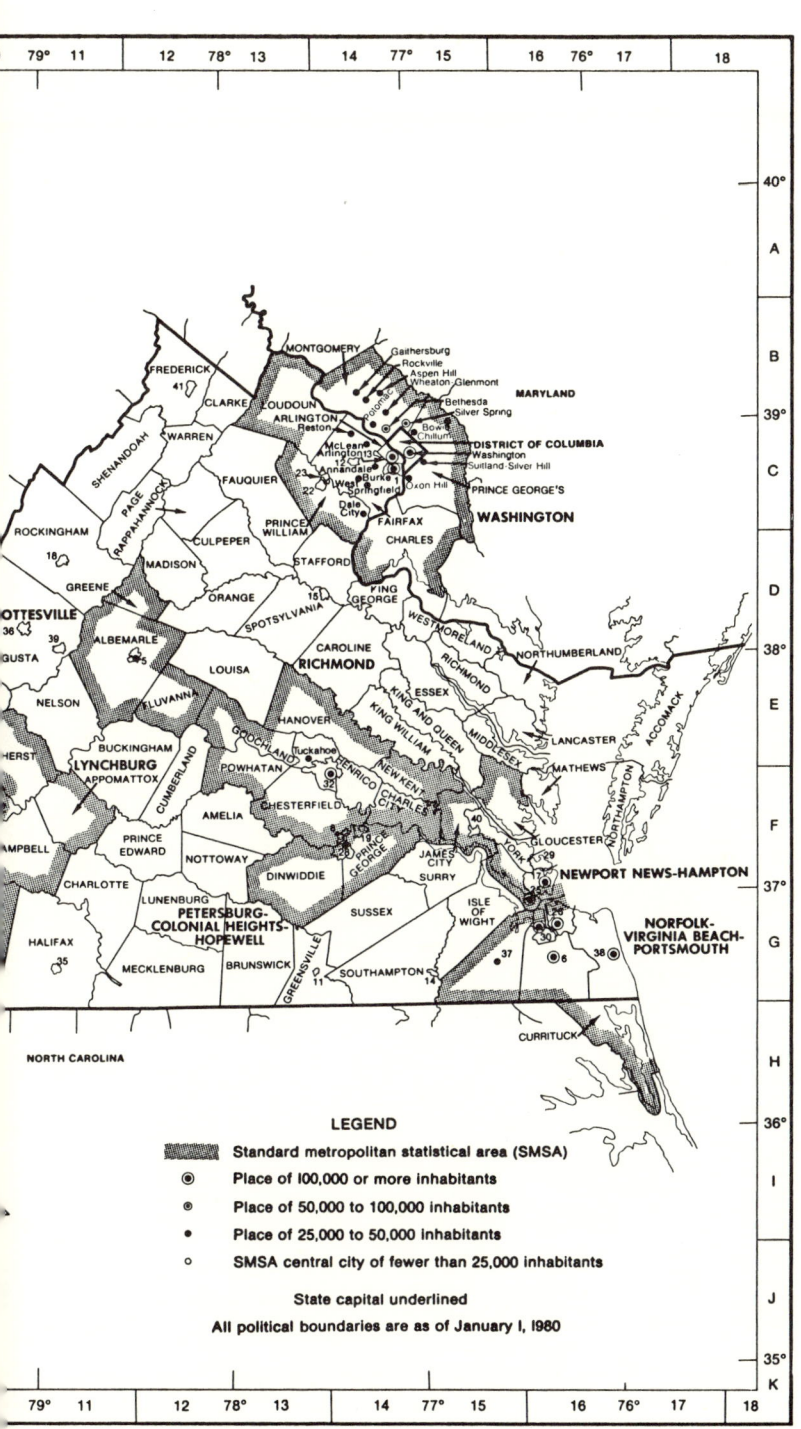